MATT AND TO

CLASSIC FOOTBALL HEROES

KLINSMANN

FROM THE PLAYGROUND
TO THE PITCH

Published by Dino Books
an imprint of John Blake Publishing
Suite 2.25, The Plaza,
535 Kings Road, Chelsea Harbour,
London, SW10 0SZ, UK

www.johnblakepublishing.co.uk

www.facebook.com/johnblakebooks ◼
twitter.com/jblakebooks ◼

This edition published in 2018

ISBN: 978 1 78606 922 1

British Library Cataloguing-in-Publication Data:

A catalogue record for this book is available from the British Library.

Design by www.envydesign.co.uk

Printed in Great Britain by Clays Ltd, St Ives plc

1 3 5 7 9 10 8 6 4 2

Papers used by John Blake Publishing are natural, recyclable products made from
wood grown in sustainable forests. The manufacturing processes conform to the
environmental regulations of the country of origin.

Every attempt has been made to contact the relevant copyright-holders, but some
were unobtainable. We would be grateful if the appropriate people could contact us.

John Blake Publishing is an imprint of Bonnier Publishing.
www.bonnierpublishing.co.uk

TABLE OF CONTENTS

CHAPTER 1

WORLD CUP WINNER

Stadio Olimpico, Italy – 8 July 1990

All football fans dream of playing in the World Cup final, especially young football fans. As he walked out onto the pitch in Rome, Jürgen was about to make his childhood dream come true. Yes, he was lucky, but he had also worked very hard for this opportunity.

Seven years earlier, Jürgen had been playing for Stuttgarter Kickers down in West Germany's second division. Over time, with goals and grit, he had raised his game higher and higher until he reached this, football's greatest event, the World Cup final.

'It doesn't get any better than this!' Jürgen thought to himself as he looked up at the 70,000 fans and listened to their chants and songs.

Deutschland! Deutschland! Deutschland!

Jürgen didn't feel nervous – just excited. Not only was he playing for West Germany, but he was also now his country's main striker. He was their big tournament hero, expected to bring home their third World Cup trophy.

So far, Jürgen wasn't letting them down. After a great start at Euro 88, he was now one of the biggest stars at the 1990 World Cup. He had that special striker's instinct:

Touch, *BANG, GOOOOAAAALLLL!*

Jürgen had already scored against Yugoslavia, United Arab Emirates and the Netherlands in the World Cup, but his game wasn't all about goals. He was everything that the fans were looking for – focused and fair, talented and tireless. West Germany knew that they could count on their Mr Consistent. When it came to chasing goals, Jürgen never stopped.

'Next time I get to a final, I'm going to win it!' he had promised himself after missing out on the 1989 UEFA Cup with Stuttgart. It wasn't going to be easy, however, especially against the best player in the world. In 1989, Diego Maradona had ruined Jürgen's night in a Napoli shirt and now, a year later, he was back to do the same in the white and blue of Argentina.

'Keep their little magician quiet and we'll win!' the West Germany manager Franz Beckenbauer told his players.

West Germany had previously also played Argentina in the 1986 World Cup final, and on that occasion, Maradona had led his country to victory. This time, things would be different for West Germany, especially with Jürgen up front. His plan was simple but very effective – to fight until he fell, to run until he couldn't run anymore.

In the first half, Jürgen battled for the ball with little success. There was nowhere for him to go, with Argentina's defenders marking him so tightly and aggressively.

'Ref, that's a blatant foul!' Jürgen argued as he fell to the floor.

'No way, he's diving!' the defenders argued back.

Although he was frustrated, he never gave up. The

World Cup trophy was definitely worth fighting for.

In the second half, Jürgen won the ball off Gabriel Calderón and played a one-two with his captain, Lothar Matthäus.

'Go on, Klinsi!' the West Germany fans cheered, their hopes lifting.

As Jürgen raced down the right wing, Pedro Monzón lunged in for a reckless tackle but didn't get anywhere near the ball. Instead, he kicked his opponent and sent him flying through the air.

'Arghhhh!' Jürgen screamed out in pain.

The referee was fed up with all the fouling. As Jürgen lay there on the grass, he rushed over and gave Monzón a straight red card. 'Off!' he pointed.

It wasn't the goal that Jürgen was looking for but hopefully that would come soon, now that West Germany were facing only ten men.

'Go on, Klinsi!' the fans cheered. 'Get us a goal!'

However, with five minutes to go, it was still West Germany 0 Argentina 0. Lothar burst forward and passed the ball forward into the path of Jürgen's strike partner, Rudi Völler. As Rudi tried to control it, the Argentina centre-back brought him down.

'Penalty!' Jürgen argued, pointing at the spot.

'No way, he's diving!' the Argentines argued back.

They surrounded the referee, but his mind was
made up. 'Penalty!' he said.

With the pressure on, Andreas Brehme stepped
up... and scored. 1–0!

As the net bulged, the stadium erupted with the
noise of 40,000 delighted West Germany supporters.
Jürgen chased after Andreas and threw his arms
around him.

'You did it!' he yelled. '*We* did it!'

After a few more minutes of tense defending, the
final was over and West Germany were the champions.
Jürgen was now a World Cup winner and he wanted to
share the amazing feeling with everyone.

'Come here!' he said, hugging each and every one
of his teammates, coaches and physios.

As Lothar lifted the trophy, Jürgen stood behind him
with his winners' medal around his neck, clapping
and cheering. The baker's boy from Göppingen didn't
want his magic moment to ever end.

CHAPTER 2

THE BAKER'S BOY

Göppingen was a small, quiet town, especially for an energetic kid like Jürgen. As soon as he was old enough, he rushed outside to explore the neighbourhood with his friends.

'Just don't go far, okay?' his parents Siegfried and Martha called after him anxiously.

'I won't!' he promised. With his blonde hair and big smile, their son bounced off down the street.

Jürgen and his friends started with playground slides and make-believe adventures. However, it wasn't long before they discovered Germany's favourite game – football. It had been regarded as the national sport ever since their captain Fritz Walter had first lifted the World Cup trophy in Switzerland in 1954. Their parents loved telling them about 'The Miracle of Berne', the unforgettable night when West Germany defeated Hungary 3–2 in the final.

So, when they found a battered old ball in a bush, they were all full of excitement. 'Awesome, let's play!'

Jürgen's first touches of the football came in crazy kickabouts at the park. There were no rules or positions; there was barely even a pitch. None of that seemed important to a bunch of lively six-year-olds. A free-for-all was much more fun anyway, with everyone kicking and then chasing, from one end of the field to the other.

Jürgen was always happiest when he was on the move. A day sat at home was a day wasted. Even in a sleepy place like Göppingen, there was always so much to see and do. Once Jürgen reached the age of seven, his dad decided to put all that energy to good use.

'Right, it's time to find you a proper sport!' Siegfried told his son.

TB Gingen was the local sports club, where young kids could try out all kinds of activities before picking their favourites.

'How about gymnastics?' Jürgen's dad suggested.

Before becoming a baker, Siegfried had been
a talented gymnast. He still helped out with the
coaching at TB Gingen, and so that seemed like a
good place to start.

Jürgen's gymnastics career didn't last long, however.
He liked the jumping but where was the action, the
competition? It was all too slow and boring for him.

'Sorry, Dad,' Jürgen said, looking down at the floor
guiltily.

'Don't worry!' Siegfried replied with a smile.
'Gymnastics isn't for everyone, I know. That's why
there are so many different sports to try!'

Jürgen's search continued. His older brother,
Horst, loved the decathlon. He practised ten different
track and field events, including the 100 metres, the
long jump and the javelin.

Jürgen's athletics career didn't last long either. He
liked the variety but where were the teammates? It
was all too lonely for him.

'Sorry!' he told his brother.

When his friends started playing handball, Jürgen

joined them. *Frisch Auf Göppingen* had a team in
Germany's top division. Perhaps he would become a
national star?

But no – Jürgen's handball career didn't last long
either. He liked the teamwork but where was the
footwork? He could kick a lot better than he could
throw.

'Sorry!' he told his friends.

Jürgen finally realised the lure of football when
West Germany stormed all the way to the 1972 final
of the UEFA European Football Championships, held
in Belgium. The seven-year-old boy watched every
game avidly on TV, especially the final against the
Soviet Union. It was so entertaining that, for once,
he was happy to stay indoors.

'Can you turn up the volume, please?' Jürgen
asked his dad. He wanted to hear the national
anthems and the roar of the crowd.

West Germany were simply unstoppable. Franz
Beckenbauer dribbled out of defence and passed to
Gerd Müller, who flicked it to Günter Netzer, who
volleyed the ball towards goal. His shot struck the

crossbar and bounced down to Jupp Heynckes. His shot was saved but Müller raced in for the rebound. 1–0!

'*Deutschland*! *Deutschland*!' Jürgen shouted from the sofa.

Siegfried was delighted to see his son enjoying himself so much. Jürgen's eyes were glued to the screen. In the second-half, Heynckes played a through-ball to Herbert Wimmer. 2–0!

'Yes, yes, YES!' Jürgen cried out, punching the air.

Then, Müller dropped deep to get the ball and dribbled forward. He passed to Heynckes and then kept running, right into the penalty area. Heynckes passed to Hans-Georg Schwarzenbeck, who passed back to Müller to complete a great team goal. 3–0!

At home in Göppingen, the Klinsmanns watched as Müller jumped up and down with his arms above his head, who then turned to share that fantastic scoring feeling with his teammates.

Jürgen's mind was made up. 'Yes, that's the sport for me!' he cheered.

CHAPTER 3

GINGEN'S GOAL MACHINE

Once Jürgen started playing football at TB Gingen, he couldn't stop. It took him a few weeks to learn all the rules but after that, he was flying. Like Gerd Müller in the national team, he was simply unstoppable.

'I can't believe we used to just chase the ball around like charging bulls,' he told his friends after training. 'What were we thinking? Real football is way more fun!'

There was one particular part of real football that Jürgen enjoyed most – scoring goals. Other players liked it, but he *loved* it. There was no feeling like it. Every time the ball crossed the line, he threw his arms up and bounced like his hero. Jürgen was born to be a striker.

The TB Gingen coaches were impressed. Only a week after his arrival, they handed him his debut. It was time for Jürgen to test his skills. He spent most of the match against FTSV Kuchen on the subs bench, but he didn't mind. It was a good chance for him to watch and learn. There was so much more to real football than just kicking and running.

'What's "offside"?' Jürgen asked one of the coaches as he warmed up.

'Don't worry, we'll work on that next week. Just enjoy yourself, kid!'

With ten minutes to go in the game, Jürgen took to the field, proudly wearing the TB Gingen's red and white shirt. His dad had arrived just in time to watch, after closing up the bakery.

'Go on, son!' Siegfried shouted from the sidelines.

On his debut, Jürgen barely touched the ball but he never stopped looking for it.

'Yes!' he called out eagerly as he sprinted towards goal.

Jürgen was desperate for that scoring feeling. He chased after everything – hopeful long balls, crosses, shots and back passes. The tired Kuchen defenders couldn't keep up with him. They tried to scare him with their height and strength but he wasn't backing down. He battled on bravely, right until the final whistle. Playing against opponents had really brought out his competitive streak.

'You've got spirit, kid!' the Gingen coach told him, patting him on the back. 'If we can channel all that energy into goals, you're going to be a superstar!'

One week later, Jürgen scored his first goal for the club against SV Altenstadt. It was the moment that he'd been waiting for – that fantastic scoring feeling. Touch, *BANG, GOOOOAAAALLLL!* As the ball crossed the line, he leapt into the air with his arms up like Müller.

'Well done, son!' his parents clapped and cheered.

Jürgen had certainly found his sport, and his skills were improving all the time, especially his shooting. It was all thanks to hours and hours of practice. Even at the age of nine, he had a special drive to succeed. He had one training session and one match each week for Gingen, but that was nowhere near enough football!

'Who wants a game?' he asked every day after

school, knocking on all the neighbours' doors until he'd found enough players.

On the rare occasions when his friends were busy, Jürgen would just kick a ball against a wall on his own instead. His technique was getting better and better.

Right foot, left foot, right foot, left foot...

It was the real matches, however, that Jürgen loved the most. He enjoyed challenging himself against the best defenders in the district. How good was he, and how good could he become? Plus, scoring in front of an audience was way more fun. He soon became Gingen's goal machine.

'How did it go?' his mum would ask when he got home from football.

'We won and I scored,' Jürgen replied, time after time.

He scored goals with his right foot, goals with his left foot, and goals with his head. He scored goal-mouth tap-ins, one-on-ones with the keeper, and long-range volleys too. Jürgen was just a natural-born finisher.

Gingen's tactics were simple but very successful – kick the ball over the top for Jürgen to chase. Against

their rivals Aichelberg, he found the net sixteen
times in one forty-minute match.

Touch, BANG, GOOOOAAAALLLL! Touch,
BANG, GOOOOAAAALLLL! Touch, BANG,
GOOOOAAAALLLL!

No-one in Göppingen had ever seen anything like it.

'That kid's going to be the next Müller!'

'He's like a smiling, blonde assassin!'

'Gingen are a one-boy team these days!'

Most strikers would have got carried away after
a hat-trick, but not Jürgen. He stayed calm and
composed throughout. There were no fancy, flashy
finishes – just strong, accurate strikes.

Most players would have slowed down after their
fifth goal, certainly by their tenth, but not Jürgen.
After his usual celebration, he just raced back for the
next restart. He always wanted more.

By the end of his first full season, Jürgen had
scored an incredible 106 goals in eighteen games.
With a record like that, word soon spread about
Gingen's goal machine.

CHAPTER 4

MORE GOALS FOR GEISLINGEN

In July 1974, just a few weeks before Jürgen's tenth birthday, West Germany won the World Cup for a second time. This time, the tournament was taking place right there on home soil. There were even games at the *Neckarstadion* in Stuttgart, less than an hour away from Göppingen. For Jürgen and his friends, this was so exciting.

'This is *our* World Cup!' they cheered joyfully.

Playing in the park, they pretended to be their heroes – Beckenbauer, Paul Breitner, Rainer Bonhof, Müller. Jürgen, of course, was always Müller. He watched his hero closely on TV and then tried to copy all his goals.

In the final in Munich, West Germany took
on Johan Cruyff's Netherlands. Late in the first
half, Bonhof dribbled down the right and crossed
to Müller. He controlled the ball and fired off a
quick shot before the Dutch defenders could block
it. Touch, *BANG, GOOOOAAAALLLL* – 2–1 to
Germany!

'*Deutschland! Deutschland!*' Jürgen shouted on
the sofa at home. He had a new goal to copy.

Before the 1974 World Cup, Jürgen had dreamed
of being a pilot when he was older. He loved the
idea of flying through the sky and travelling around
the world. But when Jürgen saw Beckenbauer
lift football's most famous trophy, he had a new
ambition.

'How cool would it be to play for my country?' he
said to himself.

Until then, Jürgen had only thought of football as
something that he did for fun, but what if he could
make that his career? He would still get to travel
around the world, but instead of flying planes, he
would be scoring goals.

Jürgen loved the sound of that. Now, he just needed to make his dream come true. The first step was finding a new club. He loved playing for Gingen, but he was in his comfort zone. He needed to get out of it and challenge himself at a higher level.

His neighbour Werner Gass was a promising youth player at SC Geislingen but in his spare time, he also coached their Under-12s team. It was a much bigger club than Gingen and it was only seven miles away. One day, Jürgen plucked up the courage to knock on Werner's front door.

'Hi there, how can I help?'

'I want to come and play for you,' the boy replied.

Werner smiled. 'Sure!'

Jürgen couldn't wait to get started. Geislingen trained three times a week and played matches every Saturday. That meant lots of extra football for him to enjoy.

At first, Werner drove him out to Geislingen for each session and then dropped him back home. That was easy, but when Werner became a professional footballer for VfB Stuttgart, Jürgen had to make his own travel plans. He rode his bike seven miles there and seven miles back, four times a week. It was a real test of his commitment, but nothing was going to stop him.

Ahead of Jürgen's first game for Geislingen, his dad gave him a good luck gift. It was a record book for writing down all his results and all his goals. On the first page, Siegfried had written a message to his son:

'Be honest in battle, humble in victory, and gracious in defeat.'

It was a message that Jürgen would never forget. He set about filling up the record book with his new footballing achievements. He proved that his goals for Gingen weren't a fluke; they kept on coming just as fast at Geislingen.

'How did it go?' his mum would ask when he got home.

'We won and I scored,' Jürgen replied, game after game.

Although he made the step-up look easy, there was lots of hard work behind it. Jürgen was always learning and looking for ways to improve. He watched as many matches as possible, from around Germany but also from Italy and England. Liverpool was his favourite team, with their quick, skilful attackers like Kevin Keegan and Kenny Dalglish.

As he followed their figures across the screen, Jürgen dared to dream. He was full of ambition. Others might be more talented, but no-one was more determined.

'Keep going!' Jürgen urged his teammates at all times. 'We fight until we fall!'

With that will to win, Geislingen hardly ever lost but when they did, Jürgen was devastated for days. He put absolutely everything into his performances out on the pitch. If he threw his kitbag down in the hallway and stormed upstairs, his parents knew that it was best to leave him alone for a little while.

Most of the time, however, it was all glory and goals. Geislingen won the Under-12 and Under-14 State Championships, with Jürgen scoring over 250 times in his four seasons at the club. His striker's instinct was growing stronger and stronger.

Touch, BANG, GOOOOAAAALLLL! Touch,

BANG, GOOOOAAAALLLL!

If there was a way to get the ball over the goal line, Jürgen would find it. Anything for that fantastic scoring feeling. He was simply unstoppable. At the age of thirteen, a regional newspaper even wrote an article about him called 'In Gerd Müller's Footsteps'.

What a headline! Jürgen, the article said, was 'as swift as an arrow, with dynamite in his legs'. The feature concluded: 'He's got a great future ahead of him.'

That future, however, would not be at Geislingen. Jürgen was destined for bigger and better things.

CHAPTER 5

MOVING TO STUTTGART

Stuttgart was less than an hour's drive from Göppingen but to Jürgen, it felt like a million miles away. Life was so different there. Jürgen was used to knowing every person and every place around him. How would he cope in a busy, industrial city with over 600,000 people?

He would soon find out because the Klinsmanns were moving to Stuttgart. Siegfried had bought a new house there with a bakery on the ground floor.

'This is a great opportunity for us,' he explained to his children enthusiastically. 'We'll have lots more customers here and we'll be able to expand the business. It's perfect!'

Jürgen was really pleased for his dad. It was the least he deserved after working so hard to look after the family. While the rest of them slept soundly in their warm beds, he stayed up all night, baking the bread, cakes and pastries for the next day. Jürgen really respected his dad's dedication, but he couldn't help worrying about what the change of location would mean for him.

'What's going to happen to my football career?' was his greatest concern.

As soon as Stuttgart's top youth clubs heard about the Klinsmann family's move, they were queuing up to sign Jürgen. They knew all about Geislingen's Goal Machine. He had terrorised their defences many times over the years.

'Come join us!' they urged him. 'We'll turn you into a superstar!'

Jürgen, however, wasn't yet ready to leave Geislingen behind. He had already moved to a new house and a new school; he didn't want to move to a new football team too.

'All my mates are there,' he told his dad, 'and

besides, we're the best team in the region!'

Siegfried listened carefully to his son. He knew that too much change could be hard for a child to deal with. Jürgen was fourteen now, and he was responsible enough to make his own decision.

'We just want you to be happy,' his dad told him. 'It's your choice.'

So, for the first six months, Jürgen chose to stay at Geislingen. Three times a week, he rushed out of school to make the long journey to practice. If there was time, he tried to catch the last train home to Stuttgart. If not, he had to stay over at a friend's house and catch the first train back in time for school the next day.

'It's worth it!' Jürgen kept telling himself. He was playing football with his best friends and he was banging in the goals for Geislingen. What more could he ask for?

The problem was that the travel was really starting to tire him out. Jürgen could barely stay awake in class, let alone do his homework on top. When his parents saw his school grades, they had to intervene.

'I'm sorry, son, but your education must come first,' his mum told him, firmly but fairly. 'We will never stop you from playing football, but you need to find a better place to do it.'

On that dreaded train ride, Jürgen passed lots of other clubs that were much closer to home. He was going to have to make new friends eventually, and football was the best way to do it. With all his goals, he'd be the most popular boy in Stuttgart in no time.

Geislingen were sad to see their superstar go but they understood. There was more to life than football.

'Good luck, kid,' the coaches said, shaking his hand. 'Just promise not to score against us next season, okay?'

Jürgen smiled. 'You know that I can't promise that!'

Geislingen, like Gingen, had become his comfort zone. It was time for a fresh start, but where? In the end, Jürgen chose the Stuttgarter Kickers, one of the teams that he had originally turned down. They hadn't given up on him and, as a tireless striker, he always admired persistence.

'Let's do this!' Jürgen told them.

From the very first training session, everyone made him feel really welcome: the Kickers coaches *and* the Kickers players. Jürgen saw straight away that this was a step forward for him, rather than a step sideways. It was a bigger club than Geislingen, with better training facilities and coaching methods. Even with his endless energy, Jürgen still found the fitness drills challenging.

'This was a smart move!' he told himself as he panted his way off the pitch.

Jürgen didn't need time to settle into his new surroundings. He was Mr Consistent. He could score goals anywhere; he could magic them out of nothing if he had to. In his first year, The Kickers won the State Championships.

Touch, BANG, GOOOOAAAALLLL! Everything Jürgen kicked seemed to turn to gold.

'This is just the start,' he told his triumphant teammates. 'Let's go on and win the national title now!'

CHAPTER 6

JUNIOR KICKER

During his first season in the Stuttgarter Kickers youth team, Jürgen often went along to the *Waldau-Stadion* to watch the seniors playing in the 2. Bundesliga, Germany's second division. The style of football wasn't always the prettiest but there was plenty of pace and power on show.

Even though Jürgen was only fourteen, he was already thinking ahead to playing at a higher level.

'That's where I want to play one day,' he told Horst, but his brother burst out laughing.

'The second division? Come on, you've got to aim higher than that!'

Secretly, Jürgen *was* aiming a lot higher than that.

His ultimate plan was to play at the highest level, for club and country, but he had to be realistic and take things one step at a time.

'Let's just wait and see,' he replied cautiously.

If Jürgen kept scoring goals and winning trophies as a junior Kicker, who knew what would happen next?

The answer to that question arrived in the post, a year later. 'There's a letter for you!' his mum called out when he got home from school.

The first thing that Jürgen noticed was the 'DFB' stamp on the envelope. Why was the West German Football Association writing to him? His hands were shaking with excitement as he opened it and read the magical words:

'Congratulations, you've been selected to play for the national youth team in Portugal.'

Jürgen read the letter five times, just to make sure, before he shared the wonderful news with his family. 'Mum! I'm going to play for West Germany!'

'What?' Martha screamed proudly. 'That's brilliant – well done you!'

Jürgen's dream was coming true. He was playing football and travelling the world at the same time. Portugal was a completely different country, where the people spoke a completely different language.

'I can't understand a single word!' Jürgen realised as he tried to listen into the conversations around him.

Every day, when his teammates went upstairs for an afternoon rest, Jürgen snuck outside to explore. The sea glistened in the sun and the water looked so inviting. He couldn't stop staring at the spectacular sight.

At first, the West Germany youth coach Berti Vogts was worried about Jürgen's bold behaviour.

'Just don't go far, okay?'

'I won't!' he promised his manager. With his blonde hair and big smile, Jürgen bounced off to the beach.

The trip to Portugal wasn't a holiday, however. As always, Jürgen was totally focused on football. He wanted to win and make his country proud. On the pitch, West Germany beat Switzerland, but lost to Spain and the Netherlands. Although Jürgen didn't score any goals, he learnt a lot from the experience. The path to the top looked clearer in the distance. He could see what he needed to work on to reach the highest level.

'I'm going to get there!' he promised himself.

Jürgen returned to Stuttgart feeling more determined than ever. He was a West German youth international now, and after that first taste of football travel, he wanted more. Where next?

Later that year, the junior Kickers visited the Netherlands for a big competition against clubs from Italy, Spain, France and Denmark. Jürgen loved every second of it. If there was that much noise and atmosphere at a European youth tournament, what would a real World Cup be like? He could only imagine the fantastic scoring feeling.

Jürgen was disappointed to lose in the semi-finals but at least he finished as his team's top scorer with seven goals in six games. His striker's instinct was back with a bang.

Touch, BANG, GOOOOAAAALLLL! Touch, BANG, GOOOOAAAALLLL!

Where other youngsters felt pressure, Jürgen saw opportunity and adventure. Tournament football was so exciting – one touch, one moment, could change everything.

'What's not to love about that?' he laughed.

As his sixteenth birthday drew near, Jürgen was the talk of the Stuttgarter Kickers Football Club. He had smashed all of their junior scoring records and he was showing no signs of slowing down. In football, a natural finisher was the most prized possession of all. Jürgen was going to be Germany's next big thing and the Kickers really didn't want to lose him to another team.

'What are we waiting for?' one coach argued. 'We need to show him how much we care. I know we can't sign him properly until he turns eighteen but we can still agree a deal now!'

Jürgen had a big decision to make.

CHAPTER 7

SENIOR KICKER

Was he ready to commit to a career in football? That was Jürgen's life ambition, but it still felt like a big and scary step. Although everything was going well so far, his fortunes could change in an instant. There were so many young Germans chasing the same dream. Surely, not everyone could achieve it.

What if he got an injury?

What if a new manager didn't like him?

What if he stopped scoring goals?

That was hard to imagine but Jürgen didn't want to take the risk. Was he just going to give up on his dreams of becoming a pilot? He didn't want to leave school at the age of fifteen; he wanted to keep learning. He had always planned to go to college, but he couldn't do that *and* become a professional footballer at the same time.

'What should I do?' he asked his dad in desperation.

Siegfried was torn too. He believed in his son's footballing talent, but that wouldn't last long – maybe fifteen years if he was really lucky. A good education, on the other hand, would set him up for life. Surely, there was a way that Jürgen could have the best of both worlds?

'Here's an idea,' his dad suggested eventually. 'You could sign for the Kickers and do a part-time apprenticeship with me at the bakery. That way, if the football stuff doesn't work out, you'll still have a useful qualification.'

Perfect! Jürgen already knew lots about baking. It was the family business, after all.

Siegfried didn't go easy on his new apprentice. Jürgen wasn't a football superstar yet and so he had to do what he was told. That meant waking up in the middle of the night to start making the bread, cakes and pastries for the next day. After a short rest and a

bite of breakfast, it was then time for Jürgen to go off
to football training.

'Play well!' his dad would shout before he left
'*Bäckerei Klinsmann*' each morning.

Those were long days for Jürgen, but the hard
work was all worthwhile. Within weeks, he was
called up to train with the Kickers' first-team squad.
Jürgen couldn't believe it; he was definitely out of
his comfort zone now. A sixteen-year-old practising
with all the experienced professionals? It was almost
unheard of!

'I can do this!' he muttered under his breath as he
arrived for his first day.

Jürgen was nervous about being the new kid
again, and this time, he was the new kid amongst
men. He was desperate to impress but next to the
big, strong defenders, he still looked like a little
boy. His skinny shoulders didn't stand a chance. As
bravely as he battled, the centre-backs pushed him
off the ball so easily. At the end of his first senior
practice, Jürgen trudged off the field, feeling very
disheartened.

'Hey, you did well out there,' said the Kickers coach Slobodan Čendić, putting an arm around his shoulder.

'No, I didn't, I was awful,' Jürgen moaned. 'I'll never be able to compete with the first-team players!'

'Of course you will!' Čendić replied. 'Those guys were all your age once. You're still growing and building up your muscle and confidence. Don't be hard on yourself. I know you, you're not a quitter. Get some sleep and I'll see you back here tomorrow!

No, Jürgen wasn't a quitter. He returned the next day, and the next day and the day after that. He just had to believe in himself and make the most of his many talents – his speed, his clever movement, his striker's instinct.

Touch, BANG, GOOOOAAAALLLL! Touch, BANG, GOOOOAAAALLLL!

'That's the striker we know and love!' the coach shouted as Jürgen strolled off the training field with his head held high.

Jürgen was on his way to the top, one determined step at a time. First, he completed his baking

41

qualification, and then he forced his way into the Kickers match-day squad.

At the *Waldau-Stadion* against SC Freiburg, he sat on the bench, watching and hoping for a run-out at the end – ten minutes, maybe even fifteen if they were winning comfortably. But when Milomir Jakovljević hobbled off injured in the middle of the first half, Čendić called for Jürgen.

'Me?' Jürgen thought to himself in shock. He couldn't believe it. On his senior debut, Jürgen was going to play sixty-five whole minutes!

'Good luck, kid,' the manager told him on the touchline. 'Run your socks off and show them what you're made of!'

Jürgen nodded eagerly; he could definitely do that. With his proud parents cheering in the crowd, he became the Kickers' youngest ever player at the age of seventeen. What an achievement! Even a 2–1 defeat couldn't dampen his spirits.

'So, how did it feel?' his dad asked afterwards.

Jürgen beamed brightly. 'It was so much fun!'

With the Kickers sitting safely in mid-table,

Čendić kept giving his young star game-time – ten minutes one week, thirty minutes the next. It was an amazing opportunity for Jürgen, but he was determined to make it count.

When he came on against SG Wattenscheid 09, the Kickers were already winning 5–1. Jürgen knew that he wouldn't get a better chance to put his name on the scoresheet.

Touch, BANG, GOOOOAAAALLLL!

He raced over to the fans in the corner with his mouth wide open and his arms up above his head. As they clapped and cheered, he bounced up and down like an excited little boy.

Jürgen was off the mark and, yes, that fantastic scoring feeling was even better in professional football.

CHAPTER 8

SPRINTING TOWARDS SUCCESS

Jürgen hoped that the 1982–83 season would be his big breakthrough. With Čendić's support, he was going to shoot his way from the subs bench to the starting line-up, and the rest would be history.

That was the plan, but it didn't work out that way. The Kickers hired a new manager, Jürgen Sundermann, and he wasn't so interested in developing young talent. Jürgen and Jürgen didn't get along. Even when the manager gave him a chance, he had to play out of position.

'No, no, no, you're not a winger!' Berti Vogts argued, shaking his head. He was now Jürgen's coach for the West Germany Under-21s and he didn't like to see top talent going to waste. 'You're a striker!'

But Jürgen only scored three times all season for the Kickers. Where had his striker's instinct gone? He was no longer the goal machine that he used to be, and that was worrying.

Jürgen hoped the arrival of another new manager, Horst Buhtz, might turn things around. But when Buhtz selected his first Kickers team, Jürgen's name wasn't there, not even on the bench. Jürgen was shocked and confused.

'What am I doing wrong?' he asked everyone he knew. 'How can I improve?'

It was his brother Horst who came up with an answer. From decathlon days, Horst knew a lot about running and he had spotted something about Jürgen's style.

'You lose so much speed towards the end of matches,' Horst explained to his brother. 'As soon as you get tired, your technique is all over the place. With all that wasted energy, it's no wonder that you're not scoring goals. What you need is some sprinting lessons!'

Jürgen was willing to try anything to get better. He asked his brother to introduce him to yet another Horst – Horst Allman, his old athletics coach.

'Right, let's see how fast you are at the moment,' Allman asked at their first secret session on the race-track.

Jürgen didn't want the Kickers to know about his extra training. With his skinny limbs swinging, he ran the 100 metres in 12.0 seconds.

'Not bad,' his new coach muttered, 'but we can make you a lot faster than that. If you're ready, let's get started!'

Yes, Jürgen was ready. On top of all his training sessions with the Kickers, he worked hard with Horst on his upper body strength and his running technique. With a stronger, smoother sprinting style, he would be able to escape from defenders with ease, all game long.

11.7, 11.5, 11.3 – month after month, his 100 metre time got quicker and quicker.

'Not bad,' Horst muttered every time, looking down at his stopwatch, 'but you can still do better!'

Jürgen kept pushing himself. He wasn't giving up on his dream without a fight. Finally, a year later, he achieved his target. He ran the 100 metres in 11.0 seconds, a whole second faster.

'Yes, yes, YES!' Jürgen cheered, jumping up and down on the finish line.

He was now ready to show off his new speed on the football field. His coaches noticed the difference straight away. 'Wow, you're flying out there!' they applauded.

After the false start of the 1982–83 season, Jürgen's big breakthrough occurred the following season instead. He was a man on a mission. He fought his way into Buhtz's starting line-up and proved himself as the Kickers' new Number 9. His striker's instinct was back. Rather than fading away towards the end of matches, he now burst into life in the box. Jürgen made those last twenty minutes his favourite scoring spell. His tired opponents didn't stand a chance.

Touch, BANG, GOOOOAAAALLLL! Touch, BANG, GOOOOAAAALLLL! Touch, BANG, GOOOOAAAALLLL!

However, while Jürgen was firing, the Kickers were struggling. Halfway through the season, they found themselves deep in a relegation dogfight.

'If we finish in the Top Ten, I'll take you all on a trip to Florida,' the club president Alex Dünnwald-Metzler promised his players.

Jürgen already had an amazing will to win but the Florida trip just added to his hunger. He had always dreamed of going on an American adventure.

'Come on, we can do this!' Jürgen told his teammates. The Kickers' young star striker was ready to save the day. He was sprinting towards success.

Touch, BANG, GOOOOAAAALLLL! Touch, BANG, GOOOOAAAALLLL! Touch, BANG, GOOOOAAAALLLL!

Jürgen finished the season with nineteen goals and the Kickers finished eighth.

'Florida, here we come!' the players cheered happily.

CHAPTER 9

STUTTGARTER TO STUTTGART

Stuttgarter and Stuttgart – the two team names were almost identical, and their stadiums were less than five miles apart. The gap in football quality, however, was much bigger than that.

Stuttgarter Kickers had been playing in Germany's second division for over twenty years, in front of 11,000 fans. *Die Blauen*, 'The Blues', had got used to living in the shadow of their more successful neighbours.

VfB Stuttgart played in the Bundesliga, Germany's top division, in front of 60,000 fans. And not just that; *Die Roten*, 'The Reds', had just become Champions of Germany for the third time.

Although 'The Blues' and 'The Reds' were big rivals, moving up to the Bundesliga was a prospect that every Kicker dreamed of. Few actually achieved it but in 1984, Jürgen became one of the lucky few.

After winning the Bundesliga title, Stuttgart were looking to strengthen their strikeforce for the next season. They had lots of goalscorers in their squad but no natural poachers, no classic Number 9s. Their scouts searched and searched until they spotted someone who fitted the bill perfectly - a skinny blonde twenty-year-old who had just scored 19 goals in 2. Bundesliga.

'The best part is – he's just down the road, playing for The Blues!'

Stuttgart and Stuttgarter agreed a transfer fee of £108,000 but at first, Jürgen didn't want to go.

'I can't do it to the fans,' he told Dünnwald-Metzler. 'I said that I would never sign for The Reds. I can't go back on my promise. They'll hate me forever!'

The club president smiled. 'You're an honest kid, so I'm going to be honest with you. This is your big chance and you might not get another one. You're too good for this league and you're ready to play at a higher level. Who cares if it's for our rivals? At least you'll be staying here in Stuttgart!'

'Really, you think I should go for it?' Jürgen asked.

'Absolutely!' Dünnwald-Metzler laughed. 'If it was me, I wouldn't even think about it. Go and do us proud!'

As soon as Jürgen signed his contract, he started preparing himself for the next step in his football journey. He had watched enough German football to know that the players in the top division were much faster and stronger. He needed to up his game and there was always room for improvement. The sprint work with Allman had shown him that.

'I want to be super fit before I even arrive for preseason training,' Jürgen told his brother Horst. 'It might make all the difference!'

Horst couldn't help admiring his brother's focus and determination. 'Just don't tire yourself out before you even kick a ball!' he warned.

The extra work certainly paid off. Jürgen wore

the Number 11 shirt for Stuttgart's first game of the season and he never looked back. In his first home game against Eintracht Braunschweig, Jürgen scored twice in a 6–1 thrashing.

Touch, *BANG, GOOOOAAAALLLL*! Touch, *BANG, GOOOOAAAALLLL*!

He celebrated each goal with the pure passion of someone who had battled all the way from the bottom to the top.

'This is where I belong!' he cried out to his teammate Karl Allgöwer.

Playing in the Bundesliga was even better than Jürgen had expected – the noise, the excitement, the emotion.

'I love it!' he told Dünnwald-Metzler. 'Thanks for telling me to go.'

'My pleasure,' the Stuttgarter manager replied. 'Your transfer fee helped us to pay the bills!'

The Stuttgart fans loved Jürgen from day one. They loved his energy and his attitude. He didn't stop chasing goals until the final whistle, even when the team was losing.

'That's it, Klinsi!' they cheered. 'I wish our other players would work that hard.'

Stuck in mid-table, Stuttgart won then lost, lost then won, but Jürgen was Mr Consistent throughout the season. He finished with fifteen goals in thirty-two matches, only four behind Karl as the team's top scorer.

'Not bad for your first season,' his brother, Horst, congratulated him.

'Yeah but I can do better next season!' Jürgen replied confidently.

Away at Fortuna Düsseldorf, Michael Spies gave Stuttgart the lead. After that, however, it became the Klinsmann Show.

Jürgen volleyed past the keeper with his right foot. 2–0!

Jürgen tapped in with his left foot. 3–0!

Jürgen jumped high for a header at the back post. 4–0!

Jürgen dribbled all the way from the halfway line and scored with his right foot. 5–0!

Jürgen dribbled all the way from the halfway line

and scored with his left foot. 6–0!

Five goals in one game! It was like the glory days at Gingen all over again. Jürgen celebrated his first three with his usual excitement but after that, it was just too tiring. For his fourth, he walked back with his arm up in the air. For his fifth, he fell to his knees and roared at the sky.

With Jürgen on fire, Stuttgart made it to the semi-final of the DFB-Pokal, the German Cup. Their opponents, Borussia Dortmund, had no chance. Jürgen collected the ball in the penalty area and poked it through the goalkeeper's legs. Nutmeg!

Goooooooooooooooooooaaaaaaaaaaaaaaaaalllllllllllll llllllllllllllll!!!!!!!!!!!!!!!!!!!

In the last minute, Jürgen turned the Dortmund defender and shot into the bottom corner.

Goooooooooooooooooooaaaaaaaaaaaaaaaaalllllllllllll llllllllllllllll!!!!!!!!!!!!!!!!!!!

Stuttgart were into the 1986 cup final, against the German champions Bayern Munich. It was Jürgen's first final as a professional footballer, the biggest match of his career so far. Could he carry on his great goalscoring form?

'We've got nothing to fear today, guys!' captain Karl encouraged his teammates before kick-off. 'If we play well, we can beat anyone.'

'Anyone!' they yelled back.

Jürgen felt really fired up as he walked out onto the pitch at the *Olympiastadion* in Berlin. He had already come so far since his move from Stuttgarter Kickers but there was still so much that he wanted to achieve. A first major trophy was top of his list.

Stuttgart started well but Bayern were clever and composed. They defended patiently and then caught their opponents out on the counter-attack, once and then twice. As Stuttgart heads began to drop, the German champions took full advantage. After sixty-five minutes, Bayern were 4–0 up.

'Don't give up!' Jürgen shouted.

Even if his team wasn't going to win, he still wanted to score in the final. With five minutes to go, Jürgen got his chance and he took it brilliantly.

He dribbled into the penalty area, beat the Bayern centre-back and slid the ball past the goalkeeper.

Goooooooooooooooooooaaaaaaaaaaaaaaaaaallllllllllll lllllllllllll!!!!!!!!!!!!!!!!!!!!! This time, Jürgen didn't celebrate at all. What was there to cheer about? Stuttgart were still 5–2 down. He just walked back to the halfway line and got on with the game.

Only after the final whistle, when he stopped running around, did Jürgen let his emotions show. As he trudged off the pitch, he cried and cried. He couldn't help it – he cared so much, and he hated losing.

Jürgen didn't know it then, but he would soon get his revenge on Bayern.

CHAPTER 10

BICYCLE KICK VS BAYERN

Fifteen league goals in one season, then sixteen in the next, then sixteen again – Jürgen really was West Germany's Mr Consistent. As the 1987–88 season started, however, he set his sights a little higher.

'My scoring record is good but "good" isn't getting me into the national team,' he told Karl. 'I'm twenty-three now and I want to get noticed!'

A hat-trick against Borussia Mönchengladbach was the perfect place to start. Touch, *BANG*, *GOOOOAAAALLLL*! Jürgen wasn't just a great goalscorer, though. He had skills that he wanted to show off. When he got the ball, he nutmegged one defender and then used his speed to dribble past two more. On the edge of the penalty area, a fourth defender slid in for the tackle and Jürgen nutmegged him too! His finish was calm and right in the corner.

Goooooooooooooooooooaaaaaaaaaaaaaaaaalllllllllllll llllllllllllll!!!!!!!!!!!!!!!!!!!

'I hope you're watching!' Jürgen wanted to scream to Franz Beckenbauer, the manager of West Germany. But instead, he let his feet do the talking.

And his head. Against Bayer Leverkusen, Jürgen jumped high at the back post to score his first goal and then dived low at the front post to score his second. He was developing into the complete striker. He was now capable of every kind of goal – tap-ins, headers, mazy dribbles, one-on-ones and volleys.

Jürgen could use his amazing leap to score acrobatic goals with his feet too. He had already been impressive and ingenious on that front. In 1985 against 1. FC Köln, the ball flew towards him in the crowded box. It was slightly behind him, so he couldn't head it. What else could he do? In a flash, he swivelled his body to the side and volleyed it in.

'What a goal!' Ásgeir Sigurvinsson yelled as Jürgen

raced away, swinging his right arm in the air.

A year later, Jürgen repeated his trick against
Werder Bremen and this time, his strike was
even more spectacular. He was so excited that he
celebrated with a forward roll! His technique was
getting better and better, as Bayern Munich would
soon find out.

In November 1987, the giants of Germany arrived
at the *Neckarstadion* feeling as confident as ever.
Bayern had beaten Stuttgart in the cup final and they
were going to do it again in the league. 'Easy!' they
thought.

However, Jürgen and his teammates hadn't
forgotten about that cup final defeat. They were out
for revenge in front of a big home crowd.

'Those Bayern players aren't going to know what's
hit them!' captain Karl roared in the dressing room.

If Jürgen wanted Beckenbauer to notice him, he
needed to do something special in a big game like
this. He sprinted around the pitch, hunting for a
chance to score. He was even more determined than
usual.

'That's it, Klinsi!' the fans cheered for their hero. 'Get us a goal!'

Stuttgart dominated the game from the very start. In the eighteenth minute, Ásgeir chipped a long diagonal pass from left to right. As it landed, Günther Schäfer decided to cross it first time on the volley. Jürgen was waiting in the penalty area, eager and alert.

The ball looped high into the air and dropped down just behind Jürgen. He had to think fast and use his striker's instinct. What was the best way to get the ball into the goal? If he swivelled his body to the side like he did against 1. FC Köln and Werder Bremen, the angle would be all wrong.

'It's more likely to hit the corner flag than the back of the net!' he thought to himself.

Rather than 90 degrees, Jürgen turned a full 180 degrees. If he got the bicycle kick wrong, it would be really embarrassing, but if he got it right, it would be really exciting.

'Why not? I have to try!' he convinced himself.

Every striker dreamed of scoring a goal like that.

Jürgen had been practising bicycle kicks in training since he was eight years old. It was time to test his talent at the top level.

With his back to goal, Jürgen sprung up with his amazing leap and swung his right foot towards the ball. The timing was perfect and so was the connection. The brilliant bicycle kick flew into the top corner.

Goooooooooooooooooooaaaaaaaaaaaaaaaaallllllllllll llllllllllllll!!!!!!!!!!!!!!!!!!!!

The Bayern goalkeeper and defenders just stood and watched in awe. What had just happened?

Jürgen, however, was off, running towards the frenzied fans behind the goal with his fists pumping. 'Come on!' he screamed.

What a moment! Jürgen felt on top of the world. He had scored a big goal in a big game, and it wasn't just any big goal. It was a goal that German football fans kept talking about, a goal that German TV channels kept replaying. It even won Germany's Best Goal of the Season award.

Stuttgart won the match 3–0 and before the final

whistle, their Number 9 did another extraordinary thing. Bayern's defender Norbert Nachtweih was already on a yellow card when he fouled Jürgen with a clumsy tackle. As the referee reached into his pocket for the red card, Jürgen rushed over, shaking his finger. He hadn't forgotten his dad's message – 'Be honest in battle, humble in victory, and gracious in defeat'.

'No, it wasn't that bad,' he argued. 'Don't send him off!'

The referee was amazed by the sportsmanship and so were the fans. 'Good on you, Klinsi!' they cheered. Jürgen was the ideal leader for the new German generation – hard-working, talented and fair.

'I just hope Beckenbauer was watching today!' Jürgen told his brother with a smile.

CHAPTER 11

GAME-TIME FOR WEST GERMANY

Only a month after that bicycle kick against Bayern Munich, Jürgen got the great news he'd been hoping for. West Germany's two main strikers, Rudi Völler and Klaus Allofs, were missing for the friendlies against Brazil and Argentina. Who else was scoring goals in Germany? The manager Franz Beckenbauer called up two replacements: Werder Bremen's Frank Ordenewitz and Stuttgart's star Number 9, Jürgen Klinsmann.

'I'm in the national squad!' Jürgen proudly announced to his family at the bakery.

'Son, that's excellent,' his dad replied. 'Congratulations!'

'Finally!' his brother Horst said with a smile. 'Why did it take them so long?'

Jürgen wasn't nervous about making his international debut. He was twenty-three years old, not seventeen, and he had already played for the Under-16s and the Under-21s. This was just the next step. His brother was right; he had earned his place in the West Germany squad, and now he had to go on and earn a starting spot. Plus, he was off on another exciting adventure. First Portugal, then North America – and now South America.

'I can do this!' Jürgen told himself as he met up with his new international teammates.

He knew Eike Immel and Guido Buchwald from Stuttgart and he had played against the others in the Bundesliga for years. Everyone was very friendly and supportive.

'What was that, Klinsi?' the captain Lothar Matthäus teased during training. 'Scoring goals is meant to be your job!'

When it came to matchday, Jürgen started up front, with Frank on the bench.

Right from kick-off, he made life as difficult as possible for the defenders. When Brazil had the ball, Jürgen chased after it like a dog chasing a stick. When West Germany had the ball, he was always on the move, calling for it.

Jürgen battled, dribbled, jumped and intercepted. In fact, the only thing he didn't do was score. Batista got the goal for Brazil, and Stefan Reuter got the goal for Germany. As the cross came in, Jürgen rose highest to win the header. He knocked it down and after a goalmouth scramble, Stefan scored.

'Yes!' Jürgen shouted, leaping into the air again.

'Great work, guys!' Lothar cheered, hugging both of West Germany's key players.

At the final whistle, Jürgen was exhausted. He had worked so hard for his country, but had he done enough to keep his place against Argentina?

Yes! Against the World Champions, he was back to do it all again. Jürgen battled, dribbled, jumped and intercepted. The only difference this time was that Argentina scored, and West Germany didn't. Diego Maradona burst down the left and crossed to

Jorge Burruchaga. 1–0! Jürgen did his best to rescue Germany but Argentina's big sweeper José Luis Brown kept barging him off the ball.

'Stay on your feet!' the referee told him when he tried to complain.

Although Jürgen was disappointed with the result, Beckenbauer certainly wasn't disappointed with his striker's performance.

'You battled really bravely out there,' his manager told him. 'I'm impressed!'

Even when Rudi and Klaus returned, Jürgen stayed in the West Germany squad. Frank Ordenewitz, on the other hand, never played for the national team again.

'How was it?' Horst asked when his brother returned home.

'It was fun,' Jürgen replied, 'but I won't feel happy until I score!'

Against Switzerland, Lothar sent a long ball over the top and Jürgen chased on to it. As it bounced, he held off the defender and lifted his shot over the diving keeper.

Goooooooooooooooooooooaaaaaaaaaaaaaaaaalllllllllllll lllllllllllllll!!!!!!!!!!!!!!!!!!!!

Jürgen stumbled to the floor and crawled to the edge of the pitch on his knees. He had scored for his country! He pumped his fists and raised them high above his head. His smile didn't fade for hours.

'Great finish, Klinsi!' Lothar shouted as they celebrated together.

Thanks to that goal, Jürgen's summer soon got very busy. First, he represented his nation at Euro 1988. The tournament took place at home in West Germany, but it still felt like a big adventure. Jürgen couldn't wait to test himself against the top nations from all over Europe.

He started every single game as one half of his country's new star strikeforce.

Against Denmark, Rudi passed and Jürgen scored.

'Thanks!' Jürgen said as they hugged.

Against Spain, Jürgen passed and Rudi scored.

'Thanks!' Rudi said as they hugged.

West Germany cruised through the group stage and into the semi-finals, where they faced the

Netherlands. It started well. Jürgen dribbled all the way into the Dutch box, where he was fouled by Frank Rijkaard. Penalty! Lothar stepped up and scored.

'Come on, let's win this!' Jürgen screamed out passionately.

After that, however, Marco van Basten stole the show and broke West German hearts. At the final whistle, Jürgen stood there with his head in his hands, trying hard not to cry. He had given everything and he had truly believed that his team would go all the way to glory.

'Not this time, Klinsi,' Beckenbauer reassured him, 'but you'll get other chances, I promise.'

Two months later, Jürgen had another football adventure to enjoy and this time, he got to travel a long way from home again. He was selected for the West Germany squad for the Summer Olympics in South Korea.

'Wow, this is going to be awesome!' Jürgen told his teammate Thomas Häßler as they arrived in South Korea's busy capital city, Seoul.

Jürgen hadn't played at a World Cup before but surely the atmosphere couldn't get any better than the Olympics? Everywhere they went, there was so much colour, excitement and national pride.

Come on, Australia!

We love you, Kenya!

Russia! Russia!

USA! USA!

Jürgen watched as many of the track and field events as he could. 'Horst would love this!' he thought to himself. His friend, Dieter Baumann, was competing in the 5000 metres race.

'Go on, Dieter!' Jürgen cheered loudly in the stadium as he raced home to a silver medal.

Next, it was the footballers' turn to try and win a medal for West Germany. Jürgen was determined to make his country proud.

'If Dieter can do it, so can we!' he told his new strike partner, Frank Mill.

Frank responded by scoring two goals against China and another against Tunisia. West Germany qualified for the quarter-finals with two wins out of three, but Jürgen was far from satisfied.

'I haven't got a single goal yet,' he moaned to Thomas. He was meant to be Mr Consistent in the penalty area.

'Don't worry, there's still plenty of time for you to score!' Thomas replied.

Against Zambia, Jürgen finally found the net and it was all thanks to Thomas. He intercepted a pass and slid the ball through to his striker. Jürgen fooled the last defender with a clever dummy and then fired a shot past the goalkeeper.

Goooooooooooooooooooooaaaaaaaaaaaaaaaaalllllllllllll llllllllllllllll!!!!!!!!!!!!!!!!!!!!!

At last! Jürgen punched the air and jumped for joy. Now, he really felt part of West Germany's Olympic success.

'Will you please stop moaning now?' Thomas laughed as they celebrated together.

Jürgen shook his head and smiled. 'No way, one goal isn't enough. I need more!'

Just before half time, Frank set him up for his second and in the last minute of the match, Jürgen stole the ball off a Zambia defender and completed his hat-trick. Touch, *BANG, GOOOOAAAALLLL!*

'Okay fine, I'll stop moaning now!' he told Thomas.

In the semi-finals, West Germany faced Jürgen's first-ever international opponents, Brazil. He was up against the tournament's other star striker, Romário. Who would take their team towards Olympic glory? After the disappointment of Euro 88, Jürgen was desperate to reach the final.

West Germany took the lead but Romário equalised for Brazil. The match went to extra-time and then to penalties. With the pressure on, Jürgen didn't shy away. 'I'll take one,' he told his manager Hannes Löhr.

Jürgen ran from the edge of the area and struck the ball low and hard. The goalkeeper dived the wrong way, but the ball bounced off the post and went wide. *Advantage to Brazil!*

With his hands on his hips, Jürgen stared down at the grass in shock. 'How did I miss that?' he kept asking himself.

His dream of Olympic Gold was over. Now, the best West Germany could win was Bronze, but any medal was better than no medal. Jürgen was eager to bounce back as quickly as possible. It only took five minutes. Frank raced down the right wing and crossed for his strike partner to score.

Goooooooooooooooooooaaaaaaaaaaaaaaaalllllllllllll lllllllllllll!!!!!!!!!!!!!!!!!!!

'Thanks!' Jürgen said with relief, giving Frank a high-five.

West Germany beat Italy 3–0 to claim the Olympic Bronze Medal. Jürgen was pleased and proud, but still never satisfied. He set his sights on winning the next big international tournament – the 1990 World Cup.

CHAPTER 12

EUROPEAN DREAMS

By the start of the 1988–89 club season, Jürgen
was a national hero. He won the West Germany
Footballer of the Year award for his performances at
the Euros and the Olympics.

'We love you, Klinsi!' the fans told their all-action,
all-effort Number 9.

Jürgen was overwhelmed with pride and joy.
What an honour! He was living out his two dreams
at the same time – footballer and explorer.

For West Germany, he travelled around the world,
playing in North America, South America, Asia and
beyond.

And for Stuttgart, he travelled around Europe,

playing in Hungary, Yugoslavia, the Netherlands and beyond.

Jürgen usually had a few hours in an unfamiliar place to be a tourist but football was, of course, the focus. The Reds were gunning for UEFA Cup glory and to achieve it, they needed his goals. Mr Consistent didn't let his team down. Jürgen scored one against Dinamo Zagreb in the second round, and then two against FC Groningen in the third round.

'Come on, there's no reason why we can't go all the way this year!' he cheered.

Stuttgart had never won a European trophy before but round after round, they got closer and closer. Although Jürgen didn't play in the quarter-final against Spanish side Real Sociedad, he was there in the crowd to cheer his team on. When it went to penalties, he could barely watch.

'Maybe it's a good thing I'm not out there!' Jürgen admitted, thinking back to his Olympic miss against Brazil.

Thankfully, Stuttgart won the shoot-out to set up a significant semi-final against Dynamo Dresden. It was

West Germany versus East Germany, the two halves of the same country, which were then still divided by the Berlin Wall.

Jürgen had made the journey to East Germany many times before to visit his grandparents. However, going there to play a big football match felt very different. With TV cameras everywhere and so much talk of politics, it was hard for the Stuttgart players to focus on the game.

'Don't even think about the draw tonight,' their manager Arie Haan told them. They were 1–0 up from the home leg. 'Let's win!'

There was a loud, tense atmosphere in the *Dynamo-Stadion*. The Dresden fans greeted them with boos, whistles and jeers, while the players greeted them with kicks, pushes and shirt-pulls. Up front, Jürgen was fouled again and again but he never gave up.

'Pass it!' he called out.

As he got the ball with his back to goal, a defender barged into him and clipped his ankle. Free kick! Jürgen bravely stood in the middle of the Dresden wall, causing trouble. At the last moment, he moved out of the way and Karl Allgöwer's shot flew into the bottom corner. 1–0! When the bruising battle came to an end, Stuttgart were the winners.

'We're in the UEFA Cup final!' Jürgen shouted with his arm around his goalkeeper, Eike Immel.

Their opponents would be Napoli, the Italian club captained by the amazing Diego Maradona. Jürgen had already faced Maradona once before, when West Germany played Argentina.

'Trust me, that guy is a genius!' he warned his teammates ahead of the first leg in Italy.

Stuttgart took the lead but Maradona and his Brazilian strike partner, Careca, eventually proved too hot to handle.

'It's not over yet!' Jürgen argued on the journey home. 'It's only 2–1 and we've got the away goal.'

At home at the *Neckarstadion*, they had 60,000 Stuttgart fans cheering them on. Unfortunately, Maradona stole the show before the match even kicked off. While Jürgen and his teammates went through a serious warm-up, the little Argentine decided to put on a juggling show. Head, shoulders, knees and toes – he didn't let the ball drop once. The crowd loved it and soon even the Stuttgart players stopped to watch.

'Look, he hasn't even done his laces up!' Karl pointed out.

As impressive as Maradona's display was, Stuttgart needed to ignore it. 'Come on, focus!' Jürgen called out.

This time, it was Napoli who took the lead and Stuttgart who needed to fight back. Where could they get a goal from? As the corner came in from the right, Jürgen lost his marker at the back post. Now, he just needed to get the contact right, both powerful and accurate. With a strong push of the neck, he headed the ball into the top corner.

Gooooooooooooooooooooaaaaaaaaaaaaaaaaalllllllllllll lllllllllllllll!!!!!!!!!!!!!!!!!!!! Jürgen raced over to the corner flag with his arms up like a champion. He had scored two goals in two finals.

'Come on!' he roared.

Sadly, however, Stuttgart couldn't complete the

comeback. At the final whistle, Napoli were the new UEFA Cup Champions.

Slowly, Jürgen made his way off the pitch and down the tunnel. It was so disappointing to get so close to glory.

'Next time I get to a final, I'm going to make sure I win it!' he promised himself.

But would Jürgen get to another final if he stayed at Stuttgart? It was a surprising person who answered that question for him.

'I think it's time for you to move on,' manager Arie Haan admitted in private a few days after the UEFA Cup defeat.

Jürgen was shocked to hear his manager speak so truthfully. 'What do you mean? Are you trying to get rid of me?' he asked.

Haan laughed. 'No, if you leave, I'll probably lose my job! I'm just giving you my honest advice. You're ready to raise your game to the next level. Here in Germany, you're comfortable and when it comes to football, comfortable is bad. I know you – you need a new challenge!'

After five successful seasons at Stuttgart, Jürgen was definitely in his comfort zone again. He was ready for a new challenge. He had proven himself as one of the Bundesliga's most consistent strikers but so far, he had no trophies to show for it, other than a top goalscorer award.

That wasn't enough for Jürgen. He always wanted more.

CHAPTER 13

ADVENTURE NUMBER ONE: ITALY

It was time to start something new, but where would Jürgen go? What about Bayern Munich, the champions of Germany?

'No, I want an adventure!' he decided.

Jürgen wanted to learn a new language and experience a new culture. Ever since that first trip to Portugal at the age of fifteen, he had dreamed of playing football in other countries. He was now nearly twenty-five and he might not get a better chance to explore the world.

The top European clubs were queuing up to buy Jürgen. A guaranteed goalscorer was hard to find and as precious as gold. In the end, Jürgen chose Italy.

Why? Because Ruud Gullit told him to.

Before the Euro 88 semi-final between West Germany and the Netherlands, the Dutch star had come over to introduce himself. He played for AC Milan and he asked Jürgen, 'So, when are you going to join me in Italy?'

At the time, he smiled and shrugged but the idea stuck in Jürgen's mind and only a year after that conversation, he decided to make the move. It was AC's rivals Inter Milan, however, who paid nearly £6 million for his shooting boots.

'We're going to win the league again!' the club president Ernesto Pellegrini cheered happily as he showed off Inter's new Number 9.

Rivals AC Milan had a deadly Dutch trio – Gullit, Frank Rijkaard and Marco van Basten. But Inter now had a gifted German trio to compete – defender Andreas Brehme, midfielder Lothar Matthäus and super-striker Jürgen.

It was nice to have his national teammates around, but Jürgen hadn't come to Italy to be just another German. As soon as he arrived, he started learning the language and adapting to the new culture. Life was a lot more relaxed in Milan. Most of the time, that was great but sometimes, it drove Jürgen mad.

'I need someone to fix my washing machine please.'

'No problem!'

'Great, when can you come?'

'Soon, my friend!'

'How soon?'

'Maybe today, maybe tomorrow!'

Jürgen didn't let that stop him from enjoying his adventure, though. He gladly swapped German beers for Italian espressos.

'Klinsi's one of us already!' the fans laughed when they saw him out drinking coffee in local cafés.

Jürgen also had to adapt to a new style of football. Serie A was a big step-up from the Bundesliga, especially for a striker. The Italian league had the best defenders in the world and the team tactics weren't geared towards attacking.

'First, make sure that our opponents don't score,' Inter's cautious coach Giovanni Trappattoni told his players.

With Walter Zenga in goal and Giuseppe Bergomi, Andreas and Lothar in defence, the team didn't concede many goals, but what about *scoring* goals? Although he had some support from Nicola Berti and Aldo Serena, Jürgen was often left to attack on his own. Inter were relying heavily on their new super-striker.

'Jürgen Klinsmann, score a goal!' the fans chanted.

On his debut against Spezia, Jürgen hardly touched the ball, but with ten minutes to go, Andreas sprinted down the left wing on the counter-attack. This was it – Jürgen's one big chance. As the cross came in, he made a great late run towards the front post. He got to the ball before his markers and volleyed it home.

Gooooooooooooooooooooaaaaaaaaaaaaaaaaalllllllllllll lllllllllllllll!!!!!!!!!!!!!!!!!!!!!

Jürgen was off the mark! He was so excited that he just kept running, off the pitch and over to the fans behind the goal. With his arms above his head, he stood there and soaked up the glory. Nothing could beat that fantastic scoring feeling.

The goals kept coming, in all shapes and sizes. Against Cosenza, Jürgen shot low and accurately from the edge of the area. Against Bologna, he jumped high for a powerful header. Against Lecce, he cut inside onto his left foot and curled the ball into the top corner. Against Juventus, he sprinted past the centre-backs and then nutmegged the goalkeeper.

Klinsmann! Klinsmann! Klinsmann!

Jürgen was loving his new life at Inter. Challenge, what challenge? Wherever he went, he was guaranteed to score goals.

Away at Verona, he scored two in the first half, one with his left foot and the other with his right. If the ball bounced in the box, Jürgen always got there first. Touch, *BANG, GOOOOAAAALLLL!* He was a predator, always ready to pounce.

'I need to get a third now!' he told himself.

The minutes ticked by and the score stayed 2–0. Jürgen didn't give up, though. With two minutes to go, he burst into the penalty area and calmly dribbled round the diving keeper.

*Gooooooooooooooooooooaaaaaaaaaaaaaaaalllllllllll
llllllllllllll!!!!!!!!!!!!!!!!!!!!*

'Hat-trick!' he cheered.

Could anyone stop Jürgen from scoring? The
answer was yes. In the important derby against AC
Milan, Franco Baresi, Paolo Maldini and Alessandro
Costacurta put on a defensive masterclass. They
marked and muscled Inter's Number 9 out of the
match.

It was a lonely and frustrating game for Jürgen.
The one chance he got, he scored.

'Yesssss!' he screamed, throwing his arms up in
the air. But as he turned around, his heart sank. The
linesman's flag was up. Offside!

'Nooooo!' Jürgen groaned, with his hands on his
head.

AC Milan went on to win the derby 3–0. It was a
big blow to Inter's title chances, but Jürgen focused
his energy on improving his game. He was always
looking to learn new skills.

'I need to get stronger!' Jürgen told Trappattoni.

With hard work, he bounced back, and so did

Inter. The team kept up the pressure on Italy's top two – AC Milan and Jürgen's old UEFA Cup enemies, Napoli.

'I can't let Maradona beat me again!' Jürgen told himself. It was time for revenge.

At the San Siro, Napoli took the lead but, in the end, Inter were too strong, and Jürgen in particular. Thanks to his extra power, he won his battle against Ciro Ferrara. The equaliser was a Ferrara own goal, but the winner definitely belonged to Jürgen. He wasn't letting defenders push him around anymore.

'That's more like it!' Trappattoni yelled out on the touchline.

Inter finished in third place but they did beat AC Milan 3–1 in the second derby of the season. After an amazing start to his Italian adventure, Jürgen had run out of steam a little towards the end. However, he finished with another fifteen goals. He was still Mr Consistent, for club and country.

CHAPTER 14

WORLD CUP 1990

Jürgen had high hopes ahead of the 1990 World Cup and so did the whole of West Germany. In 1986, they had lost to Maradona's Argentina in the final, but back then, they hadn't had Jürgen, their big tournament star, in the squad.

'This time, we're going to go all the way!' the fans boasted confidently. They couldn't wait to complete a World Cup hat-trick – 1954, 1974 and 1990.

Over a whole season, Jürgen was Mr Consistent, but tournament football was his favourite kind of football. He loved all the drama and excitement, especially in the knockout rounds. One moment could change the game. With the pressure on, West

Germany would need a cool-headed hero.

'That's me!' Jürgen told Beckenbauer.

Euro 88 had been an incredible experience and Jürgen was expecting his first World Cup to be even better. Off the pitch, he walked out into the streets of Italy to soak up the special atmosphere of so many different cultures coming together.

On the pitch, West Germany started in style against Yugoslavia. Even before the match kicked off, Jürgen knew it was going to be a good day. He was playing up front with Rudi in his home club stadium, Inter Milan's San Siro. What could possibly go wrong?

Nothing! Lothar opened the scoring with a brilliant long-range strike and after that, it was all West Germany. As Andreas dribbled down the left wing, Jürgen got himself into space between the Yugoslavia defenders. When the cross came in, he dived head-first towards the ball and glanced it into the far corner.

Goooooooooooooooooooooaaaaaaaaaaaaaaaaaalllllllllllll llllllllllllll!!!!!!!!!!!!!!!!!!!!

One game, one goal! Yes, that fantastic scoring feeling was even better at a World Cup. Jürgen was delighted. When Lothar scored again, he jumped into his captain's arms. In the end, West Germany won 4–1. It was a score-line beyond Jürgen's wildest childhood dreams but five days later, they went one better, beating the United Arab Emirates 5–1.

Jürgen set up the first goal for Rudi and then scored a brilliant header of his own. As the national flags waved all around the San Siro stadium, West Germany's star strikeforce hugged happily.

'This is going to be *our* tournament,' Rudi declared. 'I can feel it!'

Jürgen knew that it would get tougher in the knock-out rounds but he was ready for that challenge. 'Bring it on!' he roared.

First up, West Germany faced the Netherlands in a rematch of the Euro 88 semi-final. It was AC Milan's Gullit, Rijkaard and van Basten versus Inter's Andreas, Lothar and Jürgen. It was time for some German revenge.

'We *have* to win this!' Lothar screamed.

After twenty minutes, the fixture became even more fascinating. When Rudi and Rijkaard started fighting, Jürgen tried to be the peacemaker, but he was too late. The referee already had his red card ready and he sent them both off.

'Klinsi!' Beckenbauer yelled out on the touchline. 'You're our lone striker now!'

He proved to be the perfect man for the job. Jürgen ran and ran, doing the work of two, maybe even three strikers. For the Dutch defenders, it was a day that they would never forget. In their nightmares, Germany's Number 18, Jürgen Klinsmann, was still chasing them around the pitch, snapping at their heels.

'Come on, guys!' Lothar called out in the dressing room at half-time. 'We need to support Klinsi – he can't do this on his own!'

Early in the second half, Andreas played a brilliant ball over the top for his striker to chase. Jürgen sprinted away from the Dutch left-back Adri van Tiggelen and struck a fierce shot from just outside the box. It beat the goalkeeper but bounced back off the post and away to safety.

'Nooooooo!' Jürgen groaned on his knees.

What a chance to be West Germany's matchwinner! Jürgen didn't give up, however. As his old Stuttgart teammate Guido Buchwald crossed from the left, he set off on a sudden sprint towards the front post. That striker's instinct had kicked in. Again, Jürgen beat van Tiggelen to the ball and this time, his shot hit the back of the net.

Goooooooooooooooooooaaaaaaaaaaaaaaaalllllllllllll llllllllllllll!!!!!!!!!!!!!!!!!!!!

Jürgen was exhausted but in that magic moment, he could have done ten laps of the pitch. Instead, he bounced up and down in front of the German fans, all the way into Guido's arms.

'Klinsi, you legend!' his teammate cried out.

Jürgen was definitely a big game player now. He nearly grabbed a second goal but after seventy-five minutes, Beckenbauer gave him a well-deserved rest. The German fans rose to their feet to clap their man of the match.

'What a performance!' his manager said, patting

him on the back. 'I need to keep you fit for the quarter-final!'

The last fifteen minutes were unbearable. On the bench, Jürgen cheered as Andreas made it 2–0 and then groaned as Ronald Koeman made it 2–1. Could West Germany hold on for victory? Yes!

'Well played,' Gullit told Jürgen as they swapped shirts after the final whistle. 'I've never seen a striker fight like that!'

That was a huge compliment from one of the best players in the world. Wearing the orange Netherlands shirt, Jürgen ran over to his relieved strike partner.

'Thanks for saving the day!' Rudi shouted, lifting West Germany's hero high into the air.

Rudi was now suspended, so Jürgen would have to save the day in the quarter-final too, against Czechoslovakia. His country was counting on him and he didn't let them down. When he got the ball on the left wing, Jürgen had two Czechoslovakia defenders around him but he battled his way through.

'Go on, Klinsi!' the West Germany fans urged.

In the penalty area, Jürgen faced another two defenders. He was a man on a mission and the only way to stop him was to foul him. As he nutmegged one, the other pulled him to the ground. Penalty!

'Nice one, what a run!' Uwe Bein said, helping Jürgen back to his feet.

Lothar smashed the spot-kick home to send West Germany into the semi-finals. Jürgen was now, he hoped, just one game away from the final.

England, however, were not going to make things easy for West Germany. Almost every time Jürgen attacked, centre-back Des Walker was there to stop him. And even when he did escape, goalkeeper Peter Shilton was there to save his shots. After 120 minutes of football, the two teams were tied at 1–1. It was time for penalties.

West Germany kept their cool, scoring four out of four – Andreas, Lothar, Karl-Heinz Riedle and Olaf Thon.

When Chris Waddle stepped up to take England's fifth penalty, he had to score to keep his country in the World Cup. On the halfway line, Jürgen hugged his teammates and crossed his fingers. He was hoping that he wouldn't have to take one.

Waddle went for power, too much power. As his shot flew over the crossbar, he sank to his knees in despair. Paul Gascoigne tears began to flow, and the West Germany players ran over to celebrate with their goalkeeper, Bodo Illgner.

'We're in the final!' Jürgen shouted again and again.

It was West Germany against Maradona's Argentina again. Could they get their revenge for 1986?

After all the pre-game excitement, the main event was a big disappointment, but not for West Germany. Argentina sat deep and defended, hoping to win the World Cup on penalties. However, just when that looked like it might happen, they gave away a penalty and West Germany got the goal they needed.

'You did it!' Jürgen shouted, hugging Andreas, their hero. '*We* did it!'

West Germany were World Champions for the third time.

CHAPTER 15

TROPHY TIME AGAIN

After winning the World Cup with West Germany, Jürgen was eager for more glory. He couldn't wait to feel that winning feeling again in the 1990–91 season.

'Come on, let's keep our good form going!' he told his German teammates Andreas and Lothar when they arrived back at Inter Milan.

In the end, they finished joint second in Serie A, on the same points as their local rivals, AC Milan. It was a happier story, however, in Jürgen's favourite club competition, the UEFA Cup. Having lost the 1989 final, he would get the chance to make things right in 1991.

Inter started the tournament slowly. In the first round against Austrian team Rapid Vienna, the score was 3–3, even after 180 minutes of football. When the match went to extra time, Inter needed a calm-headed hero to save the day.

It was a good thing that Jürgen was still out there on the pitch. He moved from left to right, making sure that he stayed onside. He was looking for a gap in the Vienna defence and a clever pass. When both finally arrived, Jürgen used his sprint speed to burst away from his marker. Once he had the ball in the box, it was game over.

'Klinsi never misses from there!' the Inter fans said confidently.

They were right. Calm as you like, Jürgen shot straight through the goalkeeper's legs.

Gooooooooooooooooooooooaaaaaaaaaaaaaaaaaalllllllllllll llllllllllllll!!!!!!!!!!!!!!!!!!!!!

Jürgen ran along the touchline, urging the supporters to make more noise. He loved being the gamechanger.

In the second round, Jürgen was at it again. Aston

Villa were 2–0 up when he chased after a hopeful long ball. The defender had a head start but not for long. Jürgen galloped towards goal like a horse on a race track. In the penalty area, the defender panicked and tried to bring him down. Penalty? No, because as he fell, Jürgen somehow managed to kick the ball past the goalkeeper.

Goooooooooooooooooooooaaaaaaaaaaaaaaaaallllllllllll llllllllllllllll!!!!!!!!!!!!!!!!!!!!!!

'You never give up, do you!' his teammate Nicola Berti cheered happily.

Jürgen's determination inspired Inter to fight back and win the match 3–2. With their spirits lifted, they then cruised past Partizan Belgrade and Atalanta too.

'We can win this!' Jürgen kept telling the Inter players as they prepared for the UEFA Cup semi-final against Portuguese club Sporting Lisbon. After a 0–0 draw in the first leg, they just needed a win at home at the San Siro.

Lothar's early penalty helped to calm the nerves a little but Inter weren't safely through to the final yet. 1–0 was a risky score-line – what if Sporting got an away goal? They would be knocked out.

'Let's score again!' the Inter fans cried out. A second strike would help to relax the tense atmosphere around the stadium.

Jürgen leapt high at the front post but he couldn't quite reach Andreas's curling corner-kick. A Sporting defender cleared it and at that point, some strikers would have walked away. Not Jürgen, however. He stayed exactly where he was, hoping and hunting for a rebound.

On the edge of the area, Nicola chested the ball down and hit a powerful shot at goal. The goalkeeper saved it, but he could only push it straight to Jürgen. Although it looked like an easy chance to score, he had to be careful. The ball flew towards him quickly, bouncing awkwardly. With the side of his foot, Jürgen tried to guide the ball gently but it skipped up and struck the crossbar. Luckily, it landed over the line.

Gooooooooooooooooooooaaaaaaaaaaaaaaaalllllllllllll lllllllllllll!!!!!!!!!!!!!!!!!!!!

Inside, Jürgen's main emotion was relief but, on the outside, he looked as cool as ever. He just raised his right arm above his head, like a striker who was used to scoring lots and lots of goals.

At the final whistle, Jürgen threw both arms up in the air. He was through to his second UEFA Cup final and this time, he wouldn't settle for second place.

'This is our big chance, boys!' he shouted passionately.

There were two Italian teams in the final – Inter Milan and Roma – but there were a lot of top German players involved. Jürgen was up against his international strike partner, Rudi, as well as defender Thomas Berthold.

In the end, Inter's German trio beat Roma's double act. Jürgen didn't score but he still showed that he was one of the best big game players around. When he received the ball on the left wing, it looked like he was going nowhere, except off the pitch, perhaps. But with strength and skill, Jürgen fought his way past Aldair and then Thomas, before delivering a terrific cross for Nicola to tap in. 2–0!

Jürgen ran over and wrestled the goalscorer to the ground. 'Nicola, we're nearly there!' he screamed.

Inter Milan held on to win 2–1 on aggregate. The UEFA Cup was theirs.

'Us Germans win everything!' Jürgen cried out, with one arm around Andreas and the other around Lothar.

The excitement didn't quite match winning the World Cup, but it came very close. For Jürgen, it felt really satisfying to fight back and win the competition only two years after losing in the final.

'I'm always victorious in the end!' he joked with his brother.

After one more season in Italy, Jürgen decided that it was time to move on. He had learned the language, experienced the culture, won the UEFA Cup and become a fan favourite, all in the space of three years.

Now, Jürgen needed a new football adventure. There were so many other countries that he wanted to explore, but where next?

Spain? Real Madrid were looking for a top new target man to help them beat rivals Barcelona to the league title.

England? The brand new 'Premier League' was about to begin and so lots of clubs were looking for a superstar striker with goals guaranteed.

No, after much consideration, he chose the sun and romance of France. But would he sign for Marseille, Paris Saint-Germain or AS Monaco?

Before he made up his mind, though, Jürgen had another big international tournament to play with Germany.

CHAPTER 16

EURO '92

There was lots of excitement all over Germany ahead of Euro '92. It would be the first major international tournament since the 1938 World Cup where the country played as a united football team. The Berlin Wall was gone. Instead of East Germany and West Germany, they had become a reunified Germany once more – one big happy family.

'That makes our squad even better!' Rudi, the new captain, cheered happily.

Unfortunately for Jürgen, it also meant there was even more competition for a starting spot. He was now up against Andreas Thom and Thomas Doll from the East German team, as well as Rudi and

Karl-Heinz Riedle. The new Germany manager was
Berti Vogts, Jürgen's favourite old youth coach with
the Under-16s and Under-21s. However, when he
didn't score a single international goal in 1991, Vogts
took the brave decision of dropping him.

'I'm sorry but I have to pick my players on form,'
Vogts explained honestly. 'Right now, you're not
playing well enough for your club or your country.
Karl-Heinz deserves his chance.'

Jürgen was shocked and disappointed. After his
heroic performances at Euro '88 and the 1990 World
Cup, he thought the Germany striker role was his to
keep, especially with Vogts in charge. However, he
thought wrong. It was a good and important wake-
up call for Jürgen. He was twenty-seven now and if
he didn't start scoring again soon, he could be gone
from the national team for good.

'I've got to earn my place back!' he told himself
firmly.

Jürgen watched impatiently from the bench as
Germany struggled against the Soviet Union in their
first match at Euro '92. Even when Rudi went off

injured at half-time, Vogts still didn't bring him on. He brought on Andreas Möller instead.

'He really doesn't rate me anymore,' Jürgen muttered, gloomily.

It was only when Germany went 1–0 down that the manager finally sent him on. Jürgen raced onto the pitch, ready to rescue his national team. He didn't stop for a second. He ran and ran but there were no goals in sight. Just as it looked as if Germany were heading for a shock defeat, they won a free kick on the edge of the penalty area.

As Thomas Häßler, his old Olympic teammate, stepped up to take it, Jürgen was up to his usual tricks. He stood in the middle of the wall, causing as much trouble as possible. At the last moment, he ducked down low, and Thomas's shot curled up over him and into the top corner. 1–1!

'Yesss!' Jürgen screamed, bouncing up and down in front of the goal. 'You nearly took my head off!' he joked, hugging Thomas on the halfway line.

After that, Jürgen kept his place in the Germany team and carried on making a nuisance of himself up front. Yet again, the tension of a big tournament was bringing out the best in him.

Against Scotland, in their penalty area, he battled against big Richard Gough and laid the ball back for Karl-Heinz to score.

'Yesss!' Jürgen screamed, falling to knees and punching the air.

In the Dutch penalty area, he jumped high to head Thomas's corner down into the bottom corner.

Goooooooooooooooooooooaaaaaaaaaaaaaaaaaalllllllllllll llllllllllllll!!!!!!!!!!!!!!!!!!

'Come on!' Jürgen cried out, high-fiving Karl-Heinz. His goal gave Germany a lifeline but sadly, the Netherlands held on to get revenge for the 1990 World Cup.

'The good news is that we're still through to the semi-finals,' Vogts told his frustrated players the next day. 'The bad news is that if we play like that again, we'll be going home. Is that what you want?'

'No!' the players shouted back and Jürgen's was the loudest voice of all.

'Good, so let's get things right. Four years ago,

we lost in the semi-final but not this time. This time, we're going all the way!'

'Yes!' the Germany players shouted, and again, Jürgen's was the loudest voice of all.

A Euro winners' medal would go perfectly with Jürgen's World Cup winners' medal, like ice cream and sunshine, or popcorn and movies. Jürgen had fought his way back into the Germany team, forming a great attacking trio with Thomas and Karl-Heinz. It was their job to shoot their nation to victory.

It all started well in the semi-final against the tournament hosts Sweden. To the despair of the home crowd, Thomas fired in another amazing free kick, so amazing that Jürgen didn't even have to duck.

In the second half, Matthias Sammer raced into the penalty area and looked up for his star strikers. He had two excellent options – a pass to Karl-Heinz at the front post, or a cross to Jürgen at the back post. Matthias chose the pass and Karl-Heinz tapped in. 2–0!

'Come on!' Jürgen shouted. As long as Germany won, he didn't mind who got the goals. He stood in the penalty area, waving his arms and whipping the fans up into a frenzy.

Sweden fought back but Karl-Heinz grabbed another goal to secure a 3–2 win. Germany had made it into the Euro '92 final.

'*Deutschland*! *Deutschland*!' Jürgen and his teammates chanted joyfully in front of a sea of black, red and yellow national flags.

Germany were expecting to face their enemies, the Netherlands in the final, but they were beaten on penalties by the tournament's surprise package, Denmark.

'Be ready and stay focused,' Vogts warned his players before kick-off in Gothenburg. Germany were the favourites to win and that was always a dangerous position to be in. 'If they can shock the Dutch, then they can shock us too!'

Jürgen was fully focused as he walked out of the tunnel and onto the pitch. When had he ever relaxed on the football field? Never! That just wasn't his style. He was all-energy, all-action. He gave everything for his country.

When Guido Buchwald hit a long-range strike, Jürgen was ready to race in for a rebound, but the Denmark goalkeeper Peter Schmeichel held on tightly.

'Next time,' Jürgen said to himself.

A few minutes later, however, John Jensen shocked Germany with an absolute screamer. 1–0 to Denmark!

'Wake up!' their captain Andreas yelled.

Jürgen was already awake and alert. Schmeichel couldn't hold Matthias's powerful shot but he pushed it off the pitch before Germany's striker could pounce.

'Come on!' Jürgen shouted, rolling the ball over for a quick corner kick. There was no way that he was giving up until the final whistle blew.

In the second half, there were two Denmark defenders marking Jürgen but he still jumped highest at the back post. He headed the ball towards goal but Schmeichel made a super-save.

'So close!' Jürgen groaned as he picked himself up off the grass and carried on.

Just when Germany looked like they would surely equalise, Denmark hit them on the counter-attack. Kim Vilfort scored to make it 2–0 and the red and white half of the stadium went wild.

'Noooooo!' Jürgen couldn't believe it. Despite his best efforts, Germany's Euro '92 dream was over. He went up to collect his runners-up medal, but he wouldn't be putting it next to his World Cup winners' medal. They didn't go together at all – it was like ice cream on a cold, wet winter's day.

CHAPTER 17

ADVENTURE NUMBER TWO: FRANCE

When Monaco lost Liberian-born George Weah to their rivals Paris Saint-Germain, they were in urgent need of a new star striker. Who could match Weah's eighteen goals and shoot them towards another French League title? Jürgen!

That was what the Monaco manager Arsène Wenger decided during Euro '92. Now, he just had to persuade him to make the move.

'I've got big plans for this team,' Wenger explained. 'We play entertaining, attacking football and you'll score more goals than ever!'

Jürgen liked the sound of that. He was looking for a change of style, as well as a change of scenery.

The defensive Italian tactics could be so boring and frustrating, especially for a striker. It would be nice to play with freedom for once.

And live with freedom too. As Jürgen wandered through the streets of Monaco, no-one even noticed him. Business, not football, was the number one focus in the city. There were also lots of other sports attracting attention, like tennis and Formula One. That felt refreshing after the madness of Milan. Football was everything there and the fans expected so much from their stars. It was exhausting.

'Let's do this!' Jürgen decided.

He was impressed with Wenger's coaching ideas and he was also impressed with Monaco's squad. There were lots of good young French players, like defender Lilian Thuram, midfielder Emmanuel Petit and playmaker Youri Djorkaeff.

'I think we're going to have fun together!' Jürgen predicted after his very first Monaco training session.

Off the pitch, Jürgen settled in quickly by learning the French language and exploring the local culture. He believed in making the most of every opportunity in life. There was sun, sea, wealth and glamour in Monaco. What more could you want?

Jürgen settled in quickly on the pitch too. On his Ligue 1 debut against Sporting Club Toulon, he scored twice. 'The Locomotive is off!' the French newspapers declared. Jürgen loved his new nickname. It summed up his style perfectly. He was all-energy, all-action.

In late November 1992, Monaco faced PSG in the biggest game of the season. It was second place vs first place, Jürgen vs Weah. So far, the Liberian was outscoring Jürgen, ten goals to six.

'We'll see about that!' Jürgen said. When it came to a race, he was always determined to finish first.

PSG took the lead at the Stade Louis II but only thanks to a lucky own goal. The Monaco players didn't let that get them down. They charged forward and only a minute later, Jérôme Gnako crossed into the PSG box.

Jürgen followed the flight of the ball carefully and backed away from his marker. It was a high cross, but no header was too high for him. He leapt up and somehow, off balance, he steered his header past the goalkeeper.

Goooooooooooooooooooaaaaaaaaaaaaaaaaalllllllllllll lllllllllllll!!!!!!!!!!!!!!!!!!!

As the ball crossed the line, Jürgen toppled over and celebrated with a backwards roll. What an important goal! He stood up and punched the air.

'We can win this!' Jürgen screamed.

And that's exactly what they did. Luiz Henrique put Monaco ahead and then Jürgen set up Youri to seal a huge 3–1 victory. After the match, all the players hurdled the advertising boards to party in front of the delighted fans.

Monaco! Monaco! Monaco!

'Thanks, you saved us today!' Emmanuel called out over the noise, giving Jürgen a high-five.

'No way, we did it together,' he replied modestly. 'It's a team effort!'

It certainly helped to have a super-striker, though. Under Wenger's coaching, Monaco were playing fantastic, flowing football that just needed an expert finishing touch. That was Jürgen's job and if he missed one chance, he knew that he would soon get another one. Touch, *BANG, GOOOOAAAALLLL!*

'I was right – this is so much fun!' he cheered happily with Youri.

Jürgen's four goals against Auxerre bumped Monaco up to first place in the French League. By the end of January, he had already scored fourteen for the season. Mr Consistent was back!

It was all going so well but sadly, Jürgen and Monaco couldn't quite hold on to top spot. Marseille finished first, but they were later disqualified for match-fixing. So, who would be the new Champions of France? PSG and Monaco had the same number of points but in the end, the title wasn't awarded to anyone.

'What a let-down!' Jürgen complained. 'After a whole season of football, you have to have a winner.'

At least there were two pieces of good news to cheer him up. Jürgen finished as France's third top scorer with nineteen goals, one ahead of his German teammate Rudi at Marseille and five ahead of Weah at PSG. And more importantly, Monaco would now get to play in the Champions League.

'I've already won the UEFA Cup, so this is the next big challenge I've been looking for!' Jürgen told his brother Horst excitedly during the summer break.

It was another chance for him to visit lots of European countries – Greece, Romania, Turkey, Russia, Spain and Italy. Jürgen loved to travel but these weren't holidays. They were football battles that he was determined to win.

'We've got nothing to fear,' he told his Monaco teammates. 'Nothing!'

Against Spartak Moscow, Youri played a through-ball to their new signing Victor Ikpeba. His shot was saved but, in a flash, Jürgen raced in for the rebound.

Goooooooooooooooooooooaaaaaaaaaaaaaaaaallllllllllll llllllllllllllll!!!!!!!!!!!!!!!!!!!!

Jürgen had been so desperate to score that he crashed into the back of the net. Nothing was going to stop him, or Monaco. They were off! Victor got the second, Youri scored the third, and Lilian scored the fourth.

'When we play like this, we can beat anyone!' Jürgen cheered.

A few weeks later, Galatasaray received the same treatment at the Stade Louis II. This time, Jürgen got the last goal with a header at the back post. He never liked to miss out on the fun.

Despite losing to Barcelona, Monaco still made it through to the Champions League semi-finals. It was an incredible achievement for a team playing in the tournament for the first time in five years. Sadly, AC Milan were just too good for them, especially at home at the San Siro.

'I'll be back,' Jürgen told himself as he trudged off the pitch. First, he had another World Cup to win.

CHAPTER 18

1994 WORLD CUP

In 1994 in the USA, Germany were looking to do what no country had achieved since Pelé's Brazil – win back-to-back World Cups. To do that, Vogts was relying heavily on senior players such as Lothar, Andreas, Rudi and Jürgen.

At the age of twenty-nine, Jürgen had now played at two European Championships and one incredible World Cup. Not only that, but Jürgen had proved himself as a big tournament player. He could handle the extra responsibility. His country could count on him.

Just in case the Germany fans weren't convinced, Jürgen scored the matchwinner in their first match against Bolivia. Thomas beat the offside trap and chested down Lothar's long-ball. As the goalkeeper dived at Thomas's feet, Jürgen pounced and passed it into the empty net.

Goooooooooooooaaaaaaaaalllllllllllllllllllll!!!!!!!!!!!!

Jürgen was delighted – what a start for him and, more importantly, for Germany! He ran towards the corner flag with both arms above his head.

'I knew you'd save the day!' Lothar cried out, looking relieved.

Jürgen did it again in their second match against Spain. This time, however, Germany were 1–0 down when Thomas curled a free kick towards the back post. Jürgen battled Fernando Hierro for the ball and won. His header bounced down into the grass and then up over the diving goalkeeper.

Jürgen to the rescue again! He was in the best form of his international career and he felt invincible. He was playing with so much confidence, so why not try some outrageous skills? Against South Korea, Jürgen flicked the ball up with his right foot and volleyed it in with his left.

Goooooooooooooaaaaaaaaalllllllllllllllllllll!!!!!!!!!!!!

'Wow, you're on fire, Klinsi!' Thomas cheered as

he hugged his team's hero.

Three goals in three games – Jürgen really was Germany's star striker now. Just to confirm it, he scored a second volley against South Korea.

Jürgen was defending their 1990 World Cup trophy, almost single-handedly. Germany had the best squad in the tournament but where were the team's other attacking options?

Behind the scenes, all was not well in the Germany camp. There were lots of arguments between the coaches and the players. In the mornings before training, some of the stars decided to go out and play golf, as if they were on holiday. 'Don't tell us what to do!' they argued, behaving like they had already won the 1994 World Cup.

'Come on, we have to focus on football!' Jürgen urged his teammates. 'We need to work together here and win. Everything else can wait until after the tournament is over.'

In the second round against Belgium, Vogts ensured that Germany had their 1990 World Cup-winning strikeforce back; he brought Rudi into the team to partner Jürgen, and the plan worked perfectly. Rudi opened the scoring after six minutes and five minutes later, they carved through the Belgium defence together.

Rudi passed to Jürgen, who backheeled the ball for the one-two. Rudi danced past two tackles and left the ball for Jürgen to fire into the bottom corner.

Goooooooooooooaaaaaaaaalllllllllllllllllllll!!!!!!!!!!!!!

Jürgen ran to the corner flag, calling for his strike-partner to join him. When Rudi arrived, he jumped up into Jürgen's arms.

'I've missed you!'

'I've missed you too!'

Were Germany back on track? Their 3–2 win over Belgium wasn't exactly comfortable but with Jürgen in the team, anything seemed possible.

In the quarter-finals, they faced the World Cup's surprise package, Bulgaria, who had already beaten Argentina, Greece and Mexico. If Germany weren't careful, they could be next.

'Don't let this be a repeat of Denmark at Euro '92,' Vogts demanded in the dressing room before kick-off.

'You have to take this seriously because this isn't just a stepping stone to the semis. Go out there and show them what you can do!'

For seventy minutes, Germany stuck to their task. As Jürgen tried to control a bouncing ball, the Bulgaria defender clattered into him. Penalty! Lothar stepped up and scored. 1–0!

But after that, many of Germany's players decided that it was game over. As the minutes ticked by, they got slower and slower, and sloppier and sloppier.

'Keep going!' Vogts screamed on the touchline. 'This isn't over yet!'

Jürgen ran and ran but some of his teammates didn't, even when Hristo Stoichkov equalised with a brilliant free kick.

'Switch on!' captain Lothar called out but not everyone was listening.

Three minutes later, Yordan Letchkov scored a diving header. 2–1 to Bulgaria! Suddenly, the World Champions only had ten minutes to save themselves from an embarrassing exit.

'Come on, Klinsi!' the Germany fans chanted.

'Score another goal!'

Jürgen tried and tried, but it was too late. Before he knew it, the final whistle blew, and Germany were out. It was the country's worst World Cup performance for nearly twenty years.

Jürgen walked around in a daze, shaking hands with the emotional Bulgaria players. He felt numb with shock and fury.

'We threw it away!' Jürgen muttered to himself again and again.

The Germany players only had themselves to blame. It was their attitude, not their talent, which had let them down. With their egos and arrogance, they had knocked themselves out of the tournament. That's what Jürgen found so hard to accept.

It was one of the most disappointing moments of Jürgen's life. He didn't deserve to be heading home, not after scoring five brilliant goals in five brilliant games. He had been Germany's hero once again. He could hold his head up high, but that wasn't what he wanted. What he wanted was another World Cup winners' medal.

CHAPTER 19

ADVENTURE NUMBER THREE: ENGLAND

Jürgen the traveller was always looking for new experiences. After two seasons at Monaco and the disappointment of the 1994 World Cup, he was ready for a new football adventure. So, where next?

Back to Italy? Genoa needed goals and Jürgen was goals guaranteed.

Or off to Spain? Atlético Madrid offered him the chance to lead an exciting new era at the club.

No – after much consideration, Jürgen chose England. He had learned the language as a kid, in school, and also on his trips to the USA. This would be a great chance to become totally fluent. Plus, he had always dreamed of living in London, England's busy, buzzing capital city. An offer from Tottenham Hotspur, therefore, was very tempting indeed.

'Do you remember when we used to watch English football on TV when we were young?' Jürgen asked his brother. 'Glenn Hoddle, Ricky Villa, Ossie Ardiles – I loved Spurs!'

'You liar!' Horst laughed. 'You were a Liverpool fan!'

Jürgen shrugged cheekily. 'Liverpool *and* Spurs!'

Ardiles was now the Tottenham manager and he was building a talented, attacking team at White Hart Lane. Sol Campbell, Darren Anderton and Nicky Barmby were the bright young stars, while Jürgen would be playing up front with Teddy Sheringham.

'You two are a perfect match,' the Tottenham owner, Alan Sugar, told Jürgen when he showed up in Monaco one day on his luxury yacht. He wasn't sailing home until the big deal was done. 'Teddy's a very smart striker – he reminds me a lot of Rudi Völler!'

After the quiet calm of Monaco, Jürgen was ready to return to a country full of football fanatics. With the launch of the Premier League, England was the place to be. The crowds were loud and lively, and only metres away from the players on the pitch.

'Let's do this!' he told Sugar, shaking his hand.

At £2.5 million, Tottenham had got themselves a bargain with Jürgen. Their fans were delighted with their new star signing, but Jürgen didn't receive a warm welcome from the rest of the country. The England-Germany rivalry was fierce, especially after England's semi-final defeat at the 1990 World Cup. Jürgen had played in that match and to make matters worse, he had since earned a reputation as a diver.

'That guy will do anything to win a penalty!'

'He should be in a swimming pool, not on a football pitch!'

'There's no place for cheats in the English game!'

Jürgen was surprised by the cruel comments that he read in the newspapers. He would never cheat or dive. He still played by the rules that his dad had set out for him all those years ago – 'Be honest in battle, humble in victory, and gracious in defeat'. How could they judge him before he had even kicked a ball in England? Luckily, his new Tottenham teammates were there to look after him and give him good advice.

'Just ignore it,' the captain Gary Mabbutt told him. 'As soon as you score a few goals, the journalists will move on to some other story!'

Teddy, however, was more mischievous. 'Show them that you've got a sense of humour. Do an interview in a diving suit or make the dive your new goal celebration!'

Jürgen took Teddy's advice about humour. He started his first press conference with a joke:

'I'm new around here. Does anyone know if there are any good diving schools in London?'

The journalists laughed and laughed. Maybe Tottenham's new German striker wasn't such a bad guy after all.

After an open-top bus ride around the tourist sights of London, Jürgen got down to football business. It was time to prove himself in the Premier League.

On the opening day of the 1994–95 season, Spurs travelled to Sheffield Wednesday with a very attacking line-up. It was a risky tactic away from home but with eighty minutes gone, Tottenham were winning 3–2. Teddy, Darren and Nicky had all scored – but what about Jürgen? He never liked to miss out on the fun.

Darren dribbled down the right wing and chipped a cross towards the back post. Jürgen knew exactly what to do next. He had been practising the move for years. He watched the ball carefully, timed his jump perfectly and then used his neck muscles to flick the header up over the goalkeeper.

Goooooooooooooooooooooaaaaaaaaaaaaaaaalllllllllllll llllllllllllll!!!!!!!!!!!!!!!!!!!

What a way to mark his debut! Jürgen ran towards the corner flag and dived down on to the grass.

'That's for all the haters!' he thought to himself.

Some of Jürgen's teammates joined in, first Teddy, then Colin Calderwood and then Nicky. The Tottenham fans cheered wildly for their new hero.

Klinsmann! Klinsmann! Klinsmann!

After that amazing start, Jürgen just got better and better. In his first home game against Everton, he scored another of his awesome acrobatic volleys. It wasn't quite as good as his goal for Stuttgart against Bayern Munich, but the Spurs supporters still loved it.

'Come on!' Jürgen shouted joyfully.

This time, the whole Spurs team joined in with the diving celebration, even the goalkeeper.

The atmosphere at White Hart Lane was electric. Jürgen had never heard noise like it. As the stadium chanted his name, he could feel the goosebumps on the back of his neck. It was another moment that he would never forget.

Tottenham weren't a consistent team, but they were definitely entertaining. As Gary had predicted, Jürgen quickly went from villain to hero, with ten goals in his first seven games. In June, one journalist had written an article called 'Why I Hate Jürgen Klinsmann'. Two months later, he wrote another article called 'Why I Love Jürgen Klinsmann'.

'Klinsmania' soon spread across England. Jürgen was helping to change the stereotype of foreign footballers. He was humble and hard-working, rather than spoiled and lazy, and he drove a dark blue

Volkswagen Beetle, rather than a flashy Ferrari.

Jürgen was pleased with all the praise, but he wanted a trophy to go with it. In the FA Cup quarter-finals, Tottenham took on his childhood favourites, Liverpool, at Anfield. Robbie Fowler scored first but just before half-time, Jürgen laid the ball back for his partner Teddy to strike... 1–1!

'Yessss!' Jürgen cheered, sinking to his knees in the penalty area and punching the air.

He was so passionate about every single match and he loved playing with his Tottenham teammates. Now, he just needed to grab the winner. He was determined. With two minutes to go, Darren passed to Teddy, who flicked it through to Jürgen. He was in the box, with just the goalkeeper to beat...

Goooooooooooooooooooaaaaaaaaaaaaaaaaaallllllllllll llllllllllllll!!!!!!!!!!!!!!!!!!

Jürgen was soon at the bottom of a big pile of celebrating Spurs players. 'We did it!' he screamed.

At the final whistle, even some of the Liverpool fans stood and clapped the Tottenham performance.

In the end, Jürgen didn't win the FA Cup or the

Premier League that season, but he did win the Football Writers' Association Footballer of the Year award. It had been his best-ever scoring season, with twenty-one goals in the Premier League and thirty in total. He even finished second in the 1995 Ballon d'Or behind his old rival George Weah.

Jürgen loved his season in London and he wanted to stay longer. However, he was desperate to play for his country at Euro 96. The horror of the 1994 World Cup still haunted him. To stay in the Germany squad, Jürgen knew that he needed to be playing in Europe's top club competitions – the Champions League, or at least the UEFA Cup. Sadly, that wouldn't be possible at Spurs, and one of Jürgen's old managers was calling...

CHAPTER 20

GERMANY CALLING

After leading West Germany to the 1990 World Cup trophy, Franz Beckenbauer had moved to France to become the manager of Marseille. But after one year, he had returned home to become the president of his local club, Bayern Munich.

The 1994–95 season, which had gone so well for Jürgen at Tottenham, had been a disaster for Bayern. Under Jürgen's old Inter Milan boss Giovanni Trapattoni, the team finished way down in sixth place. That was their second worst league position since 1978.

'We need a new manager and a new striker,' Beckenbauer decided during the summer. Bayern had only scored fifty-five goals all year and their top scorer was their left-back, Christian Ziege.

The President had two perfect people in mind – the Werder Bremen boss Otto Rehhagel and Tottenham hitman Jürgen.

'Come home!' Beckenbauer urged him. 'Don't you dream of lifting the German title? With you up front, we can do that!'

Jürgen had a tough decision to make but in the end, he couldn't say no to 'The Kaiser', his country's greatest football hero. Beckenbauer was right; he *had* always dreamed of winning the Bundesliga. Jürgen hadn't won a single trophy for four years. This was his big chance at Germany's biggest club.

First, however, Jürgen needed to speak to his dad. Years earlier, he had promised Siegfried that he would never, ever, play for Bayern Munich.

'Please will you let me break my promise?' Jürgen asked on a trip to the family bakery. On the walls, there were proudly displayed photos of all his son's previous teams – Stuttgarter Kickers, Stuttgart, Inter Milan, Monaco and Tottenham.

His dad smiled and nodded. 'Of course, son. You

must do whatever's best for your career. I understand. Just don't expect me to hang up a picture of Bayern!'

With Siegfried's permission, Jürgen was ready to say a sad goodbye to England.

'I'm sorry, I'll be back!' he told the Spurs fans.

'Ok, let's do this!' he told 'The Kaiser'.

After six years of travel and adventure, Jürgen returned home to Germany as a national hero. Not only had he been the national team's star at the 1990 and 1994 World Cups, but he had also conquered Italy, France and Spain with his charm, energy and goals.

'Welcome back, Klinsi!' the fans cheered. 'We've missed you!'

At Bayern, Jürgen had two top targets to aim for – the Bundesliga title and his favourite club competition, the UEFA Cup.

'Come on, we can win both!' he told his new teammates eagerly.

Despite Jürgen's best efforts and sixteen goals, Bayern finished second in the German League, six points behind Matthias Sammer and Karl-Heinz Riedle's Borussia Dortmund.

'We'll beat them next year,' Jürgen declared after a few days of disappointment.

Before that, however, Bayern had a UEFA Cup final to win. In Germany, Jürgen had been solid all season, but in Europe, he had been spectacular. Two goals against Lokomotiv Moscow, then three against Raith Rovers, then four against Benfica!

On a snowy night at the Allianz Arena, Jürgen put on his gloves and ploughed through the Portuguese giants. It was a striking masterclass.

He ran onto Mehmet Scholl's pass and poked the ball past the goalkeeper. 1–0!

He steered a rebound into the bottom corner. 2–1!

He found the net in the middle of a goalmouth scramble. 3–1!

He headed home Mehmet's cross. 4–1!

Jürgen had left England behind, but he brought his famous goal celebration with him. He dived on to the frosty grass and slid all the way over to Mehmet.

'You're on fire!' his teammate told him.

'Not in this awful weather,' he joked back. 'I'm freezing!'

With another hat-trick in the quarter-final against Nottingham Forest, Jürgen was up to fourteen goals in only eight games.

'This is *my* tournament!' he said with a smile.

Could Jürgen make it to a third UEFA Cup final in seven years and win it for a second time? In the semi-final against Luís Figo's Barcelona, he didn't score, home or away, but he certainly played his part. His tireless running helped to stretch the Spanish defence and create chances for his teammates.

'I'm happy to let other people score for once,' Jürgen teased Mehmet and Marcel Witeczek. 'It's good for you guys to get some shooting practice!'

That special team spirit was crucial as Bayern pulled off a shock 2–1 win at the Nou Camp to reach their first European final in eighteen years.

'What a performance!' Beckenbauer shouted, clapping in the stands.

The last team standing in their way was Bordeaux. The French club had shocked AC Milan in the quarters and they were hoping to do the same to Bayern in the final in Munich. Mehmet and Jürgen were going head-to-head with the tournament's other deadly attacking duo – Zinedine Zidane and Christophe Dugarry.

'Let's teach those young pretenders a lesson!' Jürgen declared before kick-off.

Mehmet laughed. 'Speak for yourself, old man. They're only two years younger than me!'

In front of their home crowd, Bayern won the first leg 2–0. The fans were already celebrating a win, but Jürgen wasn't.

'Well done, we're halfway there!' he congratulated his teammates at the final whistle.

In Bordeaux, Jürgen led by example from the front. He chased after the right-back and blocked his clearance. The ball fell to Emil Kostadinov, who backheeled it to Mehmet. GOAL – 3–0!

'Keep going!' captain Lothar yelled from the back.

When Emil made it 4–0, it was game over but not for Jürgen. He couldn't let his amazing tournament finish without another goal in another final. He was only one off a new European record. He chased after every through-ball and back-pass. He raced around the penalty area, getting into as many goalscoring positions as possible.

'Yes!' he screamed on the six-yard line as Alexander Zickler crossed from the left. Alexander pulled it back to Thomas Strunz instead, but as his shot fizzed past, Jürgen stuck out his left leg and deflected it past the goalkeeper.

Goooooooooooaaaaaaaaaalllllllllllllllllllll!!!!!!!!!!!!!!

'You're such a poacher!' Thomas joked as they celebrated together.

'No way, your shot was going wide, I promise!' Jürgen replied. He wasn't letting go of his fifteenth goal of the competition.

There was no time to argue – Bayern were the 1996 UEFA Cup winners. Up on the stage, Jürgen stood with his teammates in a happy huddle, a winners' medal draped around his neck. As Lothar lifted the trophy above his head, they all whooped and cheered.

Bayern! Bayern! Bayern!

After a big night of celebrations, Jürgen moved on to his next target – Euro '96. He couldn't wait to return to England.

CHAPTER 21

EURO '96

Euro '96 would be Jürgen's fifth major tournament
for Germany, but his first as captain of his country.
It was one of the proudest days of his life when
Berti Vogts first gave him the armband during the
qualification campaign. Yet another of Jürgen's
childhood dreams had come true.

'Don't worry, I won't let you down!' he assured
his manager.

After years of working together, Vogts had full
faith in his new captain. Jürgen was Mr Consistent,
with goals guaranteed. When had Jürgen every let his
country down? With his spirit and experience, he was
the perfect man to lead Germany to European glory.
They were getting closer and closer to triumph with

every tournament – the semi-finals in 1988, then the final in 1992... and now in 1996? The final again, maybe, but hopefully this time with a happy ending.

Jürgen certainly believed in his teammates. Although Lothar, Rudi and Andreas had all retired, there was still plenty of quality in the side. There was Matthias Sammer in defence, Mehmet, Thomas Häßler and Andreas Möller in midfield, and Jürgen in attack.

'We've got what it takes to win!' their captain kept telling them.

Jürgen was determined to create a warm atmosphere amongst the Germany players and a great team spirit. Their 1994 World Cup disappointment had showed him the importance of harmony and will to win. At club level, the Bayern Munich and Borussia Dortmund players were rivals, sometimes even enemies. At international level, however, they were teammates, working together for the same united country.

Deutschland! Deutschland! Deutschland!

Euro '96 was taking place in England, Jürgen's home for that one sensational season. He was so excited to be back. Usually, the Germany squad

stayed somewhere small and peaceful, far away
from the fans and the media. However, Jürgen had a
different idea, based on his experience at Tottenham.

'I think the buzz of London life could help us,' he
argued. 'We can soak up that energy and then use it
out on the pitch!'

Vogts and Jürgen settled on a compromise;
Germany would start in the quiet countryside but if
they got to the semi-finals, the team would move to
the bright lights of the capital city.

Jürgen was suspended for the first match against the
Czech Republic but Germany got the job done without
their captain. His Bayern Munich teammate Christian
Ziege got the first goal and Andreas got the second.

'Great start, guys!' Jürgen congratulated them in
the dressing room afterwards.

He was raring to go for the second match against
Russia. His new strike partner was Oliver Bierhoff, a
powerful target man who played for Udinese in Italy.
Jürgen dropped a little deeper, using his speed and
instinct to chase after Oliver's flick-ons and knock-
downs.

The plan worked well but Jürgen's first shot soared high over the bar.

'No, no, NO!' he screamed at himself. What a waste! That wasn't like him at all. He needed to calm down and focus.

In the end, it was Matthias who broke the deadlock in the second half, but Jürgen made sure of the victory. He tapped the ball cleverly past the slow Russia centre-back and raced on to his own pass. From the edge of the penalty area, he shot with the outside of his right foot and the ball flew into the top corner.

Goooooooooooooaaaaaaaaalllllllllllllllllllll!!!!!!!!!!!!!
Another tournament, another goal! Jürgen ran past the Germany fans, roaring at the top of his voice. He never got tired of that proud feeling of scoring for his country. Goal Number Thirty was just as exciting as Goal Number One.

Germany's big game player was back, and he scored again in the last minute to make it 3–0. With two wins out of two, Germany were through to the quarter-finals.

'Keep it up!' Jürgen urged his teammates, giving them all high-fives.

Next up: Croatia. Jürgen knew the likes of Zvonimir Boban, Alen Bokšić and Slaven Bilić from his travelling days in Italy, France and England.

'Don't underestimate them,' he warned. 'There's a lot of talent in that team.'

It was Jürgen himself who put Germany ahead from the penalty spot. With Lothar gone, it was his responsibility as captain. Despite the pressure of 43,000 fans at Old Trafford, Jürgen placed it perfectly, right in the bottom corner.

Gooooooooooooaaaaaaaaallllllllllllllllllll!!!!!!!!!!!!!

The Germany fans never doubted him for a second. 'We love you, Klinsi!' they cheered.

Sadly, Jürgen's match was over before half-time. As he limped off with a hamstring injury, he just hoped that it wasn't too serious.

'We've got to keep our concentration,' Jürgen told Andreas as he handed him the captain's armband.

Davor Šuker equalised after the break but there was

no repeat of Germany's collapse against Bulgaria. They had learnt their lesson. They were so much stronger now, and they took the lead again eight minutes later. This time, they held on until the final whistle.

'Yes!' Jürgen shouted, punching the air in relief. Now, he just needed to get himself fit, if not for the semi-final, then definitely for the final.

As Vogts had promised, the Germany squad moved into a London hotel. However, Jürgen didn't spend his days off on open-top bus tours. Instead, he worked hard with the team physios to heal his injured calf.

'I have to be fit,' he said through gritted teeth on the massage table. 'I *have* to!'

Jürgen was devastated to miss Germany's semi-final against England at Wembley. What football match could be bigger than that? He watched nervously from the bench, through 120 minutes of tense football and then a nail-biting penalty shoot-out.

When Andreas eventually scored the winning spot-kick, Jürgen wanted to race out onto the field to celebrate with his teammates, but he managed to stop himself. Germany needed their captain back fit and firing for the Euro '96 final.

Jürgen worked harder than ever on his recovery. On the day before the big day, he was able to run.

'Tomorrow, I'll be able to play!' he promised Vogts.

Jürgen led the Germany team out for the final in front of 73,000 fans at Wembley. His pre-game message had been simple: 'We haven't won anything yet!'

Their opponents in the final were the Czech Republic, the team that they had beaten 2–0 in their very first game of the tournament.

'That result means nothing now,' Jürgen told his teammates. 'Remember the 1992 final against Denmark? That day, we thought we could win without even trying. We're not going to make the same mistake again, are we?'

'No!' the players yelled back like a battle cry.

After a goalless first half, the Czech Republic were awarded a penalty and scored it. Suddenly, Germany's Euro '96 glory was in real danger.

'Don't panic!' Jürgen called out. 'We've still got plenty of time!'

Mehmet went off and on came Oliver. As Christian curled a free kick into the penalty area, all Czech Republic eyes were on Jürgen and Matthias, the danger men. But they forgot about Germany's super sub, Oliver, who headed the ball home. 1–1!

'You beauty!' Jürgen screamed, hugging the team's hero.

The match went to extra time and it was golden goal time – if one team scored, the final was over immediately.

Christian dribbled down the left wing and pulled the ball back to Jürgen. This was it – his golden chance. The Germany fans got ready to celebrate... but a Czech Republic defender blocked it.

'Noooooo!' Jürgen cried out, slumping his shoulders.

Again, Christian crossed and Jürgen jumped up and flicked the ball goalwards... but it flew high over the crossbar.

It just wasn't his day but could one of his Germa

teammates be the hero instead? Jürgen turned in the penalty area and crossed the ball to Oliver. He held off his marker and managed to get a shot away.

To Jürgen, the next part seemed to play out in slow motion. Oliver's shot deflected off a defender and fooled the goalkeeper. He could only push the ball onto the post and watch as it rolled over the goal line.

Gooooooooooooaaaaaaaaallllllllllllllllllll!!!!!!!!!!!!!

Germany had the Golden Goal! Jürgen ran around, jumping and hugging everyone he could find. His teammates, the substitutes, the physios, the coaches, the manager.

'We did it!' he cheered with Vogts.

As the national team captain, Jürgen had the important job of lifting the Euro '96 trophy first. What an honour! After his moment in the limelight, he passed it on down the line to Andreas and the rest of the players. Germany's win had been one big team effort, a triumph of togetherness over talent.

Deutschland! Deutschland! Deutschland!

CHAPTER 22

BACK TO ITALY, BACK TO ENGLAND

Jürgen finally had the Euro winners' medal to go with his World Cup winners' medal. What an international career he was having with Germany! He returned home to a hero's welcome at the airport.

'Thank you, Klinsi!'

'We love you, Klinsi!'

At club level, however, he still had plenty more to achieve. Jürgen had won the UEFA Cup twice but he had still never won a league title – not in Italy, not in France, not in England, and not in Germany.

'People think I'm just a big tournament player,' he told Mehmet, 'but I'm not! Just look at my record – I score goals all season, every season.'

Jürgen was determined to prove himself once and for all. His old Inter Milan boss Trapattoni was back in charge of Bayern but he didn't let the defensive tactics get him down. If it meant that he got a Bundesliga winners' medal at the end of the season, Jürgen was happy to play the lone striker role.

'Just come and visit me up front sometimes!' he joked with Mehmet.

Bayern only lost three league matches all year and they clinched the title against Jürgen's old club, Stuttgart. He didn't score that day, but Jürgen finished as Bayern's top scorer, yet again, with fifteen goals.

'We're the champions of Germany!' he cheered with his teammates.

Jürgen had waited a long time to say those wonderful words. With another dream achieved, he was ready to head out on further international adventures.

First stop: back to Italy! Sampdoria needed a new star striker to replace the legendary Roberto Mancini. Jürgen jumped at the opportunity. He was thirty-three years old now, but he still had plenty more goals to give.

'Let's do this!' he told the club president Enrico Mantovani.

Sadly, Jürgen's second Italian adventure didn't go according to plan. First, he suffered an injury and then, just when he was finding his form, a new manager arrived. Vujadin Boškov decided to play with only one striker, and he chose Vincenzo Montella instead.

Jürgen wasn't going to stay where he wasn't wanted. He was desperate to captain Germany at the 1998 World Cup and Vogts had made his message clear: he would only pick Jürgen if he was playing regular football and scoring regular goals.

Next stop: back to England! Tottenham were in the middle of a real relegation battle. Teddy had moved to Manchester United, taking all their goals and confidence with him. Spurs were in urgent need of a new hero to rescue them. Or perhaps an old hero – who could that be? Jürgen, of course!

'Let's do this – again!' he told Alan Sugar.

Jürgen's only demand was lots and lots of game time. He wanted to be fighting fit for the World Cup.

'No problem,' agreed the Tottenham manager Christian Gross.

Jürgen made his big comeback in the North London derby. The fans were delighted to see him again. The doom and gloom lifted instantly.

Klinsmann! Klinsmann! Klinsmann!

Jürgen didn't score against Arsenal or Manchester United, but he did score in his third match against West Ham. And it wasn't just any goal; it was the winning goal.

'Come on!' Jürgen roared in front of the celebrating Tottenham fans.

The Spurs spirit was returning but with three games to go, they were still only one place above the Premier League relegation zone.

'We can't go down!' the captain Gary Mabbutt urged his players. That was unthinkable for a top club like Tottenham.

Jürgen was ready to fight until the final whistle. Against Newcastle, David Ginola dribbled forward and crossed into the six-yard box. Jürgen was there, waiting to head the ball home.

Goooooooooooooooooooooaaaaaaaaaaaaaaaalllllllllllll llllllllllllllll!!!!!!!!!!!!!!!!!!!!!

He ran towards the corner and dived across the White Hart Lane grass. It was only a start, but Spurs were now one step closer to safety.

'Nice one!' Jürgen's strike partner Les Ferdinand said, putting his arm around him.

Les got the second goal to secure a very important victory for Tottenham.

'Two more games, two more wins!' Gary demanded in the dressing room afterwards.

Next up, they faced a tricky trip to Wimbledon but luckily, Jürgen was an experienced traveller. When his team needed him most, they could always count on him.

Darren crossed from the right and Jürgen flicked the ball on for Les to score. 1–0 to Tottenham!

But Wimbledon fought back with one goal and then another. 2–1!

'Don't give up!' Jürgen called out to his shocked

teammates. 'We're going to win this!'

Jürgen was a man on a mission. Before half-time, he poked David's cross past the goalkeeper. 2–2!

'Come on!' Jürgen shouted, running into the winger's arms.

After half-time, the goals kept coming. David blocked a clearance and Jürgen ran through and scored. 3–2!

This time, he ran into the arms of the Tottenham fans behind the goal and threw his arms up in the air.

Les flicked the header on and Jürgen turned brilliantly in the box and banged a shot into the bottom corner. 4–2!

Les dribbled forward and slipped a pass through to Jürgen. He let the ball roll across to his left foot and fired it into the far corner. 5–2!

There was even time for Jürgen to set up Moussa Saïb with a brilliant backheel. 6–2!

Thanks to his four fantastic goals and two amazing assists, Tottenham were staying in the Premier League! At the end, Jürgen picked up the matchball and raised it high above his head like a trophy. The crowd roared.

Klinsmann! Klinsmann! Klinsmann!

'I knew that we'd do it!' he told Gary as they celebrated the great escape.

Tottenham vs Southampton wasn't just the last game of the 1997–98 season; it would also be the last game of Jürgen's club career. He wanted to say goodbye to Spurs in style.

When Les chested down Ian Walker's goal-kick, Jürgen hit it on the half-volley from outside the penalty area. The technique was textbook. The ball flew straight as an arrow into the top corner of the net.

Goooooooooooooooooooooaaaaaaaaaaaaaaaaalllllllllllll lllllllllllllll!!!!!!!!!!!!!!!!!!!!

Jürgen ran past the fans, urging them to make more noise. This was it. It was time for his last dive at White Hart Lane.

CHAPTER 23

WORLD CUP '98

Jürgen's incredible football career was almost over. All that remained was one last World Cup in France. Could he finish on another high?

Germany's Euro '96-winning squad was back together again. Matthias had retired but Lothar had returned as the team's thirty-seven-year-old sweeper. They had so much experience and quality all over the pitch, and that's why they were one of the favourites to lift the World Cup trophy again.

'One step at a time,' Jürgen warned his teammates.

Thanks to his late season form at Tottenham, he had kept his place as Germany's leader and goalscorer. He was so proud to be bowing out at the very top of world football, as the captain of his country.

'Enjoy it,' the national team manager Vogts urged him. 'You've earned a fairy-tale ending!'

Jürgen always saved his best form for the biggest stage. In the first match against the USA, he jumped up in between two defenders to head the ball across to Andreas Möller. 1–0!

'Come on!' Jürgen shouted, punching the air.

In the second half, he chested down Oliver's cross and calmly side-footed the ball into the bottom corner.

Goooooooooooooaaaaaaaaalllllllllllllllllllll!!!!!!!!!!!!!

Another tournament, another goal – and what a classy finish! Jürgen raced over to Oliver and jumped into his arms. Together, the Germany players were living up to the nation's great expectations.

'Good start, guys!' Jürgen congratulated them.

After a dramatic 2–2 draw with Yugoslavia, Germany's star strikeforce combined again to beat Iran. When Oliver's shot bounced back off the post, who reacted first? Jürgen, of course! With a diving header, he scored his tenth World Cup goal.

'Yes, yes, YES!' Jürgen shouted, shaking the goal-net with excitement.

The Germany fans loved to see their hero's passion and pride. Even after eleven years of international football, he still cared so much about his country.

Germany had the experience, but did they have the energy to go all the way? Tournament football was tiring, and their senior players were struggling to stay fresh in the summer sun.

Germany found it hard to cope with Mexico's fast, entertaining football. After seventy minutes, they were 1–0 down and facing another early exit.

'Keep going!' Jürgen clapped and cheered. 'We'll find a way to score!'

It wasn't pretty but eventually, Germany's captain pounced. One Mexico defender headed the ball against another and Jürgen was there in a flash to take full advantage.

Gooooooooooooaaaaaaaaalllllllllllllllllllll!!!!!!!!!!!!!

The fans waved their national flags wildly, with joy and relief. It was Jürgen to the rescue once again!

Thanks to him, their World Cup wasn't over yet. In the dying minutes, Oliver headed Germany to a hard-fought win.

'Well done but we can play so much better than that!' Vogts shouted, trying to lift his exhausted team.

In the quarter-finals, they faced Croatia. Germany had beaten them 2–1 at Euro '96 but two years on, it would be a totally different battle.

'Dig deep, guys!' Jürgen cried out. 'We've got the chance to make our country proud here.

At half-time, Germany were one goal and one player down. With ten men, it was going to take something very special to turn things around. Jürgen, however, wasn't giving up.

'We can't let the fans down,' he told the disappointed faces in the dressing room. 'If we lose, then we lose, but let's lose fighting!'

When Croatia scored their second goal, it suddenly hit Jürgen like a bolt of lightning. This was going to be his last-ever game as a professional footballer, for club or country. He ran and ran but this time, there was no goodbye goal.

At the final whistle, Jürgen shook hands and swapped shirts. With Oliver, he walked over to the Germany fans to wave and thank them for all their love and support. In that moment, Jürgen felt a powerful mix of emotions – pride, shame, regret, sadness. He had done everything he could, but his World Cup dreams were over.

Once he was back in the dressing room, Jürgen broke down in tears. He hugged Thomas and Andreas tightly as if he'd never let go.

'I'm going to miss you!' he sobbed.

From humble beginnings in Göppingen, Jürgen had risen all the way to World Cup glory. With his drive and determination, he had made the very most of his top footballing talent. Jürgen was Mr Consistent, Mr Reliable. When his team was crying out for a hero, it was he who got the goals. He did it in Italy, in France, in England and best of all, he did it for his beloved Germany, time and time again.

'We're going to miss you too!' Thomas said back, patting his shoulder.

It was the end of an incredible era for German football. Jürgen had led his country to World Cup glory in 1990 and European glory in 1996. Who would be their next national hero?

Turn the page for a sneak preview of
another brilliant football story by
Matt and Tom Oldfield. . .

MANUEL NEUER

Available now!

CHAPTER 1

WORLD CUP WINNER

Sunday, 13 July 2014

As Manuel sang the words of the German national anthem loud and proud, he tried not to look over at the famous gold trophy sitting a few metres away from him. It was so beautiful and so close. Manuel could have reached out and touched it when he walked out of the tunnel. But he didn't want to jinx it. The trophy didn't belong to them. Yet.

'Come on!' Manuel clapped as the music finished.

The famous Maracanã stadium in Rio de Janeiro was packed and ready for the 2014 World Cup Final – Germany vs Argentina. After thrashing the hosts Brazil 7-1, they were the favourites to win, but they couldn't underestimate a top team like Argentina.

Philipp Lahm, Mats Hummels, Jérôme Boateng and Benedikt Höwedes – they were more than just his teammates, for club and country. They were his friends. They believed in each other and worked together. That's why they were one game away from becoming Champions of the World.

Yes, Argentina had Lionel Messi, but Germany had Manuel. In Brazil, Manuel had consistently shown that he was the best goalkeeper in the world. It wasn't just his incredible reaction saves; it was his all-round game. Manuel was no ordinary keeper. He could catch, stop, tackle *and* pass. He was Germany's last line of defence and also their first line of attack. His teammates trusted him and relied on him.

'Jérôme, watch Messi when he drops deep!' Manuel called and pointed.

He never stopped moving, talking, organising. It all helped him to keep his concentration for the big moments, the moments when Germany would need their goalkeeper to save the day.

After thirty minutes, Argentina's Gonzalo Higuaín had the ball in the net. But Manuel already had his arm up, even while diving down. 'Offside!' he called out.

Manuel was right, of course. The linesman raised his flag. No goal – what a relief!

In the second half, Higuaín chased after a long ball. He used his speed to escape from the German defenders, but he couldn't escape from the German goalkeeper. Manuel to the rescue! He sprinted off his line to jump and punch the ball away from danger.

'Thanks, Manu!' Benedikt shouted.

Manuel nodded modestly. He was just doing his job: number one sweeper keeper.

Argentina couldn't score past Manuel, but Germany couldn't score past Sergio Romero either. The longer the match went on, the more nerve-wracking it became, for the fans and for the players. Fortunately, Manuel was Mr Nervenstärke: 'Mr Strong-Nerved'. Even though he was the last man, he stayed calm and focused.

In the last ten minutes, Germany had several chances to score.

'So close!' Manuel was groaning, putting his hands on his head.

But he didn't switch off. He had to concentrate at all times. A goalkeeper never knew when his team would need him. In extra-time, Rodrigo Palacio chested the ball down and ran into the penalty area. Manuel was out in a flash, making it hard for the striker to score. Palacio managed to chip the ball over him, but it went wide of the goal.

'No more mistakes!' Manuel told his defenders.

He was already preparing himself for his favourite battle – penalties. Goalkeeper vs striker, one on one, the pressure, the drama – Manuel loved it. He had been the shoot-out hero so many times before, for Schalke and for Bayern Munich, but never for Germany. Would this be his moment?

No, because André Schürrle crossed to Mario Götze, who volleyed the ball into the net. What a goal – Germany 1 Argentina 0!

Most of the players and fans went wild, but not Manuel. He punched the air and then returned to his goal-line. There were still six minutes of football left to play before he could celebrate properly. 'Stay organised!' he screamed out.

Lucas Biglia flicked the ball into the path of Marcos Rojo. Danger! Manuel had one last bit of sweeper keeping to do. He rushed out, lifted the ball over Rojo's head and caught it on the other side. He made it look so easy.

Neuer! Neuer! Neuer!

It was the perfect way for Manuel to end a perfect tournament. At the final whistle, he ran and jumped onto the growing pile of his Germany teammates. He hugged every single one of them.

Back in 2009, Manuel had won the Under-21 European Championships with Mats, Jérôme, Benedikt, Sami Khedira and Mesut Özil. That night, they dreamt about the future. Now, that future had arrived. They had won the World Cup together.

Manuel put on a white Germany shirt over his green goalkeeper jersey. He wanted to wear the national colours and he was no different to the outfield players anyway. But soon he had to take it off because he had a special award to collect.

'...And the Golden Glove for Best Goalkeeper goes to... MANUEL NEUER!'

Manuel had kept out Cristiano Ronaldo's Portugal, Karim Benzema's France, Hulk's Brazil and finally Messi's Argentina. He was the number one sweeper keeper, the best in the world.

Manuel raised the trophy in one big hand and punched the air with the other. What a night! He was very proud of his own achievement, but he was prouder about his team's achievement. The World Cup was the trophy that Manuel really wanted to hold. It was his childhood dream come true. 'Yesssssssssssssssssssss!' he shouted, lifting it high above his head.

The German League, the Champions League, and now the World Cup – the small, skinny kid from Gelsenkirchen had won them all.

When Manuel was younger, lots of people had made the mistake of doubting him. Would he grow tall enough to be a goalkeeper? Could he make it at the top level? Was his style too risky? But he rose to every challenge with nerves and gloves of steel. He was a leader, a winner, and a goalkeeper extraordinaire. It was like he had been born with a football in his hands.

JÜRGEN KLINSMANN HONOURS

Inter Milan

🏆 UEFA Cup: 1990-91

Bayern Munich

🏆 UEFA Cup: 1995-96

🏆 Bundesliga: 1996-97

Barcelona

🏆 Summer Olympic Games: Bronze medal 1988

🏆 FIFA World Cup: 1990

🏆 UEFA European Championship: 1996

Individual

- 🏆 Bundesliga Top Goalscorer: 1987–88
- 🏆 West German Footballer of the Year: 1988
- 🏆 FIFA World Cup All-Star Team: 1990
- 🏆 German Footballer of the Year: 1994
- 🏆 FWA Footballer of the Year: 1994–95
- 🏆 PFA Team of the Year: 1994–95
- 🏆 Ballon d'Or (Runner-up): 1995
- 🏆 UEFA Cup Top Scorer: 1995–96

KLINSMANN

9 & 18

THE FACTS

NAME: Jürgen Klinsmann

DATE OF BIRTH: 30 July 1964

AGE: 53

PLACE OF BIRTH: Göppingen

NATIONALITY: German

BEST FRIEND: Rudi Völler

CURRENT CLUB: VfB Stuttgart, Inter Milan, Monaco, Tottenham, Bayern Munich

POSITION: ST

THE STATS

Height (cm):	181
Club appearances:	614
Club goals:	282
Club trophies:	4
International appearances:	108
International goals:	47
International trophies:	2
Ballon d'Ors:	0

★ ★ ★ **HERO RATING: 88** ★ ★ ★

GREATEST MOMENTS

Type and search the web links to see the magic for yourself!

**14TH NOVEMBER 1987,
VFB STUTTGART 3-0 BAYERN MUNICH**

https://www.youtube.com/watch?v=1RxYCM3ku8I

Jürgen was already one of the top scorers in
Germany, but he needed to do something special
to impress the national team manager, Franz
Beckenbauer. This bicycle kick against Stuttgart's
rivals Bayern Munich in the Bundesliga was certainly
special. It was Jürgen's big breakthrough and a few
months later, he got the international debut that he
was looking for.

24TH JUNE 1990, WEST GERMANY 2-1 NETHERLANDS

https://www.youtube.com/watch?v=ThSAbZRzBP0&t=1s

This might be Jürgen's most famous performance of all. Jürgen had to play as a lone striker. He proved to be the perfect man for the job. Before leaving the field to a standing ovation, he even snuck in to score the first goal. West Germany went all the way and won the World Cup.

20TH AUGUST 1994, SHEFFIELD WEDNESDAY 3-4 TOTTENHAM

https://www.youtube.com/watch?v=ntJJoHTgbrY

Jürgen didn't receive a warm welcome from English football fans. His Germany team had beaten them at the 1990 World Cup, and they claimed he was a diving cheat. Jürgen was determined to prove them wrong in the best way possible. When he scored this brilliant winning header on his Tottenham debut, Jürgen celebrated with the first 'Klinsmann Dive'. The Premier League had a new hero.

4 15TH MAY 1996, BORDEAUX 1-3 BAYERN MUNICH

https://www.youtube.com/watch?v=c3HQoKT3wDU

Not only was this Jürgen's second UEFA Cup trophy
success, but it was also the night that he broke a
European scoring record. When he tapped in Bayern's
third, it was his fifteenth goal of the competition in only
twelve matches. Jürgen had showed yet again that he
was a big tournament player.

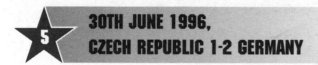

5 30TH JUNE 1996, CZECH REPUBLIC 1-2 GERMANY

https://www.youtube.com/watch?v=arrPEu7CNhE&t=59s

Oliver Bierhoff was Germany's hero in the Euro '96
final, but Jürgen was Germany's captain and leader.
After a disappointing 1994 World Cup, he led his team
all the way to victory. It was a triumph of togetherness
over talent. Lifting the trophy was one of Jürgen's
proudest moments in football.

PLAY LIKE YOUR HEROES

THE JÜRGEN KLINSMANN DIVE

SEE IT HERE You Tube

https://www.youtube.com/watch?v=-Mikgy19u20

STEP 1: Score a goal. It can be a spectacular volley or a simple tap-in; it doesn't matter as long as it goes in!

Step 2: Watch and wait for the ball to cross the line. You don't want to look like a fool, do you?

Step 3: Once it's in, race towards the corner flag, whipping the fans up into a frenzy as you pass.

Step 4: Tell your teammates what you're about to do. A big group celebration will look way better than just you on your own.

Step 5: When everyone's ready, put your arms out in front of you and throw your body forward. Make sure it's a dive, rather than a belly flop!

Step 6: Glide gleefully across the grass for as long as possible. Then lie there soaking up the applause, while the others catch up.

TEST YOUR KNOWLEDGE

QUESTIONS

1. What job did Jürgen's dad do?

2. Which sport did Jürgen's dad introduce him to first?

3. How old was Jürgen when he moved from Göppingen to Stuttgart?

4. Which country did Jürgen visit with the West German youth team, aged 15?

5. What was Jürgen's prize for keeping Stuttgarter Kickers away from relegation in 1984?

6. Which country did Jürgen face on his international debut?

7. What are the four languages that Jürgen can speak fluently?

8. How many times did Jürgen win the UEFA Cup?

9. Which club was Jürgen playing for when he won his only league title?

10. How many World Cups did Jürgen play in for West Germany and Germany?

11. Jürgen won the Ballon d'Or – true or false?

Answers below. . . No cheating!

1. *He was a baker.* **2.** *Gymnastics* **3.** *14 years old* **4.** *Portugal* **5.** *A trip to Florida, in the USA!* **6.** *Brazil* **7.** *German, Italian, French and English* **8.** *Twice – 1991 and 1996* **9.** *Bayern Munich* **10.** *Three – 1990, 1994 and 1998* **11.** *False – but he was the runner-up in 1995.*

This summer, your favourite football heroes will pull on their country's colours to go head-to-head for the ultimate prize – the World Cup.

Celebrate by making sure you have six of the best Ultimate Football Heroes, now with limited-edition international covers!

COMING 31ST MAY

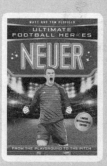

FOLLOW IN THE FOOTSTEPS OF LEGENDS. . .

Bridge the gap between past and present by stepping into the shoes of six classic World Cup heroes and reading their exciting stories – from the playground to the pitch, and to superstardom!

COMING 31ST MAY

SARA STOCKBRIDGE

The Fortunes of Grace Hammer

A Tale of the Victorian Underworld

VINTAGE BOOKS
London

Published by Vintage 2010

2 4 6 8 10 9 7 5 3 1

Copyright © Sara Stockbridge 2009

Sara Stockbridge has asserted her right under the Copyright, Designs
and Patents Act 1988 to be identified as the author of this work

Originally published as *Hammer* in Great Britain in 2009 by
Chatto & Windus

Vintage
Random House, 20 Vauxhall Bridge Road,
London SW1V 2SA

www.vintage-books.co.uk

Addresses for companies within The Random House Group Limited
can be found at: www.randomhouse.co.uk/offices.htm

The Random House Group Limited Reg. No. 954009

A CIP catalogue record for this book
is available from the British Library

ISBN 9780099520955

The Random House Group Limited supports The Forest
Stewardship Council (FSC), the leading international forest
certification organisation. All our titles that are printed on
Greenpeace approved FSC certified paper carry the FSC logo.
Our paper procurement policy can be found at:
www.rbooks.co.uk/environment

Printed and bound in Great Britain by
CPI Bookmarque, Croydon CR0 4TD

For Max and Lelu

PROLOGUE

Grace arrives as night falls, huge and black over her head. She had seen the smoke a mile off and supposed they had been burning the stubble that day; an acrid wisp hangs in the air over Pagham, of smouldering chaff, she fancies. There are no lights in the village as she makes her way up the lane, no one cooking, no shouting, no children. The Green Man is empty; abandoned jars stand huffily upon the bar, the clock ticks to itself above the mantel. A lonely dog barks her up the lane, whining at the end of its tether. No faces, no greetings – surprise! Coming home at last, as she had pictured it. She stands by the sleeping church, all alone, turning her head this way and that, and wonders, for a curious moment, if everyone is hiding. Past the juniper hedge she realises the tang is not fading, but coming thicker, on a soft breeze, every step. She stops short. And the clock, and the dog, and the turning earth. Her chest seems to hollow, horribly, and she picks up her feet and hurls herself up the hill, waves swelling and breaking in her ears, heart banging on her tongue. Something sharp in the lane bites through the sole of her shoe; sparks burst across the horizon as the still in the outhouse explodes.

Hellfire swallows the Hammer farmhouse, lighting the

sky: a raging orb lashing jagged tongues around the black bricks, cracking screaming timber like dry ribs. It rips livid into the dark as if it would tear itself loose from the ground and cast furious Judgement down across the earth. She crosses the meadow on rubber legs. Dread smoke churns into the starry sky, gathering like doom; bats, blazing horsemen, devil hounds spiral frenzied into the night. In the distance crazy figures blow, tiny, to and fro like tumbling ashes. Demons flicker at the dead windows, spewing cinders, taking human shape, watching her drown, running through treacle. She throws herself howling on the crowd, gaping into hot faces, looking for her pa, brothers, her sweet rosy sister. May was sleeping the last time she saw her – beatific – flying, evidently, on a white horse through her favourite dream (which sounded tedious, though Grace had never said so). The good people of Pagham hold fast to her arms to stop her running into the blazing house. And they watch, rigid, as the roof caves in with a mighty groan, like an elephant dying, collapsing into a million sparks.

Grace wakes, eyes wide, upright in her bed. Sleeping breath fills the room. Someone cries, 'Thief!' in the distance. All is well. She goes back to peaceful sleep. And though she will feel something amiss in the morning she will put it down to a dream she cannot quite remember, and leave it at that.

Out in the dark countryside, in his gloomy farmhouse, Mr Blunt sits upright in his oily bed, jabbering and growling in the dark. It haunts him tonight in his sleep, as it does maybe once a year now – calling, as bright as it ever was! – leading him on, like the Pole Star twinkling through a veil of cloud, only to dissolve again, and he clenches his brutal fists, and blasts the sleeping birds from the trees.

'*Damn you, Hammer! Damn you wretched bitch!*'

Sometimes he dreams, with pleasure, of slicing her throat.

CHAPTER ONE

Jack Tallis sleeps in a warehouse at London Docks whence he ventures daily to drink himself unconscious in the Queen. He is a favourite with the local ladies, who find him captivating though he is often rude. When rejected with a contemptuous glance they giggle nervously, as if in shock, and wither back into the wall, perhaps to try their luck another evening – when he might smile charmingly, flashing his full brilliance, so that the chosen girl will feel special, though she knows he does not mean it.

Handsome! How devilish can a man be? With his dark eyes, and his insolent mouth, and the cheek of him! Flashing his winning grin! He is handsome through to the very back of his head. He shines at the lucky girl, lips curling as if they know she imagines how it would be to kiss them, tender and firm, flashing strong white teeth behind.

'Good evening, Louise.' (Or any other female name you may care for.)

She lights up like Piccadilly, a little breathless. 'Hello, Jack!'

'You are dazzling tonight, if I may be so bold,' he says, grasping her round the waist with a rough hand and pulling her closer, pressing a knee between hers.

'Why, thank you, Jack.' She blushes sweetly and giggles.

'I must say I should like to tempt you into a darkened room with me, Louise.'

Speechless, she basks for a moment in the glow; it will be enough to keep her going until he acknowledges her existence again. This might take weeks, but such is the force of his appeal that she will be content to wait. Already his attention is elsewhere, upon Mrs Maybury, the landlady, who barred him only last week but has forgotten it already.

'What's it to be, you devil?'

'Hello, there he is! Oi, Jack!' Oh, God, that voice again, bobbing up behind him, every night of the week. It belongs to Miss Lucy Fear, whose company he has been hoping to avoid this evening. Her name may tell you all you need to know.

'Look, Sally, I found him!' She is lurching across the bar at him, shouting as she goes. 'She's been all over looking for you!' It is clearly Lucy who has been looking all over. Sally, who lives in oblivion, turns her head at the sound of her name and steadies herself to focus, which she manages with a nice blush when she sees it is Jack, even though she is pickled.

'Best please, Mrs M.'

'She wants to get hold of you, Jack!'

Lucy is prodding him now, brushing up against him. He can feel her breath on his cheek. He fights the urge to punch her loud fat face. Sally has fallen off her stool.

'Go on then, you silly girl!'

'I don't dare!'

Women flirt with Jack like clumsy children – they giggle stupidly, in a manner they imagine to be fetching, with their

6

eyes wide like village idiots', they ask him to repeat particular words, such as 'thoroughfare' or 'thirty-three', his age, just to see the shape his lips make when he says it, and the big wide laugh that bursts like a ripe fruit, with his head thrown back as if in the throes of some passion. His dark brown eyes might cloud in the space of a blink – hard and flat – as if the charming gent to whom you were talking just a moment before had vanished, and you had never met this cold stranger.

He breaks away to sit by the wall where he cannot be cornered, next to Archie Simmons, who will talk about his bedsores, or the damp at his lodgings if he is lucky.

Grace Hammer has no reason to be in the Queen over any other public palace that dots the corner of any other street, like a rash across the Temperance map, lighting up London town: only that she was thirsty and right outside the door. This evening she is looking rather lovely, and not because she has scrubbed up nicely but because she woke up so that morning, shining like the cherry on the cake. Her assets are not racked up underneath her chin, east and west, as if in a window-box, like every other pair there. And not big either, just a nice handful. Her legs are long and strong and shapely, hidden under her skirts. Her lips curl at the corners. Grace can change like spring weather, be stern as Queen Victoria. She looks to Jack Tallis like a missing heartbeat.

He has seen her here before, in fact, across the bar; now, as then, she pays him not a flicker of attention. This evening he takes her in properly: strong hands, clean hair, her mouth, the curve from her chin to her throat. She says something to her tatty friend and laughs, showing good teeth, the whitest in Whitechapel, except maybe his own. He stares until she turns round.

They gaze at each other for several moments, delighted, and caught, share a fleeting thought – that rare thrill: There you are! After scorching him thus she looks away. He sits still for a while, stealing a glance now and then, but she doesn't look over again, so, cocksure (or putting on a good show of it), he rises from his seat to saunter arrogantly to her table.

The men of the parish envy Jack. Though he is poor he never seems to want for much. He eats well, he never wears a desperate face. His clothes are shabby but he always finds a kind lady to wash them. He will always land on his feet. He has ease, and luck, and he has long ring fingers to prove it. Only a few who have made his intimate acquaintance will know that sometimes he feels small and foolish.

She fixes him halfway across, and he falters, tripping on an invisible nail in the floor but covering it well, making her grin, and he catches the blatant thought in her eye and bats it back so that by the time he has crossed the room and sat next to her they are almost laughing, and feel that they have jumped a few steps and don't care where they start.

So he says, 'Who might you be then?' and she says, 'What's it to you?'

'I'm Jack,' he offers, tipping his hat.

'It's nice to meet you, I'm sure.'

'You look *fine*.'

'Is that right?'

'I've seen you here before.'

'And so?'

How startling the attraction and how strangely familiar they seem – a common element of many ill-fated connections, as Grace is well aware. They sparkle mischief, letting their mucky thoughts talk and looking at each other's lips.

'Where d'you spring from, then?'

'Round the corner.'

'And me.'

'Fancy!'

'So where do you hide?'

'Indoors!'

'That's a shame.'

'I can't see that I'm missing much.' She looks right at him as she says it, with her face quite straight, which tickles Jack Tallis. He likes a girl with prickles.

'How many have you got indoors, then?'

'Plenty to be going on with, thank you.'

'No husband?'

'Ask a lot of questions don'tcha?' Grace can't help but crack her face. She likes a man with just the right bad manners.

'Chased him away, did ya? How d'you find it on your own?'

'I grit my teeth.'

'I'll bet you do!'

They laugh wide together, stop, and look. She runs her fingers up his throat and grips him softly by his handsome jaw, surprising them both, and their matching lips meet. Both note that the other's breath is sweet, though laced with smoke and gin. When their mouths part they stay with their faces close together, rapt, with a little crooked smile as if they know each other well.

'I quite like you, Jack.'

'Won't you tell me your name, then?'

'No.'

Hurrying out they draw bitter glances from the usual girls. People see them go and think: What a handsome pair! Bursting with it. And all their teeth.

'Can I follow you home?'

'Not likely!'

'Will you come with me then?'

Now let us set this straight before we carry on: Miss Grace Hammer is no unfortunate creature of night. She has no need of anything this charmer may have upon his person and, indeed, has resolved already not to fleece him. She does not make a habit of stepping out down dark and lonely streets with men who have not told her where they are going, however handsome they may be, and she has a razor in her pocket, just in case.

And so she lets him lead her up Cable Street, then left, past the Dock Street Sailors' Home, past the church. The pub at the corner is bursting with noise, fights are breaking out, Irishmen are singing merry songs about their hard luck and their heartless women. Indians play dominoes on the benches outside, dark faces in shadow, bright flashing eyes. They cross Smithfield Street and go down towards

Pennington along the forbidding wall of the London Docks. Grace has passed this wall only once before, though it is a mere spit due north from her front door; it seems to stretch a mile, made of countless bricks, laid by hordes of tiny men, slaving like ants on the scaffolding. She rarely sees the river, imprisoned as it is from Blackwall to the Tower. She never ventures further than this, to the end of the lane, to catch a glimpse of the dark water beyond.

The wide river Thames is England's jugular, busy like the heart. It brings in everything you could eat, drink, smoke, or wear, buy or sell from the far corners of the globe. As the city grows, so does its appetite: the ships grow larger and the hungry docks unfold, spreading towards the sea. The largest and newest is the Royal Albert Dock, past the Isle of Dogs: two miles long, built to harbour the biggest ships in the wide world – an ungodly hole in the ground, like the grave of some colossus, fallen to earth with a mighty crash. It was dug by such a dusty legion as built the great pyramids of Egypt, and killed very many of them in the process. Three unlucky men, who had nothing to do with its construction, rest in such peace as may be afforded in the concrete beneath the gigantic lock gates.

The first two – deep in the ditch! – had tried to rob the notorious Wilson betting shop, a bone-headed venture indeed, though to be fair they were new to the area, having docked just five days before. They had found the front office free of cash, which did not accord with their tip-off, and lurched upstairs, hoping to find something there, by which time the Wilson girl, who was minding the shop, had whistled across the street for the Wilson men, who came directly, with hatchets. The terrible two had found a small safe in the back room and, with a Herculean effort, had managed to heave it out of the window. It fell on to a very nice birdbath in the yard below, obliterating it, but no matter. These hapless idiots (their being referred to thus in the fairest and most amiable manner) were staring drunkenly after it, preparing to climb down somehow, when the hatchet men caught them. They ended up in the bottom of the trench the night before the concrete, in approximately five pieces each.

The third unfortunate fellow below the Royal Albert Dock gates joined them the very next day. It struck him as unfair as he went under – a harsh price to pay for a simple mistake. He had leaned just an inch too far over the edge to retrieve his watch. It had jumped from his hand as he took it from his pocket, arcing in slow motion into the wet cement; he had been meaning to get the chain fixed all week and cursed himself for putting it off. He was late and taking a short-cut to Canning Town. It was submerging slowly, looking at him with half a face, and he was sure he could reach it. He supposed the concrete was not too deep.

Below Whitechapel lurk the London Docks, tight behind fortress walls, high as the Tower, where our two tiny vagabonds scurry around the perimeter, sinking into shadows. By day they swarm with hungry men, sweating blood in the warehouses, toiling under haystack bales of wool, fat barrels you could drown in, sacks of coffee, green bananas, crates of lemons; they break their backs upon the landing decks and feel lucky still to have been picked out from the crowd at the gates, like winning the tombola, even if the finger that is sacrificed most days to the jealous god of commerce should be one of theirs. (Someone ought to log these sorry digits but nobody bothers; they are clean gone, ripped smartly off in cranking chains or bitten through by turning iron teeth; they turn up now and then in the foreman's lunch.) They stack tobacco, row on row of tusks, leopard– or bearskins, tiger fur; pythons from some fetid jungle hang from the rafters to the floor.

After night falls it becomes a silent and deserted place. The barrel yard is huge and empty; the warehouses loom into the black sky beyond. The sound of lapping water comes gently across the breeze, and the groaning of stacked ships, jostling each other in the great west basin. Gulls cruise the night sky, rats come out of hiding to sniff around the storerooms.

The only human beings who inhabit this strange netherworld are Jack – who resides there on the quiet, courtesy of his good friend Bill Brierley, foreman of the west dock – and the night-watchmen, of whom there are four: two for the west and two for the east and the Shadwell Basin. They are not the most vigilant guardians, preferring to take frequent tea breaks in their hut at the side of Tobacco Dock, where their beats overlap. They are supposed to patrol in pairs but split up to halve the time. They boil a little tin kettle and feel themselves very clever indeed, making rounds every hour that take them no more than seventeen minutes.

★

Handsome Jack Tallis stops suddenly by a small arch, hidden in the precipice of the dock wall, and looks up and down the wide ghost way, a million cobbles stretching into darkness, before sinking inside, feeling his way to the end. He presses his ear to the stout wooden door. Grace strikes a match. It flares with a tiny sizzling sound casting yellow light across their faces. Footsteps pass inside and they wait, holding their breath. He opens the lock and the heavy chain with a key that seems to have sprung from the palm of his hand, and they are through the portal into the secret world, locking it tight behind them.

The yard stretches away to the grand entrance of the wine vaults, with the clock above, the warehouses dark behind, and beyond, glimpsed between them, the sparkle of light on water. Jack grabs her hand and they scurry like rats across the vast empty yard. The watchman is almost back at his hut, his lantern fading into the distance, shaking on its chain. Grace follows Jack out by the water: deep Indian ink, rippling slowly in the moonlight. Banks of ships like sleeping dinosaurs hang in the great basin, their chains clanking softly, masts and prows stuck out like prehistoric limbs against the dark milky sky. He catches her hand and, turning her to face him, kisses her again. Arching together, moonlit, charmed rag and bone shadows.

She spots the boat first, among the great creaking hulls, just waiting with its oars tucked in, ready as if they had called for it – and in they go, water heaving beneath them, lapping like thick black jelly. Jack takes the oars and thrusts them outward into the pool.

The moon lights patterns around them, dancing out from

the stern, breaking with each stroke into shards of silver. The chatter and rabble are far behind, the Queen is a dream, and the peace lies around them like a blanket. It is uncommon and blissful, and Grace does not want to break it. She trails her hand in the water, wonders how deep it goes down. Far over on the dock wall the night-watchman's lantern casts a shaky halo but he is a speck in the distance. Jack stops rowing, oars poised in mid-air as if holding their breath, shining drops falling like chimes. They are mice in a newspaper hat, afloat on their own private sea.

'Let me try,' she says, taking the oars.

CHAPTER TWO

Jack Tallis did not have the pleasure of her company again that week or the next. He looked for her in the Queen and then the Britannia, the Alma, the Princess Alice, the Ten Bells, the Horn of Plenty and even the Saracen's Head. Had he known he had missed her by a few moments on Thursday outside Spitalfields Market and then again on Saturday at the top of Brick Lane he might have persevered, but he was not famous for sticking at it and gave up at last. He was sulking into his beer at the Frying Pan – she seemed to have disappeared from the face of the Earth, as if he had dreamed her – when the door swung open and in she came, followed by a small girl, maybe five years old, with a crisp blue bow in her hair. He almost rubbed his eyes to make sure he was seeing straight.

Grace Hammer marched straight past him up to the counter and banged her fist upon it, making the jars jump. It was midday and the regular rabble were not all in yet, so the landlord swung round ready to start, but laughed heartily when he saw it was Grace and lifted the hatch to let her through to the back room. The little girl caught Jack's eye as she followed them in, trailing by the hand from her mother's grip, fixing him to the wall with that cast-iron look he has seen already, only blue this time, right through him. Then the door closed behind them.

Jack waited, straining his ears, but heard nothing – he sat for a while feeling unaccountably awkward, as if he was watching himself. He was getting up to leave when they reappeared, and sat down quickly; there was hand-shaking and more joviality. The little girl ate an iced bun, looking past them at him, studying his hat and his hands, which unnerved him somehow. It seemed an awkward moment to present himself so he sank back in his seat, trying to merge with the shadow. Grace and the little girl walked out into the street. Jack drained his jug and slid after them.

Grace Hammer has four living children: Charlie, who is almost a grown man, Billy, eleven, Jake, nine, and lovely Miss Daisy, just five. The boys are a crew of fine young men with a righteous sense of justice and respect for their fellows, though they earn their daily bread and butter rifling the pockets of wealthy strangers – they are often to be found helping old Mrs Cutler to eat her meagre dinner or reading to Miss Grieve, who is dying in a cold bed. They are fiercely and utterly devoted to their little sister, though they love to tease her for their own selfish amusement.

'Who's your sweetheart Daisy? Is it Harry Harding? I saw you getting friendly on the corner.'

'Go *away*!' she shouts: a fair retort, she uses it often – for a greeting sometimes, as they enter the room, even before they have opened their mouths.

'Was you sharing secrets? Or just sugar lumps?'

Daisy does not respond in English but growls as well as any jungle creature might at such a bunch of monkeys. One day when she grows big she will be something to reckon with; for now she is small, and soft, the prettiest girl in London Town, so they laugh, and prod some more, as boys do – 'So it *is* Harry now, see! What happened to poor Joe? He was the only boy in the world last week. Ain't you gonna marry him no more?' – making her roar. Daisy beats them back and they laugh at her as they run away.

When the girls are left in peace they draw pictures, or do chains of cut-out people, holding hands. The Hammer boys keep all the things their sister makes them – careful, knotted, twisted things of string and paper, sticks and bones, and feathers she finds in the street. There are dozens, she being an extraordinarily busy little person: sheaves of drawings and maps of the world, adorned with writing of her own design, which she will read you if you ask her nicely.

Charlie lost his father at the age of three – the only decent man Grace had found. He fell into a blast furnace at the foundry where he worked and is much missed still. Billy and Jake's father fared no better, catching tuberculosis in the outbreak of 1879 and wheezing on for a few miserable months in the Union Workhouse before kicking the bucket – a fate richly deserved as he was a useless cheat, cruel and unfaithful, though he had seemed charming at first. Grace had thought herself thoroughly cured of scoundrels until Daisy's father happened along, giving her two girls. The first was Rose, who died while still new, buried in a tiny white coffin carried by her brothers while her father mourned in the pub. The second was darling Miss Daisy, after whose conception Grace kicked him out. She had embarked already on a private life of crime and had no need of him. The family thrived thereafter; they ate well, they wanted for nothing. Grace felt herself lucky every day. Poor Mrs Ratch next door had a brute who beat her twice a week and gave her a baby every year; he spent his wages on drink and Grace could see she was starving slowly to death, trying to feed her children.

Daisy was lucky enough never to meet her father. He died under the wheels of a brewery cart not a month after he'd gone; a kindly copper brought the solemn news, which made Grace laugh and clap her hands, and ask if death had been swift and merciful, or horribly brutal; and if he had suffered, how terribly and for how long. Sergeant Manley Goodwell was shocked at Grace Hammer's cruel sentiments and wondered if she had arranged the accident – which, indeed, she would have been happy to do – but he was not to know that the dead man's favourite game was to eat his fill when there was not enough for dinner before the family were allowed to start. They had to wait around the table and watch him smack his lips and lick his fingers until there was nothing left but rind and bones and potato skins. Grace wanted to stick a fork in his eye, and we must forgive her hard heart. Reluctantly she paid for a decent funeral, which might have seemed worth every penny if she had been driving the brewery cart.

And so it is their mother who has taught the Hammer children all they know. From her the boys have learned their trade, and to read and write – which sets them in some way apart from the other ragged children in the street. She is loving, and strict as the Law, which they respect as a convention though they break it every day. They have the smartest manners in London. And though Grace has a violent temper – which last exploded on Christmas Eve of 1878, driving Billy and Jake's father bare-chested from the house, beating at his charred beard, never to be seen again – she keeps it in a box and never turns it on her children, not even Charlie with his bare cheek. She had wondered if he might be better for a slap or two until her neighbour Mrs Jacob nosed across the street one day to tell her he was getting far too clever, and to recommend correction, along those very lines: iron discipline, as she had dealt her own wilful sons. Grace wouldn't have the heart anyway. She loves him, wilful as he is.

Jake doesn't say much; she keeps a special eye on him.

Billy reads the most, easily the best behaved. She loves them all as much.

Jack didn't spot Grace and Miss Blue Eyes for a minute or two, coming out into the light of day. Blinking up Brick Lane this way and that, he clocked them outside the chapel, exchanging a word with the shoe-black. He bent to pick up an imaginary penny as she turned her head his way, and when he looked up again they were on their way down the street. He hurried after them, feeling urgent suddenly, as if it were his last chance to see her. They turned right down Church Street before he reached the corner, and for the few moments that they were out of sight a strange panic held tight to his chest, until he saw them again, walking hand in hand past the tall Christ Church. He dropped back until they crossed Commercial Street, where he dived into the crowded road after them, weaving through the traffic, and caught them up, hanging close behind. At White's Row they turned right, then left into Bell Lane. He watched from the corner as they went inside and ventured up the street a little, unusually timid, to see the door. Number twenty-eight. There it was.

Now he wasn't sure what to do next, or why he had stalked her there in such a furtive manner when he might have presented himself, with his charm and his flashing teeth, as he would any other day. Upright, he liked to see himself, not skulking in the street. He drew himself tall but felt awkward still. It seemed he must turn tail and walk away – how could he knock? He stood there stupid, feeling as if he were frozen to the spot. His next move was decided by Grace, who stepped out abruptly into the street, hands upon her hips. She stood and watched him writhe, like an earthworm in salt. Her eyes did not twinkle.

'Hello, Jack,' she said. 'Fancy meeting you here.'

Inside it was dim but for a small lamp by the bed. He was surprised by the exotic scent of tuberose, though he didn't know what it was called. Glancing around, feeling uncommonly shy, he took in the clean stove, the patchwork bedspread – and sheets! He was sure they were the only decent sheets in that street, the next and the next as well. Then a small table with books upon it, not a lonely almanac or a Holy Bible, but books, in a teetering pile, stacked by some distracted intellectual. He wondered who that might be.

A red curtain half drawn across a small doorway revealed a second room; he could see the edge of a bed and a tin bath leaning against the wall beyond. Rows of paper dolls and some lively drawings of what he supposed were zoo creatures decorated the walls, signed in varying degrees of legibility by the artist, one Daisy Hammer. A lofty ballerina hung in pride of place, poised above the mantel on one toe with the other leg high in the air and her arms stretched out as if she was flying. All evidently the work of Miss Blue Eyes. He wondered how many others there were. Three at least, judging from all the washing. There were plates and clean cutlery, and by the stove a bucket of coal. The effect of entering the room from the world outside (apart from the frosty reception) was of stepping into an enchanted cave, in which to fall headlong and rest, receive comfort and refuge. She was certainly doing very nicely for herself, very nicely indeed. The woman in the back next door slept under a flour sack and ate apple cores and peelings from the gutter; a fact he did not know but would surely not have been surprised to discover.

'Charlie, this is Jack. Jack, this is my son, Charlie.'

Charlie was reading in the corner, sat regally upon a shabby armchair. He looked Jack up and down, in the way that young men have for male strangers who follow their mother home. 'How d'you do, Jack?' He stood up to kiss his ma.

'What you reading, darlin'?'

'Charles Dickens.'

'Oh, lovely.'

'*Two Cities.*'

'Where d'you find that?'

'Holywell Street.'

'Did you borrow it?'

'No, Ma!'

'Very nice indeed. Where are the boys?'

'Gone to look at Tommy's aunt again.'

'Haven't they buried her yet?'

'Tomorrow.'

'God bless her.'

Daisy pushed forward to be introduced to the stranger. He could see she remembered him, but was keeping it to herself for the moment.

'Hello,' she said from behind the stuffed dog she was clutching. 'Who are you?'

'Jack.'

'Can you draw animals?'

Now Jack, unknown but yet suspected by Grace Hammer, may be a chancer and a scoundrel but he is sweet with little children and they love him. He endeared himself thoroughly to Daisy and, to a lesser extent, with the young men of the family, when they had tired of Tommy's aunt and returned to find this stranger. They like him much better than they allow for. By the time Grace sent him home he had been invited to the next roast dinner and asked very many questions on the subjects of football, and cards, about which he seems to know a great deal.

Grace tucked Daisy into the big bed with her scruffy stuffed dog and kissed her delicious cheek.

'When is Jack coming again?'

'I couldn't tell you, darlin', I don't know. He wasn't meant to come today.'

'Why not?'

'Because no one invited him.'

'I could invite him next time.'

'Get your face washed, Jake.'

Charlie was popping out and Billy wanted to go with him.

'Course you bloody can't. He's off to see some girl, most likely. He won't want you hanging about. Sit and read that *Family Robinson*.'

'I finished it.'

'Was it any good?'

'It's all right.'

'Well, start something else, then.'

The fire snapped; Billy shuffled through the cupboard.

'And I don't want you going to the bloody Eagle anyway, not by yourself.'

'Yes, Ma.'

'Don't you cheek me.'

Jack Tallis lay on a sack of coffee in warehouse twelve, London Docks, smiling to himself in the dark. He drained his fine brandy, fresh from the barrel at the foot of his sackcloth bed – tomorrow he might sample the armagnac – and fell into contented slumber.

In Bell Lane Grace closed her eyes and pictured his strong hands, his face. He had a crease beside his mouth made by smiling, the particular smile that seems made just for you.

He was a devil indeed. She could remember such details about him, and so vividly! What a charmer.

Out in the dark countryside Mr Blunt snoozes peacefully, with a smile upon his face. He dreams of choking her, slicing her throat.

CHAPTER THREE

Long, long ago, in a fine stately home in Hampshire, Mr Horatio Blunt liberated the magnificent ruby necklace that represented the very pinnacle of his criminal career: from a secret drawer in the Honourable Lady Stanhope's armoire that gave him no trouble at all. A big crew was assembled to strip the house down – it had thirty-seven rooms and they meant to do the job properly – organised from inside with the help of a Miss Violet Chance, who would never work as a housemaid again. Mr Charles Worth himself was rumoured to have had a hand in it, though he was entertaining the lord and lady of the house that very evening at a charity ball in Mayfair. They took the best silver, porcelain, the finest pictures – leaving pale squares on the wallpaper beside the indignant family portraits – and the jewellery.

And such jewellery! A parade of shining stones to shame the night sky, sparkling against the plush velvet lining of their cases. Precious opals, like pieces of the full moon, flashing their every colour at once, as if they could not choose. A plague of sapphires – evidently Lady Stanhope's favourite, for not only did she have more than the Queen, but had arranged them in shade order, from the cornflower bud to the deep blue sea. And emeralds – immodestly green – ropes of pearls, exotic jet, a galaxy of diamonds: necklaces, tiaras, brooches, pins. Every drawer of the box hid a promise, bright like a brand new star, dazzling the crooked assembly, making them giddy, like girls. The heavy safe in which these treasures should have been tucked up tight arrived the next afternoon from the ironmonger, unluckily for Lady Stanhope, who greeted it with a kick and broke her toe upon it.

Outstanding among this confusion of riches were a necklace and drop earrings, boasting three brilliant-cut diamonds that Mr Blunt reckoned correctly, with a hasty glance, at three carats each, set around with emeralds and pearls, a diamond pin – small perhaps to you or I, beside its ostentatious neighbours, but rare blue, and flawless, and an opal ring as big as a brandy ball. But the best piece by far was the ruby necklace. It was exceptionally fine, which no one paused to consider, and indecently large, which they spotted straight.

As any good thief will know, a ruby is the rarest and most valuable stone. This ruby had more of a scarlet hue than crimson, a rare clear colour. It had been dug out of the ground in 1808 by a very poor man in Burma – the best find that year, the size of a good walnut – and caused great excitement among the miners, being a useful excuse to down tools for a minute or two. It went to France directly, where it was table cut, and then to England, where it was mounted in silver on a gold frame, edged by tiny brilliant-cut diamonds, as the centre drop of a magnificent necklace. Smaller rubies were set in the delicate silverwork that ran round the neck, in tiny claws among the silver leaves, worked with seed pearls and diamonds. The clasp at the back of the neck was studded with a two-carat diamond. It languished in the window display of Harvey and Gore for all of a week before it was purchased by the obscenely rich Earl Stanhope as an offering to his beleaguered wife after another of his indiscretions, and remained in the family for three generations.

In it went with the rest, as the alarm was sounded, and everything scattered. In the chaos the sack was dropped, and scrabbling in the dark for spilled jewels, so many men all around, piling great sacks of silver through the windows, tearing art from the walls, Blunt grabbed it on the sly from under a chair and ran out with it in his pocket, his arms full of the earl's fine pistol collection.

Now this, though he did not realise it at that moment, was Mr Blunt's finest hour. He could see it was something very pretty indeed but even he could not have known yet that Lady Stanhope's ruby was the most precious thing he would ever lay his eyes upon – outside the Tower of London, perhaps – never mind his fat, filthy hands. It was worth more than everything he had stolen that year together, with everything he had stolen the year before and the one before that. In the right market, at the right time. A jewel of such incomparable quality and size did not spring out of the ground every day, flashing so flagrantly red. He must keep it quiet a while, tread carefully, be patient. But what might a man do with such an asset! Start a new life, catch the right woman – she would look at him differently once he was rich. Let her refuse him then! He would escape the dead orchard, the broken roof, the damp and the howling wind. And leave his mother behind, under the holly tree, in the churchyard where she has been these twenty years last Tuesday.

It was later, on his own, gazing into its scarlet light, that Mr Blunt would see what he was holding, and the crudest man in all creation would melt a little, surrender to wonder and beauty, and his dreams begin to dawn upon it. And how could he have known he would be chasing them still as his hair turned grey? And that it was not he who held the treasure but, rather, the other way round?

The gang congregated in the woods some ten minutes later with the spoils. Blunt, along with all the rest, denied any knowledge of the ruby necklace that John and Jack Dean mentioned, and it was assumed first that they were exaggerating its splendour, and second, that it had been lost in the chase. A search of the undergrowth was dismissed on account of police activity in the area. Glimpsing torch beams criss-crossing in the distance, they made haste to their hideout.

It was a tense night that Mr Blunt spent, worrying that someone, on a sudden impulse, would demand to search the insides of his pockets. He felt it must show, that somehow he might emit a tiny involuntary signal that someone would sniff out through the folds of his overcoat. The sound of his name broke this private trance.

'Blunt, what do you say to these pearls?' He turned his attention to them, adopting a studious attitude.

'They are fine indeed. Round and even, lustrous. The

brooch is a quality trinket, much sought after.' He was surprised by how steady his voice sounded.

'And these diamonds?'

'Paste.'

'And which items invite the most interest?' Mr Blunt felt the ruby necklace almost burning through the lining of his coat.

'I reckon on the pearls, the emerald choker and this little diamond pin,' he held it up to the yellow glow of the gas, 'which, though small, is a rare blue, and quite flawless.' He rubbed his chin thoughtfully, affecting an air of detachment quite at odds with the fluttering wings in his stomach. Most of the company were wrestling with their own nerves still and yet to concern themselves with the market value of anything or its division thereof – too concerned with unidentified noises outside – so he need not have worried.

'There are, indeed, very many fine pieces in Lady Stanhope's collection. This set of table-cut sapphires, the opals – gems of unusual quality – and the citrines, though less precious, are large, well cut and perfectly clear. The settings are certainly French. Fine indeed. Uncommonly fine.'

It was agreed to take the haul to Ray Mathers's safe-house and to leave in half an hour. A tentative relief crawled up his back as Blunt watched the others twitching and peering through cracks in the wall, eardrums cocked into the black dark outside.

Barely a word was spoken as the hand crept round the clock, until Mathers Senior gave the word. They gathered themselves, like ugly children, in a crooked line. Hard-faced men of granite stared impassively at the wall; weasel eyes darted nervously about beneath Big Arthur Bolt's iron shoulders.

'Wait a minute,' someone said. 'There's summink missing.' A profound silence fell upon the company; owls called in the wood outside; a delirious moth slapped into the lamp. 'I can smell it.'

Blunt thought on reflection, much later, that it had been Snook, long and thin and bitter, who had uttered this vile suspicion, pointed like a bony finger at hapless Harold Whitbread – most likely to deflect attention from himself. Whitbread, indeed, *seemed* shifty: he blanched even in the dim lamplight.

'So can I,' said Charlie Fry.

Well, he's got something in his pocket for sure, thought Blunt. Piping up like that, all keen. Two or three of the crew weren't looking too smug suddenly either. In his guilty fog Blunt had quite forgotten the dishonourable thieves among the company and he wanted to laugh now that he remembered them. Even so, his heart seemed to bang against his ribs and he felt sure his colour had risen. He prayed silently and put his faith in the Lord God, whose mercy he really had no claim to, and the secret pocket deep in the lining of his greatcoat.

'Show us what you got, you sly bastard!' Poor crooked Whitbread, trembling, shook out his pockets, looking like a man with a rope already round his neck. Most of the crew were glad the suspicion had converged on someone else's head and stared intently at him, their eyes glinting with cruelty. He never did have the stomach for serious crime, thought Blunt. How quickly, in accordance with the laws of nature, does the pack turn on its weakest member! The circle tightened round Whitbread's shaking hands, eyes converging in a single beam, scorching his fluttering light-fingers. When his pockets were empty they turned to his boots, whence, after a short and futile struggle, a twinkling sapphire ring was brought forth. Just a small stone, really, set in gold, flanked by two little square-cut diamonds, and seen through Whitbread's eyes at that moment, most definitely not worth it. A moment passed before he started to whimper, horribly, for mercy – a thin, ghastly sound, it seemed to creep across the floor and clutch, wheedling, at their ankles, making them want to throw it off in revulsion and stamp upon it till it ceased. Had he known that his pleading would inspire not sympathy but murder he might have contented himself with a Hail Mary or two and repented his sins in time to enter Heaven, as he had always planned in such an eventuality. Someone struck him round the head, hard, with a heavy cudgel, making him squeal in panic and confusion like a stuck pig. And the Mathers mob piled in like hungry dogs, blunt weapons cracking at his head, a frenzy of sweat and muscle and raining blood.

They left him with his face covered, such as was left of it, a sticky pool under their boots, darkening red across the floor as they vanished into the night. Blunt thanked the devil for his luck and poor Whitbread for his diversion. The ruby necklace snoozed comfortably in the folds of his coat. He kept hold of himself, even after the company had parted, until he had locked his own front door behind him. Trembling, he leaned his back against it and allowed himself a quiet sigh of relief. He stood in the hall, listening, cast his eyes down the dark passage to see if the girl was there, suddenly, with tea. The house was still.

In his dusty library, with the heavy curtains drawn and every chink that might admit a view robustly secured, Blunt reached into his pocket, shaking a little. His clammy fingers found cold stone and he pulled it out, sparkling, into the candlelight, forgetting himself, blood red rays warming his face.

After more time than he could account for, when he thought of it afterwards – spent in rapturous delirium that he could not altogether recall or explain – Mr Blunt laid the necklace tenderly to bed in a secret nook, high behind the sleeping books, glancing over his shoulder all the while, heart in his throat. And there it hid, just an arm's reach through the hole behind *Bleak House* – the last book his dear mother had bought before she died – for all of nine days, until it was stolen, which served him right.

It is poetic to imagine that Grace might have left it well alone, had she known what she was stealing – a deadly thing, a burden and a curse. But, of course, it would have made no difference. She is a thief, after all: she will steal the priest's watch on her deathbed; that's how she was born.

You know it's not done with, says the tiny voice at the back of her head, the one that speaks at unsure moments, most often in the dark. You might walk the plank yet!

He falls out of the sky into her busy day, of pans and plates and laundry, maybe once a year now – a chill that runs down her neck, unprovoked – today, as it happens, while she is shaking out the bed. And still it makes her stop and look behind her, as if he might be there. She feels foolish and laughs at herself, but a cold hand grips her belly and the ground falls away at her feet. Then she marvels, as she does every time, at how she could forget such a thing, before she forgets it again – buried treasure, sparkling to itself in the dark – as if it had been a dream. Sometimes she imagines it rusting.

CHAPTER FOUR

Though it had all gone off nicely after the inauspicious start, Jack found himself tortured with shame when he remembered being caught lurking outside the Hammer home – a moment he had relived every twenty minutes or so throughout the last few days, causing him to wince visibly. Several of his companions asked him if he was feeling quite all right, to which he replied that someone had just walked over his grave.

He spent a great deal of time wondering what on earth had possessed him to follow Grace home, and came up with no good answer, which made him all the more uncomfortable. Jack is a creature of habit, though he may vary the order in which he visits the pubs and the women he consorts with. It would not do well with him to be trailing after any one in particular and he vowed not to do it again, leaving the next time they meet to chance, though he hoped it would be soon. Thus resolved, he ordered another jar of Truman's.

Grace kept expecting Jack to pop up outside the window, which made her uneasy. How dare he trail around after her? She was furious that he knew where she lived. Grace is a secretive soul; she is happy to hide under a rock and come out when she pleases. She has a great many secrets and an instinctive dislike of anyone too forward. Miraculously Jack has not fallen within that bracket, in spite of his clumsy manners. Daisy likes him very much. She asks when they might see him next and Grace tells her there are no plans to do so.

Tuesday afternoon the Hammer family were at large in Whitechapel, enjoying the warmth of the day. They were searching, as usual, for the next dip, but to anyone in the busy thoroughfare who cared to look they were just picking along the gutter. East London in July is barely clearer than it is in any other month, and smells a good deal worse, but at least there is light and heat. Today the sun threatened to break through the veil; there was no breeze to relieve the stink and the air hung still and thick around them. The haze had defeated the weaker members of the street race and they lay in pools of beer and other stagnant fluids among the rubbish, feet stepping round them.

The family turned into the Whitechapel Road, merging into the bustle of traders and carousers, shoving and lurching, pausing to look at a monkey in a miniature ball-gown performing a vigorous dance to the strains of 'The Boy I Love Is Up In The Gallery'. The boys bobbed off into the crowd at intervals, popping up here and there. Daisy kept a grip on her mother's hand. Where the throng became too thick for her little legs Grace hoisted her up and carried her on her hip.

'Can *we* have a monkey, Ma?'

'No.'

They walked on past the Horn of Plenty, where they spotted Sally Ann Dunn in her usual spot, rocking and vomiting into the gutter. She lurched up and looked around with a wild, glazed grin, toppling towards the gentleman with whom she was consorting that afternoon. She had split her lip the day before, from the look of it. Grace wondered whether she'd been thumped or fallen flat on her face on the cobbles.

Her attention was caught by an angry commotion, rising even above the clamour of the street: urgent shouting six or seven heads away, a shrill police whistle, a struggle. Someone had her Billy by the scruff of the neck and was shouting into the face of a burly copper. She grabbed Jake by the collar as he was diving in to help his brother.

'This little bastard had my wallet!'

'Put the boy down at once, sir, and calm yourself. Turn your pockets out, lad.'

Both complied with these fierce orders. Billy turned out a piece of wire, a stone, an apple and a shilling from his pockets. His ear burned.

'I saw him take it, I tell you! I saw him!'

'Well, where could it be now, sir?'

'How am I to know that? He will have passed it to an accomplice in the crowd.'

The man was agitated and undoubtedly German. His red face seemed to swell as he waved his cane, tracing wild circles before him as if to keep the riff-raff at bay, stabbing the air for emphasis. He wore a fine wool overcoat, best kid gloves, a nice pearl pin in his cravat, gold watch-chain and studs, and a powder-blue silk handkerchief just so in his breast pocket. Most definitely a tourist, stuck out like a sore thumb, come to see the dubious sights of London's fabled poor and rotting East End. So he got what he came for really, thought Grace. Her eyes flickered distractedly over the sea of faces.

Jack was in the crowd, having heard the to-do. There he is again! she thought. Can't shake him off nowadays! What a picture he was too, even better than she remembered; she caught herself gawping and stopped at once, a little irritated. He looked ready to jump in for Billy, watching with his handsome frown, wondering what to do, and she wanted to shout to him not to worry. There were no flies on Billy – he hadn't turned a hair. He was tip-top, better even than Charlie, who would have the wallet away by now: they were home and dry, you could smell the roses already.

Jack ran his eyes over the crowd and caught her watching him, a little crooked smile on her face. She gave him a right saucy wink and he wondered – while his nether regions stirred, without reference to the rest of him – why she made no move to help her son. He returned the secret signal, but without the reserve he would have liked, grinning idiotically, rather than enigmatically, as he had intended. People peered in from every side like beady-eyed museum visitors, chattering excitedly about the exhibits. A crow in a dusty black hat shoved her elbow into his ribs, digging in to get a better look, craning her scraggy neck, lined with dirt. The grimy ribbon on the back of her hat caught him in the eye as she climbed on her neighbour's foot. The crowd pushed and swelled, starting to boil; the policeman tried to calm the general mood, without success. He turned back to the German, grim-faced.

'Are you quite sure this lad had your wallet, sir?'

'How dare you question my integrity, Constable? I saw it in his filthy hand.'

The policeman, a kindly chap by the name of Frank Wallace, knew this scrap most likely had robbed the loud red man – in fact, he would have laid money on it – but he didn't take kindly to his loud red manner, laying down the law – as if it was he who was wearing the uniform. He would set him straight and no mistake. An intense dislike for the pompous balloon was unfolding in his chest, fuelled further by the irrelevant but nonetheless influential fact that it had been a German man his mother had run away with on the morning of his seventh birthday. Ice formed round his good heart.

'So you say. Only he doesn't seem to have it now, sir.'

The German took a deep lungful and drew up to his full height in readiness for a fresh torrent of rage.

PC Wallace chipped in, as officiously as he could manage, his generous moustache seeming to puff itself up like his chest. 'Would you be so good as to check your pockets, sir? If it's not too much trouble.'

The German spluttered but pulled forth from his pocket, dumbfounded, his wallet, with all his money present and correct. He gasped, open-mouthed, as if a bucket of cold water had been thrown in his face. The onlookers roared. His shame was not spared by PC Wallace, who insisted he apologise to the boy, with the support of the howling crowd, some of whom were delighted to see the underdog triumph for a change, and others who simply disliked large bombastic foreigners. Then our good constable dealt the final blow.

'I'm afraid you'll have to come along to the station, sir. This seems to me to be a clear case of public affray and disturbance. This way please.' And off they went to Leman Street, the German raging. A crowd of filthy children and drunks followed them, shouting and jeering down the street.

Billy slipped back in next to Grace. They exchanged a look – what it said Jack couldn't fathom. Grace looked as though she would burst into song.

'Come on,' she said. 'Let's go home.'

She looked for Charlie, who appeared at her elbow.

'Look!' said Daisy. 'There's Jack!'

At home Grace dumped the princess on the doorstep with a chunk of peanut brittle, and went inside with Charlie and Billy, whom she pulled in by the collar. She had been friendly enough on the way but did not invite Jack indoors or, indeed, so much as look at him as she shut the door. He kicked about with Jake for a minute or two, wondering whether to go or what. Daisy stared at him, sticky, and offered him a piece of brittle.

Indoors Grace reached into the secret pockets deep inside her skirts and drew out seven wallets, a gold watch and a handsome silver bracelet, which she threw upon the table. 'That was a bloody close call,' she said to Billy. 'What happened?'

'I was clumsy.'

'That's not like you.'

'He was looking at some girl,' said Charlie.

'Huh! Were you frightened?'

'No!'

'Good lad. You're a triumph incarnate.'

'Cheers, Ma.'

'Go on, then.'

As Billy came out to play in the street Jack caught a glimpse inside of Charlie and Grace hunched together. The boys lined up before the door with Daisy as it shut, peering at Jack, like a row of sparrows on a chimney-stack.

The takings spilled on the table; coins and wads of notes were sorted in a flash. Grace counted swiftly, lips moving. 'A bounteous haul today. Enough for a little extra!'

CHAPTER FIVE

'So, what will we wear for the Bank Holiday?' enquired Daisy, voicing her most urgent concern.

'What do you want to wear, darlin'?'

'A beautiful dress.'

Daisy Hammer, the only living daughter of a comfortable criminal, had the advantage of brand-new clothes, while her poor friend Emily, whose parents did honest work, had to suffer the hand-me-downs of her five sisters.

'Any particular colour?'

'Lilac. With ribbons and bows.'

'Well, you know what you want, don't you?'

So out they went to the West End (all except Charlie, who wanted to be on his own, though he said he was not in a bad mood). Grace always kept something by to splash in the shops, for fancy things they didn't need. What else was the object of devoting the family to a life of crime?

They took the Green bus west, the boys heading straight for the top deck, right at the front, Daisy tripping up the stairs in her haste to keep up. She positioned herself in the middle where she wouldn't miss anything, her eagle eyes scanning the vista. As they left Spitalfields behind she beamed at Grace, glowing, brimming with it. Faint sunshine ahead that seemed to come from the promised land of the West End lit her hair like butter melting. Grace promised herself to take outings more often, wrapped up in the joy of simple things that were there every day on the doorstep.

They passed the City and the Bank, and soon after the great dome of St Paul's loomed before them, dwarfing all around it like a great grey mountain, stunning even Daisy into momentary silence. She kept her eyes upon it as they passed, as if it might fall, but recovered quickly, and resumed her barrage of questions – 'Who lives in there?' 'Why does that man have his hair like that?' 'Will we see the Queen?' – directed mostly at Billy, who seemed to know about everything. They made their way slowly, wedged in traffic, down Fleet Street towards the West End, gazing at the scene around.

The majestic façades of Regent Street are an enchanting sight when you have money in your pocket to spend. Their eyes were like dinner plates as the omnibus turned up towards Oxford Circus. Even Jake stopped fidgeting to look at the broad sweep of the street. Elegant store fronts lined the curve of the thoroughfare, clean, cream, shining in the sun, running perfectly parallel on either side of the broad road, wide like the Amazon river, which Billy had come upon in the encyclopedia while looking up 'armadillo'. The sky was deeper here, the air sweeter, the clouds white! Billy wondered if it was like this every day in the West End, if they in East London were just idiots under a shadow. As they stopped in traffic his wandering eyes alighted on a wiry little man through an upstairs window, hunched at his desk beneath a tower of papers. A napkin was tucked into his collar and he was carving a piece of ham upon the desk before him. As Billy watched he sliced hard into his thumb, dropped the knife, yelped, silently, through the glass and shoved the bloody digit into his mouth. He shook his fist at the boys as they rolled away.

'What are you laughing at?' said Grace, leaning round from the front.

They alighted by Howell James & Company as if in a foreign land, mute and gazing round like marmosets, even Billy who had been once before at Christmas. They held hands so as not to lose each other. Diamonds glittered at them from a window.

'Look at that!' said Billy. Jake slipped between the passers-by and pressed his face to the glass; Grace held Daisy up so she could see. They gaped aghast through the glass at sparkling rocks, brilliant cut, elegant tendrils of pale gold, intertwined at the throat, dripping yellow diamonds like shining syrup. The necklace was laid on black velvet and beside were the earrings, two carats each. The family's eyes were as wide as they could go, as if it might help them see more. If they had observed themselves at that moment they would have laughed a great deal. In the next window was a tiara.

'Look, Ma, a crown! Look!'

'Yes, darlin', isn't it lovely?'

'Is it for a princess?'

'I expect so.'

'How can you be a princess?'

'You have to marry a prince.'

They admired a flamboyant brooch of flowers made from seed pearls; a citrine the size of a macaroon, a necklace and earrings set with table-cut emeralds of evil green, jet beads, opals, topaz like knuckles, clasped in golden claws. Grace led them away, up towards Oxford Circus. Their first port of call was Hamley's toy shop.

Though they had worn their best clothes that day, feeling overdressed as they waited for the bus on Whitechapel Road, Grace felt a little tawdry among the fine ladies and gentlemen of the West End, milling about at leisure. The boys had never seen so much unbroken glass. Grace kept her eye on them, though they were sworn to their very best behaviour, secured by the promise of two shillings each to spend.

'Can we buy something for Charlie?' asked Billy.

'Yes, can we?' echoed Daisy, wishing she had thought of it first. 'Because he missed the trip?'

'Yes, darlin', course we can. Shall we let Billy choose? He knows what boys like.'

They left the boys looking at fishing rods, on a strict promise to meet them in an hour, and went to see about dresses.

How wonderful it is to have a little girl, to hold her hand in yours and chatter as you wander down the street. Grace thought of her own mother, remembered walking this way. She took Daisy to Marshall & Snelgrove, grandest store on

Oxford Street, taking up a whole block to itself: swish enough for a princess.

Daisy tried several dresses on. She twirled before the mirror, charming the shop-girl, who had seemed doubtful when they had come in. Grace disarmed her with polite chatter, affecting a better accent and employing the natural air she could conjure of having some kind of status, whatever it might be, so that the girl had put her dark skirts down to Bohemian eccentricity. She was from the country herself, having been in the Smoke just two weeks, and fancied herself already a cosmopolitan lady. Her name was Tabitha Berry and one day she hoped to marry a rich man, to be a Tabitha Rothschild or a Tabitha Vanderbilt, and move in society circles. She did not yet know that, though sweet-faced enough, she had none of the requisite ruthlessness and would be back in the sticks within the year, happily hitched to a potato farmer.

Blue suited Daisy better even than lilac, though she would have looked delectable in a coal sack, to her doting mother anyhow. She chose her favourite dress the moment she put it on and did not trouble herself with a second thought about it. She wanted to wear it home but was persuaded, with the enticement of pink tissue paper, to take it wrapped. They chose a pretty little raffia hat for hand-me-down Emily, with a pair of tiny apples on the brim; and bought satin ribbon, green for Grace's eyes and blue for Daisy's.

After Grace had managed to tear Tabitha Berry and Daisy apart they joined the boys, who, to Grace's amazement, were waiting in the tea-room as instructed, quiet as church mice. They were even standing up straight. The manager was eyeing them suspiciously, looking for a reason to turf them out.

'What have you done?' she said warily.

'Nothing!'

They had bought a cricket bat for Charlie and a football for themselves, and had managed not to lose each other or venture towards shady St Giles. They did not show her the pocket-knife they had lifted in Gentlemen's Sundries. Daisy brimmed with news about her dress, to which they listened sweetly, although they had no interest in clothing. All refreshed themselves with lemonade and iced buns.

Marshall & Snelgrove was a flurry of delight, a carousel of finery and ladies shopping, buying things they had already, in the latest style, such as dinner plates or luggage or gloves. Seated at every counter in the perfume hall, where a thousand delicious scents blend into a soft cloud that wafts across the ceiling, they primped and picked and enjoyed the eager attention of the staff. This season their hats were adorned with dyed ostrich feathers, which fluttered in the perfumed air, red or blue or violet; pheasant for the country.

The family meandered through this palace of wonders, trying not to touch anything, past the crystal, the silverware, the cut glass. Grace steered them towards the door, holding her breath as they traversed the fine-china department. Rows of polished cutlery blinked ostentatiously as they went by;

a giant candelabra posed in all its pompous glory, as if it were the only thing in the shop.

They never noticed the pallid stranger who fixed his eyes upon them from behind the ostrich-leather-bound address book he was pretending to study. As they went past he put it down and moved after them towards the door.

The boys were outside already when Daisy noticed the display by the entrance and stopped. It had a rural theme: branches fanned out on either side, hung with shiny artificial fruit. At its centre was a mannequin, dressed for the next season in sumptuous velvet, standing on a cushion of moss. She wore a short tweed jacket, draped with silver fox, and a full skirt of deep berry red that matched her hat, frozen jauntily atop her upswept curls. In her gloved hands she held a fur bag and a lace handkerchief. Daisy appraised this ensemble, aping the pose, admiring the skirt, the blue glass eyes, the pink painted lips.

The stranger sidled closer, lurking behind the display. He could hear them talking. They were looking at a stuffed robin perched above the mannequin's hat, and as he crept round the plinth he glimpsed them through the branches. They never noticed him, staring, like a man who had seen a ghost. As they went out through the grand doors into Oxford Street he hurried after them.

Mr Ivor Squall is a spindly little man. He resembles an insect, with his hunched back and dark suit, cut tight and mean as befits his demeanour. In fact, his wealth is his only personal asset. His business is ostensibly bookkeeping, run from offices in Oxford Street – it launders the proceeds of his quiet export trade. He finds his offices most conveniently located for his frequent business in notorious St Giles – hive of lawless activity, just a stone's throw away – coming and going, scuttling about unnoticed. His various associates are well aware that Mr Squall has always something hidden, shifty as the woodlice in the skirting, and keep their wits about them. When he laid eyes on Grace he forgot altogether the purpose of his shopping trip, not because she caught his fancy – for Ivor Squall has none – but because a bell rang in the back of his head, from long ago.

He remembered her face as if in a dream. Compelled by this notion – under a spell – he abandoned the umbrella he had set out to purchase, and followed. There was no doubt that he knew her from somewhere. He knew he must remember where.

This was the first day all year that Grace Hammer had dropped her guard. She was not in her own manor, and in the rare delight of taking a whole day for entertainments she had abandoned her usual watchfulness. The sky was blue, the boys were behaving themselves: there was no reason to look over her shoulder.

Ivor Squall shadowed them at a discreet distance until they took the bus and, hiding at the back of the line, he slipped on unsuspected. He had been involved in many underhand things but had never actually followed anyone before, and he began to enjoy it thoroughly; as thoroughly, that is, as he could in his own miserly way – a sly tingle of excitement pinched his scrawny belly, the cloak-and-dagger thrill of his mission, though he was still unsure of its end. He stole furtive glances at the family, the little girl smiling to herself, proud of the parcel on her lap, the boys hanging out over Regent Street, pointing at things and kicking each other. The bus crawled towards Charing Cross; all the while he wrestled the clues in his head, long-ago pictures, things he thought he had seen.

He might well struggle to place her. The first and last time they had met was seventeen years to the day before. The answer buzzed around him like a fly. He realised he was staring; the little girl had noticed him and tugged at her mother's sleeve. Luckily for him, she was busy reprimanding the boys for spitting on somebody's hat. Mr Squall bent down in his seat, pretending to tie his shoelace, which took him a full minute. When he lifted his eyes above the handrail of the seat in front, the family were engaged with some new distraction, laughing among themselves. He watched more carefully this time, making a show of looking out at the view as they crossed Trafalgar Square. As the bus passed Nelson the children craned their necks to look at him, stood all alone on his great big column. The woman was smiling contentedly, taking in the scenery. A ray of sunshine crept through the clouds and she shut her eyes and tilted back her head – and then he saw it, like a flash. He almost shouted aloud with the relief of remembering.

★

Grace did not notice their shadow until Cheapside. She wondered where he had got on and decided to ignore him, for what else was there to do? They would get off by St Mary, beyond their stop, and walk back.

Now, perhaps Grace was unusually carefree that day – it might be, as he sat behind them, she had not enough time to get a good look. Whatever, we are witness to something rare, like a perfect eclipse of the sun: Grace Hammer misses a trick. She does not recall Ivor Squall. Not a penny drops, not a bell rings.

The City rumbled past, then Aldgate. A boy was standing on his hands outside the window when the bus stopped, a group round him watching as he walked about upside-down. A couple dropped coins into the hat between his feet. They passed St Botolph, then the rag market, and rolled past their stop.

By Church Lane he and they were the only passengers left from the West End. As Grace made ready to get off she turned to look at him again – just a little too long, with a quizzical air so fleeting he might have imagined it. He felt his face colour and his heart quail as he shrank into his seat. Then she was gone. He dared not get off after them but stole a glimpse over his slippery shoulder as the bus moved away again, to catch them rounding the corner into Osborn Street. Alighting at the next stop Ivor Squall tore back down the street as fast as his match-stick legs would allow but, of course, by the time he reached the turning they were nowhere to be seen. He recovered his weak breath and made his way home, trembling with impatience. Had he stayed on the corner for another minute he would have spied them coming out of the grocer's, with a bag of oranges.

Ivor Squall recorded every detail of his encounter, with his bookkeeper's pedantic efficiency, the very moment that he reached his office in order that he might not forget the smallest thing. He found he derived considerable pleasure from compiling this furtive intelligence and positively glowed with self-satisfaction at the prospect of passing it on to its intended recipient. Though he had nothing much to note he made a great deal of it on new paper, toying with the idea of small sketches before contenting himself with exhaustive descriptions of each member of the family in perfect lines of spider-crawl across the page, scratching away in his favourite uncomfortable seat at his plain desk that had spindly legs to match his own. He stopped only to dip his pen in the ink, as urgently as he could without splashing, holding his breath – as well as he was able with his meagre lungs, being sickly from birth – feverish as the drop trembled at the end of his nib. Ivor Squall had never yet splashed ink on his desk. Every day this became more significant and he was not ready to blot it, however whipped up he might feel. He finished carefully, as if he was writing important legal documents, and set down his pen with a weak sigh, before allowing himself to revel – as much as he might in his tight suit – in his own efficiency and his symmetrical desktop.

Then he rubbed his hands with glee and wrote a short message addressed to Mr Horatio Blunt, with which he caught the last post.

Dear Esteemed Friend,

I trust this letter finds you in sufficient health after these long years. I send intriguing news – brooking not a moment's delay – which I venture may be of interest. This very afternoon I have uncovered information, by fortunate chance – and artful investigation – pertaining to the whereabouts of your former employee: a Miss Hammer, if I recall correctly. I hope these efforts will serve to be of satisfaction.

Yours most faithfully, Ivor Squall Esq.

On the other side of London the Hammer family reconvened and shared gifts.

'You picked the right day to go up west,' said Charlie. 'That man from the board school's been about.'

'Look at these beautiful chocolates,' said Daisy.

The subject of Jake's education had come up in conversation not two days before between Grace and her busybody neighbour Mrs Jacob, who had raised six children – as she never tired of recounting – all of whom now lived as far away from her as was possible without leaving the country.

'Do you not think that Jake might be better at school now?' she had ventured nosily.

Grace wondered at how no one ever noticed that Billy was not at school either, most likely on account of his beautiful manners. 'Well, they do seem very crowded, Mrs Jacob. And a hotbed for typhoid.'

'A proper schooling teaches a youngster some discipline,

Miss Hammer. Prepares him for a trade, perhaps. A good, decent future.'

Grace had felt her blood begin to simmer. She put a swift, graceful end to the conversation.

'Well, the last time he went he reckoned they were still learning the alphabet, Mrs Jacob. Once they've got past that I'm sure he may consider going again. And as for a trade, well, I'm sure he's spoilt for choice. I expect you'd have him up some toff's chimney, or sewing shirts, perhaps. Jake's quite happy to be out and about with me. He's a good little helper. Good day to you.'

CHAPTER SIX

Grace Hammer was an ugly baby. She was born in Pagham, near Bognor, by the Sussex seaside, on the morning of 18 July 1853, with the sun shining on rippling waves of barley. She had a comical air, as most brand-new people do, with dark spiked hair and serious navy blue eyes that seemed to focus from the moment they opened. These changed to blonde and green respectively within six weeks to devastating effect.

Within a few short years she was asserting her natural authority over the rest of her family, at least her doting parents and four older brothers, if not her sister, who was almost six and her closest playmate as well as her worst enemy. Grace remembered playing dens under the bed, but also the time she had been tricked into eating soap, which had made her sister laugh a great deal before Ma had come in and slapped her. Baby Grace grew razor-sharp wits very quickly, ready to strike the first time she clapped her eyes upon a book. It was an illustrated edition of *Tales from the Brothers Grimm*, which had sat undisturbed for a decade or more next to *Moll Flanders* upon a dusty shelf at the very top of her grandmother's house. These lonely tomes had belonged to Great-grandfather Hammer, who had entertained scholarly aspirations, and, though treasured in his memory, had been forgotten due to their subsequent uselessness within the Hammer family – a practical bunch, more inclined towards husbandry and agricultural pursuits, which was certainly a good thing, for the farm ran like clockwork. If there was spare time they used it to sit about and drink cider.

Little Grace had climbed the stairs one day, finding no one to hand for games – the family having rushed out to the barn to watch the cow labour – and, standing on a chair, she reached the shelf and pulled out the first book, having not the slightest notion of such a thing. It fell open at the illustration of Rumpelstiltskin before the Queen, twisted and raging, his foot stuck through the floor! She could not imagine what had made him so angry. He had long, spindling legs and a chicken feather in his hat. She leafed through the pages and looked at the pictures and something started turning in her head.

Grace could read and write by her seventh birthday, having worked it out mostly for herself with the benefit of spells at the village school, thus surpassing her parents' academic achievements. By the time she turned eight she could cook for the family – roast pork and potatoes, mutton stew, apple cake – stood on a box, while her ma went to help with the lambing. She sheared sheep at nine, split logs at ten and ploughed the field at eleven. When she was twelve her proud father was entrusting her to manage certain affairs of the farm, among them the bookkeeping, which he found intolerable. At thirteen she ran an independent sideline selling vicious apple brandy she distilled in the barn. This paid for the books she ate. She enjoyed the works of Dumas: *The Three Musketeers* being the book she had read most frequently (though not in the French), Jonathan Swift and Edgar Allan Poe, but her favourite author was Charles Dickens. She thought him quite the sharpest man that ever scratched a page, having happened upon *David Copperfield* while perusing the shelves of the bookshop in town, affecting, with some success, an air of knowing what she was looking for while having no idea.

She had pulled it out from the row of spines and, reading a page or two, had quite lost herself, sunk into the world therein, until the shopkeeper had broken the spell at chapter three, with a touch on her shoulder, to enquire if there was anything in particular with which he could assist her. She came to with a little start, before she remembered where she was and paid for the book with urgency and much charming fluster, thus procuring a small discount.

Outside the shop she sat down upon the pavement and swallowed chapters four to eleven, neglecting her thirsty horse until it became too dark to read. She rode thereafter into Chichester every fourth Tuesday for fresh books, and her family thought her quite mad, though this did not diminish their enjoyment of her fireside readings – furnished as they were with different voices for each character (their favourite being the odious Uriah Heep, for whom Grace contorted her elastic face into an alarming mask, twisting her handsome features beyond recognition and frightening the dog) and piles of hot toast – which they ate in perfect silence, ears cocked, eyes wide, pausing mid-chew as Mr Bill Sykes battered Nancy to her dreadful death or poor Mr Guppy shone his lamp on Krook's grim remains.

Though she loved her happy family, by her fifteenth birthday Grace had tired of her surroundings and decided to leave them behind, if not permanently then at least without imminent plans to return. Upon the announcement of these plans her father, sick with the fear of unknown threats ahead, promptly and utterly forbade any such idea. So she stole from the house that very night, down a rope from the window, avoiding the creaks that lurked in the staircase and the attendant paternal ears, pricked in sleep. She dropped the last yard to the ground outside, next to the bag ready packed in the flowerbed, picked one last crimson camellia and was gone.

Now, young Grace had a soft spot for unlikely men, which was the very first worry on her poor pa's long list. This fancy had begun with the extra farmhands who came every summer. They were gypsy lads, fit and dark, up to no good. They looked wild and their arms and chests rippled in the sun; they had brown skin and strong hands and mischief crackling around them like a dirty halo. (Years later Grace Hammer would wonder why she found trouble so attractive and still have no answer.) She gazed up at them on top of the haystack and they grinned back down at her, bold like a red rag.

It was one of those lads she stole away with that night, taking him for company till Chichester, where reluctantly but with no significant guilt she gave him the slip, reasoning that he had been most pleasing at the top of the haystack, mystery intact, and that he made dull conversation and had bad breath to boot. A fresh breeze broke over her as she left with his wages, a scent of blossoming freedom.

Grace Hammer has been in proper employment only twice in her long life – the first a three-week stretch that November 1872, after hearing her ma was lost to scarlet fever. For a week she roamed desolate through Wiltshire before taking a position as housemaid in the grand house of Lord and Lady Davenport of Tisbury, being desperate and unwilling to return empty-handed to her family home, with no mother inside it.

She found little time for sad reflection as her job was cold and thankless and entirely at odds with her proud demeanour, most especially as the mistress was an imperious bitch who never uttered a please or a thank-you. She stalked round the house finding causes for complaint – a patch of dust that had been missed along the top of a door, an invisible tarnish on the silver – barking at creases in the table linen. She snapped orders at her staff in the morning without greeting them first and never addressed them by name, though two of them had been in her service for thirteen years, come Christmas – which would bring them nothing but an orange each and stiff new aprons, as had the twelve before. If that is a real live lady! thought Grace – how glad I am not to be one and determined not to try! They were woken at six every morning of the year, save Mothering Sunday (as if everyone had mothers to call on), to empty chamber-pots as dawn broke, followed by scrubbing and washing and polishing and running upstairs and down until they fell into hard beds at ten o'clock.

This employment ended abruptly after the mistress accused Grace of stealing pennies that she herself had set under the drawing-room rugs to test the honesty of the servants on the one hand and their attention to the sweeping on the other, leaving them guilty either way. When Grace remarked that if Mistress did not want to lose her money perhaps she would do better not to leave it lying about, she flew into a rage and dismissed her at once. Grace had not, in fact, stolen anything and took satisfaction in doubling back two miles down the road, cross-country, and hiding in the orchard till dusk when she scaled the wisteria and left with the mistress's favourite diamonds. Indeed, they were the finest stones in the jewellery case: a pair of drop earrings, two carats each. A little bird caught her eye in the next velvet compartment – a sweet thing, flashing tiny jewelled wings, a ruby berry in its slender beak; it sparkles at her but she isn't greedy.

Now, let us cast some light inside Miss Hammer's head, where a hundred forgotten trinkets languish in the dark – for it is true to say she is a magpie, and likes a shiny thing. It is her nature and her joy to steal a precious sparkling stone. She doesn't care to wear them, but holds them to the lamplight and turns them in her hand, bewitched; then she hides them in the dark, in secret places, strung across England like lost stars. Though she means to take them with her mostly she forgets. They call her, miles down the road, kicking stones, laughing at the sky; she never goes back. There are more ahead. She has stolen so many jewels that today she might be living in Belgravia, but she would not suit the company, or care to dress for dinner every evening. Grace would find herself downstairs, drinking with the servants and peeling the potatoes. And now she has a family she restricts herself to wallets and pocket watches, which are bread and butter – a different matter altogether – and she is pleased her sons seem not to have inherited her blind compulsion but go about thieving as a practical business – except perhaps Jake, who has buried treasure in his eyes sometimes. She keeps a tight rein on her magpie nature for she wants for nothing more than she can enjoy today, and should she surrender to it she would head for the Tower straight to steal the Crown. Just the Crown, mind, nothing else. Grace prefers to take the best thing in the box.

When the theft was discovered, riders were dispatched into the countryside to find the thieving hussy, who was sleeping in a hedgerow, just two miles away – having the cheek of the devil and the good sense to have left nothing behind to scent the dogs.

Lady Davenport never did recover her earrings, despite the efforts of the local men, who tired after a day or two of her demanding manner and decided that the relatively poor reward of thirty pounds could remain unclaimed. She wore out the sympathy of her visitors with her ranting – they departed with sore ears, wishing the unscrupulous, insolent girl luck, leaving Mistress Outrage to squawk at the staff instead. When she called at their houses the next day to acquaint them with the indignant details she had forgotten to mention she found no one at home.

She returned late to find the house quiet. Her best Meissen vase was gone from the mantel. The silver was missing. Someone had turned out her dressing table on the bed and made off with the rest of her jewellery. We may only imagine how our good lady's mind boggled at this heinous discovery – indeed she took several minutes to recover her breath: she gaped like a drowning fish and rubbed her eyes to make sure she was not seeing things. And where were the servants? She would see them hang for this. She discovered them locked in the cellar, drinking the armagnac to restore their shattered nerves. They could not describe the culprits, save to say they were fearsome men, gruff, four or more of them, neckerchiefs tied round their faces like olden-day highwaymen.

Three days after she had left the Davenport manor Grace arrived by means of her weary feet and fateful chance at Hatetree Farm, by Netley Marsh – a sprawling ramshackle pile at the edge of Hampshire and home to a Mr Horatio Blunt. The sky was low and thick with cloud, darkness was falling. She was spent indeed, having travelled away from the road and slept fitfully the night before, dreaming of dogs on her trail. Her steps slowed as she drew near, halting a few cautious feet from the crippled fence.

Beyond it a derelict yard, studded with bricks and bottles and broken wheels, stretched before a stone farmhouse, crouching in the gloom. Though young Grace was not much given to notions of the kind, the house seemed to watch her with one cold yellow eye, staring through the twilight, eerie silence blanketing the ground. But for her lonely breath, time itself stood still. A tortured apple tree stuck its claws up to the dead sky. The very air above this wretched homestead seemed to stall, thick and listless; she might have supposed the house abandoned but for the lighted window. Not a welcoming glow but a harbinger, burning greenish, casting slippery light. It was as clear as a sign on the gatepost that somebody lived there alone. Ghoulish creatures from the *Tales of Grimm* ran through her head. She stood by the fence as the rain started to fall, weighing the prospect of warmth and rest against her reluctance to knock at the door.

The gate creaked on its rusty hinge. She took a brave step up the tired path, brambles catching at her coat. She was not to know what the knock on the door would bring and neither was the occupant, sitting by the fire in his favourite chair. If he had he would certainly not have answered it.

The door was opened halfway after a short wait, revealing to each their first view of the other. The man seemed to fill the little porch, his coarse face leering, pork fingers in sweaty bunches. He looked to Grace as if she had disturbed him counting money.

'Good evening, sir,' she said, with all the breeze she could muster, as if she had set down at Claridges.

He took her in from head to toe before he spoke. 'Yes. What do you want?'

'I have come from the coast and I am sorely tired. I beg a bed and a rest in return for useful work, housekeeping perhaps, or whatever else you might need.'

This last part had caught Mr Blunt's imagination and stirred him somewhat – though he knew that the particular 'whatever else' that sprang immediately to mind was not what she had meant by it – so he widened the gap to let her in. She looked promising indeed: fair, despite the grime upon her skin. Without the slightest nod to civil manners he held the candle closer to inspect her, unabashed, his rude eyes raking her as if she were a fruit stall. Grace would not have been surprised if he had looked behind her ears for mould, or squeezed some piece of flesh to see if she was ripe. His hands looked clammy and the corners of his mouth were wet. His stare was greedy and repulsive, poking at her, pulling at her clothes; she clasped her shawl across her chest. Had she not been tired and cold she might well have left there and then, but the fire crackled enticingly in the grate and she longed to sit down by it.

Presently she was shown to a small room at the top of the house, bare except for a bed, a chair and a bucket, set in the corner to catch the drip above. Mr Blunt explained that she was to cook twice a day and tidy and clean, as well as run general errands, and that she might rest from all duties save cooking on Sunday. She was to confine herself to her bedroom, the kitchen or the parlour in her own time, though she might enter the library to dust. On no account was she to disturb the bedroom off the landing – which had been his dear mother's – or the outhouse, or the attic. It seemed they were indeed alone together in the house.

Grace listened patiently, thinking it best not to divulge that she would be leaving in a day or two. For a moment she let her curiosity run up to the attic but brought herself back to hear him telling her he liked his eggs soft-boiled, with pepper. When he left her alone at last she inspected the door thoroughly for chinks or cracks and put a piece of rag in the keyhole. There was no key or bolt or other means of securing the door from inside, so she wedged a chair against it. She found a short board in the corner, held down by one nail, and eased it up with her knife. Down went Lady Davenport's diamond earrings and back went the floorboard – there they lay, together in the dark: two carats each, brilliant cut, sparkling quietly, catching tiny rays of candlelight that crept through the cracks in the floor. A mouse or two came and sniffed at them but found them quite the most inedible prospect and left them alone.

Grace woke to the sound of heavy snoring on her first morning at Horatio Blunt's residence. It seemed to shudder through the walls, flabby and thick, echoing round the house. She got up and stoked the fire, made some tea, ate several slices of a large ham she found in the larder. All the while the snoring went on. She was making her way quietly back upstairs to fetch her things, having decided to leave before her host woke up, when a sparkle of light caught her eye, on the floor, a flash of red under the coat-stand. She picked it up: a delicate bird, worked in small diamonds, a brilliant-cut ruby clasped in its slender beak. The pin and settings were of white gold, with a tiny safety chain. She had seen it not four days before in Lady Davenport's jewellery box.

A cold wave swept over her, rooted to the spot with this glittering thing in her hand; the clock stopped, a tangle of questions ran through her head. The still air was shattered by an urgent hammering upon the door. Grace leaped almost out of her skin. She shrank into the back of the house, heart banging – the knocking came again, and the snoring, which had been going steadily all the while, stopped. As Mr Blunt grunted his way downstairs she was at the back door, ready to run – her only chance, and not a good one – if it was someone come for her. She could not imagine Mr Blunt had many visitors. Trembling on the back step she could hear him dusting down the caller for banging on the door so loudly, and at such an unreasonable hour of the morning when a fellow might be sleeping in. She could barely make out what the caller said but she caught 'Lady Davenport'. This was enough for Grace and she had started across the yard when she heard Mr Blunt bellow and the door slam. She froze like a deer, every nerve pricked. All was quiet. She slunk back to the door and ventured an ear across the step. She heard him pick up the poker and stab at the fire, huffing and puffing to himself. Shaking, she put on the water to boil his eggs and went into the front room. There he was, sweaty and half dressed, face bloated from sleep. His demeanour gave away nothing.

'Good morning!' she said brightly.

He scowled and scratched his groin. If he had anything to say he kept it to himself, but he looked her clean through as he dumped himself down in his chair. There he sat without speaking, staring into the fire until he had swallowed his breakfast. During this imposing silence Grace realised the brooch had disappeared. In the panic she had clean forgotten it. It was not in the kitchen or on the floor, as far as she could see. She busied herself with sweeping and tidying so that she could look more thoroughly but came up with nothing.

Later she would search her pockets, to no avail – it seemed it had flown away to its little golden nest, never to be seen again.

After a loud belch Mr Blunt pushed back his plate and turned his boorish gaze on her. She tried to look nonchalant, feeling as though she was thinking out loud.

'Where did you say you had come from?' he asked, without attempt to make his enquiry appear conversational or courteous.

'Christchurch,' she replied, as casually as possible. There was a stagnant pause. 'Who was at the door?'

'Evidently there has been a local robbery.'

'Oh?'

'Apparently, a housemaid,' – he chuckled to himself at this – 'has made off with an item of considerable value from the grand house of Lady Davenport – you may know it. Naturally Lady Davenport is keen to have it back. They gave a detailed description of the girl and asked if I might have seen such a person.' They looked at each other steadily.

'Goodness! I wonder where she might be,' said Grace at last.

'Indeed.' He lit his pipe and settled further into his greasy chair. 'You must stay here for the time being. If you leave they will pick you up within hours. And you do match her description quite remarkably.'

CHAPTER SEVEN

Grace could see from the first that Mr Blunt was a busy thief. New silver appeared on Monday, only to vanish on Tuesday. There were furtive comings and goings at irregular hours; shady visitors called. He was out till the small hours on Friday night, and made much explanation at breakfast of how he had come to be so late at the Swan, though she had not asked. Now Grace had an eye for an opportunity and she began to wonder what she might gain from this situation. Perhaps she would stay a while longer.

And so she made herself useful. She cooked and tidied, kept the stove burning, kept quiet. By the second week she was part of the furniture, picking up scraps of conversation as she served brandy and tea to his associates at cards – gloomy affairs in the back parlour with talk that stopped as she entered the room. She grew ears like a bat, caught crumbs of information. It seemed a grand plan was afoot, ambitious business indeed. Prospects seemed to open up before her. Lady Davenport's earrings faded a little, forgotten under the floor.

Mr Blunt's favourite supper, when in at his pig-pile for the evening, was liver and onions, which he ate with enormous relish, smacking his lips greedily, eyes fixed upon his plate.

He expected this feast to be served on Monday, Wednesday and Saturday, and Grace was happy to provide it, though it meant having to witness the spectacle of its consumption, her company being required at the trough. She ate her own meals in the kitchen. Blunt would look her slowly up and down as she brought in his tray, and if she turned by the door on her way out she would catch him staring at her arse, with a lascivious smile that came back to her at dead of night and made her shudder. She dreamed of walloping him around the head with the poker. And wondered how long she would give it.

It wasn't long before Mr Blunt chanced his arm. On the twelfth day he pounced, after smoking his pipe. Grabbing her by the back of the skirts as she went by with the pail for his mustard bath, he dragged her down to the gloomy depths of his armchair.

We will not relive the details of this encounter. Suffice to say that she fought him off with a gritted smile before the bounds of decency were contravened, laughing but forcing her way out with his filthy damp hand up her skirts. Grace considered leaving that very night, but decided that the time already spent in his repulsive company should not go to waste. She resolved to stab him the next time he tried it. She must make some result of her efforts, and soon.

For the next few days she kept well clear of him, leaving the room when he entered, ignoring his requests. Dinner was dumped in front of him on a cold plate. He felt sheepish, which was quite a new sensation. Indeed, he might have forced himself upon her and could not altogether understand why he had not. She seemed to glow with some enchantment; he barely dared look at her now. Perhaps after she had calmed down he might make a better approach; he had heard that women liked flowers. Perhaps that was the way to win her affections. Catching himself, he shook his head to quiet these unlikely thoughts – they seemed to have crept in through his ear, while he was asleep perhaps: like a hex cast upon him.

The week's end brought some other matter to occupy him – he grew distracted, the atmosphere drew tight around the house. People came and went, talking in low voices: a general furtiveness seized the air. Grace sensed that the grand plan was hatching at last.

There was a knock at the door late one night as she was halfway up the stairs to her bed. She opened it to a strange little man, thin like a twig, in a tall hat.

'Good evening,' he said, with an oily smile. 'I am Ivor Squall. Is Mr Blunt within?'

Grace happened to notice that Mr Blunt spent a good deal of time in his library the following week. She hadn't had him down as much of a reader before, never having seen him so much as touch a book, or, for that matter, set foot in the library, that she could recall. He seemed nervous: he would wake in his chair with a start and look towards the door, or rise to patrol the hallway, fancying he heard an unusual noise; once or twice she found him standing guard outside the library, in silent contemplation of the brass doorknob.

Mr Blunt had inherited his extensive collection of books from his mother who, bedridden, had spent her very last bean on them. She was a caustic woman who despised her lazy, stupid son but had no one else to whom she could leave her estate. Unluckily, he had no interest in literature. In spite of this he enjoyed the library for its grand associations, visiting it once a month or so to take sherry and stalk about in a lordly manner, surveying the room with satisfaction. A couple of volumes had gone on the fire when he couldn't be bothered to chop a log.

The books stretched from wall to wall and up to the lofty ceiling, perhaps six hundred of them. Grace often browsed when he was drunk and sleeping and the house was quiet. *The Memoirs of Casanova* was a rare curiosity and she had swallowed three chapters before tiring of his conquests and deciding that, at six thick volumes, perhaps he had remembered too much. She moved on after that to *The Vampyre*, which she finished before leaving the chair, and then *Jane Eyre*, which she discarded some twenty pages in, in favour of *Candide*. Currently she was enjoying *The Last Days of Pompeii* – though she thought it rather melodramatic – but had been unable so much as to glimpse a book through the keyhole for days. Mr Blunt's new-found interest in literature was as inconvenient as it was puzzling.

Harold Whitbread had come back to haunt his murderers – all except the brothers Dean, who had not a shred of conscience between them. He had howled so terribly as they beat him to death that Blunt heard it still in his nightmares. He had seen Whitbread in the garden at night, his face battered in, smiling at him, peering in at the window through one red eye. Blunt became nervous and shifty, grew restless with the dark; he watched Grace more carefully than usual. He did not like the way she seemed – too quiet of late. He knew it must be his own anxiety; he must calm himself and try to behave as normal. The ruby necklace seemed to burn a hole in his head, throbbing at night through the library walls; he wanted rid of it. He would sell it on soon, prosper, start his new life. She would look at him differently once he was rich.

It never occurred to Mr Blunt that Grace might read; he never saw her take a book from the shelves. Why would he have spared it a thought? He had learned at his mother's knee, and had read sometimes to please her, but had not opened a book since she died of consumption. The idea that one might pull out a book from the shelf to peruse it had become an alien notion to him, as strange as taking the clock down from the wall to tell the time. This oversight would cause Mr Blunt to curse himself whenever he thought of it thereafter, stupid as it was.

A few nights later he drank himself into a proper stupor. Grace slipped into the library for the first time in a week and sat back down with *The Last Days of Pompeii*. After it had gasped its last she breathed a sigh and put the book back in its place. She bent an ear towards the kitchen and was rewarded with snoring; looking up at the shelves, tall all around her, she wondered where she should start. By the stroke of extravagant fortune she picked on *Bleak House*.

As her fingers closed round the treasure it seemed to

pulse, like a beating heart in her hand, and she covered her eyes to peek at it through her fingers. Carefully, fearfully she looked, lest she drop down dead, and slowly, slowly, she dropped her hand and held up her face to bask in its enchanted rays, helpless like Eve. Scarlet light enveloped her, intoxicating, stealing her magpie heart away.

After finishing her employment with Mr Blunt – abruptly, at dead of night and with spoils as never before in her pockets – for the first time in three long years Grace Hammer set sail for her family home. She missed them sorely and had managed to fight this down by not thinking about them, and now as she made her way back she gave in to empty longing. Her sister would be grown; her brothers would be fine, strapping men. Not half a mile on she remembered Lady Davenport's diamond earrings. She laughed at the thought of them nestling still under the board in her leaky bedroom, perhaps under Mr Blunt's very feet as he paced furiously about. A shepherd watched her go by and thought her soft in the head, cackling at the sky.

Mr Blunt woke the next morning at ten o'clock with a fearful headache. He shouted, from his prone position, for tea. The house seemed unduly quiet: not a sound came up the stairs, not the chink of a plate from the kitchen or a creak in the floor. He hauled himself from his bed, still clothed, holding his throbbing head, and made his way down the stairs. There was no fire in the stove, no kettle boiling.

'GIRL!' he shouted into the still air. The birds stopped their twitter and froze in the trees, the mice held their breath in the skirting. He stood at the door of the kitchen, scowling, the story unfurling in his head.

Slowly he went, as if trying to put off the horror, his eyes fixed on the library door. He held his breath as he turned the handle and stepped inside: nothing seemed disturbed. As he crossed the room, blind panic seized him and he hurled himself towards the shelves, ripping out *Bleak House*, plunging his hands into the empty hole, scrabbling at nothing. He let out a howl of blistering rage that scattered God's creatures a mile around.

Grace woke in a hedge with a beady-eyed robin regarding her, turning his head this way and that as if sizing her up. They considered each other a short while before she took the necklace from her pocket and held it up to catch the morning light. The ruby flashed at them, a deep red wink, like an exotic dancer lifting her veil, mesmerising them for a few moments. She hid it back in her skirts and crawled out from the hedgerow, unsnagging her hair from twigs. The bird resumed his hunt for berries.

She was quite sure that Mr Blunt would kill her if he found her so Grace kept to the hedgerows and did not stop for refreshment until she reached Havant, twenty-nine miles away. She ate steak and kidney pudding and drank a pint of beer. A little brown bird flew down and pecked at pastry crumbs on the windowsill. A slice of sunlight was casting a golden stripe on the floor, a thousand tiny flecks of dust caught in its beam.

Coming out of the King's Arms, a little sleepy from the suet in her belly, she looked across the yard and nearly jumped clean out of her skin. There he was, unmistakable even with his back turned, watering his horse. She dived back inside, heart pounding. There was no other door to leave by and as she looked around again he was walking towards it. She took a seat at the back of the room, shrinking behind the bar. Luckily it was mid-afternoon and season-able, so the inn was busy with people drinking. She saw him enter the pub in the mirror on the back wall. She must take the red ribbon off her hat. She stole another glance as she snatched it from her head.

He was so gruff that he was served without delay and moved off to one side of the bar, striking up a conversa-tion presently with a young girl who didn't seem to mind his attentions. Grace made her move, edging out between the people, round the other side of the bar, holding her breath as she crossed the room. A bare space lay between her and the door, she could hear his growl in the babble of the pub; out she went, wanting to run, a prickle running up her back.

Grace did not stop shaking for half an hour. She took immediate cover and did not move so she could see which way he left. His companion evidently amused him as he spent more than an hour inside; Grace was wondering if she had missed him when she heard heavy hoofs on the path. She peered through the hedge to see him riding past, towards Chichester.

Blunt had been lucky thus far to find himself on the right road. He made another stop some miles on to refresh himself and his poor weary horse. Unluckily for them, the Hammer family were well known in that part of Sussex for their

76

business acumen and their lively parties – being part Irish. It did not take him long to find a local who claimed to know them well. After a great many drinks, much laughter and back-slapping, Mr Blunt had gathered a good deal of useful information.

A large ruddy man arrived at Pagham that afternoon, asking after the Hammer family. The good people told him nothing, feeling an instinctive mistrust towards the stranger. All except sweet imbecilic Nora Barker, the village idiot, who thought nothing of it and pointed him down the lane.

Mr Blunt skirted the village and took up a vantage-point at the edge of the wood above the Hammer farm. He bided his time until dusk, when he saw the family coming in from the fields to their dinner. Tethering his horse to a tree, he stole down the hill. He could hear laughter inside as he slunk round the house, circling it with a trail of kerosene and dry hay. It went up like a beauty.

After the fire Grace Hammer was a shrunken woman. She was taken in by neighbours – for a week she did not speak at all. She would not eat or, indeed, move, except to take sweet tea; otherwise she merely gazed through the window.

The ruby became an object of horror to her. It seemed to haunt her, beating under the floor, like the Tell-Tale Heart. She took it from its hiding-place one day, determined to be rid of it, and dug a hole in the lower field by the river; but when the time came to throw it in she could not seem to let it go. She stood a long while, looking at the ground, wishing she was down inside it.

The day after the funerals she went to the ruined house. It was a terrible sight: a blackened shell, scorched timber stumps stuck up against the sky, desolate in the rain. She left the next afternoon without warning, with the ruby necklace in her deepest pocket, wrapped in a charred page of Grimms' *Tales*.

CHAPTER EIGHT

It was only after Ivor Squall had deposited his letter safely in the post-box – stamp end first, according to his ritual, making sure it did not touch the sides – and was scurrying back to his office, wiping his fussy hands on his handkerchief, which was the only thing about him that may be called generous, that his thoughts turned to what it had all been about. He had been rather carried away with the intrigue and his own congratulations and only now did he reach back through his dusty cranium, to dig up old bones, balance old accounts he had forgotten.

It was Ivor Squall who had arranged for the disposal of goods from the Stanhope robbery, among others that had taken place that distant year at the hands of the Mathers mob; though this association had been profitable, he did not last the winter. By that November Ivor was a nervous wreck, being thoroughly afraid of most of them – he found the business troublesome, too much so for his liking, and intolerably complicated. Come December he had extricated himself and slithered off to London, where he found a little hole and went quietly about his business. Ivor trusted no one, but preferred to deal with people more his own size; he had seen none of the Mathers mob in ten years or more and he hoped to see none of them ever again – something he failed to consider fully until after his letter was safely in the post-box. He remembered with a shiver what he had heard of sorry Harold Whitbread; he had done well, he told himself, to get away. Ray Mathers's brutish face floated before his mind's eye, Big Arthur Bolt's heavy hands, and the Dean brothers, with their vulpine teeth, as clear as last week.

Any passing acquaintance of Mr Blunt that year knew the name Hammer: her disappearance had been at the forefront of Mr Blunt's concerns to an extent that one might fairly call obsessive. They had heard of nothing else. No one had managed to elicit quite why it vexed him so – he raved and tore his hair, or sat and watched the wall, as if to petrify himself – or why he wanted so urgently to find her, or should grieve so bitterly over the silver tankard that had apparently departed with her, even if it had been his beloved mother's. Most decided he must have been smitten, which in fact was true. Ivor had his own suspicions. She had left after the Stanhope robbery – abruptly, he would wager. Not for the first time he wondered what she had taken with her.

The thought came back to Ivor Squall the next evening as he scurried out to meet an associate in St Giles: if there was anyone at all to ask it was Emmeline Spragg. She would know the Hammer family or find them out. Even so, he had decided against it once already and, turning the idea over, rejected it again. Though Ivor Squall is straight in his own crooked way, and does a great deal of good criminal business – and much of it with Miss Spragg – he is not a man to share, unnecessarily, any extra profit that might fall from the tree, in the way of a reward, for instance. On the other hand, if it came to that, he might enquire casually, by way of conversation – he would have to make more than usual. Scheming made him itch and he decided, scratching along Fleet Street, to put it aside for the moment.

Ivor Squall cannot be expected to know that Grace Hammer is no ordinary mortal who may be traced with a few local enquiries, but rather a name that no one recalls, who has just left the room, who may not have been there at all. She is invisible even to the all-seeing eye of his associate. He may as well look for a black cat in a coal-hole, blindfold.

Miss Emmeline Spragg keeps her business as quiet as possible: she comes and goes without attention, her appearance doing nothing to announce her considerable wealth. In fact, she is often mistaken for a bundle of rags, should she be lurking in a quiet corner or crouched beside a wall. This suits her well, allowing her to hear all manner of useful information. She keeps tabs on the mobs that run London, each to their own piece, and her evil eye over the East End, where her network runs down every street, pushing sly tendrils through the keyholes and around the sleeping children – dreaming fitfully of Newgate prison, where their mothers stay for now. It winds like bindweed in at broken windows, beneath floorboards, into secret meetings, confidences: into anyone's affairs she cares to know. She has a hundred pairs of faithful eyes to cover Shoreditch, Whitechapel, Stepney, Bethnal Green, Wapping and Limehouse; and a hundred and ninety-seven pricked ears. Miss Spragg can account for only one of the lost ears – indeed she keeps it close about her person, hidden in her deepest pocket, where she squeezes it sometimes for comfort. Of the other two she knows nothing. This particular ear belonged to one Arthur Cuttle before her, who kept it cocked at the London docks, where he worked when last he had a pair. Arthur squealed to the foreman who caught him, at the back of Shadwell Basin, piling furs over the wall, and named names, like a leaky bucket – Miss Spragg's among them – at the prospect of losing his fingers on a block in the skin house, one by one. (Mr Muster, the devil's foreman, took a couple off in any event. He had meant to remove just the one but, unluckily for Arthur, he misjudged it.)

Miss Spragg had Happy Harry Harding chop the ear off – clean enough for the Queen, and flush with his scalp – leaving Arthur two fingers and an ear down on the deal. It was soft and barely cold when Harry presented it; she put it in a deep pocket and forgot about it altogether, until she saw its brother twelve weeks later, in the Alma, on the side of Arthur's head.

The ear had turned quite shiny in her pocket, and shrunk a good deal, hard and brown; she thought it charming and kept it about her from that day on, as a sort of lucky token; thus she invested it with superstitious importance, more every day, until she could not leave it behind. She has grown more attached to it than Arthur Cuttle ever was, and it is right and proper she should have it; evidently she needs it more than he, for he gets along nicely without it, and does not seem to care that it is gone. Miss Spragg and he are back on terms, and he keeps the ear he has left to the ground.

And so the wicked witch maintains the respect and loyalty of her trusty band of criminal accomplices, and runs a profitable empire, cornering the stolen-goods market east of the Tower. She never spends her money but keeps it in a tin chest, buried in a crumbling recess behind the chimney-breast. One day the wall will sink into the Thames, taking her fortune with it.

St Giles was not the rat-hole Ivor Squall remembered when first he knew it: it grew brighter and drier every year. This rotten log was all but torn up, the vermin scattered, to Clerkenwell, or Saffron Hill. Off Drury Lane, around Seven Dials the last dark spots remained. It was to shady Nottingham Court he made his way that evening – stronghold of the criminal element, unspoilt by sunlight or civic improvement – to the usual bolt-hole, an expedient spot upstairs at Willie the Stick's knocking shop, where Miss Spragg and he might conduct their business undisturbed. A gaggle of filthy children threw stones at him on the corner as he scuttled past. Cursing, he knocked at a mildewed door, handkerchief wrapped round his scrawny knuckles. A hatch snapped open and a beady eye poked out.

'Let me in,' said Ivor irritably, the filthy children closing in, cat-calling down the street behind him. He beetled up the dark stairs, past a dead rat on the landing. She was waiting in the back room, crouched in a gloomy armchair, black eyes glittering in the shadow. 'Good evening, Emmeline,' he said, with his best grimace.

Now, St Giles is not strictly Miss Spragg's patch – it reminds her of her mother, whom she prefers not to think about – but she would come up if she had something of particular quality that might suit Mr Squall's foreign clients. She would be in a good mood only after she was home again, with the money.

'What so, Mr Squall,' she croaked. 'You are late.'

'I do beg your pardon,' simpered Ivor.

Spragg looked him up and down as if he were a stuffed sheep. 'I do hope the exertion will be my worth my while,' she said, though she had come not four miles. She pulled a bunched handkerchief from her skirts and unwrapped it in her wizened palm, holding it towards the lamp for his inspection. He peered at it gingerly, recoiling inwardly at the greasy rag. A shiny thing it was too: a jewelled cross, unusually ornate, fine yellow gold, certainly Russian. It had surely come from a church. Divine light seemed to radiate from the holy thing, incongruous in the goblin's cursed hand. He wondered that it did not scorch her with its goodness, drive her shrieking underground.

Ivor Squall does not believe in God, but allows for the possibility for his own insurance – he repents his sins once a week, in case he is hit by a bus unexpectedly and finds it is all true. His name would be marked – especially dark for this – in the book of reckoning. Reparation must be made on Sunday. His foreign client, on the other hand, would be pleased as punch.

He lifted the cross, piously, with the very tips of his fingers, and adopted a doubtful air, as if it were not up to scratch – which was a struggle to maintain as it flashed its golden light, brilliant in his face. He did manage to convey a sense of disappointment, though it fell some way short of the effect he had intended; Spragg, in any case, is no fool. She knows exactly what is what. Ivor opened his mouth, thought better of it and shut it again.

'You seem bewildered, Mr Squall.'

'Merely wondering how best to proceed, Miss Spragg.'

'Is the business not clear to you, sir? Straightforward, indeed.'

'Perfectly so.' Ivor stalled, searching for hairs to split, something to bargain the price down, though it was fixed already and he saw it was a tidy deal. 'Did we fix upon a price?' he ventured, hoping to negotiate it.

Grace, boiling the kettle for tea in Bell Lane, felt a sudden disquiet, blowing over her feet, like a draught under the door. She looked up from her trance and into the fire, to capture the thought. Who was the little man on the bus? Why did he trouble her?

In dark and desperate Miller's Court, Sally Ann Dunn leaned against the wall of the passage, her arms swinging limp by her sides, mouth hanging open. She was fighting the urge to collapse upon her favourite spot and give in to unconsciousness. The pavement blurred, swaying beneath her. Summoning all her strength and will, and remembering dimly how cold she had been in the morning the last time she had slept in the passage, she lurched upright and staggered into the darkness in the direction of her filthy bed. A fortuitous choice, indeed – perchance her guardian angel was watching, and sober.

That night a cold wind blew. A monster was abroad; he

walked right past the archway, on the very paving where she might have been sleeping. He did not find the right moment to act that night, which evidently irked him, as he accomplished his task the next, finding conditions more favourable.

CHAPTER NINE

The morning of the Bank Holiday, Monday, 6 August 1888, also, incidentally and much less importantly, the forty-fourth birthday of the Duke of Edinburgh, dawned blue and bright. Sun soaked through the curtain and lit the room with the glow of a special day beginning. The Hammers leaped out of bed and into a flurry of dressing and shoe polish and ribbons. Even the boys washed in honour of the occasion. Daisy put on her new dress and everyone admired her as she turned in the middle of the room to show them, a little shy but beaming, delighted at herself with her clean rosy face and her pretty hat. It had a pansy like a tiny face and a velvet ribbon.

Grace took in the scene: the boys, all scrubbed and shiny, Daisy twirling at the centre. She must have the family picture taken. What a marvel, to capture and keep them! Breaking from this reverie she said, 'Let's go!' The family cheered. 'And keep your mitts to yourselves today, my boys,' she added, as they went out of the door.

'What do you mean "keep your mitts to yourselves"?' asked Daisy, who wasn't meant to hear.

'I mean be good.'

★

They were to meet Jack outside the Britannia at eleven – an arrangement Daisy had made – and Grace was glad to see that he had not disappointed her. There he was, freshly shaven, with a clean shirt and shiny boots. The cheeky peaked cap he had worn the first time she saw him was pushed back from his handsome face in the same distracted manner, as if he knew nothing of his devastating charm. Grace managed not to seem too eager; Daisy bounded up to him with transparent delight. After he had admired her hat and dress, and she his boots, they made their way with the milling crowd towards Victoria Park.

The Bank Holiday was a feast of merriment. Wondrous diversions were everywhere they looked and they spent the day pointing at things and trying to win coconuts. The little ones rode a donkey, ate ice cream and cockles and dough-nuts and went twelve times on the merry-go-round. As Grace got down from her painted horse Jack sprang forward to help her, though there really was no need, as close as he could, taking her hand, with his other round her waist; a little current passed between them for a moment, with Daisy watching in fascination and the boys nudging and giggling behind.

It was true that Jack had thought about Grace a great many times that week, and feared he was losing his head, the feeling growing every day. He could not remember the last time he had polished his boots or thought much about a woman he had already hooked, and he did not altogether like it – though he had urged the Bank Holiday to come. And he liked her better every time he saw her, he supposed – on account of his obstinate nature – because she didn't seem all that keen. When the children got back on the merry-go-round he caught her by the green ribbon round her neck, gently, and kissed her hard. A curious sensation came over him, blood flowing to his boots and his hands, an agitation. They watched Daisy go round again.

When he handed Grace hot tea with sugar she smiled at him as though she would take him to a private room. Daisy was clamouring to go on the Big Wheel – a hypnotic confection, turning above them with its pink and green seats, the footboards adorned with painted flowers.

The wheel went up slowly, stopping every few feet to let people on at the bottom. They chattered, excited, as they went higher, picked out the boys in the crowd, thrilled at the park stretching all around. When the wheel was full it started to turn at speed, flying them over the drop, and as their seat swung down to earth, Daisy felt as though she was falling and clung to her mother as though her life depended on it. 'I don't like it,' she said urgently.

Oh, bloody hell, thought Grace, it's only just started. 'It's all right, darlin', it'll stop in a minute.'

'I hate it.'

'Don't worry, girl. Look at all the things around – there's Charlie, see?' She tucked her comforting arm further round Daisy. She didn't like it too much herself. It seemed to go on and on, with the lurch of your stomach each time as you dropped down forwards, making you clench your hands and jaw though you know there is no need. What use indeed would that be should you fall, heaven forbid, or the wheel should break, or the bolt that your seat hangs on? she thought, as she did it once more.

'I hate it,' Daisy said, as they went round again.

'It's all right, baby, just sit still. Look up at the sky.'

They wandered home among the happy debris with the crowd, thinning out now in the darkness, stall lamps lighting their way. Daisy invited Jack back for a cup of tea and he duly obliged her, though Grace gave him gin instead. Jake fell asleep on the bed straight away so she took off his boots and breeches and pulled the blanket over him. Charlie wanted to go out and asked if Billy could come, which was kind, leaving, as it did, Grace and Jack to be alone. After Daisy had gone to sleep, that was, which took a full twelve minutes.

'Come here and kiss me,' he said.

'But you're ugly.'

'Don't make me come and get you!'

Grace did as she was told for only the second time since he had known her and sat on Jack's knee, one hand on his chest, just resting there while the other unbuttoned his fly. They did not tear off their garments with abandon and fuck each other senseless, as they might have liked, but slowly, under her skirt, pressing together, in silence, looking at each other all the while.

Billy was enjoying himself thoroughly at the Paragon. The Sisters De Laine were on the bill, and something called Devil Bird; and they had just seen Miss Vesta Tilley, queen of the music-hall stage. He had even been allowed a gin, which was swimming round his head. The thick smoke stank; rowdy chat and laughter filled the room. Suddenly he felt a bit sick.

Charlie had spied a pretty girl and was oblivious to Billy's discomfort. She had huge brown eyes and ruby lips like a china doll's; her hair was tied back from her flushed cheek with stray tendrils falling round her face. When she looked over he smiled bashfully, wishing he could make a more confident impression, but she smiled bashfully back. Her name was Elsie Brown and she worked at Bryant & May, which Charlie would find out later, when he dredged up the courage to talk to her, aided by a good many beers. Billy struggled with his nausea, trying not to vomit.

An Alpine Vesuvian is the best match money can buy – indeed, it is the king of matches – being sturdy and highly explosive in its own diminutive way. You can strike it in heavy wind and it will not fail you, making it an excellent companion for camping expeditions or country jaunts. Elsie cleared four hundred boxes a day through her part of the dipping table alone. She did not know it yet but the phosphorus will kill her.

Daisy and Jake slept peacefully on into the night, dreaming of toffee apples and the merry-go-round. The day was blighted only by terrible events in George Yard Buildings, scene of horrible murder that night as the festivities rolled into the early hours, the bloody corpse undiscovered till dawn.

★

Out in the country, near the little town of Netley Marsh, Mr Ivor Squall's letter lay upon Mr Blunt's doormat, next to an unpaid bill from his solicitor. It remained there for a week or more, gathering dust, its recipient being abroad in Berkshire, where there were many fine country houses.

CHAPTER TEN

Mrs Atkins from Hanbury Street was a fading flower, just twenty-four and without Mr Atkins now for three months or more. He had found himself unequal to the responsibilities of family life and left her to it, with their three children and her opium habit to feed (the latter taking priority as is customary in this tortured world) and a baby on the way – having been busy up until the very moment of his departure, that particular aspect of their relations unaffected by the wretchedness of the rest.

The baby, when his turn came, was very small and took several minutes to draw his first sickly breath. He seemed doomed from the start and died before the week was out, having neither hunger nor interest in living to inspire him. The others, meanwhile, suffered their betrayed and broken slap-happy mother, scratching around for their own food, lifting her head from puddles in the gutter when they found her. They would sit and guard her until she came to and cried at them for being there, hugging them too hard, and then, guilt done for another day, would scrape herself up off the pavement and back into the crowd, promising to come back in a moment with ice cream.

Daisy had spotted the Atkins girls, and remarked that

they walked sadly and looked as though they were frightened and had no friends. Grace had seen their mother talking to Sally Ann in the Ten Bells and she looked much as the girls did. The next week Billy reported that there was also a small boy in the Atkins house, not more than two or three years old. He was evidently alone, left to the care of his sisters, whom Billy had seen begging in Brick Lane – their ma had not been home for two days, and they had left him as they were all hungry and he was too heavy to carry. Grace and Daisy went to Hanbury Street and found him chewing an old mutton bone, damp and reeking. They gathered him up and left a note, with their address, hoping the recipient could read it.

'His name is Tom,' said Daisy, helpfully.

'Have you seen him before?'

'Only through the window. He was playing by himself.'

'Come on, Tom. Come and have a nice bath.'

'Can we wash him?'

'Yes, we can. He seems to like us all right.'

'He smells. Can we keep him?'

'Hold your horses there, Miss Daisy. Let's wash him first and talk to his ma.'

If Tom had ever had a bath before he had forgotten it: he shrieked with fear at first and then delight as he felt the warm water. Daisy and Jake found this hilarious and they caught the giggles. They washed him sweetly with a flannel, carefully around the scabby patches, and showed him how to splash. It made a very cosy scene and Grace quietly prayed she wasn't up the duff. Then they got him out and dried him by the fire, and combed the lice out of his hair.

'Jake, can you run round to Hanbury Street and wait for his sisters to come home?'

'They're called Annie and Kate. Annie is nine and Kate is seven.'

'Thank you, Daisy. When they come home, bring them here. When Billy gets back I'll send him to wait with you.'

And so it was that the Atkins children came to stay with the Hammers. When Jake returned with the girls, wide-eyed like rabbits, she sent Billy to wait for Mrs Atkins to come home.

'Her name is Mary Jane,' said Daisy, 'but I don't know how old she is.'

Mary Jane never got home that night or the next. The landlord came to throw her out on Wednesday but went away again. The children found her dead in her bed on Thursday morning. Tom still hadn't seemed to notice she wasn't there. The thin, haunted girls came back with Billy's arms round them.

'Will you go over, Ma? I'll watch them.'

Grace found Mary Jane Atkins stone cold and stiff on her filthy bed in her boots and hat. She had choked on the vomit that had dried down her dead neck, and her face was waxen and grey. Mercifully her eyes were shut. A fly droned above them, banging into the windowpane. Grace took her possessions, such as they were: a hat with a tattered bird perched on the brim, ragged children's clothes, some shells from the seaside. She looked at Mary Jane's fingers for a wedding ring but, of course, it had gone to the pawn-shop long ago. Then she stroked her, just lightly, on the arm and the cheek, to touch her before she went into the earth. Her skin was frigid, blood pooled along the back of her hands and arms, turning a purple pattern on the pale flesh. She was taken away the next morning, in a box with rope handles.

For the next three days Annie and Kate, who was the image of her mother, were ghostly figures who drifted round the Hammer home, soundless, with empty faces. Daisy exerted the full power of her hospitality, making encouraging conversation, involving them in games and anything else she thought would make them feel better. They could not be persuaded to leave the house, not for cricket or catch, or even just to sit in the street, and clung round Grace as close as they could without actually touching her. Charlie had given up his bed quite cheerfully to his brothers, who with Grace, had forgone their place in the big bed so that tiny Tom and the girls could be comfort-able together. This left Charlie and Grace on the floor, which was the only place they could stretch out, and they couldn't do that for ever. Billy insisted on each of them taking a turn in his place for a night at least, his ma first on Sunday, Charlie Monday. Tuesday they made up a cot for Tom, put the girls top to toe and got back into their beds. Grace lay in the dark in the sleeping room, wondering how they would manage and what she should do for the best.

The Atkins children had not been with the Hammers a week before there was trouble. It came in the vile shape

96

of Mirabel Trotter as she passed by the end of Thrawl Street.

She is a sly piece of work, Mrs Mirabel Trotter, like a great flabby toad lurking under a dank rock, staring out from the gloom at her dinner. She is solid, and square, with the strength of a man to match her temper. She wears a great deal of gold, all of her jewellery at once, it seems, to show off – it does nothing to enhance her appearance save to dazzle the spectator in sunlight. Although she is vulgar in this respect she has a good few impressive connections: various baronets and a duke or two, among other esteemed clients, for whom she herself is the model of discretion, and she leads an enviable life of comfort, her empire stretching across East London. In addition to her quieter interests she owns the greater part of Thrawl, and Flower and Dean Streets, chunks of Hoxton, a lodging-house or two in Bow. She has every-thing, in fact, except true love, which she heard about long ago and has pursued ever since, finding it elusive, which is not only, as she thinks, because she cannot buy it but also because she is so unfortunate as to lack any personal appeal whatever.

She had spotted the Atkins girls out and about and, not knowing who was looking after them, had engaged the poor innocents in conversation, from which she deduced that their mother was dead and they were staying with a local family for now. They told Grace about the fat, fright-ening lady in the fancy carriage who had spoken to them, though they tried not to say much; how she had watched after them down the street, waving as they hurried away. Grace knew why the old sow was sizing them up, though they might be all of eight and nine. She told them to stay away from Thrawl Street and asked the boys to keep an eye open.

Sure enough, two days later Billy came racing home, in a breathless panic.

'Annie's gone, she's been snatched.' He was near to tears, Kate by his side, her eyes like empty dinner plates. Grace grabbed her little hand. 'Where?'

'Dorset Street.'

'What in *God's* name were you doing in Dorset Street?'

'We was taking a short-cut.'

Now Dorset Street, dear reader, is no likely avenue for a quiet stroll or a short-cut to anywhere, though it runs not a hundred and fifty yards long, between Crispin and Commercial Street. It is said by some to be the most notorious street in London. Policemen rarely patrol it and only in pairs. You can find a man for the dirtiest job here; cutthroats and thieves rub shoulders with the grimiest brasses, smoking opium and drinking their filthy London gin. Near one end is an archway that leads through to Miller's Court, which sounds cheery enough but is really a warren of mouldy rooms and passages, so neglected by sunlight that not even moss can grow on the wet walls, never mind a pot plant – if there was anybody here who might keep such a thing: hideout for the Blind Beggar mob, bitter rivals of the Nicholses, and squalid home to other shady operations and some of the most wretched girls in the parish. A century ago Dorset Street was a clean thoroughfare with fresh air, the wide blue sky and flowers growing at the windows; a century before that, a country lane. It is doomed to be the scene of dark events, though no one can know these things yet. Grace was down there like a flash.

Miss Kelly was the first voice of reason: she had spotted the children round about twelve and told them to get themselves home. Then she'd gone into Miller's Court for a minute, only just inside the archway, to see that Sally Ann was breathing – she had stumbled in a half-hour before and fallen asleep in the passage. No one wanted to move her as she had walloped Nelly Holland last time for trying to put her to bed, and her eye was still black. Coming out again she had spotted Billy racing down the street with the little one in tow, stumbling to keep up, all the commotion behind them, and Busy Liz Stride hammering with her long arms on the door of MacMurphy's lodging-house, wailing in Swedish.

Mrs Mirabel Trotter, in all her glittering gold, has plucked Annie Atkins, along with two other girls that day, from the street and they are on their way, terrified, in a plain carriage, to an address in Shoreditch. The journey is tortured and silent. She receives them at the inner door once the gate is firmly locked behind them. She tells them they will be put to work straight away at general household tasks and that they are there by order of the Metropolitan Board of Works. Two of them do not know that this is untrue.

★

There was one person who could help poor Annie Atkins, and Grace had wasted no time in looking for her. She searched every pub the length of the Whitechapel Road, which was no mean feat, and returned home, where Billy was minding the little ones, to find Charlie and Jake on the doorstep, having scoured Commercial Street all the way to the station and back down Brick Lane, with no joy either. Trixie May Turner, lady of leisure, East End society queen, was not in the neighbourhood that afternoon. Grace wanted to sit down in the road and cry with hopelessness. It was Daisy who suggested the next step: 'You could ask Jack.'

It was true that he knew everyone. And he seemed a reliable sort, strangely enough, the kind you might turn to in times of trouble.

'That's a good idea, darlin'.' And so it was her turn to find him.

He turned up in the Saracen's Head, luckily at that moment not charming a lady but cracking rude jokes with Michael Robinson, the landlord. She grasped him by the elbow, a little breathless.

'Will you run an errand with me, Jack?'

As it happened, Jack knew a thing or two about Miss Trotter; not, as Grace suspected, because he frequents her brothel but because Trixie May Turner was his best friend for drinking and sometime associate. He did not divulge this information for now, expecting she would make something of it, as women in his experience are wont to do. And he happened to know that Trixie was in Canning Town and not due back until after dinner. He had never met the vile Mrs Trotter but her reputation preceded her for miles around, and he felt as if he knew her already more intimately than he would like.

He rejected Grace's plan to find Mrs Trotter and confront her – a brave idea, but foolish. Mirabel Trotter runs a tight racket and casual callers rub her up the wrong way, which nobody wants to do. Those with troublesome enquiries or pointy fingers are likely to be shown through to the yard, to be dealt with where no one can hear them. Jack was not about to go knocking on the door at Thrawl Street or her fortress in Shoreditch. Furthermore, Annie might not be at either, but at Trotter's premises in Mile End. Or – though he refrained from saying it – dead in a ditch already. He proposed instead that they visit an acquaintance of his in Limehouse, who is the best source of information on any business in the criminal world, if you can get her to talk. He drained his beer and they left at once.

Jack is a city boy, born and bred in St Olave. His great-grandmother had kept a beautiful tidy cottage in Hanbury Street in the days when Whitechapel had clean air and birdsong, and fields still skirted the district. He remembers her faintly, as if in a dream, her window-boxes the last flash of colour in their street. He may be an unsuitable choice for a consort but he can be a solid friend. He has saved many a day, rescued many a damsel in distress – and not just the young, pretty ones.

He was surprised that Grace asked for his help, having supposed that she was cast iron. They stormed down

Commercial Road heading for Limehouse: scene of human degradation, lair of the wicked, axis of criminal activity. It was one of the blacker spots on East London's face, dark and grey and damp. The wood had rotted on the windows in these bleak streets, eating itself; the buildings were slipping slowly into the marsh, with the people still inside, clustering and scuttling like silverfish.

As they walked past the workhouse at the end of Thomas Street they saw a dead dog in the road.

'It's just round the corner and down the alley now,' he said.

They rounded the corner and stepped from their grimy, stinking surroundings into a rotten place. A narrow, crooked passage, slick with condensation from the sewage on the floor, the sound of thick drops dripping. It smelled of dead things and sickness and shit. Tunnel-like alleyways led off in other directions ahead. This was Blight Street, St Anne, notorious den of thieves and miscreants.

As they picked their way through the slime they passed tiny windows, some dark and soundless, some patched with pathetic rags or greasy brown paper, with a faint light inside and the sound of crying. Just inside a half-open doorway, a baby was asleep on the floor, sucking breaths of fetid air into rattling lungs. Their footsteps squelched under them, someone shrieked in the distance. They climbed some stairs that appeared suddenly from the gloom, feeling the way, passing figures slumped unconscious or dead on the steps. Grace was certain she had stood on someone's hand. A rotten door appeared at the top and upon knocking they were admitted, after a gruff inquisition through the keyhole.

The creature who opened the door to them was more goblin than woman in appearance and demeanour. She greeted them with a smile that was neither warm nor friendly and hollow black eyes.

'Good day, Miss Spragg, how nice it is to see you,' said Jack, tipping his hat, plainly lying but doing very well at it. 'May I beg a moment of your valuable time?'

'Why, charming Mr Tallis, can it really be you after all these weeks?' she replied, with a sickening grin. 'I had quite forgotten you! What could you be wanting this fine day, I wonder? And who's this pretty piece?' She jabbed a vicious claw in Grace's direction. Grace swallowed the urge to smack her rotten teeth down her throat.

'This is my good friend Miss Jane Hanbury,' said he. 'One of her girls has been taken this morning, in Dorset Street. I'm sure you've heard something about it.'

The goblin Spragg laughed nastily, creature of hell, black-hearted. 'Oh, sure indeed, are you?' she rasped, through her fit of merriment.

'I'm sure you will think of something to say,' he said quietly, 'when you have heard me out in private.'

She looked a little uneasy suddenly and stepped aside to let them in. Her long skirts covered her feet so she seemed to glide or, rather, to scuttle along. They entered a damp passageway and ascended a flight of rotting stairs, the reek of mildew closing round them. Upstairs a fire hissed in the grate, burning green wood, like the poison tree Grace had read about in some tale or other, most likely Grimm.

'You. Wait here,' the goblin told Grace, her eyes cold,

black like a spider's. She waved Jack up another flight. Grace watched their feet disappear. Footsteps crossed the floor above and faded away.

Now Jack, in fact, had nothing on Miss Spragg at all. He was blessed, however, with hypnotic eyes, the crooked gift of effortless deception as he spilled from his mother's womb. He employs it often for his own casual amusement, dropping confusion here and there like litter: a curse that his sorry victims struggle with, brows knit, until they are buried with it, doubt worrying them under the ground – so that even before the gates of Heaven, as they declare their tally before St Peter, a part of them is caught in perpetual distraction, perplexed by something they cannot remember, wondering what he meant.

Jack fixed Emmeline Spragg with his deep dark eyes.

'Do you know where Arthur Cuttle's been this last week?' he said. Not a question but a foregone conclusion that she did not and would want to. 'You might keep a special eye on him.' Pity poor Arthur Cuttle, who had nothing to do with anything underhand but loyal service to his goblin mistress.

The glassy black eyes glittered back at him in the gloom. Jack smiled affably as he watched the cogs tick behind them, chewing on his words.

As she and Jack share a fair few connections, the wicked witch was wondering who he had been talking to and what they had said – the unfortunate consequence of living as a dishonourable criminal, without loyalty even to one's own associates.

Jack adopted his best mysterious face. 'Tell me about Mirabel Trotter,' he said, 'what business she has been about this week.'

The goblin's ears pricked at the mention of Mrs Trotter. She was expecting something altogether trickier from him, and had no idea why Jack should be asking after her business. However, Mrs Trotter and Miss Spragg have their own private bone, which she is always keen to gnaw on. So, to his satisfaction, she indulged his enquiries. She wondered what to do for the best about Arthur Cuttle. And who exactly the woman downstairs might be. With the green ribbon round her neck.

Meanwhile in Shoreditch, Annie Atkins, showing more spine than we may give her credit for, is plotting her escape. Though she has been in the Shoreditch house not more than four hours she has already noticed that the keys are kept on a chain by bone-fingered Miss Craven, vile keeper of their prison, who sleeps downstairs with her glass eye open, and that the only window without bars is on the third floor: in fat Mrs Trotter's private office. She resolved to keep her eyes peeled and her spirits up. The other girls are a Maureen O'Dowd, a pretty Irish thing, and a little Polish girl called Nina, who speaks about six words of English, none of which can help her, being things like 'fire' and 'baby'. The most helpful words she has are 'Thank you', which she has no occasion whatsoever to use here. She is younger even than Annie Atkins and, like Maureen, is lost in confusion and will cry herself to sleep in the narrow beds to which they are shown that night, after the door has been bolted, while Annie lies awake, listening to their jailers carousing below.

It is rumoured that Mirabel Trotter once kept a man in her cellar for a month, chained to the wall, whom she flogged every morning until he begged, weeping, for his life and she threw him bleeding and penniless on to the street. His name was Sam Miller and he had a wife and three young children and owed Mrs Trotter twelve shillings. Foolishly, he had attempted to hide when he was unable to repay it, rather than explain his difficulties – which in truth would have made little difference to the treatment he received. She had to make an example of somebody once in a while to maintain her credibility, and that time it happened to be him.

He crawled home to find his family gone. The landlord had thrown them out a week before and, having survived upon the kindness of her neighbours for a day or two, Mrs Miller had turned to hawking the only asset she had left, believing her husband to be dead. He was a good man, not given to disappearing, she told her friends. He must have met some dreadful fate. They nodded sympathetic agreement but secretly thought not. The day before Sam Miller returned, his wife decided she could not carry on without him. She was a fragile soul and unable to bear the shame of her new situation. No one saw the family go. The next person to lay eyes on them was the lighterman who pulled them out of the Thames at Tilbury, still clinging together, little dead hands entwined in her hair.

Mrs Trotter has a finger in every pie in the criminal world. Her own mother sold her to a travelling show of wonders as she was such an extraordinarily large and odd-looking baby. She was trained to juggle and perform acrobatics in a troupe of girls, four of them, with strange faces and muscular arms, in yellow satin gowns. The Daffodil Sisters was their stage name and they went down very well all over London for a time.

After this brief but exhilarating career had run its course she made an important decision. She would never allow her circumstances to revert to their former humble state; on the contrary, she would make something important of herself – acquire position and power, pursue the high life she had tasted. This meant clearing seven hundred pounds per annum by her most conservative estimate. The only serious way to achieve such an ambition seemed to be through organised crime. Starting with minor robbery and prostitution – at which she enjoyed surprising success – she progressed to extortion and brothel-keeping, by virtue of the contacts she had made. Within a year she had twin sons by Alfie Skinner, notorious villain and scourge of Hatton Garden, kept fifteen girls on her books and protected the interests of several other local concerns for a monthly fee, helped by her associates the Wilsons and Mr Harry Harding. Thus she carved her own way through East London until she controlled a good part of it, vanquishing her enemies (not least Mr Trotter, a hapless little man with his trousers an inch or two short – she forgets why she married or, indeed, killed him: he rests peacefully under the vegetable bed at her country retreat near Harlow). She feels lonely sometimes, but she knows she will never have everything.

She and Miss Spragg tolerate each other, having separate patches. Miss Spragg's line is more in goods: she can sell anything of quality, the finer the better, having more connections than the Queen herself, an unusual circumstance for someone who looks as if they live under the ground.

Jack emerged from the lair at last. He said nothing until they had left the crumbling kingdom behind.

'What now?' she said.

'Annie's in Shoreditch. Locked up tighter than Newgate. There's only one person can help you with that.'

They happened upon Trixie May Turner at last, after dark, propping up the bar of the Grave Maurice. She embraced them both with exuberant fondness and bought them a drink.

'You could do better!' she said to Grace.

'I can't shake him off.'

'Try rat poison.'

Jack revelled in this appreciation, knowing he was the handsomest cad in the parish. After these greetings were done they took a corner table and Trixie settled down to listen.

Trixie May Turner (which is not her real name) was born to a rich family, who disowned her, in shame and disgrace, pregnant by a bricklayer named Arthur Blakey, who was devilish charming. He stole her heart clean away, costing Trix her rightful inheritance of the family pile. Less than three minutes after she had imparted this news he was out of the door and away, never to return. This had happened twenty-three years ago last Wednesday, but though he was a distant memory that popped up less often than her birthday, Trixie could see his face still, and feel the pain, as sharp as if he had left yesterday. She had drunk like a whale at first to dull the sorrow but had tired of the company and reverted to her lively self: she likes to talk, and eat well, and knows everybody.

She finances her moderately hedonistic lifestyle through a steady business in opiates, which has gone along nicely since 1872, by way of a good Asian connection and a friend at Custom House, who manages to overlook the import tax on her goods. She knows Mirabel Trotter from long ago; they dine together often, sharing a taste for good wine and caviar. They never do business, or talk about it, which is why they get on so well, restricting their badinage to matters of entertainment. Vile Mrs Trotter has been seen, on occasion, gazing rapt as Trixie talks, like a little girl watching the Queen.

Stripe Wilkins seemed to enter the room without opening the door, as he always did, and hovered silently before his mistress, waiting for the word.

'Jack Tallis was here not an hour ago,' said the goblin Spragg. 'He brought company. A tall woman, handsome, good teeth. I've not seen her before.'

He slid from the room, gone as she turned from the grimy window, without a squeak, through the keyhole, into the slippery street.

★

After the matter at hand was discussed, Jack and Grace sat down to roast beef and potatoes, at Trixie's insistence; they must eat and there was nothing more to be done for now. Grace forced down her dinner and left at ten – Jack saw her to the door. His kiss was coarse; he tasted of stale beer. She shoved him back into the pub and went on her way.

London was slick with rain, black and grey. The street-lamps glowed sickly yellow on the Yorkshire stones, showing up the dirt and shit, the rotten leaves pasted flat, mixing slime and grit, sticky city.

Back in Bell Lane the family were tidying the rooms and folding their clothes as a surprise for Ma so she wouldn't have to fuss at them or shout. Jake and Tom fell asleep after pie and mash at seven o'clock. When everything was nice Billy read to Daisy in bed and Charlie stoked a nice cosy fire. Twenty minutes passed peacefully so, till poor Billy burst suddenly into tears. He was racked with guilt about Annie and, though he had been holding it well all day, he cried his heart out, with Charlie's arm around him.

'Come on Billy,' he said, 'you musn't blame yourself.'

'It's all my fault' sobbed Billy.

'No it ain't.'

Daisy hugged his head and wiped away his tears. She was sure that Annie would be back at any moment.

'It'll all come out in the wash, Billy,' she said. This made him laugh a bit and she was pleased to have cheered him up. Then she tucked him into bed next to her. Charlie stayed up to see his ma home, and tried to immerse himself in a new serial, which he could not, despite having a fancy for the heroine. He had read several pages without taking in a word when Grace came home, knocking softly on the window. As he opened the door Mrs Jacob's curtain twitched across the way and prying eyes clocked Grace as she went in.

Charlie looked at her expectantly but Grace just shrugged her shoulders in a gesture of despair and exhaustion. Then she took off her boots and fell fast asleep with all her clothes on.

CHAPTER ELEVEN

The very next day Trixie May Turner called at the Shore-ditch residence of Mrs Mirabel Trotter, dining partner and acquaintance of early days, dressed in a fancy bonnet to amuse herself and anyone else who might be looking. The bell was answered by Miss Isobel Craven, fastidious housekeeper and devout reader of the Holy Bible, naturally drawn to suffering and punishment. Her hair was scraped back tightly from her gaunt face, tied in a painful knot and stuck with a sharp comb. She regarded Trixie with utter indifference, as if she had no idea who she was or what she might want, or the slightest interest in finding out. Her glass eye fixed upon something invisible beyond Trixie's left shoulder, rolling slightly in its socket, making Trixie want to laugh out loud.

'Good day,' said Trixie, haughtily. 'Would you announce me to the mistress?' Trixie knew Miss Craven quite well and loathed her thoroughly. She enjoyed getting under her tight, witless skin – being possessed of an unusual taste in amusement – so much so that she indulged this impulse every time she called at the house. The drollery mostly took Miss Craven's neurotic domestic routine as its inspiration: in light of the recent chimney-sweeping Trixie had planned something special for today.

She ascended the stairs (after being made to wait) with a flounce and a toss of her head because she knew it irked Miss Craven when she put on airs and graces. At the top was Mrs Trotter, toad woman, at the helm of her empire. She glowered from behind her desk, heavy eyebrows knitted, trying not to look as though she was pleased to see Trixie, who dissolved her with a beatific smile, a feat that only she could perform. There was truth in the rumour that Trotter preferred women for love, and no one exploited this better than Trixie, being in the unique position of her equal, from the start of their long acquaintance in the days when Trotter turned tricks in the graveyard at St Botolph. She has severed connections with all others who remember her so, thus bestowing on Trixie a singular omnipotence that she wields on occasion to her own advantage. Mrs Trotter regrets this soft spot, but is unable to resist her. And so Trixie May can flirt with the toad and extract things with charm without resort to the unthinkable. And though Mrs Trotter has been in love, as much as she is able, with Trixie for these last fifteen years, despite getting nowhere, they are friends of a sort still.

'So,' said Trixie, brightly, dropping into the easy chair, 'what news?'

'I might ask you the same,' said Mrs Trotter, 'having heard neither hide nor hair of you all this week.'

'Oh, come now, Mirabel, don't sulk. You know I've had my hands full with Mr Worth being over.'

'I know you've been drinking yourself sick in the Grave Maurice. I have eyes at every corner, you know.'

'You sound just as my mother would if she were breathing.'

They glared at each other for a moment. Trixie lit her pipe.

'Tell me, Mirabel,' she said, after a lengthy pause – in which they waited, quite at ease, as if the other were not there, to see who would speak next, one contemplating the condition of her fingernails while the other wondered idly where to dine that evening. 'What of the new girls?'

Mirabel Trotter sat up quite straight in her French leather chair. Trixie May Turner never mentioned the girls, new or not, having a distaste for the business that she had laid upon the table long ago, with typical candour, resulting in the understanding that the subject never came up again. Why she should toss it into the air now, after twelve years or more, in such a casual manner, Mrs Trotter could not imagine.

'What of them?'

'I heard tell you've found a new one in Dorset Street.'

Mirabel Trotter took a good look at Trixie May. There was something about her this afternoon. She did not like the angle, more rakish than usual, at which she was wearing her hat, which, now she happened to notice it, sported a new peacock feather. She smelled a rat. 'That may be so,' she ventured, with what she hoped was a cryptic air.

'One Annie Atkins, if I recall correctly,' continued Trixie, smoothly, cutting directly to the point without regard for Mrs Trotter's aura of mystery. 'Unluckily you have picked upon quite the wrong girl.' She took a long draw on her pipe for effect, and looked out of the window as if composing difficult news.

Mrs Trotter held fast to her nerves.

'The problem with Annie,' said Trixie at last, 'is her royal connection.' She had been studying a hoarding outside and had not completely planned what she was to say; she wanted to reel the words back in as soon as they had escaped her lips.

They sounded so utterly far-fetched, however, that Mirabel Trotter was reluctant to dismiss them, the truth being, in her wide experience, much stranger than fiction. She waited instead for what might follow, while Trixie's mind somersaulted, paddling, like swan's feet, beneath her composed exterior, scrabbling for the next words to say. They came out by themselves, as they ever seemed to do, by virtue of her disregard for the cares of the world, a happy quality born of a broken heart.

'She happens to be the bastard child of one Robert Samms, Master of Command and most esteemed counsel – the chief courtier to Her Majesty the Queen herself, and protected therefore, though it may be at arm's length, by the might of the Crown. When Scotland Yard become involved they shall certainly find their way into your affairs, whatever your connections may be.'

Mrs Trotter digested this, weighing it, wondering how much a fool she might be, looking all the while at Trixie May Turner, who kept her gaze steady. The clock ticked on the mantelpiece. 'And what might this have to do with you?' she ventured at last.

'Nothing at all,' replied Trixie, employing her most

innocent expression of concern, which she heightened further by leaning earnestly forward, stopping just short of clasping the flabby hand upon the desk. 'I am merely passing on what news I have heard, out of care for a dear friend. I am only sorry that I know nothing more.'

Mirabel Trotter looked doubtful, but not confidently so.

'Do with it as you wish,' said Trixie, rising from her chair and making for the door. 'I shall see myself out.' By rights she should have pursued a career on the stage. She left the room with a sweep of her skirt and a glance over her shoulder as she closed the door behind her, leaving Mrs Trotter standing, feeling unaccountably stupid, behind her great desk.

As Trixie descended the stairs she remembered the delicious surprise she had in store for Miss Craven and stopped short of the front door, opening and shutting it with an energetic slam as if she had left. Looking around furtively she pulled a fresh herring wrapped in newspaper from her coat pocket and silently crossed the hall to the drawing room. Peering round the door she saw her at the bureau under the window. She had her back to Trixie and was searching for something, opening and shutting each drawer, somewhat irritably, stirring their contents with a bony finger. Trixie shrank back behind the door, watching through the gap between its hinges. Presently Miss Craven seemed to find what she was looking for; she stopped scrabbling and held up a small brass key, shook her head and tutted loudly to herself.

'That wretched *woman*!' Trixie heard her spit, and stifled

a burst of laughter. She was clearly not the only one who made a hobby of vexing Miss Craven. The 'wretched woman' could only be Isobel Craven's nemesis: one Miss Rosalind Pinch. Miss Pinch held the position of Mrs Trotter's personal secretary so the two were constant competitors for seniority within the household, daily treading on each other's toes, interfering in each other's responsibilities. They had been sworn enemies for so long now that neither could remember why exactly, but kept up their mutual hatred as both had invested so much effort in it already. Trixie watched as Miss Craven unlocked the bottom door of the bureau to reveal a squat iron safe. She stopped for a moment, key in hand, apparently in thought, before placing it in another drawer. So, hiding the key was a household game! Then she seemed to feel she was being observed – she stiffened, and lifted her sharp nose as if to sniff the air.

Miss Pinch's voice floated down from the room above. Trixie could not make out what she said but it seemed she was reprimanding some poor soul, who was no doubt imagining the pleasure of killing her in her bed. Miss Craven seemed satisfied that she was alone, for she turned back to the bureau and, reaching above it to the picture hanging there – a small Canaletto if Trixie was not mistaken, very fine and surely original – she took another key, from behind the gilt frame, and opened the safe.

Trixie never bothered to leave the herring up the chimney. She forgot it altogether, in fact, until she was halfway home with a small ensemble of hungry cats behind her.

★

Mirabel Trotter sat at her desk for a full ten minutes after Trixie May Turner had flounced out, in deep thought, which she was not good at – after which things were no clearer. Failing to decipher what this strange visit had been about, much less what the truth might have been, she decided to give Trixie's intelligence the benefit of the doubt, just in case. She would wait till tomorrow and turn the girl out on the street, with a crown for her trouble. Kidnapping was becoming a precarious business. She resolved to confine her attentions, for the time being, to more reliable concerns: extortion, running the older girls, a little smuggling. And there were new interests to pursue: ventures involving the workhouse mortuary at Whitechapel and a surgeon at the London Hospital, whose recent acquaintance she had made at one of Mr Worth's parties. Dead people, she surmised, with solid reason, would be easier to steal. This was becoming more apparent every day. She bellowed loudly for Miss Pinch, making the pictures jump against the wall, and ordered her carriage.

Annie Atkins was not woken for work the next morning but allowed to remain in bed. The other girls set to, airing the upper floors of the house and sweeping the rugs. She woke to the sound of Nina crying, footsteps running down the stairs. She sat up, wondering why she was still in bed and if she was in trouble. It was quiet again so she dressed quickly and crept down the narrow stairs. As she reached the next flight a dreadful commotion struck up downstairs, making her jump, a banging and thudding as if someone was throwing furniture. The door of foul Mrs Trotter's room swung open across the landing. Annie stopped still, shrinking into the corner.

The racket seemed to involve Miss Craven and poor Maureen O'Dowd, who had thrown herself into a cupboard to escape the lashes of Miss Craven's stick – an unwise move, for now she found herself locked in and, terrified of small dark spaces, was hammering on the inside of the door and howling in panic, to the sadistic delight of her glass-eyed jailer. Most importantly, it brought Miss Pinch out of the Trotter office where, no doubt, she had been fixing the books in her own interest. The commotion had startled her; she was jumpy already from poking her fingers in while the boss was out, and she came raging out from behind Mrs Trotter's desk, forgetting, in her haste and fury, to lock the office door. The windows were open inside; a gentle breeze ruffled the curtain. Miss Pinch flew down the stairs like an angry dart and Annie Atkins took her chance.

She crossed the landing and stepped gingerly inside the lion's den, stomach turning as she crossed the threshold, her breath rattling like an old woman's teacup. The room was huge and stern; the furniture seemed to watch her.

When she looked down from the window she saw why it had not been fitted with bars as every other. There was a sheer thirty-five-foot drop to the paving below, the wall stretching away without a ledge or any other feature that might serve as a foothold or grip to hang your life upon, save a thin drainpipe running straight down that you would not trust with half your weight, even if you had the bottle for the climb. She stared at this prospect, dumbstruck. She only noticed that the commotion downstairs had stopped when the stair creaked below the landing, and again: another step, coming towards the open door. She found herself climbing out, legs first, gripping the sill, swinging a foot over to meet the pipe, grasping it with white knuckles. She flattened herself to the wall as someone inside closed the window. The urge to scream welled in her throat and she swallowed it, trembling like a dry leaf.

The drainpipe held fast enough till the first floor, when a part came away from the wall above her, as it had threatened, with creaks and groans, all the way thus far. She pushed away as it started to give, landing in a laurel bush on the far side of the garden wall. She opened her eyes slowly in case there was something terrible to see – an impossibly twisted leg, or a bone sticking out through her skin. Finding only scratches and a bruise or two she thanked heaven, then untangled herself from the shrubbery and ran.

Downstairs the commotion raged on and no one noticed she was gone. Misses Craven and Pinch vented their mutual loathing, full force, like valves shooting livid steam, with poor Maureen O'Dowd still locked in the cupboard, her desperate screams ignored. The butler and cook came up to watch and found themselves restraining the combatants, and soon the whole household was involved.

Once the fuss had died down the staff busied themselves

tidying, and attending to minor injuries sustained in the excitement. It took the rest of the morning to restore order. Annie was only found missing when Miss Craven, at Mrs Trotter's bidding, came to find her at noon to set her – reluctantly – free without question. Cursing herself for not having locked the harlot into her room, she turned the house over, raging all the while, the other girls trying to hide their delight.

Mrs Trotter suspected immediately that Trixie May Turner had had a hand in it. As the girl was leaving them anyway it mattered none but put the devil's fury up her all the same. She took it out on the unfortunate girls who were left behind, making them scrub the chamber-pots with soda till their hands bled, and waking them at half past five on Sunday morning to make ready her bath and her boots, in the event that she might ride that afternoon – which she had done only twice in her life. It had been an unsuccessful exercise on both occasions, horses seeming to have an instinctive dislike of her. A bad humour settled upon the house in Shoreditch where it remained for several weeks.

Annie found her way back by those faculties that are employed only when one is left to survive all alone. She fell through the door into the arms of Charlie and Grace, and was presently tucked up in bed, attended by Daisy and Kate, who fussed over her every need for the rest of the day, tiring of servitude the next.

Mirabel Trotter reviewed the security provision at her Shoreditch premises and, concluding it was watertight, laid the blame – to Miss Pinch's relief and delight – on Miss Craven's head, which was not strictly fair, though Miss Craven dared not say so. She was happy enough to escape with a most severe warning. The slightest error was intolerable, Mrs Trotter told her. It had taken her many years and a great deal of personal sacrifice to build up her business. She simply could not run the operation with less than completely dependable associates and would consider any slipping of standards to be a personal affront. Miss Craven bit her tongue and said she would make it her utmost endeavour to ensure that no such thing would happen again. Mrs Trotter said that indeed she hoped it so.

Thereafter she left the Hammer family and their houseguests alone, and they, in their turn, avoided Dorset Street, Thrawl, or Flower and Dean, to which they had no call to go anyhow, and settled the next week into a reasonable, though cramped, state of play. The girls made themselves helpful and things were tidy enough; but Grace sat down after all were in bed and thought hard about their prospects.

The next day she sent the girls with Charlie and a fruit cake to visit the Cherrys, a sweet, decent couple in Cannon Street Road. Mrs Cherry used to watch the boys when Jake was just a baby. She was a kindly woman, always smiling, and devoted to Mr Cherry, a smart little man with clean cuffs who worked for the railway. They had lost their own children two years before to influenza.

Grace had hit the nail on the head. The very next day Mrs Cherry came to visit Bell Lane. She took tea and admired the girls' animal drawings, and their pretty hair, marvelled at how big and handsome Charlie had grown, the clever books Billy read, Jake's beautiful manners (which had never appeared before), how charming their home was, and what lovely moss roses. Then she took Tom on to her lap and cut to the chase. She could see that Grace was doing admirably for them all – and she took her hat off to her for it – but had her hands full indeed, and not an inch of space to spare, while she and Mr Cherry fair rattled around in their empty house. Might the Atkins children come to stay with them? Grace accepted this gracious proposal without hesitation. Daisy, who had been eavesdropping, considered it rather more intently and had a few questions of her own: where did Mrs Cherry live, was Mr Cherry nice, and how were her lodgings? And – before Grace could stop her – how old was she? Mrs Cherry answered Cannon Street Road, yes, he was, and that Daisy might come and see for herself if she liked. And she was as old as her tongue and a little older than her teeth.

Billy had to take Tom over and settle him in, as he cried without him, having grown attached these last two weeks. He came back with red eyes, visiting again the very next morning to see that Tom had slept all right.

Trixie May sat with her feet up on the silk chaise, alone in her rooms on Wilton Square. She sipped her pink gin and contemplated recent events. She had come a little too close to Mirabel Trotter's business for her own liking, these last few days. It was something she usually thought nothing about and now she felt ashamed for she found it distasteful indeed. She resolved to distance herself from Mrs Trotter for the time being. Perhaps she might spend some time in Hampstead with friends she had neglected lately. Or take a few days in Surrey. It was just the weather for riding out.

CHAPTER TWELVE

The rain does not wash London clean, not East London anyway. It gathers in filthy puddles among the spewing rubbish, bringing up the smell, filling the gutters, painting the streets slick and grey. It drips off the edges of every filthy roof in thick gobs of dirty water, pooling at your feet, seeping in round your collar, unseasonable enough even to keep the Irish indoors.

It was chucking down in bucketfuls as Grace took refuge in the Britannia. There was Mary Kelly, pretty thing, sat at the bar, unusually sober for that time of the evening. She spotted Grace and smiled radiantly. Save for a purple bruise on her cheek she looked right enough.

'How's tricks, Miss Mary?'

'Oh, I can't complain,' she replied sweetly, in her County Cork accent, as if she had stepped off the boat last week.

Off she went to prowl her usual spot, across the street outside the Ten Bells. Grace watched the rain run down the window in little rivulets, like turgid veins, and wondered when she might see Jack next. After their visit to Limehouse he had disappeared and she had been too occupied all week to think much about him. She made a dip, an elderly gent who mistook her for a brass; she let him ply her with gin, then relieved him of his wallet and melted into the street as he visited the bar.

The rain had slowed to a fine drizzle, whipping around in the thick night air, poking her with clammy fingers. The street was thick with people, chattering and pointing, children running, moving like a tide down towards the docks. She caught a wisp of smoke in the air, a dark smell as if it was November. A little unconscious, she drifted with the crowd down Leman Street. In the distance a thick orange glow spread against the night sky, drawing them on, like a spell. At Cable Street they could hear a rumble, ominous like Judgement Day, growing louder, roaring down Dock Street. An acrid scent blew on the breeze like a ghost; waves broke in Grace's ears and she was running through the village again, past the juniper bush, up the lane, watching herself go. Licks of flame escaped and blazed into the dark. London Docks was a raging ball, scorching their dumb faces.

An explosion split the air, drawing synchronised gasps from the crowd, bursting like fireworks over Grace's head – belching heavy black smoke from the warehouse on Spirit Quay, which houses the East India Company's fine brandy and, under cover of darkness, our handsome Jack Tallis. Her heart seemed to shrink and drag down through her guts, as if she were back on the Big Wheel.

People were turning out from Garrick's, and the Pavilion, pushing in from the back. Sally Ann's vacant face bobbed up a few feet away. The drunken theatre mob would have been tempting to dip any other day but Grace didn't spare it a thought. She watched in horror at the gates as the ware-houses burned to the ground.

Of course Jack wouldn't be at the docks at this hour! He'd be drinking in the Queen or the Saracen's Head. She stopped off at both to put her mind at rest. He was at neither, and no one had seen him since six o'clock, when he had been spotted leaving the Camel, lurching off in the direction of the river in need of a lie-down. Michael Robinson poured her a gin and told her he hadn't seen Jack since yesterday, which Grace knew was true. Michael Robinson has handsome hands, dependable, that look as though they make things and as if he tells the truth – which, indeed, he always does, though he chose not to divulge his suspicion that Jack might be entertaining a lady friend.

Assuring herself that this must indeed be what he was up to, she walked home, sunk in her own thoughts. At the corner of Cable and Cannon Street Road she came upon Nelly Holland. Nelly was a good girl. She kept herself clean and sober for the most part and looked after her ragged friends. She was searching for Polly Nichols, who had been thrown out of her lodgings the day before and had been seen that very afternoon, blind drunk, in a brand-new bonnet. Nelly was worried and wanted to put her to bed. Grace said she hadn't seen Polly all week and they parted company. Not five minutes later whom should she come upon, staggering, clutching the wall?

'Polly!' she said, gripping her by the shoulders, trying to

penetrate her glassy eyes. 'Nelly's out looking for you. You must go back to MacMurphy's. She's a bed for you there.'

Polly Nichols struggled to focus upon the apparition before her, trying to make sense of what she was saying. She got Grace sharp for long enough to recognise her – though she couldn't have told you her name – before she saw two of her again, and laughed helplessly, a private fit, making sense impossible. Pointing her back the way Nelly had gone, Grace watched her weave down the road, cackling at nothing.

She listened to her own footsteps for another hundred yards or so, her brow knitted; told herself again she mustn't fret about him, he'd be safe somewhere. If only he would turn up. She was sure she wouldn't sleep until she saw him.

Drawing near to the lights of the Frying Pan she picked out a silhouette, unmistakable through the steam on the window, and stopped on the kerb. He was laughing, in his charming way, flashing his beautiful teeth. She saw him leaning in close to the girl, slipping an arm round her waist. Grace held her breath, frozen to the pavement, quite, quite foolish.

The London Docks raged until midnight when the blaze began to die down. There were scattered fires still as morning broke; the usual crowd formed, to see if there would be work today clearing the wreckage. They pressed their faces to the gate, staring in at the smoking ruin.

Some twenty-three miles away, resting his stout legs by the road and peeling an apple with all the meticulousness of a surgeon dissecting a rat, sat Mr Horatio Blunt. He was on his way into London to settle an ancient score, and meant to be there today. Now Mr Blunt might be an altogether crooked man, remorseless and greedy, but the very worst part of his character was the bitter grudge that he held, hardened with time, and he longed for the sweet taste of revenge. He might look from a distance a jovial sort of fellow – being large and ruddy – but if you'd asked him for directions you would spot the ugly glint in his eye. He crushed a small beetle underfoot before hoisting himself upright, and pressing on towards London.

CHAPTER THIRTEEN

The very first view that Grace had of London looked like a great grey cloud laying low across the horizon. As she saw it she wondered if she really wanted to go any closer. But she did, and was swallowed into a tangle of streets where the colour drained from the scenery, dim as if some giant had put a lid on the sky. Grey walls towered in the gloom at every turn, damp and rotting; rats and sewage ran in the alleys; dark and desperate people lurked in the streets having nowhere to go.

She spent the first night in Bermondsey, having encountered it almost directly. Our Grace was a resourceful woman. She could learn to fit with anybody and blended into the scenery. She kept the necklace next to her skin for the first week until she had found lodgings and connections. She meant to sell it, but she knew she'd have to wait. It wasn't the sort of thing you might shift in a week or two.

And then she read about it in the paper – or rather, a page of the *Echo* that was wrapped around the pudding she'd just bought: 'the centrepiece of Lady Stanhope's fine collection,' it said; '. . . thought likely to have been taken overseas,' it said, '. . . sure to surface on the international market in time'.

So down it went, under the floor again, and there it stayed. Grace was chased through her nightmares by Mr Blunt, and worried – at quiet moments – whether he was out in the dark somewhere, hunting her down. But the days passed without a sign of him, and little by little she stopped looking over her shoulder. A million people lived in London. She took a job at the market and, after a month, was breathing easy again.

It was in Bermondsey that she learned her trade under the most thorough instruction of one Harry Tate, whom she met in the Cherry Tree one dark evening as she took refuge from the cold wet world. She was in the habit of sitting face to the door so she saw him come in. He stopped short and stared at her, on account of her fresh country face and that she was in his seat. They got talking and hit it off straight away.

Harry was a fine professional thief and in a very short time Grace acquired new tricks: her natural criminal talent was smoothed and perfected. They worked different patches around Southwark Park or the Old Kent Road. Grace watched her back but not for Mr Blunt any more. She thought of him less and less, swallowed in the great black city, dense warren of streets and brick, of tunnels and bridges and squares, with train tracks cutting over the buildings and the silver river snaking through its dark heart.

Blunt did make several fruitless attempts to find her: indeed, he was not satisfied. He seemed to hear his stolen treasure call to him at night, flashing red rays through his cloudy dreams from far away, and he would wake tormented, bilious with rage. The closest he came was Wandsworth, at the edge of the city. Though he knew she had come this way he saw plainly that there were a thousand places to look and his heart sank. He pressed on for a while, but within another mile London seemed bigger still. He drew his poor horse up, then turned away, vowing to return.

When he arrived at his gloomy home he sat brooding in his armchair, plotting his next move, his furious retribution. Presently a knock on the door revealed Ivor Squall, with intelligence regarding their next venture, gathered through the daily running of his accountancy firm – which, although small and somewhat mean, like Squall himself, had several considerable clients, providing him with invaluable scraps of information, details he exploited to their greatest effect. He acquainted Mr Blunt with the latest, and then listened, patiently enough – though he really had no choice, much less interest, in the matter – to the tale of indignation that followed, which he had heard already. He failed to understand quite why Mr Blunt was seething so – why such a rage over a silver tankard, even if it had belonged to his dear late mother? Though the girl would seem certainly to be a most insolent type.

He comes creeping through the dark, under the door in Bell Lane, towards the bed – as he does maybe once a year now – a malevolent shadow approaching. Grace struggles awake, swimming up through wet concrete. And she is fearful of closing her eyes again and fights sleep till it overwhelms her. Tonight she finds herself rising from her bed, haunted by a red shining light. Peaceful breathing fills the room. Her mind wanders down a crack in the floor, behind the stove, among the rubble and into a secret corner that only mice and cockroaches know, to see the deep red beauty, sparkling to itself in the dark.

She hasn't looked for five years or more. The thought that it may not be there makes her want to laugh out loud, or vomit. She stoops and prises up the short board. It groans sharply but the children don't stir. Placing it delicately aside she reaches under the stove, gingerly, as she is not fond of spiders, fingers searching the rubble. They close on cold hard stone and she pulls it from its grave and holds it up to catch the chinks of light from the street, forgetting herself, scarlet rays dancing on her face.

CHAPTER FOURTEEN

First thing the next morning Mr Horatio Blunt came at last to his destination, after ninety-nine long miles and seventeen years of waiting. He was in a filthy temper, having entered London the day before to encounter, almost immediately, roadworks at Wandsworth, which had delayed him – with bitter regret and loud cursing – late enough to miss office hours, even supposing he had not found himself lost at Nine Elms and again at Victoria. Kicking his horse, he had gone growling east to find a room – which had fleas.

He stopped outside 133 Oxford Street, and rang the little brass bell marked 'Squall.' After some moments shuffling footsteps were heard within and a pockmarked youth with shoes several sizes too large opened the door. His mouth hung open stupidly and he wore a threadbare dark suit he had outgrown two years ago, giving him the overall appearance of a lost and rather shabby penguin. He stared dumbly at Mr Blunt.

'I am looking for Ivor Squall. Is he within?' demanded Mr Blunt, glaring at the dull boy – he hated slow-witted people. The spotty youth stepped aside to let him in and indicated the staircase, his mouth hanging open all the while.

Mr Blunt took this dumb gesture to mean that Mr Squall's offices were situated on the upper floors of the building and ascended the stairs.

'Who is that idiot?' he enquired of his accomplice, once they had greeted each other.

'My nephew. He's slow.'

'Indeed.'

With rather mean glasses of sherry in hand they settled themselves into Spartan armchairs by the grey window, and Mr Squall began. In great detail and with considerable embellishment of his own central role, he recounted how he had single-handedly tracked the target to her very door, this last point somewhat let down by the absence of a specific address. 'I know for certain they reside within two streets either side of the hay market,' he said hopefully. 'I have made further enquiries around the district,' this was a barefaced lie, 'and can pinpoint a very particular district with some confidence.'

His confidence was waning fast, in fact, under the relentless pressure of Mr Blunt's stare: blank but somehow expectant, as if he was still waiting for the part he wanted to hear. As Mr Squall had already told him everything, he dried up, his voice trailing away weakly, and was possessed of a completely unanticipated sense of failure. He felt small and weak – which indeed he was, but now in his very own office! Though he had business with Mr Blunt from time to time, it was never in person (indeed the best way, he mused to himself ruefully).

He had certainly not remembered Mr Blunt to be quite such an intimidating figure. He seemed to cast a shadow over the room: the furniture seemed small suddenly; the desk had lost its meagre authority. Had he foreseen this he might have thought twice about bringing this beast of a man into his private office, to invade it thus, grunting quietly and staring into space, as if Mr Squall was not there! How dare he? It was in Mr Blunt's own interest that he had been good enough to invite him there in the first place – quite apart from the prospect of a decent reward. Indeed, he had banked on something handsome in it for him – which he was not so sure of now, as he sat on the edge of his chair, feeling as though he was made of matchsticks.

Mr Blunt continued to stare for an interminable two minutes without speaking while Mr Squall wondered where he should look, thought of a few possible things to say, which he quickly decided against, and remarked to himself how loud the clock ticked. At last Mr Blunt rose from his chair, Mr Squall stumbling up beside him, seeming to have shrunk since he last stood up.

'You can show me there now,' said Mr Blunt, 'while the iron is hot.'

'I am afraid I have some extremely pressing matters to attend to this afternoon, appointments that have been fixed for some time that must be seen to without delay,' ventured Ivor Squall, timidly. 'Would five o'clock be convenient for you?'

This futile assertion was met by another granite stare as Mr Blunt made for the door, Mr Squall dripping in his wake.

If you have ever woken to find that the ceiling seems too close, the cracks and dirt all too clear as you open your eyes, and instead of getting about your daily business, protected under the collective illusion that what we do matters at all, you want to spill hot tears at the hard world, and for time lost, and for how wrong you have been and just how sharp everything feels, you will know how that Wednesday morning was for Grace. She covered it well by bustling around the fire and generally busying herself with chores.

Jack was all over her thoughts and she was dismayed to find that she missed him. She saw now what a tricky position she might be in. Already it seemed she had gone too far to avoid heartache and she kicked herself for indulging in such a nonsense, becoming lost in its charm. She felt as if she had been cheated at cards. When one is miserable, she reasoned, one cannot mope about the house: one must do something simple and useful or jump in the Thames and be done with it. She went out with Daisy for apple fritters.

Not five minutes after they had left, Jack Tallis happened along to knock at number twenty-eight. He had woken that morning with Grace in his head and come to find her as soon as he had swallowed his breakfast pint. He was met by Jake, who pushed his grubby face out of the door to say that he didn't know where his ma had gone. She had told him but he had not been listening. He slammed the door before Jack could leave any message, not out of rudeness but an urge to finish his marble practice before she returned to shout at him for not sweeping. Jack considered the outside of the door, reflecting on how he seemed unable to find her when he wanted to.

★

As August was fair and quite warm, so September was a dark, heavy blanket. The sun struggled through the cloud as if it was going out. The dark air seemed fitting for the dreadful news. Nelly had not found Polly Nichols in time to take her indoors to bed. She turned up, all right, on the front page of every paper. It was difficult to avoid the ghastly details – they were thrust in your face, shouted on every corner.

'What happened, Ma?'

'Don't worry about it, darlin'.'

'Is it a murder?'

'Let's go and get cake.'

Ivor Squall took a hansom cab to Whitechapel with Mr Blunt – reluctantly. He made it as plain as he could that he really must get back to his desk by twelve. One o'clock at the absolute latest.

The Hammer girls wandered along hand in hand and ate seed cake, looked at pigeons and sat on the bench by the churchyard, like matching gloves in different sizes, watching the local girls go round.

The wide Whitechapel Road was full as usual, populated this morning with relentless haycarts and country bumpkins, fat and swarthy, with their arms like great hams. Grace didn't dip farmers often, they always had dogs for one thing, but one particular turnip did take her fancy, sat on his cart, large as a barge. A ragged knot of brasses had gathered at his feet, hung on his every word, as he supposed, with awe and wonderment, as he related details of his farm, two hundred acres — so he said — with trout in the river and plums on the trees. He had plainly used the trip to the city as an occasion to drink himself stupid before nine o'clock and did not feel the eyes fixed on his pockets. Grace had robbed him not a month before. She watched as he barked at his cowering dog, clocked his wan-faced daughter sitting on the cart in her thin dirty dress that may have been pink once. They crossed the street towards him.

'Watch your toes under the cart, darlin'.'

Grace and Daisy drew in and joined the circle, waiting for the group to break a little, some distraction or movement. It happened presently. The farmer made a grab at the heaving female flesh in front of him and caught a handful that happened to be Lucy Fear's breast. She slapped him hard.

'Dog face!' cried the drunken farmer, and a small riot broke out, scuffling and slapping between him and the girls, screeches, and shouts — 'I'll put your eyes out!' 'Stick that, you filthy cur!' As they struggled, Grace threw herself against him, as if she had been shoved from behind, and lifted the farmer's wad from his waistcoat. Daisy, with her little eyes at pocket level, saw everything, lightning fast though it was. This was the first time she had noticed her mother dip somebody's pockets. Being a clever girl she knew instinctively not to say anything just then, but Grace was in for it after.

'Ma, why did you take that man's money?'

For the first time in her long life Grace was dumbstruck. The only sensible response she could muster: 'Do you think I shouldn't have?'

'No.'

'Never mind it now.'

Ivor Squall became nervous as they approached Whitechapel, knowing with dreadful inevitability that what he had to show for his bluff would be inadequate, and seeing no way out of this imminent difficulty. He tried to cover this by talking a lot about the area as they went along, most of which he made up as he did not know it well.

Horatio's Blunt's face was stone, not remotely impressed or, indeed, giving any visible sign of having heard a word. He looked out of the window at the slurry of East London: puddles of horse piss, wretched children, sleeping bundles of rag. Somewhere in this pigsty he would find that bitch and take his revenge. 'Are we nearby?' he barked, cutting quite across what Mr Squall was telling him about the local vegetable market – which, to be fair, was not interesting.

'. . . they really are very good with cold meats or even . . . Oh, yes, quite near, quite near now, yes, we are.'

'How near *exactly*?'

'Just another half-mile or so,' stammered Mr Squall, peering down the road.

The foul air had not dissuaded the crowds from Petticoat Lane, tramping through the filthy puddles, with fine drizzle dampening their clothes and their lungs like cold steam; the Hammers poked about the market unconcerned. The boys ducked about in the fog but it was too early for their sort of mark to be out. They never stole from traders – they were hard-working people who deserved every penny, and if you were caught fleecing one you were in boiling water. Grace and the boys were so tidy that most of the locals never knew how they got along – they supposed she ran a brothel in Wentworth Street.

They stopped and bought chestnuts and hot tea. The baked-potato man leered at Grace, which put her off buying any. He was handsome enough but a touch grizzly and she'd had a bellyful with Jack and couldn't be bothered. Daisy wanted to warm her hands by his cart so Billy went with her. Potato Man offered her a slice of toast, which she accepted graciously.

Spitalfields seemed to drip with gloom that morning, damp and filthy, in mourning it seemed for poor Polly Nichols. Grace didn't want to think about her. Or Jack, though she knew full well he had been carrying on. She wished she hadn't seen him at it.

'Come on, Ma,' said Daisy, pulling her down Goulston Street towards the sweet-shop. Ten yards behind her a dark carriage rolled past. Its occupants: a wild boar of a man and a woodlouse. The back of her neck prickled; she shuddered as she might sucking lemon drops. The black clouds crowded overhead; a curious breeze caught her.

'Let's take a trip,' she said.

'Where?' said Daisy, after cheering loudly.

'To the Crystal Palace,' said Grace.

★

The carriage crawled along the kerb as the traffic stuck up Whitechapel Road, attracting several girls, reaching in at the window, smiling, thrusting their wares and then cursing them as they drove past. Deciding they were attracting too much attention, they alighted and carried on by foot, Ivor Squall reluctant, yet tempted by the prospect of more creeping about. Mr Blunt strode along behind him, stamping to hurry him up. He wore a cruel sneer upon his flabby face, which repelled everyone in his path. They reached the corner where Ivor had last seen the Hammers. He slowed and wondered how best to proceed. It took Mr Blunt not a moment to realise that he was engaged in a wild-goose chase and he was not favourably impressed.

'Am I to take it that this is where your information falls short?'

'This is the very spot where I saw them last.' Ivor tried to make his voice sound authoritative. 'They were heading in that direction.' He pointed down Osborn Street, boiling with carriages and crowds, bargaining, shouting, drinking, a great din rising in the gloom, a thousand voices chattering. Mr Blunt gave Ivor a look that turned his last shred of good hope to stone.

Daisy was impressed with this ready answer, though she knew nothing of such a place. A crystal palace! Why had Ma not mentioned this before? It sounded like something from a fairytale and she was wondering if she had heard right.

This proposal was a stroke of genius on Grace's part.

The Crystal Palace being not a figment of fantasy, but the vision of a divine lunatic made manifest, as solid as you like: a confection of steel and glass so colossal that one must stand a mile off to see it all at once, as if, having drawn up the plans at its conception, a rabid frenzy had seized the architect, inspiring him to triple its every dimension. A magnificent, superfluous creation, it was built for no other purpose than to house its vast collection of wonders and to take one's breath away. No practical necessity troubled its invention. So was cricket born, and mountain climbing, art and seed cake. All that we are that is special and precious and extra.

To be pedantic the palace is not truly crystal, and houses no royal personage, but it is magnificent beyond one's wildest dreams; fit indeed for the Queen. The surrounding park counts among its attractions life-sized representations of the dinosaurs that were supposed to have walked the Earth before men – paling a little perhaps in comparison to the palace, but certainly worth a look. Everyone was eager for such novel sensation and fairly clamoured to visit; they washed their faces and put on their best hats. By eleven o'clock they were on the train.

The hands crawled round the clock for poor Ivor, dragged on a tour of the district, from pub to pub, into the afternoon. One o'clock came, and then two: his feeble assertions – he really must get back to his books as a matter of urgency, catch the post, the paper would be piling up on his desk – were swatted aside; by three o'clock he had given them up. Mr Blunt drank and glared at the company; he said nothing, but spat odd words under his breath. Ivor couldn't make them out but it made him jump and unnerved him thoroughly. He glanced at the ogre, brooding silently into his jug.

In the Princess Alice the Wilson girl – she of the hatchet clan – spotted them. She had an eagle eye for a new face and pointed them out to her boyfriend, who was a member of the Wilson gang and went by the name of Dog Brown, on account of his thick neck and pointed teeth. From time to time he ran errands for a particular lady (if we might call her that for now) in Limehouse.

They were a strange-looking pair, sitting in the corner side by side. Few words were exchanged between them; the little rat-like man wore an expression of utter despair. His brutish companion sat staring ahead, gulping rudely at his ale. A cloud of menace hung around him. The rat man twitched in his shadow, eyes darting here and there. Dog Brown wondered what they were after and if he might help.

The dinosaurs most certainly did not disappoint the children, or Grace for that matter. They crouched in the park, in shallow pools, with spiny backs and grey-green skin, big mouths full of teeth, frozen mid-roar, in perpetual attack. Large aquatic beasts with elongated jaws devoured the smaller ones, their children, so it appeared.

'Look at that duck,' said Jake.

'Did they have ducks then, Ma?'

'No, darlin', I don't think so.'

'Well, they didn't have people,' said Jake, with some authority.

'No people?'

'No, not even one.'

And there was the Crystal Palace, tall above them, a million sparkling panes, spectacular enough even to knock Grace out of her black mood. The weather had cleared – although it might well have been raining still in Whitechapel – and sunlight twinkled at them, caught in the glass. To Daisy this constituted a real princess's castle and she stood below it in awe and wonder, gazing at this vision, better even than she had imagined it from what Billy had told her on the train. (She was somewhat disappointed not to find a princess's bedchamber or throne, though there were very many other things that compensated for this oversight.) The fountains and cascades that lined the walk gave way to wonders inside; they stopped as they came through the grand entrance and gazed around them at the great hall, spacious beyond their imagination, shining with light. Displays of every modern endeavour were here, every marvel of the industrial age, treasures from every corner of the Empire. The boys looked at machines, the girls preferred the stuffed animals. They wandered through the Greek court, the Renaissance and the Alhambra, taking in the fountains, the statues and the exotic plants; they looked at silver and brass and brocade and spears, and as they came through the Indian jungle there were jewels, sparkling at Grace on silk cushions in shining cases, sunlit through the great glass ceiling high above her head.

'Look!' she said. 'An elephant!' complete with howdah and a stuffed monkey on his back. And just when they thought nothing could top that, the aquarium! They sat down to take refreshments in the Palm Court, eliciting snooty looks from a well-dressed couple at the next table. Grace gave them the dead-eye and Daisy bestowed her sweetest smile upon them. Fancy cakes came, and sandwiches with the crusts cut off, on a tiered stand with paper doilies.

Grace clocked Jake sizing up their neighbours as they dropped sugar lumps into their tea with silver tongs. 'Jake. Don't you dare,' she said.

'Dare what?' said Daisy.

'Dip that macaroon in your cup.'

He looked at her with his eyebrows up, feigning innocence. 'Yes, Ma.'

Little Jake Hammer had noticed that Grace has not involved Daisy in the family line of business as yet. He had asked her why but had no satisfactory answer. This confused him, as he could see no reason why Daisy should not be allowed to join in, and he felt a little sorry for her. He had started to learn the family trade at four, and he was sure Daisy was older than that now. Maybe girls were a little stupid, he surmised, and came to things later. Though Daisy could read already better than he. He decided he might teach her himself, so they could surprise their ma one day.

★

When the Hammer family could eat no more buns they wandered away across the grass, looking back every few steps, the autumn sun shining out from behind the clouds, tingeing their edges with gold. Grace and Daisy held hands, the boys laughed and dodged around them, wrestling each other to the ground.

They took the train home once Grace had sworn they would came again, and before too long. At Aldgate they stopped to buy pink spray roses from Lily Dixon. Lily Dixon has a sharp little face with huge eyes, spaced far apart, like the creatures children see at the bottom of the garden. She sells only one variety a day, but always beautiful, fresh and properly conditioned. If you changed the water every other day they would last for a week, a tip she would have been better not giving her customers.

'Hello, Charlie!' she said.

Charlie went a bit pink. The family made faces at each other.

'Hello,' he mumbled.

'Why are you shy?' said Daisy, to her poor brother, who grimaced at Lily and went a good deal pinker. Matching the roses, in fact. The family stood around in an expectant circle, making no sign of small-talk among themselves.

'Let's get these home and put them in water, then!' said Grace, to his relief. Lily said goodbye sweetly to everyone and on they went, Charlie trudging along trying not to look at anyone, the others trying not to snigger. Down Commercial Street they came upon Sally Ann Dunn who was upright at least. Daisy gave her a rose and an apple dumpling, which she dropped in the road. When they got back, there was handsome Jack Tallis on the doorstep, with nothing but a saucy grin.

As she watched him fast asleep, like the king of the bed, Grace marvelled at how this circumstance had come about and how she had not managed, though she had promised it to herself, to field the little tricks with which he had edged his way back in, to resist that smile, the silver tongue. He was just too damned charming. Even as you knew it wasn't true. He had made no mention of where he had been and Grace had not asked. She was sure she did not want to know. He had an angry cut above his eye, maybe three days old, and another across his cheek. He always looked like trouble coming. She slid under the blanket, musing on what it was that made such a man so attractive and how he looked so innocent asleep.

Ivor Squall got away from his imposing new companion as the clock struck eight, which was good going but seemed not a moment too soon. He could feel Blunt's blank stare on his back all the way down Folgate Street as he skittered away. Round the corner he collected himself, breath rattling alarmingly in his delicate lungs. Mr Blunt was a difficult customer. Dread set in Ivor's empty belly. He had stirred up something indeed. Much more than he had bargained for.

Mr Blunt returned to his fleapit lodgings, after letting his disappointment be thoroughly known, and sat on his infested bed with his head in his hands. He ground his teeth together, made fists in his hair, raged to himself inside at the impotence of his efforts.

Ivor Squall went to sleep in his office, which he liked to do on occasion: it made him feel safe. Peacefully, curled up under his desk, next to his precious stationery.

CHAPTER FIFTEEN

When the family woke up, faint sunshine was creeping into the room. Daisy made a beeline for Jack, jumping up next to him. 'Hello,' she said, with a savvy little smile, delighted to see him but keeping it reserved.

'Hello,' he said back, playing the same game.

Then they sat and beamed at each other. Daisy proposed first: 'Do you want to play?'

'What should we play?'

'Wolves.'

Mr Blunt woke to the sound of traffic, with a fresh feeling of urgency. He lay still for a moment, staring intently at the ceiling. The rage that had kept him up till late had subsided enough for him to think. He would comb the district methodically, street by street. Within a day or two he would surely come up with something. First he must call upon Squall, just to keep him on his toes, though he did not plan to enlist his help today, useless as it was. He rose, dressed and consumed a large breakfast of eggs and sausage.

He caught Ivor skulking from his office, surprising him.

'Argh! Good morning, Mr Blunt!' he grimaced, dropping the packages he was carrying. 'Did you sleep well?'

'I did not.'

'Oh,' said Ivor, scrabbling around Mr Blunt's great feet for his parcels. 'I am sorry to hear it.' Gathering them together at last, he drew himself upright, tentatively, into view, withering under Blunt's stare, along with several nice begonias in the window-box behind him.

'I shall be abroad in East London this morning,' said Mr Blunt, 'expecting satisfaction. We shall see.' And, with an ugly smirk, he turned towards Whitechapel and stalked off into the crowd.

'Ma killed this man once, you know. I saw her.'

Something so matter-of-fact in the tone of Daisy's definite little voice, stating this information as if it were not so very different from any other noteworthy topic, breathed a chill up the back of Jack's neck. It came smack out of the blue, into the middle of a game of Snap. He wondered what in hell had set such a thought in motion. He knew it was surely true and couldn't find a word to say.

'She hit him with a bottle. Bang! And then he fell down and she hit him again. Don't tell because she doesn't want anyone to know.' Jack fixed on a corner of the carpet. It had a faded blue leaf pattern, the intricacies of which he had never fully appreciated, and a hole he had not noticed before. Then, from Daisy, not to reassure him but because it was the next thing that occurred to her: 'He was trying to steal us.'

'Oh,' he said.

'Do you want to do drawing now?'

'What should we draw?'

'Well, I don't know, do I? Let's get the paper and think of something.'

And so Jack drew dinosaurs, glancing at his clean clothes and wondering how soon they might be dry.

At the end of Bell Lane Mr Blunt was commencing a thorough search of the area in its tiniest detail. He drew himself up determinedly and even sniffed the air. He knew that Grace must dwell within a stone's throw of where he stood. On the corner of Commercial Street stood a couple of local girls. He thought he might ask them first. 'Good morning,' he said.

'Good morning to you!' said Mary Kelly, pretty thing. 'You're a nice rosy gent, aren't ya?'

'I'm looking for a woman. Perhaps you know her,' began Horatio. 'I—'

'Special, is she?'

'Is it a special woman you're after?' They cackled loudly. 'What's so special about her then?' Mary leaned down and tugged up the edge of her skirt; he caught a flash of her thigh under the black stocking, soft and luminous, lily-white, like the light of the full moon.

He thought of that white thigh again, several unsuccessful hours later, as he came back round to the same spot. Mr Blunt had never encountered such a labyrinth of alleyways and ramshackle dwellings as made up the East End of London. It had seemed a good idea to divide his map into sections and do without Squall's help; he saw now that he had underestimated the task altogether, having covered just a crumpled inch or two, which, furthermore, did not seem to correspond entirely with the tangle of streets before him. Lost and thoroughly irritated, he resolved to drag Squall along with him tomorrow and retired to ease his worries for a short while in the Britannia, situated on the next corner. Solace from the wretched stinking hard world. In he went and ordered a pint of ale.

Now, sitting in the Britannia was a wise old man who could spot a scoundrel through the back of his head, and he clocked Mr Blunt directly, having not seen him about before. I wonder who he's after, he thought, for it seemed perfectly obvious to him the fellow was missing something. His drink stood neglected upon the table – from time to time he cast his eyes wildly around the room, settling on nothing. His cheek twitched of its own accord, he ground his teeth, his fists clenched as if they longed to strangle someone – he fairly brewed inside, boiling some awful grudge. The fellow evidently felt the attention for he stirred and looked around the bar again. His eyes settled contemptuously on Mr Byron Stanley, travelled from his green felt hat to his drink and away without interest. Then he drained his jar and rose from his seat to leave. The old man resolved to follow, though he was not usually given to interfering in other people's business. He had an ominous feeling about this restless fellow, what with the recent attacks. As Mr Blunt vanished into the street Mr Stanley slipped out after him.

He followed him to the edge of the City, where he watched him vanish down Barge Street, from the shadow of the Tower.

★

Mr Blunt made straight for Ivor Squall's office, where he rang the bell as hard as he could. Ivor, who was expecting a late delivery, answered the door himself, recoiling with horror when he saw Mr Blunt, glowering at him in the darkness.

'No joy?' said Ivor.

'I am not happy, Mr Squall.' A heavy gloom seemed to gather round the porch; the air grew cold, Ivor quaked in the doorway. 'Well, it is early days yet, Mr Blunt.' Oxford Street was ghostly quiet. 'Do forgive me for not inviting you inside. I am about to leave the office myself, you see,' he said, in his slippers. Blunt grasped him by the collar and pulled him up until poor Ivor's feet were barely touching the floor. He whimpered, shrivelling under the hot breath.

'I shall call on you every day, Mr Squall. You may be sure of it. Every day until I am satisfied.' He dropped Ivor on his doorstep and strode away into the night.

Across the city Charlie popped out, his hair combed, to see his new girl again, deaf to the queries and taunts of his merciless family, who assumed he was off to see Lily Dixon. He let them think so as it was better than having no privacy at all. He picked Elsie Brown up at the door of her lodgings in New Street and they went to the Oriental, where he spotted Jack Tallis in the smoky crowd, his arm round a woman, laughing his wide laugh, drinking beer and gin.

★

Stripe Wilkins entered the room so silently Miss Emmeline Spragg could swear he'd blown in through the window.

'The woman with Jack Tallis,' he said. 'She lives in Bell Lane with four children. She operates a family concern. Her name is Hammer. Grace Hammer.'

CHAPTER SIXTEEN

One might have imagined that the carnival of horror parading across the front pages every day now, fresh in the newspapers each morning, was some novel new entertainment for the delectation of the hungry public, such was the lurid detail and melodrama with which they competed for the ravenous audience. The *Illustrated Police News* ran a full three pages on the recent murders, including several pictures, depicting the grisly scenes of discovery, for the apparent purpose of their vivid imagining. What on earth will they print tomorrow? thought Grace. As if there wasn't enough sensation already for people disposed to such things, if not on their very doorsteps then surely a short ride away from their perfumed gardens to the scrag-end of their fair city. Grace was haunted by her last sight of poor Polly Nichols, in her brand-new bonnet, weaving down the Whitechapel Road into darkness. Once or twice she had dreamed of running after her, only to find she was gone.

Ivor Squall hid in his office for three days, breaking cover only to scurry home – very early or very late – while Mr Blunt scoured Whitechapel, loitering at street corners, engaging the locals, making what he hoped were casual enquiries, without any luck at all. This infuriated him on many counts, the least of which was that he loathed the district, though he suited it well. It beggared belief that of the very few who thought they might know a Grace Hammer, none was able to be specific about where she lived, or any more informative than to enthuse about what a lovely family the Hammers were. He felt himself sicken as he smiled along, keeping up whatever long-lost-relative story he had invented. *Where was she?* Had she given him the slip? Waiting and failure were feeding his viciousness. He felt he would grab her by the throat when he found her and shake her like a rat.

He stopped at the end of Church Street and clenched his fists. He would catch Ivor Squall before he left his office tonight. Outside the Ten Bells Mary Kelly was basking in the lamplight.

She took him down Red Lion Court, rather than to her room. She didn't like the look of him. Down the dark alley past the heaving shadows, white thighs in black stockings. He was rough and his hands felt damp. After soiling poor Mary's skirts he felt not soothed but rather stoked; he strode down Brick Lane, growling at the evening, and fuelled himself in the Frying Pan. Mr Byron Stanley watched him go from under his green felt hat.

Ivor Squall was tidying away his stationery for the night, with difficulty – he had taken to working in the back room (which was more of a large cupboard) so that his candle would not be visible from the street, and nothing was in order – when the bell rang. The sound shrilled up the back of his ears and tugged at his scalp. He froze, with his precious envelopes clutched to his chest. He need not ask himself who that might be. Trembling, he crept upon his hands and knees to the front window and peeped out. Below on the step was the dread shape of Mr Blunt – unmistakable even from Ivor's curious aerial view – grunting and cursing at the door. Ivor cowered below the still and listened to his own heart thumping until he heard the heavy steps retreat, rumbling east.

A knocking, weak but urgent, brought the goblin to her door, cursing the absent fellow she had posted to answer it while she took stock upstairs. Ivor Squall was lurking on the slick stairs, undulating.

'Good evening, Emmeline,' said he, with a glutinous smile, little rodent hands clenching as if he was counting invisible money. 'I wonder if you might spare me a moment.'

It was most unusual for Ivor to call upon Miss Spragg at home. She looked him up and down, shrinking him a good foot further as he writhed on the step.

'Why, of course, Mr Squall. Do come in. I've some sausages cooking. Perhaps you might eat with me.'

'How kind, thank you, but no,' said Ivor, who never ate in company.

'Now,' she said, settling herself into a bundle, poking at the rancid frying pan, 'what brings you to Limehouse, Mr Squall?' She knew it was something desperate. 'An unexpected pleasure indeed!' She beamed with such glee at Ivor that he quite mistook her meaning and the awful notion flashed through his mind that she had taken a shine to him. He wanted to turn tail and run but he was, indeed, desperate.

'There's a woman I'm looking for,' he said, surprising himself, and Emmeline Spragg, with his boldness, 'by the name of Hammer.'

She looked inside his head with her black eyes. 'Hammer,' she said. 'Hammer.' The sausages hissed in the pan. 'I'm afraid I shall disappoint you, Mr Squall. I know no Hammers.'

Ivor seemed to deflate as she said this, the weight of the world on his shoulders.

'Is it very important Mr Squall?'

She never seems to blink, he thought. 'Perhaps,' he said, carefully. 'She is wanted most urgently on the business of a special client. Most urgently indeed.'

'Evidently.'

Miss Spragg took a sausage from the pan. Brown grease dripped down the fork on to the putrid wool of her gloves.

'Won't you sit down and make yourself comfortable, Mr Squall?' He did so, touching as little of the chair as was reasonably possible. 'I expect your special client will be offering some reward. On such important business!'

'Well, yes, perhaps, I expect so, yes, they might.'

'So, who is it wants to know?'

He found he was quite unable to sit up straight, much less look Miss Spragg in the evil eye. 'Ah, ha ha ha ha!' was his best effort.

Her eyes twinkled black at him. 'Are you not at liberty to say?'

'Well, exactly the point I was coming to, Emmeline,' he said. 'Most regrettably not.'

'Regrettable indeed.'

Ivor Squall is a tiresome little man, thought Miss Spragg,

after he had scuttled out – with a little sympathy perhaps for his predicament: he seemed so very agitated. She was human, after all. She cackled at the very idea, black blood oozing through her veins. Tiring of this whimsy she turned her villainous thoughts to the woman Hammer – such a private creature – and why the business had thrown Mr Squall into such a frenzy. He would crack for sure, eventually. She might keep a special eye on the Hammer family.

CHAPTER SEVENTEEN

Mr Blunt had spent a fruitless week in Whitechapel. Grace was known to most in the district by her first name only, being a secretive soul, and he had had no luck so far. He was a changed man – indeed, a different colour altogether, the country bloom fading in his cheeks. He had been tempted down several dark alleys and enjoyed the local female company, which soothed his temper in short bursts. At night he stalked the district, a great looming shadow, glowering and muttering to himself. He growled at people on street corners; women felt afraid and crossed the road. Grace heard talk of this sinister fellow; she didn't pay it much attention. She felt glad she hadn't come across him.

Blunt does not know that on Saturday he walked past Jake playing marbles in Brushfield Street, and on Thursday he would have come face to face with the entire family at the market, if he had kept on down Wentworth Street instead of ducking into the Princess for a quick one. He had missed Grace again just that morning outside the butcher's.

All the week, as he pursued his task, Mr Byron Stanley – who could spot a scoundrel through the back of his head

– traced his every move, from under his green felt hat. More than once he was almost discovered.

'So! How's Lily?' said Grace over Sunday dinner, in the way that mothers do, which makes you want not to tell them anything. Charlie cringed. A blush started but didn't bother past his ears. 'She's keen on you! I saw her by the pawn shop and she asked after you. Told me to give you this.' She presented him with a red rosebud from Lily – clearly a wicked sort, given to teasing.

'She's not my girl!' he protested.

'Do you think she's pretty?' This, of course, from Daisy who was fascinated by the strange adult world of courting and secrets, having recently become aware that sometimes things were going on to which she was not party. She knew how to flirt as all little girls do, and loved handsome men, but knew that there was some other mystery attached just for grown-ups. She wondered what it was that made them laugh that way, and knew she was not in on the joke. However, this is the way of things for small children and, equipped with cast-iron perseverance to deal with their daily ridicule, they are hardened to it. So, instead of feeling left out, she pursued her enquiries.

'Did you kiss her?'

Everyone laughed and she wondered why it was quite that funny. Charlie thought he had dodged the question when Jake dived in.

'Well, did ya?'

'Not Lily!'

'Elsie, then!'

'Which one's Elsie?'

'I might 'ave.'

Daisy wondered how he didn't know.

'He did. He did! He kissed her!'

'Leave him alone!' said Grace — a fine thing for her to say since it was she who had started it. The brothers jeered on for a moment or two. Daisy watched intently, with her serious button face.

'All right, it was Elsie and I did kiss her.'

Further riotous enjoyment was had from this admission, only Daisy fully retaining her composure. Incisively she cut straight to the next relevant point. 'Can we see her?'

'No!'

'Why? Is she ugly?'

'No!'

'Where does she live?'

'New Street. St Philip.'

'Oh.'

Daisy had not reckoned on getting an answer to any of her questions and had no idea where New Street was anyway so she was flummoxed into silence. For a moment.

'Which house?'

The whole room laughed again; someone touched her hair; she waited patiently for them to calm down. She was formulating her next line of enquiry when there was a sharp knock at the door.

They opened it to find Nelly Holland, red-faced and breathless with news. 'Grace they've found another one this morning! In Hanbury Street. With her heart torn clean out of her chest!'

Jake was already halfway out of the door. She grabbed him by the scruff. 'And where are you off to, young man?'

'I want to have a look.'

'I'm sure you do, but you'd only be satisfying your nasty curiosity.'

'Oh, Ma!'

As she turned away from him, to catch Daisy jumping off the table, he slipped out through the door, just too quick to catch.

'JAKE!'

'Don't worry, Ma, I won't be long!'

'Oh, Charlie, sweetheart, will you go after him?'

Miss Annie Chapman had lost her two front teeth courtesy of a customer in a dark alley. Now she was hanging by a hook on the mortuary wall having her photograph taken, for it was she who had perished in the back yard of twenty-nine Hanbury Street, discovered by poor John Davis, who was still reeling from the shock. When the boys reached the scene of the crime they found the landlady selling tickets by the passage door to enter and see the bloodstains. They didn't go in, though Jake was ready to lift the sixpence.

'I've seen him lurking about by St Mary's lately. You want to watch out for him. He's that smart type who likes to slum it – coat tails, stick, all that. Most of the girls have shied well off and so should you. He's a nasty fucker. Mary Kelly entertained him last week. God knows, she'll consort with any piece of scum for a shiny coin. Though she barely remembers a thing after eleven o'clock any day, she said she wouldn't have him the next time – she couldn't say why. Just that he was cruel. I asked her what he'd done and she said nothing in particular, just that he'd made a very strange proposal, something she didn't want to repeat. Well, what that could be if Miss Kelly doesn't want to repeat it you can't imagine, can you? He comes from Belgravia, she says. I'd stay well away from him, and so should you.'

Nelly Holland leaned back against the wall and sighed, wondering if any of this was going into Sally Ann Dunn's stupid head. The gentleman to whom she referred had been seen about a few times of late and had given one or two of the girls quite a turn. He had grabbed Busy Liz from behind in George Yard, stepping out from the shadows. As she struggled free and fled, he laughed her down the street – a sickening laugh by all accounts, varying from brutish to inhuman with the storyteller. Though Grace had managed to escape the finer details, she had heard he'd asked Mary if he might wrap his hands round her throat and squeeze just a little while he was about his business. As many of the gentlemen slummers made unusual requests this wouldn't normally be worth a mention, but in the current chill wind it cloaked him in suspicion, along with every second man in the street.

Sally Ann Dunn cared nothing for what was round the corner but her next drink. She wasn't one to fret about troubles ahead or hope for better luck next time – it never came. This much she could count on. She had never had a present or a surprise that she could remember and didn't want to start now. The hollow girls who haunt the alleys, clutch at straws, lost each in their own world kept her company: making desperate alliances, loud threats, and sleeping where they dropped, fights breaking out round their blissful heads.

That evening she was conscious still, it being barely seven o'clock. She had done well that day, having earned two shillings and drunk but half of it. Now Nelly was intent on telling her about poor Polly Nichols and this monster on the loose and she didn't want to think of it. She was careful enough anyhow, she reckoned; you could tell a strange fellow by the look in his eye. She stood up to get another drink, the blood rushing to her feet, the tiles spinning round her.

Ivor Squall had managed to give Mr Blunt the slip that afternoon, or so he thought, which made him feel rather clever. In truth, his usefulness had been exhausted now that Mr Blunt could find his own way around Whitechapel and he had not tried particularly hard to locate him for the last couple of days, or even drop by his office to torment him further. Ivor had been asked so many times if he was quite sure it was Grace he had seen that now he was not. That evening he had anticipated a visit and left the office early, and was at that moment on his way home to enjoy a nice piece of boiled beef he had left over from yesterday. He prefers his food simple and holds no truck with fancy seasoning, though he likes a bit of mustard. He twisted his wiry mouth into as much of a smile as it would go at the satisfaction of being alone for dinner, and rubbed his rat hands together, again.

★

Mr Blunt, too, was dining alone in the Britannia, on steak and kidney pudding, which was sufficiently delicious to have distracted him from all else. Lucky for Grace, though she knew nothing of it, except for a shiver that ran through her – as if someone was digging her grave. As Mr Blunt was lost in his gravy she passed right outside the window: if he could have reached through the glass he might have touched her head – though it was up in the clouds, thinking about Jack Tallis: who else? Grace had met him that day and had a drink or two, and more besides to remember him by; she found an idiotic grin on her face, as she had at intervals all afternoon. She'd been keeping Jack away from the house: Charlie had given him a frosty reception at his last visit and wouldn't say why. Grace wondered idly what he knew but she was sure she didn't want to ask. She drifted down Commercial Street, in a wistful bubble. As she neared the corner she felt someone skulking behind her. He hung back, measuring his steps, and quickened his pace as she did.

She turned left deliberately, away from home, and crossed the road heading for the Ten Bells. Sally Ann was inside the door, leering at a dusty bricklayer. He turned away from her broken grin back towards the bar, leaving her hazily forlorn. She spotted Grace coming in and latched on.

'Evening, Miss Sally,' said Grace, glancing behind her. Sally Ann started on the story of her latest misfortune. She's getting tiresome, thought Grace. She'd better not ask me for money today. Grace's shadow came in behind her and she met him with a hard stare. He was tall and well dressed, with greying hair and a groomed moustache, and looked not the slightest bit brutish or sinister but, rather, returned her look with startled embarrassment and averted his eyes. She watched him all the way to the bar and slipped out as he ordered a pint of ale. As she looked back through the door, Sally Ann was lurching after him, spilling someone's drink.

Red Lion Court was pitch black and quiet, save for the bestial grunting of two or three brides and their clients. Trying not to hear she made her way through, glancing behind her as she reached the bend. No one was following; just the dark shapes of the couples moved slowly behind. Grace Hammer had not carved out a decent life for herself among the flotsam of East London by waiting for someone to bite her first. Her safety after dark was secured by the clear head she kept on her shoulders and the razor that lived in her pocket.

Sally Ann took all of a minute to discourage the mystery gentleman from staying or buying her a drink, with her missing teeth and her Hell's breath. Outside the door he looked this way and that, wondering where Grace had gone.

Grace came out into Hanbury Street and kept to the shadows all the way down to Brick Lane where she turned right, then right again at the church, heading for home. She was halfway down White's Row when she heard footsteps and looked behind to see a tall figure marching briskly towards her in the gloom.

'Excuse me, Miss,' he said, in a smart accent, not six feet away now. As he closed in, she swung round and smacked him in the face with a furious fist and before he could catch his breath she followed it with the other, bloodying his nose all the way down his starched shirt-front. Then she took off down the alley, grasping the razor in case he gave chase, which he did not.

In fact, he was a gentleman of unusual tastes, who was rather shy and had been hanging around the district hoping for satisfaction. He had seen Grace earlier in the day and mistaken her for a lady who might help him, choosing her largely on account of her kind, direct face. This seemed ironic to him as he knelt in the street, blood dripping from his nose. He was sure he would find it amusing one day.

At home, Daisy and Jake were wide awake though they were not supposed to be, in the back room, whispering. Billy had fallen asleep in front of the fire and Charlie was out. Jake was showing Daisy new games – magic tricks: how to fan the mark, brush against them to find the wallet; how to sandwich, distraction, sleight of hand.

Mr Blunt finished his dinner and shoved aside his plate, belching soundly.

Across town Ivor Squall finished his also, and washed his plate and cutlery fastidiously in his tiny sink. After tidying his desk, he sat down to enjoy the peace and quiet.

In the Britannia Mr Blunt stared into his beer, fuming silently at Squall's disappearance, plotting to catch him the next day. Such an air of simmering rage surrounded him that no one sat near. Into the pub fell Miss Lucy Fear. She had been thrown out of the Ten Bells after baring her tits for the customers' delectation. Staggering by the door she surveyed the bar, which was swimming before her, and made a beeline for the stranger by the window.

'Hello, love, buy a girl a drink?' she slurred.

Blunt glowered at her from under his eyebrows. Without a word he rose and struck her hard across the face, one way, then the other, and left her on the floor of the pub, the landlord gaping after him like a drowning fish.

CHAPTER EIGHTEEN

◆◆◆◆

The Hammers did so well on Monday that they knocked off early and bought a chicken. They had gone home and got it roasting and Grace had run out to get potatoes. On her way back she was crossing Commercial Street, thinking about browning chicken skin – and there he was. Just his head and shoulders through a pane of glass as her eyes wandered across the road, unmistakable, ominous, mean as a prize pig. She gasped and almost pissed herself, right there in the street. Horror ran up her back like a swarm of ants, crawling through her hair. He was sitting at the window in the Britannia, and who should be across the table from him but Jack. If they had looked out at that moment instead of lifting their beers to their greedy gullets they would have seen her, frozen to the spot, narrowly missed by the brewery cart. As it rumbled past, Jack glanced up and saw her. He did not wave or smile but widened his eyes, staring urgently at her for a second. Then she turned about-face and walked away.

The first thing she did, as if in a dream, was to look for the children. She ran straight home where Charlie was keeping an eye on the bird.

'Where are they?'

'Somewhere about. What's the matter?'

'Go and get them in.'

He came back with Billy and Daisy just as the secret board behind the stove was back in its place.

'What are you doing, Ma?'

'Nothing.' They looked at her funny, she thought.

'Where's Jake?'

'He's gone again,' said Daisy, rolling her eyes as if she was his mother. Grace told them to pack useful things for a short trip and their favourite toy, and not to ask questions for now. Then she flew to the Frying Pan to speak to Horace Daley.

Mr Horace Daley is the sort of man with whom you would entrust your very head if you had to leave it somewhere. If you had some extremely valuable item that you did not want to lose, a fine piece of jewellery, for instance, you could wrap it in rag and string and hide it in his cellar, in the sure knowledge that it would be there when you wanted it next. You could even be sure that not only would he keep it safe, but also that if you put it into his hands he would not unwrap it to see what he was hiding, though you could hardly expect such restraint.

'Horace, I must leave London today,' she said, in the privacy of the back room. 'If anyone asks for me in the next week or two, tell them you never heard of me.'

'Right you are,' he said, clenching his red hands.

'And can you keep something for me?'

'Is it something special?'

'Very special indeed.'

'You can put it downstairs.'

In the back room of the Frying Pan, under the carpet, is a trapdoor which leads to the cellar. Down in the far corner a low passageway runs under the next building. Without a lantern you cannot see your hand in front of your face. If you cared to crawl with your head down to the end of the tunnel you would come out into the cellar of the house across the street, which connects to the shop next door and from there all the way under Brick Lane to Whitechapel Road. You have to squeeze through parts of the tunnel so it is not for the faint-hearted, or the fat, but you can stay down there, all right, if you don't mind a spider or two. It is said to have been used by Dick Turpin himself. No one bothers with it much any more. It is, however, a fine hiding-place: Grace makes use of it now and then, reckoning it the safest place in all the maze of London Town.

So down the stairs she went, under the trapdoor – while Mr Daley saw to his customers – trying not to touch the damp bricks.

As she kissed the beauty goodnight she fancied she heard it breathing, pulsing in time with her blood. And then, a sigh – or a rustle – behind her: a mouse! Or perhaps the edge of her skirt, brushing the wall; and she looked sharply into the darkness, into nothing and felt foolish. For now she could hear her own heart beating, and her own breath. Silence.

Then she bricked the ruby, still warm, into the wall.

★

'Where are you heading for?'

'I don't know yet.' She hadn't thought further than getting away. 'Wherever the first train goes.'

'From Whitechapel?'

'No.' Her hands were still trembling round her brandy glass. 'Liverpool Street's safer. Or St Pancras.'

Horace Daley regarded her quietly for a moment as if he was reading her mind. 'The railway system is a marvellous convenience,' he said at last. 'Busy, too.' He sipped his ale delicately, like a lady taking tea, setting the jar down as if it was a china cup. 'Why don't you take one of Big Roy's boats? Who would think of that?'

The idea hit her like an anvil falling from the sky. The river! Who *would* think of that?

Roy Harman is the nearest thing to a giant in the real world: you have to crane your neck to get a proper look at him. At the last count he stood seven foot two in his size-sixteen boots, and half as wide across. He had started growing in earnest when he was two, outstripping his big brother the following year – people thought him stupid as they assumed he was the elder. He topped five foot as he turned six and earned a man's wage at the docks by the time he was twelve. He'd done well for himself: the boats that Mr Daley mentioned were a fleet of lighters and barges that unloaded cargo for the East India Company. Roy was handsome enough but had had only one woman in his life, on account of his sensitive heart and her being the only girl big enough, at six foot three, to consider taking him on. It was fortunate indeed that they made a perfect match, still standing sixteen years last week.

As Grace left the Frying Pan she skulked along the street, uncomfortable as if she were naked. She hurried home. Outside the Ten Bells were Sally Ann and Mary Kelly, who shouted greetings to her as she passed – they were in good spirits, having had no money for gin the night before and just earned the first that evening. She tried to wave inconspicuously, hurrying away as they called after her down the street.

They were to leave under cover of darkness that evening – Grace spent the rest of the day indoors with the curtains drawn. When Daisy asked her why she would not come outside she replied that she was spring-cleaning the house and enlisted her help. Never had the hours ticked by so slowly for Grace, who looked at the clock every seven minutes. By two they had swept and dusted everything and made the beds and Grace had to feign exhaustion as an excuse to stay in and read the paper. She avoided looking at the clock for as long as she could bear it in the hope that the time would pass more quickly but it did not. They folded the laundry, played rummy, sat on the bed. Daisy grew bored with Grace and ran outside with Billy to play, with strict instructions to stay where Grace would see them if she put her head outside the door.

Happily, she had no intention of doing so. Not ten minutes later Mr Blunt turned the corner from Wentworth Street and started up Bell Lane. He was in an uncommonly good mood, having caught up with poor Ivor Squall that morning and left him a gibbering wreck. This was the third street in his section for the next day – his search had begun again, a little wider, and he was getting ahead of his schedule as his enjoyment in prowling the neighbourhood grew. It tickled him to give people a turn in the gloomy alleyways at dusk, pulling his hat down and glaring menacingly from under the brim as he went past, revelling in the ominous sound of his footsteps, heavy and slow, imagining he heard feet skittering away before him, like nervous animals. And so his search had become less tiresome and more thorough. He had walked up Bell Lane just two days ago, quite early, and it had been much busier. Today there were just a few grubby children in the street and one or two old women on their doorsteps.

Though Mr Blunt had never doubted before that Grace Hammer's likeness was burned into his memory and that he would know her anywhere, his conviction had begun to waver. He had looked at too many women – his head spun with faces; they blended into each other. Once or twice he had thought he saw her, only to be confounded. Sometimes he could not picture him: which frightened him: he felt he was losing pieces of his mind, breaking up and drifting away from him like Madeira cake in a stream. He prowled up the street, scowling, past the little girl with the blue ribbon. She watched his feet approach, frowning at him as if he was a stormcloud, his bulk casting a gloom over her game.

Across East London Ivor Squall wrung his handkerchief, twisting it round his spindly hands, dabbing it against his bursting head.

'He is a most persuasive man. Imposing.' Here he shuddered from his shoulders to his restless fingers and back again. 'A *most* imposing man. He has called upon me again only this morning, without announcement. He really is most insistent.'

Miss Spragg eyed the sweating brow and the jittery hands. 'I only wish I was able to help you, Mr Squall,' she said, 'but certainly I shall keep my ears to the ground. Will you have an egg?'

'Thank you, Emmeline, no.'

'It is a shame indeed that you must keep your client secret.'

'Why, Emmeline, I am sure you must understand,' slimed Ivor Squall. He was going on to suggest that he was acting out of personal integrity but stopped short with a feeble laugh. 'I really must protect my own interests, you see. Of course, for the right information I should certainly cut someone in for a share of the benefits. If only someone knew where to find this cursed Hammer woman.'

'If only,' said Miss Spragg.

'I shall certainly not let go of it, you see.'

'Indeed.'

At seven o'clock the Hammer family left their home, managing somehow to elude the watchful eye of nosy Mrs Jacob, who was giving her twitching curtain a rest. Grace set a brisk pace and kept her head down. The pubs were full and most people merry, paying them no heed. They looked as though they had been evicted from their lodgings that evening. Grace carried Daisy for some of the way as she was tired and wanted to go nowhere and the boys carried the luggage:

Charlie blankets and clothes, Billy their personal things and Daisy's scruffy dog, and Jake some cheese and bread, and the roast chicken, trickling warm grease down his chest.

Never had she felt so conspicuous than on that walk from Bell Lane to the Eagle Wharf, Wapping, as if she was spot-lit: people seemed to look at her strangely as they went by, as though they knew something. The children, except Charlie, had no idea that anything might be wrong: she had told them they were taking a surprise trip and that they were to ask no more questions, a ploy that had worked a treat so far.

Every step towards the river seemed to take them further into a foreign land. The buildings loomed higher, warehouse blocks climbing as Whitechapel vanished behind them, their steps advancing into darkness. At Cable Street they crossed the edge of their patch. How we live in the same square mile every day, she marvelled. What village idiots we are, though we may live in the sprawling metropolis! She kept straight on down Dock Street, wondering at the relief that started to fill up her lungs, walking into this exotic world as though she no longer had command of her feet. Out of the inn before them, springing out of the gloom like a lighthouse, piled a bunch of Chinamen. At the front of the group was Genghis Khan, roaring at the night, baring his teeth. His hair sprang in a thick dark plait from the top of his head, shaved all around like an island. Daisy clung to her hand, and they hurried past in a tight little bunch.

The next corner was Smithfield Street. Billy was struggling so Charlie took one of his bags and they stopped to get their breath, sitting on their luggage on the kerb. Grace cast her eyes over the moonlit street. Just across the cobbles was the spot where she and handsome Jack Tallis had kissed, that first night, on their way down to London Docks. She pictured herself, caught by the waist on the corner, in his strong arms. She got to her feet.

'Let's keep going.'

'Where to, Ma?'

'You'll see.'

Mr Blunt was back in Bell Lane. Unfortunately he had spent some of the afternoon in the company of a friendly but rather stupid girl named Molly Whelk, who visited an aunt in Bethnal Green every Thursday, much to the old lady's irritation, and enjoyed a port in the Princess Alice after. She told him quite innocently that she did remember a very nice Grace who lived on the Aldgate side of Commercial Street: she thought her name might be Hammer – on Goulston Street, perhaps, or Middlesex. Or Bell Lane.

It was dark now and lights had appeared in some of the windows. The sound of chatter floated out as Blunt stalked quietly past. No one else was in the street. He stopped by one of the dark houses and peered through the letterbox. All he could see was a bundle of laundry, or what may be a corpse. He moved past. Someone came running down the street. They slowed as they saw him, then hurried past. The next house was quiet and dark. He looked in at the window. Up the street ahead of him a dark figure knocked at someone's door. No one answered. They knocked again, and waited, then turned away.

★

Nightingale Lane was long and dark, warehouses on either side, dwarfing the family, casting them into gloom. At the feet of the great walls huddled dark shapes, in bunches, a small fire here and there, prehistoric figures in flickering relief. Grace's imagination tortured her as they went past, the sound of footsteps behind them, dark shadows lurking ahead. She could see Blunt's face, leering at her. As they neared the bottom of the street they caught a glimpse of the river, shining like the light at the end of a tunnel. It vanished between towers of brick as they turned into the high street, the smell of it following them, lurking on the other side of the warehouses that lined the way, strange and enticing. As they came out on Wapping New Stairs the Thames opened out before them and they stopped still and held their breath.

The grimy buildings had fallen away, and sparkling water stretched away at their feet; the air hung clear around them. Lights on the opposite bank glittered like stars. For a moment nobody made a sound. Then they started pointing at things floating by.

'Look, a crocodile,' said Daisy.

'It's a dead person', retorted Jake.

'No, it isn't,' said Grace.

Sure enough Roy Harman was there. The children, deducing that they were to go on a boat, were consumed with excitement. They had never been on one before, never mind at night. Roy helped them in – it was sturdy but, as he put it, not too bloody heavy to row – settling Daisy with her dog in the stern, which had a little bench with a back to it so that she could make a nest with the blankets. The boys piled in and jumped about until Roy told them to sit still. He gave Grace directions, and wished them all the best of British luck.

'If you go east you'll have the tide with you till about one but you'll get more traffic, and bigger ships, which are a risky prospect, and you'll have to take a turn at Canvey Island before it grows too wide and the currents get tricky. If I were you, I'd go west.' He gave Charlie a friendly slap on the back that nearly knocked him overboard. 'You can row for your ma, you're a proper lad.'

They pushed away from the stairs, Charlie trying the oars, sculling away over the river, waving at Roy as he disappeared into the dark.

As they slid past Eagle Wharf a lonely figure on the quayside watched the boat glide away. From the shadow of the warehouse wall the goblin Spragg remembered the woman with the green ribbon. The mean eyes tracked the boat down the river, heading west.

CHAPTER NINETEEN

'That's it, there.' Billy pointed. They peered into the gloom at Bermondsey on the south bank, gliding by on their left. Was that port or starboard? thought Grace absently, missing what Billy was saying, her attention brought back by noticing how intently Daisy was listening.

'He took himself there when his ma died.'

'Who?'

'Tommy Hanley.'

'Where?'

'To the Bermondsey casual ward.'

'What did she die of?'

'Drink.'

'Oh.' She digested this, wishing she had been listening, trying to remember who Tommy Hanley might be. 'How do you know where it is?'

'I went.'

'By boat?'

'No!'

'You went through that bloody tunnel?' exclaimed Grace, so that the boat rocked slightly.

'Yes.'

'What tunnel?' enquired Daisy.

'It's a tunnel under the river, darlin'.'

'What's wrong with the tunnel?' piped up Jake.

'It's under the bloody river! What if it leaks?'

'It's perfectly safe, Ma,' said Billy, patiently.

'Never mind that. So what were you and Tommy Hanley up to in Bermondsey anyway? How d'you know it so well?'

'Nothin'! I don't! I seen a map of the river! We're just going into the Upper Pool, see, that's Fountain Dock there, and once we're through that and past London Bridge we'll go west till Waterloo, that's about two mile away, and then round the big bend south, down past Westminster, right next to the Houses of Parliament, then Lambeth and Vauxhall where it bends west again, on towards Battersea, Wandsworth, Putney, Hammersmith and so on.' The family gazed at him with wonder.

'No flies on you, are there, my Billy?' Grace found nothing more to say, and marvelled at how her brilliant son could see London in his head as if he had grown wings and flown into the very sky above the Thames. 'So after Hammersmith what comes next?'

'Barnes and Chiswick, then Kew.'

'You're a good lad.'

'Thanks, Ma.'

'Don't you be going to Bermondsey any more, son.'

'Why, Ma?' he said, as if he didn't know.

'I'm sure you know very well.'

'Why shouldn't he go?' demanded Daisy.

'Because the people are unfriendly and most likely dangerous, my beautiful girl.'

'It's not as if we live in Mayfair ourselves,' observed Charlie.

'None of my children are to go to Bermondsey *or* in that bloody tunnel,' said Grace, loud and firm, sealing the subject shut. She remembered very well what a pit it was, unpopular even with gentlemen slummers. In fact, it was no rougher than parts of Spitalfields, but Londoners must always have some district they imagine to be worse than their own. She watched Jacob's Island drift past, notorious decaying rat-hole. Faint cries and shouting came from the rotten maze of timber, crazy world the colour of Thames mud.

Charlie did well at the rowing, though Grace was sure he had not done it before. They slid past the docks, sheltered in the dark. Odd lights in riverside windows and the faint glow of the moon through the grey paper sky lit the way. Daisy and Jake were mostly speechless, but Billy had plenty to say, keeping up a helpful commentary on the passing landscape: how the cranes worked, the new bridge, half built, the Tower of London.

'That'll never be a bridge,' said Charlie, as they passed by the Tower. 'The sides are going up too high.'

'It's a bascule bridge,' said Billy. 'It goes up when a tall ship comes in.'

'How?' said Daisy, razor-sharp as usual.

'I believe it's something to do with hydraulic power,' he replied, hoping to confuse her as he did not fully understand the idea himself.

How does he know all these things? thought Grace. There

was traffic on the river but no police. Just past London Bridge she took the oars.

'Can I row the boat?' said Jake.

'Can I?' pleaded Daisy, chiming in straight away.

'Not now,' said Grace. 'Maybe tomorrow.'

'Will we go on this boat tomorrow?'

'Well, who knows?' she said mysteriously, confounding the little face.

They passed quickly under the railway and then South-wark Bridge, the wall high beside them, dwarfing the boat. They stared up at the ironwork arches, vast above them, stretching out to great stone piers that rose from the turgid water, and the river seemed huge now, stretching across to the other bank like an ocean, a great surging grey serpent writhing under them. Even Billy was quiet for a while as they pushed on.

Grace Hammer had a peculiar gift for rowing, which was just as well because there was a long way to go. Bridges followed – Blackfriars, Waterloo, Hungerford, Westminster – each a monument to the miracle of man, a soft creature of flesh without claws or significant teeth or strength, who commanded steel girders and great blocks of stone. The family fell each into their own thoughts. As they slid past Big Ben towards Lambeth the great bell struck ten. An uneasy feeling crept up through Grace's belly and settled in her chest – she felt small, a matchbox person in a tiny boat, under a giant eyeglass. The children were craning their necks up to the clock; they had forgotten their cold feet. She wondered when she ought to tell them that they were not turning back.

'Let me take a turn Ma,' said Charlie.

Daisy fell asleep first, of course, after crawling on to Grace's lap. She covered her with a blanket and stroked her warm head. When he saw this Jake huddled next to her and fell into deep slumber not ten minutes later. Billy fought it for a while and gave in. Charlie rowed on into the night.

In a nook in the damp wall, warming her twisted hands before a poisonous fire that crackled and hissed with mouldy wood, sat the goblin of Blight Street, contemplating the events of the day. She had spent it well, being out for most of the evening on business down by the docks and as happy to return home as a scorpion might be to scuttle back to its carcass-strewn nest. But Miss Spragg did not savour its comforts: she crouched in the dark, musing upon the little group on the river. What a curious business. Such an hour to take a pleasure cruise! She would wager Jack Tallis knew nothing of it. There is something at stake indeed, she thought. She must squeeze Mr Squall yet harder for the name of his private client.

These musings were interrupted by a knocking downstairs – four slow knocks, a pause, two fast and two more. Dog Brown was at the door. He was expected.

After their business was concluded Dog assumed his best air of mystery. 'Something's come up that may interest you,' he said, pausing for effect. She waited, poker-faced, for him to get on with it. She was sure that what he had to say would be a disappointment. Dog Brown was not famous for his brain.

'The gent I saw last week in the Princess Alice, imposing fellow, you'll remember me mentioning him.' Indeed she did, and glared at him to save him telling her about it again. 'Name, he said, was Belmarsh.'

Another tedious pause.

'Will you finish this tale today or will I beat it from you?' she growled.

'Well,' said Dog, triumphantly, 'I happened upon him in the Britannia this afternoon, drinking by himself, muttering and staring out the window, a proper madman he looked. Anyhow, I got talking to him and he's frantic to get his hands on this woman he was asking about before – Hammer, her name was – and did I know of her, he asks me again. Well, I'd still never heard of her, I told him.'

Miss Spragg's ears pricked and a curious nerve twitched in her neck. She maintained her air of indifference as Dog Brown blundered on.

'He wouldn't let it rest. And I was wondering who she was and what he was after, thinking it must be a matter of life or death the way he talked about her, eyes bulging – popping out of his head, they were. Never seen nothing like it. Life or death or a lot of money.'

'And then what?'

'Well, I'll tell ya. As he's got up to leave this paper's fallen out of his wallet. And I've had a proper look at it and it turns out he's not Mr Belmarsh at all.'

'There's a surprise,' said Miss Spragg.

'He's a Mr Blunt. Horatio Blunt. And I thought, Don't I know that name from somewhere? And then I remembered . . .'

Dog Brown droned on for several minutes more but the goblin was not listening. She herself had never made Mr Blunt's acquaintance but she knew exactly who he was, through the tentacles she spread over the south. Little wonder Ivor Squall was keeping his private client to his chest. Every top-rate fence knew the name: his reputation went before him with his bulging stomach. He was known for the superior quality of his merchandise – most particularly the fine jewellery in which he specialised, his area of expertise over the course of a long and distinguished career, for he was a lazy thief and would rather not run about the countryside with heavy silver if he could help it. Mr Blunt is renowned for carrying the very best pieces: flawless diamonds and purest gold. She kept this from faithful Dog Brown for the moment, disappointing him with her lack of excitement at his revelations.

'Could you find him again?' was all she said.

After Dog Brown had left, Miss Spragg sat very still for several minutes, like a crocodile watching its supper, as the pieces of the picture started to fit. Mr Blunt's urgent business must be something special indeed. Something very shiny.

Now, Miss Spragg was not to know that Mr Blunt had lost his pretty prize seventeen years ago and, supposing it long gone, was merely seeking his revenge. She assumed, reasonably enough, that the goods were knocking around somewhere, most likely in Grace Hammer's pocket. And knowing Ivor Squall quite well, she assumed, reasonably enough – but barking up entirely the wrong tree – that he meant to find the treasure and side-step Mr Blunt. Miss Spragg fairly boiled with curiosity: what fine rare things might tempt Ivor Squall to cross such a fellow? Her imagination ran wild in her head, flashing diamonds in her black eyes, sparkling treasures in her greasy claw.

And so she decided, reasonably enough, to go after the treasure herself. And perhaps the reward as well, if she played her cards right. She would find Mr Blunt tomorrow, and hear what he might have to say.

Emmeline Spragg made her way out, slipping like a dirty vapour through the broken landscape, plotting the chase. She would send a man on horseback: he could go ahead to Hammersmith Bridge and watch for the Hammers' boat. She stopped off at the Queen to see who might be about.

Grace took the oars again after Chelsea Bridge, settling Daisy gently into her blanket nest and giving poor Charlie a rest.

'You've done well, son,' she said. 'You know I couldn't manage without you.'

He moved next to Billy and shut his eyes. 'It's all right, Ma,' he said. 'I like rowing.'

Chelsea went by on the north bank, rows of clean

houses, ornate like jewellery boxes. As they approached Albert Bridge Daisy woke, with a little animal noise, as if coming out of hibernation, and lifted her tangled blonde head to see a vision before her, coming closer, shining in the moonlight like a birthday cake. She gazed up as they passed beneath. Grace thought she was making a wish. She watched the lamps shrink into the distance for a while, then laid her head down again. They started round the big bend towards Battersea.

'Ma, where are we going?' said Jake.

'Up the river, son.'

'Are we in trouble?'

'Only if we get caught.'

Billy stirred in his sleep just then, talking nonsense, making them laugh and letting her off the hook. Charlie tucked the blanket round his brother and gazed out over the water. 'It's pretty, isn't it, though?' he muttered, before he fell asleep.

Jack Tallis visited the Hammer family home that evening and found it quiet and dark. He stood in the street for a while, wondering where they could be, if not here, at half past eight. It seemed very strange. He thought of the country gent he had met that morning in the Britannia, who had asked after her, and an uneasy feeling turned in his stomach. From the moment Mr Belmarsh had struck up conversation Jack had thought it fishy. He had been minding his own business in the corner when he had noticed the fellow looking over, so he had given him a nod, out of courtesy, which the fat country gent seemed to take as an invitation to sit at his table. And it was odd how quickly he had divulged a good part of his life story while managing to ask a great deal of questions. He had long-lost family in the area, he said. Jack had been surprised when he mentioned a Grace Hammer, though he had covered it well and pretended complete ignorance of her. Grace had never told Jack her family name, leaving him to find it out from Nelly Holland, who could tell you anything about anybody.

When Grace had appeared outside the window not two minutes later he had nearly choked on his beer. She had stared at Mr Belmarsh for what seemed an age while Jack struggled to distract him with chatter. When Grace saw Jack at last he managed to throw her a look and then she vanished. He bombarded his companion with local information, trying to divert him – even volunteering himself as a guide for the afternoon. This offer was declined, to his relief, after a lengthy pause during which Belmarsh showed no sign that he had heard this generous proposition, but ground his teeth, and rocked slowly, staring at a spot on the wall. Jack had thought to call on Grace, once he had moved along. In the event he was distracted by a pretty thing who came in a few minutes after Belmarsh had left.

Suddenly he missed her, wistfully, as one does with something elusive. He turned away from the cold house and wandered forlornly down the street.

After Battersea came the railway bridge, then Wandsworth and Putney, sliding by ghostlike, faint through the silver mist that clung to the banks. It seemed easier now, as if the river had decided to help, carrying them along. Maybe the tide had come in. She cast her mind back to where she had come from, tried to count the miles and gave up. No rest for the wicked, she thought. Not in a lifetime. She rowed between the trees, standing tall and dark, rustling in the night breeze, breathing the fresh air, heading west.

As they passed up the river away from London it began to narrow and what little light there had been to guide them had faded away with the city. The full moon cast a silver halo on the water as they glided soundlessly towards Hammersmith Bridge. It seemed through the gloom to be a mythical creation, as if it had stood on the earth since the dawn of time. The tops of its four grand towers were lost in the mist; the suspension curved down in a huge iron sweep to the centre and back up into the cloud again. She looked up along the great pillars into the night sky, to the pointed tips of the very top of the bridge, then down to the great feet in the water, as they passed beneath, missing Miss Spragg's watchman, who was relieving himself in the undergrowth, having a touch of the runs and being unable to wait any longer. Only Charlie opened his eye a chink and blinked at her. The air grew cleaner with each new breath, keeping time with the dip and the splash that propelled them onwards. Grace went to sleep in a clump of bulrushes towards Richmond, falling down next to the oars, arms aching as if beaten by the devil.

★

Mr Blunt slept fitfully, pictures turning in his head. He dreamed of the girls by St Botolph, their sticky white thighs, and of Grace Hammer – kissing her, slicing her throat.

CHAPTER TWENTY

Daisy opened her eyes first, to see the branches of a great beech tree spreading above her, twinkling green with a million leaves. She wondered where on earth she was, then remembered the day before and that she was on a boat. She tugged at Jake's sleeve to wake him, as excited as if it was Christmas.

Beyond the bank of reeds and bulrushes a green meadow sloped up towards an enormous house, bright white against the trees, the windows sparkling clean. The landscape rolled away in waves like none they saw in London, not even in Victoria Park. And the air! It was fresh and clean; it slid through the lungs like sweet ether, pure, intoxicating. Charlie woke with sore shoulders. He lay for a minute listening to the little ones chattering, and wondered what on earth they were doing in a boat far from home.

Soon the whole family was alive and exclaiming at fishes and dragonflies, and other country wonders. The boys splashed at each other, unable, as boys are, to stay dry. Sunshine lit the water, the children laughed at something, and a fearless spirit took hold of Grace again. The prospect was thrilling! Up the river to who knows where! She laughed at her sore arms, feeling a trifle mad, watching the dancing light on the water as she rowed the boat along.

After a while her arms hurt unbearably. 'Who wants to row?'

'Me!' shouted the young ones. So they bounced from bank to bank for a while and ate cold chicken. A mile on they came upon Teddington Lock. Now Grace, though she was a country girl, could not remember having been through a lock in her life. She had seen them and thought she knew how to work one but she didn't want to ask the keeper for fear of striking up conversation.

Thank goodness for Billy, who knew exactly what to do, though he had only seen one in a book.

'Look, Ma, Teddington Lock. Can I wind it?'

'Yes, darlin'.'

After a seemingly interminable wait, Miss Spragg's errand boy decided that they must have eluded him in the small hours when he had nodded off for a minute or two. He was making good progress up the river, gaining on the Hammers, having called already upon Miss Spragg's associates in Brentford and the ferry near Isleworth. He was heading for Hampton Wick now, trying to stick by the river as much as possible and to keep his eyes peeled for the family, as he had been ordered to do. This last part he found difficult since much of the water was teeming with traffic, most of it families in rowing-boats, enjoying the sunshine. He felt unsure of what he was looking for.

Just five miles up the river, in Kingston, Grace bought

provisions. They ate buns and cheese as Hampton Court glided by.

Miss Spragg had intelligence, not yet cold, that Mr Blunt was enjoying a drink in the Commercial, and within minutes she was on the corner, sneaking a look through the window. There was Archie Simmons, talking about the damp at his lodgings, no doubt, Big Roy Harman, Busy Liz and a small crowd of children from Dorset Street. A solid red man was swatting them away with heavy hands. He wore dirty brown tweed, just as Dog Brown had said: a solid man, no hat and a bright angry boil on his brow. This was surely Mr Blunt. And there in the very next seat, popping up like a rash again, was Ivor Squall. He was telling Mr Blunt something urgent, in a state of some excitement, waving his arms; or – indeed more animated than she had ever seen him. Up to something, for sure. And he looked to mean business about it.

In fact, poor Ivor was only trying to extricate himself from the whole affair, pleading, in effect, for mercy, which was why he was waving his arms more than usual.

What to do about Mr Squall? she thought, watching him through the glass. He is making a good deal of nuisance. There will be no easy way round him. And intent as he is on this business, she thought – barking still further up the wrong tree – there'll be no shaking him off it. Lurking at the corner Miss Spragg considered how far Ivor Squall might cramp her interests, and how much that might weigh against his merits.

★

She found him later at his offices, peering nervously from a chink in the top window. 'I can see you, Mr Squall. Let me in.'

Ivor came to the door in quite a state, wondering why his fortunes had turned so, these last weeks, and why he must endure so many gruesome visitors.

'I've seen her,' she said, once she was through the door and all the locks were fast again, which was quite a procedure. Had Miss Spragg called by just an hour before, his extravagant precautionary system would have been quite useless to him, for she had planned at first to kill him there. The cruel absurdity of his big bunch of keys and his safety ballet would surely not have been lost on him in his final moments. But he was luckier than he felt, for now: she had abandoned this plan as careless, and adopted another.

'Not an hour ago,' she lied. 'By Wapping Stairs. With all the children.' Ivor almost dropped dead upon the mat anyway. 'On the river they were, heading east.'

He took some time to recover his breath. 'I must contact my client,' he stammered at last, wondering how he might do so without Miss Spragg's involvement. He groped for a ploy to excuse himself, scraping around the inside of his head.

'Never mind that for now,' she said, relieving and confounding him in equal measure. 'She won't be far. We'll go and have a look first, just to make sure of it, eh? I'll arrange horses. We'll leave at four o'clock.'

Perhaps it was sensible, thought Ivor, twitching quietly to himself behind his bony desk, worrying it all over. It was best to make sure. He didn't want to lead Mr Blunt up the garden path, after all. Indeed, he decided – generosity flooding his delicate heart at the happy prospect of closing the matter for ever – if Miss Spragg had her woman she could keep the reward.

That day the Hammer children saw a great many things they had never laid eyes on before: fields of wheat, apple orchards and hop-pickers at work glided by. The boys swam – or, rather, Charlie swam while Billy and Jake clung to the side of the boat. Daisy wanted to go in but Grace wouldn't let her as they were in the middle of the river and she didn't want to go in herself. She could swim all right but she didn't like to be wet afterwards.

They stopped by a bank so that Daisy could paddle. The light came down in ripples through the leaves above, dappled on the water and the children, casting sparks around them. They caught tiny minnows and frogs and beetles like shiny buttons. At Sunbury Lock they were passed by Miss Spragg's errand boy, though he failed to spot them. He had become half-hearted in pursuit of his task and was more interested in riding as fast as possible to his next port of call, having several visits to make before Windsor where he was to turn back. He thundered past the lock at break-neck speed, thrashing his unfortunate mount. The family rowed on serenely, past the small island in the middle of the river.

'Do people live there?' asked Daisy.

'Yes,' chimed Charlie and Billy. 'Little tiny ones,' added Charlie.

'With webbed feet.'

'Where are they?'

'In the bushes,' said Charlie.

'Or asleep,' said Billy, knowing she wasn't that daft. 'They sleep in little houses under the ground.'

'Do they, Ma?' she asked, hoping for a straight answer.

'They might.'

Daisy scanned the trees intently. 'A lot of ducks live there.'

'That's what the little people eat.'

'Do they, Ma?'

'Most likely ducks and berries.'

'Berries?'

'Yes. But don't you go eating berries, you ask me first.'

'Why?'

'Because some of them are poisonous.'

'Where are we going Ma?' said Jake.

'You'll see.'

As the afternoon mellowed Grace turned her thoughts to where they might sleep. Charlie must have read her mind because he said, 'Ma, when are we going to stop?'

'When we get somewhere nice and quiet, son.'

The river wound on, past a field of sheep, a great weeping willow, past Shepperton, where the children clamoured to stop but were refused. A couple more locks appeared to entertain them until they reached the next town. A perfect row of riverside gardens slid past, then a long stretch of mooring. Behind it they could see a road, lined with shops, another inn, people walking along the riverside, enjoying the warm afternoon. It seemed too busy, and in spite of the children, who pleaded to get off the boat, she kept on past, ignoring their protests. The houses thinned behind them; the day began to fade.

'Are there lions in the country?'

'No, darlin', only cows and horses. And sheep, too.'

'And bears,' offered Jake.

'Stop it, Jake.'

'Are there bears?'

'No, darlin', there's no bears.'

They rowed quietly along for a while.

'Or wolves?'

'No wolves either.'

As if to prove the point, a couple of cows floated by, looming on the banks, mooing gently to announce themselves.

'Do you think we'll find a house to sleep in?'

'Perhaps an inn,' said Grace.

'A nice one?'

'Now that I don't know.'

'Hm. There are nice houses in the country.'

'Yes, darlin'. You shout when you see one you like.'

'How many days will we go on this boat?'

'Are you tired of it already?'

'No. I think we should go on it every day.'

The light was fading in earnest now.

'We could build a shelter,' suggested Billy.

You bloody could, too, thought Grace.

Daisy proposed the building of a house, which Grace explained would take too long and, although a fine idea in principle, was further hampered by their not having any bricks. A couple of riverside inns had been passed and she suggested stopping at the next. Everyone watched the banks intently, to be the first to spot the new scene of adventure. It didn't appear for some time, after all the children, save Billy, had grown bored of the anticipation.

'There it is,' he said quite calmly. They all scrambled to look, rocking the boat.

Their Nirvana was a small stone cottage, set back from the river behind a charming garden – like a picture on a chocolate box, from the fluffy smoke coming out of the chimney, clean and white like cotton balls, to the roses round the door. Foxgloves fringed the path that led down to the river and an old lady, rosy like an apple, was cutting pinks as the sun set. The scene was unbearably quaint. She is surely a witch, thought Grace, as she waved them in.

Miss Spragg arranged for horses at four and Ivor Squall joined her reluctantly, being thoroughly uncomfortable with animals in general but horses in particular. He was keen to get it over with. Steeling himself – as much as he might with his poor constitution – he resolved to hold on tight and hoped they would not go too far or too fast. Perhaps it might be worth his while, after all. Having recovered from his heady flight of generous fancy, he had revised his position, allowing fair shares with the goblin – an even split, should there be profit. He was happy enough thus deluded. Ivor Squall was not usually so far behind the game. He was a wily fellow and could make a great deal of nuisance. He wondered idly if his goodwill had been tallied in the great Book of Judgement and if it counted in his credit, being given so grudgingly.

Another thing he couldn't hope to know was that his horse, which looked neither too big nor too frisky, was the devil's steed in disguise. His stable boys called him Lucifer and swore blind he understood English. Indeed, he seemed to – he made no noise at all, stood still in his stall, casting his sharp eyes around as if he was thinking human thoughts. He needed a fierce hand to ride him but kept his temper mostly in check, finding good behaviour paid – balanced on a tight string, ready to tip, with the right provocation. Miss Spragg had chosen him especially for Mr Squall.

'I have word they stopped off at Deptford, not an hour ago,' said she, as they made ready to leave. 'We can cut across the bend, by West India Docks, and head them off.'

Though she looked an unlikely tangle of rag she mounted her horse robustly and took its head with a firm hand. Ivor was not so assertive. He did not feel in control at all, and though he made a fair show of it, Lucifer the devil horse knew it straight. So poor Ivor had lost the game before he started; he struggled upright in the saddle, remarking to himself how much higher it seemed from this vantage-point, and took the reins as if there was a rabid dog at the end of them.

The first mile went by tolerably well, he thought – he managed to hold on all right and keep up with Miss Spragg. They were cutting across by the West India Docks now, the houses and shops dropping away, dusk falling, the docks closing. Presently he saw the river, winding back to join them, black and shining – looking, he thought absently, quite remarkably like Indian ink. He thought wistfully of his little desk. So absorbed was he in matters of blotting-paper, pencils and stamps that he barely noticed Miss Spragg drop back, and thought nothing of it until she was behind him. He felt suddenly uneasy. His delicate stomach slid round his ribs and curled into a ball.

'No sign of them yet, then,' he twittered, through the dark.

'No, indeed,' she said.

Ivor was wondering what he should say next when Miss Spragg struck, jabbing Lucifer hard with a sharp stick just below the tail. He kicked out and took off like a thunderbolt, snarling, which he alone among horses could do. Ivor clung on desperately, losing his stirrups and his hold of the reins, grasping handfuls of satanic horsehair. Miss Spragg watched from a distance as Lucifer hurled Ivor from his back on to the bank with a good crack as he landed on his head. He wasn't moving, as far as she could see. She trotted up to have a look.

Ivor was certainly not moving unless you counted his desperate face, and the fluttering of his hands as he tried to reach for help – perhaps he thought she might save him! Blood pooled on the ground beneath his skull as he stared, crazed and hopeless, at her, like some wretched dumb animal; in fact the Book of Judgement had swum before his eyes and he was wondering if his account was in credit – he had not anticipated dying today and felt unprepared. And terrified. She stood patiently for a whole minute but still he stared, writhing a little as he tried to sit up. Miss Spragg had had enough. Grasping his useless arms she dragged him to the river's edge. Then she took him by the hair and pushed his head under. She held it there for a good two minutes, enjoying the view and the fresh air until he was still.

'Why didn't we come before?' Daisy wanted to know.

'Because we didn't know it was here.'

'Do you think Mrs Robertson was here all the time?'

'Yes. Lucky for us.'

'We're lucky, ain't we?'

'Yes, darlin', we are.'

'Do you like this bed? It's made of feathers.'

'Very much. Do you?'

'Yes, I like everything.'

I hope that keeps up, thought Grace. Daisy's attitude was comforting: she slept a beautiful ten hours in the clean feather bed.

Grace's head was uneasy on the pillow. She dreamed Blunt was coming down the towpath that followed the river. His face was indistinct, just a space in the dark shape that advanced towards her. She found herself unable to get out of bed, even to move or scream. She woke with a struggle, sweating and gasping for air.

In fact, Miss Spragg was much nearer Grace's tail than Mr Blunt. She had sent word to a number of acquaintances along the river: the lock-keeper at Penton Hook, and Chertsey, and various innkeepers, and should they have information she would hear of it soon enough. She sat by the greasy lantern in her lair in Limehouse, awaiting developments.

★

Mr Blunt, meanwhile, prowled the noisome streets of Whitechapel, finding himself back in Bell Lane again. As he paused by the darkened windows of number twenty-eight a curtain twitched across the street.

CHAPTER TWENTY-ONE

Madeleine Robertson had been married a long time ago, to a man she loved with all her heart; he had loved her back for twelve happy years until he disappeared into the sunset with a milkmaid who had started work at the farm not three weeks before. Maidie had never bothered having another man, though she was a handsome woman and could have wed again. She simply never considered it. She was in love with Mr Robertson and that was that. She did not wallow in her miseries for long but sold the farm and got on with a good life by the river.

When the Hammers woke up to the sound of birdsong, she had a handsome breakfast ready. Though they ate well in London they had never had breakfast like this, with eggs and bacon and sausage all at once, and the children were silent, fixed on devouring it. Maidie Robertson chatted sociably to Grace, showing an interest without being too nosy.

'So you came from London, you say?'

'That's right. We live there.'

'I've a sister in London. I went once to see her. She lives in Brixton – do you know it? It's dreadfully busy. You can't hear yourself think for the chatter and the carriages. I saw a fire engine there, all the bells ringing and people jumping out of the way, such a commotion! Still, I expect you're used to all the hustle and bustle.'

'You do become accustomed to it, it's true. That doesn't mean we don't like a bit of peace and quiet.'

'We like the country,' interjected Daisy.

'Do you, young miss?'

'Yes. We like it very much.'

'You're a good girl. Would you like to feed the chickens?'

They trooped out with Billy and Jake in tow, trying to get in on the chicken-feeding. Charlie and Grace washed the dishes.

'So, what are you up to, then, Ma?' he asked her, as if he expected a decent answer.

Go on, then, and tell him, he's big enough, she thought. 'We're getting away from someone in London.'

'Who?'

'His name's Mr Blunt. I knew him before you were born. I stole something from him, years ago, something very precious, and he has found me out after all this time. You go along with me in everything, in trust, as you always have.'

'I know, Ma.'

'Do you, though?'

'Yes,' he said, solid as a brick wall. 'Don't worry, Ma. We'll be all right. He won't get past Daisy.'

They were laughing as the troops came back into the kitchen.

'Why are you laughing?' demanded Daisy, straight away. They laughed more then, and she shot them one of her hard stares.

After roast lamb and potatoes and a look at *The Water Babies*,

Grace felt the itch to move and on they went, packed into their trusty boat, laden with food. They waved until they had rounded the bend, entreaties to return at any time and to take care ringing in their ears.

The day was not as bright as the one before, and it seemed that the moment Mrs Robertson's cottage was out of sight it began to rain, as if encouraging them to turn back. Grace struck up a chorus of 'The Fireman's Dog' to raise flagging spirits. They pushed on for a while, taking shelter under a huge willow tree some half a mile on as the day grew wetter. Under the branches was a green kingdom, enchanted and dry, the leafy roof curving round them. They waited for the rain to stop.

Jack was nursing a pint in the Ten Bells, wondering where Grace had gone. He had been busy the last day or two with some casual work and various unexpected but pleasing female distractions. Now that these were finished, and he was bored, he was annoyed to find her unavailable for entertainment. With complete disregard for his own comings and goings the last week, he mulled possessively over where she could have gone without so much as a nod in his direction, and whether she had another fancy man. How could she! He felt, with a stab, that hard truth, that you can't have your cake and eat it.

Many miles away, tucked under a tarpaulin in the rain with her children, Grace suddenly thought of him. More a picture than a thought: his hands, his jaw, his melting grin. She felt a pang of sadness until she remembered he was no good.

★

In a lonely house in Shoreditch Mirabel Trotter sat before the fire in her darkened room, counting the days since she had seen Trixie May Turner; she reckoned it at eleven. She sensed something was up – there had been not a word – and she missed her. She calmed herself by having a little brandy, and then another. Her burly sons were downstairs but she didn't want their company. Mrs Trotter poured herself one more and swallowed it straight, listening to shouts and laughter below. Staring into the fire, she saw blue dragons, devil-heads, burning buildings.

CHAPTER TWENTY-TWO

The footsteps came from behind, as the ones that you notice do. She remarked to herself the moment they began to follow that they rang dull in the ears, flat and sinister. They stayed close behind in the shadow, neither over-taking nor falling back, and she gripped the neck of the bottle in her pocket, squeezing Daisy's hand, keeping her eyes on the end of the street. Her tormentor hung behind them another twenty yards, another fifty. Just the soles of his shoes and a soft, wheezing breath, which she caught as she strained the very nerves of her eardrums.

Just as she thought she could bear it no longer she heard the footsteps quicken, and as time slowed she mar-velled at how he had still surprised her, though she had been poised on a nerve string. She turned as he leaped towards her, pushing Daisy aside, and swung the bottle, still half full, into the side of his head. It shattered into pieces that flew through the air, a shower of glass and gin, catching the gaslight, twinkling and falling to the ground, leaving a vicious jagged dagger in her hand. As if in a trance she heard Daisy scream, looked round to find her crouched by the wall and gathered her up. They glanced back at him once, staring dumbly at them, mouth hanging open, blood running down his face into the puddle of gin.

Grace came to with a start and a little gasp, knuckles white on the side of the boat. The family were sleeping. She took in the reeds, the birds, the chirping riverscape.

The family woke early and cold fingers of sunshine fought through the canopy. Billy rowed them into the weak morning sun. Charlie broke out breakfast – rolls, butter, cheese, ham. He gave the first roll to his sister. And on they went. Whitechapel seemed far away. The sky grew blue, the children spotted sheep, the birds sang. It was all very nice but she knew they made quite a picture: they must keep moving. Maybe they should get off the river soon.

They stopped past the next town, and tied up the boat. After they had tidied their few effects, prompted by Charlie, and eaten, they sat on the riverbank and tried to catch fish with long switches and a line they found in the bottom of the boat, though Daisy was content to imagine hers. Their eyes fixed on the water, every ripple and splash. Within five minutes Daisy tired of this. Grace and she walked up the bank to the lane at the top and over the bridge.

'I know a good game,' said Grace. 'You get a stick and drop it in the water, then run the other side and see whose comes out first.' Daisy found herself a fine stick and a large twig for Grace.

After Daisy had won four times, and lost two, and they were playing with blades of grass as the good sticks were becoming harder to find, Grace suggested a foray into the village, though Daisy wanted to play on. She was lured by the possibility of bull's-eyes and the promise that they would play sticks again on the way back. Though only once.

They took a little footpath that ran behind the town. As they wandered up it, Grace filled her lungs with the sweet, clean air and imagined how it would be to live in the countryside, spending every day among the rolling green fields instead of grey streets and human wreckage. Maybe in a little house like that one on the hill ahead, with its apple trees and its thatched roof. She pictured herself inside, baking, or making jam perhaps, the children running around outside, picking blackberries and apples. Daisy skipped ahead, plucking wild flowers from the hedgerow as if participating in this idyllic fantasy. And suddenly Mr Blunt, never far from her thoughts lately, swam into them again, spoiling the scene. She saw him thundering down the footpath towards them, breath grunting, coat tails flapping, heavy boots kicking up stones. She felt uneasy and looked about her, and though she knew he could not be near them, not yet at least, her nerves crackled, as if she was being watched. She remarked to herself then that the only way she could be free of this shadow was if Mr Blunt was dead and buried. A cold notion that dropped out of the sky on to her head. She was surprised she had not thought it before.

They came upon a winding road that appeared to be the main street. A sign said Runney Mead. The sky was blue between the billowing clouds, white like Maidie Robertson's feather pillows. Two shops huddled together opposite a miniature pub.

'What's mead?' said Daisy.

'Some funny old drink they used to have in the olden days.'

'Is it nice?'

'Dunno, darlin'. I've never had it.'

'Everything's so small, ain't it?'

They bought plums, bull's-eyes and sweet tobacco, and walked through the village, munching, lost in thought. A woman watched them across the square. As Grace looked over she lowered her head and went inside her shop. The windows all around seemed to stare like dead men. She hurried Daisy on.

By the boat the boys were talking about some girl with red hair they had seen in the last town. When Grace and Daisy reappeared they had given up fishing and were eyeing up a fancy skiff moored at the other bank.

'What are you doing?' Grace said.

'Nothing.'

All the way from Datchet to Boveney Lock, Grace sank into herself, the children chattering around her. They must leave the boat soon. Supposing someone knew they had left London on the river, and had merely to follow it along? She had felt sure before of their secret escape, now she was not. At Romney Lock the keeper seemed to watch them for all the time it took the water to fill. Grace could see him peering from his little booth as the boat came up.

Now, our Grace is a handsome woman and it may be the lock-keeper was merely sneaking a good look at her – he is a lonely fellow, and though he spends his days in this idyllic spot, with the birdsong all around, and eats fresh country eggs and ham every morning, he finds it interminably tedious and longs to see the lights of Piccadilly; so who knows how he whiles away the hours in that little booth of his – but the running and hiding and secrecy had drawn Grace tight as piano wire. She could hear the grass grow, smell fox in the hedgerow, see through skin, and this had quite skewed her judgement of everyday things, which is the problem, of course, with suspicion. So, he was not a lonely lock-keeper but a spy, piercing her with sharp eyes. She turned her back.

'Look, Daisy, a windmill.' Even that seemed to watch them, looming dark across the fields.

'Why doesn't it go round?'

'There's no wind.'

'What's it for?'

'Making flour.'

'Oh!' Flour was not something Daisy had thought much about; it came in bags and never troubled her. But she was pleased to know anyhow, and to solve the matter of windmills, which she had seen on china cups but never considered properly either. 'Can we wait until the wind comes?'

'No, we can't.'

They made a stop presently at Maidenhead, which seemed a bit risky, but the children were clamouring for food and they had none. They moored on the quieter side of the river, at the end of the landing.

'We're not stopping long!' Grace shouted after them, as they leaped out of the boat and ran down the jetty.

The children were hoping to find another Mrs Robertson and were cruelly disappointed by the surly fellow who was landlord at the Orkney Arms. They sat down to chops and boiled potatoes and were quiet for some time, the landlord scowling in the background, before Grace ventured conversation with him. 'Do you see many travellers around these parts?'

'No,' was the gruff reply.

Even Daisy did not melt his rude manner. 'May I have a cup of milk, please?' she asked him politely.

'Get your nasty hands off the bar, little girl,' he said, under his breath, so that her mother could not hear, which she did. Grace bit her lip.

They wolfed their food, making surreptitious faces at each other all the while, paid their bill and left. The landlord watched them until they disappeared round the next bend, staring intently from the upper floor of the inn, beard bristling as he sucked his front teeth – a habit he had indulged since childhood – which made his chin protrude, giving him a pugnacious yet ridiculous air. He stood on the small balcony as if it were the prow of a ship, imagining himself to be Lord Nelson, before he had lost his arm. He enjoyed this fantasy for a few moments, until his wife, who was even more disagreeable than he and bedridden with colic, shouted for him to empty her pot.

Where do you think you are going? said the tiny voice at the back of Grace's head – the one that spoke at unsure moments such as this. In the rush to escape London she had not thought past the end of her nose. When she looked at their prospects she felt that she had been labouring under a wishful delusion: did she imagine that he might simply abandon his search after a week or two and go home again? How stupid. You are sleepwalking! You knew he would come, the voice scolded. You have made a pig's ear of it.

They stopped for a nap not a mile on, concealed by a great bank of alder, and Grace went back and robbed Landlord Nelson while Charlie watched the little ones, who were sleeping peacefully as she came running through the orchard, night falling behind her, Charlie turning the boat to row back the way they had come.

She shivered in the night air, punting silently past the Orkney Arms. Charlie kept his head down and steered them away from the bank with the other oar. The river was empty; they kept to the shadows on the far bank and disappeared under the bridge. Grace would get her family off the river as soon as they woke, before Laleham and Maidie Robertson's cottage. If Daisy went there again she would never get her away.

Jack was turning away from the house in Bell Lane once more. They were gone for sure. It must have something to do with Mr Belmarsh. He had the uncomfortable feeling that he had failed her – a sentiment she might have appreciated, though there really was nothing he could do – and tried to content himself with the thought that she could get by nicely without his help. Trixie May Turner might know something.

It didn't take him long to find her. She was on good form, though precious about her recent exploits. They had several jars in the Britannia. She hadn't seen Grace since all the business with Mirabel Trotter, or so she said.

'Where do you reckon she is, then?' he asked, for the second time, possessed of the irrational theory that all women are part of some general conspiracy, as many men are, especially the ones who are up to something themselves.

'I've really no idea,' she replied again.

'Do you think something happened to her?'

'No!' She felt sorry for him suddenly, staring moodily into his jar. He needed diversion, perhaps a little venture. Trixie and Jack had a modest history of partnership in crime; certain occasions when an opportunity had presented itself. She needed help with a few tricky tabs that were owing. 'Don't sulk, Jack. Listen to this . . .'

Mr Blunt had taken to drinking in the Frying Pan lately, finding it the quietest place for a beer at certain times of the day. He has asked, of course, after his long-lost cousin, a Miss Grace Hammer: bringing solemn family news, most regretfully – and notice, on a happier note, of a financial nature – but Mr Daley, the landlord, amenable fellow though he was, could not attest to having heard of such a person. He did, come to think of it, remember some Hammers from years back – they lived west, he was sure of it, Hammersmith way. Mr Blunt was sure these were not his Hammers and ignored him. He wondered about the tunnel that was rumoured to run beneath the building, stretching under the street and beyond. The idea of this subterranean network appealed to his devious nature. He wondered how one might get in.

CHAPTER TWENTY-THREE

'I've seen your lady friend,' said Miss Spragg to Jack, the next time she met him.

He gave just the reaction she had hoped for. 'Where?' said he, trying not to look as if he wanted to know too much, but failing entirely upon showing that he knew whom she meant. Miss Spragg smiled hideously at him, baring a graveyard of rotten pegs, making him want a stiff drink.

She had asked Jack about the charming companion he had brought so carelessly to her private residence in Blight Street; he was not forthcoming, of course (being loyal to Grace in that particular at least), but she hardly needed him to be. There had been a sighting of the family near Maidenhead yesterday; she'd had word of it this morning, and was quite sure the information was reliable.

'I'm sure there must be something you could help me with in return,' she said. 'There are a great many services a fine lad like yourself could offer a poor old woman such as me, all alone in the world.'

It is true to say that Miss Spragg has wide-ranging interests of a business kind. It is certain that many of these involve dirty work indeed. She has a good deal of use for a man like Jack, rough and ready, not too curious.

Maidie Robertson was thrilled to see the Hammers again and ran down the garden in her apron.

'We came back!' exclaimed Daisy, as if it was a surprise to her as well.

'Yes, here you are!' beamed Mrs Robertson. 'Come indoors and eat something.'

When the children had gone to play – 'Stay in the garden.' 'Yes, Ma.' 'Away from the river!' – the women sat down to talk.

'Now, dear, what are you up to?' said Mrs Robertson, sharp as a new pin.

So Grace recounted the whole story, omitting not the slightest relevant detail. 'And what do you plan to do now, dear?'

'Go back to London.'

'Whatever for?'

'To get shot of the necklace.'

'What will you do with the children?'

'Put them with a family I know in Harrow.'

'I think it would be best to leave them here with me.'

Grace thought this over in less than a minute, looking at Maidie Robertson. Then she gave her Landlord Nelson's money. 'I will,' she said. 'Stay away from the Orkney Arms down the river.'

'Good luck, dear.'

And so it was that Grace Hammer left her children, who didn't seem to mind much, in the care of kindly Maidie

Robertson early the next morning, kissing them on the way out, mist clinging round the boat as she glided across the water, oars lapping stealthily.

Two miles away, as the crow flies, in the charming Norman village of Halliford, Miss Emmeline Spragg was enjoying her breakfast alone in a private room at the Plough Inn. Chewing on her bacon she contemplated the day before her. When the plate was clean she pushed it aside and smoothed a tattered map upon the tablecloth. She reckoned on taking the towpath to Shepperton, to call in on the landlord of the Anchor, before cutting across country and up towards Maidenhead.

Grace had not been without the company of any, or all, of her children since the day she had had Charlie, and although she felt a pang of emptiness at the thought of them, she was surprised to find herself content to be alone. It was novel indeed to be so free, with no little voices asking for things, and she thought guiltily that she might not miss them as much as she had imagined – at least, not all of the time. A lonely moorhen regarded her, floating along like a tiny coracle a cautious distance away. With her mouth full of ham sandwich Grace's thoughts turned to London: shifting the necklace was a tall order in two weeks, never mind two days, which was all she planned to stay, three at the most. She must make some house calls. Suddenly the inside of her head seemed a vast and unfathomable place. Perhaps he was gone already. Perhaps she was getting in a knot about nothing. The moorhen watched her glide away, shrinking into the distance.

She made good progress, though the river twisted after a mile, writhing round innumerable bends. The boat was a lot bloody lighter without all the family but there was no Charlie to take a turn, so she tired after a few miles and slowed down, going with the current. As she drifted along, lost in thought, a ragged figure on horseback made its way along the towpath, coming towards her. The horse slowed and stopped. Grace recovered her arms and started to row again. As the boat slid by, two goblin eyes watched it go from behind a great bank of nettles.

Miss Spragg smiled grotesquely to herself, rubbing her spiny chin with glee. What a chance sighting! Grace Hammer, London bound. She noted with particular interest that her family were not with her. After a moment's pause she urged her horse on down the path, towards Maidenhead.

CHAPTER TWENTY-FOUR

Grace drifted into London like a ghost as 16 September was dawning. The filthy Thames was swathed in mist and a cold blue glow lit the riverbanks, bearing no apparent relation to the rays of any burning orb. How hot the sun must be, she mused, to light our every detail through the blanket of cloud that covered London, settled on it like a giant sleeping animal, with the bustling hardy people beneath, damp like rags. She saw them as she drifted past, catching glimpses through windows of private scenes, flashes of the street in the gaps between warehouses and loading bays, in perfect detail but misty like a dream.

At half past six she pulled the boat in under Eagle Dock. A lamp was burning in the office window above. She tied up beneath the jetty and scurried up the harbour steps. A furtive knock upon the door at the top of the stairs brought forth Big Roy Harman.

He was surprised to see the family were not with her and pleased the boat had not sunk. They had hot tea in chipped cups in his rickety office.

'Listen Roy,' she said. 'You haven't seen me.'

She set off down Cable Street. The pubs were filling and the bustle made her feel safe. She even stopped at the Queen for a shot of rum. She would chance a little look up Bell Lane first and pick up a few things, if the coast was clear.

Commercial Street was just the same, going on as normal. She wondered what she had expected. She stopped at Betsey's bake stall to buy treacle tart. Betsey had not been asked searching questions by any suspicious gentlemen – perhaps Grace was making a great meal of nothing. She turned cautiously into Bell Lane; nothing looked untoward.

As she approached her front door her stomach turned over. It stood ajar, just a crack; the lock was broken. She stopped still. And her heart, and the traffic. The city babble seemed to hold its breath. She crossed the street, and pushed the door open with shaking hands.

As if in a dream, the wreckage of her home and possessions spilled across the room before her like a burst tomato: the contents of every shelf and drawer strewn round the room. The coal bucket was upturned on the bed; splashes of black dust defaced the sheets; books lay like dead birds across the scene. And Daisy's best blue dress, torn like a rag.

The perpetrator of this chaos had withdrawn an hour ago, foul-tempered and bored of waiting, taking by way of compensation the pleasure of pissing on the wreckage and smashing her china as he left.

Grace took Daisy's dress, and the cricket bat, which Charlie had forgotten, being too busy helping the others.

It was Jack who had dropped her in it. Blunt had been suspicious when he had denied all knowledge of the Hammer family or, indeed, anyone who might help him find them: he had been rather too keen about it. And when he saw Jack again that very morning, knocking at a door in Bell Lane – which seemed to draw him back every day – he did not catch up and greet him, but kept a distance and went up after Jack had gone to see the door from which he had come. Through the window he spied a child's drawing on the wall: a ballerina, balanced on one pointed toe. The artist was evidently proud of her efforts – she had signed the picture with her name. 'Daisy Hammer', it said.

Jack, yawning and useless, with his handsome face, had shambled to the end of the street to sit in the Britannia and never noticed a thing.

Shaking, Grace made her way to the Frying Pan to see Horace Daley. The shock was engulfing her now. She wept hot tears, trudging away in the drizzle, feeling further than ever from her children, sick at the thought of their broken things. Up Thrawl Street she went, kicking herself all the way.

As she rounded the corner she glanced in through the window of the Frying Pan. And who should be in her favourite seat at that very moment but Mr Horatio Blunt himself. She froze mid-step, struck by lightning.

He was fully engaged in constructing a sandwich from a slice of sausage and a crusty roll and did not lift his head to see the stricken figure through the glass not ten yards away. (Had Mr Blunt known that the interest he took in feeding his fat gut had foiled him for the second time he might have indulged it a little less, and done a good deal better but, of course, there was no one to tell him.)

Grace pulled herself together as he raised the sandwich to his mouth and slid back round the corner, heart shrinking, pulse banging in her ears.

Big Roy Harman was not in his office but she found him in the yard breaking rocks for ballast. He sat her on a crate with a bucket of tea and listened to the tale that unfolded. When she had finished, he picked up his hammer and put a big lump of flint in his pocket. 'Let's see if he's still about.'

She followed him out of the yard feeling like a small child, hurrying after his giant strides. Crowds seemed to part like waves before him as they made their way up Osborn Street into Brick Lane.

Blunt was gone. Grace felt a sudden irrational panic that he might pop up behind her. After a few deep breaths this subsided, leaving the feeling that comes when a big spider you have been tolerating on the wall has vanished from the spot it has occupied for the last day or two.

'There's been a gentleman asking after you,' said Horace.

'I know,' she said. 'I saw him in my seat.'

'He's a nosy fellow. Started on about a secret tunnel. Reckoned he'd heard it went through my cellar.'

'What did you tell him?'

'I told him it was a fairytale. Now, let's get you out of sight.'

In the back room, after a nip with Horace (to start the day properly as he put it), she sized up her prospects. She must get her skates on. First to Canning Town, to call on a gentleman who was known to deal in especially shiny things. She would come back for the necklace if he was interested. She wasn't about to go running around with a twelve-carat ruby in her pocket on the off-chance.

As she crossed Brick Lane she came upon Trixie, who took her straight into the Alma. Grace sat in a corner seat and had another gin.

'Someone's looking for you,' Trixie said.

'I know. What did he say?'

'I haven't seen him myself but he's been all over asking.' She watched Grace swallow her gin. 'Who is he?'

'A nightmare.'

'I could help you with that.'

Grace skulked from the Alma with her hat pulled down and her face buried in her scarf, which looked a little odd, as it was a seasonable day. At the corner of George Street she clocked an old man filling his pipe. He wore a little green felt hat; she could swear he was watching her. Perhaps she imagined it. She glanced back at him, feeling eyes on her back, but he was tucking his tobacco into a pocket.

At every corner she held her breath, expecting to see Mr Blunt. It seemed as if everyone she knew was in the street at once this morning, stopping to greet her and ask where she had been; she kept conversation short, eyes darting up and down. Crossing Hanbury Street she bumped into Lily Dixon, with sweet williams today, deep pink, purple and white, like little friendly faces. On the next corner she walked smack into Mary Kelly, whom she had not seen for at least a month, and was engaged in unavoidable conversation, Mary being delighted to see her and interested in all the family news, as the Irish generally are. As they chatted Grace felt as though someone was aiming a gun at her; people seemed to look at her searchingly as they went past. After they had talked about the children, and what a shame it was they weren't out with her – Grace trying to chat without telling her anything much – Mary went on her way. Going up past the Jewish club Grace saw Nelly Holland but thought better of saying hello. Nelly talked too much to everybody. Grace liked her, though, and felt deceitful as she hurried past with her head down.

Mr Rubenstein, the gentleman who dealt in especially shiny things, was unavailable that afternoon. She made enquiries after him but was told nothing more helpful than that he was up west and not about for business until tomorrow. He was a private sort so she didn't push it. As she skulked back to the Frying Pan her mind drifted down the dank stairs beneath the trapdoor – she would take a look this evening, just to make sure.

Unhappily the back room was occupied when she returned – a private card game in progress. Thwarted, she retired upstairs to wait. Ten o'clock came and went, then eleven and midnight. Evidently the players had deep pockets. She fell asleep at last, in a warm bed. A tap at the door woke her. She sat bolt upright in the dark.

'Grace,' came a voice through the keyhole. It was Jack. She threw open the door and pulled him in.

Once the door was locked he was greeted with a long, enthusiastic kiss. 'I missed you, Jack,' she said.

'Where have you been?'

'Never mind that. Tell me what happened in the Britannia.'

She quizzed him thoroughly about what Mr Blunt had said, and everything else he knew, giving him no chance to ask where she had been. She watched his mouth as he talked. She had made resolutions that hadn't lasted past the first crooked smile before. She remembered this later as they pounced upon each other, urgently, with their matching lips, moonlit: making butterfly love. It was then that she began to sense Jack Tallis was a bad bet. Just a feeling. Not in the charming way she had first been attracted to, but darker altogether, something she couldn't explain.

Three miles away, in Bethnal Green, Mr Stanley shadowed Mr Blunt, following his every move. He had gone after him into the Camel and watched as he drank beer and leered at unfortunate girls. Before long he had one on his knee and was buying her gin. She looked much the worse for wear, but had most of her teeth and was charming enough. She said her name was Sally Ann.

CHAPTER TWENTY-FIVE

◆◆◆◆

Miss Spragg's goblin fingers stretched far across the country. She had tracked the progress of the Hammer family as far as Maidenhead, and had come in person, on the hearsay of an acquaintance who ran the Orkney Arms and would surely regret it if the journey should prove fruitless for her.

She had slithered into his pub the day before, startling the regulars.

Landlord Nelson had taken her through to the back and spilled what he knew, keen to send her on her way. She was more fearsome even than when he had seen her last, which was four years ago if not more. Her face was withered with lines, her evil soul drawn on it for anyone who could stand to look at her long enough. Her eyes were mean, her mouth a cavern of foul tombstones. Her back had hunched still further, and though she had shrunk, her sinister authority seemed to have grown.

She asked him about the children particularly, how old they were, the colour of their hair. It made Landlord Nelson's skin creep a little but he was soothed by a generous tip. He told her they had gone upriver towards Henley and that the bitch had stolen his takings practically from under his nose – the truth being that she had taken them from the drawer in his bureau, through the open window, and by the time he had noticed, it was the next day, given as he was to drinking alone after hours. They could be in Oxford by now, he told the goblin. He was keen to wring Grace Hammer's wretched neck himself.

For just a moment as she opened her eyes Grace wondered where she was. Her dreams had been busy and strange, playing the last few days over, twisting events in her head. She must take care of business and get back to the family.

And so under the trapdoor she went, trying not to brush against the damp walls. She set down her lamp and clapped her hands to chase away the spiders. The wall was dark and pockmarked with hollows and holes, black bricks stacked as if by some great subterranean insect. She counted seven from the corner, three from the top, and pulled one out. Then, telling herself she was a grown woman and ought not to take on so, she slid her cold hand in.

Her fingers groped blind into the dark space, crawled into the corners, panicked, frisked the bricks. She pulled them out and counted again, plunged her hand back into the hole, grasping at nothing.

In the back room, head in hands, she pieced together the awful truth. 'He must have come in at the other end.'

'No one's used that tunnel in fifty years,' said Horace, shaking his head.

'He was down there with me. I heard him.'

The blood seemed to stall in her veins, and then a strange current stirred it: like swelling poison, pumping through her magpie heart — and she knew she couldn't let him get away with it.

It took little more than a few calls upon various local acquaintances to find out that Mr Blunt had been enquiring after her whereabouts for the past fortnight or so, most often claiming to be a long-lost member of the family with news of a bequest to which she was entitled. Most of them, acquainted well enough to know that Grace had no distant wealthy relatives, had seen him off at the door. Mrs Crackit at the corner coffee house had been sweetly concerned that Grace might miss out, but had thought it best to confer with her personally before giving out her address. Grace reassured her that she had done right, and that there was no fortune, and tried to impress upon her as plain as she could that Mr Blunt was a dangerous man who was on no account to be entertained, if not in so many words. Poor nervous Mrs Crackit trembled visibly, eyes chasing over the door bolts, imagination running wild.

'Please don't worry yourself, Winifred,' Grace said, trying in vain to soothe her. 'He won't hurt you, he's looking for me.' Oh, God, that sounds all wrong, she thought.

At Mrs Jacob's door she felt a cold current. She told Grace that a Mr Belmarsh had called, but had nothing else particularly to say about him. She mentioned nothing about an inheritance. After an awkward pause Mrs Jacob asked after the children, affecting a casual air, betraying nothing. Grace left, wondering what she had told him and what enticement he had offered.

Now to call on Sally Ann. Sally would have seen him if he'd been about.

Back in St Giles Mr Blunt awoke from a deep stupor with a crippling headache. He had never had a hatchet buried in his head before but, he reflected as best he could, if he ever did it would surely feel very much like this. He could not recall coming back last night and had fallen asleep with his coat and hat on. There was blood on his cuffs, lots of it, dried in the fibres of the wool.

It took him several minutes to remember the events of the night before. As it flooded back to him he recalled the girl: her dress, her tattered bonnet; the pattern on the wallpaper; the ugly mole between her collarbone and her throat. When he had seen her he had wanted to take out all his rage upon her.

Sally Ann Dunn was the easiest target in the pub, if not the parish, born eager to please. She never turned a man down if he might buy her a drink. Adrift on that particular evening she had caught the piggy eye of Mr Blunt and it was not long before he had her full attention. Mr Blunt was not a charmer on his best days, but Sally Ann's perpetual stupor rendered her impervious to the dark cloud around him, his clenched fists and his furious contempt – boiling especially hot that evening. Sally had merely laughed as he raged drunkenly to himself, mistaking his growling for jest. She barely understood English, these days, if truth be told. Neither did she mind when he grabbed a handful of her breast or thigh, rough and spiteful, not once looking at her face. She had only grinned wider and leaned down for him to get a better view. It is no surprise, of course, that she took him back to her lodgings.

As they had left the pub Byron Stanley had drifted after them. He had last seen them on the corner of Commercial and Dorset Street, where he had vanished into the night, feeling suddenly afraid.

Once Mr Blunt had relived the full horror of the night before, he rose from bed and dressed, then proceeded to the nearest good coffee house where he devoured a cooked breakfast of eggs and bacon, with brown crusted bread and butter. He ate greedily, smacking his lips, spraying crumbs, as if he were at home by himself – causing his fellow diners to push their plates away and have coffee instead. He leered at the serving girl and goosed her when she came to clear the table. After settling his bill, he swaggered out. Luckily for him he never went there again, for she would certainly have seen him coming and spat in his gravy.

Grace found Sally Ann Dunn dead upon the bed, her throat slit. The blood had dried on the sheet to a brown-black colour and her body was pale and stiff. Grace stared for what seemed an age before she went near. Strange how shock is, she thought. Numb, like looking at pictures or through glass. She took a clean rag from the trunk and laid it upon Sally's dead face. Then she left quietly and went to sit by the riverside. She had known this would happen one day, and it seemed to her that, regrettably, death was in most instances a relief for the lost girl. She pictured Sally Ann's blue eyes, bloodshot and innocent, her rotten grin, and remembered the day she had broken her teeth on the kerb outside the Ten Bells, getting up without a care and, finding one still intact in the gutter, shoving it back into its bleeding socket and heading inside for a gin. Grace wished she could float Sally's corpse on the Thames and set it alight.

Daisy and Billy would be inconsolable. She would not tell them the whole awful truth and hoped they would not find out. Neither would she alert the police: she had been wily enough thus far in her career to avoid their attention altogether, unknown at the local station, a rare position for a London criminal. The children had followed her shining example in maintaining the clean family slate – no hasty risks must be taken. But there were no friends who might call by to discover Sally's corpse and raise the alarm, and she couldn't leave her until the landlord came on Friday. She decided to keep an eye open, and if Sally Ann was not found by Tuesday, she would drag her outside in the small hours of Wednesday morning and leave her in the street.

After reflecting on the harsh and comfortless life of Sally Ann Dunn, Grace rose from her spot by the river, where the mudlarks scratched through the stinking rubbish at low tide for any scrap they might sell. One had found a rusty trowel and was holding it up triumphantly for all to see, which was not what he might have done had he thought more about it. Several vagabond figures, flapping in ragged shirtsleeves like demented ravens, were making their way across the prehistoric landscape towards him.

As she turned down George Yard she saw the green felt hat again and marched straight up to him with her chin jutting. 'Why are you with me wherever I go?' she said.

'Are you looking for a large, ruddy man, with old-fashioned clothes and a cruel sneer for a smile?' said Mr Byron Stanley.

'I might be.'

'Come with me.'

The curious little man in the green hat proved to be divine intervention. He was a member of the Whitechapel Vigilance Committee, active since the murders had begun that summer. He had trailed Horatio Blunt all week and seen him break down her door.

They skulked to the White Hart and into the corner seat where he gave Grace full details of Mr Blunt's every movement and with whom he had spoken. Apparently he had spent the day drinking in Whitechapel before falling asleep on a bench in St Mary's graveyard. He had not called on anyone about business, or made any move to leave London. Grace shrank back in her seat. A cold hand crept round her heart. Mr Blunt might have his necklace but he was not satisfied yet. She made plans to meet Byron Stanley the next day, for further intelligence.

A moment of clarity visited her that evening as she drank tea at Mrs Cherry's table, with Tom on her lap; he was much better now, and heavy. There is no way round it, said the tiny voice at the back of her head. You must kill Mr Blunt or the game will never end. Sally Ann's dead face swam before her. She knew who to ask as well.

Grace cursed herself for her weakness, the glitter in her

stupid eyes. What had she made of her fortune? The ruby was a useless trophy, a forgotten thing under the floor – as good as if she had thrown it away. It seemed to matter less than Daisy's torn dress.

London has always been brown and grey, not least in autumn. In warmer months it wears the colours you could swear had never been there – purple, yellow and blue – in crevices and cracks, sprouting forth again to blossom in the city. From October until March, London Town is bleak and unrelenting, a gloomy place where the poor never get properly dry or warm. The sky is dark, the work is hard, the going heavy. And so life in Whitechapel rolls on, people battling against the elements, scuttling between the damp buildings, brick towers slick with rain, blank cracked windows staring. The poor witless souls who had caroused away the summer with their bar-fellows – as if the warmth and ease would last for ever – were caught without a bed, like last year, trying to keep warm without a coat.

Out in the countryside Mrs Robertson and the Hammer children ate apple pies, shot rabbits and read a great many new books. They taught Daisy to spell complicated words, such as 'octopus', which she would surely never have occasion to write but which were nice to know.

Down by the river, Mrs Robertson was calling Jake for his bath. She had a great tub of warm, soapy water waiting for him and had determined to wash him thoroughly. Daisy had been scrubbed already and was drying before the stove, savouring the aroma of rabbit stew, her maiden kill.

'Jake! *Jake!*' called Maidie Robertson, to no avail.

At the bottom of the garden Jake Hammer crouched in a space between the hedge and a gnarled wisteria that grew into the pear tree above. In his hand a twelve-carat ruby, swinging on its sparkling chain, caught the last rays of sunlight, flashing red stars across his face.

CHAPTER TWENTY-SIX

The next morning Grace went looking for Miss Trixie May Turner, and found her carousing in the Horn of Plenty, as she scurried in with her hat jammed down and her scarf round her face as if she was freezing. She grabbed Trixie and took her to the back room.

Of course, Trixie was ready to oblige. She knew just the man, she said, to help Grace with her difficulties. He was certainly experienced, and though he was not cheap she would pay on dispatch. And, yes, she was confident that he would have no trouble with the task in hand, notwithstanding the size and ferocity of the problem. Grace gave a thorough description of the subject, her account of his movements, and departed for the Cherrys', leaving Trixie to take care of the rest.

To Landlord Nelson's horror Miss Spragg had decided to make the Orkney Arms the base for her investigations, having no further intelligence, and had been with them now for two nights, with no talk of her departure. He began to wish he had never told her anything. Mercifully she was out for most of the day, returning at nightfall to disconcert his customers. He served her in her room, whenever possible, to the effect that he had become a slave to her every whim. His wife continued to bellow at him from upstairs, causing the company to feel sorry for him, though they did not like him much, and to wonder how an invalid might be so loud. Of course, his wife told Landlord Nelson that he should take the situation in hand and turn the goblin out, but how could he explain why he couldn't seem to do it? If she was on her feet, his wife told him, she would have seen her off by now. Why was he so weak and lazy? As she berated him he watched her lips move, hearing not a word, while he wondered how it was that he had ended in servitude to two witches, and wished that she were dead.

Miss Spragg detested the countryside and was unhappy to find herself there for longer than she had hoped. There was no word from London, and no sign of the children, though she fancied she could smell them on the breeze. Her colleague had made a definite sighting and he swore blind they had departed west. After searching some way up the river she had tired of horseback and the mixed welcome she was receiving at her door-to-door enquiries, and had decided, quite correctly, that they must have gone back beyond Maidenhead together. This enraged her, and made her saddle sores worse.

The next day she rode back the other way. Taking the west bank of the river she reached Bray, where she started her furtive enquiries again. The houses were fewer for the next hour and she made rapid progress.

It must be noted that Miss Spragg was unlikely to have

much luck by this strategy, on account of her dreadful coun-
tenance, which made people recoil, some more visibly than
others. One or two slammed their doors as soon as they
saw her, or even screamed. No one claimed to have seen
the family she described.

Emmeline Spragg knew they were along this stretch of
the river – she had seen the mother near Laleham, with her
own eyes, and all alone. She urged her horse onward with
a vicious slap, making such good time over the next few
miles that she resolved to push on to Chertsey and cross
the river there, going back on the other bank. Little did she
know how close this would bring her, scowling in the drizzle
at the milestone.

Trixie sat at her dressing-table, brushing her hair. She had
decided she was finished with Mirabel Trotter. She had
managed to avoid her for two weeks or more and shuddered to think of her now. And she had hatched a tidy
plan involving the office safe and the dancing key that
she had seen at her last visit to Mirabel Trotter's grand
residence. The problem was the need of an accomplice:
she herself would have to be prominent somewhere else,
in public, with a sound alibi – and she could think of no
one who would dare to break and enter the Trotter house.
It occurred to her now that this Blunt fellow might pave
the way. Burglary was his trade, after all, and he knew
nothing of Mirabel Trotter's reputation. Trixie might kill
two birds with the one stone. Suppose Mirabel was at
home, she thought, perchance with her sons, who knows
what might occur? She might save Happy Harry Harding's

fee for one thing – and if Jack could happen along after the rumpus had died down, to find the house unsecured, that would be most timely.

The very next day Trixie tracked down Mr Blunt and was ready to meet him as he turned up in the Frying Pan. Acquainted most thoroughly with the facts, she recognised her target at fifty paces and affected appropriate non-chalance, positioning herself next to where he would land at the bar. It did not take her long to strike up conversation. Within ten minutes they had moved through to the back room, with the kind permission of Horace Daley. They smoked Havana cigars and just a little opium. She needed the help of a certain type of gentleman, as she put it to him over several gins and a hand of twenty-one.

The job seemed simple enough; indeed, he was wondering whether he would bother with it at all when Trixie said something that made him prick up his ears, not in connection with the business at hand but some chatter in which she knew he would have no interest.

She was not daft and knew perfectly well that she would have to bait him with something, and so, with the casual air of the born liar, she dropped her 'very dear friend' Grace Hammer's name. She saw the lights flicker behind his eyes, which had been glazing over just a moment before.

An hour later she had furnished him with certain information, pertaining to the layout of the Trotter residence at Shoreditch: how he might gain entry, where he would find the safe and the key.

★

Jack was sitting in the Saracen's Head when Trixie walked in with news. 'You'll never guess what I know,' she challenged him.

'No, but I'll wager it's something good by the look on your face.'

She sat down across the table from him, rather pleased with herself.

'Well?'

'I've a nice little job for you.'

They huddled into a booth and she told him what he needed to know about the Shoreditch house and its secret treasures. He was to go at ten o'clock sharp, Thursday next. On Thursdays the rent collections were made, rounds that stretched from Hoxton to the river, and from there to Mile End, and by evening the safe would be fit to burst. After scaling the back wall, he must follow the side of the building round to the garden door. He would find it open.

Jack was reluctant, to say the least. 'The Trotter house? You must be off your rocker. I'd sooner pull my own teeth.'

'Listen to me. Mirabel Trotter will be accounted for. Did you think I hadn't thought of it? You insult me, Jack.' Here she shot him a reproachful look, tinged with hurt, to show how wounded she felt at his faithlessness. 'Now, then. I've got a girl on the inside – her name doesn't matter. She'll leave the door unlocked and take care of the diversion. All you've to do is empty the safe. Don't you mind anything else.'

He was schooled thoroughly in the arrangement of the

rooms, and where to find the safe, and the key. He assured her he could do without it in any event. He was taught to pick locks at his grandfather's knee. Then they drank gin as though they would die tomorrow and sang into the night.

Of course Trixie did not tell him the whole story. She did not feel the need to disclose the fact that Mr Blunt would also be visiting the premises that evening. With the benefit of her careful planning, she regarded it as an irrelevance. If Jack went at ten sharp, she reckoned, all attention would be elsewhere. She would meet him an hour later, at eleven o'clock, at Liverpool Street, whence she would get out of town for a day or two.

Out in the country Daisy woke from a bad dream and sat with Maidie Robertson by a low, glowing fire, listening to *Alice's Adventures in Wonderland*. As they turned the page a sharp knock came at the door. They looked at it.

'Go and get in with Charlie upstairs and bolt the door, Daisy,' said Maidie Robertson, very quietly. Daisy had heard her mother talk like this and did as she was told without question.

Mrs Robertson went to the front door and opened it, feigning sleepiness. 'Who's there?' she asked, blinking as if confused. The cloaked figure on the doorstep turned to the lamplight, casting a faint glow upon the creature inside the dark hood. Miss Spragg, the goblin creature, flashed her most hideous grin. Unsettling enough to behold in the broad daylight, looking as she did like a ghoul from a dark fairytale, never mind in deep shadow on the doorstep, she gave Maidie Robertson quite a turn; but she composed herself, and smiled politely.

'I am so sorry to wake you at this hour,' said the cloaked horror, in an oily voice, and it was as if a cold wind had swept in at the door. The hairs stood up at the back of Mrs Robertson's neck. 'I am leading a local search for a woman believed to be at large in this parish. She may be in the company of some unfortunate children whom she claims are her own, going by the name of Hammer. We are seeking them most urgently or any information relating to their whereabouts.'

There followed an impressive silence as Maidie Robertson looked suitably overawed, as she supposed typical country folk would to a city rat, but said not a word, as if dumb-struck.

Miss Spragg grew impatient and pushed for more. 'This woman is a dangerous criminal, holding them to ransom. Their poor parents are naturally distraught. May I ask if you might have seen any such party passing by this way?'

As she spoke her cold black eyes wandered into the cosy room. She had assumed that country people were simple creatures, used only to hoeing and reaping and other such agricultural pursuits, and did not suppose they would doubt her ludicrous story for a moment.

Maidie Robertson, of course, saw through her straight away. 'Well, goodness me, no,' she said. 'What a terrible thing. I've seen no one out of the ordinary. How many are they?'

'Four,' said the goblin. 'Three boys and a girl. The little

girl has golden hair.' She looked along the top of the bureau, her eyes like mice crawling over each object, the china cat, the pansies, a teacup.

'No, I've seen no such family about, no one at all. But perchance my sons have. I could wake them if you'd like, though they've been working in the fields all day.'

Miss Spragg's eyes landed on a blue satin hair ribbon on the floor. 'No. That won't be necessary,' she said. 'Thank you kindly for your trouble.'

After she'd left Maidie Robertson made fast all the windows and doors, which she was unaccustomed to doing. She packed a carpet bag with a few clothes, Daisy's hairbrush, a bar of soap and a revolver, and put it by the door. She planned to rise at dawn with the family and call upon Mr Mullins at the farm, who would be up milking.

Miss Spragg rode directly to the next village where, though it was the middle of the night, she found a light burning and banged on the window. She brought forth a disgruntled farmer who quieted upon seeing her and duly obliged with a room till morning. After sleeping but three hours she rose and went out into the dawn mist, certain to find help in the form of a sturdy man, as everyone, in her considerable experience, had their price.

She happened upon him just ten minutes later at the edge of the village, herding cows into the milking shed, a large dull fellow in a brown cloth cap. When she waved money under his nose he was interested enough to listen, though it required a good effort as he was quite stupid. Not fully understanding the finer points of the goblin's plan, but grasping enough to know that it did not involve murder and that he was to be richly rewarded, he found himself saddling a horse and leaving the cows to wander in their field. They started back towards Laleham, to the little house by the river.

CHAPTER TWENTY-SEVEN

◆◆◆

Sneaky Jake Hammer woke early, and went about the house quietly on his own, as he liked to do when the opportunity arose, pretending for his own amusement that he had no family and was alone in the wide world. He pulled on his boots and ventured outside to look at the horses over the way. He had reached the garden hedge when he caught the sound of hoofs coming up the lane. They stopped some way off and he peered out cautiously. Two figures on horseback were talking: one pointed down the lane, a small withered figure in a ragged cloak – clearly a wicked witch – waving a crooked arm towards the house.

Jake fled back up the garden path, heart racing, flinging himself inside the door and slamming it as the riders approached the house. It was only as they drew level with the hedge that he saw them. And it was then that he saw Daisy, wandering down the path, picking rosehips. As she reached the end, beyond which she knew she wasn't to go, two horses stopped outside the gate.

Looking up she saw a surly man, and another creature such as she had only seen in nightmares, wizened and bent, with black eyes. Frightened, she backed towards the house and at that moment Jake opened the door and tore down the path shouting to her to run inside. She turned, and the man was off his horse, up the path and grabbed her. She did well to kick him in the shins with the heels of her boots, struggling as he hauled her up and away. Within a moment they were gone.

Maidie Robertson might have been an old lady but she was on the neighbour's horse directly, hard down the road the way they had left. Charlie followed her with the farmer not five minutes behind. They met at the crossroads, looking desperately for signs of which way to follow, and decided to split up and ride for two miles, then to turn back if nothing was found, converging again at the milestone.

Twenty minutes later they were all headed for Datchet, where they refreshed their horses. Mrs Robertson went into the inn to ask the barmaid while the men made enquiries around the square. Little did she know that Daisy was but a few feet away, through the floor. They had caught up with the goblin and her dull henchman, hiding in the cellar of the Bird in Hand.

Unluckily it was the landlady who had put up the strange party earlier that morning, before retiring to bed with a crashing headache, leaving the poor barmaid with all the cleaning to do and strict instructions not to disturb her on any account. Miss Spragg had presented herself alone, and while her visage had alarmed the good landlady at first sight, she would take anybody's money and so, although she had no decent accommodation left, she had offered the base-ment room behind the beer cellar, referred to among her

248

family rather aptly as the dungeon, having been the object of threats made to her naughty children when they were young.

It was small and damp, with one tiny window that looked out at ground level on to the yard and admitted so little light that the room must be lit with a greasy oil-lamp that hung from the joists above, if the occupant was to see anything at all. She had expected the wizened creature to refuse it, but, seeming perfectly content with the arrangement – if such a thing could be expressed upon such a face – she explained that she had been riding all night and needed to rest.

Once installed in the dungeon she had smuggled in her accomplice with Daisy, distracting the good landlady by requesting a clean blanket, which should have aroused her suspicion, but only irked her. She had gone upstairs to suffer in bed as her girl arrived for work and no one was any the wiser.

After exhausting their enquiries the search party moved on to the next village. Daisy heard hoofs above but didn't dare scream; she wondered if she would be rescued soon, if she might escape.

The search party were still out when a ransom note fell through the door of Mrs Robertson's cottage, brought expressly by a village youth who was happy to be woken by a strange hag with a sovereign, having recovered from the initial shock. Billy read the note. It demanded the surrender of the family spoils for the safe return of their little girl. No one but Jake had any idea what this might mean, though Billy was sure it had something to do with his mother. The old lady was to show herself, alone, at the crossroads at Hythe End, at precisely half past six that evening, to deliver the treasure. Until the matter was settled they would not see Daisy alive. They were urged not to play games or test the resolve of her captors.

Poor Jake fetched the necklace from under the wisteria. Now he understood what the game was about. He was sure that everything was his fault. Billy swallowed his horror as he was presented with the treasure, flashing in the sunlight; blood red stars across his face. They waited for news, together on the stairs, the door locked and bolted, the windows barred.

Daisy was bearing up well during her dreadful ordeal – she was a plucky little thing. Her captors had not hurt her but she believed their terrible threats and dared not shout for help. Luckily she had faith in her eventual rescue, trusting in divine justice, as small children tend to do, bravely, with no proof at all of such a phenomenon. The large dull fellow in the brown cloth cap paid her little attention, having chained her by the foot to the rusted iron bedstead. To Daisy's relief the witch had been out for an hour or more, leaving her under his watchful eye. So, there they lurked, in silence, behind the barrels, the little girl with her back to the wall, eyes wide, expecting the witch to appear again at any moment, perhaps from thin air.

Until that day Daisy had believed that such creatures existed only in fairy tales – Now she could see for herself that they lived outside the pages of Grimms' *Tales* and walked among us in the real world. She wanted to cry but dared not. The hours crawled past. If only Ma or Charlie would come.

Charlie was in a desperate state. They had had no lead of any kind, and he was beginning to grasp the futility of their efforts. At four o'clock he sent Mrs Robertson back to Laleham to see if the boys had heard anything, and pushed on for an hour or so with Farmer Mullins. At Slough he stopped suddenly. He looked as though he would throw himself upon the stones and cry his heart out. He knew he must turn back.

'Come on, lad,' said good Farmer Mullins, speaking his very thoughts. 'They can't have come this far. Let's go back by Wraysbury and search from there. You must eat as well or you'll be of no use to her.'

Indeed Charlie was weak with hunger, though he would refuse to eat until he found his sister. They started back along the road.

Miss Spragg's hired help was wavering in his resolve; in truth, he was not altogether comfortable taking young children from their mother, and the more time he spent with the woman the more distasteful he found her, especially now that she had returned and they were shut up in the same small room together. He could almost feel the chilly malevolent cloud that hung in the air, as she flicked her little black lizard eyes back and forth, smiling nastily every now and then at some dark, private thought. The girl, who refused to tell her name, was a sweet creature and he meant her no harm; neither did he want his wages now. He could see how frightened she was and tried to give her secret looks – though there was no chance she might trust him – wanting to cheer her a little.

Though he might seem to have had a good heart, he fell short of overpowering Spragg, as he could easily have done, and rescuing the little girl; he was a weak man who wanted no trouble with the law. The sentiment made him feel better about his part in the affair nonetheless, and so he watched her keeping quiet in the corner, praying for deliverance.

He had reckoned without Daisy's special resolve and, indeed, her new skills. She had forgotten nothing her sneaky brother had taught her and had already pilfered the key to the padlock that chained her foot to the bed. She had taken it from Cloth Cap's pocket when he brought her meagre supper – so neatly that he never suspected a thing. She tucked the key under the edge of the damp rug she sat upon and there it remained all afternoon. She kept quiet and resisted the urge to piss, as she would have had to ask Cloth Cap to unlock her for that. The witch had instructed him not to do so under any circumstances, but in her absence this morning he had taken pity and smuggled Daisy outside to spend a penny. This small kindness would prove to be his undoing, which would serve him right.

Charlie and Farmer Mullins had intended to return by a different route, thus widening the scope of their search, but the hand of Fate and the winding anonymous lanes sent them back again by Datchet, a circumstance they considered unfortunate, which, of course, was not so. They stopped to water the horses in the square and Farmer Mullins, a faithful companion indeed, persuaded Charlie to take a beer in the Bird in Hand, with a whisky to follow.

Now, the good landlady of the Bird had recovered her health and come down to the bar to make ready for the evening. As they had made their enquiries here already, it seemed futile to ask her but Charlie thought it worth a try. 'I wonder if you might help me, Madam,' said he, his face desperate, his voice shaking as she filled his jug. 'I'm looking for my sister who was snatched early this morning. She is a pretty little thing, just five years old, with blue eyes and fair hair. Might you have seen her?'

'You poor dear, how dreadful!' said our good lady, sympathy swelling in her heart. 'I'm afraid I've seen no children all day long. I've been upstairs with my lumbago, which gives me such distress. You must be frantic.'

'She is likely in the company of an old woman, a rather fearsome creature, if the truth be told. I haven't seen her myself but I understand she is short and wizened, dressed in ragged black and resembling, according to my young brother who is the only witness, a crone from Grimms' *Tales*, though you may allow for some exaggeration on his part.'

Now the landlady had never heard of Grimms' *Tales*, having no interest in books, but she knew immediately whom Charlie was talking about. Unfortunately she had more loyalty to Miss Spragg than to Charlie, having taken her money this morning with the promise of a handsome bonus if she was left in peace; this now served the purpose Miss Spragg had intended. Had our good lady actually seen the child with her guest she might have given Charlie a different answer, but as she had not, she persuaded herself that it could not be the same woman, after all.

'I'm afraid I've seen no such person,' she told him. Charlie sank into his beer, a picture of despair. Farmer Mullins put a strong arm round his shoulder.

'Excuse me,' piped up a sweet female voice. It belonged to a mousy girl named Alice Beakey, who had a habit of picking up on other people's conversation, which on this occasion would prove to be a virtue. 'I believe I have seen the woman you describe so vividly, riding out this morning. It gave me quite a turn to see her face! She was all alone, but I'm sure she must have been the one you're looking for. I don't expect there's another with such a fearsome appearance in the whole of England, or anywhere else for that matter. Is she a criminal? She certainly looks it! Might she be dangerous, do you think?'

Now, Miss Beakey is a lonely soul, due in the most part to her habit of talking too much, if given the opportunity, and asking rather too many questions. If she had looked hard enough at herself she would have found that her interest in disclosing what she knew had as much to do with involving herself in the affair as helping to find any lost children. Indeed, her information was of limited value, stopping short at the edge of the village, where she had been surprised by the goblin while picking wild celery. She had seen neither where the mysterious hag had come from nor where she had gone.

But her noisy chatter had prompted someone else's memory: a Miss Bunn had seen no fearsome crones, but had noticed a dull-looking fellow in a brown cloth cap this morning, with a small fair girl she had not recognised as being from the village. They had been behind the outhouse of the inn. He had looked about him in a rather surreptitious manner, she had remarked to herself at the time, and, now she thought of it, had definitely seemed to be up to no good. The question of why she had thought to do nothing more than watch out of the window and feel suspicious was passed over.

By now the blacksmith's wife had joined in; she, too, had seen the dull fellow in the brown cloth cap, though she could have sworn it was blue. It was possible he may have taken a room in the village, but certainly none of hers. She said she would ask about, and sent her daughter to see if the Beehive had taken in any latecomers last night.

Maidie Robertson was on her way to Hythe End, alone, as the ransom note demanded. She had no time to find Charlie and Farmer Mullins. She carried a twelve-carat ruby necklace and a Colt revolver, concealed in her skirts.

Downstairs the goblin had fallen asleep on the mildewed bed, her evil breath rasping in her throat. Daisy closed her eyes. She heard Cloth Cap shift in his seat. He sighed heavily, kicked at the chair-leg and scratched. Then, after a few minutes of huffing and fidgeting, he rose and approached the bed. Daisy peeped through her eyelashes, her heart pounding. He was standing over the witch, his face a picture of distaste, as if he were regarding a mighty spider on the wall. Daisy wondered what he was up to — afraid, yet glad of any disruption to her appalling circumstances. She felt as if she had been there, under the ground, for ever, though she knew it couldn't have been more than a day.

In fact, he was not preparing to kill the witch in her sleep, as Daisy supposed, merely assessing the depth of her slumber. Her mouth hung open; he could almost see the poisoned vapour that passed for her breath, hanging in the air like a toxic particular. Her skin seemed flayed from a corpse, pale and dirty, as if she had been dug up from cursed ground. She was asleep, all right. He had been instructed to stay out of sight and to wake her at six, but thirst overcame him and he could not bear to remain in that hole a moment longer. He decided that one jar and a few minutes couldn't hurt. She need never know. A glance at the little one confirmed her asleep as well, so he removed his cap and combed his hair, in an effort to disguise himself, then crept out, locking the door behind him.

Daisy did not waste one second. She knew he might be back directly and that this could be her only chance. Her little fingers shaking, she unlocked the padlock and unwound the chain from her leg, slowly, so it made no noise, though she wanted to throw it off and run. The witch stirred. Daisy held her breath, her heart bursting in her chest. She freed herself at last and made her way on tiptoe to the tiny window. Silently, silently, she lifted the chair and put it below the sill, stealing a glance back at the bundle of rags upon the bed. As she stepped on to it, the chair creaked. She screwed up her little face, frozen, but the witch snored on. She reached up and tried the window latch. It wouldn't budge – having rusted together years before. She tried it harder, to no avail.

Daisy Hammer wanted to cry and scream but with an iron will she resisted this urge. As far as she knew there was no one to hear her: no sound came through the flagstones above – she wondered if the witch had turned the people to stone. She must save herself. At that moment she noticed that Cloth Cap had left his rifle behind. It was leaning innocently against the doorframe, as if waiting for an omnibus.

It seemed that the entire village had passed through the Bird in Hand, adding to the conjecture the possibility that Miss Trebor, who was due back from town at six, had taken them in, or that they were hiding in Mr Piggot's derelict outhouse. At the end of the bar skulked Cloth Cap, bare-headed, ears burning. He sneaked a glance at the boy, the farmer's arm round his shoulder: he looked as though he would drown himself in his jug. A guilty heartstring twanged in Cloth Cap's chest. Louder still was his self-interest. He was a spineless fellow, who would fail to redeem his sins on this occasion. Abandoning Daisy to her fate, he slipped away into the night.

Mrs Trent, the butcher's wife, arrived; after confirming she knew nothing of a dull fellow in a cloth cap, brown or blue, she offered the theory that the kidnappers were hiding in the woods behind the village. Lively speculation followed among the throng, which was perhaps fifty strong now. They were preparing a search party when the rabble was silenced by a gunshot from downstairs.

The last thing that Miss Emmeline Spragg saw was her small, fair-haired prisoner levelling a rifle at her head. She had been woken by the click as Daisy cocked it, and in the scant time she had to reflect before Daisy blew a fatal hole in her head she remarked to herself how well the child handled it – how inventive to have propped the heavy barrel upon the bedstead! – and wondered where she had learned such a skill.

Charlie was down there directly – Farmer Mullins putting the door through with one good boot – and swept his little sister into his arms, where she cried as though she would drown him in tears. Wrapped in a blanket she went home on the front of Mrs Robertson's horse, as Charlie and Farmer Mullins scoured the town for the mysterious dull fellow, who had left his brown cloth cap behind him. He was never seen again, even though they traced him back to Canker Farm. He had simply melted into thin air.

Our good landlady was left to clean the goblin's brains from the wall, after which she barred the doorway, vowing never to use the room again. A week or two later she opened it once more to desperate guests, who found it impossible to pass the night there; they were woken in the early hours by a sinister rattling sound, accompanied by a curious smell.

CHAPTER TWENTY-EIGHT

◆◆◆◆

In London Grace was blissfully ignorant of all the carry-on. She found herself hankering after Jack, having laid low in an upstairs room at the Frying Pan for the last couple of days. Trixie had seen him at the Commercial tavern and said he had asked after her, though Grace did not know if this was true.

Unknown to Grace, Jack the Lad was in St Giles, away from his East London haunts and the usual crowd, constructing his own plan for that night. Since Trixie had proposed the Shoreditch robbery, he had been wondering what the catch might be. No one in East London was honest: if they were, they wouldn't survive. Deceit was a way of life from Aldgate to Mile End, and no one held it much against their fellows. Surely there was something more to be had from this venture, he thought. This might be considered greedy or enterprising on Jack's part, according to one's point of view: the safe would certainly contain a tidy pile of cash on a Thursday evening.

Jack was going out to do the job, as intended, except that he had decided to leave an hour early. He had not consulted Trixie and he did not mean to share the proceeds. In fact, he planned to get out of town himself for a day or two, before she had a chance to catch up with him. He arrived at the house in Shoreditch and scaled the wall behind the magnolia tree.

After a quiet moment, listening, sheltered from view in the bushes, he crept out and crossed the lawn. Crouching below the level of the windows he sneaked a look inside, round the edge of the curtain, to see the darkened study, light from the hall leaking in through the chink in the doorway. He crept round to the garden door, taking a crowbar from his belt. To his surprise it was already open.

The clock had just struck nine when Mirabel Trotter heard the first creak on the stair. She had drunk half a bottle of cognac and fallen asleep in front of the fire in her drawing room some three hours ago. It sobered her immediately, as if a bucket of cold water had been thrown over her head. She gripped the poker that was still in her hand and turned towards the door. Someone was creeping very quietly up the stairs.

She rose from her chair slowly, crossed the room, graceful as a prima ballerina, and positioned herself behind the door. The footsteps reached the landing and paused. Not a sound but the clock. Then a tiny creak, directly outside, which made her jump. Seconds passed as the intruder listened at the door. Mrs Trotter held her breath. Then the handle turned slowly as somebody tried it, rattling softly.

Mrs Trotter gripped the poker ever tighter as a key turned

in the lock and the door opened. A dark furtive figure sniffed his way over the threshold and was met by an iron bar, glancing across his head, followed by a small hatchet that she ever kept upon her person. She was not one to mess about and she realised immediately that she had never seen this person in her life before and was ready to swear to it. Her sons were downstairs, smoking and playing cards, but she hardly needed them. She laid about the intruder until he stopped moving. Then she wiped her face with the back of her butcher's arms and stood panting and sweating in the darkness.

The cries had brought the Trotter men forth from the kitchen and hurled them up the stairs. They found their ma dripping with sweat and gore. She put down the poker. 'We'd best tidy up,' she said.

It took Mirabel Trotter, one of her burly sons (the other was faint at the sight of blood) and two men from the yard to clear up the terrible scene and restore order to the room. They took up the carpet and burned it in a brazier outside, an expensive silk carpet with an elephant-foot pattern, in deep red and black, that had come all the way from Afghanland. They took the dead man downstairs in a sack, with a cloth round his oozing head, and dumped him by the back door. Then they returned with a horse and cart and dragged him off to Canning Town, where they chopped him into several pieces with a bandsaw. Mrs Trotter rewarded them all with a handsome bonus.

The first London heard of the violent demise of Horatio Blunt was the baying of dogs as his remains were dispatched to the swine and the canine fraternity in Mrs Trotter's Mile End yard the next morning.

Jack had crept in through the open garden door and, finding the drawing room opposite, had ventured inside. He found the bureau without trouble and set to searching the tiny drawers. He found everything as Trixie had said it would be.

He had the key and was congratulating himself, before turning his attention to the safe, when the door swung open silently and in came Miss Craven, who was not afraid of bumps in the night. She held up a rifle as he swung round and pointed it at his head. He dropped the crowbar and put his hands in the air.

Miss Craven was the type who would kill an intruder without losing sleep at night. She would have shot this stranger without hesitation if not for the fact that the trigger had jammed. She braved it out, advancing towards him slowly with the barrel aimed between his eyes, while he wondered why she did not shoot and then concluded, quite correctly – though not in the way he thought – that she couldn't. In a second he was across the floor and had grabbed the gun by the barrel, swinging it round and down on her skull like a thundercrack. She fell to her knees and Jack hit her again, so violently that her glass eye popped out of its socket and rolled under the bureau, where it stared indignantly at his boots.

With his heart bursting in his mouth, he fumbled with the key, twisting it into the lock. A thick pool was forming around Miss Craven's head, stretching across the floor to his feet. His hands shook. He opened the safe door to see great wads of notes, rolled round with black rubber bands. At that moment he heard a dreadful wailing shout that shook the house and came so suddenly that he almost jumped out of his skin, heart pounding as if he was winning the Derby. It frightened him even more than murdering Miss Craven. He looked down at her – the blood had reached his boots, and the screaming had stopped upstairs. There was just a whimpering, like someone's last breath. Footsteps came hurrying up from below. Jack took to his heels and ran.

Rumours spread round the district of a double murder, but died as quickly as they had begun. There was no mention of such an event in any newspaper, no front pages with lurid scenes and sketches of the house with the murder sites marked, not even in the *Daily News*. The Trotter fiend had tidied her mess well away. Jack held his breath for a day or two, hiding out in Shad Thames. The company was gruff and evil: hyena people congregating in dens below the street to watch dog-fights, drink meths. Jack fitted into this scene well, much better than his mother would have liked. He took to smoking opium, played cards, started to lose his mind. After a week he had become the colour of Limehouse itself, forgetting a little more each day about the world above.

Trixie, of course, true to her name, was nowhere about while all of this was going on. She breezed into town a day or two later, as if she knew nothing of it. She was, of course, privately furious at Jack's betrayal but decided to bide her time, for she was sure he was stupid enough to turn up again when he had spent the money, having underestimated her regard for loyalty. One benefit of this unplanned turn of events was that Miss Craven was out of the way for good. Trixie sent word to Grace that the deed was done, then ordered rack of lamb and more champagne.

Grace went home to set it straight. She picked up the scattered papers and books, threw away the broken plates; it was dusk by the time she had scrubbed everything. She waved at Mrs Jacob behind her twitching curtain as she tipped her dirty bucket down the gully.

'Grace,' came that voice down the street, like a ghost. A cocky dark shape in the shadow, and there he was, like the King of Arabia himself – unbelievable! – coming through the rain as if he had heard her thoughts calling. He walked up to her, dripping, with his ragged grin, and she let him in. In the morning he was gone. Perhaps it was best. She left with a spring in her step to collect the children.

Some fifty-two miles away, in the picturesque seaside town of Whitstable, Miss Rosalind Pinch was toasting her success. She peeped inside the carpet bag again, just to see that the money was still there. She giggled girlishly, exactly as she had the last time she looked, then lifted the brandy to her lips, thanking the good Lord once again for her heavenly luck. She set down the glass and perused the map, planning her agenda for tomorrow. Perhaps she would take a carriage and ride down the coast to Brighton, or maybe see a show. She put her feet on the table before her, sighed contentedly and lit a large Havana cigar.

CHAPTER TWENTY-NINE

✦✦✦✦

'I want to knock you into tomorrow and kiss you all at once, son.'

'Sorry Ma,' said Jake, hanging his head.

'Don't you sorry me, you tricky little bastard.'

'I won't do it again.'

'I expect you'll do as you please.' She wrapped her arms around him. Jake looked confused. 'What else are you up to that I don't know about. Eh?'

The family settled back as though they had never been away, but they talked of the country often and wrote letters to Maidie Robertson. If one of them came over quiet and gazed out of the window Grace knew they were dreaming of the riverside. One day soon they might move to the country for good, not so far, perhaps, from Mrs Robertson. She wouldn't tell them that for a while.

Charlie took his handsome face straight round to Elsie Brown's, his hands a little sweaty in his pockets, and they took up where they had left off. Daisy was happy to see her friends, though she wept for three miles after leaving her country home. When she asked where Sally Ann was, Grace said she'd gone home, back up north. Where was north? Far, she said – when she'd be back she couldn't say. It was hand-me-down Emily who told her, the very next day.

Daisy ran home with her little face tied in knots. 'Ma, Em said Sally had her head cut off. Did she, Ma?'

'No, my sweetheart, she didn't.'

'Is she dead, though?'

'Yes, she is, darlin'.'

It was back to business as usual in the district. Whitechapel had turned up no butchered women on its streets for three whole weeks, and started to breathe again, as easy as it ever did. Talk returned to hard luck and money trouble – even the papers had run out of things to say about the horrors. And then, at the end of September, just as the boys at the newsstands were shuffling their listless feet, two more were found, on the very same night.

The first was Busy Liz Stride, still warm, in a yard off Berners Street, outside the Jewish club, stirring Gentile outrage to fever pitch. It seemed the fiend has been disturbed at work; he hadn't done the full job on her. The second was slit from belly to throat, sewn together at the mortuary with thick black stitches like Frankenstein's monster. She had been gutted, her nose slashed, her eyelids cut – in your ears at every newsstand, shouted loud in the street. Every man, woman and child of the rotten East End talked of nothing else. Every stranger was suspect, each shadow hid a fiend, and terror lurked in every doorway, especially now night came early. The women went about in pairs, which made business tricky for the brasses. None had thought too much about the uselessness of their patrol companion in the event of trouble, being dependent on the meagre spoils of their only commodity, and for the most part having a heavy drink habit to drown. Some chose not to care.

Grace went to see Busy Liz Stride into the ground, holding Nelly Holland to keep her upright as she convulsed in loud, drunken sobs over the chaplain's voice and then stared numbly past the headstones, as if lost, most likely thinking about her next tipple. Grace thought about Sally Ann, and Polly, whose meagre funeral seemed so long ago now. The Whitechapel girls were disappearing one by one.

Grace was haunted sometimes by dark moments when she wondered if she knew the devil. Sometimes she dreamed of him coming, a dark shape at the end of a tunnel with the river behind him, and she tried to run, waking with a start. Not for the first time in her long life she counted the blessing that she did not turn tricks.

CHAPTER THIRTY

London clay makes yellow-grey bricks, the blocks that built the East End. If you venture to the finer parts of London you may find the Oxford clay, red and rich, moulded in intricate designs, floral patterns and curves; the houses stretch away in a straight matching line. How long will a brick last? A hundred years? Two hundred? Long after the building has bitten the dust if the mortar is not mixed right. To cut his costs, Mr Weevil of Norbury made his with too much sand, endangering the occupants of his cheaply built dwellings. It was a miracle indeed that those structures stood as long as they did before they fell down upon the sleeping heads of the people inside them. Mercifully they knew nothing of it, save old Mrs Tallis, who was smoking opium and did not care. Mr Weevil was chased out of the building game long ago and a factory stands on the site; and here, directed by a reliable friend, with a note of recommendation, Grace came to call upon a gentleman with the right connections. She stood at the back door, looking this way and that, chewing her lip as she waited for it to open, praying not to be robbed. Lady Stanhope's ruby necklace lay in her pocket, wrapped in a silk handkerchief.

Autumn had set in over London, the bitter wind was

blowing, the time of year when inmates of workhouse or prison were most glad of the shelter. It was dark by five o'clock. People huddled together; less chatter was heard in the street. Everybody drank more than usual, claiming it kept them warm on the way home, crowding into the pub needing comfort and good cheer. They found a hundred reasons not to leave just yet: it may have started to rain outside, say, or someone had come in whom they must see about business.

If the ruby weighed heavy in her pocket on the way out, it was a lump of lead on the way back: now she knew what it was worth. Enough to move to the country, all right. She scurried down Whitechapel Road, beneath the great walls of the hospital, the rows of dark windows watching her down in the street.

The buildings seemed to drop away at the crossroads and the vista opened out before her, the wide sweep of the thoroughfare and the darkening sky, and she breathed in the night air, intoxicated, standing on the corner gazing down Whitechapel Road. Perhaps she saw trouble coming, or Polly's ghost, in her new bonnet – who can know these things? – for she decided to turn off, down Thomas Street.

The Union Workhouse loomed at the end, dark and forbidding, to discourage the downtrodden. She shuddered at its gloomy façade, scowling down at her as if it would snatch her up with a stone hand and pull her in through the barred windows. Grace was alone on the street and felt a prickle of fear. A gas lamp threw a warm sphere of light ahead; she gathered her nerves but quickened her step.

As she drew nearer the globe of light there was a rustle in the darkness. The back of her scalp contracted and she stopped short in the shadow and listened. It came again, from the side of the yard, near the mortuary; urgent whispering and cursing. It's Mary Kelly or one of the other girls working, thought Grace, and had turned to go when the voices rose and she heard they belonged to two men. Horror stories rang in her ears – she had an urgent feeling that she did not want to be seen. Holding her breath she moved closer to the wall, crouching into the shadow.

For a few moments there was silence and Grace wondered whether she should run for it. Then came the voices again, drawing closer. Panic swelled in her chest. There was muttering and the sound of something heavy being dragged along the ground – the men were exerting themselves a great deal. One must be fat: he huffed and puffed and had to stop for little rests, his accomplice cursing all the while. Did she know that voice? She held her breath, straining to hear. The gas light snuffed out, making her jump. Never was she so glad to be left in the dark.

She stood up cautiously – and ducked back down again: the men stood, with their backs half turned to her, not ten feet from the wall. They were engrossed in lifting what was plainly a fresh corpse, wrapped in sackcloth, on to a hand-cart. She peeped back over the wall. They were piling crates of rotten fruit on top. Crates of fruit! With a last shifty look round they made to leave, and as the taller man turned his head Grace glimpsed him in the moonlight.

It was Jack. Jesus Christ. Tin cans clanged in her ears –

she could taste them like blood at the back of her throat. She had an urge to stand up and shout to him, but she shrank back against the wall, staring into a spot on the black paving, listening to the cart creak away.

Where would they take the corpse? she wondered. Who was it? She hoped he had not done such a thing before they were together last, watching the kettle boil, frowning at the stove. How could such a man have worked his charm on her? She felt shocked and stupid. The children noticed she was quiet and made her a card, with a bird on the front and paper frills they had cut from a picture.

Sure enough he came again, just a few days later, at two o'clock in the morning. He rattled the window stealthily as she sat reading and she knew straight away it was him. 'Go away,' she said, round the curtain, then shut it again.

He stood puzzled for a moment, watching his cloudy breath in the winter air, condensing on the window-pane; not sure what to do now that his charm had misfired. This was a situation for which he had made no provision. He decided, for reasons known only to himself, to knock again, at the door this time.

Grace appeared with a cricket bat in her hand, ready to batter him with it. The smile dropped off his face, making him look like a small child. She glared at him, familiar but strange. There seemed nothing to say. Jack shrank away into the night.

Grace put the bat down, kissed the sleeping children again and went back to her book. A little piece of her ran down the street after him, breathless, slipping on the cobbles, bursting with life.

After Jack left he wondered who had told her what. Or who she'd seen him out with. He was not surprised to find she hated him at last and did not blame her. Then he turned his thoughts to where he was to sleep that night.

On visiting a lady friend in Bow he discovered that the Metropolitan Police had been at her door, enquiring after his whereabouts. She had told them nothing, of course, but was not given to lying and could not be sure she hadn't blushed.

Jack reminded himself never again to consort with a girl just for her pretty face. He kissed her sweetly and went his way. Unfortunately he found the same welcome at Ruby Richardson's door when he called on her over in Cable Street. Ruby was a most voluptuous specimen of womankind, dark and mysterious, and one of his favourites. She painted her lips red and hitched up her skirt at the side into her garter, and was always pleased to see him, this evening being no exception, but she had the same story to tell. A detective from Scotland Yard, no less, had been asking after his whereabouts and she, a savvy lass, had told them he had gone to his mother's in Crewe – if, indeed, they were talking of the same fellow – and that she had not seen him since he had left. She had told them she would dearly like to get her hands on him too. She gave Jack a quick kiss and told him to be on his way.

The same story followed at every safe-house. He grew tired after a while, and went into the Prodigal Son for refreshment, where the landlord refused him, having been visited also, and not best pleased with the sudden attention for himself or his customers.

What Jack did not know was that Trixie May Turner, having been questioned by the police in connection with a certain murder, had pinned the ticket firmly on him. She had had them at her door before and they knew she always had something to tell. It was not for nothing that she kept her eyes peeled. She planned well ahead, saved people up for when she needed them most. She was loyal to her friends; it was a grave mistake indeed to cross her.

Mirabel Trotter enjoyed a sojourn at the seaside. Although the weather was unseasonable the air was bracing and invigorating and she had the opportunity to visit several colleagues and her sister, who was fat also. They ate many fine meals and watched the waves lash the pier. She thought fondly of Trixie, made plans to forgive her if she ever saw her again. This made her wistful and she stared out at the crashing sea through the rain on the window.

CHAPTER THIRTY-ONE

Newgate Prison is a bleak, dark structure, squatting like a giant anvil next to the Old Bailey, whence many of its wretched tenants have come direct. The heavenly dome of St Paul's Cathedral, rising above it, might serve to lift their spirits or inspire some repentance if only they could see it from the vantage-point afforded by the mean windows. The people who pass down Newgate Street, going about their daily business, carefree, laughing perhaps, or enjoying ice cream, have no notion of the despair just the other side of the walls they brush as they hurry past, within a spit of the hopeless souls locked inside.

Inside Newgate's walls the air seems to crush you, thick as you breathe it in; a heavy stench hangs in the atmosphere that reluctant visitors try not to swallow, hoping somehow not to draw breath until they escape. The cells are separate now for the most part and gone are the days when a prisoner could get a beer. For exercise they trudge in a circle, in a yard that was built to make a man feel small indeed.

Shuffling in this line Jack Tallis found himself – proud conman and dweller of night, a thin man. He would spend the rest of his days languishing in his cell, worn out like a rag.

'Will they hang him?'

'Yes, son. Don't tell Daisy.' It's a shame we can't watch, Grace thought, in a burst of spite. I wonder where they'll bury him.

Jack Tallis was hanged by the neck until dead on 6 November 1888, a day short of his thirty-fourth birthday, and an uncommonly fine one for that time of the year. He woke in his cell to the sound of the chaplain, who had several last rites to deliver that morning and was consequently in a bad mood, banging on the door. As he opened his eyes he remembered, like a lump hammer striking him full in the face, that he was to die today and marvelled at how well he had slept, then burst into terrified laughter. The Reverend Mr Cane, the filthiest rat ever to have been admitted into the ranks of the clergy, decided, upon hearing this private commotion, that he was too busy to be bothered with this irredeemable sinner and so passed by cell ninety-nine, abandoning Jack Tallis's soul without a care to the fires of hell for ever. Thus Jack found himself on his knees on the caked stone floor, begging God, in whom he had never previously believed, for forgiveness.

Over in Christ Church, Spitalfields, at that very moment Grace, who had never believed in God either and still did not, was on her knees before the altar, praying fervently for mercy on Jack's soul.

He must have heard her somehow for he thought of her suddenly and wished in that very moment, with all his heart, that things had been different. Overwhelmed with loneliness he sprang hot tears.

She wiped her face and went out thieving.

They came for him an hour later and found him peaceful, whistling 'I'm A Young Man From The Country'.

'Tell my mother I'm sorry,' he said, and spoke not another word.

The cold was vicious now, coming into winter, forcing itself through your clothes, sharp like a knife. Enough to make desperate girls do anything for warmth and comfort. And so they went round the church, praying for a crumb, entertaining anyone.

London life was shades of brown and grey. Brown and grey through the ages with a little red mixed in. Brown and grey endures for ever.

EPILOGUE

Life was sweet without the tell-tale heart, since Grace had found the man to deal with her interests. He had international connections, in America and Asia, and counted the famous Mr Worth among his associates. Grace trusted him as far as she could afford to. She waited for word to spread round the market. Sometimes she spotted Mr Byron Stanley in the Frying Pan and they had a quiet beer.

'So what will we wear to the Lord Mayor's Parade?' enquired Daisy, voicing her most important concern.

'I don't suppose it matters, darlin'. Everyone will be lookin' at the mayor. What do you want to wear?'

'A beautiful hat. With feathers. Can we go to Brixton?'

'We can go tomorrow.'

ACKNOWLEDGEMENTS

Thank you Vivienne Schuster, Clara Farmer, Juliet Brooke, the Chatto team, Jill Bialosky, Jane Gelfman and Keith Thomas. Also Gill, Derek, and everyone who put a penny in.

www.vintage-books.co.uk

Step-by-Step Competitive Strategy

Dave Francis

London and New York

First published 1994
by Routledge
11 New Fetter Lane, London EC4P 4EE

Simultaneously published in the USA and Canada
by Routledge
29 West 35th Street, New York, NY 10001

Typeset in Times by Solidus (Bristol) Limited
Printed and bound in Great Britain by
Biddles Ltd, Guildford and King's Lynn

British Library Cataloguing in Publication Data

A catalogue reference for this book is available from the British Library.

Library of Congress Cataloging in Publication Data
Francis, Dave.
    Step by step competitive strategy/Dave Francis.
    p. cm. – (Self-development for managers)
    Includes index.
    1. Strategic planning.   I. Title.   II. Series.
    HD30.28.F716 1994   93–42359
    658.4′012 – dc20   CIP

ISBN 0–415–08698–1

Contents

—— *Figures*

Series editor's preface

In the last decade organisations and managers have been forced to take a much more outwardly focused approach to help face the challenges in the marketplace. These changes have not been confined to the private sector. Many organisations have found themselves for the first time required to develop a competitive strategy. This trend is becoming increasingly important as organisations compete globally.

Some people might think that only senior managers need concern themselves with the tools and techniques for developing competitive strategy. They are, however, a must for any manager wanting to make a worthwhile contribution to their own part of the organisation. Without this broader view, managers become blinkered and insular, and unable to contribute effectively to organisational success.

Step-by-Step Competitive Strategy has been written in a logical, down-to-earth way and can be used not only by top teams to conduct a strategic review of the business, but also by more junior managers to help develop strategic awareness. The approach can also be used by consultants and facilitators helping teams develop their strategies.

Dave Francis is a well known author and has already written *Effective Problem Solving* in the Routledge Self-Development for Managers Series. He has worked as a strategy consultant in the UK and internationally for many years. I was first introduced to a structured approach to Competitive Strategy just over four years ago when developing the strategy for company programmes with my team, facilitated by Dave. The approach worked well and I encouraged him to write it up in the form of a workbook. *Step-by-*

Step Competitive Strategy offers a well tried and tested framework which has developed over the years and will be of great value to many managers.

Step-by-Step Competitive Strategy will join a cluster of books in the Self-Development Series aimed at providing managers with a self-development approach. Earlier books in the series have addressed personal skills; later topics will cover functional areas and develop strategic skills.

Jane Cranwell-Ward
Series Editor

Introduction

You will not be short of advice if you're interested in competitive strategy! There are hundreds of books and thousands of articles on the subject. Why, you ask wearily, another?

Let me tell you about this book – why it was written, the intended audience, what is distinctive about the approach – where *Step-by-Step Competitive Strategy* offers something new.

As a coach to strategy level teams as they shape their business future, I began by borrowing theories from academics to help managers resolve their strategic dilemmas. Sometimes the theories worked well; sometimes they didn't – so new theories had to be developed. Gradually a distinctive and integrated approach to strategy development emerged from hundreds of workshops held with managers in many cultures. These managers were my teachers: *Step-by-Step Competitive Strategy* contains the ideas and techniques which they found effective. The principle of selection used was that if managers couldn't use an idea then it isn't in the book.

I have sought to demystify strategy development and present the process in a 'do-able' form – as a straightforward if demanding senior management project. The book, therefore, has a workbook format: disciplined, wide ranging and practical.

You will find that *Step-by-Step Competitive Strategy* is arranged in two parts. Part I has three chapters. The first gives an overview of the step-by-step structure (this section provides a route map), the second chapter offers guidance about how to form a strategy development team and the final chapter introduces the concept of strategy (useful for those who are new to the task). Part II has ten steps – work through each, in sequence, and you will have analysed your strategic position, developed a competitive strategy for your business and formulated an organisation development plan.

It used to be thought that strategy was too complex and important for most managers. This book's philosophy is completely the opposite. Managers (not consultants) must determine their business's future.

The book is written for three audiences:

1   *Managers* finding answers to the four elemental strategic questions: 'Where will we compete?' 'What value will we create?' 'How can we be superior?' and 'How can our strategy be implemented successfully?'
2   *Students* of management who aspire, one day, to answer these four key strategic questions.
3   *Teachers and consultants* who help managers to answer these four key strategic questions.

This book is written as a ten step strategy project for a senior team in a real business.[1] The term 'business' has a wide definition. Schools, TV stations, charities and hospitals are businesses – they all need a competitive strategy.

Management development specialists will find *Step-by-Step Competitive Strategy* provides a powerful framework for what is called (excuse the jargon) 'action-reflective learning'. Since the mid-1970s it has been widely realised that managers learn best through achievement in the real world. Projects are the usual vehicle for this form of management development but these tend to be marginal, narrow or abstract. For the development of general management skills it is better to use the strategic opportunities of the business as a whole as the 'project'. The learning benefits are enormous.

The step-by-step process requires that the strategy review team undertake a series of structured workshops. Each workshop requires preparation and follow up. The firm becomes its own case study. The workshops result in a complete strategic review and formulation of a broad organisation development plan.

The approach is particularly useful in corporations with several businesses if the corporate planning system has been aligned to match the *Step-by-Step Competitive Strategy* process. Support and facilitation should be provided from the top of the corporation to add expertise and direction to each business unit.

The process described in this book has another use. Teachers of business policy or strategic management, perhaps running an MBA course, will find that the step-by-step approach can be used with little amendment for case work, assignments and industry studies. By referring to the keyword list, it can be used as a reference for students in understanding the essential concepts in strategy. This book is written in a 'user friendly' style which opens an author to the criticism of being excessively simplistic. Hopefully readers will enjoy the informality of the approach, forgive my prescriptive style and excuse me for omitting a myriad of alternative viewpoints.

Some of the strategic concepts are new. For example, there is a distinctive definition of core competitive strategies. However, if there is anything revolutionary about this book it is the structured, multi-disciplinary 'tool-kit' approach.

Structure gives logic, rigour and confidence. But a structure must not become a straitjacket. An open mind is always required: one can never substitute intelligence with discipline. Managers who begin to work through *Step-by-Step Competitive Strategy* sometimes feel that they know the outcome before they start; they are always wrong! Something new can always be learnt.

The weakness of the approach (a reverse of one of the strengths) is that this *is* a 'step-by-step' approach. Breaking a complex whole into bite-sized chunks is ideal for analysis but can mean that connections are overlooked and the interactiveness of the elements is under-explored. Managers will need to integrate the insights from each step into a whole (there are suggestions about how to do this in the text).

The book does not use all of the currently available strategic frameworks – for example, the powerful product lifecycle model is ignored. The reason is that the step-by-step approach has proven to be as much as managers can handle. More concepts overwhelm; a selective approach is more effective in practice.

The book argues that a winning competitive strategy is rarely a brilliant idea – more often hundreds of ideas aligned in the same strategic direction. The aim is to provoke a series of high level debates between all those who shape the future of the business.

Step-by-Step Competitive Strategy owes a tremendous debt to many teachers and writers. In particular: Professor Michael Porter of Harvard University, whose structured analysis was the launch pad for my own work; Professor Henry Mintzberg of McGill University, Professor Yves Doz and Professor Dominick Heao of INSEAD who are great teachers for me. However, the responsibility for this book rests solely with myself.

My colleagues, including Don Young, Helen Price, John Ward and Marcus Alexander have given their advice and support over many years. Jane Cranwell-Ward, the series editor, encouraged me to write this book and provided many helpful comments.

Many managers have worked with me defining their strategic future. In particular, teams from the following companies and organisations worked on earlier versions of the approach: British Steel Computer Services, Commercial Union Assurance, EMI, Ericsson Telecommunications, GEC Marconi, Henley Management College, Hindustan Construction Company, Hong Kong Mass Transit Authority, Hong Kong Telephones, Inmos, Jardine Pacific, Northern Ireland Office, Oberoi Hotels, Picture Music International, Save the Children Fund, SmithKline Beecham, Software Sciences and Thorn EMI.

The guidance and creativity of my wife has been invaluable. Her comments and criticism have added many ideas and helped me prepare a more coherent and 'user-friendly' text.

Perhaps the right place to close this introduction is with the comments of a Chief Executive who worked through the *Step-by-Step Competitive Strategy* approach and, at the end of the project, said, 'I'd thought about our strategy a great deal, but in a totally unstructured way. Then I worked through the step-by-step process. Slowly a notion of where to go arose. It took much more discussion than I imagined. Some of the best ideas came to me in the shower! In the last two years we have changed many things and it shows in the results. My bonus is the best it's ever been.'

May the same happen for you!

Dave Francis
Hove, England
September 1993

Part I
Getting Started

1 How to use this book

Step-by-Step Competitive Strategy is a practical manual for a strategic project team. It structures a complete strategic reappraisal of a business. The overall objective is to answer four elemental strategic questions:

- 'Where will we compete?'
- 'What value will we create?'
- 'How can we be superior?'
- 'How can our strategy be successfully implemented?'

These four questions are answered as you work step-by-step through the process defined in this book. You cannot benefit from the power of the approach unless you use the techniques in practice. The book is written as an extended project for a senior management team developing a competitive strategy for itself. However, all of the techniques can be used by a task force, a consulting team or by students of management working on case studies. Simply adapt the questions – the framework stays the same.

SUCCESSFUL STRATEGY DEVELOPMENT

Although luck is needed to implement a winning competitive strategy we need ways to help lucky people become fortunate. This requires six attributes which are best understood on a diagram (Figure 1).

These six elements are links in a chain – when all are present the business is able to craft strategy in an effective way:

Figure 1 The six attributes for a winning competitive strategy

■ Organisational support to give permission for people to devote their energies to strategising with confidence that it will make a difference.

■ A structured strategic framework to make a complex task achievable.

■ An effective team process to integrate many people's input and ideas.

■ Well developed strategic skills so team members can contribute to the process.

■ A comprehensive data base to give valid raw material for strategic debates.

■ Creativity, intuition and 'gut feel' to provide the elusive – but vital – human factor.

The step-by-step structured approach has proved to be an effective way of linking these six elements. It provides a discipline which ensures that the strategy development will be completed with quality. The structure provides an interrelated kit of conceptual tools lodged in an evolutionary framework. Each separate theory, idea and technique has power. The impact is cumulative. Once you start you need to finish. The approach has checks and balances built in. Stopping halfway can be demoralising, even dangerous, because insight is developed without resolution. One team member brilliantly described the structure as 'a series of meditations on the nature of the business'.

PRECONDITIONS

There are four preconditions for successful implementation of the approach. These are:

1   A distinct business (strategic business unit) not a corporate group is being reviewed.
2   The general manager is willing to devote his or her personal time directly to the project (at least ten days).
3   There are real strategic dilemmas which need an answer.
4   There is a logical link between the *Step-by-Step Competitive Strategy* approach and current corporate strategic planning systems.

If you can't answer 'yes' to these four preconditions it is worth spending time influencing those whose informed support is needed so that you have the maximum chance to succeed.

WHAT IS 'THE STRATEGY REVIEW PROJECT'?

The completion of the ten workshops in Part II of this book is 'the project'. Most workshops take about half a day and each requires preparation and follow up. Figure 2 shows the ten steps in sequence.

Competitive strategy emerges as you work through this process. Ideas accumulate during the first seven steps; the new competitive strategy is defined in Steps 8 and 9 and elaborated into a strategic organisation development programme in Step 10. The aim is to review your business as if you were an award winning consultant with total objectivity, breadth of vision and analytical prowess.

The rationale for the step-by-step nature of the project needs to be carefully explained to members of the core team. It must not be seen as an academic exercise. Managers can resent spending time thinking about strategy – they see it as an unwelcome interruption to 'real' work. The strategy development process must be given stature, priority and meaning within the firm.

WHAT COMMITMENT IS REQUIRED?

How long will it all take? The short answer is 'at least ten days over a two or four month period for each team member'. But this

The Ten Steps

STEP 1
> **EXPLORING INDUSTRY SCENARIOS**
>
> *Assesses opportunities and threats for firms similar to yours*

STEP 2
> **ASSESSING MARKET DYNAMICS**
>
> *Defines customer groupings*

STEP 3
> **EVALUATING STRUCTURAL PROFITABILITY**
>
> *Answers the question 'Can we make money?'*

STEP 4
> **ANALYSING COMPETITORS**
>
> *Helps you know your enemy*

STEP 5
> **COLLECTING EXTERNAL PERCEPTIONS**
>
> *Challenges your assumptions*

STEP 6
> **CLARIFYING VALUES**
>
> *Clarifies what you believe in*

STEP 7
> **GENERATING IDEAS**
>
> *Explores all the things you could do*

STEP 8
> **DEVELOPING STRATEGIC OPTIONS**
>
> *Clarifies alternative futures*

STEP 9
> **DEFINING A COMPETITIVE STRATEGY**
>
> *Identifies your formula for gaining superiority*

STEP 10
> **IMPLEMENTING STRATEGY SYSTEMATICALLY**
>
> *Specifies your strategic organisational development plan*

Figure 2 The ten steps to competitive strategy

varies. The less data you have on customers, markets, competitors and industry forces the longer will the project take – all gaps must be filled. A typical business will take several months to go through the process. Senior managers need to give the project between 10 and 20 per cent of their time; other managers will be called in to help. Consultants and facilitators may also be required.

This is a demanding task, not to be undertaken lightly. However, in addition to the strategic development output, there is a strong team building and educational benefit. Team members learn a great deal about the skills of general management as they contribute.

Will the team get it exactly right? Probably not. The future is too full of unknowns to predict with certainty. But, as one team member said after they completed *Step-by-Step Competitive Strategy*: 'You never really know what will happen in business. Because we had done the research required by the book about a year ago we were ready to react quickly and positively when a totally unforeseen crisis came along.'

WHAT NEXT?

If you can answer 'yes' to each of these five questions you can skip the next two chapters and go on to Part II.

■ Have all the members of the strategy development team been selected?
■ Have they worked together extensively in the past?
■ Does the team have an open and questioning climate?
■ Is the team efficient in: tuning in to new tasks, setting objectives, establishing success criteria, collecting and managing information, making decisions, planning, taking action and reviewing to improve?
■ Do all members of the team really understand 'strategy' and how strategic analysis differs from operational analysis?

If the answer is 'no' to one or more of these five questions, you should work through the two remaining chapters of Part I which will prepare your team for the series of demanding strategy development sessions which are to come.

2 Building the strategy development team

A core team should drive the *Step-by-Step Competitive Strategy* project. Early investment in a team development workshop can pay off handsomely: poor teamwork means progress slows to a snail's pace and the output is uninspired and slipshod. Let us review how the core team should be selected and developed.

WHO SHOULD BE A MEMBER OF THE STRATEGY REVIEW TEAM?

The membership of this team normally includes the general manager (as team leader), key functional or business directors and others who can contribute because of their knowledge, expertise or analytical capacity. The team normally has between five and ten members. Sub-teams, with additional members, can be constructed for specific tasks; perhaps including trade union officials and younger managers on an accelerated development programme. Ideally the process should include all those whose views shape the direction of the firm (the 'opinion leaders') and who need to 'buy in' to the strategy. From time to time there is a need for divergent ideas, specialist data and input from people with distinctly different mind sets. For this reason the membership of the core team and sub-teams can be supplemented or changed as the project progresses.

Should anyone else contribute to the process? The glib answer is 'everybody who can add an observation or an idea'. Managers have received brilliant suggestions from strangers in the adjacent airline seat. Customers, trade unionists, shop floor workers, sales people, middle managers, bosses, suppliers, industry specialists, professors and, even, consultants can make a contribution. You will need to gather and harvest all relevant observations and ideas (there are mechanisms to do this in Part II).

HOW CAN A POSITIVE TEAM CLIMATE BE CREATED?

Some team climates are more conducive to strategy development than others. Four key characteristics of a positive team climate for the strategy development project are:

- All demonstrate by their actions that strategic thinking is important and are willing to dedicate a great deal of time to the process.
- Team members show themselves to be open to new ideas and are non-defensive.
- Everyone is prepared to contribute fully and openly.
- The following values are prized: analysis, argument, challenge, decisiveness, debate, innovative thinking, listening, directness, option exploration, prudence and respect for difference.

A healthy climate enables team members to share thinking and explore information, ideas and assumptions. Teams develop a set of informal rules which shape the behaviour of every individual member. Often these 'norms' are subterranean but it is vital that they are positive. Team norms need to support openness, energy, trust, authenticity, intellectual rigour and creativity.

HOW SHOULD THE TEAM BE LED?

A high order of leadership and chairmanship is needed to keep the project moving. *Step-by-Step Competitive Strategy* is not a bureaucratic or form-filling exercise. The process is as important as the outcome. Informed debate is essential. Conflict, abrasion and contention are resources to be cultivated. The process must be kept vibrant and alive. The team leader must sustain an environment which facilitates input, creativity, realism, thoroughness and challenge throughout each of the ten steps of the process.

It is important that all members of the team realise that *Step-by-Step Competitive Strategy* advocates a consultative but not a democratic approach to strategy formulation. False expectations should not be raised. Strategy development is one task that cannot be delegated; the general manager is always directly responsible.

Leadership should be directed towards ensuring that all members of the team feel supported and encouraged – especially when 'the going gets tough'. The strategy development process requires an extended period of far-sighted thinking which few managers find easy. There is always a tendency to return to the comfort of the known rather than the void of the possible. It is the primary task of the leader to motivate and encourage the team to deal with stretching strategic questions.

HOW CAN THE TEAM BE EFFECTIVE?

Your project team will need to become an efficient and effective working group. In particular, everyone must give their full participation. When John Harvey-Jones became Chief Executive of ICI, one of Europe's largest companies, he insisted that board meetings were conducted with structure and strong discipline. No one was allowed to pass on a subject and everyone was expected to give their views openly, cogently and succinctly. The ICI board learned to work together efficiently and effectively. Your project team will need to do the same. Team building and all the paraphernalia of project management are relevant: activity charts, time plans, task specifications, critical paths and so on.

The key features of effective teamwork are:

- Conducting regular and frequent reviews of team performance with improvement ideas listed on a flip chart (it is often helpful to record some team meetings on video tape so that the process can be fully reviewed).
- Working as a team – not a group of individuals – so that all members are working for the common good rather than their own partisan interests.
- Using such techniques as brainstorming, flip charting, and structured discussion to help the team become more efficient.
- Setting targets to be achieved in the time available and reviewing performance against these targets.
- Always having a leader to manage the process of the team – this may not be the formal manager in charge of the team.

HOW TO BUILD THE TEAM?

Here is a checklist of five action points for the formation of the core strategy development team:

1   Define the core team's terms of reference (normally these are 'to complete all the steps in *Step-by-Step Competitive Strategy* by ...').
2   Select core team members for both technical ability and personal qualities.
3   Develop the core team as an effective work group.[1]
4   Ensure that the disciplines of project management are used to schedule tasks.
5   Give time and resources to support the project – a budget is sometimes required.

STRATEGIC TEAM SKILLS

A bewildering list of skills are required by management teams as they formulate competitive strategies. In a recent research project conducted by the author[2] more than 100 distinct skill areas were identified. However, merely understanding that strategy development is a complex topic will not help us. In order to simplify the process my 'top twenty' strategic team skills are shown on Figure 3.

Insight into the skills required help us to realise that the step-by-step project described in this book will challenge the team emotionally, intellectually and managerially. It is useful to audit the team that you have established to see whether they are strong in each of these twenty areas. If not, you will need to strengthen the team before you proceed. Sometimes an experienced facilitator can add value. He or she can act as a coach, catalyst, mirror and goad. It is essential, however, that the work is done by the managers concerned.

WHAT NEXT?

These guidelines on team effectiveness scratch the surface of a vital topic. The step-by-step process only works effectively if the work is undertaken by a strong and close team with a positive climate. You will find Part II begins with a brief team building module.

	SKILL	INDICATOR
1	Analytically Precise	'This is the situation, these are the trends and these are the threats and opportunities'
2	Confident with Complexity	'These are all the elements which affect this situation'
3	Focused on Competitive Performance	'This is how our performance compares with our competitors'
4	Economic Analysts	'This is how we can make a profit in this industry'
5	Opportunity Seekers	'These are opportunities for us'
6	Competitive Strategists	'This is our competitive strategy and this is how it will affect each part of our business'
7	Business Builders	'This is the way that we build lasting strength into the organisation'
8	Orientated to Add Value	'This is where we are providing real valued benefits to the customer'
9	Customer Directed	'We know our customers, what they really want and this is what we do for them'
10	Idea Collectors	'We collect ideas from all of these sources'
11	Vision Builders	'This is where we want to be in the next five years'
12	Network Developers	'This is how we influence people'
13	Organisation Developers	'We develop the type of organisation we need'
14	Empowerers	'We help people to take initiatives'
15	Unblockers	'We detect and clear organisational "blockages"'
16	Learners	'We learn from feedback and manage our own development'
17	Organisational Leaders	'We attract people to follow'
18	Team Skilled	'The top team works well'
19	Strategy Process Managers	'This is the process we use to develop our strategy'
20	Believers	'We can make it happen!'

Figure 3 Top twenty strategic team skills

However, if you are uncertain as to whether your team is ready then undertake a team building event (perhaps for two days) before you begin the step-by-step process.

3 What is strategy?

In Part II you will be asked to develop something called 'a competitive strategy'. This chapter introduces a concept of strategy that has evolved to meet the needs of the twenty-first century. You should read and discuss these ideas if you have not studied the subject before or learnt your strategic theory before 1990.

This chapter will introduce you to:

- The concept of 'strategy'.
- The nature of competitive strategies.
- The interests of stakeholders.
- The organisation as a system of competencies.
- Constraints on strategic freedom.
- Guidelines for strategy formation.

THE CONCEPT OF STRATEGY

The word 'strategy' causes confusion. For example, some managers use the term 'strategy' to describe a set of broad objectives ('our strategy is to produce a series of state-of-the-art products for office automation') whilst others think of a 'strategy' as the means of accomplishing an objective ('our objective is to distribute in China and our strategy is to find a joint-venture partner').

Since there is no consensus about the meaning of the word we must define our terms before we begin. In this book 'strategy' is used to mean 'an underlying logic beneath the flow of decisions which create the future'.

This definition requires explanation. The deeper meaning of

strategy becomes clear when we consider an example. Imagine it's an August morning and you are watching the golden light spill over a deserted bay in a remote part of Crete. You are at a retreat called The Practice Place to learn Astanga Yoga, Tai Chi and other Eastern Arts – six kilometres from the nearest phone.

The centre has twelve twin bedrooms, a substantial kitchen and two airy exercise rooms. It represents the fulfilment of ten years' effort by the founders, Derek and Rhada Ireland. They have invested their capital and energy to make the centre a reality. For this couple, founding The Practice Place was one of the most important strategic initiatives of their lives.

Their strategic decision had a profound impact. Before they went to Crete in 1991 Derek and Rhada had a very different life-style. They taught yoga in London, New York, Nassau and in Greece, coached private students and spent several months each year studying in India. Now they plan marketing campaigns, design their 'product', continuously develop the business, pay staff, keep records and turn down requests to teach in exotic locations.

Derek and Rhada believed in sharing their yoga. This belief energised them. They took big decisions. The Practice Place began with an idea which grew into a vision, solidified into an intention and evolved into a plan. Figure 4 captures three main stages of strategy formulation which requires a combination of achievable possibilities, willpower and relevant competencies.

Many changes of tactics were necessary as the concept took form. New constraints and opportunities demanded a reaction. Derek and Rhada committed substantial resources and fundamentally changed the nature of their business in ways that would be difficult or impossible to reverse. They cannot rest – other competitors come along and markets change – a stream of innovation is needed.

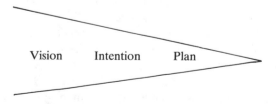

Vision   Intention   Plan

Figure 4 Three main stages of strategy formulation

This last paragraph captures the essence of strategy which (to remind you) we define as 'an underlying logic beneath the flow of decisions which create the future'.

The line between strategic and operational decisions is blurred. If Derek and Rhada decide to build another twenty bedrooms they will be taking a strategic decision (the fundamental nature of their business would change) but would it be strategic if they decide to build two? Or four? The line is fuzzy.

Strategic decisions have an interesting quality. They are as powerful in their absence as in their presence. Consider this example: a firm has a thriving business as a retailer of utility sports wear but fashions change and designer sports clothing becomes the 'in-scene'. Our retailer continues to sell his long established ranges. He loses business and fails to react until the inevitable closing down sale marks the end. The retailer, although he might deny it, took strategic decisions by failing to adapt the business to a new environment. He shaped his fortunes just as surely as if he had decided to reposition his business as a supplier of antique sports equipment for museums. Edward Wrapp[1] wisely observed strategies can be formed in 'the corridors of relative indifference'.

THE NATURE OF WINNING COMPETITIVE STRATEGIES

Business strategies are quintessentially competitive. The Practice Place competes with other 'alternative' holiday options. Save the Children competes with other charities in their fund-raising efforts. Competition is more than an add-on: it is a way of life. Global competition is the business reality.

'It is surely the case that competition is our fundamental economic policy'[2] says the American Supreme Court. That wise observer of capitalism, Adam Smith,[3] added that rivalry imposes discipline on the social order: competition is the great motivator, the spur which drives firms beyond self-imposed limits and creates an overarching logic for all business activities.

What are businesses competing for? The answer is always the same. There are three vital and interdependent elements. A business thrives because:

■ Sufficient numbers of customers want or need their products or services and are able to pay for them.

■ These can be provided with a substantial profit margin.
■ Customers choose to buy from that firm rather than another.

We can, therefore, define a winning competitive strategy as the 'bundle of advantages provided at sustainable cost which impel sufficient numbers of customers to choose your firm over its rivals'.

All firms are attempting to provide this 'bundle of advantages' – technically called 'value' – a term we will explore in detail in Part II of this book. Value is always defined by the customer (or groups of customers that we call 'market segments'). Value must be understood by the firm. If a business can provide greater value than its accumulated costs the business will prosper – if not, oblivion beckons.

Competitive strategy requires keeping these three balls in the air at the same time – providing superior value, winning sufficient customers and managing costs. Implicit in this definition is the concept of timing. Competitive strategies are 'a series of races against the clock'[4] to deliver survival and advantage.

An effective competitive strategy will:

1 Create and recreate your business.
2 Provide clarity about what is important.
3 Specify your formula for 'adding value faster than cost'.
4 Tell you where to compete.
5 Define your superiority.
6 Become a management action plan.
7 Be constantly evolving.

THE INTERESTS OF STAKEHOLDERS

There is an interesting question – 'who is strategy for?' If your firm is unionised do the trade union officials want the same things as the chairman of the board? Do the institutional shareholders of a multinational want the same as the major customers of the same firm?

The intentions of interest groups are relevant to understanding the dynamic forces which shape the strategy of a firm. Stakeholders include shareholders, customers, employees, suppliers, bankers and government, and they have different, sometimes conflicting, values. Analysis of their needs and wants is an important part of the strategy development process. A useful way to unravel the sources of influence is 'stakeholder analysis'. This requires that you:

1 List the stakeholders in your firm.
2 Rank the stakeholders' intentions in order of significance to the strategic direction of the firm.
3 Analyse the stakeholders' motives and intentions by answering two questions: 'What would they really want for this firm?' 'What would be the minimum they would be prepared to accept?'

The primary purpose of competitive strategy can be defined as 'to satisfy as many stakeholders as possible – especially the important ones'.

IMPLEMENTING STRATEGY

Strategies are nothing unless they are systematically implemented. In the final step in Part II of this book you will be introduced to the powerful concept of 'competencies'.[5] These are building blocks which transform competitive strategies into life. A strategic competency simply expressed, is 'everything it takes to perform to world class standards'. Competencies can provide a competitive edge – at least until rivals catch up. Also, competencies don't last forever unless they are continuously updated. Some examples make the point:

■ In the 1920s Ford developed the competencies to mass produce motor cars at prices ordinary people could afford and gained competitive advantage, but later other firms achieved the same competencies.
■ In the 1940s Caterpillar developed the competencies to supply the world with reliable earth moving equipment and gained competitive advantage, but later other firms achieved the same competencies.
■ In the 1960s Michelin developed the competencies to construct superior tyres for motor vehicles and gained competitive advantage, but later other firms achieved the same competencies.
■ In the 1980s Canon developed the competencies to supply low cost but superior photocopiers and gained competitive advantage, but later other firms achieved the same competencies.

Consider the final example in the list above. Canon correctly identified that there was a huge potential market for low cost, small and reliable copiers. Their competitive strategy was to develop a new range of plain paper copiers and attack Xerox's virtual monopoly. However, this strategy would be merely an aspiration unless the company had the competencies to deliver the new products with their leapfrog technologies and low costs of manufacture. It would take a long time to tell the full story of how they acquired the 'right' portfolio of competencies but here are some of the key points: Cannon had a well funded research team, a portfolio of patents, advanced optical knowhow, precision engineering capability, low cost manufacturing, various routes to market and a strategic intention to dominate the world's photocopier industry. They had 'everything it takes to perform to world class standards'.

Strategies and competencies are a conceptual see-saw. Competencies are needed to implement strategies and the possession of competencies opens strategic opportunities. Many organisations have developed a competencies approach as a principle for the implementation of strategy. The British army have a world-class competence in urban warfare honed by decades of combating the IRA in Northern Ireland. In the 1980s Apple developed an awesome competence in designing user-friendly computer tools as an aid to intellectual workers. A competence brings a degree of stability in uncertainty. It enables some types of unpredictable events to be planned for. The British army do not know where they will be asked to fight in the next five years but there is a high probability that their competence in urban warfare will be needed.

There are generic competencies which apply to most firms. For example, it is likely that success in the next industrial era will require the competence to exploit accumulated relevant knowledge. No longer are capital and size the sole arbiters of achievement. More important is the organisational competence to learn and adapt.

Competencies give a flexible capability that enables opportunities to be exploited as they occur. They are the bedrock of competitive strength and open strategic opportunities. In Step 10 – the final stage of the step-by-step process – we will design your business as a coherent system of interrelated competencies aligned behind a clear competitive strategy.

STRATEGY AND ORGANISATION DEVELOPMENT

In the introduction to this book you were promised that your competitive strategy would flow into an organisation development plan. The notion of competencies we have just discussed takes strategies one big step towards implementation. However, this is still too generalised for practical managers to know what they should actually do differently. We need a more elaborate and systematic model of an organisation as a tool for conceptualising an organisation development plan.

Strategy envelops every aspect of the firm and is, therefore, the foundation on which each aspect of the organisation is built. Remember strategy is 'an *underlying* logic beneath the flow of decisions which create the future'. In Part II you will learn how to take your competitive strategy and apply it to the processes,

Figure 5 The 'twelve box' model

competencies, tasks and systems of the firm. This is done using a specially developed[6] framework which is best introduced as a diagram (Figure 5).

There are twelve headings on the diagram (which is, as you would expect, usually called 'the twelve box model'). Taken together these headings cover all of the areas of a strategic organisation development plan. Let's work through each of the areas briefly – you will cover them in much more detail later (in Step 10).

In the centre of the diagram is a triangle with three strategic activities:

1 *Direction* – defines the firm's competitive strategy.
2 *Learning* – the accumulating knowledge of the firm.
3 *Cash management* – ensures money is well used.

Within the circle there are five core activities:

4 *Marketing* – aligns the firm to customers' real needs.
5 *Operations* – makes what you sell.
6 *Logistics* – moves materials and products.
7 *Sales* – encourages the customer to buy.
8 *After sales* – ensures customers get best use from purchases.

The outer box has four support activities:

9 *People management* – provides excellent human resources.
10 *Product development* – creates tomorrow's offerings.
11 *Technology* – develops systems for efficiency and effectiveness.
12 *External interfaces* – provides positive linkages with the outside world.

We use these twelve headings to explore in detail what our strategic decisions will mean to the organisation. Strategies provide an underlying logic to drive the business forward. Each 'box' has to play its part in both the formulation and the implementation of strategy. As the 'boxes' must be interconnected by linkages into systems almost all strategies require that organisational processes are managed. Hence fundamental issues about organisation structure must be debated once a new strategic direction is determined.

CONSTRAINTS ON STRATEGIC FREEDOM

Firms do not have total strategic freedom (although 'the exception proves the rule' occasionally!). A taxi partnership in Sydney Australia cannot be transformed into a pharmaceutical giant. Someone running a nightclub in Manila cannot rival Kodak – although Kodak could open nightclubs in Manila.

There are five primary categories of constraints which limit our choices:

1   Constrained by lack of understanding (specific knowhow is lacking).
2   Constrained by lack of imagination (creativity is lacking).
3   Constrained by lack of permission (a higher authority says 'no').
4   Constrained by lack of resources (insufficient funds or other essential resources).
5   Constrained by lack of willpower (the top team are not willing to drive through changes).

These five constraints may return to haunt us. Some are under the control of the top team in an organisation whilst others are susceptible to influence. It is important to assess each perceived constraint and ask 'is this a mirage or a real barrier?'

GUIDELINES FOR STRATEGY FORMATION

In Part II you will be formulating a competitive strategy for an individual business (in strategy-speak this is called a 'strategic business unit' – SBU for short). For all but enlightened companies, the result will be very different from the annual business plan required by corporate parents, shareholders or bankers. Mostly owners are interested in financial ratios and most business plans have many pages of numbers. The output from the step-by-step process is conceptual – not numerical. We are concerned with finding a winning competitive strategy rather than measuring it. Financial appraisal is used later to validate your proposed strategy and provide ongoing discipline.

SBU strategies may be very different from the statements written down in the annual planning documents. Strategy is about what actually happens, not what is stated. As Peter Drucker[7] said, 'strategy is nothing until it degenerates into work'.

Strategy development is demanding because we are dealing with such intangibles as concepts, intentions, meanings, logic and futures. Here are seven guidelines which assist the team to ready themselves for the strategy development task.

GUIDELINES FOR STRATEGY FORMATION

1 *Realise that the formation and implementation of wise strategy in an SBU is the core leadership process*

Leadership provides vision which energises and directs. For this reason strategy must be a deep consensus about ends and means by those who shape the future of the organisation. Strategies are devised by people whose motives make a real difference. In the 1960s an insignificant Japanese company called Komatsu[8] was making dumper trucks for the local market with the support of the trade ministry. Their chairman, Ryoichi Kawai, developed an ambition to 'encircle Caterpillar'. This intention was to shape the development of the company for two decades until, in the 1980s, Komatsu emerged as Caterpillar's most serious global rival.

2 *Be prepared for set-backs*

Strategies emerge; two steps forward, one back. As we learn about the process of strategy formation we learn about ourselves: our weaknesses and strengths. The step-by-step process is long, painstaking, difficult and exhausting. You will be asked to provide a well researched foundation of data before you are 'allowed' to go on to the heady task of generating strategic options. 'So why don't you make it simpler?' you will ask. The reason is that strategies plucked from the air are as likely to be fantasies as inspirations. Thoroughness pays off.

3   *Collect information widely*

Strategies often emerge from deep within organisations. Each customer contact, employee, system and input is a source of intelligence. Organisations are 'distributed systems' – wisdom is everywhere. The task of the strategy development team is to harvest ideas as well as generate them.

It is ironic that some of the best ideas never flower because they are developed too low down the organisation. In 1985 the author was told by several IBM employees that 'this company is a megalith – it needs to be broken down into stand-alone businesses able to compete on price and performance'. Seven years and billions of dollars later IBM did precisely that.

4   *Be willing to 'think the unthinkable'*

The aim is to be poised and strong in a bewildering confusion of aims, possibilities and difficulties. Strategic people bring their beliefs, values and assumptions into question. This is easier said than done – we all tend to take things for granted. Questioning is necessary because every management orthodoxy has the weaknesses of its strengths.

5   *Think tough!*

Business strategy is a polite martial art – a form of warfare. Aggression is the underlying orientation of successful strategic managers. For example, many of the winning strategies currently used by Japanese firms can be traced to the precepts of the Samurai tradition.

6   *Win friends!*

Strategic skills are not just belligerent: they are also persuasive. All strategies are 'political'. People with influence need to be convinced and give their active support (often this means opening their cheque books). Brilliant ideas founder because they were not sold. Many times the importance of politics is under-estimated.

Personality also affects strategic decision making: engineers tend to prefer engineering-based strategies, financial people support financial strategies and so on. If we underestimate the importance of politics and personality all our good work can be rendered impotent.

7 *Be flexible*

Strategies, like performing karate, often require a rapid response to a new situation. An opportunity occurs or a threat menaces and managers must react – perhaps to exploit a 'window of opportunity'. Being reactive is widely, but incorrectly, considered to be dishonourable. We are wrong to believe that everything can be planned; that certainty about the future is possible. As Eastern teachings emphasise 'everything changes – the shrewd person bends with the wind and deals with the realities of the moment'.

The view of strategy encapsulated in these seven points is quite different to the control/planning orientation advocated in many older academic texts. We are not trying to plan down to the last decimal place the revenues for five years in the future. Strength in uncertainty requires personal capabilities more readily learned in the judo hall than the library (perhaps this is why some Japanese companies expect their young executives to become experts in a martial art).

Business strategy is never easy. In 1991, 100 of the USA's Fortune 500 companies lost money. They all spent endless time on strategic development. But there is no choice but to work at it: we take strategic decisions whether we act or not. Struggle is indivisible from strategy.

Part II
Step-by-step competitive strategy

Introduction

The remainder of this book contains the ten workshops that enable you to develop and review your existing competitive strategy and decide where you want to take the business in the future. The guidelines below will help you get started and use the ten workshops successfully.

Each step begins with a definition of the prework required, has a workshop briefing which describes the strategic tools you will use and concludes with detailed guidelines about how to run the workshop.

You will find the process works effectively if you:

- Undertake the workshops in sequence.
- Review the prework at least one week before the workshop to assess what is required and assign tasks to team members. Sometimes prework can be undertaken by small groups rather than by individuals.
- Insist on the best sources of data being used to supply information.
- Ensure that everyone reads the workshop briefing notes before the workshop is held.
- Appoint a chairperson to lead each workshop.
- Schedule the meetings to last the time suggested.
- Keep all of the flip charts etc. that you generate – have these typed as a record of the sessions.
- Ensure that the workshop time is protected – no interruptions or absences.

'GETTING STARTED' TEAM WORKSHOP

Before you begin the ten steps it is often worth holding a mini-workshop to launch the process. Here is a format for a 'getting started' workshop.

You will need a room with a flip chart, marker pens, Blu-Tack and one copy of *Step-by-Step Competitive Strategy* for each member of the team. The team leader should pre-prepare flip charts covering item 1 below. The workshop will take approximately 1 hour and 45 minutes.

WORKSHOP PLAN

1 The team leader (normally the general manager) introduces the session, presents the objectives of the project and establishes a time frame. The process should be put in the context of threats and opportunities facing the business at the present time. Any constraints facing the team should be brought to the surface. The priority of the project is clarified. The personal commitment of the team leader should be stated. Flip charts covering these points should be posted. (30 minutes)

2 If members of the team do not know each other then a 'getting acquainted' session should be structured. (time as required)

3 Each member of the team takes two minutes to outline their personal interest in the project, and, in detail, describe what they hope will happen and what they fear could happen. Key points are recorded on a flip chart. Questions for clarification are allowed at this stage. Flip charts should be posted. (20 minutes)

4 The team discuss the points raised under item 3 and answer the question 'what are all the things that we can do to increase the chances that the project will be a success?' These are listed on a flip chart. (10 minutes)

5 Under the direction of the chair the team answers the question: 'How can we establish a productive team climate?' A team mission statement is generated and

recorded on a flip chart. This should be displayed at subsequent meetings. (20 minutes)

6   Diaries are required for this next task. A series of ten workshops needs to be planned (each should to be scheduled for half a day – but sessions 8 and 9 are longer and are best arranged as a residential two day workshop). These should be approximately fortnightly. (10 minutes)

7   A copy of *Step-by-Step Competitive Strategy* should be given to each member of the team and the prework task allocated for the first workshop. (10 minutes)

8   All flip charts should be collected and typed as a record of the first meeting.

Step 1
Exploring industry
scenarios

PREPARATION

Each member of the team should talk (separately) to at least one different 'expert' on your industry and ask the questions below. Take full notes. Supplement your notes by reading journal articles etc. You will be expected to make separate presentations lasting no longer than 2 minutes on each of the twelve questions in Workshop 1 on this step. Please bring your analysis pre-prepared on OHP slides.

The twelve questions are as follows:

1. What are the forces driving change in the industry today? What is their effect? Consider these ten categories:
   a Political factors.
   b Legal constraints.
   c Economic policy.
   d Sociological changes.
   e Environment issues.
   f Innovative products or services.
   g Possible impact of information technology.
   h Investors' attitudes.
   i Management philosophies of industry leaders.
   j Other relevant forces.
2. How have these forces changed over the last three years?
3. What new forces may affect the industry over the next three to five years? What could result?
4. Who are the winning firms in the industry now? How sustainable is their dominance? What is the pattern of entries and exits? Why are these occurring?

5　Who will be the winning firms in the industry in three to five years' time? Why?

6　What political, environmental and social forces (including lifestyles, demographic, age structure, trade unions, skill levels) may re-shape the industry in three to five years' time? Why?

7　What industry issues including technology, industry structure, economics and patterns of competition may shape the industry in three to five years' time? What significant changes are taking place in the cost structure of running a successful firm? Why?

8　What changes in customers' demand patterns are taking place? Are new market segments developing (or capable of being created) and are existing market segments changing their buying behaviour? How?

9　What products or services may be needed in three to five years' time? Why?

10　How is your own firm placed in the industry?

11　Is this an attractive industry? Give the reasons for and against.

12　What are the possible ways in which a firm in this industry can realise opportunities and minimise threats?

WORKSHOP BRIEFING

In this step we analyse your[1] industry and project trends into the future using the techniques of scenario planning. This begins the analytical work that underpins your strategic review. In this step you will:

- Use a straightforward approach to scenario planning.
- Undertake an industry analysis.
- Develop industry scenarios to help you spin off ideas for your strategy development.

SCENARIO PLANNING

In the early 1990s the Pentagon[2] launched a major initiative. We can learn much about strategy from their approach. The Pentagon presented to government six scenarios that, they believed, could draw American troops into conflict within ten years. The six scenarios were developed by the Joint Chiefs of Staff and defense experts. They were:

1   War against Iraq which might again attack the oilfields of Kuwait and Saudi Arabia.
2   War against North Korea which could attack Seoul with an army of more than one million men.
3   War against both at the same time.
4   Containment of a resurgent Russia attacking the Baltic nations and Eastern Europe.
5   In Panama a hostile far-right government denying access to the canal.
6   Deter a new 'global adversarial rival' or 'an international coalition with an aggressive expansionist security policy'.

The Pentagon called the scenarios 'illustrative and not predictive'. They served as the foundation for long-range budget planning and, once agreed, determine the number and kinds of troops and weapons that the USA needs to maintain. In effect, the scenarios help the US military to identify the portfolio of competencies that it will need to fight any likely future war.

Strategists say that scenarios are 'descriptions of possible archetypal futures'. For the rest of us it is helpful to think of a scenario as a 'faction' novelette – a story weaving fact and possibility set some time in the future – but, hopefully, not a piece of romantic fiction.

Scenarios encourage us to think about the unthinkable. Chaos theory tells us that we can never predict the future: it is too complex. But we can make conditional predictions. This provokes a creative debate needed for strategy development.

We write stories to transform unstructured thoughts of what could happen into something useful. A story about each possibility – a mini-novel really – is the best way to explore alternative possible futures. It is important that scenario stories are internally consistent and highlight trends and challenges. The story should have a 150 word summary.

The task of writing scenarios gives an opportunity to explore uncertainty, shakes existing perceptions, widens thinking, reduces complexity and enables us to explore possibilities. Those who study scenarios will be better able to recognise signs that the future is unfolding in an unforeseen way (a 'radical discontinuity').

Business scenario planning is helped by the equipment of science, with complex mathematical models being crunched by powerful computers. It is, in the last analysis, an art. The currency of scenarios is probabilities and possibilities. Strategies flow from an informed mind willing to think beyond the normal limits.[3]

There are six primary levels of scenarios. The levels that will be the most useful to your strategy development project are:

1 *Grand scenarios* (global issues including political, environmental, social, lifestyle, economic and cultural. Answers questions like 'what is the future of the motor car in the context of global warming?')

2 *Regional scenarios* (regional issues including political initiatives, environmental, social etc. Answers questions like 'what will be the pattern on motor car use in ASEAN countries over the next twenty years?')

3 *Industry scenarios* (industry issues including technology, industry structure, economics, patterns of competition etc. Answers questions like 'what types of motor manufacturer will make above average profits over the next ten years?')

4 *Market scenarios* (market issues including lifestyles, market structure, segmentation etc. Answers questions like 'what types of motor car will retired people buy over the next ten years?')

5 *Product scenarios* (product issues including technology, design, functionality etc. Answers questions like 'what will an ambulance look like in ten years?')

6 *Organisation scenarios* (organisation issues including competitive strategy, competencies and strategic alliances etc. Answers questions like 'what will Ford be like in ten years?')

Not all levels of scenarios are relevant for every business. It makes little sense for a shop owner selling American comics in Singapore to invest intellectual effort in predicting the economic and political changes in South East Asia over the next ten years. He would gain more from looking at local product and market scenarios.

It is helpful to develop a matrix with two axes. On one axis we place the six levels and on the other we indicate the degree of radical thinking that we will adopt by showing two principal types

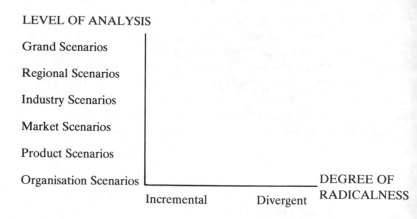

LEVEL OF ANALYSIS

Grand Scenarios

Regional Scenarios

Industry Scenarios

Market Scenarios

Product Scenarios

Organisation Scenarios

Incremental   Divergent

DEGREE OF
RADICALNESS

Figure 6 Matrix showing incremental and divergent scenarios

of scenario: incremental and divergent (Figure 6). We need to spend some time considering what 'the degree of radicalness' means. For the sake of simplicity we have identified only two principal types of scenario: incremental and divergent. Both are relevant but they need a different approach by the workshop team.

Incremental scenarios

Incremental scenarios result from the *rational* projections of trends. For example, if we look at the pattern of motor car ownership it is apparent that there is a steady growth in almost every country in the world. This means that more roads will be needed, larger car parks, more replacement tyres and so on. Sometimes changes are known well in advance; it has been decided that 5 per cent of cars sold in California by 2005 must be emission free. We can rationally project such trends forward for maybe twenty years and predict the future of the industries which serve motor car ownership.

Incremental scenarios begin with historical analysis. We look at the pattern of motor car ownership over the last ten years and try to find ways to explain variations in the annual statistics. Then comes the tough bit. We extrapolate the past into the future. As soon as we start to do this we find that we have to make a number of assumptions (like GNP will grow at 2 per cent per annum, train passenger miles will continue to decline by 1 per cent p.a., there will be no increases in subsidies for buses and so on). Based on these assumptions we will be able to make logical and reasonable extrapolations: normally, a 'best' case, 'worst' case and 'expected' case. In order to make the analysis useful we have to 'take a time horizon snapshot' at some fixed times in the future – normally two years from today, five years from today, and ten years from today.

Divergent scenarios

Sometimes the future is not a logical or incremental extrapolation of the past. Something radical happens: a *discontinuity* occurs. Cigarette manufacturers woke up one morning in the 1950s to find the newspapers full of medical evidence linking smoking and cancer. In Uganda in the 1970s, many thousands of Asian business people were told overnight to shut their business and leave the country. The 1990 invasion of Kuwait by Iraq led to virtually every oilwell in Kuwait being set on fire. Such events are a sudden break from the past – perhaps the best example is when the Berlin Wall was destroyed in 1989.

Radical discontinuities often create grand-scale threats and opportunities. Cigarette manufacturers used their fabled wealth to diversify into new industries; Ugandan Asians saw their fortunes destroyed; oilwell firefighters had almost unlimited demand for their services in Kuwait, and the integration of East and West Germany created a need for major infrastructure development projects.

There are many hundreds of plausible discontinuity scenarios. Divergent thinking is needed to think about them. It is possible that a gigantic meteor may wipe out your office as you read this book! We need to generate divergent scenarios, categorise them, assess the likelihood, reflect on the probable impact and channel the insights gained into our strategy development process. In practice, we cannot think of every possible eventuality and so develop a number of illustrative cases.

This will help us to recognise new options, assess the impact on existing strategies and highlight major dilemmas. Questions and issues emerge; they swim into focus. It is important that the workshop team do not allow themselves to be prematurely dragged back from the future. We are looking for a genuine mind-expanding experience which is intellectually challenging.

All high impact scenarios, no matter how unlikely, deserve to be considered. We need to ask three questions:

■ What will be the impact of the scenario on firms within our industry? Who will be better off? Why?
■ What will be the likely impact on us?
■ What are all the possible ways in which the opportunities can be realised and the threats minimised?

INDUSTRY ANALYSIS

Scenarios need to be developed for 'industries'. An industry is 'a group of firms whose products or services, from the customer's point of view, offer substitute products or services'.[4] So, firms which provide business travellers with away-from-home accommodation are in the 'commercial hotel industry' and firms which sell smells in bottles are the 'fragrance industry'.

Usually it is easy to determine what industry you are in – but not always. Managers in a firm making cutting tools using the flame cutting process may define their industry as 'steel flame cutting' but this is incorrect because steel can be cut by methods other than flame (for example: by laser, saw and so on): they are in the steel cutting industry – they compete with these other technologies. A manufacturer of gold pens is not (as it might appear) in the 'writing implements' industry but the 'gift' industry – since most gold pens are given as gifts. The key question is 'from the customer's point of view what are the substitute products or services?'

Firms in an industry are subject to similar, but not identical, forces; some firms may be better protected than others. For example, all firms in the television programme making industry are influenced by satellite systems, reducing entry costs, global alliances, new technology, lower costs of equipment and so on. (These forces are shown diagramatically in Figure 7.) This affects Earthworm Productions (two people in Australia making nature films through a microscope) differently from CNN – the global news station: firms are affected differently by industry forces (as we shall see later insightful strategies position a firm to exploit industry forces – just as a sailor takes advantage of currents and winds).

All firms must try to predict the forces which will influence their industry so that they can wisely take the following decisions:

- Do we want to stay in the industry?
- How do we protect ourselves against industry threats?
- What opportunities are created by the evolution of the industry?
- Can we lead the industry the way we want it to go?
- How would we need to change to be an industry leader?

Industry analysis can be a matter of life and death to a business. In the early 1980s the office-automation firm Wang failed to forecast industry trends and keep up to date with the rapidly emerging personal computer technology. In 1992 they were technically

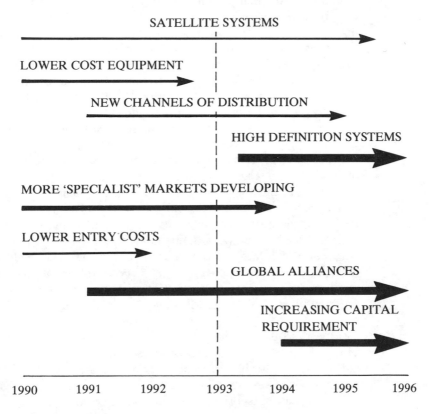

Figure 7 Industry forces map

bankrupt and sought protection from their creditors in the US courts.

There are two common errors in industry analysis. The first is analysing your own situation rather the situation affecting all firms in the industry. The second is analysing the past and present but neglecting the future (which is a much greater intellectual challenge).

Every force which may affect a firm in an industry needs to be defined as precisely as possible. Then each force must be ranked in terms of their likely impact on firms in the industry . One way is to grade each force high, medium or low. My favourite way to do this is to draw an 'industry forces map'. A simple example, showing the television programme making industry, explains the principle (Figure 7).

Although the map is simplistic – only eight forces are shown – the principle is clear. The map was produced in 1993 (hence the dotted vertical line). Forces which have affected the industry are shown as arrows starting when the force became significant and stopping when its impact had waned. The impact of the forces is indicated by the thickness of the arrows. The forces are projected forward. By taking a vertical line up from 1996 it is possible to see what forces will be influencing the industry at that time. We can now begin to answer the five basic questions with precision: Do we want to stay in the industry? How do we protect ourselves against industry threats? What opportunities are created by the evolution of the industry? Can we lead the industry the way we want it to go? And how must we change to be an industry leader?

The arrow diagram does not show the interdependence of forces which can best be analysed on a 'weather map' or system diagram which shows (at a defined date in the future) the possible interaction of forces. As the future is always uncertain – fortune telling is an inexact science – several scenarios are needed. Such predictions are almost always wrong, but the activity of trying to forecast future industry trends is an essential discipline.

External industry change drivers

There are many interdependent forces which drive change in an industry. It is possible to spend one's whole life tracking industry changes. However, to make an analysis possible we will group these into nine categories which are shown on the diagram on the next page (Figure 8).

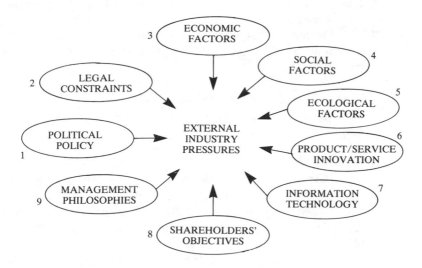

Figure 8 The nine external industry change drivers

Each category of external change driver may have a crucial impact. For example:

- Government may decide to encourage investment in your industry and give a ten year tax break.
- It may become illegal to sell the traditional product.
- Economic policy may put up interest rates to squeeze inflation out of the system.
- An increase in numbers of old people creates a new requirement for health care facilities.
- Concern about the environment may force you to move towards sustainable use of the earth's resources.
- Someone may come up with a new idea. For example, in 1993 a British inventor announced that he had discovered how to make a plastic that was virtually indestructible. This could drive major changes to many firms in the defence, steel, security and auto-motive (and many other!) industries.
- New ways of managing complexity may reshape an industry. For example, computerised booking systems permitted the growth of global airlines.

■ Shareholders may flood your industry with funds so promoting growth and innovation.

■ Management philosophies may change. For example, the insurance industry used to be staid and conservative but is now aggressive and ambitious.

These change drivers are powerful stimulants to identifying strategic opportunities and threats. Hence we will examine each one in relation to your own firm.

Industry definition

There are always ways to redefine an industry, even if the industry is deemed mature. Consider the concept of a railway station. This used to be thought of as a place to catch trains: with a few decrepit travellers' services available for the valiant. Now a railway station is reconceptualised as a shopping centre with a railway to guarantee customer traffic. Even the left luggage department is fundamentally changed – with automated luggage lockers, twenty-four hour service etc.

It is worth reflecting on the stage of evolution of your industry. Many industries develop in predictable ways. Mostly industries begin by being fragmented (like the early days of the motor car when there were hundreds of small manufacturers) and then become concentrated into the hands of a few firms. The insurance industry and the air-conditioner industry are good examples. However, the opposite may also be true. For example, the television film industry used to have a few large players but ENG technology permits much smaller companies to make highly professional films.

As we develop industry analysis it is often possible to group competing firms together as they follow the same broad strategy. The notion of strategic groups is very powerful. If we can plot current strategic group strategies against a 'map' of the industry it is sometimes possible to find 'strategic gaps' – spaces which permit a firm to move in a new direction. For example, in the USA the growth in long term hotel residents displeased with conventional hotels created a strategic space which was filled by 'apartment' hotels, like the Residence Inn.

The development of industry scenarios is an intellectually demanding activity but one which is at the heart of strategic analysis. The task may seem remote from day-by-day challenges but insightful industry scenarios are money in the bank. They permit strategic positioning to become deliberate.

WORKSHOP 1: EXPLORING INDUSTRY SCENARIOS

Preparation
You will need an overhead projector, screen, flip chart, marker pens and Blu-Tack.

Time required
The workshop takes approximately 4 hours.

WORKSHOP PLAN

---

1   The team leader opens the workshop by sharing the objectives which are:

■ To undertake an industry scenario analysis.
■ To spin off ideas for strategy development.

The team leader reminds the group that each team member should help in the process of generating and capturing ideas.

2   Presentations are made by individuals question by question. Discussion and argument should be prevented. Notes are taken of salient points and recorded on flip charts which should be displayed around the room. (2 hours in total)

3   Based on the input given by individuals answer the ten items below in discussion. Record your answers to each question on separate flip charts. (1 hour 45 minutes for all ten questions)

a   The key substitute products or services for our current products or services are ...
b   We answer the question: 'What industry(ies) are we in?' this way ...
c   Average growth rate and profitability of firms within our defined industry(ies) is ...

d Our performance compared with industry norms over a three year period is ...

e Exhaustively define and plot industry forces as suggested in the text.

f Look at each industry force. Does it present an opportunity and/or a threat? Determine all possible offensive and defensive strategies.

g Who are the principal players in the industry? Which firms do you believe will be industry winners in the future? How are successful firms positioning themselves? How sustainable is their dominance?

h What is the pattern of entries and exits? Why are these occurring?

i Are acquisitions, mergers or other factors changing the structure of ownership of firms in the industry? How?

j How significant are concerns about the environment (social, economic and physical), governmental and legislative initiatives or requirements? (Include constraints and opportunities caused by sociological factors – demographic, age structure, trade unions, skill levels etc.)

k What technological and other innovative changes are affecting product development, cash management, procurement, marketing, manufacturing, logistics, sales and aftersales, systems, people management and organisation development?

l What changes are taking place in customers' demand patterns? Are new market segments developing (or capable of being created) and are existing market segments changing their buying behaviour?

4 In conclusion, the most important task of all! You must capture *all* the ideas that have emerged, provisionally categorise them and place the ideas into one of four conceptual 'buckets'. Sometimes ideas will not fall neatly into one of the categories but choose the best fit. The four conceptual buckets are:

Bucket 1 Improvement Ideas (enhancing what we do now).

Bucket 2 Opportunities (ideas someone might exploit).
Bucket 3 Threats (hazards to growth, security and/or profitability).
Bucket 4 Uncertainties (issues which need further analysis or debate).
(15 minutes)

Ensure that your buckets are safely stored, enjoy a few moments to celebrate the success of your workshop and agree how to manage the prework for the next session.

Step 2
Assessing market dynamics

PREPARATION

Before you come to the workshop on Market Dynamics you should answer these questions:

1 How do you define 'market segments'? What market segments (groups of customers with similar needs and wants) do you serve *and* could serve?
2 What are the economic characteristics of each (served now and possible) segment? How big a share is it necessary to have in order to maintain a superior return on investment?
3 What are the key decision making criteria which shape the purchasing decisions of customers in each of the market (served now and possible) segments?
4 Are there new ways to access market segments that you serve at the present time? What would be their advantages and disadvantages?
5 Are there new market segments waiting to be recognised? What could they be?
6 How are market segments that you serve at the present time changing?
7 Could you create a new market segment? What could it be?
8 Who is competing in each market segment? What are their strengths and weaknesses compared with you?

WORKSHOP BRIEFING

The industry analysis completed in the previous step looked at 'the game'. In this step we look at 'the reasons why the game is played'.

This is crucial because the sole purpose of business is attracting customers. In this step we concentrate on markets from a strategic viewpoint. The purposes of this step are:

■ To understand how analysis of market dynamics has become the pre-eminent creative strategic tool.
■ To develop skills in segmenting markets.
■ To develop a mind-set of being able to shape the market.
■ To deepen insight into the ways a firm needs to be configured to be market orientated.

MARKET DYNAMICS: A CREATIVE STRATEGIC TOOL

Marketing is a core business profession. Huge sums are spent on researching, conceptualising and developing markets. A great deal of this work is excellent and helps us take sound business decisions. With all of this market data available why is it important for a strategy development team to think afresh about markets? The reason is that most market analysis is 'today orientated'. Competitive strategy is about underlying logic, patterns and creating the future. We need to use market data for different purposes than everyday marketing planning.

Let me give you an example. The author was consulting with a firm offering marketing services in the USA to Scotch Whisky exporters. Their market analysis of the position of Scotch Whisky in the US spirit market was superb – they knew market shares to a fraction of a per cent. But the firm knew virtually nothing about vodka, gin or brandy since these were spirits they didn't carry. Yet their competencies would permit them to market other imported liquors. Their market analysis reflected their current mind-set: a total preoccupation with Scotch Whisky.

A strategic market analysis should be:

■ *Fundamental* – not taking existing markets served as a *conceptual* limitation.
■ *Orientated* to the longer term – looking more than two years ahead.
■ *Creative* – questioning current definitions of markets and market segments.
■ *Analytical* – identifying the key success factors for market success.

■ *Dynamic* – detecting changes which create opportunities or impose threats.

What is 'a market'? From some points of view talking about 'markets' is dangerous because it encourages us to take an intellectual stance towards customers who respond individually and emotionally.[1]

'Markets' don't exist. They are a sociological abstraction. Their purpose is to help us to think about something otherwise too complex to imagine. For example, we talk about DINKs (dual income, no kids) as a market. But within this group there are yoga buffs, mormons and scuba divers – all of whom have different needs and wants. But DINKs have an important characteristic – which is that they have lots of disposable income. This helps us define the category but we should never assume that the category label tells the whole story.

We might wish to know the needs, wants and valuing criteria of every DINK household – but this is impossible. So we must generalise. Since every generalisation is based on assumptions, your conceptual abstraction is always a conditional hypothesis. This means that when your marketing director says 'this is the way the market is segmented' you should ask 'what are the other ways of segmenting the market that you have rejected?' Strategic market analysis must (for a period of time) throw conventional market definitions up into the air.

Market segmentation

The reason why we segment a market is to reduce the risk of marketing generalisations which are so bland that they breed simplistic strategies. Much modern strategic creativity comes from increasingly precise definitions of small groups of customers' needs: this has become known as 'micro-marketing'. From this fine-cut analysis firms are capable of generating highly creative strategies.

Let us explore this uniquely revealing strategic concept by considering a category of humanity – unattached adults. Few people would dispute that there is a deep human need for companionship. Those who want to meet others with romance in mind are a 'market' which is 'segmented' in interesting ways.

For the 'exclusive' segment the most upmarket service is offered by Helena International VIP Club of Beverley Hills which uses psychoanalysts, handwriting experts and private detectives to probe into a potential clients past life. This can cost up to $20 000 for each hopeful and, once accepted, a date often takes six weeks to set up.

Another market segment which could be described as the 'mature unattached' can be accessed using new technology. Phone dating has arrived in the US. The system works this way: fifty word personal ads appear in magazines. The prospective suitor phones a number and listens to a recorded message. He or she may choose to leave a reply. The advertiser listens to the recorded messages and may ring back if they like the suitor's blandishments. Dates within the hour can sometimes be arranged. The cost? About $1.50 a minute for the phone call.

Market segments vary in their characteristics geographically. In Japan there is a market segment of mobile young Japanese who are no longer able to use the services of traditional matchmakers. Innovative ways to access this market segment have been developed. One-day matchmaking tours are run by a tour firm called NEAT which schedules trips each weekend. The highlight of one such trip was a visit to an aquarium. At the end of the day everybody gathers in two lines for 'proposal time'. What happens? About a quarter of each group usually pair off.

Another Japanese firm is creating a new market segment – urban Japanese women who are seeking low-cost dates. This segment is accessed by a recent innovation in Tokyo – dating vending machines. They offer profiles of 450 young men with their name, height, weight, job, phone number and photo. The Japanese women use the discreetly placed vending machines and then they can peruse the profiles at their leisure and make a call if they feel attracted.

Market segment strategies

The analysis of the date making industry reveals some important insights into market segmentation. Market segments are groups of customers with similar needs and wants – so far as this affects their purchasing behaviour. For example, urban Japanese women who are seeking low-cost dates are a market segment.

Customers within a market segment have similar (but not identical) decision making criteria. This means that all customers in the segment can be treated *to a large extent* alike. Remember that there are real differences between customers who we have categorised together as a single market segment. One person may buy cherry yoghurt because they believe that cherries are a cure for gout whereas someone else may buy the same pot of yoghurt because it makes a marvellous substitute for cream on chocolate cake.

Within market segments there are often very different valuing and decision making criteria. For example, Marks & Spencer reported in 1992 that the sales of vichyssoise soup doubled when they renamed it 'leek and potato soup' – customers found the down-to-earth name fitted their lifestyle better.

Market segments are accessed in particular ways (what works in one segment may not work for another). They are influenced by many factors; social, economic, geographical, lifestyle and so on. The firm that understands how these factors shape buying behaviour has real advantage. New ways to access segments do arise: through technology, creativity and so on. For example, city radio has opened up new channels of communication for local suppliers and contractors.

Market segments may be brief 'windows of opportunity'. For example, in 1992 one firm sold 100,000 chocolate orang-utans on St Valentine's Day with the motif 'don't make a monkey out of me'. Sometimes market segments are waiting to be recognised. When planes from Europe and North America land in Hong Kong the discarded newspapers used to be thrown away as happens in most airports. Now, somehow the newspapers are spirited away, diligently ironed in cramped flats and then sold by street vendors at a discount on airmail express charges – a price sensitive foreign newspaper market segment was detected.

New market segments can sometimes be created. It is said that the idea of Beaujolais Nouveau was developed by a marketing man who asked the question 'what can we do with this rather rough new wine that does not keep well'? The concept of desk top publishing was conceived by Apple Computers and created several new market segments. Before Federal Express started there was no market for a reliable overnight parcel service – just a latent need. It took a brilliant insight to spot the opportunity and a bold strategy to make it a reality.

Market segments change – sometimes very quickly. This is the reason why we call this step market *dynamics*. Lifestyles are more diverse today than they were twenty years ago. The 'one-dimensional' products of the past are no longer acceptable to today's mass market. Innovations are needed, even in basic products. For example, in the 1990s Sanyo introduced a 'multi-dimensional' refrigerator with revolving shelves and 'fuzzy logic' controls: a real innovation in a product that most people considered to be mature.

Segmentation is subtle. In England there are thousands of pubs which sell beer, other alcoholic drinks and food. You might think that pub users were a distinct market segment. Not so. The drinker in Mayfair has very different wants and needs from a pub user in a country village. Every pub demands its own strategy because its local market and competitive environment is distinctive. The key question that the publican must answer for potential customers in his or her catchment area is: 'Supposing you have £5. Where will you spend it if you want an evening out?'

One product can actually appeal to a number of market segments at the same time. Consider a 747 flying between London and Tokyo. There are perhaps a dozen people flying in first class who are receiving personal treatment and watching their personal video selection on an individual TV screen. Further back are the business class passengers who are comfortable (not as comfortable of course) and are being treated as if they were staying in a four star hotel. Right at the back of the plane are the economy passengers who are queuing for the toilet and trying to get comfortable in seats that feel as if they were designed for people who are one size smaller than they are. It is the same plane for all three classes yet the airline has succeeded in customising their product so that it meets the needs of three distinctive market segments at once. Clever!

Market segmentation uncovers the valuing and decision making processes of 'typical' customers. A firms market segment strategy is influenced by its competitors. They can destroy differentiation by replicating advantages, finding innovative other ways to win the customer or redefining the customers needs and wants.

Market segments have distinct needs and wants but these can be filled in different ways. In Bombay the office workers like to have their lunch cooked by their wives. An incredible system to collect dinners in the morning and transport the lunches by bike, train, bus and wheel barrow ensures that each colour-coded container reaches its hungry target just in time for lunch. Urchins pedal around the crowded streets of Bombay peering around huge stacks of tenderly prepared dinners. After lunch the system goes into reverse and the container is returned to the home kitchen. Most of the carriers are illiterate yet there are sophisticated backup mechanisms in case anything goes wrong. This complex Bombay system illustrates that there is a direct connection between a need and a business solution. Yet, if the system did not exist other ways would be found to meet that need – the office workers of Bombay would be eating from lunch boxes carried in their briefcases.

When you have time there is another aspect of market segmentation to explore. You can look at the strategies that competitors follow in different market segments. Often unexpected opportunities are uncovered by this process of detailed analysis. For example, a hotel may compete in a dozen major segments – each needs to be reviewed, as a competitor may be strong in several of the segments but weak in others.

We should not allow our emphasis on market segmentation to shape our thinking entirely. Markets can be ignorant, conservative and plain wrong. Listening to the market yields ideas which reflect the present. When asked, in 1970 most people did not see a use for a fax machine. Now they are ubiquitous.

Segmenting markets

Market segmentation is a technique for strategic analysis and a tool for planning the future. The first question is 'how do we segment the market?' This may sound easy but, in reality, is a highly creative task. Remember that a market segment does not really exist – it is a sociological abstraction. Let's take a simple example. Consider people who buy household insurance through an insurance agent. From the point of view of the insurance company how should they segment this market? There is the obvious segmentation by class of business; household, fire, motor etc. Let's have a look at some of the other options. Ten segmentation criteria spring to mind:

1 Segmentation by location (some places have a much higher incidence of house breaking than others).

2 Segmentation by occupation of customer (teachers have a lower loss rate than florists).

3 Segmentation by age of customer (young people have double the number of motor accidents than people over 30 years).

4 Segmentation by education of customer (professionally qualified people buy more travel insurance).

5 Segmentation by race of customer (although they are loath to admit it most insurance companies price themselves out of the market when asked to insure property in inner city areas).

6 Segmentation by whether the customer has other insurances of certain types.

7 Segmentation by the type of insurance broker (some are national, others are part time one-man bands).

8 Segmentation by the loss ratio of the insurance broker (some brokers find much better risks than others).

9 Segmentation by the amount of commission paid to the insurance broker.

10 Segmentation by the degree of fit between the insurance company's systems and the insurance broker's systems.

We could go on! These possible segmentation criteria for household insurance are less than half of the available options. Each segmentation option has strengths and weaknesses. There is no right answer. It is necessary to brainstorm all of the possible segmentation options and try to see which ones seem both practical and powerful. In practice, it is difficult to use more than three segmentation criteria. So, for example, in the insurance example the company might choose to segment its household market by type of customer, by the loss ratio of the insurance broker and by geographical areas. This segmentation model is shown as a cube. Figure 9 is a simple example.

In the example cube the type of customer is shown as four socio-economic classes, AB, C, D and E; the loss ratio as those brokers whose claims exceed their accumulated premium income compared with those who have the opposite track record, and three simple geographical categories. Even on this chart there are twenty-four segments (four customer type multiplied by two loss categories multiplied by three areas). A real example will have dozens of distinct segments, each with different economic drivers, competitive environments and attractiveness. This changes over

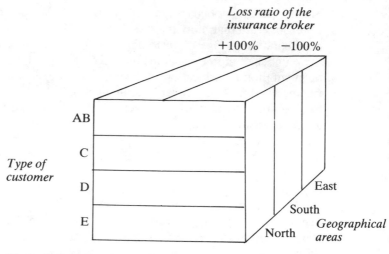

Figure 9 Segmentation model (cube)

time. For example, today the car market is conventionally split into twenty-three major segments as compared with eight in the 1960s.

Purposes of market segmentation

Market segmentation is a key step for strategy development. The argument has four stages:

1   Competitive strategies are only effective if they provide superior value.
2   Value is determined by customers.
3   We can conceptually group customers into categories called 'markets' and then again into 'market segments'. These are sufficiently unitary for firms' strategic planning.
4   Firms must be configured to meet the needs and wants of different market segments more effectively than competitors. (The firm as a chameleon!).

This requires that you:

■ Critically evaluate your current philosophy of market segmentation (the principles on which you have categorised customers into groups) and test its validity.

■ Understand the valuing and decision making processes of customers within each segment – this helps to assess your strategic strengths and weaknesses in each market segment.

■ Assess whether you are serving 'attractive' market segments. This requires an understanding of segment economics.

■ Map how 'your' market segments are changing – this will include both speed and direction of change.

■ Detect opportunities to gain advantage through serving related market segments. A firm which sells books by post to speleologists (cavers) could gain access to mountain climbers (who use the same shops) more cheaply than a firm which makes dog food.

■ Track changes in existing market segments to identify market dynamics – both opportunities and threats.

■ Identify whether there are market segments which you need to enter to achieve your long term strategic intention.

WORKSHOP 2: ASSESSING MARKET DYNAMICS

Preparation

You will need an overhead projector, screen, flip chart, marker pens and Blu-Tack.

Copy these onto a flip chart or OHP foil in advance:

■ Possible segmentation criteria table (below)
■ Segmentation cube (below)

Time required
The workshop takes approximately five hours.

WORKSHOP PLAN

---

1   The team leader opens the workshop by sharing the objectives which are:

■ To undertake a strategic market analysis.
■ To review segmentation criteria.
■ To develop a creative and assertive mind set towards shaping the market.
■ To explore ways your firm needs to configure itself to be more market orientated.

The team leader reminds the group that each team member should help in the process of generating, building on and capturing ideas. (5 minutes)

2   Presentations are made by sub-groups. Presentations should last about 20 minutes and be followed by 15 minutes' discussion. Notes are taken of salient points and recorded on flip charts which should be displayed around the room. (2 hours in total)

3   Based on the input given by sub-groups answer these five questions in discussion. Record your answers to each question on separate flip charts. (Allow 2 hours 30 minutes for all five questions)

a   Brainstorm *all* possible segmentation criteria. There is a list of possible criteria below (Figure 10) but add additional ideas for segmentation as they occur to you. Go on to separate pages if there is no room on the chart. Many groups can think of at least twenty segmentation criteria.

Figure 10 Possible segmentation criteria chart

POSSIBLE SEGMENTATION CRITERIA	POTENTIAL BENEFITS	POTENTIAL DISADVANTAGES
1 By geography		
2 By income of customer		
3 By lifestyle of customer		
4 By size of customer		
5 By nature of customer's business		
6 By financial strength of customer		
7 By technology of customer		
8 By how purchasing decisions are made by customers		

9		
10		
11		
12		
13		
14		
15		

b Select the three most useful segmentation criteria and place one on each axis of the cube. Develop the cube so that it represents a picture of your market (Figure 11). Each box is a market segment.

SEGMENTATION CUBE

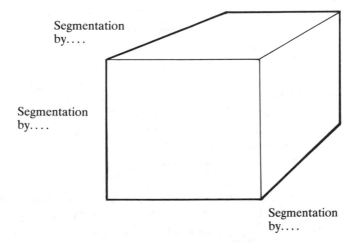

Segmentation by....

Segmentation by....

Segmentation by....

Figure 11 Segmentation cube showing three most useful criteria

c Who are the current segment leaders?

■ Name up to five firms, you may include your own firm.

■ What are their current strengths and weaknesses of these competing firms segment by segment?

■ What are these firm's strategic intentions in each of

the segments? Where do you think they will be in say three years' time?

d   Analyse *all* those segments in which you now compete *and* may wish to compete by producing a segment specific strategy (SSS) for each. Cover:

■ Segment description – all of the factors which are reshaping the segment's buying behaviour.

■ Segment size and profitability (historic and projected) – shown with historical trends projected forwards.

■ Entrants – who are they? Why are they entering? Who else may enter?

■ Nature of rivalry – how do you believe that competing firms will react over the next two or so years?

e   Develop three 'Market Scenarios' for a date three years from now using the scenario planning technique that you learnt in Step 4.

4   In conclusion, the most important task of all! You must capture all the ideas that have emerged, provisionally categorise them and place the ideas into one of four conceptual 'buckets'. Sometimes ideas will not fall neatly into one of the categories but choose the best fit. The four conceptual buckets are:

Bucket 1 Improvement Ideas (enhancing what we do now).

Bucket 2 Opportunities (ideas someone might exploit).

Bucket 3 Threats (hazards to growth, security and/or profitability).

Bucket 4 Uncertainties (issues which need further analysis or debate).

(30 minutes)

Ensure that your buckets are safely stored, enjoy a few moments to celebrate the success of your workshop and agree how to manage the prework for the next session.

Step 3
Evaluating structural profitability

PREPARATION

Before you come to the workshop on this step you should read the workshop brief and consider the checklists which relate to the seven structural forces driving profitability. Draw a force field chart (this is explained in the text) of the seven forces affecting your industry on an OHP foil. Then take each of these forces and draw a separate force field diagram as suggested in the text (again on an OHP foil). Bring your completed OHPs to the workshop.

WORKSHOP BRIEFING

In this step we analyse the preconditions for profitability. So far we have conducted an industry and market analysis. Now we explore the factors which make industries attractive or not. This can be a crucial step; measures of comparative profitability[1] suggest that at least 40 per cent of a firm's profits come from competing in an inherently profitable industry. The remaining profit percentage is the result of strategic positioning within an industry and operational effectiveness in innovation, quality, responsiveness and efficiency. In this step you will:

- Study the seven forces which structure the profitability of an industry.
- Analyse the impact of these forces on your own firm.
- Assess whether you can shape your competitive strategy to avoid structural threats and seize structural opportunities.

This is about profitability – the major preoccupation of strategic managers world-wide. Without going deeply into the realm of philosophy, it is worth asking 'what is profit?' For the time being we take a conventional view and define profit as 'the reward for meeting customers' needs at a sustainable cost'. This is our starting point. The statement makes three assumptions:

■ That potential customers are able to buy.
■ That potential customers are willing to buy.
■ The structure of the industry permits firms to make a profit.

Able and willing to buy?

Not all customers with needs are able to buy. Industries only thrive where there is a sizeable potential market of people who can afford to pay. This is well understood, for example, by pharmaceutical companies who invest far less research budget into drug development for third world diseases because most sufferers cannot pay to cure their complaints. Many more research dollars go into the diseases of the wealthy.

Sometimes potential customers have a need but are not willing to pay: most people accept that they should have a fire extinguisher in the house but few buy one. The concept of 'market readiness' tells us that a real need can exist but, because this need is either not perceived or valued, customers won't reach into their pockets. One of the most insightful realisations of market readiness was when Apple computers defined their competition not as IBM but as 'public ignorance'.

Industry structure

The analysis of structural profitability was given a giant conceptual prod by Professor Michael Porter[2] who argued that the attractiveness of an industry is the result of the composite strength of negative industry forces. The model we use grew directly from Michael Porter's work but includes environmental and market factors to provides a comprehensive framework.

You recall that we define an industry as a group of firms offering products or services which are substitutes for each other. Some industries are much more profitable than others. Why? We will assume that the profitability of an industry is the result of seven forces. These are shown on the diagram below (Figure 12).

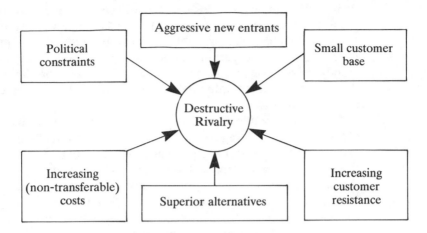

Figure 12 The seven forces that determine industry attractiveness

Our argument is efficient firms that have the right economic scale will be outstandingly profitable in an industry which enjoys – political support, transferable costs, benign new entrants, constructive rivalry, low customer resistance, a large customer base and no attractive substitute products. However, if one, or more of the forces is negative then industry profitability will be reduced. The stronger the negative forces the more anxious your bank manager becomes.

The seven forces shown on the diagram (Figure 12) fundamentally determine industry attractiveness and they change continuously. A word of caution is appropriate. Some firms can succeed in an unattractive industry whilst others produce doleful results in the most benign circumstances. Firms can 'buck the system', but, like backing an outsider in a horse race, the odds are against the maverick.

We examine each of the seven forces below. Pay particular attention to the checklists which conclude each of the sections. You need to refer to these in preparation for the workshop on this step.

Force 1: Political forces
'Political forces' are all restrictions on commercial freedom caused by social forces reflected either directly through institutions or

indirectly through sociological forces. Usually the impact of
political forces are profit limiting: British Gas cannot raise prices
to the extent that the market will bear because a government
watchdog will not permit the company to exploit its virtual
monopoly position. Many firms would enjoy higher profits if they
discharged pollutants into the nearest stream – but they are not
allowed to do this.

Sometimes political and social forces enhance profitability.
Governments encourage some firms by allowing them to make
extraordinary profits: many governments offer tax holidays to new
firms setting up in unpopular regions. The Kingdom of Saudi
Arabia has a thriving agricultural industry even though the desert
is inhospitable to the farmer. Why? The government has decided
to support the farming industry so that it is now economic to run
air-conditioned cow sheds even though the costs of imported
products are much less. Political logic has overtaken commercial
logic.

Politics impacts in indirect ways. Social stability attracts investment. Governments can create a climate for enterprise. Singapore,
for example, in the 1980s was a good place to manufacture hi-tech
products because a strong government created all the necessary
conditions. If politics are in your favour the following things will be
happening:

- Government 'approves' of your product or service.
- Legislation supports preferential or free trade.
- Government accepts your profit margins.
- Government is not favouring rival industries.
- 'Foreign' suppliers have no special advantages or are disadvan-
  taged.
- Government supplies a suitable infrastructure for the industry
  (transport, education, training, financing etc.).
- Social forces (e.g. consumer bodies) are innocuous.

Force 2: Non-transferable costs
There is a small grocer's that has served a local community for
many years. Two miles away a brand new 'mega-superstore' with
parking for 2,000 cars was opened two years ago. The grocer, who
sells exactly the same brands as the mega-superstore, was visited
recently by the supplier of canned beans and told that wholesale

prices would be rising by 7 per cent. The grocer replied: 'You can't do that. I hardly make a margin as it is. The mega-superstore sets the prices. I can only go 5 per cent above otherwise people won't shop here. If you raise your prices I can't pass it on.' The representative shrugged and replied: 'You don't have to have these goods if you don't want them. It costs us too much to supply the small fry like you.'

The grocer was incurring costs that he could not transfer to his customers. His margins were squeezed and, if this pattern is repeated with other suppliers, the profit potential of firms in the neighbourhood grocery retail industry is reduced (unless someone can think of a smart way to mitigate the problem).

Industries are often constructed by chains of firms – each handling a stage of product development (for example, baked beans are grown, harvested, cooked, canned, advertised, distributed and sold). Powerful suppliers are sometimes capable of squeezing the profit out of their customers.

There are other sources of non-transferable costs. For example, wage inflation in Hong Kong was 11 per cent in 1992 – far higher than in other ASEAN countries. Since Hong Kong manufacturers are selling to the world market they cannot transfer their increasing wage costs to their customers – either their margins shrink or they decide to manufacture in a low cost area.

Non-transferable costs may not equally affect all firms in an industry: small firms may suffer more than big, some countries suffer more than others. It is possible to map the impact of non-transferable costs on groups within industries and, thereby, bring into focus which categories are most disadvantaged. A strategic objective is always to avoid the disadvantaged parts of the industry (or maybe the whole industry).

If non-transferable costs are insignificant the following things will be happening:

- You can obtain supplies of inputs from many sources.
- Your suppliers compete with each other on price.
- Those who supply you value you as a customer.
- You would have low costs of switching to other suppliers.
- Your input costs are as low as anyone in your industry.
- Your variable costs (energy, labour etc.) are as low as anyone in your industry.

■ Your fixed costs (buildings, equipment etc.) are as low as anyone in your industry.

Force 3: New entrants

A profitable industry attracts new firms to enter. When home video players became popular thousands of street corner video libraries were established. The prospect of windfall profits caused many investors to enter the industry: so many, in fact, that many video hire shops became unprofitable and went out of business.

New entrants frequently drive down margins – especially where profitable firms enjoy economies of scale. Why is this? If unit prices can be reduced by taking a large market share then all new entrants will seek to grab a major share as soon as possible. Sometimes offering superior products achieves this. Commonly, a new entrant comes in with lower prices which attract customers away from the existing suppliers. Firms with a large market share respond with anxiety and aggression: they reduce their prices, a war develops, and the industry becomes less profitable.

New entrants are discouraged by these factors:

1 Existing products (often brands) have loyal customers.
2 Economies of scale are significant.
3 Capital requirements are high.
4 Existing firms have an established reputation.
5 Access to distribution will be expensive to acquire.
6 Existing firms have accumulated experience and so are outstandingly efficient or innovative.
7 Proprietary technology prevents new entrants from duplicating existing products (through patents, copyrights etc.).
8 Suppliers are unwilling to sell to new entrants.
9 Existing firms are in the best locations.
10 Government policy supports existing players.

Not all new entrants destroy industry profitability. There is a small town in England called Ross-on-Wye. Many years ago a second-hand bookshop opened, then another and another. Soon the town became inundated with antiquarian bookshops many specialising in such esoteric subjects as Civil War memoirs or scholarly works on oriental tapestries. But the new entrants were benign: book collectors came from all over the world to stay in Ross-on-Wye and browse. The proliferation of competitors adds to the profitability of each competent firm.

Sometimes a new entrant can add to the stature of an industry and bring about a huge increase in profitability. Until IBM entered the personal computing industry few of the competing firms were significantly profitable. IBM created a new market; from the competitors' viewpoint, little could have been better than the then industry leader legitimising the product and setting high prices. The new entrant was welcomed with open arms.

If new entrants are benign the following things will be happening:

- There are modest industry profit margins so possible new entrants are not attracted.
- Entry costs are high so possible entrants are deterred.
- Economies of scale are significant (so an entrant cannot start small).
- It is difficult to 'learn the business'.
- Existing products/services are 'differentiated' – regarded by customers as special or unique.
- Channels of distribution will be expensive to acquire.
- New entrants add to the stature of the industry and increase general profitability.

Force 4: Rivalry
It is a principle of capitalism that competitive rivalry between firms is the mainspring of progress. Rivalry drives prices down which favours the consumer; acts as a spur to innovation and weeds out weaker players who do not survive. But competition is a blunt instrument. Sometimes rivalry mutates from being a condition of a healthy organism into a cancerous growth.

For several years in the 1980s many of the airlines of the world reported huge losses. Few were profitable. Why should an industry which has so much business be less profitable than a small chain of fast food restaurants? The answer, of course, is rivalry. Airlines require massive investments of capital, once committed an airline company cannot easily metamorphose itself into another kind of firm, utilisation of capacity determines profitability and it is impossible to really differentiate the product. All of these factors ensure that competition will be price driven and whenever there is over-capacity in the airline industry, hey presto, price competition drives down industry margins to abysmal levels. A few, well positioned firms may be able to escape the general malaise but most are dragged down towards unprofitability.

Many industries are in this situation. At the time of writing few of the world's motor tyre manufacturing firms are profitable: rivalry in the industry has destroyed profitability for almost all the players.

Rivalry is most damaging when:

1 There are many small firms but a large firm would enjoy substantial advantages, especially economies of scale.
2 Some of the players are overseas firms – which operate under different rules.
3 There is slow market growth.
4 Some firms believe that getting a dominant market share now will gain a superior long term position.
5 Rival firms fear each other and do not want to be in an exposed position.
6 There is no clear industry leader and there are several firms aspiring to dominate.
7 Fixed costs are high.
8 Entry costs are low.
9 Industry economics are capacity utilisation driven.
10 Customers are price sensitive.

Rivalry can become a way of life. Firms fight each other because they fight each other. Governments may encourage toe to toe combat in the interest of the consumer. Cartels are illegal in many parts of the world. Managers are caught in a 'Catch 22' situation – if they match the prices of their competitors they lose money and if they don't they lose more money. Why not sell up or close down? Sometimes this is possible, but the costs of getting out (technically called 'exit costs') can be so high that firms stay in hoping that weaker players are forced out and the industry returns to profitability.

If rivalry is low the following things will be happening:

■ There are insignificant economies of scale so small firms can thrive.

- Exit costs are small so that unprofitable firms can leave painlessly.
- Industry growth is high so that there are rich pickings for all the existing players.
- No firms are staying in for long term strategic reasons – all the players are seeking normal profits.
- Firms don't compete head-to-head.
- Products or services are 'differentiated' – regarded as special or unique.
- There is a history of firms avoiding strong price competition.

Force 5: Customer resistance

Some customers are much more effective purchasers than others. An analogy with a normally frugal family on holiday makes the point. Say they go to a foreign country for the first time. The family do not know how much it is reasonable to pay for a bottle of wine, a meal or a night's accommodation. The currency is unfamiliar and looks like Monopoly money. The family are likely to pay too much for everything and adopt an attitude of 'why worry – it's only two weeks a year'. This is in sharp contrast to their purchasing at home when the cheapest supermarkets are chosen and sandwiches are taken for low cost outings to the zoo.

Purchasing is a business discipline that attracts intelligent people. The stakes are high, the work is challenging and there is a legitimate opportunity to use one's aggressive instincts. Increasingly, suppliers cannot get away with inflated prices or inferior offerings because the customers know too well what they are buying.

In hard times firms examine their costs with aggressive intent. Brought-in supplies are a major cost and so are squeezed. For example, in the UK recession of 1992 the 90 per cent of users[3] of consulting services sought to contain or reduce the daily rate for consultants they hired.

This applies in many industries. For example, firms supplying military equipment to governments find that generals are expert in design, development and costing. Therefore defence industry profits are held down by the monopoly buying position and sagacity of the customer.

If customer resistance is low the following things will be happening:

- You have many different customers (hundreds or more).
- Customers are uninformed (so they do not assess the value of what they are buying).
- Customers are unorganised into buying groups.
- Products are differentiated (i.e. price is a minor criterion on which the customer takes a buying decision).
- 'Switching costs' are high (so customers cannot readily go to a competitor).
- Customers are not suffering from low margins themselves, so don't watch every cost.
- Your supplies are essential to the customer.

Force 6: Customer base
The size, wealth and accessibility of the customer base affects industry profitability. Small markets have less spending power so total industry profitability is reduced. Oil companies make more profit than artists' oil paint manufacturers: slimming food suppliers make more than sheep dog trainers. This is not to say that small markets are inherently unprofitable for a firm – a Mexican restaurant can make larger profits than General Motors. In fact, the 'focus' competitive strategy is based on exploiting confined markets.

The wealth of markets is a key factor. There are millions of Africans who want advanced consumer electronic goods but cannot afford them. In the Philippines many businesses still use typewriters because word processors are too expensive. Without the ability to pay, the market shrinks and, therefore, the overall profitability of the industry falls.

The accessibility of the customer base is important. Some markets are unprofitable because the costs of access are high. Selling ornamental carp to Australian sheep farmers is likely to be unprofitable because the market is tiny with high costs of marketing, stock and distribution. On the other hand, selling sheep dip to these farmers has a much greater profit potential as the customer base is greater.

If the customer base is sufficient the following things will be happening:

- There are many potential customers.
- Customers need and want your products or services.

- Customers can and will pay for your products or services.
- It is economical to access customers.

Force 7: Alternatives
There are industries that have seen their business swept away by alternative products or services. Quill pen manufacturers went into receivership when the steel nib was invented. Today optical shop owners are anxious because micro-laser surgery could correct many sight problems without a need for glasses.

An alternative may have a different form from the product it replaces. For example, in the 1980s teenagers sat around for hours listening to record players. Now they play their computer games whilst the compact disc player gathers dust. Computer games, so far as many teenagers are concerned, are a superior alternative to rock 'n' roll.

This applies for many purchases. A packaging buyer in a mineral water plant can use paper, plastic, aluminium, or steel materials. If one material becomes more expensive then the buyer will switch. A navy procurement team may decide to buy a frigate or a missile system. A husband could weigh up the relative merits of a subscription to a health club or a holiday as a gift for his wife.

Products can substitute for other categories of costs. An example makes the point. Investment in an electronic mail system encourages people to type their own internal correspondence. The number of secretaries required dwindles and staff costs fall significantly. The electronic mail system is substituting for labour. This situation is repeated many times over: artificial intelligence computer systems are replacing insurance underwriters and industrial robots are replacing production operators.

Superior alternatives do not exist in all industries. There are no substitutes for champagne at weddings, flowers for anniversaries and life insurance for family security. But watch this space! Someone may think of a new way to meet these traditional needs.

If there are no superior alternatives the following things will be happening:

- Technological product or service breakthroughs are unlikely.
- There is little expenditure on research in parallel industries so no radical new ideas are expected which could replace your products or services.

■ No other industries could migrate into 'your' industry with cost advantages.
■ You are not under pressure from customers or others to supply more effective products/services.
■ There are few creative people running your industry.
■ Firms in your industry cannot defend or patent their technological breakthroughs.

Analysis of structural profitability

Structural profitability may look abstract but it often is the spring-board for many innovative strategic ideas. We will analyse structural profitability at two levels – firstly a coarse cut and then a fine cut study.

For the 'coarse cut' analysis we use a technique called 'force field analysis'. This presents any situation as being held in equi-

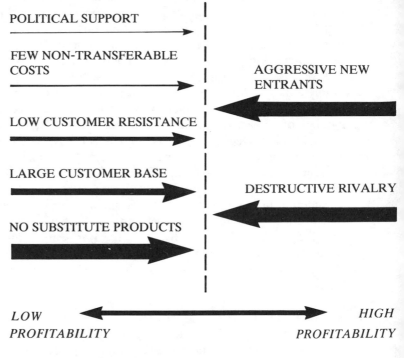

Figure 13 Force field analysis

librium at a moment of time by forces pushing in opposite directions. In the diagram (Figure 13) the equilibrium is shown by the vertical dotted line. The forces are shown by arrows.

You notice there are five forces on the left which are driving up industry profitability. The current relative strength of these forces is indicated by the thickness of the arrows. On the right there are two hostile forces – aggressive new entrants and destructive rivalry. These are the *bêtes noires* of firms in the industry. Firms need to mitigate these forces (or, judo-style, turn them to advantage) as a fundamental part of their strategy.

The primary force field analysis gives us the big picture. But each force is made up of sub-forces – which require a much more detailed ('fine cut') analysis. This should be done by taking the seven forces (even if they are positive so far as you are concerned or apparently of minor importance) and drawing a separate force-field diagram for each.

Remember that this is an *industry* wide analysis so you should consider the forces which are affecting all the firms in your industry – not just those which are acting upon your firm now. Later you could use the same techniques to analyse how the different forces affect the groups of firms within your industry and also analyse industries that you could move into. Many strategic ideas will emerge.

We close this step with a true story. The top team of a firm specialising in marine surveying undertook the seven forces analysis and recognised that aggressive new entrants working from a low cost base posed the most significant threat to existing players. So they computerised ship surveying with their own proprietary software to cut their costs over a three year period and set a new standard for professionalism. It worked. Entrants were disadvantaged and the firm became outstandingly profitable.

WORKSHOP 3: EVALUATING STRUCTURAL PROFITABILITY

Preparation

You will need an overhead projector, screen, flip chart, marker pens and Blu-Tack.

Time required

The workshop takes approximately four hours.

WORKSHOP PLAN

1   The team leader opens the workshop by sharing the objectives which are:

- Understand the seven forces which structure profitability in your industry.
- Analyse the impact of these seven forces on your own firm.
- Assess whether you can shape your competitive strategy to avoid structural threats and seize structural opportunities.

The team leader reminds the group that each team member should help in the process of generating, building on and capturing ideas. (5 minutes)

2   Presentations are made by sub-groups. The first presentation is the 'coarse cut' analysis and should consider all of the seven forces. Ask one group to present and the others to share their analysis and debate differences. Conclude with an agreed diagram. (40 minutes)

3   Further presentations are taken on each of the seven forces (the 'fine cut' analysis). Again ask one group to present and the others to share their analysis and debate differences. Conclude with an agreed diagram in each case. (3 hours)

4   In conclusion, the most important task of all! You must capture all the ideas that have emerged, provisionally categorise them and place the ideas into one of four conceptual 'buckets'. Sometimes ideas will not fall neatly into one of the categories but choose the best fit. The four conceptual buckets are:

Bucket 1 Improvement ideas (enhancing what we do now).

Bucket 2 Opportunities (ideas someone might exploit).

Bucket 3 Threats (hazards to growth, security and/or profitability).

Bucket 4 Uncertainties (issues which need further analysis or debate).

(15 minutes)

Ensure that your buckets are safely stored, enjoy a few moments to celebrate the success of your workshop and agree how to manage the prework for the next session.

Step 4
Analysing competitors

PREPARATION

The purpose of this step is to undertake a structured analysis of several 'bad' competitors. Pick three or four 'bad' competitors after reading about the difference between a 'good' and a 'bad' competitor in the text. Gather the information however you can. Answer the questions below. Data should be presented in graphical form wherever possible. Give sources of data and your view of its validity. A presentation should be prepared on each 'bad' competitor. Suggested questions are below.

1 Collect research data on the defined competitor which contains:
   a Their annual reports for last three years.
   b All relevant press cuttings. Include assessments from the financial press/experts in stockbroking companies.
   c Any specialised studies available (consult the computer data bases).
   d If relevant, patents and pending patents.
   e Company specific information (e.g. journals, their internal newspaper, trade associations etc.).
   f Reports on discussions with employees and ex-employees to discover their strategies, strengths and weaknesses.
   g Intelligence from equipment suppliers to establish their intended new investments.
   h Visit reports and photographs of their facilities.
   i Biographical information on their key executives.
   j Interview reports on: break-even points, capital utilisation,

exit costs, advantages of economies of scale, overcapacity, demand cycles, effects of currency fluctuations, numbers of equivalent competitors, maturity of markets and degree of informal/formal collusion between key companies.

k Comparative costs as compared with yourselves (show, if logical, on a per unit basis for typical products or services). Include raw materials (itemise), direct labour, indirect labour, other costs of manufacture, distribution, sales, marketing, research, development, and management overhead.

2 Prepare a recent history of the competitor and show key points on graphs and tables.

3 What markets and market segments does the competitor serve now? (Draw as a series of pie charts, show geographical differences, slices represent contribution to turnover/profit).

4 What markets and market segments did the competitor serve three years ago? (Draw as a series of pie charts, show geographical differences, slices represent contribution to turnover/profit).

5 Look at the pattern of investment decisions they have made and show this information on a chart which also shows financial performance.

6 Show your costs and prices of sample products or services in constant currency against the competitor over last three years. Use graphs to illustrate trends. What investment plans are being considered by the competitor now? What capabilities do you think that the competitor will have in five years' time? What advantages will this give them?

7 Study data on your competitor's products and services. Prepare sample product comparison charts showing comparative strengths and weaknesses compared with yourselves. To what extent does the competitor have systematic strengths in his products or services? How far does this vary across different market segments?

8 Study the competitor's top management team
   a Who has power?
   b What are their business histories?
   c What are their top team strengths and weaknesses?
   d What are their ambitions for their business? What do you think that they would define as 'success'?

Draw an organisation chart of your competitor and summarise this information on it. Put photographs of key executives on the chart summarising the strengths and track records of their key managers.

9 Study your competitor's culture.

   a Is their culture focusing energy on the important issues for success?

   b What are their orthodoxies ('recipes' they use for success)? Which do you believe are vulnerable?

   c What is their status and reward system? Is it motivating high performance?

   d What major changes in their organisation have occurred over the last ten years? Why did these occur? (Draw annotated organisation charts)

   e What are the strengths/weaknesses of the competitors current organisational culture?

      Consider: ease of control, visibility of performance, strength of attack in distinct market segments, ability to make good use of expensive resources, ability to retain and motivate staff and capability to fulfil a chosen competitive strategy.

10   Be ready to role play your competitor's top team.

   a Talking about their strategy.

   b Talking about you and how they will damage you.

Prior to the role play try to ensure factual support for each assertion. Consider your competitor's and imagine that you were their top team.

WORKSHOP BRIEFING

Almost all firms operate in a competitive environment. Competitors affect each other in myriad ways. We cannot formulate a competitive strategy without understanding the dynamics of competition and, most importantly, predicting how competitors' future strategies may unfold.

This is easier said than done! Like Las Vagas poker players competitors keep their hands secret and indulge in bluff and slight of hand. As Sun Tzu wrote over 2,300 years ago: 'The enemy must not know where I intend to attack. For if he does not know he must defend in many places, so the more scattered are his forces and the weaker is his force at any one point.'[1]

In this step you will:

■ Identify your competitors.
■ Learn how to conduct a competitor analysis.
■ Practise mapping how competitors may move – competitive positioning.

WHO ARE YOUR COMPETITORS?

Consider the yoga retreat that we looked at in the first step. Who are their competitors? The answer is not as easy as it may appear. Firstly, there are other yoga residential retreats, secondly, there are 'alternative' holiday centres which teach arts like aromatherapy or shiatsu massage, and thirdly, there are general 'activity' holidays. These firms are trying to attract people who want to combine a holiday with a personal growth experience.

Competitors offer substitute products or services which meet the same human need or want. Some of these offer similar substitutes (like the other yoga residential retreats) whereas others offer dissimilar substitutes which are alternative ways of meeting the same need. Both similar and dissimilar substitutes are competitors. It helps to show the circles of competition on a diagram (Figure 14).

Exploring the wider reaches of competition is exciting, salutary and provocative. A firm selling video games is a competitor to a compact disc manufacturer – both of them are competing for the weekend spending power of teenagers. If the nature of this competitive threat had been fully realised by music company executives in the 1980s 'we would have got into bed with Nintendo or Sega rather than ignoring them'.[2] Strategies need to be forged in relation to a wide definition of substitutes.

COMPETITOR ANALYSIS

The reasons for studying competitors are well known. As Sun Tzu[3] wrote:

He who has a thorough knowledge of himself and the enemy is

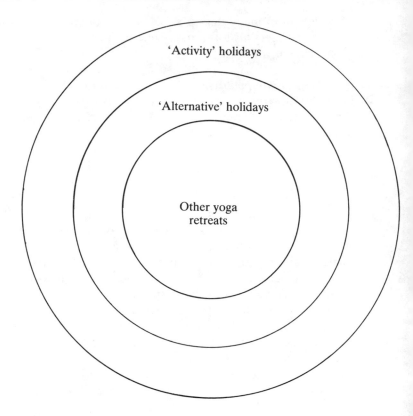

Figure 14 Circles of competition diagram

bound to win all battles. He who knows himself but not the enemy has only an even chance of winning. He who knows not himself and the enemy is bound to perish in all battles.

However, the principle is rarely put into practice. In more than two hundred strategy workshops conducted by the author none of the firms had a full competitor analysis at the start of the process.

The four key benefits of competitor analysis are:

1   Industry benchmarking (comparing yourself, in detail, with similar firms so that you can identify your strengths and weaknesses).

2   Learning (competitors are excellent teachers: they are performing experiments for you in similar market segments).

3   Positioning (knowing competitors' strategies helps you to choose how to compete).
4   Identifying opportunities and threats (competitors' actions threaten you and create opportunities: being forewarned enables you to be forearmed; this will be analysed in the workshop for this step).

INDUSTRY BENCHMARKING

Industry benchmarking requires a detailed comparison of your own performance with similar firms in your industry. For example, if you make semi-conductors and produce on a 6-inch wafer line there is a world 'entitlement' standard for the yields you should achieve. If you are below your entitlement standard then your production process is inefficient and, in that cost competitive business, you are at a serious competitive disadvantage.

The first step is to identify all meaningful success measures. A haulage firm may have 'cost per tonne per kilometre' as its primary measure whereas a television station may have audience size as its key yardstick. Often dozens of success measures can be set but, for the purpose of strategic analysis, only a handful will be significant.

Benchmarking requires use of the 'cost structure' approach. This is a particularly powerful strategic analysis tool which takes some time to learn how to use in practice – so persevere!

The principles of 'cost structures' are straightforward. Let me explain the concept in theory and then work through an example. We have defined competitive strategy as 'adding value faster than cost'.[4] If we take a unit of value (for example, a hair piece) costs accrue as the hair pieces are manufactured, packed, advertised and sold. If we accurately show these costs as a pillar chart, avoiding unattributable lumps of cost called 'overhead', then we have a cost structure analysis. Compare cost structures between competing firms and you have a powerful technique for competitor analysis.

Consider an example of three 'alternative' holiday centres: the unit of value is a two week holiday for one person. Centre A offers two hours' yoga each day and books accommodation in the local Inn. Centre B offers two hours' yoga, two hours' aromatherapy and one hour of reflexology (foot massage therapy) each day and provides accommodation and macrobiotic food in a simple hotel which has been leased for the season. Centre C offers windsurfing,

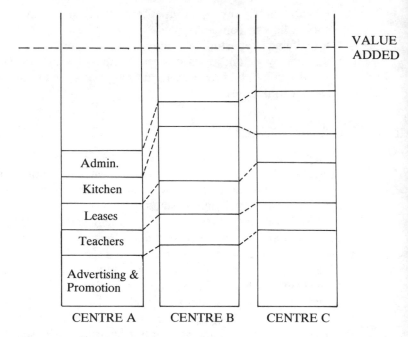

Figure 15 Cost structure of competitors chart

hang-gliding, aerobics and fifteen other sports in a purpose-built holiday village. Let us assume that they all achieve an 80 per cent occupancy rate and look at a simplified cost structure comparison (Figure 15).

This is an over-simplified example; we have only shown five blocks of costs. In reality there are many more categories. You notice that the size of each box in the pillar accurately represents the quantity of cost. With this chart we can really compare the cost structure of competitors. Another line, labelled 'value added' has been added to the diagram. Assume that all three holidays were equally attractive to those seeking an alternative holiday so the three holiday firms can charge exactly the same price (i.e. they add the same value). Based on the example, Centre A makes considerably more profit per head than the others but Centre C could still be the most profitable overall: they may attract many more people each summer. Comparative cost structures show us the different ways of investing to add value.

Learning

The benchmarking technique provides many insights and ideas but we are looking for strategic insights. We want to find how each significant competitor answers the four elemental strategic questions: 'Where will we compete'? 'What value will we create?' 'How can we be superior?' and 'How should we organise?'

Every good spy needs to know what intelligence is required. There are many subsidiary questions to be explored. These are listed in the preparation for Workshop 3 (at the end of the previous chapter).

Sometimes competitors describe their strategies in reports or newspaper articles. Perhaps they will tell us about their strategy if we ask them. Or we may meet someone in a bar who will share details of his or her company's strategy for a sucession of malt whiskies. All manner of intelligence gathering techniques are relevant. Komatsu, the Japanese earth moving equipment company, have a man based in Peoria, the home town of their great rival Caterpillar.

There is another subtlety. Not all competitors are dangerous. There are 'good' competitors who provide a firm with advantage. Their characteristics are:

- They offer equivalent goods or services with higher costs and at a high price.
- They offer sub-standard goods or services but at an equivalent price.
- They are passive (not innovative).
- They have demanding short-term oriented shareholders so mortgage the future to meet the avaricious needs of their shareholders.

Like military officers we must collect intelligence about each of our significant competitors. A 'significant' competitor is defined as 'a competitor who could threaten us or teach us'.

How is this done? The best way is to appoint one person to act as a permanent 'collecting point'. He or she gathers information including press cuttings, annual reports, promotional material, price lists, comments from employees and ex-employees and any other available data. From this a 'competitor profile' is produced which includes:

- A 'history' chart (we will explain what this is shortly).
- Performance assessment (include measures of their financial strength).
- Evaluation of their top management (evaluate the capabilities and motivations of key managers).
- A competencies assessment (a list will be sufficient for this step: later you will learn to undertake a full competency systems analysis in Step 10).
- A strategy evaluation (undertake this market segment by market segment).
- A cultural review (define their cultural strengths and policies).
- Product analysis and comparative cost structure examples (explore the strength of their product range, quality and brands).
- Technology audit (assess what technologies they have access to and what advantages this gives).
- Organisation analysis (the strengths and weaknesses of their organisation).

We mentioned a 'history chart' above. The chart should be completed for each significant competitor and relates together three different kinds of data – turnover, profit before tax and, most importantly, key strategic forces and decisions (Figure 16). Let's consider a simplistic example to gather insight into the value of this tool. Along the base of the chart we have the past five years (assume that the analysis was completed in 1998). The financial data is sometimes published but often has to be estimated. The real power of the history chart are the notes which explain all significant variations in the financial history. The noting process is speculative but it forces you to understand the competitor's situation and past strategic decisions.

How do you learn from your competitors? The best way (once you have developed a competitor profile and history chart) is to role play (for say 20 minutes) their top team discussing future strategy and how they will compete with you. You put yourself in their shoes. Don't forget to tape record the session for future analysis. Later you will consider the possible effects of their strategies on you.

Competitor role plays are a variation of military war games. When British Telecom[5] first faced the competition from Mercury they set up a shadow team to play out all Mercury's possible

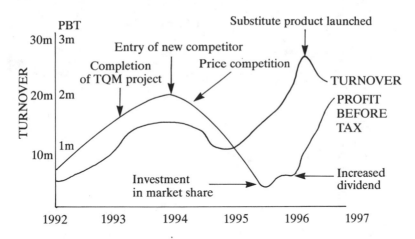

Figure 16 History chart

strategies. Responses could then be tested to provide a portfolio of possible outcomes.

The competitor role play is a tool that can be used in non-commercial organisations. A colleague used the technique with a police force which operated in a Chinese community. The officers took the local Triad gangs as their competitors. The policemen played the role of Triad members debating their strategies against the police.

Positioning

Competitors do not act in isolation: like wolves, they hunt in packs! It is always fruitful to 'map' competitors and see how they position themselves against the others.

Let us take a simple and imaginary example to clarify the process. Consider installers of fire alarms in the town of Brighton near where I live. There are nine firms competing. If we map them the result is as in Figure 17.

You will notice that the nine firms are clustered. Smith and Jones are small players at the cheap end of the market. Young is also at the low end but has been more successful. Fighter and Zeist are low-to-mid price and have achieved good market penetration. Tack is an interesting player – the most successful at the high priced end, probably being attacked by Zip. Ancient and Pike are

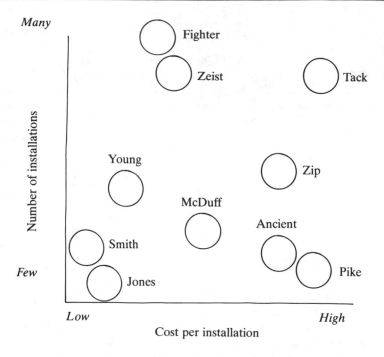

Figure 17 Map of competitors showing relative positions

high priced players who have fared badly in market share but may focus on specialised segments like banks and jewellery stores. Now let us impose on the chart our best estimate of where each competitor is moving (Figure 18). The length of the arrow represents the vigour of movement.

Young and Fighter are intending to battle aggressively for the low cost installation market segment. Whereas Pike, Zip, Tack and Zeist are hoping to take the premier installations – but it will be crowded! Ancient is either going out of business or focusing on an extremely specialised market.

Let us assume that you are McDuff. What could you do? There are a number of alternatives. You could slug it out with Young and Fighter, move to Zeist's old position, take on Ancient and Pike in the select premium segment and so on. Opportunities exist in the 'white space' where no one is competing.

Sometimes people ask 'what are the best titles for the axes on

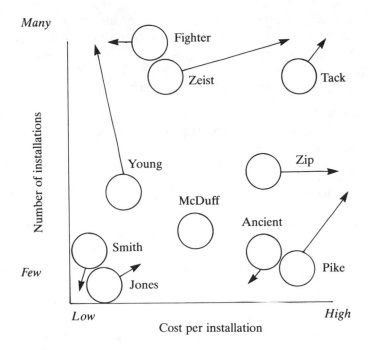

Figure 18 Map of competitors showing relative movement

the competitor map?' No one really knows. For example, we could compare quality with price or range of services with size of installation. The best answer is to try a number of alternatives and see which provides the most useful insights.

Often it is not possible to predict competitors' initiatives. This morning I opened a newspaper to find that Compaq were offering three years' on-site warranty with their new computers. I'm sure that Compaq's competitors are engaged in hurried discussions as to whether to match this service initiative. Perhaps we should all follow Field Marshal Montgomery who had a picture of General Rommel on the wall of his headquarters. From time to time he would look at the portrait and ask 'What would he do?'

It always pays to study competitors. The analysis is never easy. The aim is to determine where the competitor wants to be, and could be. But be cautious. Some of the competitors may have taken Sun Tzu's advice to 'be as shy as a maiden in the beginning of battle to entice the enemy to lower his defences and, as the battle progresses, be as swift as the hare to take advantage of his unpreparedness'.[6]

WORKSHOP 4: ANALYSING COMPETITORS

Preparation

You will need an overhead projector, screen, flip chart, marker pens, and Blu-Tack.

Time required

The workshop takes approximately 4 hours.

WORKSHOP PLAN

1   The team leader opens the workshop by sharing the objectives which are to:

■ Analyse the current strategies of selected 'bad' competitors.

■ Project forward the likely strategies of these 'bad' competitors.

■ Draw a competitor map to show how competitors are positioning themselves now and project forwards into the future.

The team leader reminds the group that each team member should help in the process of generating, building on and capturing ideas. (5 minutes)

2   Presentations are made by sub-groups. All should present their analysis and answer questions of clarification only. (1 hour for three groups)

3   Draw a 'history chart' for each competitor. Try to infer what strategies were being followed over the past five years. (1 hour)

4   Which animal does the competitor remind you of? Produce a drawing! (15 minutes)

5   Role play the top team of each competitor. Answer the question: 'If we were the chief executive of the competi-

tor what ten actions would you initiate over the next three to five years?' The observers take notes and the role plays should be recorded for later analysis. (1 hour and 30 minutes for three groups)

6   In conclusion, the most important task of all! You must capture all the ideas that have emerged, provisionally categorise them and place the ideas into one of four conceptual 'buckets'. Sometimes ideas will not fall neatly into one of the categories but choose the best fit. The four conceptual buckets are:

Bucket 1 Improvement ideas (enhancing what we do now).

Bucket 2 Opportunities (ideas someone might exploit).

Bucket 3 Threats (hazards to growth, security and/or profitability).

Bucket 4 Uncertainties (issues which need further analysis or debate).

(15 minutes)

Ensure that your buckets are safely stored, enjoy a few moments to celebrate the success of your workshop and agree how to manage the prework for the next session.

Step 5
Collecting external perspectives

PREPARATION

Before you undertake this workshop considerable prework is required (more than for any other step). This will need to be organised and the best way to do this is to plan a further short coordinating meeting in a week or so when everyone has read Step 5 and absorbed the task to be completed.

You must conduct four surveys as directed in the text. The best way to do this is to break the team into four groups, each of whom can enlist additional support as needed. There is merit in undertaking surveys with analytical rigour and managers who are not used to the techniques of behavioural science research will benefit from coaching throughout the process.

It is helpful to establish four teams now:

Team 1 Customer research.
Team 2 Supplier research.
Team 3 Employee research.
Team 4 Adviser research.

Each team should research their area and prepare a presentation (each lasting 30 minutes) for the workshop on their findings. Groups should interpret data independently so as to obtain the most objective analysis. It is best to schedule up to six weeks for the completion of the research phase.

WORKSHOP BRIEFING

The most vicious and destructive enemies of effective strategic thinking are complacency, arrogance and groupthink. In order to prevent any risk of insularity undermining the step-by-step process you will conduct four surveys to gather feedback from customers, suppliers, employees and advisers. We will go and ask them what they think of us!

In this step you will:

- Explore the value of feedback as part of the strategy development process.
- Conduct four surveys to gather feedback from customers, employees, suppliers and advisers.
- Evaluate the extent to which feedback should cause you to question your assumptions.

WHY COLLECT FEEDBACK?

Feedback reduces the risk of 'groupthink' – the most serious potential hazard in the strategy development process. Groupthink is a psychological phenomenon which results in members of a close group making blunders of judgement. This menace was identified by a political scientist, Professor Janis,[1] who studied political and military catastrophes and asked: 'Why did these intelligent people not see the obvious flaws in their arguments?' The answer was that members of the ruling group looked to other members for confirmation that their viewpoints were correct. As the group became closer something interesting happened: dissonant thinkers were expelled, contradictory opinions were derided and individual perspectives became increasingly alike. 'Reality' became defined by what the other group members thought rather than what the facts indicated. In such situations it is easy to see how the analytical and judgmental capability becomes seriously flawed.

Valid feedback helps you to:

- 'See yourself as others see you.'
- Evaluate your capability compared with rivals.
- Gather ideas for new strategies and tactics.

■ Identify blockages to effectiveness.
■ Develop a responsive, outward-looking approach.

CUSTOMER FEEDBACK

There is a wall poster that used to be in many offices and work-places. It shows a lion sitting proud looking directly at the camera. The slogan printed underneath is 'The Customer is King'. I recall waiting for several minutes for service in a tool shop whilst three assistants excitedly gossiped about their amorous adventures the night before – standing under that very poster. It is easy for a firm to want to be customer-orientated, difficult to make it happen.

By the time I was finally served in that tool shop I had obser-vations and ideas that could have been helpful to the management. The layout of the tools confused me, the choice of electric drills lacked one with an extra-large chuck, only one checkout was operating despite the fact that it was a very busy time and the sales staff treated the customers as unwelcome interruptions to their more important duties.

No one asked me for my views, I left without making a purchase and never went back. A few months later I drove past the shop which had a closing down sale and, coincidentally, met the proprietor socially that evening who told me that he was 'getting out because the local economic downturn had taken the profit out of the business'.

Great ideas come from customers. In some industries, more than 60 per cent of improvement suggestions can be directly traced back to customers' comments. We cannot understand the strategic position of a firm without knowing how customers perceive its strengths and weaknesses.

Some firms have used knowledge of their customers as the foundation of their competitive strategy. Perhaps the best example is a UK road transport firm, Heron Distribution,[2] who recognised that the conventional approach to developing a road transpor-tation business through aggressive purchasing and tight cost control wouldn't be effective and hit on the idea of gaining competitive advantage through meeting the unique transportation requirements of each of their clients. This required the develop-ment of a set of management concepts they called 'culture matching'. Essentially the idea was simple; Heron had to under-

stand the unique corporate culture of each client and, chameleon-like, provide systems which matched the clients' individual needs. Heron managers embarked on a huge sociological survey which included intensive observation, interviews with drivers and customer surveys. They found that customers' culture could be defined on five dimensions. These were:

1   How rigidly does the customer require adherence to agreed standards?
2   How adaptable does the customer expect the distribution company to be when urgent needs require a change in plans?
3   How dependant is the customer prepared to be on one distribution company?
4   How far did the client feel that personal relationships and joint problem solving was important?
5   How much information did the customer require?

Heron's research showed that customers varied on each of these five dimensions much more than they imagined. Specifying *precisely* the cultural requirements of each client (note my emphasis) meant that a huge programme of training, selection, systems development and objective setting enabled Heron to become the preferred provider of distribution services to many top UK firms. The results? In three years following the initiative Heron's turnover grew by 50 per cent in a declining market.

Managers believe they understand their customers; yet, as the Heron managers showed, systematic customer analysis provided unexpected benefits. Theories about customer behaviour are too important not to be tested. For example, it was believed by insurance companies that a person requiring an insurance renewal would be more likely to stay with their present insurer if they received a reminder phone call just before the renewal date. Customer research revealed that the theory was false; a lower proportion actually renewed when they received a reminder call. The reminder actually stimulated insured people to search for a better deal!

Why conduct a customer analysis? There are six key reasons:

1   To understand what the customer values.
2   To understand the customer's decision making processes.

3   To learn how the customer perceives you.
4   To learn how the customer perceives your competitors.
5   To gather improvement ideas from your competitors.
6   To understand the customer's latent needs and wants.

Customer analysis must be broad based for strategy development. Often the people who can give you the best feedback are those who could be your customers but have chosen to buy from a rival firm. Ford, for example, learn much from someone who has just gone out and purchased a Honda motor car.

Conducting a customer survey

We ask you to identify a champion to see the research project through to completion. You will need to visit your customers (and potential customers) and interview them using the questions below. Here are some guidelines which will help you gather useful data.

1   Don't be defensive – be open to having your ideas questioned and assume that you know nothing.
2   Enrol sales staff, management trainees etc. as researchers. Ensure that they are trained.
3   Before you collect information think about how you will process the collected data and decide what format you will probably use to present the data. Lay out questionnaires for easy analysis. Pilot the questionnaire (perhaps twice) before undertaking the full survey – then fully review to improve.
4   Ask standard 'core' questions – to provide a standardised analysis. Avoid asking too many questions (more than ten). Record detail – probe into important areas.
5   Identify a valid sample (include possible as well as actual customers) – get sufficient data to form valid conclusions. Try to survey all of your market segments (remember the work you did in Step 2). Most firms find that they need to survey between 10 and 30 customers. Firms with many small customers may need much larger samples.
6   Think about your customers' interests as you conduct the interviews – don't take too much time. Agree a win-win 'contract' with each informant – see what he or she wants from

the session. Summarise at the end of the meeting – check your understanding of the key points.

7   Ask questions which will yield 'rich data'. For example, not 'do you like our service?' but 'what aspects of our service meet your requirements and what aspects do not? Please give examples in each case'. Invite customers to prioritise views and opinions.

8   Collect as many ideas for improvement from each informant as possible.

9   Develop customer files on large individual customers or categories of small customers. Try to differentiate between customer groups.

10 When you analyse the data draw a schematic chart representing customers' decision making processes. Revise your views on market segmentation following the survey.

Questions to ask

It is never easy to decide what questions to ask. We tend to work from an existing mind-set. Sometimes questions that you haven't considered would give the best results. Here are some questions to get you started. By all means adapt them to your particular needs.

1   What do you buy from us?

2   What could you buy from us but choose to buy from another supplier? What are the factors influencing your decision?

3   What do you wish that we would do differently or better? (Collect as many ideas for improvement from each informant as possible.)

4   In the next five years how do you expect your business to change, and how do you want us to respond? (Probe how the customers' needs and wants will change – try to do this year by year.)

5   How thoroughly do we understand your business? Are there systematic gaps in our understanding? What are they?

6   Where do we fall down? Please give as many examples as you can.

7   Where do we succeed? Please give as many examples as you can.

8   Have you complained about us? How was your complaint handled?

9   What would we need to do to be the best in our field? Please be precise.
10 Can you think of any other points that would help us improve?

SUPPLIERS' FEEDBACK

Suppliers can provide important feedback. Consider a pharmacist selling a wide range of drugs, medical supplies and toiletry items. The suppliers of these items visit thousands of similar outlets and usually operate internationally. They probably know more about running a successful pharmacy than anyone else. Yet firms hardly ever systematically tap this rich vein of knowhow.

Feedback from suppliers is important for three key reasons:

1   They provide data which will allow you to compare yourself with similar firms.
2   They suggest ways in which firms of your type may need to develop in the future.
3   They suggest ways in which you can build closer relationships with them and, thereby, gain strategic advantages.

The final point in this list requires explanation. Many firms have gained advantage by improving the quality of the linkages between themselves and their suppliers. Toyota in Japan have developed very close relationships with their suppliers which allow for 'Just-in-Time' delivery of quality tested products. Marks & Spencer share their strategic thinking openly with their suppliers and develop a symbiotic approach which permits two firms with different core competencies to work together for mutual advantage.

Conducting a supplier survey

Arrange to interview the senior people in firms or other organisations which provide inputs into you. Ask the questions listed below (adapt for your particular needs).

1   What aspects of our operation make it easy for you to work with us? Please be precise.
2   From your observation, what would you say are our strengths? How would you compare our strengths with other firms that are similar to us?

3   From your observation, what prevents us from being excellent? How would you compare our weaknesses with other firms that are similar to us?
4   In what ways do firms of our type need to develop in the future?
5   How do you help us achieve our business strategy at the present time?
6   How could you help us achieve our business strategy in the future?
7   What practical actions could we take to improve relationships between us?
8   Is there anything that you would like to add that would be helpful?

EMPLOYEE FEEDBACK

The people that work for you are a boundless source of new ideas. The author was once invited to facilitate a strategy workshop with a firm making semi-conductors. As part of the preparatory work 500 engineers were asked to give their views on technical development options. More than 4,000 ideas were received and the resulting display filled a room! A new strategy emerged as these ideas were explored.

Don't forget that we are undertaking a strategic review and so don't want to get involved in asking what colour should the rest room be painted. Our aim is to collect data on the strategic strengths and weaknesses of the firm and where people feel that it should be heading.

Conducting an employee survey

Experience suggests that the best way to collect this data is through focus groups, not questionnaires. A 'focus group' is about six people, perhaps gathered randomly, who are asked to meet and discuss a number of questions. Each question should be discussed for about 10 minutes. The administrator takes anonymous notes but does not seek to influence the discussion.

Questions to ask include:

1   What are we really good at?
2   Where do we fall down?

3   What should we be doing in the future?
4   How are we going to beat the competition?
5   If you were the chief executive of this firm what would you do over the next year?

ADVISERS' RESEARCH

Sometimes the best strategic ideas are developed by people who are one step removed from an industry. They may be in a university, consultancy or research centre. Such people have time to study, make links with apparently unrelated industries, and watch the behaviour of the most advanced companies around the world. For example, technologies can be taken from one application to another; the non-stick frying pan was a technological spin-off from the US space programme.

Conducting an adviser survey

Arrange to meet at least two 'experts' who might be able to give you an informed viewpoint on how your firm might need to change over the next three years and ask the questions below. Record the answers and push for as much detail as possible.

1   What new products or services will the firm be expected to make or supply in say three years' time?
2   What current products or services will need to be improved over the next three years?
3   What changes in organisation, systems, methods, and management may be necessary in say three years' time?
4   What different pressures will we be under in three years' time?
5   What are the most important challenges that we face over the next three years?
6   How do you see our industry developing in the longer term (more than three years)? What are the implications for firms like ours?

WORKSHOP 5: COLLECTING EXTERNAL PERSPECTIVES

Preparation

You will need an overhead projector, screen, flip chart, marker pens and Blu-Tack.

Time required

The workshop takes approximately four hours.

WORKSHOP PLAN

1   The team leader opens the workshop by sharing the objectives which are:

■ To understand the collected feedback.

■ To identify where the collective mind-set of the top team is biased.

■ To harvest ideas from the collected feedback.

The team leader reminds the group that each team member should help in the process of generating, building on and capturing ideas. (5 minutes)

2   Presentations are made by sub-groups. Presentations should last about 30 minutes and be followed by 30 minutes discussion. Notes are taken of salient points and recorded on flip charts which should be displayed around the room. (3 hours in total)

3   Based on the input given by all of the sub-groups answer these questions in discussion. Record your answers to each question on separate flip charts. (1 hour for all questions)

a   How are you perceived by each of the groups of informants?

b   From the feedback received what is your current capability compared with your rivals?

c   Where are the feedback items consistent?

d   Where are the feedback items not consistent? Why?

e   What have we learned about the current mind set of the top team? Are there any systematic biases? What are they? How can these be eliminated in future?

4   In conclusion, the most important task of all! You must capture all the ideas that have emerged, provisionally categorise them and place the ideas into one of four conceptual 'buckets'. Sometimes ideas will not fall neatly into one of the categories but choose the best fit. The four conceptual buckets are:

> Bucket 1 Improvement Ideas (enhancing what we do now).
> Bucket 2 Opportunities (ideas someone might exploit).
> Bucket 3 Threats (hazards to growth, security and/or profitability).
> Bucket 4 Uncertainties (issues which need further analysis or debate).
> (15 minutes)
>
> Ensure that your buckets are safely stored, enjoy a few moments to celebrate the success of your workshop and agree how to manage the prework for the next session.

Step 6
Clarifying values

PREPARATION

The preparation for this workshop is very different from that required for the previous five. Each member of the team is asked to look inwards at his or her personal values. You are asked to read this step and answer the 35 questions in the text – they are listed in 7 groups of 5. Questions should be answered privately and not discussed. Notes should be made and brought to the workshop. You will be relieved to know that formal presentations are not required!

WORKSHOP BRIEFING

We are more than half way through the strategy development project and we have paid no attention to what you really *want* to accomplish. Our focus has been on capabilities, industries, markets and competitors – rational issues. But, in the last analysis, many of the great strategies have been based on passions, values and beliefs.[1]

We need to consider 'what contribution does our firm want to make to the world?' Your values (principles you will fight for) are as important for strategy formulation as a bookshelf of strategic research. My friend and colleague, Roger Harrison, says that 'strategy is a search for meaning: not a search for advantage'.

In this step you will:

- Understand the role of values in strategy development.
- Clarify your own values.
- Quiz your values to provide more strategic ideas.

VALUES IN STRATEGY DEVELOPMENT

The phenomenal global success of the Body Shop in the 1980s provides an excellent example of the importance of values in business. Anita and Gordon Roddick set up a tiny shop in Brighton in the summer of 1976 selling cosmetics and skin care products which were natural and kind to the environment. Anita and Gordon believed that people had a right to buy products which conformed to new age values. The venture proved to be a case study in retailing history. Anita Roddick explains: 'We are innovative, we are passionate, and we care ... The image, goals and values of our company are as important as our products. What is our mission-statement? It's easy – we will be the most honest cosmetic company around. How will we do it? That's easy too – we will go diametrically in the opposite direction to the cosmetic industry.'[2]

The Roddicks did not spend months analysing the market, competitors and industry before they went to the bank manager to borrow £4,000. They did what they believed in – and on the way the Body Shop created a new market, found new ways to compete with established players and redefined the cosmetic industry. They succeeded in achieving an elusive strategic initiative – redefining 'the rules of the game'.

Of course, passion is not enough. Heart must be supplemented with reason and logic: especially as the firm grows. By 1990 things had changed: competitors had woken up and the Body Shop was a global company. The Roddicks needed to analyse competitors who sought to exploit the same rich market seam. A new phase of development was initiated. Commitment had to make friends with strategic analysis.

No formula lasts forever in an unchanging form. Unless the Body Shop continues to evolve they will be a dated retailing case study rather than a profitable pioneer by the time this book is read.

Values about what?

Values are beliefs about what is important and unimportant, good and bad. Values tell us what to fight for and what to neglect: what to cherish and what to despise. Without values a person becomes a cipher, a zombie.

What values do top managers need to clarify? The model we

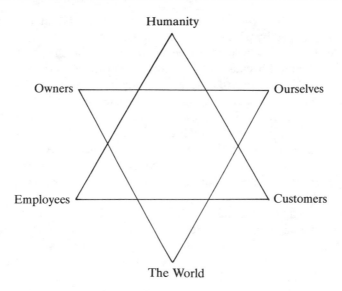

Figure 19 The six value domains of top managers

use has six 'domains' – areas within which managers must clarify their values. These are shown as Figure 19 (by the way, there is no mystical significance in the shape of the diagram!). We will briefly explore each of these six value domains.

1 VALUES TOWARDS THE WORLD

At home yesterday the door bell rang and I was confronted with a man trying to sell me double glazing. At one point he said to me 'all the mahogany we use comes from sustainable forests in Indonesia – we plant three trees for every one we fell.' I felt relieved as frequent travel has shown me just how much damage we are doing to the fragile ecology of the world.

Despite his apparent environmental concern I wondered whether it was only skin deep. This double glazing salesman and his bosses are solely measured on their capacity to generate profit according to current conventions of accounting and economics. Yet, most accounting conventions are based on early twentieth century assumptions about what wealth actually is. We must ask 'are these right for the twenty-first century?' The world is being pillaged by people who want to consume like Hollywood film stars. Is an ivory poacher to be applauded as he slaughters the last wild elephant because his revenue exceeds his costs?

Values towards the environment are seeping into the decision making processes of leaders. In the early 1990s Al Gore, Vice President in President Clinton's Administration, wrote a book titled *Earth in the Balance: Ecology and the Human Spirit*. Later, speaking about his experience of writing the book he said 'writing this book was a journey of self discovery ... I believe ecology is the defining issue of our time. The experience has led me to redefine what I want to do'.[3]

Environmental carnage has not being done by 'them'. It is managers who have taken the decisions which hurt the environment; it is managers who have changed the world's climate; it is managers who have developed the organisational technology for mankind to dominate the world.

There is no defensible argument for cash generation being the sole arbiter of business[4] success – otherwise we would make Mafia Godfathers businessmen of the year. Other values are necessary. For anyone with a conscience there seems no alternative but adopt the principle that everyone with resources to dispense needs to play a part in healing our world damaged by the excesses of mankind in the twentieth century. This will require knowledge, commitment and a redefinition of the meaning of 'profit'. We will come back to this theme several times in this step.

There are five questions to answer (if you can):

a   What are the negative effects on the environment of all of the resources that your firm consumes?

b   What are the negative effects on the environment of all of the products you produce?

c   What are you doing to heal the damage done to the world over the past fifty years?

d   What are you doing to avoid damaging the world in the future?

e   What are you doing to promote environmental awareness amongst employees and the public?

2 VALUES TO HUMANITY

A deep understanding of the human purpose of business is a source of inspiration and a dominating principle for coherence within the firm. Isao Nakauchi founder DAIEI, Japan's largest supermarket chain, illustrated this when he wrote: 'I began to think about the purpose of selling medicines. I realised that I was selling health. I expanded, and developed the concept that my business was to provide the "software" for human happiness.'[5] For Isao Nakauchi profit is not the goal of business but a reward for serving a human need with intelligence, dedication and efficiency.

The principle that business is a service to mankind has a nineteenth century ring. Yet it is more relevant today than a hundred years ago. The pure market economy substitutes machines for labour[6] and engenders a society deeply cleaved by discord. It is the view of this author that a love for humanity is necessary to minimise the abrasiveness of the harsh mistress of capitalism.

If we believe that will, intent, desire, values and a sense of serving humanity are a vital part of a firm's strategy then we must move away from simplistic notions of the purpose of business. At a recent lecture the students answer to my question 'What is the purpose of business?' was unequivocally 'profit'. A myopic focus on profit is dangerous because it shifts attention from the customer to the accountant: then greed replaces prudence and short termism elbows out commitment. In the end 'profit' is a benefit a firm enjoys for providing real value at a sustainable cost. From this point of view 'profit' is a cost of staying in business.

There are five questions to answer:

a   What human needs does your firm serve?
b   In what ways does your firm enrich people's lives?
c   In what ways does your firm damage people's lives?
d   What further could you do to add value to humanity?
e   To what extent are you, personally, proud of your firm's values?

3 VALUES TO EMPLOYEES

Values do more than orientate the firm towards its contribution to the world they also shape organisational competencies (the building blocks of competitive strength). For example, the British retailer, Marks & Spencer, has achieved an outstanding competence in staff relations. This provides a superior level of customer service and is driven by the values of the top management group. One of the characteristics of truly great business builders is their capacity to take decisive action following an apparently trivial incident. Israel Sieff, ex-chairman of Marks & Spencer, wrote:

> One day I was in one of our stores and I asked a girl to pack something for me ... Simon (the co-founder) glanced at the clock and saw that lunch time had already begun. 'Don't start on that' he said 'or you'll be late for your lunch'. 'Oh', she said, 'that's all right, I won't be having any lunch ... I can't afford it'. We were very shocked. We were doing our best with our wage scheme ... That night I sat up late with Simon talking ... there would be cases in which individuals, possibly because they had extra demands at home ... would go home without lunch or tea. There was only one thing that could cope with this, and that was to provide a hot meal at such low cost that an employee would have to recognise that it was uneconomic not to pay for it and eat it. Out of that chance encounter with the girl in the store developed an expansion of our whole welfare apparatus.[7]

This powerful story demonstrates that values towards employees profoundly shape organisations and create strategic capability.

The theme is echoed by many experienced business leaders. It may be a surprise to learn that one of the gurus of world business, Dr W.E. Deming, frequently quotes a passage about taking joy in labour from the Book of Ecclesiastes. The 'right' way to treat others is an ancient art. Core values have not changed by a jot or tittle since the works of Greek philosophers first spelled out the principles.

There are five questions to answer:

a   What values does your firm adopt towards employees?
b   How consistently are these values expressed?
c   To what extent are your employee values felt to be fair by the staff themselves?
d   How do your values support your aim to achieve world class performance?

e   To what extent are you, personally, proud of your firm's values towards employees?

4 VALUES TO OWNERS

Every firm has owners. They are vital stakeholders in the firm. Divisions of larger businesses owe allegiance to their corporate parent. Ultimately firms are responsible to their shareholders and, sometimes, statutory bodies as well.

Many ultimate owners are financial institutions who have a daily flow of funds from ordinary people to place in lucrative and secure investments. These funds are as essential as any other resource to a firm and owners have an absolute right to be fairly treated.

Owners have two principal rights; firstly, to have access to honest and full information about the health of the firm; and, secondly, they need to receive a fair apportionment of the profit flowing from business success.

The right to honest information is well understood, but practice sometimes falls short of the ideal. It is a matter of public record that a firm can submit audited accounts which show that it is financially healthy only to become insolvent within a matter of months. Accounting standards are a bulwark against exploitative managers but the values of directors are even more crucial. Any system can be abused by the cynical or unscrupulous. Ethics of openness and disclosure are the only ways that the firms owners can feel secure.

There are five questions to answer:

a   What values does your firm adopt towards shareholders?
b   To what extent do your reports and accounts faithfully present the status of the firm?
c   To what extent do shareholders receive a fair return on their investment?
d   How effectively are shareholders' wishes canvassed so they form part of the strategic decision making system?
e   To what extent are you, personally, proud of your firm's values towards owners?

5 VALUES TOWARDS CUSTOMERS

There is little to add in this section that we have not said before in this book. The dedication of the firm to the present and emerging needs of the customer is the overarching recipe for business success. This requires much more than a commitment to the customer. Love of the product is equally important. An example makes the point. John H.C. Chan,[8] an entrepreneur whose firm Handsome now makes millions of shirts a year including the top ranges for Christian Dior said:

> Thirty years ago we worked as a team and would rip up various types of garments and find out how they were made – this was how we learned our trade ... we wondered why it was that some people could carry a shirt with aplomb and why others looked terrible in the same shirt ... Even today we are still learning.

The company comes up with ten new pattern designs a month.

There are five questions to answer:

a   What values does your firm adopt towards customers?
b   To what extent do your staff really dedicate themselves to customer satisfaction?
c   To what extent do your customers find that their expectations are exceeded by your products and service?
d   What is the evidence that your managers and staff really love the products (or services) that you offer?
e   To what extent are you, personally, proud of your firm's values towards customers?

6 VALUES TOWARDS YOURSELVES

In the last analysis it is the values of powerful leaders that shape strategies. It is important to believe in what you are doing. An example makes the point. Jim Maxmin became chief executive of the ailing fashion firm Laura Ashley in 1991 and changed its strategy, structure and culture in a heady push towards redefining the firm as a global brand with an unreplicatable mystique rather than just another chain of fashion shops. Jim's humanistic, expansive and somewhat quirky values (he once ran a £1 billion company using a Mickey Mouse telephone) rushed through the staid and doleful Laura Ashley culture like a forest fire.

What values should leaders adopt? The principles of holistic management can be helpful. These were first articulated by the ancient Greeks who believed that any healthy community (a family, a community, or an organisation) needs to be whole: that is, to provide a balanced nourishment, for the five needs – the physical, mental, emotional, social and spiritual sides of mankind. The true leader, therefore, was a person who could find ways for people to meet all the five needs. Symmetry, balance and order were considered to be essential for wellbeing.

It may sound remote from the cut and thrust of real management but the massive new Saturn car plant in the USA is being run totally in accord with these principles of symmetry, balance and order laid down two and a half thousand years ago. If GM see this as the best way to keep indigenous motor manufacturing in the USA then maybe we should all take it seriously!

There are five questions to answer:

a What values excite you as a person?
b To what extent are your values shared by your colleagues?
c Are your organisational values fulfilling the physical, mental, emotional, social and spiritual sides of mankind?
d Do your values support the principles of symmetry, balance and order?
e To what extent are you, personally, proud of your firm's values?

CLARIFYING VALUES

A 'value' is not a behaviourial entity; you can't directly see it, touch it, feel it. But values are there; like the foundations of a building. Organisations are governed, for good or ill, by the shared or conflicted values of those who have power within the system. As part of the strategy development process decision makers need to clarify, refine, integrate and honour their values. Unclear, contradictory or damaging values are a poor basis for strategic thinking.

Values exist only when they are actualised. Words are not enough – only deeds count. For several years Apple Computers said that they valued the individual above all. Then came an economic downturn and more than 20 per cent of the workforce had to go. John Sculley, the CEO at that time said:

Affected employees were notified in one-on-one meetings with managers and given liberal severance allowances. Psychiatric counsellors met privately with people who might suffer great emotional stress ... There was amazingly little bitterness and rancour ... it reinforced my belief that Apple didn't deserve to be turned into another fine-tuned, expense-controlled company in corporate America.[9]

For Apple, values flowed into strategic decisions and through into action. The power of the decision and the integrity of action came because the elemental values were clear and consistent. Values are the fundamental elements in the corporate genetic code which we usually call 'organisational culture'. It is far from easy to measure, clarify or confront managers' values. Partly because values are subterranean – they manifest themselves indirectly through symbols, myths, legends and behaviour.

Clarifying (and later communicating) values often needs to be undertaken systematically. Of course, much of the information comes from within the personal experience, beliefs and feelings of the managers developing strategy. Values clarification is one of the few topics in which inner beliefs are more important than external analysis.

Values clarification is a process which helps to ensure that people hold values which meet these seven criteria:

1   The chosen value has been chosen from alternatives. Only values that have been positively chosen will be firmly held. The act of choosing strengthens commitment.
2   Values need to be consistent with each other. Values should support each other. Values pulling in different directions are destructive.
3   Core values need to be few in number. Trying to adopt an excessive number of core values dissipates effort and is confusing. Core values are broad, deep and general.
4   Values need to be actionable. A value that cannot be put into effect becomes a weakness: we should not be committed to an impossibility.
5   For organisations, values need to be performance enhancing. Values are 'an enabling device'; they are a means of shaping contribution to achieve performance objectives.
6   Values must be attractive and 'pride giving'. People need to be

uplifted by their values. Values must be capable of being respected.

7 Values need to be capable of being communicated. Values align behaviour behind strategic intentions.

This is a brief overview of the 'technology' of values clarification; a process dedicated to helping each strategic manager to become clearer about where he or she stands. The task is to find inner sureness; to find where we stand; to find who and what we serve.

Values are deeply rooted in society. It is the prevailing value system that shapes how people think and feel. Some of the attributes of a successful firm can be traced back to the social origins of their leaders. Here are some examples:

- From the Samurai the Japanese have learnt the qualities of endurance.
- From Confucius the Chinese have learnt the qualities of respect and harmony.
- From Protestantism the West has learnt the qualities of hard work.
- From Judaism the Israelis have learnt the qualities of trustworthiness.
- From Islam the Arab peoples have learnt the qualities of commitment.

Clarifying or changing values will never be easy. Much inertia is built into us. Habits run deep and are resistant to change. But, somehow, when we work with our true values we are energised, enlivened and empowered. It is the task of every top team to identify where they stand on each of the six values domains we have explored.

WORKSHOP 6: CLARIFYING VALUES

Preparation

You will need an overhead projector, screen, flip chart, marker pens and Blu-Tack.

Time required

The workshop takes approximately four hours.

WORKSHOP PLAN

1   The team leader opens the workshop by sharing the objectives which are:

■ To understand the importance of values in strategy development.
■ To clarify our own values.
■ To use values to provide more strategic ideas.

The team leader reminds the group that each team member should help in the process of generating, building on and capturing ideas. (5 minutes)

2   Take the six values domains described in the text separately. Ask each person to share their notes. List on a flip-chart ideas that everyone agrees upon and debate issues of disagreement. Try to come to a consensus on each item. (2 hours)

3   Take each agreed value and brainstorm 'if we put this value fully into effect what will be the implications on our business?' (1 hour 30 minutes)

4   In conclusion, the most important task of all! You must capture all the ideas that have emerged, provisionally categorise them and place the ideas the conceptual 'buckets'. Remember, sometimes ideas will not fall neatly into one of the categories but choose the best fit. (25 minutes)

To remind you, the five conceptual buckets are:
Bucket 1   Improvement ideas.
Bucket 2   Repositioning ideas.
Bucket 3   Opportunities.
Bucket 4   Threats.
Bucket 5   Uncertainties.

Ensure that your buckets are safely stored, enjoy a few moments to celebrate the success of your workshop and agree how to manage the prework for the next session.

Step 7
Idea generation

PREPARATION

How do you prepare for the next workshop? This one is easy! There is no formal preparation except to read the workshop briefing on this step and come to workshop in the right frame of mind to contribute in an open and unfettered way.

Consider carefully two points.

1 Where will you hold the event? Sometimes creativity is enhanced by an exciting offsite venue. Once we held a great creativity workshop on a sailing barge off the coast of Holland – a flip chart in the cabin. So why not take a day off, go somewhere where the phone is switched off, and let it rip!

2 There is another possibility. It can make sense for Steps 7, 8 and 9 to be completed together over a two day period. Look through them both and see whether this makes sense for you.

WORKSHOP BRIEFING

We've reached a turning point in the strategy development process. The previous steps were concerned with analysis. You spun off ideas and captured them from each workshop but, deliberately, you have not systematically explored the future direction of the firm. It's foolhardy to initiate a new strategic direction until you've have taken a totally fresh look at yourselves: our work so far has been preparatory. Now we are going to begin the process of creating a future. This is the exciting and awesome part of the process.

In this step you will:

■ Create additional strategic ideas to add to those sitting in your conceptual buckets.

■ Cluster ideas into categories.

In any firm there are a myriad of strategic ideas. A customer asks a salesman 'why doesn't your company offer an installation and maintenance service?' Two engineers are talking in a bar and one says 'I've been reading about gallium arsenide semi-conductors. If we used these we could produce a civil version of the 110'. The managing director attends a conference and is impressed by a lecture on 'time based competition' and thinks 'this is something we can use'. Such fragments are the germs of strategic ideas but few firms have any effective procedure for capturing them. Fortunately this has not happened to us! We have collected ideas systematically and started the important process of categorising them (in those buckets).

This step will challenge everyone. Before we describe the nuts-and-bolts of the task it is helpful to consider how we can create a climate in which strategic creativity can thrive. You will need seven strategic skills:

1   True independence of thought – being intellectually free.
2   Openness to others' ideas – no one has a monopoly of insight.
3   A long time perspective – strategies concern long term positioning.
4   Genuine creativity – sometimes it is necessary to 'think the unthinkable'.
5   Boldness of vision – avoids the trap of small-mindedness.
6   Prudence – avoiding foolish optimism.
7   Data intelligence – taking data and transforming it into wisdom.

These seven qualities sit easily on a sheet of paper but are hard to acquire in practice (how does a timid person become bold or a foolish person learn prudence?). Senior managers should try to acquire all these strategic skills themselves but a balanced strategic team with these seven strategic skills – under a skilful chairperson – this is the most reliable way to develop strategic options.[1]

CREATIVE TEAM CLIMATE

The strategy team needs to adopt a distinctive team climate during this step. In the previous steps scientific research and intellectual rigour were prized attributes. Now we need a vibrant climate of tolerance, openness, supportiveness and optimism (the pessimism comes later!).

All too often ideas are discarded because they require a new mind-set. An accepting team climate must be developed to value radical thinking. Judgement must be postponed: free flowing creativity is required.

Interestingly the physical context for developing strategic options can be important. The environment has to signal 'space and opportunity'. Some teams find that a chateau in France, a colonial hotel in Macau or a boat cruising the Caribbean creates the right atmosphere to encourage risk taking and openness (although it's difficult to convince the auditors that a week in Bali is an essential business expense!).

The physical and psychological environment needs to enhance the ability to dream; to access the subconscious. Creativity, more than most other human attributes, has an element of magic. It requires quieting the left side of the brain (the part that deals with analysis, thought and logic) and allowing participation from the usually somnambulant right side of the brain (the part that is conceptual, artistic and intuitive).

No one really knows where new ideas will come from. The story is told that during the late 1970s an American MBA student called Dan Bricklin had to copy complex accounting case studies from the blackboard. When the lecturer started to use different assumptions Dan found it difficult to keep up and errors began to occur. He asked his friend, Robert Frankston, if it would be possible to recreate the blackboard on a computer and enter the relationship between numbers such that when one number changed all the dependent numbers changed automatically. Frankston used his Apple II computer and developed Visicalc, the first spreadsheet. The rest, as they say, is history.

COLLECTING IDEAS

If you ask the question 'where do good ideas come from?' the

Customers	33%
Staff	19%
Market Studies	17%
Top Team Members	14%
Sales	7%
Suppliers	6%
Consultants	3%
Shows and Conferences	2%

Figure 20 The sources of good ideas

results are striking. From a survey with many types of firm[2] the following analysis has been made (Figure 20). From Figure 20 it is apparent that well over three-quarters of good ideas come from people other than top team members – that is why we did so much research in the earlier stages of this strategy development process. Now the challenge is to build on the ideas bank you have accumulated with an effective idea generating and information processing system within your team.

CREATIVE MEETINGS

The strategy development team must hold a creativity session (maybe several). Initially we need to generate as many strategic ideas as possible; in the next step we will elaborate those which have any prospect of being feasible.

We need what Neil Rackham[3] rightly calls 'amplifier' meetings to encourage divergent thinking. The team manager should encourage everyone to:

- Be supportive.
- Withhold criticisms until the last possible moment.

- Recognise the value of others' ideas.
- Build on the ideas of others.
- Draw others out.
- Summarise.
- Test for understanding.
- Encourage intuitive thinking.
- Stretch their own imagination.
- Avoid ridicule.
- Question assumptions and 'the givens'.

In amplifier meetings managers are tempted to stop the creative process when they come to the first idea. The tendency to be satisfied with the initial answer is a profound creative weakness. Often a deeper study reveals quite unexpected nuances and options. We have to learn to live (for a time) with a void of uncertainty.

STRUCTURING CREATIVITY MEETINGS

You can sit around a flip chart (maybe on the deck of that yacht in the Caribbean) and ask 'what strategy do we want to adopt?' This is unlikely to be effective. Rather you will use four creativity techniques (described later) on twenty-one strategic questions – a methodology developed by the author which has been proven to generate ideas systematically. You will need to understand the rationale behind the twenty-one questions and then the creativity techniques.

THE TWENTY-ONE STRATEGIC QUESTIONS

These twenty-one questions cover the types of major strategic initiatives taken by hundreds of firms[4] and so provide a mind-expanding checklist. They fall (not always neatly) into four categories as shown on the diagram (Figure 21).

The twenty-one questions relate to these four categories:

- Questions 1 to 8 are product related.
- Questions 9 to 13 are market related.
- Questions 14 to 19 are organisation related.
- Questions 20 and 21 are competitor related.

STRATEGIC CATEGORIES

Figure 21 The four categories of strategic questions

Some questions are obvious, others more obscure. The benefit lies in answering *all* the questions creatively.

CREATIVE PRODUCT STRATEGIES

Strategic question 1: How could you enhance or improve 'the product'?

The product – what you have to sell – is the first place to look for strategic development ideas. You may develop a feature or adapt the product to the needs of specific market segments. A theatre that produces superior plays or a laptop computer with a huge memory attracts customers – sometimes the inventor of a better mousetrap does find that the world will beat a path to his or her door.

Strategic question 2: How could you enhance or improve 'service'?

Service – the way you offer your product – is a way of gaining competitive advantage. Some firms, airlines for example, have little ability to differentiate their product but they can offer better service. There are many opportunities to enhance service – a computer with a three-year warranty is more attractive than one with a ninety-day cover. A motor car that you can return within a month for full refund has more appeal than one that you must keep once the purchase decision is made.

Strategic question 3: How can you lower your costs?

A superior cost structure creates strategic space. Resources become available for product enhancement, price reduction or both together. When costs can be reduced, without disadvantaging the customer, the firm gains strategic flexibility. For example, Bic's capacity to produce precision pens with extraordinary low costs enabled them to enter successfully the razor and lighter markets.

Strategic question 4: How could you lower the cost to the customer of acquiring and owning 'the product'?

Why do many Japanese ladies travel to Hong Kong twice a year? They go to shop and many of the things they buy are global brands, like Christian Dior perfume, which are considerably cheaper than in Tokyo. Savings exceed the costs of the airfare. Stores in Hong Kong gain competitive strength from being able to lower the cost of ownership to the customer.

Strategic question 5: What new valued products could you create?

New things to offer are a 'classic' outcome of a strategic initiative. Sometimes evolution of products is sufficient. In 1993 Sony introduced the digital mini-disk walkman in Japan which gave them a winning position with the high-end customer. Often it is necessary to produce genuinely innovative products. Products include services in this definition – so the offer of a new computer cleaning service by an office cleaning specialist is a new 'product'.

Strategic question 6: How could you supply an 'integrated offering'?

This is a less obvious question. One source of competitive advantage is the ability to supply an integrated offering. A customer will go to Harrods for his Christmas shopping because virtually everything can be brought under one roof. A small shopkeeper will go to one large cash-and-carry store because she can pick up all the supplies she needs in a single trip. Integration cuts the buyers' costs because purchasing takes less time.

Strategic question 7: How could you innovate faster than your rivals?

We live in a time when virtually everything can be copied. Almost all competitive strategies can be imitated and so their value is time bound. The only recipe for success is continuous innovation. Speed of adaptation can be a major source of competitive advantage – perhaps the most important challenge of the twenty-first century. Swiftness of innovation (called the 'wave' theory of competitive advantage) is a profound source of strategic strength.

Strategic question 8: How could you sell your knowhow?

Firms have based their strategy on their ability to sell their knowhow. Some hotels, restaurant chains, copy shops, research establishments, sell their 'technology' often in the form of franchises or licences. Accumulated expertise can be an extremely valuable resource.

CREATIVE MARKET STRATEGIES

Strategic question 9: How can you deepen your market penetration?

If you look at the research[5] on successful businesses you will find that for many industries (but not all) it pays to have a large market share. Getting to a position of dominance in defined markets is a fundamental aim of many businesses. Almost always this requires gaining a larger share of the existing market. Sometimes this can be done by changing the customers' perception of the value of the product through marketing and advertising.

Strategic question 10: How can you find parallel market segments?

Once you have something to sell it can make sense to sell to new markets, for example, firms in defence electronics found that they could sell their detectors of battlefield poison gases to airports for the detection of explosives. Moving into parallel segments is a 'classic' strategic initiative.

Strategic question 11: How could you move to new geographical territories?

Moving into a new geographical area offers many advantages. It can represent an opportunity to expand with only a small addition to your cost structure (mainly in the sales and marketing area). As products and services become global it could be said that there is a risk to remaining local: other players have the opportunity to become dominant. Despite these strategic advantages some of the most spectacular strategic failures have been caused by unwise geographical expansion.

Strategic question 12: How can you create new market segments?

Some firms actually create and reshape the market. For example, Apple created a market for desktop publishing that did not exist. They saw their enemy not as IBM but as the ignorance of people who were possible customers. Apple created a new market segment which they succeeded in dominating for ten years.

Strategic question 13: Could you focus your business on specific market segments?

Sometimes it makes sense to focus on a particular market segment or a definite technology. The author, for example, has not tried to be an expert in every branch of management consulting; rather, he specialises in coaching top teams who are seeking to strengthen their competitive strategy. Focus reduces costs and enables the firm to know its market intimately. Sometimes it is sensible to get smaller – either to reduce risks or find a more economic scale of operation. For example, in the early 1990s Union Carbide reduced its commodity chemicals business as this had become unattractive through the intensity of competition.

CREATIVE ORGANISATIONAL STRATEGIES

Strategic question 14: How could you exploit your existing resources or competencies in new ways?

Sometimes it is possible to find new ways to exploit existing competencies. Very often this is a route to competitive advantage. The major UK broadcasting organisation, the BBC, found that they could supply a daily news programme for passengers on long haul flights. Nippon Bearings found that their skill in manufacturing in clean room conditions very close tolerances in micro-bearings gave them an edge in the mass manufacture of semi-conductors. New ways to exploit existing competencies are a potent source of strategic options.

Strategic question 15: How could you acquire new resources or competencies?

New competencies are often needed for strategic development. For example, in 1993, Chrysler completed their $1 billion development centre which enabled them to take a new car from concept to showroom in three years rather than the previous five year wait. They had acquired a new competence in rapid product development which opened a range of previously inaccessible strategic opportunities.

Strategic question 16: Could you reorganise for strategic innovation?

At first sight reorganisation seems to be an errant suggestion in a strategy analysis. Yet this is not the case. In New Zealand many government organisations were privatised in the 1980s. This energised many organisations as teams began to see their role as seizing opportunities rather than maintaining rules. New strategies emerged from the middle of the organisation and created waves of strategic initiatives.

Strategic question 17: Should you build alliances with complementary firms?

There are many situations when it makes sense for firms to combine their resources. This may be with joint ventures, shared ownership, technical or marketing agreements and so on. The fundamental purpose of alliances is to combine competencies to the advantage of each partner.

Strategic question 18: Should you acquire other businesses?

There is a time when the right thing to do is to acquire other firms. This is the fastest way of gaining new capability, often acquiring new competencies. But beware, some studies suggest that about half the firms that acquire regret their decision three years later.

Strategic question 19: Could you get help?

From time to time firms get help: sometimes from unexpected sources. There have been cases when huge sums of money have been invested by public sources, foundations and charities which have enhanced strategic options. For example, one of the strategies being pursued by Oxford University is to raise £60 million which will give this magnificent university a whole range of strategic possibilities.

CREATIVE COMPETITIVE STRATEGIES

Strategic question 20: Could you grip upstream or downstream channels?

Some firms have achieved competitive advantage because they have a special relationship with a desirable supplier. The lady who owns the Body Shop Franchise in South East Asia made a fortune in the 1980s. Also important are downstream channels – the way a firm gets goods or services to the end users. Gripping such channels it is difficult for competitors to get in. For example, Mercedes-Benz impose strict conditions on their agents which enables them to ensure that the customer receives superior service.

Strategic question 21: Could you weaken competition?

It may be possible to reduce competition; some firms have deliberately squeezed their weaker rivals out of business. This can be done by methods fair and foul – price wars, legal actions, poaching key staff, smear campaigns and financial raids have all been used. Sometimes lobbying government is effective. In the early 1990s British Airways sought to damage their rivals Virgin Atlantic by using proprietary information to approach customers. To an extent the initiative succeeded. Other firms have sought to reduce rivalry by warfare.

FOUR CREATIVITY TECHNIQUES

These are the questions: you will use four creativity techniques on each question – that's eighty-four mini-creativity sessions!

Creativity technique 1: Solo brainstorming

In this technique everyone makes an input untainted by the views of the others. The advantages? Each individual makes an independent contribution and avoids the risk that a few vocal group members contribute unfairly.

Creativity technique 2: Group brainstorming

Totally new ideas can be divined through group interplay. The advantages? Group brainstorming is especially useful when individual contributions are exhausted and new energy is required in the creativity process.

Creativity technique 3: Benchmarking

In 1972 the Xerox Corporation was one of the world's richest companies with a net worth of $11.8 billion. Then Cannon, and a host of new competitors, with attractive substitute products invaded Xerox's traditional market. Margins were cut and Xerox saw its profit stream virtually dry up. David Kearns took over as CEO in 1982 and said 'we were in danger of going out of business ... we were becoming a dinosaur that couldn't get out of its own way'.[6]

Every area of Xerox's business needed to be re-examined and radically improved – from manufacturing to research. The management approach that Xerox adopted was 'benchmarking' – each senior manager was charged with looking for firms with similar processes in the outside world and systematically comparing the Xerox systems with the comparison firms. A wide range of firms were chosen; for example, Fuji was the exemplar for manufacturing, American Express for billing and Proctor and Gamble for marketing. The insights that resulted from this process helped transform Xerox from being a flabby giant into an innovative and exciting business. Benchmarking is an honest way to 'steal' good ideas from other firms and industries.

Creativity technique 4: Wish lists

This approach attacks fundamental assumptions by looking at the business from the customers' point of view. The advantages? Firms gain a new perspective on their strategic possibilities by considering the customers' wants and needs anew.

WORKSHOP 7: GENERATING IDEAS

Preparation

You will need plenty of flip chart paper, six packs of large post-it notes, marker pens, scotch tape and Blu-Tack. Find a large room which can be locked to prevent your competitors from spying! All interruptions must be prevented. The twenty-one strategic questions (see above) should be written on separate sheets of flip chart paper – one question as the title for each chart.

Time required
The workshop takes 1 day.

WORKSHOP PLAN

---

1 The team leader opens the workshop by sharing the objectives which are:

■ To create additional strategic ideas to add to those sitting in your conceptual buckets.

■ To cluster ideas into categories.

The team leader reminds the group that each team member should help in the process of generating, building on and capturing ideas. (5 minutes)

2 Put up twenty-one sheets of flip chart around the room each with one of the strategic questions written on it. (5 minutes)

3 Go through each of the proceeding steps and empty the 'buckets'. Put each idea on a separate post-it note and stick it on one of the twenty-one flip charts as appropriate. (The post-it notes will permit you to cluster the ideas easily in the next step). (1 hour)

4 Discuss how you will use each of the four creativity techniques (see the text) on the twenty-one questions to generate additional ideas. Each new idea should be written on a separate post-it note and added to one of the flip charts as appropriate. This may seem a tiresome process but experience suggests that unexpected and valuable ideas are generated by the vigour of the approach. The ideas must be captured. Beware of assuming that you know the answers before you start; try to tackle each question without preconceptions – as if you are a group of super-able strategy consultants taking a look at the business for the first time. (5 minutes)

5   Solo brainstorming. (1 hour 30 minutes)

   a Take each strategic question in turn.
   b Allocate a fixed time for idea generation. (say 5 minutes)
   c No talking.
   d Each group member is asked to generate as many ideas as possible on the topic. Only one idea should be written per post-it.
   e When all have finished, clarify uncertainties, categorise the post-its and add the ideas to your wall charts.

6   Group brainstorming. (1 hour 30 minutes)

   a Take each strategic question in turn.
   b Appoint a scribe and say 'we will brainstorm this question. We will take five minutes initially. All ideas, no matter how wild, will be recorded on flip charts. No one is permitted to evaluate anyone's ideas until later. Let's go!'
   c Generate ideas and write them on the flip chart.
   d No evaluation is allowed during the brainstorming process.
   e When finished, clarify uncertainties and prepare a post-it note of each idea.
   f Categorise the post-its and add the ideas to your wall charts.

7   Benchmarking. (1 hour 30 minutes)

   a List your processes – things that you do which add value.
   b List organisations with similar processes to you.
   c Select excellent examples of their organisational processes.
   d Ask 'Where are they the same as us?' 'Where are they different?' 'What can we learn?'
   e When finished, clarify uncertainties and categorise the ideas in a coherent way. List 'good' ideas on separate post-it notes. Categorise the post-its and add the ideas to your wall charts.

8   Wish lists. (1 hour 30 minutes)

a Have real customers, or objective customer research, available for this session.

b The leader says 'let's put ourselves in the position of our customer and ask "what would he wish us to do?"' For example, self-loading cameras were developed from market research information which said that more than 50% of camera users were apprehensive of loading films by hand.

c Brainstorm (individually then in a group) 'what would customers really like firms like ours to do differently?'

d List all ideas on flip charts.

e Take each suggestion and ask 'what could we do to improve the situation from the customers' point of view?'

f When finished, clarify uncertainties and categorise the ideas in a coherent way. List 'good' ideas on separate post-it notes. Categorise the post-its and add the ideas to your wall charts.

9 Capture your ideas. By the way, it helps to stick them firmly to the flip charts. You are now ready to move on to the next step. (1 hour)

Step 8
Developing strategic options

PREPARATION

Once again you have got off lightly! There is no formal preparation for the workshop except to read the briefing for the step in advance and come to the workshop ready to contribute.

WORKSHOP BRIEFING

You are sitting in a room with twenty-one sheets of flip chart paper festooning the walls containing your 'ideas bank'. Experience suggests that you have between one and three hundred ideas; some radical, others pedestrian; some revolutionary, others evolutionary; some feasible and others fantastic.

In this step you will:

■ Cluster the ideas in the ideas bank.
■ Develop several strategic options.
■ Determine measurement criteria to assess your options.
■ Decide your broad competitive strategy – the 'moment of truth'.

STRATEGIC OPTIONS

Strategic decision making is a form of gambling. As any punter knows, you can assess the form of the horses in the race, choose the runner with the best form and sometimes nobble the opposition. But in the end there is an element of risk. Even the favourite can lose on the day.

We cannot expect to foresee the future exactly but we can

formulate a strategy with a high probability of success – then develop flexible competencies that give us the strength to exploit opportunities as they occur. The future is not a blank page, rather a series of out of focus images, some of which are clearer than others.

Consider the notebook computer industry. This a growth segment. Notebook computers will get smaller, lighter, more capable and more user friendly. Yet no one knows what will be the impact of parallel processing, exactly what competitors are planning and when concepts like voice control will be proven. Guesses, approximations, hunches and beliefs are needed to fill the gaps. Sometimes it is possible to actually create the future – just as IBM did with the personal computer in the 1980s.

Top managers have a murky crystal ball, but cannot abandon the corporate future to chance. They must be solidly committed to a vision of the future and yet open to radically redefining their viewpoint. Managing dualities is at the heart of strategic development.

A word of caution! Each industry has its individual logic. For example, Ooh La Lagerfield of Chanel said of the fashion industry: 'When luxury goods become an institution they become boring.'[1] Yet banks do precisely the opposite – they seek to become institutions to fill the deep need for customers to feel secure. Ideas are situational: they only make sense in context.

CLUSTERING IDEAS

Clustering begins with the clarification of ideas. Creativity is untidy. Duplicate ideas must be rationalised and suggestions which offend your core values should be removed. Structuring information so that its meaning becomes apparent is vital. You must group ideas into clusters (meaningful groups). You will be pleased that you wrote the ideas on separate post-it notes – it makes it easy to move them around.

No one can advise you how to cluster your ideas – so much depends on the nature of your business. A firm hiring dredging equipment has very different strategic possibilities than a manufacturer of women's corsets. These are four standard ways of clustering ideas: why not try each and see what works best for you? The principles are:

1   Grouping consistent ideas together (for example, all ideas relating to competing on the basis of superior service).
2   Grouping ideas on the basis of their degree of 'radicalness'.
3   Grouping ideas on the basis of likely appeal to stakeholders.
4   Grouping ideas on the basis of likely appeal to the top management team.

Move your ideas around and explore different patterns. Don't rush this stage – the future of your firm may be recorded on just one scrap of paper. Finally, decide on the most useful clustering and tape the notes down (later these will be typed as a record of the session).

STRATEGIC OPTIONS

You now have the raw material to generate strategic options. A 'strategic option' is 'an elaborated, internally consistent and feasible possible future' – sorry that the definition reads like computer code but an example helps to clarify the concept. A sixteen year old student may identify three strategic options for her career – becoming a fashion designer, working with deprived children or entering the family firm as a thatcher. Each will require different competencies and lead to different outcomes and are often (but not always) contradictory.

Strategic options fall into two categories. Some are evolutionary – such as 'to sell our existing insurance products direct to end-user customers as well as our present route to market through insurance brokers'. Other strategic options are revolutionary, perhaps involving a whole new area of business – such as 'to set up a business selling satellite telephone exchanges in Russia'.

The fishbone technique[2] is the way we explore strategic options. Consider the example of a small training consultancy. They have amassed dozens of ideas as they worked through the previous steps. These ideas fell into six clusters. Each grows into a strategic option. Our consulting friends could:

1   Link with an overseas business school accessing skills which would enable additional value to be added to their clients.
2   Develop a unique methodology to provide a distinctive approach.

3   Focus on a defined organisational level: for example, supervisors, and develop programmes specifically for this group.
4   Focus on their geographical area and develop services for local organisations dealing with local issues.
5   Focus on a defined industry: for example, food processing, and develop programmes for this category of firm.
6   Develop a popular product (they are thinking about video assisted learning packages) and try to sell these by the thousand.

Let us look at these six options displayed on a fishbone (Figure 22).

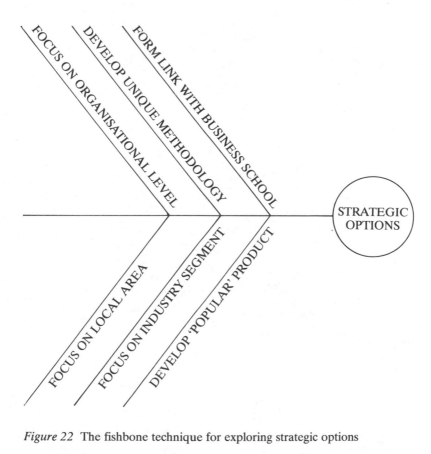

Figure 22 The fishbone technique for exploring strategic options

The main bones of the fish are defined. Next, strategic ideas will be added to become minor bones as in the example below (which only shows two of the six main 'bones'). You will see that the ideas are cryptic – but they mean a great deal to the people involved. Consider the idea of forming a link with an overseas business school. The team have come up with four ideas: they could act as a marketing arm for the business school, form a joint venture in an area where they have expertise, provide research facilities at a fee or use materials under licence which will give access to high quality resources at low cost. The team have also three additional ideas for developing popular products which have been added to the example chart (Figure 23).

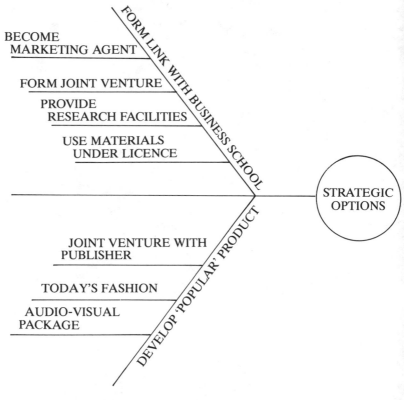

Figure 23 Fishbone with additional ideas ('minor bones')

To mix a metaphor, the fishbone is the coat rack on which you hang all the strategic ideas (Figure 23). Sometimes an idea can be on several bones. Here we are concerned with elaborating *all* of the options to the point when they can be fairly evaluated. Notice that we are not assessing ideas at the present time – simply structuring and elaborating them.

EVALUATING STRATEGIC OPTIONS

You will have several strategic options and need to move towards the vital task of choosing. In the final analysis this will be a long process: often many people need to be convinced and much time spent in discussion. Since many firms have watchful bank managers or cynical corporate headquarters the decision rarely rests with the top team. It is worthwhile reminding yourself what are the stakeholders' criteria for assessing the strategic plans of the business. This information is vital as no strategic proposal, no matter how brilliant, will be accepted if it offends the criteria of the key decision makers.

It is wrong to agree a strategy unless the economic and financial implications are well explored. All too often the financial justification of a strategy becomes a game played with corporate headquarters to 'play the system'. The creativity of the strategic process needs to be balanced by a vigorous financial analysis. The problem is not to find something to invest in; there are hundreds of ideas. The important question is, 'What will lead to the strongest businesses and the best returns?'

We make progress towards decision making by specifying criteria to evaluate the options. This is, perhaps, the most important activity in decision making. Essentially the idea is simple: to make a choice we need to define precisely the criteria which will be used for assessment. Articulating criteria clarifies choice.

You need to decide whether a criterion is essential or desirable. An essential criterion is one that if an option did not have this attribute it would be automatically excluded. A desirable attribute is one that gives advantage but is not decisive: some desirable attributes are more enticing than others and so should be rated on a 1 to 10 scale.

Defining and weighing criteria may seem like an unnecessary

ATTRACTIVE BATTLEGROUNDS	UNATTACTIVE BATTLEGROUNDS
Where you can occupy first	Where you are fighting your own people
Where you can choose how to fight	
	Where your efforts are dispersed
Where your weapons are superior	Where the enemy occupies the high ground
Where you can dominate others	
Where the enemy is weak	Where you can be trapped – only escaping at huge cost
Ground ignored by the enemy	
Ground that you know well	Where you cannot gain a decisive advantage
Ground that fits your capability	Where your lines of supply are long
Ground that is costly for the enemy to fight for	
	Where the local population detest you
Where you have the good will of the population	

Figure 24 Formulating battleground criteria

and burdensome waste of time but, in reality, the opposite is the case; the rigour and discipline given by this technique adds greatly to the quality of decision making.

Criteria used to select a strategic option may include:

- Superior profit potential (measured on a defined return on capital employed formula).
- Coherence with group strategy (measured against stated corporate policy objectives).
- An opportunity to strengthen long term viability (assessed by management judgement).
- A good fit with existing competencies and infrastructure (assessed by technology audits and management judgement).
- Low exit costs (estimated £, $ or ¥ figure).
- A close breakeven date (by a specified date).
- The effect of raising the image of the business to the customer (measurable by market research).

Criteria must help us decide where to compete. Some industries and markets are much more attactive than others. We can obtain further insight from an old source. The ancient warrior-philosopher, Sun Tzu, wrote in *The Art of War*[3] about where to fight. Interestingly, his advice is still read in army staff colleges around the world and, increasingly, in the board rooms of Asian businesses. Sun Tzu's description of types of battleground helps us avoid age-old blunders. Figure 24 gives useful ideas for formulating criteria.

In essence, the process of identifying criteria is straightforward (but rarely simple). Three questions need to be answered:

1   What are the essential criteria that our choice must meet?
2   What are the desirable criteria that our choice should meet?
3   How important are each of the desirable criteria?

When you have the options and the essential and desirable criteria to assess each option, all that remains is to put both together. This is best done on a matrix. The matrix technique does not take the decision for you. If it was so simple then a computer could do it without anyone's intervention. But a decision matrix increases objectivity. The technique also permits wide participation and is a useful tool for facilitating group approaches to strategic decision making.

Decision review questions

There is a need to stand back and reflect before making a strategic commitment.[4] This ensures that every possible avenue has been explored. Take all of the options that are viable (not just the one that you have selected) and ask the seven questions below:

1   How much will the decision cost?
2   What are the probable negative consequences of taking this decision?
3   What are all the things that could go wrong if we take this decision?
4   What could prevent us from putting this decision into effect?
5   What strategic advantages (e.g. providing an improved competitive advantage) does this decision offer?
6   How will people inside the organisation interpret this decision?
7   How will people outside the organisation interpret this decision?

After all the questioning, debating and exploring you make a decision. Sometimes this will be a 'pure' strategy like 'to sell our watercress company and invest the proceeds in expanding the designer cheese business'. More often a hybrid strategy emerges which combines options and provides a platform for opportunism like 'to develop a range of organic vegetable products and new cheeses in a joint venture if a suitable partner can be found'. At this stage strategies are directional rather than precise; they provide an intention rather than a presciption. In the next step we will develop the broad strategy into a coherent vision.

WORKSHOP 8: DEVELOPING STRATEGIC OPTIONS

Preparation

You will need an overhead projector, screen, flip chart, marker pens, scotch tape and Blu-Tack.

Time required

The workshop takes approximately 4 hours and 30 minutes.

WORKSHOP PLAN

1   The team leader opens the workshop by sharing the objectives which are:
- To cluster the ideas in the 'bank'.
- To develop strategic options.
- To determine measurement criteria to assess your options.
- To decide our broad competitive strategy.
(5 minutes)

2   Try these ways of clustering ideas:
a   Group consistent ideas together.
b   Grouping ideas on their degree of 'radicalness'.
c   Grouping ideas on appeal to the stakeholders.
d   Grouping ideas on appeal to the top management team.
(40 minutes)

3   Decide on the most useful clustering and tape the notes down (later these will be typed as a record of the session). (15 minutes)

4   Use the fishbone technique as suggested in the text to develop *each* strategic option. (1 hour 30 minutes)

5   Identifying criteria for choosing between options

   a   Specify essential criteria (be precise if possible).
   b   Specify desirable criteria (be precise if possible).
   c   Decide how important are each of the desirable criteria. Give a weighting factor from 1 to 10 for each item.

   (45 minutes)

6   Draw a matrix showing options against criteria as suggested in the text. (30 minutes)

7   Answer the seven decision review questions as suggested in the text. (30 minutes)

8   Select one option which you feel gives you the most exciting and positive future. Give it a 'name'. Find a way to draw a picture of your selected option. Take your picture to the next workshop. (15 minutes)

Step 9
Defining a competitive strategy

PREPARATION

Read the workshop briefing carefully and understand the requirements of the competitive strategy task. Here are some points that you should think about as you read the step.

1 What competitive strategy is your firm following at the moment?
2 How effectively has your firm implemented its chosen competitive strategy?
3 What competitive strategy will your firm follow in the future?

Come to the workshop ready to discuss these points.

WORKSHOP BRIEFING

At the end of the last step you decided on your business strategy. It was a definite choice from a very well researched set of ideas. But it wasn't a *competitive* strategy. This needs to be developed.

What exactly is a competitive strategy? There are hundreds of business schools in the world, each with professors of strategy whose task is to enable students to answer the question 'why do some firms win and others lose'? Their answers have been codified into a theory of competitive strategy.[1] We define a competitive strategy as 'the bundle of advantages which impels a customer to choose your firm's products rather than another's'.

In this step you will build on the broad strategic commitment that you made in the last step and:

■ Explore the principles of competitive strategy.
■ Identify what competitive strategy you intend to use.
■ Assess what you will need to change to implement your chosen competitive strategy.

Consider an example that everyone can understand from their own experience. Reflect on hotels in any capital city in the world. A visitor will have a wide choice – from bare rooms with threadbare bedding to de-luxe apartments with fitted jacuzzis and dedicated butlers.

The theory of competitive strategy is based on the customer's perception of value. The concept of 'value' differs from customer to customer. A student seeing Europe on $30 a day wants a clean cheap room where he can safely leave his rucksack and 'do the town'. The Ambassador to Ruritania wants a luxury hotel with a secure fax in her room, separate dressing room for her husband and ten different kinds of whisky to offer guests.

All the hotels must be adequate (i.e. 'fit for purpose') as a minimum. No one will knowingly stay in a hotel with unclean bed linen, mice in the wardrobe and a rock group practising across the hall – it is not adequate. Defining what adequate means is important. The minimum requirements for any hotel probably include cleanliness, security, and accessibility.

Let us return to the student. Assume that there are three hotels that meet these criteria: how does he choose? The answer is, of course, on the basis of price. The cheapest – Hotel Tourist – is selected. The competitive strategy that the Hotel Tourist is following is a *price leadership strategy* – an adequate product at a low price.

The Ambassador to Ruritania is unlikely to stay in the Hotel Tourist. She wants a superior experience (the fax, dressing room, cocktail cabinet and so on) and is prepared to pay as her expense account will bear the charge which might be thirty times higher than the Hotel Tourist. She stays at the Hotel Splendide which offers the experience she desires. Her night's sleep is just as refreshing as the student at the Hotel Tourist but in palatial surroundings. The competitive strategy that the Hotel Splendide is following is a *benefits leadership strategy* – an enhanced product at an acceptable price.

Can a hotel follow these two competitive strategies at the same time? Well, it is hard to imagine – the fax, dressing room, and cocktail cabinet add to the cost base of the hotel. Even though the Hotel Splendide charges a price that is thirty times higher its costs are twenty times higher, so it can't offer adequate accommodation at rock-bottom prices. But does this argument apply to all firms? As it happens the Hotel Splendide owns Franco Video, the largest chain of video shops in the country. They can buy video films much more cheaply (through their increased purchasing power), use better computer systems and employ true retail experts (these costs are spread out over a bigger business). From the customers' point of view Franco Video is more professional and better stocked than its rivals (it offers an enhanced product) and, because its costs per unit are lower than its rivals its prices are lower to the customer. The competitive strategy that Franco Video is following is a *dual benefits and price leadership strategy* – an enhanced product at a low price.

We can show the three competitive strategies on a diagram (Figure 25). Because we can apply them to all firms we call them

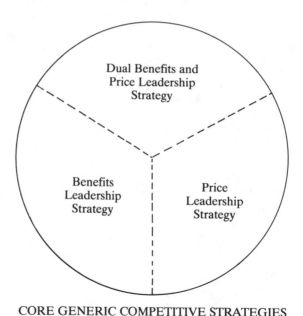

CORE GENERIC COMPETITIVE STRATEGIES

Figure 25 The three core generic competitive strategies

'generic' competitive strategies. Each will be explored in more detail below.

This all seems logical and is the principle that successful street traders operate by. From the customers' point of view the best situation is to obtain superior value at a knock-down price (if this were not true then sales in stores would not be popular). Thereafter, people will go for a 'fit for purpose' product at the lowest price unless they feel that enhancements are worth paying for. If a firm has neither price or benefits leadership it lacks a core competitive strategy and will be outclassed by others.

From the firm's point of view the analysis is flawed: there is a missing dimension – market. Ask a managing director 'what is your firm's competitive strategy?' If she replies 'we are price leaders' the statement is incomplete. However, if she says 'we are price leaders in supplying generic drugs to hospitals' the competitive strategy becomes clear. The full definition of competitive strategies must include a definition of market focus.

I have found that the most useful way to classify a market is in

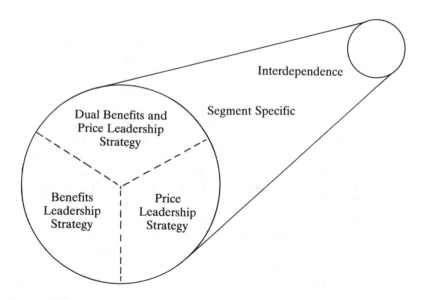

Figure 26 The generic competitive strategies showing market size dimension

terms of the numbers of customers. Some firms, selling military equipment, for example, have no more than five customers. Others, selling soap, for example, have millions of customers. Somewhere in the middle are firms selling to tightly defined market segments, customer groups like fishermen, people with cosmetic dentistry or teachers of art to children. Based on this insight we can add the market size[2] dimension to the diagram (Figure 26).

There is little difficulty in seeing how the three generic competitive strategies apply for the mass market. In the pen industry Bic follow a price leadership strategy, Mont Blanc follow a benefits leadership strategy and Pentil seem to be pursuing a dual benefits and price strategy.

What about segment specific strategies? Let us return to the hotels example. A few who come to town will make their way to the Hotel Vegan which is located in an obscure part of town. Why do they pass several cheaper and adequate hotels on the way? The Hotel Vegan advertises in journals called *Vegetarian Life* and *Wholesome Living*. It offers some of the best vegan food in town and attracts true vegetarians. People go to the Hotel Vegan because it meets their specialist needs – a vegan is rarely happy in an ordinary hotel no matter how expensive. Guests sit down to lentil casseroles and nut roasts feeling well cared for. The competitive strategy the Hotel Vegan is following a *segment specific strategy* – a product which meets special needs at an acceptable price.

At the end of the diagram a new word has appeared – interdependence. This is the competitive strategy used by firms which are selling a capability rather than a finished product. Such firms work closely with their customers to evolve products or services with their customers – each contributes and learns. Consider, for example, Hotsoft, a computer software company specialising in tailor-made products for the hotel industry. The Hotel Splendide decide they want a computer system which recalls personal details of clients – the pillows they like, kind of tea and so on. Hotsoft win the contract and their senior consultant sits down with the manager of the Hotel Splendide and asks 'let's brainstorm all the characteristics you want in your new system'. Gradually the design of the computer system emerges through collaborative effort. The competitive strategy Hotsoft is following is an *interdependence strategy* – a capability to collaborate which meets special needs at an acceptable price.

Of course, there are overlaps. Following a price leadership strategy for a large market segment (like women with children under the age of ten) is little different than mass marketing children's clothing. For this reason we simplify the analysis by describing the three core strategies and the two limited market categories – five competitive strategies in all. Now we need to examine each in more detail.

PRICE LEADERSHIP STRATEGY

The price leadership strategy[3] enables customers to buy 'an adequate product at a low price'. Let's dissect this statement. Firstly, the concept 'adequate' – this is a 'must' criterion. In effect, the customer is saying 'it must have this attribute otherwise I won't buy it.' The definition of adequacy is affected by psychological and sociological forces and varies over time. Two generations ago a child would be happy with a small toy for his Christmas presents. Now two sackfuls of toys are viewed as barely satisfactory. One of the most important strategic tasks (once you have selected your market) is to define what 'adequate' means to your target customers.

Secondly, the concept of 'price'. If I am on holiday in the USA, I might go into the local supermarket and choose to buy a tin of anchovies for $5 even though the hotel Bell Boy has told me that an identical tin can be purchased for $4 in another supermarket ten miles down the road. Is the local supermarket using a price leadership strategy when they offer to sell me a tin of anchovies for $5? The answer, paradoxically, is 'yes' because my costs of getting to the next town will exceed $1 and so I am buying a tin of anchovies for the lowest 'cost of ownership'.

Cost of ownership are more significant when I make a capital investment. The cost of owning a car includes maintenance and repair costs, less the car's value on resale. I may buy an expensive car but end up paying less in total because the ownership costs are much lower. Another example from medical products industry makes the point. Second generation anti-depressants cost £1,000 per patient per annum whereas the old treatment cost £800, but the rate of attempted suicide and emotional distress on the old drugs means that the actual cost of the old drugs is five times more expensive than the new.

A price leadership strategy has great strength. This is especially true when a product becomes a commodity. Consider IBM's unhappy experience with a market they pioneered – personal computers. 'For years IBM ... repeatedly charged higher prices than the competition. No longer. In launching its own low-cost PC line IBM is vowing to match its competitors – price for price, feature for feature – across the globe. "We are tired of watching from the side lines," said William E. McCracken, general manager of IBM's new personal systems business in Europe, "IBM is going to stay with the market place. And if the competitors cut prices we will too." '[4]

Here's a test question for you: 'is a firm following a price leadership strategy if it has:

■ Selected a market which has profit potential.
■ Correctly judged what customers define as "adequate".
■ Is able to supply a product which meets the customers' basic requirements.
■ Offers the lowest cost of ownership?'

The answer is 'almost!' There is a missing element: 'signalling'.[5] Only when the firm signals that it is the price leader and the customer believes that his costs of ownership will be less can a price leadership strategy be effective.

If a firm is genuinely following a price leadership strategy will it make a profit? The answer is 'Yes, if ...' And, it's a big 'if'. If the firm's total costs are lower than the revenue received the answer will be 'yes'. Since costs are such a crucial element, a price leadership strategy can only be delivered when your costs are equal or lower than your competitors.

The argument is complete. A price leadership strategy requires:

1 Finding a market with profit potential.
2 Correctly judging what customers define as 'adequate'.
3 Supplying a product which meets the customers' basic requirements.
4 Offering the lowest cost of ownership to the customer.
5 Signalling lower costs of ownership.

6   Understanding the factors which drive costs.
7   Sustaining low costs for every activity.
8   Enjoying superior economies of scale.
9   Installing efficient manufacturing and service philosophies.
10   Constantly experimenting to find better/cheaper ways.

BENEFITS LEADERSHIP

The benefits leadership[6] strategy enables customers to buy 'an enhanced product at an acceptable price'. Let's dissect the definition.

The Ambassador to Ruritania wanted enhancements from her hotel. We have mentioned a number already but she also wanted to be near the Palace (handy for lunch) and enjoy a restaurant that served bortsch soup (which they love in Ruritania). In fact, if the Ambassador was asked to brainstorm what she wanted from a hotel she could fill several sheets of paper without pausing for breath.

To attract the Ambassador the Hotel Splendide needed to meet all (or all the important items) of her requirements in an integrated and harmonious way. It would be jarring if the hotel's public rooms were designer-perfect but the waiters spoke with the gruff familiarity of attendants in a sailors' mission. Most importantly, none of the services could fall beneath an 'acceptable' level for that class of hotel. They could get a thousand things right but if the switchboard fail to give the Ambassador a wake-up call and she misses her audience with the Queen then all the other provided enhancements become devalued and worthless.

The notion that enhancements need to be integrated and harmonised into a cocktail (the technical term is 'gestalt') is one of the most useful ideas in competitive strategy: so important that we will devote step 10 to explaining how to develop the competencies of your firm behind an integrated and harmonious strategy.

Let's explore another element in the definition of a benefits leadership strategy – the word 'product'. Two firms, John's and Jack's, try to sell me exactly the same photocopier but Jack's offers free after sales service. As a customer I chose Jack's because his product is enhanced – it includes additional value that a firm of his type can provide – after sales service. The 'product' is both the asset acquired and the service that surrounds it.

The third element in the definition of a benefits leadership strategy is 'at an acceptable price'. Enhancements are what people feel is worth paying extra for, but they will not pay an infinite amount extra. An example, also from the hotel industry, demonstrates the principle. I was told that in the Kowloon Tong area of Hong Kong there are hotels where couples hire rooms by the hour. As each car enters the compound a smartly dressed attendant leaps out from a booth and places discreet covers over the car's number plates. In one police raid they found that every room had a different theme. There was a Viking ship in one room that pitched like a real boat, another room had a Rolls Royce with a bed in the back whilst a third was a room with a swimming pool on which floated a large mattress. It is reliably reported that the best of such establishments are 'money making machines'. The lovers of Hong Kong (often married couples) will pay about three times the price of a standard hotel for the enhancements offered in the Kowloon Tong area but not five times as much. Enhancements have added only limited additional value.

The most popular way to enhance one's product is through 'branding'. At best a brand is provides a virtuous circle. People associate a brand with quality, pay extra, and remain loyal – which gives the firm a superior return on investment from which it can fund further product and brand enhancement. Some of the impact of a brand is perceived rather than real. In a sense, the firm is signalling messages which exaggerate the value of the brand using techniques of psychological persuasion. Brands can be redefined: for example, Lucozade was repositioned from a sickness to health drink. Brands need to be nurtured as the image can be devalued. This happened to Gucci in the early 1990s. Schlitz, an American lager, went from $48 million net profit to a $50 million loss after they cut prices and skimped on quality. The beer lost its position as the premier lager. Brands offer the prospect of providing long term value enhancement – 19 of 22 top brands in standard product categories are the same today as in 1925.[7]

If a firm is genuinely following a benefits leadership strategy will it make a profit? The answer, again, is 'Yes, if ...' If the firm's total costs are lower than the revenue received the answer will be 'yes'. Enhancements must cost less to add than the value added. Also, once again, signalling is vital. Only when the firm successfully signals that it is the benefits leader and the customer believes that the enhancements are worth higher costs of ownership can a benefits leadership strategy be effective.

The argument is complete. A benefits leadership strategy requires:

1 Finding a market with superior profit potential.
2 Correctly judging what customers define as 'enhancements which add value'.
3 Supplying a product which meets the customers' enhancements requirements.
4 Building a strong reputation for the firm and its brands.
5 Researching to provide leapfrog products and innovating in design and development.
6 Constant comparing with competitors' products and monitoring competitors' strengths and weaknesses.
7 Maintaining an integrated organisation with strong coordination between departments.
8 Attracting highly able and creative staff.
9 Respecting the marketing function which creates an 'enterprise' organisational culture and is influential in decision making.
10 Successfully signalling superior value.

DUAL BENEFITS AND PRICE STRATEGY

The dual benefits and price strategy enables customers to buy 'an enhanced product at a low price'. Let's dissect the definition.

All competitive strategies are constantly under attack. Out there someone is planning to take your business away from you. How can you defend? We have established that there are two generic strategies – do it cheaper or do it better. Both are an effective form of defence. Can you use both strategies at the same time? Working on the principle brings security – wearing both a belt and braces makes it less likely that a man's trousers will fall down unexpectedly! As we explained above (the Franco Video example) the answer is sometimes 'yes' but more often 'no'. When firms opt for a benefits leadership strategy they generally increase costs to add enhancements and so cannot become price leaders and operate at a profit. But some enhancements are either free or the added value derived more than meets any additional costs. A dual benefits and price strategy can sometimes be implemented – it offers the strong-est form of defence (and attack).

Consider two airlines flying between London and Paris. Both are flying the same planes from the same airports so their costs are very similar. Both airlines make a profit if their load factor reaches 63 per cent. Airline A has a charismatic chairman who has convinced the airline's staff to be super-attentive to their passengers. Airline B has a deserved reputation for surly staff. Passengers prefer Airline A so its load factor is 81 per cent whereas Airline B scrapes along with 66 per cent. The service orientated strategy of Airline A is free – the training costs are paid for by fewer errors. Their profits are higher so they offer improved meals, more check-in staff, discounts, user clubs, excursions and cheaper business fares. Airline A's dual benefits and price strategy is strangling Airline B.

Opportunities to move towards a dual benefits and price strategy can be created by technology. For example, now hotel television sets can send messages, sell films, give customised welcome messages, show advertisements, enable bills to be checked, give fire information if the fire alarm sounds, provide a facility to order breakfast (with graphics of eggs etc.), show photos of staff, provide multi-language instructions, and so on. The hotel that possesses such a system cuts costs (less time debating items on bills) and through automated service provides an intriguing enhancement to the guest.

Perhaps the most effective route to a dual benefits and price strategy is 'time-based competition' – the innovative strategic theme of the 1990s. The argument is this: where equally com-petent firms compete, the winner will be the firm that gets the next generation of product faster to market. The concepts were devel-oped largely in Japan where most firms are seeking a 50 per cent reduction in new product development time. Since the resources needed are low cost or free – process re-engineering, team working, cell working, JIT supplies, parallel processing, empower-ment and organising for communication – product enhancements can be added, output increased and costs reduced: a virtuous circle. Land Rover produced their Discovery vehicle in 3 years rather than the typical 5 or 6 years taken by European manufac-turers. They scooped the market for semi-rugged off-road vehicles in the early 1990s. Seiko can design a new watch and manufacture a prototype in three weeks. It can be done.

It is always necessary to be ahead of competitors. In 1815 the Rothschild family had a carrier pigeon service operating from near the battle of Waterloo, thereby learning who had won the battle hours before the London stock market, and so made a fortune on the London Stock Exchange. Time-based competition is a way that local companies can have advantage over bigger distant firms. However, it requires a revolution in thinking within the firm. Historically firms have concentrated on managing cost not time. The intention of competitive strategy becomes to create a dynamic firm that acts like a karate player not a machine. Security is gained through the management of constant change – not the pursuit of stability.

For a dual benefits and price strategy we will not need an additional checklist – the items are a combination of the two lists above. When this strategy can be followed it is the strongest available; but the most difficult to achieve.

SEGMENT SPECIFIC STRATEGIES

The segment specific[8] strategy enables customers to buy 'a product which meets special needs at an acceptable price '. Let's dissect the definition.

We've defined the word 'product' – no need to go over that again! Let's look at the term 'special needs'. Firms can develop a competitive strategy which focuses on the needs and wants of specific market segments. This has several advantages:

- Costs can be contained since the strategic focus is limited.
- The precise needs and wants of the market segment can be exhaustively studied.
- It is possible to have a dominant position whilst not becoming an industry giant.
- The firm can lead the market segment without entering into toe-to-toe combat with the big guys.

China provides some good examples of segment-specific service strategies. Let us consider a highly focused example from the service industry. There is a restaurant in Guangzhou that special-ises in all kinds of rat dishes. The Jia Lu ('Superior Deer' in

Chinese) has seventeen tables. Rats are described as 'virus free from the countryside' and 'high in protein and amino acids'. The benefits? According to the restaurateur there is a Chinese saying 'one rat surpasses three chickens', and he adds that rat meat 'improves resistance to exhaustion, tension, allergies, hardening of the arteries and premature senility'.

Other examples of a segment specific product strategy include:

- A business which sells goats' genitalia is based in Hong Kong.[9] The firm is Desert Oak Goats and they sell the item either fresh or dried. Some say that delicious soup can be made by boiling the meat with rosemary and coriander.
- The Taiwanese company Saho, which is reputed to manufacture the embossing and encoding machines used by gangs of forgers who produce counterfeit credit cards.
- Artagraph Reproduction Technology[10] (ART), an Ontario-based company, laser scans great masters to reproduce the colours, shadings and brush strokes so that the final result is almost indistinguishable from the original painting. Marketing director, Ms Chrissie Fellowes, said 'there is a definite niche in the market for top quality, limited edition numbered reproductions of old masters'. Access to the originals was essential. Range now includes Picasso, Renoir, Monet, Van Gogh and Cezanne. The price? About US $8,000 each.

But some products are bought because they offer unique advantages. I am sitting on an aeroplane getting towards the end of a long flight and I am keying in the text to a tiny Agenda computer which works like an electronic version of one of those clever shorthand machines that you see in the background in old court room drama movies (it's called Microwriting). The Agenda is unique: there is no other baby computer which operates in the same way. I bought it because I felt that it was a brilliant solution to my needs as a writer on the move. The text will move painlessly to my office computer when I return home. How does the Agenda remain a unique product? The answer is, probably, that they have found a market niche that no one else is willing to pay the costs to enter. But if microwriting really caught on in a big way then a host of competitors would emerge. The Agenda wins because it is a specialist product – its limited appeal is its defence. Of course, the niche can become a tomb: someone may invent a more elegant, effective or cheaper solution and the Agenda becomes a quaint staging post in the evolution of an industry as the innovative firm that developed the product lacks the depth of technical resources to be a big player.

A segment specific strategy requires:

1 Adopting a creative philosophy of market segmentation.
2 Serving 'attractive' market segments.
3 Deliberately limiting the scope of competition.
4 Developing specialised product/market strategies.
5 Getting close to your markets and identifying customers' existing and emerging needs.
6 Understand the valuing and decision making processes of customers within each segment.
7 Identifying potential customers and related niche markets (which provide the opportunity for growth).
8 Developing specific key success factors (KSFs) for chosen market segments.
9 Analyzing changes in chosen market segments and mapping how 'your' market segments are changing – speed and direction of change.
10 Tracking competitors' strategies in chosen market segments; if possible, raising costs of entry to new competitors in chosen market segments.

INTERDEPENDENCE STRATEGY

The interdependence strategy was quaintly but accurately described by a group of managers in the Far East as 'the bondage approach'. More technically this strategy enables customers to buy 'a capability to collaborate which meets their special needs at an acceptable price'. Let's dissect the definition.

Insurance companies customers are often brokers. Usually the relationship is distant; the company develop the products and try to sell them to the brokers. The Stork Insurance Company adopted a different strategy. They formed a close association with a broker to develop a range of new products for the farming industry in the broker's territory. The insurance company offered their underwriting expertise and the broker matched this with local market knowhow. Between both businesses a new range of products was developed – which neither could have developed alone. The insurance company was following an interdependence strategy with this broker – they were offering a capability to collaborate which meets special needs at an acceptable price.

An interdependence strategy is particulary relevant to selling advisory, intellectual or consultancy services. I follow this strategy with some clients myself. It is almost as if a new, temporary organisation is constructed to fulfil a series of assignments. The client gets:

■ A tailor-made solution which meets his specific needs.
■ Low costs of tuning in new consultants.
■ Ability to put pressure on fees (as the consultant is deeply committed).
■ Ability to take over high cost activities and perform these more cheaply.

The consultant also benefits. He or she enjoys:

■ Continuity of work (the client would incur major switching costs if they changed consultant).
■ Developmental work – both sides learn.
■ Being close to opportunities.

An interdependence strategy requires:

1 Limiting the numbers of clients so each customer is unique.
2 Working with each customer to identify precise needs.
3 Building personal, smooth, open, trustworthy, collaborative relationships.
4 Taking a long term perspective.
5 Providing dedicated staff and an integrated service.
6 Indoctrinating all staff to be committed to providing customer satisfaction.
7 Obtaining full participation from the customer.
8 Developing specialised services which are expensive for the customer to replicate.
9 Learning with the customer.
10 Adopting the ethic of 'continuous improvement'.

MULTI-STRATEGIES

In practice strategy development is never as straightforward as a conceptual model presents. For example, some products can be reconfigured as the need arises. A pub, for example, may be following one competitive strategy at lunch time and another in the evening. Firms usually offer more than one product or service. Consider Sony who make the professional walkman (a recording walkman with appeal to the professional user or specialist amateur). But Sony also sell several walkmans that are truly basic and compete at the low end – they are following several competitive strategies within one product range at the same time.

British Airways pride themselves on the quality of their first class service; each passenger is addressed by name, can enjoy a personal movie channel and sleeps in a seat that very nearly transforms into a bed. At the back of the same plane there may be travellers who brought their tickets from a 'bucket shop' simply because BA was the cheapest available fare on that route: they are following several competitive strategies with one product at the same time.

VISIONING

Once a firm has chosen its competitive strategy the next task is to begin to develop a 'vision'. Don't be concerned – the concept is not mysterious. A business 'vision' is a 'mental picture' of what the organisation should become. Visions that attract others are the quintessence of leadership. Every part of the organisation must develop its own vision within the scope of the firms chosen competitive strategy – a subtle leadership process that we call 'alignment'. The principle of alignment means that people are both confined and liberated by the corporate competitive strategy which provides integrity, a framework for decision making, and is a motivating force.

The principle of alignment was well described by Peter Benton[11] who, as ex-Chairman of British Telecom (BT), wrote:

> The ten year strategic plan ... was primarily conceptual ... The purpose of the document was to create through the business a conceptual framework within which the personal initiatives of many thousands of individuals could be caused to converge – by

the spontaneous goodwill of newly freed managers, rather than by specific direction from the top.

Competitive strategy requires two forms of visions: 'enduring' and 'time bound'. The former captures the quintessence of the organisation, the latter is a systematic visualisation of the organisation on particular dates in the future which we will develop in the next step.

ENDURING VISION

Enduring visions integrate the permanent characteristics of the competitive strategy of the organisation. They incorporate the core values or mission and encapsulate the 'heart' of the company providing a sense of pride – people should feel uplifted by an enduring vision.

An excellent example is the Boeing Company which aims 'to build aircraft that are safe enough for our families to fly in'. This brief statement brilliantly captures values, standards and direction to provide a competitive strategy which could last a thousand years.

Visions are, by definition, aspirational. They describe the fundamental competitive strategy so should be 'realistically idealistic'. A vision gives confidence to people to move into uncertainty; it is a conceptual security blanket which gives courage to move forwards from the known.

The leader must fully explore and believe the vision. This needs to be felt beneath the mind. The expression 'walk the talk' captures the sentiment. The competitive strategy vision should gather a critical mass of people who become avid supporters.

WORKSHOP 9: DEFINING A COMPETITIVE STRATEGY

Preparation

You will need an overhead projector, screen, flip chart, marker pens, and Blu-Tack.

Time required

The workshop takes approximately 3 hours.

WORKSHOP PLAN

1   The team leader opens the workshop by sharing the objectives which are to:

■ Explore the principles of competitive strategy.
■ Identify what competitive strategy you intend to use.
■ Assess what you will need to change to implement your chosen competitive strategy.

The team leader reminds the group that each team member should help in the process of generating, building on and capturing ideas. (5 minutes)

2   Check your understanding of the principles of competitive strategy by finding three examples for each of the five strategies listed (different from those in the text!). (10 minutes)

3   Agree which is the primary overall competitive strategy followed by your firm at the present time. (15 minutes)

4   Agree which is the competitive strategy followed by your firm at the present time for each of the main products/services (or product families) you offer. (30 minutes)

5   Audit your capability to deliver the competitive strategy by scoring yourselves out of ten for the relevant items in the check lists above. Consider your existing strengths and weaknesses. (1 hour)

6   Reflect on the strategic option that you developed at the end of the previous step. Develop an 'enduring vision statement' as suggested in the text. (1 hour)

Step 10
Implementing strategy systematically

PREPARATION

There is a very important task to complete before the next workshop – you are asked to read and understand the competency systems analysis theory and complete an analysis (this is fully explained in the workshop briefing) of your business as it is today. By all means work in pairs or trios on the task but ensure that you have at least two different analyses to consider. Bring your completed diagram with you to the workshop.

This is quite complex so there is a lot to do!

WORKSHOP BRIEFING

We're doing well. We have defined a competitive strategy. Our prework provides us with confidence that our strategy is achievable and sustainable. The big question is 'how to get there?'

In this step we will:

- Reflect on what the competitive strategy means to the organisation.
- Identify what needs to be done to implement the chosen strategy.
- Develop a systematic and 'time bound' vision of the business.
- Specify a strategic action plan.

We are about to enter into the field of organisation development (OD) – a topic that needs a whole book to give it justice. In this step we develop a *strategic* organisation development plan to implement your chosen competitive strategy but we cannot cover the detailed process of managing change.[1]

IMPLEMENTATION

We have clarified values, formulated a competitive strategy and developed a vision of the future. We have woven analysis, imagination and passion to give the organisation a 'heart' and a 'head'. So, you ask wearily, 'isn't that enough?'

More needs to be done. Strategies and visions are, by definition, broad brush. An enduring vision is too imprecise a tool to be a template for organisation development. We need systematically to develop the broad vision so that we know what the organisation will be like at some specified time in the future; this is done through the process of 'competency systems' analysis.

People's eyes glaze over at this point. 'Systems analysis' looks dull but 'competency systems analysis' appears incomprehensible. Writing this step is a particular challenge for the author because the competency systems analysis method is one of the most valuable tools for the strategic manager that has yet been developed.[2] However, it will take you some hours to understand the technique and, later, applying the tool to your own firm will take half a day at least.

Competency systems analysis is two theories intertwined. Firstly, we use systems concepts which are drawn from theoretical physics and, secondly, we employ competency models which were developed from military strategy. The approach is easier to understand if we look at these two strands separately. We will begin with systems concepts.

STRATEGIC SYSTEMS ANALYSIS

Let's assume that you are a captain working for Global Dredgers Inc. digging a trench for a sewer somewhere off Singapore. A fax arrives in your cabin telling you that the company is adopting a new corporate strategy of 'total harbour solutions'. You look at the brief message and wonder 'what will this mean to me?' You puzzle, but the implications are obscure, so you file the document under 'pending' and go back to chivvying the deckhands.

Global Dredgers Inc. must transform their strategic intent into a full organisation development plan which has coherence and harmony. This is best done by conceptualising of the firm *as a system* and ensuring that every activity supports the overall strategy. Hence the rationale for systems analysis.

The overall business system, like a Russian doll, is made up of sub-systems. These we will group as to whether they directly or indirectly add value to the product or service offered.

Systems thinkers' eyes light up when they talk about 'core processes' which are the *direct* ways in which a firm adds value. Our dredger captain is supervising operations – a core process – every kilometre of sewer laid directly generates revenue for the firm. Global Dredging's personnel manager is *indirectly* adding value by sustaining an organisation which selects, trains and rewards the dredger's crew.

All firms – product or service orientated – can be conceptualised as having five core-process sub-systems and seven support sub-systems – 'the twelve box model'. Each of the 'boxes' is inter-related but has specialised functions – that is, makes a distinct contribution to the organisation. There is some overlap between the boxes so that sharp lines cannot always be drawn.

Before we get into detail it is helpful to see the total model laid out diagrammatically (Figure 27). Begin by taking a good look at the twelve box model. The first thing that you will notice is that the diagram is shaped like an arrow.[3] In the head of the arrow is the word 'margin'. This represents the economic motive of the firm

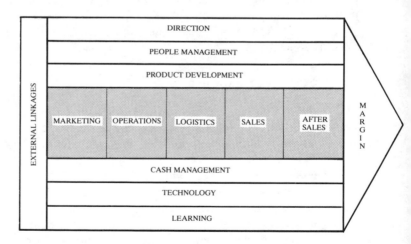

Figure 27 The 'twelve box' competency systems model

which is to add value faster than cost. Each of the twelve sub-systems adds cost; the essence is to add value faster and make a healthy margin.

In many organisations there is a complex interrelationship between sub-systems as processes cross boundaries between the 'boxes'. For example, Scoff is a company that manufactures peanut butter. They must buy peanuts, glass etc. through their supply chain, define target markets, manufacture their product, get the product to market, sell the special benefits of Scoff peanut butter and continue to enhance value even after the product has been sold. Simply drawing a flow chart of their current business process illustrates to Scoff's managers the interrelated complexities of their systems. The managers at Scoff must review their business system as a whole[4] to ensure that it is an efficient and effective device for implementing their chosen competitive strategy.[5] This requires:

■ Understanding and mapping how the current business system operates (this is a far more difficult task than it may appear as sub-systems grow uncontrolled over the years).
■ Developing a vision of the needed system at a point in the future.
■ Planning how to change from the present to achieve the 'system vision'.

Now consider each of the sub-systems. The five core process sub-systems are shown as shaded boxes in the diagram above (Figure 27). They are:

1 *Marketing* – ensuring that the firm understands the customer's valuing system.
2 *Operations* – transforming inputs into outputs.
3 *Logistics* – moving inputs and outputs.
4 *Sales* – inducing potential customers to buy.
5 *After sales* – enhancing value after sale.

The seven support sub-systems are:

6 *Direction* – determining strategy and resourcing.
7 *People management* – all aspects of the management of people.
8 *Product development* – creating tomorrow's offerings.

9   *Cash management* – spending money wisely.
10   *Technology* – developing systems and methods.
11   *Learning* – sustaining an open organisation.
12   *External linkages* – sustaining positive interfaces with the outside world.

We will take a more detailed look at each of these twelve sub-systems but remember that you will need to consider how they relate together later.

1 Marketing

The primary function of the marketing sub-system is 'ensuring that the firm understands the customer's valuing system'. Firms must create products and services which are needed or wanted by customers above competitors' offerings. Marketing has two dimensions: firstly, defining and assessing customers' valuing systems, and, secondly, aligning the organisation to deliver real value. The following activities are undertaken by the marketing sub-system:

- Market definition, research and analysis.
- Identifying existing and potential customer needs and wants.
- Product/service positioning.
- Advertising and promotion.
- Channel relationships.
- Pricing.
- Shaping product development.

2 Operations

The primary function of the operations sub-system is 'transforming inputs into outputs'. Firms have to transform something into something else otherwise they are not adding value. Operations are hugely varied so may include producing products, giving advice, cleaning streets, writing TV scripts and go-go dancing. A firm, like an insurance company, may find it difficult to define its operations, but careful thought reveals the core operations function is 'writing contracts' (underwriting). It is worth persevering. The following activities are undertaken by the operations sub-system:

- Manufacture (all stages) of the product or service offered.

■ Breaking operations tasks into manageable elements.
■ Setting and maintaining standards.
■ Integrating people and machines (designing socio-technical systems).
■ Managing for efficiency, flexibility and reliability.
■ Customising products or services to customers' particular needs.
■ Testing and continuous improvement.
■ Resources scheduling and planning.

3 Logistics

The primary function of the logistics sub-system is 'moving inputs and outputs'. Most, but not all, firms acquire tangible inputs (this includes data) and distribute their outputs. A supermarket chain, for example, has an enormous logistical task in getting thousands of products on the shelves but customers handle most of the outbound logistics themselves. A company supplying oxygen to thousands of nursing homes will have few inbound logistical headaches but a complex outbound distribution system. But how about our friend the TV scriptwriter who only needs half a dozen pencils, a notebook and an envelope for sending his work to the producer – not much logistical complexity here!

The following activities are undertaken by the logistics subsystem:

■ Finding sources of supply of necessary inputs.
■ Managing suppliers' efficiency, flexibility and responsiveness.
■ Receiving, storing and moving inputs, work in progress and finished output.
■ Inventory control and scheduling.
■ Delivery efficiency, flexibility and responsiveness.

4 Sales

The primary function of the sales sub-system is 'inducing potential customers to buy'. Sales activities have become hugely varied in the last thirty years so that, today, a computerised voice may call everyone in California who has purchased a lawnmower in the last six months to sell them grass seed. The line between marketing and sales activities can be indistinct. For example, a wine distributor in Japan may take a hundred *mamasans* (female bar managers) on an outing to Kyoto – is this a marketing promotion or a sales initiative – since the *mamasans* influence their customers' choice of wine? However, the centre of gravity of the sales sub-system is always distinct: the primary concern is 'this month's figures'.

The following activities are undertaken by the sales sub-system:

■ Influencing the organisation to meet customer needs.
■ Selecting sales techniques and technologies.
■ Sales force: selection, management, training and motivation.
■ Accessing potential customers.
■ Quoting and negotiating.
■ Order processing.

5 After sales

The primary function of the after-sales sub-system is 'enhancing value after sale'. Many firms do not find it easy to add significant value after the sale has been made. For example, you have a meal in a restaurant, pay the bill and leave. Where is the opportunity for after-sales added value? Let's say you forget your umbrella, you phone and the restaurant manager drops it off for you later that day. Some value is added since an emotional bond has been forged between you and that restaurant.

Some firms make after-sales service a strong feature of their competitive strategy. People buy a Mercedes-Benz car because they believe their servicing requirements will be met by better trained and well mannered staff and Mercedes' three-year break-down warranty gives added security of mind. The same argument is used by several computer software companies who have made their 'customer hotlines' a key feature.

The following activities are undertaken by the after-sales sub-system:

■ Installation.
■ Product adjustment.
■ Enhancing and maintaining the value of the product or service.
■ Training and support.
■ Dealing with customer complaints.
■ Providing maintenance network.
■ Repair and parts supply.

6 Direction

The primary function of the direction sub-system is 'determining strategy and resourcing'. You will need no introduction to these activities – they are the subject matter of this book. The resourcing function is widely defined to include the provision of funds, intellectual capital, joint venture expertise, key policies and the provision of leadership direction.

The following activities are undertaken by the direction sub-system:

- Giving the organisation leadership, focus and integration.
- Developing a viable competitive strategy.
- General and financial management.
- Supply of working capital and overall management of cash flow.
- Maintaining planning, management information and monitoring systems.
- Meeting legal requirements.
- Choice of partners, joint venture agreements etc.
- Maintaining positive relations with environment and stakeholders.
- Influencing powerful people in the wider corporation.

7 People management

The primary function of the people management sub-system is 'all aspects of the management of people'. This is the most disparate of the twelve sub-systems; every supervisor and manager plays a role in the task of ensuring that people are well-motivated, competent and directed. Generally, it is helpful to analyse the systematic and standardised aspects of human resource management which are directed and controlled by a group of professionals in human resource development departments.

The following activities are undertaken by the people management sub-system:

- Manpower requirements planning.
- Identifying skill and competency requirements.
- Structuring the organisation.
- Sustaining a positive organisational culture.
- Motivation and communication.
- Recruitment and selection.
- Training and personnel development.

- Compensation and reward planning.
- Trades union and staff relationships.
- Team building.

8 Product development

The primary function of the product development sub-system is 'creating tomorrow offerings'. This includes all of the work necessary to maintain a stream of new products and services; some of which may be minor enhancements whilst others are truly revolutionary. Product development usually has an organisational focus (the R&D department) but the function is much more widely spread across the organisation – for example, sales people often suggest great new ideas.

The following activities are undertaken by the product development sub-system:

- Acquiring core technological competencies and enabling technologies.
- Transforming inputs from marketing into products.
- Product and service research, design and development.
- Product testing.
- Designing for manufacturability or deliverability.
- Process development to deliver waves of innovation ahead of the competition.

9 Cost management

The primary function of the cost management sub-system is 'spending money wisely'. This is a vital area; for some firms up to 80 per cent of their costs are brought in. Expertise in managing costs gives many advantages. In recent years we have seen considerable development in the ability of finance specialists to actually provide information which helps managers take better decisions. Cost management includes the basic requirement of knowing the cost structure of every significant product or service (and being able to compare this with competitors). Additionally, the function of procurement is included under this heading. Waterstones is a UK bookstore that browsers love – with plenty of books and late night opening. In 1992 they controlled 11.5 per cent of the UK book market and employed 1,300 staff. Waterstones started with one shop in 1981 in a busy London street. By

1992 there were 88 stores, including one in Boston, USA. Brilliant procurement was one of the main reasons. By paying invoices on 80 days rather than the typical 30 days given to other booksellers Tim Waterstone could fund a large part of his stock on what was, in effect, borrowed money. It is books that attract book buyers – so the stores were full.

The following activities are undertaken by the cost management sub-system:

■ Analysis and improvement of cost structures.
■ Provision of accurate cost information for managerial decision making.
■ Purchasing raw materials and components.
■ Purchasing all services, supplies and consumables.
■ Purchasing machinery and equipment.
■ Purchasing buildings or space.

10 Technology

The primary function of the technology sub-system is 'developing systems and methods'. The term 'systems and methods' must not be interpreted narrowly; often people think of computer systems, but there is much more to it than that. Imagine that you arrive for cocktails at a big hotel. Immediately you interface with the systems of the organisation. The doorman whisks open your taxi door and greets you with a subtle blend of friendliness and servility (the training system); you walk into the lobby and are seated by an attentive waiter (the supervisory system); your order is fed into a computerised unit (the loading, billing and stock control systems) and you sit and enjoy your drink until the man at the next table is ejected for throwing a drink over his wife whilst angrily disputing her accusation that he is having an affair with his secretary (the security system).

Systems and methods are the accumulated wisdom of the organisation in a codified form. Some systems are huge – it costs at least US $100 million to develop an airline booking system – whilst others are small – Harrods have a system for looking after customers' dogs whilst they shop.

The following activities are undertaken by the systems and methods sub-system:

- Enhancing and codifying knowhow.
- Developing procedures, methodologies and technologies for all aspects of the organisations functioning including customer interfaces.
- Completing systems analysis.
- Developing, commissioning and enhancing systems.
- Installing and upgrading communication and linking systems.

11 Learning

The primary function of the learning sub-system is 'sustaining an open organisation'. Openness is the key; think of the organisation as a living organism capable of learning. Organisational learning is facilitated both from within, normally driven by the energy of key individuals, and without, normally from contact with others whose ideas are demonstrably superior.

This is not an easy 'box' to explain. The notion that organisations learn is strange to many. But consider a straightforward example. For many years APL Cine were a small Swedish film production company making advertisements, industrial films etc. Their production standards were, frankly, adequate at best. Then Ruscar, a brilliant but bankrupt Russian cartoon production company proposed a joint venture which required totally interdependent working at every level. From this association APL Cine became a world-class film maker: they learnt a vast array of new techniques from Ruscar and the creativity of their staff was liberated. The organisation had learned.

The following activities are undertaken by the learning sub-system:

- Structuring exposure to new ideas.
- Tracking competitors.
- Tracking innovations.
- Learning from comparable companies.
- Capturing ideas from all employees.
- Setting up innovation groups.
- Investing in learning and experimentation.
- Creating a climate in which it is OK to take risks.

12 External linkages

The primary function of the external linkages sub-system is 'sustaining positive interfaces with the outside world'. No organisation is an island. Linkages are backward, forward, upward, sideways and outward. These sub-divide into eight major external interfaces that must be managed for sustained competitive advantage. The eight are: suppliers, partners, distribution channels, owners, customers, 'teachers', government and the public.

The following activities are undertaken by the external linkages sub-system:

- Identifying excellent suppliers and developing 'win-win' relationships.
- Identifying excellent partners and developing 'win-win' relationships.
- Identifying excellent distribution channels and developing 'win-win' relationships.
- Exceeding the owners' requirements.
- Exceeding the customers' requirements.
- Developing learning relationships with organisations that can act as 'teachers'.
- Meeting government's needs and influencing them to help you.
- Building public understanding and support.

COMPETENCIES

When Napoleon built up the armed might of France after the Revolution of 1789 he realised that it was impossible to predict every situation that his army might encounter. Napoleon solved the problem, as other great generals have done, by developing multi-capable units which would use their skills flexibly to thrive in many testing situations. Napoleon conceptualised his army in terms of 'competencies'. The formula works today – NATO needs a desert warfare capability, a quick reaction force, a second strike capability and so on.

It is helpful to conceptualise a firm as an integrated bundle of competencies. This enables management to plan for innovation and uncertainty. An additional benefit is that a competency model offers a standardised assessment method for structuring competitor analysis. Competencies are the foundation on which competitive strength is built.

We defined a 'competency' as 'everything it takes to perform to world class standards'. We need a fuller understanding of the concept for this section and elaborate the definition to 'a combination of motives, values, knowledge, skills, systems, equipment, standards, resources, organisation and people that enables a firm to deliver a superior product or service'.

Some examples are as follows:

- Winning oil companies have a deep geotechnical competence.
- Winning department stores have an innovative buying competence.
- Winning electronics companies have a strong digital competence.
- Winning security companies have a competence in maintaining discipline over staff.
- Winning insurance companies have a deep skill in underwriting.

'Yes' I can hear you saying 'but how does this relate to all that stuff about systems that we have just waded through?' Competencies are attributes of the organisational system lodged in one or more of the twelve boxes. This becomes clear when we take a simple example. Consider Wong's Direct Trading Ltd – a firm with four market stalls in Hong Kong's Natham Road. Imagine Wong's barrows piled high with lookalike Polo Shirts and Pringle Pullovers selling for a fraction of shop prices and ask 'what competencies does Mr Wong need?' Some of the primary competencies required are:

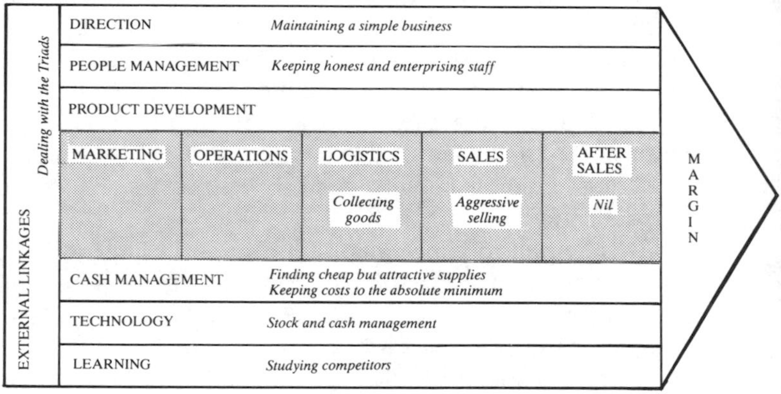

Figure 28 Competency systems analysis (Wong's Direct Trading)

■ Finding cheap and attractive supplies.
■ Keeping costs to the absolute minimum.
■ Keeping honest and enterprising staff.
■ Dealing with unlawful protectors.

Let's see where these competencies fit into the twelve box model (Figure 28). This is Mr Wong's Competency Systems Analysis. Each of the activities shown on the twelve box model are essential and you will notice that they are consistent – all serve to enable Mr Wong to pursue his price leadership strategy.

As Mr Wong's brother-in-law pushes his barrow to Natham Road every morning he passes the exclusive Rainbow Fashions which is known as the place for wealthy *tai tais* (wives) to shop for their special dresses. Of course, Rainbow needs many different competencies from Mr Wong. Some of Rainbow's primary competencies are:

■ Finding exclusive and fashionable supplies.
■ Avoiding too much 'old' stock.
■ Maintaining a stylish image.
■ Introducing innovative new lines.
■ Keeping persuasive and attentive staff.
■ Knowing customers personally.
■ Making every customer feel special.

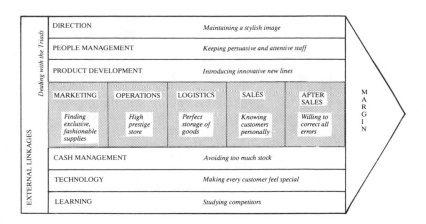

Figure 29 Competency systems analysis (Rainbow Fashion)

■ Dealing with unlawful protectors.

Rainbow's twelve box chart looks different in many, but not all respects, from Wong's Direct Trading Ltd. In fact, there are some competencies which all retailers must possess (see Figure 29). The first thing that you notice is that Rainbow's competencies absorb much greater costs. This is because they are following a benefits competitive strategy. Hopefully, their profit margins are sufficient to cover their inflated cost structure. In fact, Mr Wong makes about $3 gross on each item sold and Rainbow make $3,500 gross – but people queue at Wong's whereas the staff queue to serve customers at Rainbow.

Let us take the argument a step further with a more elaborate example. One of the best hotels in Hong Kong is the Helenestat which has excellent rooms but competes on the basis of superior customer service. This is a competency which touches almost every one of the twelve boxes.

Consider the competency systems model for the Helenestat. Here we see how a single competency (customer service) requires the orchestrated development of each of the sub-systems. Of course, the diagram (Figure 30) is a huge oversimplification: hundreds of initiatives are needed across the organisation. The process mapping approach which we discussed earlier is the best way to weave all of the integrated activities needed to create an integrated business system.

EXTERNAL LINKAGES	Shared strategy with suppliers							
		DIRECTION	Elaborate controls and policies for customer care					
		PEOPLE MANAGEMENT	Training staff in customer care					
		PRODUCT DEVELOPMENT	New services to please customers					
		MARKETING	OPERATIONS	LOGISTICS	SALES		AFTER SALES	M A R G I N
		Emphasis on image	Total dedication to customers		Relationship selling concept		All complaints put right	
		CASH MANAGEMENT	Investing in customer care programmes					
		TECHNOLOGY	Adoption of ISO 9000 standard					
		LEARNING	Studying other service excellence companies					

Figure 30 Competency systems analysis (Helenestat Hotel)

VISIONING USING THE COMPETENCY SYSTEMS APPROACH

We began the process of visioning in the previous step. The competency systems model enables us to finish the job. We will need a systematic 'time bound vision' to translate our competitive strategy into an action plan. Time bound visions are a tool for taking an enduring vision and transforming it into the 'bones' of an action plan. Consider the example of two talented trainers setting up a company in New Zealand. They decide their vision is to 'become the largest training consultancy in the country'. Then they need to ask questions like 'What will our company look like in one year's time?' 'What policies will we adopt towards our employees?' 'What services will we offer?' 'How will we manage our cost structures?' Systematically answering these questions, and many more like them, become a time bound vision.

Time bound visions begin with milestones. The best example was President Kennedy's statement 'We will put a man on the moon by the end of the decade.' From these fourteen words NASA was created and thousands of scientific programmes instituted. Truly Kennedy's statement was a tool for taking a grand vision (domination of space by the USA) and transforming it into the bones of an action plan.

Time bound visions are snap-shots in time – usually between one and five years ahead. The aim is to develop coherent elaborated 'pictures' which can be visualised by stakeholders and people within the organisation. We do this is by preparing a time bound vision diagram for defined dates in the future. The business should be shown as a flow diagram. Let's have a look at a simple example – Computer-Kings, a computer retailer (Figure 31).

This is a schematic of Computer-King's business time bound vision showing the next eighteen months. In reality they would extend the diagram for at least three years. The thick arrow is their core business (selling computers) and the kinks in the arrow indicate changes of direction – they are intending to introduce a new range of software products. Also shown on the chart are a business that the firm has decided to exit (desktop publishing); a new business to start in eight months' time (selling nationally a computer program for lawyers); a new market to exploit (schools); and a spin-off business to be established – they are going to service other suppliers' computer equipment under contract. The time

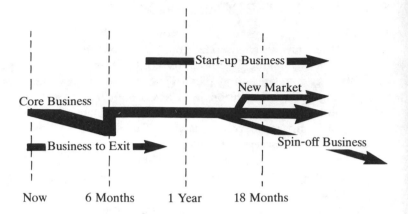

Figure 31 Time bound vision diagram

based vision diagram describes the 'broad brush' strategy. But this is too vague to be an action plan.

We take the next step by combining the principles of competency systems analysis and time based visioning to develop a strategic organisation development plan. Tasks now have to be specified and processes developed. Your strategy needs to become operational. How to do this? Draw a series of competency systems models for next year, the year after, the third year and so on.

But don't breath a sigh of relief too soon. Strategies need to be sold and that will require a good deal of effort. Also, your strategic thinking should evolve continuously and you will need use all of the strategic techniques that you have learned to renew and regenerate. But before you go on there is one piece of advice from the author – have a party! You've worked hard and you deserve it.

WORKSHOP 10: IMPLEMENTING STRATEGY SYSTEMATICALLY

Preparation

You will need an overhead projector, screen, flip chart, marker pens and Blu-Tack. Two blank 'twelve box models' (see diagrams above) should be drawn full size and landscape on a sheet of flip chart paper.

Time required

The workshop takes approximately 6 hours 30 minutes (but why not take a full day – it is worth it!)

WORKSHOP PLAN

1 The leader begins by reviewing the purpose of the session which is:

■ To reflect on what the competitive strategy means to the organisation.

■ To identify what needs to be done to implement the chosen strategy.

■ Develop a systematic vision of the business.

■ To prepare a strategic action plan.

The team leader reminds the group that each team member should help in the process of generating, building on and capturing ideas. (5 minutes)

2 Prepare a time-based vision diagram as shown in the text. (30 minutes)

3 Ask each individual or group who has completed a competency systems analysis of the business today to present their findings. Agree a common definition of the business system on the preprepared flip chart. Write with a normal (not marker) pen. (1 hour)

4 Take the second pre-prepared blank flip chart and complete a competency systems analysis to expand your preferred strategic option for three years' time. This will be your 'time-based vision'. Define your needed core process and support competencies in great depth. Take every box and list all of the activities that will be needed. Ensure that every competency that you need to fulfil your competitive strategy is reflected by activities on the chart. Show interrelationships between the 'boxes' by means of arrows or an overlay.

Answer the questions: On 1 January in *x* years' time:

■ What will be being done more of or better?

■ What will be done less of or stopped?

■ What new things will be happening?

■ What will be continuing?

Be exhaustive (continue on separate sheets if necessary). (2 hours)

5   Underline on the competency systems chart all those activities that could provide you with an opportunity to be stronger than your competitors – the differentiating benefits you provide. (30 minutes)

6   List activities to be driven for lowest industry cost, activities that need remedial attention and new activities needed. (30 minutes)

7   Develop a comprehensive action plan. Answer the following questions:

■ What programmes need to be initiated or strengthened?

■ What objectives should be set?

■ Who is accountable?

■ What management mechanisms are necessary?

Set milestones as to what needs to be achieved by key dates. (1 hour)

8   Reflect on your stakeholders. You are clear what you want to achieve but how are you going to sell your ideas to them? Develop an influencing plan for each of the stakeholders. (1 hour)

9   Get out your diaries and arrange a celebratory party! You deserve it. And why not invite your partners? They have sacrificed a great deal as you have ploughed through your strategic project.

— *Notes*

INTRODUCTION

1 Further guidance for those who wish to develop strategy level teams can be found in Dave Francis and Don Young, *The Top Team Audit*, Aldershot, Gower, 1993.

CHAPTER 2

1 For further insight into structured team work see Dave Francis, *Effective Problem Solving*, London, Routledge, 1990, and a wider approach to team development is described in *Improving Work Groups* by Dave Francis and D. Young, San Diego, Pfeiffer and Co, 1993.
2 Client confidential report by Richmond Consultants Ltd.

CHAPTER 3

1 Edward Wrapp 'Good Managers Don't Make Policy Decisions', *Harvard Business Review*, Sept.–Oct., 1967, pp. 91–9.
2 Supreme Court of USA 374 US 321 372 1963.
3 *The Wealth of Nations*, by Adam Smith.
4 K.G. Smith, C.M. Grimm and M.J. Gannon, *The Dynamics of Competitive Strategy*, London, Sage, 1992.
5 For a discussion of this concept refer to Richard E. Boyatzis, *The Competent Manager*, New York, John Wiley & Sons, 1982.
6 The author acknowledges that several elements of this framework are based on the work of other authors, especially Professor Michael Porter, *Competitive Strategy*, New York, Free Press, 1980.
7 Peter Drucker, *Management: Tasks, Responsibilities Practices*, New York, Harper & Row, 1973, p. 128.
8 See Komatsu Ltd, Harvard Business School Case Study, number 9-385-277, 9/88, Boston, Mass.

STEP 1

1 You should also repeat the analysis for any industry that you could enter if you have the opportunity to compete in a new industry sector.
2 A 70-page restricted document leaked to the *International Herald Tribune*, 18 February 1992.
3 Peter Schwartz, *The Art of the Long View: Planning for an Uncertain World*, New York, Doubleday Currency, 1991.
4 This definition is close to that used by Michael Porter in his book *Competitive Strategy*, New York, Free Press, 1980.

STEP 2

1 This point was well made by Tom Peters in his book *Thriving on Chaos*, London, Pan, 1992.

STEP 3

1 R.D. Buzzell and B.T. Gale, *The PIMS Principles: Linking Strategy to Performance*, New York, Free Press, 1987.
2 Michael Porter, *Competitive Strategy*, New York, Free Press, 1980.
3 *Management Consultancy*, VNU Business Publications, London, March 1993, p. 38.

STEP 4

1 Sun Tzu, *War and Management*, by Wee Chow Hou, Lee Khai Sheang and Bambang Walujo Hidajat, Singapore, Addison Wesley, 1992.
2 Private conversation by the author with CEO of a global music company.
3 Sun Tzu, *War and Management*, by Wee Chow Hou, Lee Khai Sheang and Bambang Walujo Hidajat, Singapore, Addison Wesley, 1992.
4 I would like to thank Marcus Alexander for introducing this concept to me.
5 Peter Benton, *Riding the Whirlwind*, Oxford, Blackwell, 1990, p. 156.
6 Sun Tzu, *The Art of War*, London, Hodder & Stoughton, 1981, p. 211.

STEP 5

1 See Irving L. Janus, *Victims of Group Think: a Psychological Study of Foreign Policy Decisions and Fiascos*, Boston, Mass., Houghton Mifflin, 1972.
2 See Michael Wellin, 'Delivering the Goods on Customer Care', *Personnel Management* 25(3): 34–6, 1993.

STEP 6

1 For a fuller discussion of values see Dave Francis and M. Woodcock, *Unblocking Organisational Values*, San Diego, Cal., University Associates and Simon & Schuster, 1990.
2 Gilly McKay and Alison Corke, *The Body Shop, Franchising a Philosophy*, London, Pan, 1986.
3 *Fortune Magazine*, editorial item, February 1993.
4 The author would like to thank Daniel Francis and other students of Environmental Management at Brunel University, West London, for telling the author he was 'a fossil and a dinosaur' and helping him see the importance of taking proactive values towards caring for the world.
5 *South China Morning Post*, p. 18, 26 March 1992.
6 In the 1980s the GNP of all European countries increased faster than the rate of employment. In four countries GNP increased as employment fell: EC Statistics, 1993.
7 Israel Sieff, *Memoirs*, London, Weidenfeld & Nicolson, 1973.
8 See 'A Study in Shirts', *Macau Image*, p. 10, autumn 1992.
9 John Scully, *Odyssey*, London, Fontana, 1991.

STEP 7

1 Further advice on top team building is in D.L. Francis and D. Young, *Top Team Audit*, Aldershot, Gower, 1993.
2 Conducted by Dave Francis 1986–91, unpublished.
3 Neil Rackham has written several books on this topic.
4 Data collected on 183 firms by Dave Francis, unpublished.
5 For example, the PIMS data base: *The Strategy Handbook* by Michael Hay and Peter Williamson, Oxford, Blackwell, 1991, pp. 197–8.
6 *Fortune Magazine*, editorial note, May 1993.

STEP 8

1 *Vanity Fair*, p. 34, September 1992.
2 This is described in Dave Francis, *Effective Problem Solving*, London, Routledge, 1990.
3 Adapted by the author from Sun Tzu, *War and Management*, by Wee Chow Hou, Lee Khai Sheang, Bambang Walujo Hidajat, Singapore, Addison Wesley, 1992.
4 The author recommends that a full financial appraisal takes place at this stage.

STEP 9

1 A theory of competitive strategy on which this chapter is based owes

much to the work of Professor Michael Porter in his book *Competitive Strategy*, New York, Free Press, 1980. However, the conceptual model in this chapter differs considerably from Michael Porter's pioneer work (in some ways it is contradictory) and the author wishes to emphasise that he is responsible for the redefinition of the theory in this chapter.

2 Michael Porter calls this dimension 'competitive scope'.

3 Some authors refer to this as a 'cost leadership' strategy. This is misleading because the customer is not interested in the supplier's costs but in the price he has to pay. Therefore price leadership is a more accurate term. Price includes all of the costs associated with ownership.

4 Tom Redburn, 'IBM Starts to Get Down and Dirty on PCs', *International Herald Tribune*, 6 October 1992, p. 11.

5 This term was coined by Michael Porter who uses it in a similar way.

6 Some authors have called this a 'differentiation strategy'. This is a misleading term since customers do not buy things because they are different but because they perceive them to offer superior benefits.

7 See David A. Aaker, *Managing Brand Equity*, New York, Free Press 1991.

8 This strategy is similar to, but not the same as, the 'focus strategy' as described by Michael Porter.

9 *South China Morning Post*, 7 May 1993, p. 7.

10 *South China Post*, 23 February 1992, p. 4.

11 Peter Benton, *Riding the Whirlwind*, Oxford, Blackwell, 1990, p. 60.

STEP 10

1 Another book in this series *Managing Change* by Colin Carnal deals with this topic.

2 The author gratefully acknowledges the inspiration of Michael Porter (see *Competitive Strategy*, New York, Free Press, 1980). Many of the ideas in this chapter are based on Michael Porter's original work.

3 Figure 27 is based on the value chain model developed by Michael Porter, *Competitive Strategy*.

4 For a further explanation of the importance of systemic thinking see M. Hammer and J. Champy, *Re-engineering the Corporation*, London, Nicholas Brealey Publishing, 1993.

5 The techniques for doing this are sometimes called 'business process re-engineering'.

Further reading

There are thousands of books and articles which are relevant to those seeking to polish their skills in competitive strategy. These (in addition to the books listed in footnotes) are my favourites.

The General Managers by John Kotter, London, Collins, 1982.
Corporate Culture and Performance by John Kotter, Oxford, Free Press, 1991.
The 5th Discipline: The Art and Practice of the Learning Organisation by Peter Senge, New York, Doubleday, 1990.
Leaders by W.G. Bennis and B. Nanus, New York, Harper & Row, 1985.
Commitment: The Dynamics of Strategy by P. Ghemawat, Oxford, Free Press, 1991.
The Mind of the Strategist by Kenichi Ohmae, Harmondsworth, Penguin, 1982.
Made in Japan by Akio Morita, London, Fontana, 1987.
The Change Masters by Rosabeth Moss Kanter, London, Routledge, 1985.
Making it Happen by John Harvey-Jones, London, Fontana, 1988.
Earth in the Balance by Al Gore, London, Earthscan, 1992.
Visionary Leadership by Bert Nanus, New York, Jossey-Bass, 1992.
Riding the Whirlwind by Peter Benton, Oxford, Blackwell, 1990.
The Strategic Process: Concepts, Contexts and Cases by J.M. Quinn, H. Mintzberg and James, New York, Prentice Hall, 1988.
G. Hamel and C.K. Pralahad, 'Strategic Intent' in *Strategic Management Journal*, May/June 1989, pp. 63–76.

Keyword index

TAKING UP SPACE

*The Black Girl's
Manifesto for Change*

Chelsea Kwakye and Ọrẹ Ogunbiyi

1 3 5 7 9 10 8 6 4 2

#Merky Books
20 Vauxhall Bridge Road
London SW1V 2SA

#Merky Books is part of the Penguin Random House group of companies
whose addresses can be found at global.penguinrandomhouse.com.

Penguin
Random House
UK

First published by #Merky Books in 2019
This paperback edition published by #Merky Books in 2020

www.penguin.co.uk

A CIP catalogue record for this book is available from the British Library.

ISBN 9781529118544

Printed and bound in Great Britain by Clays Ltd, Elcograf S.p.A.

Penguin Random House is committed to a sustainable future
for our business, our readers and our planet. This book is made from
Forest Stewardship Council® certified paper.

Contents

Interviewees

Adaobi. (she/her)
g. 2019 University of Manchester. BEng Electrical and Electronic Engineering.

Adaobi Adibe was the lead Venture Capitalist at Campus Capital, a £2.5 million fund investing in early stage technology companies. Her work in Venture Capital and clean energy led to her being awarded the number one black student in the UK by the prestigious Future Leaders magazine, and nominated by the U.S. embassy as one of the top six rising entrepreneurs in the UK. She is now an Interact Fellow and is working full time on her business.

Arenike. (she/her)
g. 2018 Emmanuel College, University of Cambridge. BA English.

After graduating with a first class, Arenike Adebajo is now a content producer and writer working across the arts and publishing industries. At university, she served as the facilitator for FLY, a forum for women and non-binary people of colour and co-edited the group's first zine.

Ayomide. (she/her)
g. 2021 Imperial College London. MBBS Medicine (with BSc Management).

Alongside working for the Imperial College Outreach Team, Ayomide Ayorinde was the director of the 2017/18 Afrogala – Imperial College ACS's annual cultural show. Before this, she was the Vice-President of the society.

Barbara. (she/her)
g. 2021 King's College London. MBBS Medicine (with iBSc Management).

Barbara Falana works closely with the student access and social mobility team within her university and is also interested in innovation technology. She is currently the beneficiary director for Step Forward, a social enterprise with the intention of preventing soil-transmitted diseases, such as Mossy Foot, which is prevalent in underdeveloped countries. She has also co-founded a social enterprise called The Ladder Project, which works with young students to develop vital skills for higher education and work.

Courtney. (she/her)

g. 2018 Robinson College, University of Cambridge. BA Human, Social and Political Sciences.

Courtney Daniella Boateng has a love for honest and relatable content creation and has spoken at multiple universities and featured in Vogue, Buzzfeed, BBC and many others. Alongside running her hair and beauty business CDBeautyCo full-time, she also provides advice on business development for other beauty brands focussing on Black hair and beauty. She also consults for 10 Downing Street and the National Union of Students (NUS) on how best to aid young entrepreneurs and financially support students in poverty.

Eireann. (she/her)

g. 2017 Homerton College, University of Cambridge. BA Education.

g. 2019 Lady Margaret Hall, University of Oxford. MSc Education (Higher Education).

Growing up in a single parent working class household in South London, Eireann Attridge became concerned with factors that influenced educational disadvantage. She later went on to serve as the Student Unions' Access and Funding Officer, running the country's largest student led access initiative and also established the

Cambridge Class Act campaign, a campaign for students who identify as being from working class and educationally disadvantaged backgrounds. She currently works at the University of Cambridge as part of the Widening Participation team.

Fope. (they/them)

g. 2019 Newcastle University. BA Politics.

During their time at university Fope Olaleye was elected BAME Network President, Feminist Society President and NUSU Part Time Officer. They also sat on the NUS Black Students' Committee and National Executive Council as Black Students Campaign second place, and they are now the NUS Black Students' Officer. In these roles Fope has campaigned to improve the experiences of BAME students across the UK with a particular focus on black womxn and QTIPOC. They have been featured in *Dazed*, *i-D*, the *Guardian* and on BBC Radio 1Xtra, and are a regular guest speaker and workshop facilitator at universities across the country.

Kenya. (she/her)

g. 2018 Jesus College, University of Cambridge. BA Human, Social and Political Sciences.

While at university, Kenya Greenidge served as Cambridge ACS's Secretary (2016/17) and played an active role in the society's executive committee. She has a particular interest in the sociology of race and gender.

Micha. (she/her)
g. 2017 Corpus Christi College, University of Cambridge. BA Psychological and Behavioural Sciences.

Micha Frazer-Carroll is an award-nominated journalist writing on race, feminism and mental health. Formerly working at HuffPost UK, she is the Opinions Editor at gal-dem, a magazine created by women and non-binary people of colour, and also founded Blueprint, a magazine on mental health. With bylines in *ROOKIE*, *Black Ballad* and *Dazed*, she now writes regularly for the *Guardian*. She graduated with a first class and served as Cambridge University's Welfare and Rights Officer in 2017-18, a role in which she lobbied the University Counselling Service to introduce a counselling scheme catered specifically to students of colour.

Mikai. (she/her)
g. 2018 Warwick University. BA English Literature
g. 2020 London School of Economics and Political Science. MSc Empires, Colonialism and Globalisation.

Mikai McDermott is a digital content creator and entrepreneur offering 'life advice, beauty and the tablespoon of honesty you need.' Her growing cult following has earned her over 2 million YouTube views, over 40k subscribers and over 50k followers on Instagram. A bold and proud advocate for women's issues, fashion and beauty, the University of Warwick graduate has crafted a niche for herself as a trusted opinion among the underground beauty community. Having collaborated with BBC Stories, Tangle Teezer and Schwarzkopf (among others), she has worked on authentic collaborations with high engagement rates anchored by informative content. Alongside building an online presence, Mikai runs a hair and beauty brand, Cipher Co, which has amassed more than 20k followers.

Nathania. (she/her)
g. 2020 Trinity College, Cambridge. BA History.

Nathania Williams is of Jamaican heritage but most of her family now live in Manchester, which is where she's from. She is passionate about access to higher education and mental health issues in the black community. She was Cambridge ACS's Welfare Officer and now serves as the society's Vice President. She is currently active in her college's Feminist Society and FLY, a forum for women and non-binary people of colour, as well as a member of Trinity College's History Society.

Renée. (she/her)
g. 2018 Keble College, University of Oxford. BA History

g. 2019 Harvard University Graduate School of Education. MEd International Education Policy.

While at Oxford, Renée Kapuku was elected as the first BME representative at her college, and worked with the Oxford Campaign for Racial Equality to tackle racial discrimination on campus. She was also elected president of the Oxford African and Caribbean society in her second year, hosting Oxford's first black history month showcase with Reggie Yates, and organising the #BlackMenAndWomenOfOxford viral campaign. She also coordinated the UK's largest student-led conference for high-achieving Year 12 state-school students of African and Caribbean heritage, receiving critical acclaim from the BBC, general media, and support from the elected Person of the Year, Stormzy. In 2018, she was awarded full funding by the Kennedy Memorial Trust to support her studies at Harvard.

Saredo. (she/her)

g. 2017 Western University, Ontario. Double Major BA Sociology and Women's Studies.

g. 2019 London School of Economics and Political Science. MSc International Migration and Public Policy.

Saredo Qassim Mohamed is a Somali-Canadian writer and photographer. During her undergraduate years, she became a Canadian National Youth Poetry champion and represented the city of Toronto in international poetry festivals. As the President of Western University's Black Students' Association, Saredo worked to create spaces of healing and community for black students on her campus. After graduating, she worked with a local NGO in Somalia to promote the social and political empowerment of vulnerable Somali women and girls. She recently won the UK's first podcast competition with a story-based podcast called 'On Things We Left Behind' and she is currently consulting on European Policy.

Saskia. (they/them)

g. 2018 St. Catherine's College, University of Cambridge. BA Human, Social and Political Sciences.

g. 2020 London Academy of Music and Dramatic Art. MFA Professional Acting.

While at university, Saskia Ross primarily worked in theatrical spaces and laid the groundwork for a more diverse and welcoming scene, becoming dedicated to widening participation in a historically elite and white community. They created the Cambridge BME Group, an online space where students of colour could share ideas, promote their work and find a safe community of like-minded people. They then directed Cambridge's inaugural BME Shakespeare performance, and one of Cambridge's largest all-black casts in a production of Fences by August Wilson. They also facilitated the creation of BME Footlights smokers and musical theatre bar nights.

A Letter to My Fresher Self

In December 2017, inspired by her own experiences and those of her peers and mentees, Ọrẹ wrote a letter to her fresher self about what it means to be a black girl at Cambridge. The letter was published in her student newspaper, *Varsity*, and read as follows:

> **When you walk into your first supervision, you will probably be the only black girl in the room. Get used to it, because it won't get much better. But don't let that scare you and, more importantly, don't let anyone make you feel small or misplaced. Don't be silent in attempts to assuage your white**

peers and supervisors. You've earned your place there, so make your presence known. Don't ever feel the need to make yourself palatable, or bite-size. Instead, fill the room with examples of Nkrumah and Mobutu that your supervisor thinks are 'adventurous', and enjoy unpacking the racism in the works of Kant that your degree so glorifies. *Their* discomfort is not your problem.

You will have supervisors who will call you defensive and angry, and who will project their own prejudiced stereotypes onto you as you walk into the room. Cry in private, write a killer essay, and prove them wrong. You will also have supervisors who will understand and appreciate your need to veil your work in your own experiences, who will recognise its value and reward you for it. So, bathe every essay in black girl magic and write in resistance to the Eurocentrism of academia that did not see you coming.

It's not always easy, though. The Black Jacobins you really want to read probably won't be on your reading lists, you won't find the support you need when you want to write your dissertation on Nigeria, and trying to go the extra mile to show your supervisors what a decolonised curriculum *could* look like will exhaust you. But where you can, do it anyway.

Don't be surprised when your lecture on industrialisation makes no mention of slavery, or when your white friends don't understand why that's a problem. Don't be afraid to ask the unnerving questions at the end of the lecture and leave them shook.

You will arrive and feel a pressure to be someone else. You won't realise as you subconsciously try to play up to what you think a typical Cambridge student does. You'll change your accent, go to events you know you don't enjoy, and try to befriend people that aren't like you in attempts to conform – but you'll only be able to keep this up for so long. When the real you resurfaces and you find the courage to admit to your new friends, and to yourself, that you actually hate Wednesday Cindies [a terrible Cambridge student club night] and VKs, you'll be okay.

When you come back next term with braids, don't let your housemates smell and touch your hair. It may take you a while to muster up the courage to tell people to stop, and to remind people that you are not some exotic creature to be caressed – but when you find the strength, do it anyway.

Oh. Boys? Don't bother. Tell every aunty that is telling you that you are going to Cambridge to find yourself a husband, that much to their disappointment, it's not going to happen. You'll learn quickly that desirability is racialised and that not everyone loves your dark skin as much as you do, that society's beauty standards don't include people that look like you. So, when someone hits you with 'you're fit for a black girl', tell them that's not a compliment. You are beautiful, and to the people who don't see that, even your own, let it be their loss. Find the beauty in your blackness in spite of the people who can't.

Don't forget that, regardless, you belong here. You'll have people who think you are here to tick a 'diversity' box. You will also be asked time and time again whether or not you go to the *other* university in Cambridge because people will have a tough time conceptualising the fact that you could possibly have earned your place here. You won't find people who look like you memorialised on the walls and that won't make it any easier – but don't forget that you belong.

You will stand out and be made conscious of your difference for your whole time here and not everyone will get it. Not everyone will get what it is about existing in Cambridge as a black girl that makes it difficult or why. You will meet a lot of people who proclaim they are 'not racist' but don't recognise how their inaction makes them complicit, why you value safe spaces, or even why your experience of Cambridge is necessarily different. Remember that it isn't your duty to lecture and to explain because the emotional labour will take its toll. You are not the appointed spokesperson for black people, and don't feel the pressure to be.

Remember that you are not alone. Black women may be few and far between here, but find them, build a sisterhood and strengthen each other. Find shoulders to cry on because you will need them. Find support systems that work for you, and take solace in them. Communities like the African Caribbean Society will be there to make you feel at home again. Take time to look after yourself. Bake and cook jollof even amid the stress that tries to break you.

It will get better. I don't know if that's because you will become immune to the blows, or because you will get stronger – but it will get better. You'll find ways to make Cambridge work for you and you will be fine. In fact, you'll be more than fine. You'll make friends for life, you'll leave your mark and eventually, you'll enjoy it.

Behind that letter were two years of navigating the white-dominated spaces of Cambridge, and learning how to survive and thrive in an environment that at times felt as if it had been expressly designed to make life harder for black women. But even before arriving at university, we had been given more than a hint that we weren't going to get an easy ride.

Introduction

Chelsea

'Cheers!'

One summer night in 2015, I came downstairs to find my dad and five men I had never met before having a party in my dining room: bottles of whisky and schnapps, laughter and a lot of chatter. My dad was celebrating the fact that I had got into the University of Cambridge. It was an important night for my parents. After years of hard work and sacrifice, I had *made it* – for all of us. I poked my head around my dining room door to find out what was going on, and was met with congratulatory applause. I joined the party, was reminded every ten seconds that I shouldn't take the opportunity for granted, and accepted a £50 note from one of the men (thanks uncle). We celebrated what was meant to be the end of something. Really, it was just the beginning.

My mum and dad came to the UK from Ghana during the Margaret Thatcher years with only 70p between them. After moving around in East London for a while, by the time I was born they had made a conscious decision to settle in Chingford, East London (or Essex). In comparison to inner-London's concrete jungles, Chingford was green and leafy, and despite being small, has raised the likes of David Beckham and Blazin' Squad. Growing up as the youngest child, I absorbed influences from all directions. I would sit wedged between my mum and dad eating banku and pepper, trying to follow the Twi that rolled off their tongues. Through them, I developed a strong sense of what it meant to be proud and Ghanaian. From an early age they made sure I never lost my connection with our mother country's food, culture, language or customs. Respect your elders, never use your left hand to receive *anything*, and when you enter a room, always greet people from right to left.

By the time I reached the age of eleven, I had started begging my older brother and sister to take me to garage raves with them. I would wait until they got home from nights out, and screw my face with envy when they both came home late boasting about Jay-Z and

Kanye West's 'Watch the Throne' concert. But once I was old enough to realise that they weren't just being mean siblings and I was actually too young, I saw just how much they were my idols (and still are). I spent the next few years calculating the steps it would take to be *exactly* like both of them. They were both elite athletes, so I planned to be an elite athlete. Jeanette liked house and garage music, so I started listening to house and garage music. Louie studied sports science at Loughborough University, so naturally, I would also do the same.

For as long as I can remember, I've loved the fact that no one could pin down my identity. I never wanted to have one defining characteristic. I wanted people to see that I could be all of them at once. I wanted to be complex, be able to change my mind, have opinions and interests that didn't necessarily make sense all the time. My identity was never just me: it was the perfect distillation of everyone and everything around me.

So when university finally came around, a few weeks after my dad's party, I was excited. Maybe a little bit too excited. I imagined it as the perfect opportunity to explore whether I had any other interests to add to my mélange of a personality. Once I got there, I drank red wine from a cow's horn while shouting Anglo-Saxon phrases to others as part of a college initiation; regularly wore a gown to eat dinner; was hospitalised for a potential heart defect brought on by eating too much pasta; and almost ran over an old lady while learning how to ride a bike on the road.

But throughout my whole experience, something my dad said to me after my first term at Cambridge stuck in my head: '**If I was walking past a bus-stop and I saw you sitting there, I would never believe that you went to Cambridge.**' Still tinged with a sense of disbelief, he never failed to remind me: I still look very young, and there's something about me that doesn't seem quite Cambridge. We both knew that I didn't fit the typical narrative of Oxbridge: privately educated, middle-class and, of course, white. In fact, I was a walking conundrum – black, a woman and working class. My university experience was never going to be 'normal'. There was a constant feeling of being a burden, and that my identity forced people to 'tolerate' or 'accommodate' me. If it wasn't a pity-party for 'poor black students', it was someone attributing all your successes to tick-box quotas.

More than anything, it was a stark reminder that I had no control over my identity. As an eighteen-year-old, it was hard to grapple with the fact that I had entered an environment which meant that I was black before I was anything else. Not only black in being, but black in theory, stereotypes, principle and reality. It would soon become my most defining characteristic, in a place in which I had thought I would have the licence to explore every facet of my identity.

Ọrẹ

My name is Ọrẹ. Not 'or-ray' or 'or-ee' or 'or'. It's Ọrẹ. With a short 'e', like the first 'e' in elephant.

A teacher at secondary school once told me that she struggled to pronounce my name because it sounded unfinished, like something should come after it. Well, she was half right – my name is actually Oreoluwa Hannah Ngozichukwuka Oluwafunmilayo Ogunbiyi. But I let everyone call me Ọrẹ, as long as they at least *try* to say it right.

I was born in Croydon. I went to school here until I was seven. For my first few years of school, everyone called me 'Or-ee'.

Then my family moved from Croydon to Nigeria. We stayed there for six years. For six years everyone pronounced my name the way my parents did. For once, my name was not something that immediately cast me into an outlier category – if anything, it did quite the opposite. I now knew what it felt like to be part of a norm, and not made to stand out due to my racial and cultural identity.

We moved back to England in 2010, and I told myself that I wouldn't let anyone mispronounce my name any more. I came back surer of who I was, who I am: Ọrẹ and not Or-ee. I had reached a stage where my name was no longer a source of insecurity but one of pride, and a story in itself. But what I couldn't bring back to England with me was that sense of inclusion and normalness that came with being part of a community where almost everyone had long names with deep meanings – more explicitly, where almost everyone was black.

When I moved back, I was black. I came back with a sense of security in my identity as a Yoruba woman, and as a Nigerian woman, but equally, I had to come to terms with what it meant to be black in Britain. I went to a very diverse boarding school, and although I loved it, it fooled me into thinking that everywhere would be just as diverse, just as readily accepting of my Nigerianness, my blackness and all the intricacies that come with those traits. In my final year there, I gave a lecture to the other sixth formers and my teachers on the history of Pan-Africanism, I interviewed the Nigerian Nobel Laureate Wole Soyinka for my school's magazine, and I would spend the weekends cooking Nigerian food in our boarding house kitchen – but at no point did I feel that I was being 'too black'.

University would change that for me. As soon as I accepted my place, I felt the return of the identity crisis that I had not felt since I had reclaimed my name. The closer I got to Cambridge, the clearer it became that my blackness would mediate my university experience. I wish that I had been better prepared for what that would actually mean.

Cambridge put 'being black' into new terms for me. My blackness became something I had to protect, fight for, defend and explain. It isn't news that Cambridge, like most of the UK's other top universities, is particularly white. I was one of three black girls in my year group at Jesus College, a group that comprised some 150 people, and time and time again, black students at other colleges would tell me how lucky I was because they were the only black person that their college had accepted that year. I got used to the questions about 'where I'm from'; and got used to the follow-up question about 'where I'm *really* from'; I got used to the attendant confusion of me saying that I was born in the UK. Being a black girl at Cambridge left me with no hope of blending into the background.

As a minority in a predominantly white space, to take up space is itself an act of resistance.

Taking Up Space

Regardless of who you are and where you go, your university years are transformative. They are your first taste of independence and they are the beginning of a difficult transition into adulthood. Above all, we're told the *experience* is life-changing: friends for life, venturing out of your comfort zone and learning all the different ways you can cook pasta.

As if university weren't enough of a challenge, navigating university as a black girl is a unique experience, especially when you go to one of the whitest universities in the country (77.1 per cent of the student population identified as white). It wasn't until we met other black women at Cambridge that we realised that we weren't the only ones facing challenges. Despite the fact that we all had different experiences, there was always something that drew us back into the epicentre. Over food, drinks, lots of laughter and genuine company, we felt part of a sisterhood – one that we knew would be unique to the environment that we were in.

So from the beginning, we always wanted *Taking Up Space* to offer that sisterhood: brutally honest whilst reassuring, almost like an older sister telling you what fashion trends to avoid because she's been there and done that. It is now a book laced with personal anecdotes, as well as more general commentary from a wide group of black female and non-binary students on how their identity as black women and students has mediated their experiences of university – with the hope that black girls everywhere will find solace in their stories.

For black girls: understand that your journey through university is unique. Use this book as a guide to help figure out how you want to 'do' university. Our wish for you is that you read this and feel empowered, comforted and validated in every emotion you experience, or decision that you make. For everyone else: we can only hope that reading this helps you to be a better friend, parent, sibling or teacher to black girls living through what we did. It's time we stepped away from seeing this as a problem that black people are charged with solving on their own. It's a collective effort that everyone has a role to play in. The sure result is that our education system will be the better for it, and students of all backgrounds will benefit. The thought of enriched histories, expansive curricula and inclusive environments alone should be enough to spur us all on.

Getting In

Chelsea

On the way back from my open day at Cambridge's Corpus Christi College, I cried non-stop until I got home.

The University of Cambridge was never on my radar at school; when I heard it mentioned, it was never in reference to me. At the beginning of Year 12, I had narrowly missed out on gaining a place in the 'exclusive' form group made up of a small number of students who got the best GCSE grades and who would receive special help when applying to Oxbridge. Their morning tutor sessions were informative and inquisitive, and exceeded the expectations of the academic curriculum. Most importantly, they would have direct application and interview help. A few steps down the corridor, my form group was debating football teams and haircuts, and planning how to clean up on sports day. I tried to brush it off, pretend that I didn't care about getting into that group, but I was upset. I had worked so hard – only to find out on results day that I was one A* short. My confidence was at an all-time low, and I limited my aspirations from early on.

At the end of Year 12, however, I discovered that I had been predicted A*A*A* for A-levels – the only pupil in my school not in that exclusive form group to receive that prediction. Even at that moment, going to Cambridge seemed like a distant dream: it wasn't expected. Yet I was told by a teacher that if I got to interview stage, my personality would guarantee me a place. I thought about it for a while, and decided I had nothing to lose. It would only be one university choice after all, and I would hate for there to be a niggling voice in the back of my mind constantly asking, 'What if you had applied, and got in?'

So I applied. But I had left it so late that all of the college open days were full, with the exception of one: Corpus Christi College. Without hesitating I submitted my request form. Once the panic was over, I decided to read a bit about the college I was going to visit. I read that Corpus Christi was established in 1352, making it one of the oldest colleges in Cambridge. There was a chapel, courts and a 'Master' of the college, apparently. I read that you weren't allowed to walk on the grass. I laughed. What was this place? I soon fell into a Wikipedia hole reading all about famous Cambridge alumni like Charles Darwin, Stephen Hawking and Prince Charles – not to marvel at them, but to remind myself that I had nothing in common with them.

The day for the visit arrived soon enough. In the morning, I promised myself I wouldn't get too attached, and told myself over and over again, 'If you don't expect anything, you won't be disappointed.' I decided to wear my older sister's blue and pink Aztec blazer from Primark, because I had no smart clothes apart from my sixth form school uniform. I already knew that I wasn't going to get in, so I thought I may as well look cool.

My mum and my brother-in-law drove me up. I was completely overwhelmed by how antiquated, quaint and cobbled everything was. My mum and brother-in-law were packed off with the parents, and I was left with other hopeful applicants. After a small introductory lecture and a tour of the Corpus Christi grounds, I started talking to a girl around my age about our different backgrounds and how nervous we were to apply to Cambridge because it was so competitive. Throughout the open day, we clung to each other, and I remember thinking to myself, 'I can't believe I've made a friend already! Maybe I do actually belong here?' My expectations had been so low that I was shocked to find I was actually having a good time. The staff were friendly, the students were helpful, and the college was very pretty. Chelsea 1 – Cambridge 0!

When my new friend and I split up for our subject-focused workshops, I felt an ounce of confidence. I sat up straight in my chair, eyes bright and ready to contribute. But the feeling didn't last for long. The first applicant introduced himself as 'educated in Surrey with a particular interest in thirteenth-century history', and it was only a short moment before the black cloud of imposter syndrome gathered over my head. My inner self screamed, 'See! These are the people who have *a lot* in common with Darwin, Hawking and Prince Charles. I do not *belong* here.' When it was my turn to introduce myself, I coughed, masked my Essex-London accent, and quietly said that I had a 'particular interest in modern British political history'. I lied. I couldn't believe that I felt so insecure that I had to *lie*. As I listened to everyone else talking eloquently about historical theories and obscure historical figures, I kept quiet. I felt so stupid – but I was even more upset with myself for ever believing that I could fit in here. Chelsea 1 – Cambridge 1.

I was relieved to bump into my new friend after the session. She was beaming as she told me how fun and engaging her workshop had been. I lied, again, and told her that mine was also really fun. By then parents and relatives had arrived back from the family tour. As we approached them, the girl's mum shot me a disgusted look. I smiled, but her expression didn't change. It seemed to say, 'What are you doing here?' – and I'm pretty sure it wasn't directed at my blazer, because Aztec was in fashion then. After staring at me for a good five seconds, she swiftly guided her daughter away without giving us a chance to say goodbye.

I shrank. I was silent on the walk to the car, as my mum told me about all the facts she had learnt about all the other Cambridge colleges. She had had so much fun – how could I possibly tell her that I hated it? That I had already started snowballing lies to fit in? That this was the first time I had been made to feel *other*?

I managed to keep it together at first. But then I got a call from my sister, excitedly asking how it went, and the wailing started. 'I HATE IT SO MUCH,' I sobbed into the car speaker. Once I was able to talk without bursting into tears, I thanked my mum and brother-in-law for coming with me, and told them that they didn't need to worry about me, because I was never going to set foot in Cambridge again.

Chelsea 1 – Cambridge 2.

Game over.

*

Black women are entering higher education in the UK in larger numbers every year. In 2017-18, UK domiciled students who identified as black totalled 77,000 and had the largest gender disparity of any ethnic group with women comprising 59.2 per cent. It is undeniable that there has been a consistent and persistent desire amongst black women to be formally educated.

For me, education was a form of armour, which later would become a strategy of resistance. It was a space in which I could critique frameworks of knowledge and begin my own process of self-actualisation. At fourteen years old, I had made it my mission to learn a little bit about everything after a lesson on *Macbeth* given by a temporary English teacher. Every time we shot him a question, he knew the answer. I wanted to be so smart that there could never be a reason for me to fail. And I truly believed that education was meritocratic: translation, if I worked hard enough, I could be anything that I wanted to be, and no one could stop me. Picture fourteen-year-old me wagging a finger at my older brother in the car: 'They can take your car and your house, Louie, but they can never take your education!' Wise words from such a young soul.

But as Professor of Race and Gender Heidi Mirza states, higher education represents a contradiction for black women. Despite black women wanting to be educated and demonstrating immense will in doing so, our energy is never matched by a corresponding enthusiasm from larger institutions like universities. We're made to believe that we are the problem: underachieving, misunderstood and not 'hardworking' enough. The narrative of meritocracy, which runs through the core of universities, has created a justification for inequality – a dangerous justification, which ignores the intricacies in what it means to be a black woman in higher education.

Barriers to Entry

Let's start by looking at what shapes the educational choices a lot of black girls make today. A quick flick through an A-level sociology book will tell you that sorting students in bands or sets according to ability is only one of the ways that our education system sets up teacher and pupil relations. Labelling some as 'able' and others as 'less able' can create a self-fulfilling prophecy, in ways that can be detrimental to pupils and their educational futures. Primary and secondary school teachers' expectations can have a lasting impact on their pupils, making some black students feel unable to attend top universities. One of the primary factors in most of us being able to apply to the universities we want to attend is our predicted grades. These predicted grades rest largely on expectations that drive a wedge between those who are deemed deserving or undeserving of 'success'.

Long before the 'exclusive' form group became a possibility, I was picked to be part of a school programme called 'Beyond Horizons', in which a group of 'more able' Year 10 students followed a ten-week programme of Saturday morning sessions. I was chosen for my optimistic attitude to learning, which I was told was seen as a promising mark of early character development. The Saturday morning sessions were actually a lot of fun. We had sessions on critical thinking, learnt a small bit of Cantonese and went on field trips across the country. Through Beyond Horizons, I was given the opportunity to make a lasting impression on school life. I was Head Girl when, during Year 12, the deputy headteacher of my school proudly unveiled a shiny new 'Russell Group' board, which had engraved on it all the names of the students who had got into a Russell Group university, and their chosen subjects.

However, I've come to realise that my secondary school experience was something of an anomaly. It wasn't 'normal' to have teachers rooting for you and your ambitions. Before you even get to the application stage, you will probably find that you're already limited in what you can do. Barbara and I went to the same school, and I remember how upset she was when a few teachers tried to convince her to apply to Oxbridge to do English instead of medicine. Despite volunteering at a surgery and at care homes, and researching medical papers, apparently her skillset pointed to all things English – despite the fact that she repeatedly said she didn't want to study it. We couldn't believe it.

'Don't do medicine, do English at Oxbridge,' they said . . . I liked English, I liked reading the books and I could write an essay. But I wasn't

**talented at English to the point where it was like,
go to Oxbridge. – Barbara**

It's easy to believe that your school and teachers know what is best for you – because they're professionals, right? We see them as unquestionably objective and rational in their thinking and advice. But the reality is that teachers can be highly influential in limiting our expectations and ambitions.

You would think that as teachers, there would be more accountability in ensuring that students reach their potential but oftentimes, they're facilitating and even reinforcing these institutional barriers. – Renée

Racialised language and tropes all seem to emphasise what black students can *realistically* achieve – especially when applying to university. Most of the ideas about black students originate from a place of authority, with underpredictions of grades explained away as a safe and well-intentioned protection mechanism. But with black Caribbean students three times more likely to be excluded from school than their white counterparts, it is clear that the way parts of the education system are set up disadvantages most black students. Lower expectations for black students have always been simply accepted by parents and students alike, because of the teacher's claim to know our abilities the best. And what remit are we given to challenge those views?

The reality is that teachers of all races – but particularly those who are non-black – are unable to detach their subconscious biases around black students and what we're capable of. It's almost as if we're being trained for specific functions within society. As black women, our ambitions are always capped.

> **I wanted to go to the London School of Economics, and at the time my grades were pretty competitive. I had the references and I was a competitive candidate – but the first thing that [the postgraduate applications advisor] let me know was that it was a difficult school to get into. – Saredo**

> **Even the teachers were like, 'Are you sure that this environment will be conducive for you?' and I was like, 'It's one of the best universities in the world, why wouldn't it be a place for me?' – Renée**

With black girls, there's a fine line between claiming to know what's best for us and deterring us from things that we are genuinely capable of. It's at this crossroads that you realise that our education system doesn't exist in a vacuum. As Saredo later went on to say, it's as if teachers are **'obsessed with not letting black girls dream'.**

It was only once I arrived at university that I became aware of the possibilities enabled by private schools. I would come to realise that in many ways, these were the students who *had* been given the licence to dream. I went from an environment of not knowing a single soul who went to private school to going to a university so exclusive that they 'recruit more students from eight top schools than almost 3,000 other English state schools put together'. From teaching style to pastoral care and resources, private schooling is a fundamentally different experience – academically and socially. Around 7 per cent of all UK school pupils attend independent schools. Statistics also show that over 50 per cent of GCSE entries from independent schools are awarded a grade A/A*, compared to a national average of 20 per cent.

The difference between private and state schools extends beyond the student, flagging up key differences between the knowledge of teachers and parents as well. It was only on a recent visit back to my secondary school that the annual sixth-form magazine *APPLY* was brought to my attention. I couldn't believe I'd never heard of it. The magazine discusses everything from apprenticeships to current news, and includes almost everything you might need to know about universities.

Crucially, it wasn't just for state-educated students, but also for their parents and teachers, who were unlikely to know much about the university process.

When I first met Ọrẹ, I couldn't help but compare our experiences. At her school, it seemed that every single student was given every chance to flourish academically. Excellence was expected of everybody, not just the few students who performed well in exams. When she reached Year 12, she sat down, as every student did, with her head teacher to discuss her future options. There was also extra help available for all those who expressed an interest in applying for Oxbridge.

Anyone applying to Oxbridge at my school also had an Oxbridge mentor. – Ọrẹ

However, Ọrẹ continued and said **'I don't think a lot of people at my school were putting money on me'** to get into Oxbridge. Despite access to resources, networks and financial advantages, it would be wrong to assume that a homogenous experience of private schools exists amongst all students. Kenya went on to say:

'Having attended a private school for most of my education I'm grateful for everything that it allowed me to achieve but I also think there can be similar patterns of expectations for black

29

students. When I moved to a state school, I definitely felt more encouraged. My experience might not be typical, but I do think it's important to recognise the diversity of experiences for black students even if they are in private schools.'

For the first time in my life, I was face to face with a real and complex class divide, and struggling to work out what the experiences of black students at private and grammar schools meant for me. To me, it seemed that private schools were always extending a 'helping hand' in the shape of scholarships, charities and trusts to students from minority ethnic backgrounds. Yet since forever, 'black' and 'disadvantaged' had always been in the same sentence.

In reality, there has always been a silent minority of middle-class black students, who have been regularly crammed into the same category of ethnicity in diversity reports. The majority of these students are well-versed on how to navigate white-dominated spaces and assert themselves. While speaking to another black girl who went to my university, but previously attended a prestigious private school in London, she explained to me how she had 'always been told that [she's] the best'. And trust me, she believed it. It's important to stress in plain English that black doesn't always mean working-class. Little has been done to challenge the cultural positioning of black students as a homogenous group, because these conversations, which fail to recognise nuances within our experiences, still persist.

Entering elite institutions that are fundamentally separatist on matters regarding race *and* class is difficult. It only took a few weeks for me to realise that I wasn't able to relate to many of the black students there either. If you type my name into Google, one of the first things to come up is a BBC article entitled 'What it's like being black and working class at Cambridge' (famous, I know). My mum's a cardiology nurse and my dad has worked in a post office depot since I was born. When my mum wanted to study for her nursing degree, my dad made the sacrifice to go part-time because we couldn't afford childcare. Ever since then, money definitely hasn't been in excess. My working class identity, to me, has always been based primarily on my parents' income, and most importantly, how I have chosen to identify. It's not a trend or a fashion statement, but how I and the people around me have navigated through life.

It was only recently that St Hugh's College Student Union in Oxford thought it was appropriate to have a 'Romans and Roadmen' Bop (college party). The description jokingly said: 'pls [sic] do not bring knives or large swords as part of either your roadman or roman costume'. At the height of a knife-crime epidemic that is largely killing young black working-class people, it's beyond me how anyone would even be able to write something like that – just to be 'edgy' and cool. Within hours, the sentence was swiftly deleted and replaced with a *Dazed* article entitled 'How to culturally appreciate and not culturally appropriate'.

I realise that for some of you reading this, class inequality may be a more present and pressing issue than race. Many people aren't able to simply take for granted the ability to pay the £24 UCAS fee (or £60 per university for a Master's application), access to the internet and parental buy-in to our education. They might yelp to learn that on average, a university student in the UK receives around £3,090 from their parents a year. In particular, Durham University students received on average around £500 a month from their beloved parents.

Even though the Bank of Mum and Dad can be nice, parents are above all seen as playing a vital part in our educational attainment. Parents and carers are our 'first teachers', helping us navigate through school and pre-university choices. Some parents take an interest not only in the behavioural attitudes of their children but also in developing skills, school policy and organisation.

I remember the lecturer saying, 'Children from middle-class families are usually read to every

night just like your parents would have,' and that was my first taste of Imposter syndrome because I was like, 'Wow, OK. Like, not only should I be middle class, but I should have two parents – and if I don't fit that criteria, should I even be here?' – Eireann

For the majority of black children, parental buy-in to educational development is complicated by matters of race and class. From languages and accents which provoke racial assumptions to unfamiliarity with the UK's education system, studies all point to the fact that the majority of black parents are at a disadvantage when it comes to parental engagement. Reni Eddo-Lodge sums this up perfectly in *Why I'm No Longer Talking to White People About Race* when talking about the intersection between race, class and expectations:

Children of immigrants are often assured by well-meaning parents that educational access to the middle classes can absolve them from racism. We are told to work hard, go to a good university, and get a good job.

My parents' work schedules meant that they did not have the time to support and supplement my education. This is true of many parents. My mum and dad were always excited when I came home beaming with my end of term report, but they couldn't invest in my education in the way that they might have liked to. Parents' and information evenings, for example, almost always clashed with my mum's night shifts and my dad's late shifts. Luckily for me, my older brother and sister would step in as my parent-designates for the night. For working-class students and our parents alike, educational attainment becomes a mechanism whereby we can escape the cycle of poverty when given an opportunity to. The Sutton Trust found that some groups, including black Africans, appear to have higher levels of aspiration than others, with pupils showing greater interest in schooling, despite relatively high levels of poverty and being more likely to have free school meals.

My mind was elsewhere. My mum had been diagnosed with a blood clot and she couldn't work so my stress was that I need to go to work and I'm in school. Who's going to provide for me? Who's going to provide for my family? – Courtney

In such an environment, you don't have the luxury of time, or the luxury to prioritise your own development – financial matters are much more pressing. Before applying to university, the prospect of a huge student debt was a massive put-off that made me seriously question whether it was worth it. I couldn't see the fairness in my brother and sister only paying £3,000 a year while I was made to buck the cost of a £9,000 bill. Worst of all, they were *still* paying off their loans, so I pretty much imagined myself going to the grave with my debt. But one day I saw Martin Lewis, the MoneySavingExpert. com founder, on TV, successfully 'myth-busting' student loans. He explained so many things that I wished I could have known for myself and shared with some of my friends, who thought that the debt wasn't worth it. For example, after thirty years any and all remaining debt is wiped. Many people who earn under £25,000 are unlikely to pay it all back within thirty years anyway. Furthermore, I had no idea about all the scholarships and bursaries that I was eligible for. Nowadays, I'd sadly describe my relationship with student finance as like having a temporary boyfriend – you get excited every time you get that occasional text: *Your money will arrive in your Bank Account within three working days*. But when you break up for good, you get hit with a massive bill asking you for everything he gave you back. I know. It's tragic.

If you're a black girl who is working-class, you'll understand that the relationship between class and race is far from simple. Moreover, when speaking to Nathania, who's from Manchester, it dawned on me how ignorant I had been about the huge discrepancies between regions across the UK. For example, in Northern Ireland, black ethnic groups make up less than 0.1% of the population meaning that whilst almost all of the students in Northern Ireland are white, less than half in London are. Regional disparities serve to highlight the vast gulf of inequality between black students who live anywhere other than the capital and those in London. If you're a black student who's grown up *outside* London, you're probably familiar with being overlooked in conversations to do with access. Most access events that focus specifically on black working-class students happen in London, or in partnership with schools in inner-city London. That means if you're from the north of England, you'll realistically have to travel down on an £80 ticket for an event that might last for only two or three hours. Unfortunately, this results in a bit of a paradox: an access barrier to access.

Add to this the very real prejudice against regional accents, which are often associated with negative aspects of being working-class. Nathania, now in her third year at Trinity College, Cambridge, felt that people immediately formed a negative impression of her simply because of her accent, automatically questioning her right to attend an elite academic institution, and contributing to her struggle to 'fit in':

> **I think it's a lot to do with my [Mancunian] accent. People just presume that I haven't got a brain.**

The intersection of class and region can be a huge deterrent to following your desired path. But crucially, recognising this at least puts you on a stronger footing to find a way to plan and confront these issues in the best way possible.

*

When applying to university, one 'deal-breaker' for me was culture. Academic credentials aside, I was eager to find somewhere that had at least some remnants of the culture I knew and loved in London – somewhere with food markets where I could buy plantain, places to get my braids done, and some diversity in the local population. So . . . I planned to apply to only London universities. Call it regional privilege, maybe, but I didn't know anywhere else, and London for me was a safe bet. I grew up in and around the city. It was my home. To be completely honest, the thought of leaving it scared me. The three universities with the biggest black student populations are all in London: London Metropolitan, the University of East London and the University of West London, where black students make up more than a third of all first-year undergraduates. After students from Bangladeshi backgrounds, black Caribbean students are most concentrated in the most diverse universities, which have tended to be in London or Birmingham. Young black Londoners have *created* a culture through music, dance and language that is so specific to London that it would be hard to imagine yourself anywhere else.

A lack of relatable culture at university has a direct correlation with the drop-out rates of black students. The University Partnerships Programme Foundation and Social Market Foundation found that more than one in ten (10.3 per cent) black students drop out of university, in comparison with 6.9 per cent of the whole student population. I was not surprised to read that the main factors were 'lack of cultural connection to the curriculum' and difficulty in making friends with students from other ethnicities. This isn't to assume that all black people are likely to be friends – but going to a university where hardly anyone looks like you signifies a massive problem. You feel as if every single other black student knew something that you didn't, and that's why none of them are here. You might begin to question whether you could be happier somewhere else (or even not in higher education at all).

It becomes a self-perpetuating choice to pick a university that you know other black students will be at, regardless of whether it's a top one. This has led some to claim a form of 'self-segregation' due to lack of 'ethnic mixing' in the UK's universities, in terms not only of the student body but also academics, support staff and culture. This creates a system in which white middle class students go to certain universities, and poor ethnic minority students go to others. Universities like these which are more ethnically diverse tend to be 'less wealthy universities which provide higher education for large numbers of first-generation university students'. Moreover, universities in ethnically diverse cities attract an ethnically diverse student body. That in turn encourages greater diversity. The student population of Coventry University, for example, is 54.5 per cent white and 44.5 per cent BME. From the outset, there's strength in numbers.

With the retention of black students at an all time low, being selective about university choices becomes a mechanism for insulating yourself from entering institutions that aren't looking out for your best interests. You even get to skip the feeling that your presence is just another way of ticking a few boxes. Instead, there's comfort in being surrounded by other black students – more so than in choosing the 'best' universities.

School of Institutional Racism

Professor David Gillborn, Director of the Centre for Research in Race and Education at the University of Birmingham, believes that England's education system is home to 'insidious institutionalised racism'. And he's right. Institutional racism can be defined as the collective failure of an organisation or institution to provide the appropriate framework for people because of their colour, culture or ethnic origin. From attitudes and behaviours to ignorance and racist stereotyping, all processes work to systematically disadvantage minority ethnic people. Black students have to work to identify and highlight subtle forms of racism that operate against the common belief that racism is easily recognisable. This very fact is what makes the institutionalisation of racism within our education system so insidious. It's easy to deny when it's woven in with privilege and power.

In 2018, the *Independent* reported on data which revealed that black students are twenty-two times more likely to have their university applications investigated for possible fraudulent activity. The UK-based organisation dealing with the application process for British universities, UCAS, claims it is 'at the heart of connecting people to higher education'. However, between

2013 and 2017, a Freedom of Information request found that the applications of 2,675 black British undergraduate applicants were flagged in comparison to 995 white British applicants. In response to the criticism, UCAS attributed blame to the fraud detection software it uses to screen applications, which 'uses historical data as a reference'.

The UCAS example is at the crux of why institutional racism has managed to persist today. Institutional racism is faceless – by which I mean, the individual motive of racism is removed from the institution, resulting in depersonalisation. How can an *institution* possibly be racist? As students, we're left fighting a system within which no one person or institution is willing to admit to their failures. Instead, we're directed to failings of 'systems' and 'operations' as a way of rationalising it.

In 2015, the number of black students accepted by Russell Group universities stood at 2,740. Before you ask: yes, this is comparatively low. Yet a BBC 'Reality Check' article, including 'five charts that tell the story of diversity in UK universities', said: 'Black and minority ethnic students of all backgrounds are actually punching above their weight when it comes to representation at university.' Black students make up 8 per cent of the UK university population, despite accounting for 4 per cent of young people aged eighteen to twenty-four in

England and Wales. However, this 'overrepresentation' is not reflected within the UK's redbrick universities (typically regarded as the top institutions).

Every so often, a headline about the underrepresentation of black students in elite academic institutions rears its ugly head in national news. Around every six months, it seems as though every major newspaper has an alarm set. During my time at Cambridge, those moments were the worst. Journalists flooded your inboxes on every social media site. All the black students became hyper-visible, and all the white students were reminded to pity you and exclaim that they 'didn't know you were the *only* one!' – despite facing that fact every day. Or, my personal favourite, being constantly asked, 'Are you sure the lack of diversity at Oxbridge is not because black students aren't applying?' Probably. But have you ever thought to question *why* they're not applying? The journalists who write these stories continue to have no regard for the black students who are actually in these institutions. These very stories also have an effect on our experiences at university. It's exhausting.

As it stands, the decentralised administration system at Oxbridge falters when it comes to access and outreach. It turns it into a game of who can get more black students into their universities, so that they can avoid the tabloids. Despite a genuine commitment from some school liaison officers and access staff, this rat race actually overlooks inclusion issues, such as how welcome black students feel on university grounds once they arrive. Universities view themselves as liberal and progressive places that are at the forefront of society. Formal education is still believed to be a sure means of gaining that social mobility passport. Clinging on to this vision of what our educational system *could* be, universities are prone to ignoring the fact that racism can still be at the core of the same institution that is offering platforms to discuss and learn about it.

The challenge universities now face is addressing an access problem under constant scrutiny. Here lurks the word 'diversity', which has become a catch-all cliché – one that points to inclusivity and representation, without ever taking in what it really *means*. Let's take the strategic objectives from the University of York's Equality, Diversity and Inclusion Strategy 2017-2022:

- Objective 1: Embed equality into all aspects of university life.

- Objective 2: Attract, attain and succeed.

- Objective 3: Be flexible and adaptive to the needs of our diverse university community.

- Objective 4: Adopt an inclusive campus approach.

I searched. And searched. I wanted to make sure that the above hadn't really been published as an equality, diversity *and* inclusion scheme that was supposed to span five years? There is no strategy within the report, no mention of *how* the university would 'monitor and address differences in degree outcomes', or *how* the university would be committed to 'promoting a culture based on the principles of respect, dignity and inclusion'. If you think I'm being harsh, have a look at SOAS University of London's Equality, Diversity and Inclusion Strategy (2016-2020). Its report not only includes detailed and specific strategic objectives for 2016-2020, but individual stories of students who are most affected by 'diversity and inclusion' policies. Most importantly, the ways in which progress will be measured and maintained. Point 10, 'Ensuring Progress', demonstrates the sophistication of acknowledging that as staff and students, we all serve different roles and responsibilities when it comes to these issues. Rather than suggesting a widespread commitment to 'equality', there is an understanding that Diversity and Inclusion Managers have a fundamentally different role to the Board of Trustees. By pinpointing specific groups, this at least ensures a standardised and coherent commitment to strategic objectives.

It seems as if most universities are stringing sentences together in an attempt to prove that they are doing something – *anything.* We're left with vague strategic papers that lack critique, discussion and direction. Sadly, it's the students who fall under the 'diverse' umbrella who suffer when universities send a clear message that equality is an afterthought.

The Racial Equality Charter (REC) is just one example of a 'gold star' sticker system that has been put in place for institutions. The REC aims to improve the 'representation, progression and success of minority ethnic staff and students within higher education'. A report by Professor Kalwant Bhopal and Clare Pitkin, detailing the experiences of the individuals responsible for the implementation of the REC in their institutions, found that all interviewees welcomed the REC. However, many felt that institutions were slow to respond to the fact that additional resources needed to be invested 'to provide adequate provision and support when applying for the REC'. I wasn't surprised to learn that institutions could be deemed as 'proactive and working towards the REC' while still employing staff who demonstrated negative attitudes towards BME students.

Oxford and Cambridge are both universities that are regularly associated with elitism, bastions of social privilege that groom the future leaders of today. In particular, Labour MP for Tottenham David Lammy has been persistent in challenging Oxbridge to admit to and rectify its diversity problem. In 2016, 1.5 per cent of the Cambridge intake was black and 1.2 per cent of the intake at Oxford, according to the Higher Education

Statistics Agency. In response to Lammy's criticisms, Professor Graham Virgo, Pro-Vice-Chancellor for Education at Cambridge, together with senior colleagues from the Admissions Office, published an open letter addressing diversity in admissions. The letter stated that Cambridge had admitted fifty-eight black students in 2017, representing 33 per cent of all black students admitted to higher education in the UK that year who had attained A*A*A at A-level. But if we're playing the numbers game, how many of those black students went to private school or high-performing grammar schools? Or, how many were based in London? More pressing, how many of those students come from international schools? In the absence of answers, it's difficult not to feel that statistics may have been interpreted to present a 'not-that-bad picture'. What we do know though is that the careful placing of statistics can do much to damage and distort facts.

The current standard of black representation at Oxbridge is not something to be celebrated. At times, black students are met with hostility from other Oxbridge students when we try to do our own bit for access and inclusion. Most notably, when BME students call for a BME representative on a college union, some colleges' voting systems mean that students who *do not* identify as BME have a significant hand in deciding whether a BME officer is 'needed' – often voting the motion down.

At Pembroke College, a BME student created and submitted a proposal for a 'White Majority Ethnic' officer, satirising the arguments that a BME officer patronises, infantilises and ghettoises BME students. It read:

How could people who come from Three Different Continents AND then some more, be categorised in this manner? How could someone who might refer to home (or homes) located in Adelaide or Middlesbrough, Johannesburg or Minneapolis, Rio de Janeiro or Zurich, stand to represent the struggles and the grievances of the entire WME community?

Yep. Some people have a *lot* of time on their hands.

Conversations surrounding Oxbridge can be entirely regressive. The two universities nonchalantly claim to be strongholds of excellence and exceptional standards. Yet in the same sentence, they can allude to black students as not achieving *enough* – suggesting that we don't meet those standards of excellence. This isn't a conversation that is happening in isolation. It's something that parents see, prospective black students see, and current black students understand.

As a black student, you're being seen as someone who's really taking a stand on diversity. But

47

middle-class white people are not the only audience. You have kids that are interested in going to Oxbridge, who are watching and reading these things and thinking, 'Wow, there's only one black student in, I don't know, Worcester College. I'm definitely not applying to Oxford'. You're perpetuating the same system. – Renée

Renée Kapuku, former President of the University of Oxford's African and Caribbean Society (ACS), has been a trailblazer in disrupting the narrative that Oxbridge isn't for black students. She has been involved in several student-led and some university-supported access and outreach programmes. Oxford ACS's Annual Access Conference is the UK's largest higher education access conference for African and Caribbean students. The conference has a specific focus on black state-school students from disadvantaged backgrounds, and aims to deconstruct Oxford stereotypes through a 'highly personalised social lens'. Since the ACS developed its access framework, applications from black students to Oxford have increased by 24.1 per cent. Clearly, there is strength in having something communicated by someone who looks like you – no glamorisation or sugar-coating, just honesty.

It's students doing this work where the university is falling short. – Ọrẹ

As black women, we're never afforded complexity in these narratives about black underrepresentation. Our voices are left outside the conversation. Access is more than trying to pump us in as fast as possible; there has been a lack of nuance and practical suggestions for change. It's always been, 'You're not doing enough,' and never a question of, 'What can we do? How can we help you?' As Renée writes for the Huffington Post, we as black students are 'turned into poor caricatures of the quintessential "black student experience" condensed into one of suffering, strife and "social apartheid"'. Black students taking hold of this narrative regarding access and race is a chance for us to demonstrate that our experiences at elite institutions are far from monolithic. They're colourful and unique.

Where Do We Go from Here?

I'm definitely not qualified to be the next Minister of Education. However, having spent most of my life in full-time education (seventeen years, to be exact), believe it or not, my experiences have taught me, and the others in this book, a few things about our educational system: some negative and positive, but crucially, all *very* different, stemming from the ways in which we have experienced and tackled institutional racism within various higher education institutions.

Universities are currently run like businesses, with marketisation increasing the role of the student as a consumer: you pay a certain amount, and you expect to leave with a solid grade and a job six months postgraduation. From league table positioning to student satisfaction surveys, it's easy to see this part of marketisation as a form of educational expansion, and potentially a means of reducing inequality by providing more opportunities for people from disadvantaged backgrounds. But the fallout of this is huge.

At present, there is a wide disparity between how much we talk about diversity and how much actual change is happening. Universities have become sophisticated in non-performative 'institutional speech acts' which make commitments to diversity and 'equality'. Your institution may claim to be driving racial equality – while your everyday interactions are telling you something *very* different. Ultimately, the question remains as to whether we can really label an institution as more 'diverse' if its commitment to racial equality is based on the meeting of racial equality targets, rather than listening to the lived experiences of its black students.

So, what can we do?

> **I think people who aren't part of these [racial] groups should be equally concerned and giving a helping hand. – Eireann**

The proactiveness of black students on the ground has meant more BME-specific targeting when it comes to matters regarding access before and within university. Bristol Student Union BME network, for example, has created its own influential platform through leading its own discussions and campaigns on topics such as intersectionality, religion and mental health. Without the persistent and collective drive of student labour and voices, I am sure little would be done to change the current status quo of ensuring black students feel integrated before and within the university environment.

Oxford and Cambridge have also both partnered with Target Oxbridge, a free programme which takes on 160 black African and Caribbean students in Year 12 who want help with their applications to the two universities, and provides more opportunities for prospective black students to speak to and ask questions of black students who are already at Oxbridge. The first event I ever went to in Cambridge was hosted by the founder of Target Oxbridge, Naomi Kellman. Target Oxbridge's partnership with both universities has proved to be invaluable in demystifying Oxbridge life.

However, it's clear that methods of tackling inequality and racial disparity within education are still mostly outsourced. Universities are more likely to work with organisations such as Target Oxbridge, Sponsors for Educational Opportunity, IntoUniversity or Future Leaders as a way of fulfilling their diversity pledges. They offload their responsibilities to tackle systemic inequalities within their institutions to privately-run, non-governmental organisations as a tokenistic means of making 'progress', without properly addressing the root causes of these inequalities within their walls.

To some, outsourcing may seem to be a step in the right direction, showing through financial investment and a reliance on experienced organisations a real and specific commitment to rectifying inequalities. Providing a platform for these organisations is also a way of allowing professionals who understand and are black themselves to address specific black issues. But I question the authenticity of many of these diversity schemes.

It's easier to adopt the argument that black students are making conscious choices when navigating the higher education landscape than to ask: *why*? Why are black students 'self-segregating'? Why do we feel a sense of Imposter syndrome before we've even started our university applications? Why do we cry in the car on our way home from open days? Why do we still feel the need to drop out of universities because we don't feel welcome? These questions require *practical* answers – answers that don't start or end with black students, but with the institutions in which they are struggling.

It would be misleading to claim that I have all the answers. I am no expert. I have just about scratched the surface of why so many black girls fail to apply to university, and what awaits them if they do. Most importantly, I can only hope my experiences, and those of others in this book, can colour the conversation on access into – and whilst at – university. If nothing else, foregrounding the lived experiences of black university students paints a more complex picture. It also highlights the fact that there is not one single factor producing the profound gendered and racialised inequalities within our higher education system, but many.

Cambridge may have won on my open day. But I didn't stop playing. By October of that year, I was driving back up to the city again, but this time with all my stuff, ready to move in to my college. Cambridge would score a few more goals over the next year, but it was one of the best decisions I would ever make.

2

#AcademiaSoWhite

Ọrẹ

As the UK's national curriculum currently stands, it is possible to go through education without encountering Africa at all. The history curriculum, for example, groups 'non-European societies' in a way that encourages them to be viewed as homogenous despite their diverse characters. As a result, students are taught to view the world through a lens of Europe and 'the rest'. Primary schools are only required to look at one non-European society, and the early secondary school curriculum does little to improve on this, despite its aims to teach 'local, regional and international history'. Although universities in the UK have autonomy over how their curricula are set, it is no surprise that their history curricula rarely do a better job than our national curriculum of looking beyond the centrality of European history.

The implications of this whiteness and Eurocentrism go beyond history. This state of affairs mediates our whole educational experiences considerably, so much so that attempting to study anything outside of the white and Eurocentric requires going the extra mile. The contents of the British curriculum have implications for class-rooms far beyond the UK, and affect more broadly what is considered to be worthy of academic study. I first became aware of the power of curricula around Year 7. I was in secondary school in Nigeria, and we had spent most of our history lessons that year learning about the Battle of Hastings and the struggles that led up to it – instead of any Nigerian or West African history. It's possible to be in a Nigerian classroom, and yet have your curriculum dictated by powers almost 5,000 miles away.

Inevitably, moving back to England meant that I would only face this curriculum even more directly. After years of learning extensively about the World Wars, I had still had no lessons on the transatlantic slave trade or the colonisation of African states. It became clear that I wasn't going to get a diverse learning experience from my school's curriculum, and that I would have to seek out the extra knowledge on my own. I hoped that going to university would change that.

At my Cambridge interview for human, social and political sciences (HSPS), my red-orange blazer – and my race – were not the only things that made me stand out. All the interviewees for HSPS sat in one room, and around a table there were about five other applicants reading the exact same neon-green politics book. I panicked – I had never, ever seen this book that they all seemed to be really familiar with. I asked someone to see what was inside (even though I really should have been minding my own business, if we're being honest); it was filled with predominantly British political history that I hadn't come across, especially since I didn't even study history at GCSE. There were things inside about the Concert of Europe and Clement Attlee that I knew I could only waffle about for a minute at best. Instead, I went back to my corner of the room and re-read Frantz Fanon's *The Wretched of the Earth* and the pile of JSTOR articles on Pan-Africanism, Kwame Nkrumah and the Négritude that I had been mulling over for the past few months. I hadn't even started Cambridge yet but *that* was when the imposter syndrome kicked in for me. My experiences and my existence felt at odds with the university as a physical space, and as an intellectual one too.

In my first interview, I was asked what I thought was the most significant event of the twentieth century. I stopped and thought: *she must want me to say something like the Second World War*. I had let that stupid green politics book get to me and make me doubt myself. But I paused, and remembered the advice that I had received from my mentor to always steer the question to my strengths. I knew nothing about the Second World War. I did, however, know a lot about the wave of decolonisation that came after it. For me, the fact that a post-war wave of self-determination enabled about one third of the world to ramp up the struggles for their independence, was *way* more significant than a war that I personally felt quite disconnected from.

In my second interview, I was given a piece to read by Isaiah Berlin, discussing the conflict between politics as an art and politics as a science. Based on this, I was asked to decide who Berlin might consider a good leader. The piece had mentioned Otto von Bismarck numerous times and so I felt that if there was a right answer, it had to be him. But again, I had no clue who he was. So I said, 'Well, I know who Berlin might consider a *bad* leader.' I proceeded to talk about how Nkrumah had an understanding of what politics was as a science, but his failure to marry this with the 'art' of politics and apply it to the contentious geopolitical context of the Cold War would make someone like Berlin consider him a bad political leader. I had no idea how that would play out, but I had no choice but to focus on what I knew: the histories that felt close to me, the histories that I could relate to.

It felt like a risky decision, but luckily it paid off. However, the constant struggle of trying to fit my interests, experiences and history into a degree which wasn't always so accommodating was something I grappled with for my whole time at university.

I was reconciling the parts of my identity that I thought were othered, and I came to understand that being othered is not necessarily a disadvantage but your superpower. – Renée

Renée puts it best, but it wasn't easy. I didn't just feel like an imposter because I was black in this predominantly white university; I also felt excluded by the nature of my experiences, and in turn, the interests that had developed from those experiences. Histories like mine, and those to which I can more easily relate, are absent on curricula everywhere.

The experience of confronting curricula that don't do enough to acknowledge our experiences as black girls is othering. This experience has its inception in our national curriculum, and has implications for the subjects we choose to study, how we interact (or don't) with our university lectures, and eventually, how well we perform by the end of our degrees. We are dealing with a black attainment gap at university level that doesn't correlate with how well black students perform at GCSE stage, and the lack of black academics at professorial level is at crisis point.

In anticipation of the critics who will say that we are liberal snowflakes complaining about an issue that isn't there, or that this is about black students asking for 'special treatment', I am packing this chapter with data, figures and research that prove that the issue of whiteness in academia is not one that I've constructed in my imagination.

I think we feel a lot of pressure that we have to produce some kind of evidence as to why you feel marginalised, or some sort of statistical data. But if you feel some type of way, it's truth on its own. Your feelings are its own truth. – Saredo

But the burden of proof shouldn't be on us. The idea that black students have to go further to show that their experiences are real is recurrent in academic spaces, and this chapter reveals similar issues. Our experiences of grappling with the whiteness in academia are valid, and highlight how black students are being failed by the education system.

Subjects

Black students make up 7 per cent of the UK university population. However, they are not evenly distributed in proportion across all subjects. Only 2.4 per cent of students who study history are black; the proportion is about 3 per cent for languages, and 5 per cent for the creative arts. To understand why this may be the case, we have to look further back, to the motivations behind our subject choices.

For many students, being attracted to a curriculum is why you might choose to study a particular subject, or even go to a particular university. But most ethnic minority students are thinking about more than just the subject and its content when we choose what to study.

When you think of English, what are you thinking of? Is it not middle-class white people? – Mikai

I agree with Mikai. However, I don't think it's because only middle-class white people are good at English, but more because English is a degree that does not have an obvious career path attached to it, and so isn't an obvious choice for those going to university for the sole purpose of improving their career prospects. Being able to study whatever you want without having to think ahead to what careers it might set you up for is a privilege that few have. There are all sorts of challenges and obstacles in the job market for black women, so from as early on as A-levels, you find yourself wanting to study something that seems safe – something that will guarantee stability and security in a society where those things don't come easily. The pressures of a job market that seems to consider some degrees more marketable than others kick in while we choose what to study at university – and in the end, degrees such as English, history, modern languages and the creative arts suffer for it.

Even if we aren't thinking along these lines, our parents are. By the time I approached Year 12, my dad had made it clear that he thought it would be a good idea for me to study law. At one point in my life, I thought a law degree was a good idea too. I regularly watched *Suits* and *The Good Wife* with my mum, and being that kind of corporate lawyer seemed, at that time, to be so *me*. I loved arguing. I debated throughout my secondary school career, and although I took maths, French, politics and economics at A-level, I was clearly tending towards the humanities. I wasn't doing medicine, that was for sure; I had no interest in doing economics either, and so law was the only other vocational-ish degree left. My whole career was planned out: I would study law at Cambridge, qualify in the UK, work in corporate law for a bit. Then I would move back to Nigeria, become a qualified lawyer there, practise for ten years and become a Senior Advocate of Nigeria, something akin to being a Queen's Counsel. But a two-week summer school and a bit of research made me realise that I had zero interest in the law, and that in fact, I loved politics. I had to come home and tell my dad that I wanted to apply for HSPS at Cambridge, a course that felt perfectly curated for me and my broad range of interests, in a way that law wasn't. I told him I would (possibly) do a law conversion once I graduated. (I later abandoned that mission.)

Being relatively privileged in terms of class meant that my experience was slightly different to the norm. My mum went to university, and my dad is an academic (and many of his best friends are too). My challenge was not that I lacked role models, or that my parents didn't appreciate the value of a university degree. The problem was that, in *spite* of my parents' backgrounds, my dad still felt that for me to get my foot in the door as a black woman in today's world, I needed a vocational degree – specifically, a law degree. As I write this, I'm currently doing a master's in journalism at Columbia University in New York. Even now, my dad *still* thinks it would be a good idea for me to go to law school!

I know that my dad's position comes from a place of love and that he only wants the best for me, but I'm also glad that I found the courage to defend my interests and my strengths. Many of my friends were not so fortunate, and have ended up graduating with degrees (a lot of them law degrees) that they are unsatisfied with because they were literally forced to do them by their parents. Over 10 per cent of students who study law in the UK are black, and that's great. While I'm sure that many of them have a genuine love for the law, I have no doubt that equally, many of them are in the same boat that I almost was, studying a degree that they hope will please their parents, and land them a job straight after graduation and, hopefully, financial security.

The role of financial incentives in choosing to study particular subjects at university should not be under-estimated. According to research by the Resolution Foundation, black African graduates are twice as likely to work in low-paying occupations as Indian, Chinese and white graduates. We know that the odds are against us, and so we hedge our bets in the hope that the qualification will lead directly to a higher-paying job, so that we don't become part of that damning statistic.

But if you are going to go to university and endure three, four or even six years of excruciating hard work and general stress, you owe it to yourself to choose a degree that you love. You may have parents who are paying for your degree and think that as a result, they have a say in what you study. Yet you are entitled to freedom in that choice. Any degree you earn is meant to teach you transferable skills that can be applied to a whole host of jobs. This might take some extra explaining to your parents, who may not see that now, but you don't have to do a whole law degree to be a lawyer, or politics to be a politician. What makes you scream? What makes you angry? What excites you? What keeps you up at night? What do you want to rant about for hours on end? For me, it wasn't law. I wanted to study a degree that would let me be myself, explore my diverse range of interests, and make me a more rounded person; I found that in HSPS.

HSPS is one of Cambridge's more diverse courses, and I am grateful for that, don't get me wrong. Nevertheless, that's still not saying very much – it just means it's slightly less shocking than the others. In my first year, I studied politics, international relations, sociology and social anthropology. In politics, I learned about what felt like all the white men under the sun, and then I had one lecture on Gandhi (without any mention of his history of anti-blackness, of course, but I digress). The only political theorists that were considered worthy of academic critique, according to my curriculum, were white. Although the course has now changed, my international relations course at the time involved a whole lecture on industrialisation that made no mention of slavery. Someone, somewhere decided that students at one of the world's best universities could accurately study Britain's industrial revolution without acknowledging that it was built off the backs of slaves. International relations, in addition to its theoretical aspects, should also address difficult questions about who does and does not benefit from the ideas and ideologies that dominate our international system. But in this regard, my course sometimes fell short.

Then there is social anthropology. The whole idea of the subject revolves around white 'explorers' studying black and brown people, and I struggled with that as a notion. In these lectures, non-European people are conveyed as something to gawk at, a mysterious subject of intrigue. That objectification made me uncomfortable.

Anthropology as a whole has a really colonial, negative, horrifying history, and I think that the fact that the people who propagated that are still at the top of the reading lists is incredibly unnecessary. There are amazing anthropologists who are either not those people, or who are actually black and brown anthropologists who have greater cultural respect, and also still fully understand the ideas of [celebrated anthropologists] like Lévi-Strauss and Malinowski. Reading

the word 'savage' in Lévi-Strauss's work a hundred thousand times is not the way that I want to spend my time at university. – Saskia

If you choose to study a humanities subject at university, there are high chances that you're going to be forced to work within the confines of a very white curriculum. Your histories, where they do appear on curricula, will be add-ons, or thrown into collective 'liberation' lectures as afterthoughts. The problem of the white, Eurocentric curriculum isn't unique to HSPS.

The Cambridge curriculum for English is very Eurocentric, very canonical . . . English at Cambridge was very white, very dry and very non-political. – Arenike

Although curricula are normally set by senior faculty staff within universities, the 'literary canon' is a set of texts that scholars across the world have effectively agreed are great and special. It typically includes the works of Shakespeare, Homer, a couple of Brontë sisters, and so on, and consists of mostly white, European, male writers. It's presented as an objective list, and is said to be 'representative' of a period. But we have to challenge who gets to decide what is considered 'great' enough to be included in the literary canon, and the conditions under which these kinds of decisions are made. We have to challenge which writers are privileged enough to have their works memorialised in this magical way. Who are the gatekeepers?

On further interrogation, it's clear that the canon is not objective at all. The books that it includes are meant to be 'authoritative' – and therefore end up aligning with socio-political ideas of the time about who could and could not have authority. The early dictators of the canon were white clergymen in the nineteenth century and beyond. Black people were largely not in positions that granted access to education, let alone able to have their works considered worthy of being canonised. This same power dynamic still exists, and as such, the canon hardly includes writers who look like me. The idea that black writers haven't written works great enough to be included in the canon is a myth that is used to justify and perpetuate their exclusion. Cambridge's *Varsity* newspaper featured a 'Rethinking the canon' column by Jonathan Chan that makes a lot of headway in grappling with the issue of the rigidity of the literary canon. But this is not just a university thing. The literary canon is a body of literature that is presented as universal, and is the basis for English curricula across the world and at all levels. You're probably going to study more Brontë sisters than black women in your academic lifetime. That is a problem for everyone.

> **It's almost as if these African and black writers were a side dish to the main meal as opposed to really exploring their own work critically. – Saredo**

Chelsea studied history. In her first year, there were ten British history papers, six European history papers, one on empires and world history, and one on 'World' history:

> **[On the world history paper] there would be one lecture on Africa, one lecture on Asia, one lecture on Latin America, but then you would have British history, which would be broken down into different areas. It was very specific when it came to European history and British history. – Chelsea**

In studying British history and the atrocities of its empire, we must study more than white and European histories, and we must study them in full. But even for the departments that have acknowledged this need, and gradually introduced the histories of non-white people to their curricula, the topics are obsessively centred around slavery and colonisation. For example, we may discuss the economics of slavery and the role of William Wilberforce in its eventual abolition, or we may speak of former colonies only in terms of their viability for European metropoles. This suggests that non-white people are only worth studying for the occasions in which they are forced to confront white power. But why? Slaves were people before they were enslaved. Black people have existed in history in roles other than those of slaves and subjects of colonialism, but you probably won't get that from your textbooks.

The [history] curriculum is so dehumanising for black people. It's really othering. – Nathania

The only times you might see someone who looks like you represented in your curriculum will be at the mention of slavery, colonisation, lynching and maybe political corruption in African states – a dehumanising experience. It is hard to believe that heads of departments think about, or care to think about, what that does to our psyches as black people. Our history books glorify the very people who profited from our exploitation. If we are told in Year 4 that Winston Churchill 'won the war', we should be reminded in the same breath that he was also, as suggested by some, a genocidal racist – given that he was largely responsible for the deaths of some 3 million people during the 1943 Bengal famine. If we're taught about Auschwitz and Nazi concentration camps, we should also be reminded that concentration camps were a tactic first used by the British in the Second Boer War and later against the

Mau Mau in Kenya. How can a university truly pride itself on being at the forefront of knowledge production when the only ideas and theories that they consider worthy of study are white and European, and most likely, propagated by men?

We struggle to find room for our identities in both our curricula and the lectures that stem from them, and that's something that affects black people in a unique way. Lecturers have a duty to be sensitive to that, too. The use of photographs of Ku Klux Klan lynchings in a history lecture could be triggering for black students, who can identify with victims of lynchings in a way that non-black students can't. Lecturers shouldn't lump a lesson on black liberation into an animal liberation lecture without considering what that juxtaposition feels like to someone black. Many BME students are already being made to feel that they are squeezing into spaces that weren't made for them. Lecture halls should not be one of those spaces.

The curricula of natural and clinical sciences have also failed to confront racism. Despite the focus on how race manifests in the social sciences, the essentialist notions of race that many of the natural and clinical sciences have traditionally adopted affects scientific research, and for medical students, it also affects how they go on to interact with their patients. Ayomide is a black medical student at Imperial College. The only time that her cohort was taught how the black experience may be different from that of white patients was in discussions about sickle cell disease, and the fact that black people have an increased risk of high blood pressure. This gap in teaching is part of a trend of medical students being taught to look at race as anything other than a biologically-determined, epidemiological risk factor.

Not once has anyone taught me how to approach my black patients outside of their disease, to approach them as a human, and that's something that I think medicine lacks in general.
–Ayomide

This is a problem for two reasons: doctors may ignore that race is a lived experience which needs to be approached as a social factor; moreover, it reinforces the idea that race is a fixed, biological category. Addressing the role of racial categories is directly relevant to how doctors should interact with the diverse range of patients that they are going to encounter. We are doing future black patients a disservice by not educating doctors on what the black experience, and the black body, might mean for healthcare. Many black people are also more likely to get strokes, diabetes and heart disease. I'm not a medical student, and I won't pretend that I can intricately explain why that is the case – but it is, and our future doctors should be equipped to deal with that reality.

Academics such as Lundy Braun and Barry Saunders have extensively researched the ways in which medical students are still taught to 'correct' for race in a way that suggests that there are innate differences between races. These differences are more accurately described as social and environmental factors that have become genetically embedded in ancestral lines. For example, sickle cell disease and approaches to it have been racialised; it is viewed as a 'black disease', although the patterns of sickle cell incidence have more to do with the genetic evolutions of people who lived in malaria-endemic areas, because people with sickle cell are protected against malaria. While most people who fall into this category *are* black, it's not a black disease, and suggesting it is reinforces outdated notions of race as something innate and biological.

Legacies of scientific racism from the Enlightenment era, when black people were 'proven' to be three-fifths human, inherently different and incapable of acquiring 'higher faculties', still have implications for how the sciences are studied today. Race is not a biological category, it's a socially constructed one, and science curricula should respond to these changing ideas. Professors of science and medicine have as much of a duty as the academic staff in the social sciences to adapt their teaching and settings accordingly, introducing critical race theory to offset the racist assumptions that often permeate medical research.

Unfortunately, science is not value-neutral, and its research is affected by socio-political contexts which we know are racialised and gendered. The context affects the questions we ask in our research, the analytical categories we use, the perspectives we take and the assumptions we begin with. It also creates a problem for the things scientific research will miss – who it does not include, and the inevitable blind spots from the position of the researcher.

We must also question the origins of modern science as we know it. Too often, we are taught that science and technology are concepts that are *introduced* to non-Western societies. An idea such as that can be constructed as true only because we aren't ever taught where science really comes from. Our curriculum ignores the history of science at its inception, in which people of colour also played a monumental role. Chanda Prescod-Weinstein expands on this in her 'Decolonising Science Reading List', Akala spoke about it at the Oxford Union, and I'm glad that there appears to be a growing awareness of the fact that science also, in spite of its claims of 'objectivity', leaves much room to be diversified. Books, articles and videos on things like inclusive astronomy, black mathematicians and the feminist philosophy of physics are vital for deconstructing how we view science, its origins and the credibility of scientific contributions. Science and its curricula are not exempt from the critical reflexivity with which we should approach all our subject content.

The 'Liberating the Curriculum' working group at University College London (UCL) has partnered with the Medical School to explore what a diverse medical curriculum might look like. Dermatology, for example, is currently taught almost exclusively using images of how conditions manifest on white skin. 'It is generally far more difficult for myself and my medical student peers to identify a condition if you've never seen it on a darker skin colour before,' observe Gemma Wells and Maihma Lamba in a post on the project's website. The site has much more to say on being taught how symptoms may look different on black and brown bodies, the importance of ethnically diverse evidence bases, and being aware of factors to look out for in the test results of black patients.

However, alongside physical differences, medical students have to be educated on how a black person's relationship with mental health might differ from that of white people. Experiences of racism and discrimination have been linked to chronic conditions of stress by psychologist associations across the world. But according to a 2018 NHS report, black people are also four times more likely to be 'sectioned' than white people – that is, detained and treated against their will under the UK's mental health law. They are also more likely to be misdiagnosed with psychotic disorders and placed in secure wards. Moreover, there are cultural factors to be considered: for example, traditionally, many West African societies would ostracise people who suffered from mental illnesses. This can lead black people to be less forward with their doctors about any mental health challenges they're experiencing. Black people are also statistically more likely to be poorer, in many Western countries at least, and that comes with a range of associated stress-inducing factors.

When you have a black patient, how do you approach that? This is a big thing in medicine that we don't do. The mental health aspect of a black person is a completely different thing from [that of] a white person. – Barbara

University medical schools have a duty to prepare their students to treat *all* patients, including black patients, and their curriculum should reflect a willingness to do that. That almost a third of UK graduate doctors are BME is a statistic to be proud of – but the battle isn't won if their curriculum doesn't reflect that diversity too. (It is also relevant to add, however, that the BME category distorts this statistic in relation to black doctors, as it also includes a large proportion of Asian doctors.)

The needs of my black patient are so different from the needs of my white patient because my white patient has not had to go through institutionalised racism or discrimination. – Ayomide

Ayomide told me that after three years of medicine, she had learnt more about black mental health from the student-led ACS than she had from her medical degree. While we should be grateful that there are ACSs around the country that are making black mental health a priority, why should that be the job of black students, who have enough to deal with already?

*

While we wait on our curricula to catch up with us, most university courses offer the option to submit a dissertation, a long essay, or some other form of independent study. It's one aspect that can allow you to explore a topic in depth that your curriculum might not. This was something I looked forward to. At last, I thought: a space where I could finally write about whatever I wanted and take some ownership of my degree. I wanted to look at the role of international organisations like the World Bank in Nigeria's energy sector. I had become really interested in how Nigeria's grid and off-grid energy worked and how it was funded. I began research, reached out to experts in the area while I was in Nigeria, and set up interviews, but before all of that, I needed to find a supervisor. I went to see my Director of Studies, [the equivalent to an academic tutor] Duncan Kelly, who was always very supportive and entertained every single one of my rants about how hard it was to fit my African interests into the confines of my degree. I told him about my plans and he told me quite frankly, both to his regret and my disappointment, it would not be feasible. There was apparently no one in the entire politics department who specialised in anything even broadly West African. If I wanted to pursue a dissertation on this, I would have to change the angle to effectively make it less Nigerian. I met with a supervisor who said he could supervise me if I took Nigeria out of the equation, and another who said they had experience studying oil-producing states, but hadn't specifically studied any in West Africa.

I made the decision not to pursue it; it was made abundantly clear that I wouldn't be able to get the support that I needed. I managed to write, instead, two long essays for my African politics paper that I thoroughly enjoyed. But ultimately, I felt I had been limited by my own choices. Most of my peers had no issue finding supervisors for their interests in Schmitt and Marx and a whole bunch of other German political philosophers. But if you had interests in studying anything broadly West African, you would face issues.

A lot of black students had similar problems. Micha encountered difficulties when it was time to carry out her psychology research project:

> **Originally I really want[ed] to do something on race and potentially on implicit bias, and when I told my supervisor she was, like, 'I don't think there's anyone within PBS [psychological and behavioural studies] who could supervise you on that.' – Micha**

Some girls, like Arenike, push on with their plans despite the lack of support. Arenike ended up looking on Twitter for resources.

> **My dissertation was called formally, 'An Exploration of Racial Trauma in the Work of Solange Knowles, Claudia Rankine and Morgan Parker' . . . and that was basically a big 'fuck you' to the three years of my degree, where I hadn't been able to do anything political. [My dissertation was] not for an institution like Cambridge. It's speaking to black women and black non-binary people. That's who my target**

**audience was, but you know, there are no black
academics in Cambridge, really, who could have
looked at it. – Arenike.**

When our interests fall outside of what these institutions consider to be the norm, the onus is on us, the
students, to sort ourselves out. The labour is outsourced
to us because there's no one who is willing to explore
our niches with us – especially given the scarcity of
black academics. When it comes to topics that are centred around the black experience in particular, this is
made even harder: you're probably going to have a white
supervisor who has the privilege of being detached
from the topic, and doesn't feel what you feel when
you're working on it.

**My dissertation was on Caribbean identity
formation, so essentially, how do Caribbean
slaves operate under the scope of slavery in
Jamaica . . . my supervisor was a white middle-
aged guy. Lovely guy but distant from what I was
researching. – Mikai**

You may even find that your white supervisor is afraid
to criticise you, fearful that their position might be
misconstrued. It's a hard balance to find. Given just
how many academic staff reach professorial level without ever having to have these discussions about race,

this is something you're very likely to encounter as a black student. And again, our academic experience suffers for it.

> **I'm learning as well . . . Just because I've chosen this topic and because it's personal to my identity, I'm not the expert on it and I expect to be given the same amount of conscientious critique as my peers – but by virtue of being a black woman writing about black women, I didn't. – Renée**

Another factor that influenced my decision on whether or not to do a dissertation was thinking about who would be grading it. Pursuing your 'adventurous' interests becomes a risk. You might find yourself writing about something that no one has studied in that depth before, and that is radical by virtue of its very existence. Renée wrote her dissertation on black transnational feminism:

> **As I predicted, one of my markers marked it ridiculously high and one of my markers marked it ridiculously low.**

One half of you wants to write fearlessly, but the other half of you is very scared, and justifiably so, that this might be marked by someone with little knowledge of your area of interest. Moreover, if your work involves any exploration of racism, you may be concerned that it will be scrutinised by someone who has never experienced racism or worse still, by someone who does not consider racism worthy of academic critique.

You can't write unapologetically and with confidence about blackness and hope that your paper blends into the background. It's going to stand out. It's hard to predict whether that will work in your favour because chances are, not many people have done it before. If you find yourself considering writing a dissertation on black issues, do it because you will produce something that you're proud of, not because you think it will get a high grade. It might not. And although quite a few of us ended up disappointed, and feeling that our labour hadn't attracted the reward it deserved, we produced pieces that we're still proud of. That feeling lasts much longer.

Peers and Professors

It's not just the reading lists that may make you feel isolated at university. Your lectures, the people in them and the people delivering them play a key role in your academic experience, and can serve as another reminder of your minority status in this space.

I had an accident with plantain five days before freshers' week, and I was in hospital when I should have been in my first few lectures (in hindsight, this is quite a funny story, but I will bore you with it later). When I finally went to my first lecture, I was on a mission to find anyone and everyone black. It actually wasn't that bad – there were a few of us. I sat in front of Courtney, who I had met at a careers event a few weeks earlier. I wanted to lock in that black girl solidarity nice and early because I knew I was going to need it.

Lectures are central to your academic experience of university. In the day-to-day of lectures and essays, I came to realise that for the most part, HSPS was anomalous in the relative diversity not just of its curriculum but also of its students. For most people, the unequal representations in their curricula were replicated in the student makeup.

I've never seen a black British person do engineering in my school. – Adaobi

Adaobi went to Manchester. Chelsea was the only black girl in her history lectures. Nathania is one of two. Mikai was one of three.

Diversity in lectures and seminars isn't just about who you sit with, and how you make friends. For most of the time, as a black student you're largely invisible within the curriculum. Going back to my very questionable industrialisation lecture that completely left out the role of slavery, my worries were compounded by the fact that I was surrounded by largely non-black people who couldn't see what was wrong with it.

I went to a lecture on gender which was part of HAP [historical argument and practice] and the lecturer only spoke about white men and white women. I remember leaving that lecture and I was so angry. I did not go to another HAP lecture after that. – Chelsea

We could be sitting right under a lecturer's nose, and yet he or she would still manage to look over us, over our blackness and over our histories. It's one thing to be constantly isolated by your lecture content, but having to deal with that alone, in silence, stings more.

You feel invisible when you're left off the syllabus, but the moment a topic slightly related to black people comes up in a lecture, you are suddenly hypervisible. You're just as much a subject of intrigue as the black person on the PowerPoint slide. You are now seen, but not in a way over which you have any control. Meanwhile, the white students around you are doing mental gymnastics trying to project the story of this black subject of your lecture onto you. They are learning something that's going to mediate how they see and experience other black people, and you, being one of the only black people in your lecture, are their first victim, the unelected and unwilling representative of the whole black population.

This might be uncomfortable. Discussing anything mildly black-ish can lead people to assume that you are well-versed on the topic simply because it includes people with the same colour skin as you. Sometimes, you might actually be knowledgeable about the topic, or have experiences that mean that you can speak with some kind of authority. But equally, your opinion on it may be held in an exceptionally high esteem that you haven't really earned. You're no expert – you're there to learn too. Don't turn around and stare at me when the lecturer starts talking about the Rwandan genocide because I know as little as you do.

That's one way it might go. Some budding racists might think that now is a great time to argue with you, shrouding their prejudices in so much academic jargon that you almost think they've said something of value. Colonialism is a common one. I would be very surprised if you got through a lecture on colonialism without someone suggesting that actually colonialism was great, and implying that there is something inherently wrong with the millions of victims of empire.

In this seminar, one boy piped up ... 'But at what point do we think Africans will take responsibility and stop blaming neocolonialism for everything?' – Chelsea.

There are always going to be provocative students. But the point is that their questionable views are validated and given weight in these environments, especially in instances when the lecturer lets it slide. Fope had it in their political geography module:

One person in class was like, 'You know what? Colonialism wasn't that bad; they gave us trains, you know.' For the rest of the lecture, I just felt like [I had] indigestion, because it pissed me off ... [The lecturer] was just like, 'That's an interesting perspective. Let's move on.' I could tell he probably was really uncomfortable with

what the guy said, but if you have privilege, call it out. And the fact that he didn't really frustrated me.

In seminars or other forms of small-group teaching that thrive on student interaction, a lot of black girls would retreat. We would hold our points back because we didn't want to come across as loud or angry, thereby living up to the tropes that society repeatedly projects onto us. You also don't want be accused of 'playing the race card', and as the Imposter syndrome begins to kick in again, you find yourself retreating.

When these things happen again and again, you just check out. And I think for a long time in Cambridge, that's what I did. – Arenike

I would almost make an effort *not* to contribute.* – Eireann

I don't want people to view me as angry. I don't want people to view me as too loud. I don't want people to think I'm always making it about race. But also . . . I didn't want to come across as stupid and let down my fellow black women . . . carrying that on your shoulders at eighteen

* Emphasis added.

**when you're trying to get your degree is quite a
lot to put on yourself. – Courtney**

Black representation figures are even worse when it
comes to teaching staff. Data released by the Higher
Education Statistics Agency in 2017 shows that British
universities employ more black staff as cleaners, porters
and receptionists than they do as lecturers and professors. In my three years at Cambridge, I had only *one*
black lecturer, a Mexican woman named Mónica
Figueroa, who was in charge of my sociology of race
paper. I knew of only *one* black supervisor in African
politics – Njoki Wamai. I had heard of another black
faculty member, Malachi McIntosh, but he left before I
could meet him. He once posted a tweet that compared
his time at Cambridge to the 2017 horror film *Get
Out** – hardly a compliment. Given how hard it can be
to be a black student at Cambridge, I can only imagine
what that experience might be like as a member of staff.
When I heard that he had left, I was hardly surprised.

**Why would you want to work somewhere where
you don't feel comfortable? Because I wanted to
leave Cambridge after a week. – Kenya**

* If you are unfamiliar with Jordan Peele's film, among many other
themes it explores different levels of racism, from the subtle sort veiled
in liberal ignorance to the more overtly violent kind.

A shockingly small 1.8 per cent of all academic staff in the UK are black, according to Advance HE, an independent organisation focused on research in higher education. We represent a lower proportion than any other ethnic group; Asian staff make up 6 per cent and white staff almost 90 per cent. The proportion of black staff shrinks further, to 1.4 per cent, if we look only at those who are British. It shrinks further still if we look at those who are at professorial level – to 0.6 per cent. Considering just black women takes us down to 0.13 per cent – of almost 19,000 professors in the UK, only twenty-five are black women. Most of the people we interviewed for this book had not been taught by anyone black at all during their whole degree.

Patricia Daley, the one that we call on every single Black History Month to come and give her thoughts, she's the only black female faculty staff that I know of. – Renée

I don't know if it's that [fewer] black people are becoming professors or [fewer] black people are being employed as professors even when they're qualified. Whichever one it is, they're both problems. – Ayomide

I refuse to believe that this is because there are no black academics who are qualified – because the truth is, there are. But these numbers are largely a result of a cycle of underrepresentation. For as long as we continue to see academic spaces as places that black people cannot penetrate and cannot excel in, we perpetuate the cycle of self-exclusion. The ivory tower of academia is still pretty ivory, and it is evidenced in our curricula, our reading lists and our lecture content. Before they've climbed high enough to be able to penetrate the system, a lot of black academics find they have had enough of the structural and systemic racism in the field – and frankly, I don't blame them.

For the few who find ways to stick around, we are grateful. Having black, or even broadly BME, supervisors and lecturers is refreshing. They get it. They don't think your black examples are 'adventurous'; they understand why they're necessary. They encourage the use of these examples, and appreciate their importance in a way that not all white supervisors do. Micha wrote a sociology essay on black hair for her black supervisor, Tanisha Spratt:

> **Firstly, I get to study this? But secondly, I think even if I wrote about this for a white supervisor, they might be like, 'What are you talking about?' It's so cool that she just gets it. – Micha**

For once, we are relieved of the burden of having to teach our own supervisors what it means to be black.

There was a time when I genuinely thought I wanted to go into academia, and I still kind of do – but I've not seen black professors. I have never even had a black school teacher before. - Ayomide

When Ayomide said this, it really upset me, because academia needs more people like her – it needs more people like us. This is how underrepresentation reproduces itself. I'm lucky enough to have my dad, whose academic career reminds me that this is something within my reach, but I also recognise that this is an uncommon privilege. We should never, as black girls, feel limited by the lack of black academics we are likely to encounter at university. If we ever feel called upon to go into academia, I hope that we will find people who can support us along the way, and believe that we can be just as qualified as any, anywhere: be the Monicas and the Malachis and the Tanishas that we so need. They remind us that we *can*, even when the numbers are ranged against us.

For as long as the people making decisions on what to include and what not to include in our reading lists are largely old, white men who don't understand what it feels like for us to encounter Eurocentric curricula, it will be difficult to create change. While I'm sure that the minority of black staff are doing their best to make change from within, their underrepresentation is helpful context for understanding why many of the efforts to liberate our curricula are coming from student-led movements.

#DecolonisetheCurriculum

We have a right, as black students, to have our stories accurately and completely represented in our curricula. To take ownership over our degrees requires us to show our senior faculty staff what it is that they may not be able to see from their ivory towers. 'Decolonise the Curriculum', 'Why is My Curriculum White', and 'Liberate My Degree' are some of the student-led movements working to make these changes, made up of students across the country, and the world, trying to make sure that their negative experiences with their curricula are not reproduced.

The impact of the #DecolonisetheCurriculum movement has varied by university. We welcomed the announcement in 2017 that Oxford University had made it compulsory for history undergraduates to take a non-European paper, in response to the Why is My Curriculum White? movement. Departments across Cambridge also put together working groups that held almost-weekly open forums and events, in which students could highlight issues with curricula, propose solutions and alternatives, and draft letters for the consideration of senior faculty staff. The work of the 'Decolonise English' group culminated in an open letter addressed to the university's English faculty.

We believe that for the English department to truly boast academically rigorous thought and practice, non-white authors and postcolonial thought must be incorporated meaningfully into the curriculum. This is not a call for the exclusion of white men from reading lists, needless to say: it is a call to re-centre the lives of other marginalized writers who have been silenced by the canon. It is a call to not be arrogant enough to assume civilization began with the writing of white men.

Over 150 people signed the letter, which also included a list of practical suggestions that the faculty could incorporate in order to diversify their curriculum, including diversity training for supervisors and making the postcolonial and related literatures paper a mandatory requirement for first year students.

The 'Decolonise HSPS' group has been working with the HSPS faculty for years on specific modifications to the reading lists. The extent of the changes to the first-year politics paper in the past three years is a testament to their hard work. Frantz Fanon, for example, is no longer included as an add-on in a lecture on violence, but is studied as a theorist in his own right.

The working group drew up an 'Alternative Reading List', which was shared widely online. It opens with a lengthy introduction outlining its goals, beginning:

> **In the context of academic learning, decolonization may be understood as the intellectually rigorous and honest acknowledgement and recognition of the histories of violence that underlie present systems of power and knowledge. Among its key aims is a disentanglement from, and decentring of, hegemonic epistemologies and ways of knowing.**

The twenty-eight-page document was the work of students, many of whom were in their final year and drowning in exam revision, but who gave up their time regardless. Featured on the curriculum are books on racism in the Enlightenment, literature on the Cold War from the perspectives of countries in the global south, and broader critical race theory. The resource has received an incredible response. Lucy Mayblin, a senior lecturer at Sheffield University (ranked second in the country for sociology), has included the resource in an online 'global social theory' reading list. The online resource pool is available for staff everywhere seeking to decolonise their departments' curricula and for the students seeking to do the decolonising that the departments may not be.

The thing with these movements is that they work. Thanks to student efforts, and to the staff who are open to supporting them, there are some exemplary, less white curricula out there that are leading the pack. Sociology at Cambridge was refreshing. I got to write essays about race and gender and intersectionality, and my experiences didn't feel as marginalised as they had for so long. In my final year, even though I had specialised in politics and international relations, I took a sociology of race paper. In my final exams, I wrote an essay in which I explored the power dynamics perpetuated by black natural hair YouTubers. I felt I could bring my full self to every supervision and every assignment. This was the one paper where I felt that my experiences were welcomed and encouraged.

When Mikai spoke about the English degree at Warwick, I was shocked to learn that English wasn't as canonical everywhere, and that some university departments had an awareness and appreciation for books other than Homer's:

My English degree differed to a lot of people's – that's why I'm glad I ended up at Warwick. [On our reading lists,] we had Assata [Shakur]'s autobiography, we had a lot of South American women writers. We had quite a few black writers, black women writers.

In the same paper at Warwick for which you can study Homer's *Iliad* – seen as an iconic, canonical part of ancient Greek literature – you can also study Ngugi wa Thiong'o's *Petals of Blood*. This piece of social and political criticism of Kenya's post-colonial context, written in the form of an allegorical crime story, was so radical for its time that wa Thiong'o was arrested in the months after its publication. Rarely do I encounter curricula that acknowledge that writers such as Homer and wa Thiong'o belong in the same category of greatness – so rarely, that I am in disbelief each time I do.

For curricula that aren't quite there yet, we as students can work to decolonise our own academic pathways. In my international relations essays, I would introduce examples of how the United Nations has been complicit in propagating neocolonialism under the guise of African 'development' narratives, and discuss how the role of the United States in sponsoring tyrannical dictators should disqualify them from being able to call themselves anything near liberal. I would write about the Cold War, but also discuss what the precarious political situation meant for African political leaders. This was my personal battle of resistance. I didn't have it in me to fight the whole system, but I did what I could from the confines of my own desk. I didn't give World War I *or* II any more time than the minimum I had to. Without question, World War I and II were monumental events

in history, and their outcomes have shaped the ideo-
logical climate that has since persisted. However, it's
not all the history that there is.

Offering diverse curricula is not always easy. Sometimes I would find that faculties had attempted to
'diversify' by introducing ideas from postcolonial contexts that did not easily fit. In order to study these
topics, it often felt as if the onus was on us, as the few
BME students, to create tenuous links between white
and non-white contexts when they weren't always obvious, or even there at all. In my third year, for example, I
had the opportunity to study patriotism, nationalism
and postcolonialism – or at least, so it seemed. In reality, it was an attempt to throw Frantz Fanon and Aimé
Césaire into a lecture on liberal and republican nationalism. (If you have no clue what any of those words
mean: it's hard, made deliberately so, and there's a very
limited amount of available literature to guide you.)

While many of my white colleagues could choose to
answer another question or do another essay, I felt compelled to answer anything that allowed me to engage
with the black authors that were so few and far between
on our syllabuses. If I spent so much time complaining
that they weren't present enough, then surely I had to
take full advantage of the rare occasions in which they
were? I felt I had an obligation to do black theorists and
writers justice, even as they were forcefully squeezed in

as 'add-ons' to a curriculum that is still very white. And it was another instance in which I was alienated from my peers, who didn't share this sense of duty and obligation, and felt that they had true freedom in the paper choices that they made. We're fighting for curricula that allow us to also study black people in their own rights, not just as add-ons to tick a 'diversity' box.

The key point here is to speak out. If you find yourself in a position in which you can be heard, let your lecturers and your supervisors know that they will get more out of you if your curriculum is inclusive, and also reflects your reality. I would give my supervisors recommendations and ask them why we were not exploring the fact that all but one of the countries tried by the International Criminal Court have been African. There are, after all, war criminals to be found in places other than African countries who haven't been brought to justice in this way. I would ask my supervisors why we studied governments from a perspective that assumed that Western liberal democracy is the only formula for good governance. I challenged my curriculum because I felt that the movement started with me.

Arenike tried to speak up too:

I was like, 'Why haven't we studied anyone who's not white?' And he was like, 'Oh yeah, I don't know, I don't really like, read those things' – bla

bla bla. I'm just looking at him like, 'Wow. You're a PhD student. How have you gotten to where you are without reading these texts? How? How am I, an undergrad, smarter than you?'

That's when I knew university was a scam. – Arenike

You may also find supervisors who are willing to listen to your complaints. They may not always know exactly how to help, but they want to learn. My Director of Studies would always ask for suggestions; where he couldn't help me explore particular interests, he would direct me to the people and literature that could. I had a supervisor, Ali Meghji, who would send me articles and texts that weren't on my reading lists but which enabled me to develop those interests that weren't given space on my curriculum.

My Director of Studies, Deborah [Thom], she was really nice. I remember one day I said 'misogynoir'* and she was like, 'What's that? I've never heard of that. Explain it to me.' You'd have

---

* Misogynoir is a term used to describe misogyny, i.e. prejudice against women, that is specifically directed at black women. The term attributed to the American queer black feminist Moya Bailey who used it to discuss the way race and gender oppression co-exist specifically in pop culture.

to explain a lot of things to her, but what I liked was she was willing to listen. – Courtney

It's hard to say what a decolonised curriculum might look like. While some who would ask that question are often seeking to belittle the movement and the need for it, it is still worth asking. Are we trying to study the world in terms of what it might have looked like in a pre-colonial context? Because if that's the case, how do we access non-written histories, or histories in dead languages, or oral histories that have been lost and transformed through generations? If it's clear how much of our very existences, and the ideas that we have developed while existing, are products of colonialism, then what room is there for us in a decolonised curriculum? To truly 'decolonise' our curriculum requires a radical overthrow of what we even consider knowledge and how it is produced.

We assume decolonising the curriculum is just adding a few more black writers or Asian writers or whoever. I think to truly decolonise might mean a different system all together, and I don't know what that looks like. – Eireann

The same question should be asked of the way we use the word 'intersectional'. The term was coined by Kimberlé Crenshaw, and sets out an analytical framework for us to understand that the different axes of our identity cannot be considered in isolation. It was developed specifically in reference to black women, whose dual burdens of racism and sexism interact to create a unique experience of oppression. More broadly, it is now used to refer to how we approach 'diversity' for those whose layers of oppression are compounded. But what does a truly intersectional approach to a topic really look like? Chanda Prescod-Weinstein writes:

> **Theorizing about what an intersectional perspective does to our discourse and remembering that Black women exist are simply not the same thing. The former requires effort, and the latter should be your baseline.**

It requires us to go beyond merely acknowledging that black women and their histories are worthy of study, and beyond including them merely to meet an arbitrary requirement.

As black women who have experienced all of the above, we should rally round any efforts made by different groups or movements to promote a more diversified curriculum in all the different disciplines. The work that such groups do is extremely necessary for a future in which black girls aren't shocked to find themselves on curricula, and can truly identify with the authors they're made to read.

The Black Attainment Gap

The whiteness of academia is ruining our experience of university. It isolates any non-white interests that we may have before we arrive, it establishes an environment that is not conducive for us to pursue those interests, it affects the subjects that we choose to study and the industries that we are able to penetrate, and it dissuades many of us from staying the course of academia until we are in positions high enough to fix the issues ourselves.

Fundamentally, for as long as academia stays this white, black students will continue to fall short. If everything I have said so far isn't enough to show that, the 24 per cent attainment gap between black and white students should be. According to a 2018 report by Advance HE, 79.6 per cent of white UK undergraduates achieved a first or a 2:1 – but the number drops 24 percentage points to 55.5 per cent for black UK students. I know that this isn't because we aren't capable. It is because several factors – among them lopsided curricula, the lack of black academics and the difficulty finding support in navigating these institutions – are holding us back from reaching our full potential. If not properly handled, the impact these structures uniquely have on us can persist long after we graduate.

Changing these statistics is going to involve more than just black students working hard. Academic staff, from those charged with setting and teaching the national curriculum, to those at universities who have autonomy in drawing up reading lists, must listen to students and work alongside them for the betterment of our academic experience. Even though the odds are stacked against us as black students, I hope that others find strength in knowing that we have all been there, and that we've got firsts and 2:1s in spite of these odds – and that we can begin to change these statistics.

3

Mental Health

Chelsea

One morning at the beginning of my second year at university, I bounced out of bed and knocked on my best friend Holly's door. She lived next to me on our tiny narrow corridor at college, and I patiently waited for her to open up so that we could align our schedules for the day. Within seconds of her letting me in, the contraband coffee machine on her desk was already sputtering out two espresso shots. I was in love with this coffee machine and had become mildly obsessed with my morning coffee hit. *It even frothed milk* . . . If I'm honest, I was sure it wouldn't be long before we owned T-shirts saying, 'Don't talk to me until I've had my coffee!' or 'Rise and Grind!' Drinking coffee at university signified peak adulting and sophistication, not to mention endless social opportunities to meet friends in really expensive cafés. (Not that I did that any more.)

I gulped down the espresso, said goodbye to Holly and went back to my room to study. My room was my sanctuary. Sitting at my desk, lost in work, allowed me to temporarily escape the pressure bubble of Cambridge life. And it wasn't as if I really needed to leave: the canteen and college café were downstairs; my supervisions were upstairs, and the launderette was down the corridor. My room was where I was the most productive, unlike most of my fellow students, who had set up a shifting camp in the twenty-four-hour library, armed with their own cardboard cups of coffee, modafinil and rollies for the rare cigarette break.

As you can imagine, however, staying in my room didn't create the most outgoing of lifestyles. By that morning, I had missed around three weeks of lectures. I hadn't even left the college in nine days. The strange thing was, no one batted an eyelid. It was so easy to slip under the radar. We were all working, and we all had our own deadlines to meet. It wasn't weird that the corridors were silent throughout the day. It wasn't weird if you hadn't seen someone in a few days.

Back at my desk, it didn't take long for the caffeine to hit me. But this time, rather than feeling energised, I felt jittery. I was finding it increasingly hard to concentrate, and became very conscious that I was alone from the familiar silence in the halls. I headed downstairs to the café to fill up my water bottle and buy a sandwich. As I went to pay, I was offered a free latte by one of the staff members. Really, I should have declined but the student in me popped out. A *free* coffee? Unheard of. It also had a smiley face carefully stencilled on top of the frothed milk. How could I say no?

But I should have done. Twenty minutes later, I was experiencing one of the worst anxiety attacks that I have ever had in my life. It was debilitating. For around six hours I stayed in my room alone – not out of choice, but because I couldn't move. I sat at my desk shaking profusely, still trying to push through my weekly task of reading seven articles and completing a 2,500-word essay. Wave after wave of panic hit me. My heart was beating so hard I feared that I was likely to drop down dead any minute, and no one would find me until it was too late. Death by coffee.

How would I explain to someone that this crisis was triggered by coffee? Everyone drinks coffee, every day! It felt ridiculous. But perhaps most worrying was that I didn't even know who to go to in the first place. Was it my own belief that this crisis wasn't *serious enough*? Or was it that I still wasn't ready to admit that my anxiety had reached a worrying level? Over the past few years, it had become increasingly bad: stress-induced panic attacks, overthinking and bouts of self-doubt. I had absorbed it as part of my personality, thinking that it was just another character trait.

Eventually, I built up the courage to text a friend and ask if I could sit in her room. Luckily, she was in and we sat down on her bed and watched season 10 of *Ru Paul's Drag Race*, my heart still thumping worryingly fast. I cursed the coffee gods, and made a promise to never put myself in that position again.

Black Effect: Mental Health at University

Universities across the country are currently in the grip of a mental health crisis. In 2015–16, over 15,000 first-year students (UK-based) disclosed mental health issues. Yet a Freedom of Information request by the Liberal Democrat Norman Lamb revealed that at 100 universities, students had to wait up to four months to access counselling and mental health support. Suicide rates among university students in England and Wales have risen to seriously concerning levels, with ninety-five students committing suicide between 2016 and 2017 – one every four days. At the University of Bristol alone, there were ten suspected suicides in the space of eighteen months.

This comes at a time when conversations regarding mental health are opening up. Society, it seems, is beginning to realise that mental health is important. And nowhere is the question of mental health more important than at university. Most people with a mental illness first develop symptoms between the ages of sixteen and twenty-five.

By third year if I met someone who hadn't experienced a mental health problem, I thought that that was more notable than meeting someone who had. – Micha

Each university has been left to its own devices to decide how best to tackle mental health issues within their own student populations. The University of Cumbria, for example, made suicide prevention and awareness training available for all staff in a bid to create 'compassionate campuses'. Over 12 per cent of all staff have now been trained. Similarly, the University of Brunel's security officers have been trained by the disability and counselling services to adequately respond to mental health crises among students.

There are, however, significant variations in provision surrounding mental health care within UK universities, with some universities doing much more than others. This signifies the varying ideas of what mental health actually is, and when it warrants external attention. As a result, some universities experience dramatic increases in demand. With the breaking down of the stigma of mental health and disabilities, it is clear that more students are starting to come forward and seek help. It's one thing to acknowledge that a university is addressing mental health – but just how well are they really doing it?

Some might say that the university environment and culture thrive on self-inflicted suffering. In my case, it was promising myself that I would eat breakfast only *after* I finished the chapter that I had failed to finish the night before; promising myself that I would sleep only *after* I finished everything on my to-do list for that day. For the first few weeks of university, it was all about keeping up, and that meant spending hours in the college library. This lifestyle was continuously validated every time I logged into Instagram to see the obligatory 3-a.m.-in-the-library-and-I-haven't-slept-in-forty-eight-hours photo of other students. It was a constant reminder that if I thought that I was working hard, there was always someone working harder. But by the end of a week-long stint in the library, I was snapped fast asleep on the library desk with my laptop next to me. Clearly, I just couldn't keep up.

At university, I experienced some of the worst mental health issues I have ever faced. I'm still unsure whether these issues developed as a result of university, or whether the transition process unearthed pre-existing conditions. In my first year, I remember being totally overwhelmed by Cambridge's email system. I hadn't really used email before university, believe it or not (my princesskwakye@hotmail.com account was exclusively for MSN Messenger). When I received an email from my supervisor asking what date and time I'd like to meet, I would draft a response. Then re-draft. Then delete it all and start again. Then re-draft. Then Google 'how do you sign off an email when you don't know the person?' Then call a friend to check what they had sent to their supervisor. Then ask them to read my attempt.

Only *then* would it be safe to send. I also spent an unnecessary amount of time worrying about cycling. My route to lectures became an imagined race course that would, I was certain, result in death-by-car at any moment. I returned to Cambridge after my first term with an extreme sports helmet clamped on my head . . . you know, just in case. My point is, the way I learnt to understand my own mental health was unexpected. There wasn't a 'sudden' change.

But something was going on – for me, and for others like me. And like many people, I didn't have a clue who was the best person to go to when I felt that I needed to talk. As expected, the added stresses associated with transitioning into a new environment definitely had an impact, as well as moving away from home, loneliness, deadlines, finances and getting to grips with this thing called 'email'.

*

There is already substantial evidence to suggest that racial discrimination and marginalisation contribute to mental illnesses within young black people in the UK. The 2014 Adult Psychiatric Morbidity Survey (APMS) discovered that the prevalence of common mental health problems varied dramatically by ethnic group for women, but not for men. Black British and non-British women were both found to be more likely to have a 'common mental health problem' (29.3 per cent) by comparison with white British women (20.9 per cent).

Black women are seen as the epitome of self-sacrifice, holding it down for everyone around them and always considering themselves last – a glamorised stereotype. Simultaneously, the 'strong black woman' is also policed to make sure she doesn't come across as *too* strong. We all know that we can't possibly be the *angry* one or the *loud* one. In fact, we're constantly told to hold it all in – the emotion (and/or rage). There is no licence to show emotion that allows us to be vulnerable, especially when many of our mental health issues are rooted in daily experiences of racism.

I don't want to be strong all the time. And it's not even a strength in myself, I have to be strong for my people, strong for my community, strong in relationships. The black woman always has to be the strong one and that's a silencing mechanism because it means we're not able to express weakness, we're not allowed to express vulnerability, and I think that's a fundamental flaw in our conceptions of black women. – Renée

How such tropes play out in university environments is rarely spoken about. In December 2018, the *Guardian* began its 'Racial Bias' series, which aimed to document racial inequalities within the UK. If you're a person of colour in Britain, I'm sure its report didn't come as a shock. In fact, I pretty much scrolled past it. It revealed that black students in England are 1.5 times more likely to drop out than their white and Asian counterparts.

The uncomfortable truth is that universities in the UK are hotbeds for explicit and implicit racism. From the words 'MONKEY' and 'NIGGA' found written on Warwick student Faramade Ifaturoti's bunch of bananas to fellow students chanting 'we hate the blacks' outside Rufaro Chisango's room at Nottingham Trent University, issues such as these are *not* isolated. On my first day at Cambridge, I was asked whether I could dance because 'black people are really good at dancing' – as if I was a minstrel ready to spring into action at the clap of a hand. For anyone still wondering: no, I can't dance. Not all black people can. Thank you for coming to my TED Talk.

On my first day, someone asked me if I was in a gang – Kenya

We had a post office on campus. The post office guy said, 'Oh, do you work here?' . . . I get that a lot on campus, 'Do you work here?' or 'Excuse me, could you show me where this is?' Am I a sales assistant of Warwick? – Mikai

The problem is not limited to overt instances of racism. Racial microaggressions are commonplace for most black girls at universities. The term 'microaggressions' was coined by Harvard professor Chester M. Pierce in 1970 to describe the insults and dismissals he witnessed non-black Americans inflicting on African Americans. Since then, the term has been revised to include commonplace and daily exchanges – not being acknowledged, or complimenting good use of English. For me, what was most tiresome was having to always consider whether something was a microaggression or not. Imagine going through your day-to-day life and having to wonder whether someone has treated you differently because you're black – because more often than not, the answer is yes.

The majority of the UK's top universities are rife with environmental microaggressions. In the not-too-distant past, a lot of people actively didn't want you here. The remnants of those beliefs are still very much apparent and play an active part in our daily university experiences, from the portraits of white, heterosexual, upper-class men on the walls to still being the only black student in a year group.

You want to talk about other political and structural reasons why your mental health can be severely affected. But when you bring those

things up, it's like, 'Oh, you're making it political. . .' And there's often a failure to acknowledge that they're really intertwined. – Micha

Understanding of mental health cannot be detached from daily racial experiences, which in turn means that the mental health of black women is largely political. Racial microaggressions are subtle yet significant forms of racism that may seem harmless, but their cumulative and constant burden can lead to a dramatic impact on mental wellbeing. Sadly, many fail to recognise or acknowledge this fundamental fact, because to them if it can't quantified or measured, it doesn't exist.

Black Excellence?

As a black girl, you are subject to a number of expectations: the expectation to be strong, for example – but also, if you manage to get into university, and especially one of the top universities in the country, the expectation to excel. For those unfamiliar with it: the term 'Black Excellence' can be used to commend or congratulate someone black for achieving a certain goal. Alternatively, it can be used in a communal sense, as a means of furthering a positive perception of black people. Think Diddy's Instagram captions: 'It's bigger than being billionaires, it's about owning our culture and leading the revolution #blackexcellence' or simply, 'B L A C K E X C E L L E N C E'. Black Excellence characterises everything that mainstream media has taught us *not* to believe. It draws on a golden thread running throughout the black community, stirring up a sense of pride and inspiration around anyone who succeeds in generating a positive perception.

At Bath Spa University, a photo exhibition entitled 'Black Excellence' displayed the faces of what they called 'the incredible array of BME talent' at the university. Staff, students and alumni were all included as a way of bringing attention to why Black History Month is so important and why it should continue to be celebrated. One of the subjects was Dr Olivette Otele, the first black, female history professor in the UK. Representation has to start somewhere, and from my own social echo chamber, black excellence narratives highlight the beauty in black people sharing a moment together. Yet some of our understandings of black excellence still revolve around white validation. It's hard to define, by our own standards, what it means to be successful. It becomes a form of respectability politics, whereby only a certain *type* of black student or person can be 'successful'. There is an extra shout-out or an even louder toot for a young black person who gains a place at Oxford or Cambridge. Taking up space in traditionally white institutions is heralded as the epitome of resistance – in reality, it's more likely to be acquiescence, accommodation and compromise. Black people (in this case black students) subsequently feel the pressure to live up to unrealistic expectations of self. This pressure all too often impacts our mental health.

All of a sudden, your actions and very existence become the blueprint for all things black. For me, that meant not showing my tutors, lecturers and support staff any signs of my anxiety, because I wanted to prove to people that Cambridge wasn't *too* hard for me and that *I* didn't struggle. Throughout my degree, I tried to demonstrate that I wasn't 'just' a black student that they had let in as part of some access ploy, that I was as good as everyone else.

Simply existing in white spaces can be exhausting – so you can only imagine the pressure of the added cloud of Black Excellence hanging over your every move. Excellence doesn't give you the opportunity to fail and disappoint, nor the room for trial and error. Ọrẹ admitted that from the outset many may have viewed her as an example of Black Excellence. As a Cambridge student and chair of one of the most successful ACSs in the UK, she has continued to push a positive perception of black students, and was vocal about what else needed to be done to ensure that black students are fully included at traditionally white universities. But often the reality was that:

> **Everyone is watching you. The eyes are on you. Don't just be the black person who got in . . . be the black person who got in and got a first. The black person who got in, got a first and got a training contract. Got in, got a first, and got five training contracts!**

Black Excellence pressure does not stop when you accept your university place. The narrative means that many black students are automatically expected to stand for the whole black community. Mikai spoke about how this understanding of acceptability is a constant cycle:

> **I think that black students always have to be proving something to someone, which is very damaging. If you're not proving to your parents, you're proving to your tutor, you're proving to your examiner, proving to somebody that what you stand for is worth it, is worth attention, is worth glory.**

Most of this behavioural pattern is engendered by a feeling of 'gratitude' experienced by most black students. There's a belief that you've been given a *chance*. You can't be the one to mess it up. But what happens if you are struggling? Or think that you are messing up? The 24 per cent black attainment gap at university reveals a downward spiral: it is clear that there is a faltering point (or phase) between black students entering university on a par with other students, and yet leaving with lower grades.

If I'm honest, I'm still conflicted around the Black Excellence narrative. I found it destructive at times, and used it as an excuse to push myself to impossible heights. At other times, I saw how far the narrative encouraged students to fulfil their existing potential, knowing that there is a whole community rooting for them. Either way, as long as success is defined on your own terms and beliefs, I give you permission to write your own Diddy Instagram captions.

Getting Help

One weekend in between exams, I decided to go home. I sat quietly in the kitchen and watched my mum wash plates in the sink. She could tell that I was tired. I had huge bags under my eyes and had fallen asleep at least two times that day. After five minutes of silence, she turned to face me and said, 'I'm proud of you no matter what. The end grade doesn't matter as long as you try your best, you've done enough.' I can't explain how perfectly timed those words were. My philosophy as the youngest child had always been, 'Chelsea, you need to work hard and sort yourself out, so your parents can go back to Ghana. They can't be worrying about you.' I wanted to, and still plan to, look after my parents. But with that comes a heightened level of stress, commitment and pressure.

For many students, it's easy to imagine families or support systems as sponges, ready to absorb our traumas and problems, helping us to feel better. But for many black families, 'strong' is valued, and persistence and resilience are favoured. The cultural understanding of mental health is different, and so is the language to conceptualise it, meaning that when mental health problems appear, African and Caribbean parents can be slow to respond. Parents or relatives may start to blame themselves and ask what they have done to 'fail' you. Some parents might tell you to pray and strengthen your relationship with God. Many parents or carers may wonder what you have to complain about: you should be *grateful*. Most of our parents came from places where mental health problems were hardly spoken of, to the point that they were made invisible. Yet here we are: educated, likely to become employable, the world at our feet, pretty much – but we *still* have something to moan about.

When I was younger a family friend said, 'Oh, anorexia is a white person's disease.' So, it just feels like if you are suffering from a mental health issue, then you're being weak or you're too Westernised. I think definitely now, at least amongst my parents' generation, the kids are getting more literate in the language of mental health. It's getting better. – Arenike

African and Caribbean communities in the UK deal with mental health problems differently to white British society. The relationship between mental health provision in the UK and the black community is complex. For starters, black men and women are more likely to engage with mental health services through the courts or the police than on their own terms.

I've always thought that with being Caribbean, a lot comes from legacies of slavery. The idea about having been through so much historical trauma, probably as a collective . . . you haven't had a chance or time to be vulnerable, to be weak, because you have to just keep pushing on. Especially if [you're] living in the UK and enduring racism. – Micha

You can't expect them [African parents] to be perfect when nobody has paid them any attention, no one has even told them that you're allowed to feel these emotions, they don't even have the room to be upset. My parents actually knew I was depressed before I knew. – Adaobi

The link between mental illness and racial trauma is something that most black people are very familiar with. Conversations surrounding mental health tend to skirt over the various elements that explain the position of black people today. The system's inability to work with socio-political forces that disproportionately affect black people renders our unique experiences invisible. Despite being less likely to receive the support we need and facing isolation within wider society, we're yet to consider how black people would benefit from a wholly inclusive service. It's time we stepped away from the assumption that mental health is apolitical.

Students are starting to seek professional support such as counselling a lot earlier, rather than having to do so when reaching crisis point. Upon reaching an agreement with yourself that help is needed, counselling can be a good way to air existing issues or past traumas. However, many black students, particularly black women, may find that counselling at university is not always the best option when dealing with mental health problems – most of which originate and continue to exist because of issues to do with race. The ease with which we talk about counselling and 'talking to someone' as a viable option shows how far from an inter-cultural health system we really are. With few (sometimes no) black counsellors working in universities across the country, this provides another huge barrier to addressing the mental health problems of black women. I always took comfort when I didn't have to *explain* why I thought something was racist. My black friends just knew it, and most had experienced the exact same feelings. But your friends shouldn't have to be a last-resort option.

You can't just give any counsellor to anyone. You will be telling your [white] counsellor things and she will be thinking, 'Why are you upset? This is not a big deal' . . . It puts you off wanting to even seek help in the first place,

which is a big step to take: to admit that you need help. – Mikai

Micha, who was previously Cambridge Student Union's Welfare and Rights Officer, played a significant role in ensuring that for the first time, black and minority ethnic students could request to see BME counsellors. In pushing for the change, she found that words such as 'explaining', 'lecturing' and 'teaching' came up more than once in students' testimonials, demonstrating how therapy can quickly slip into providing emotional and educational labour just to get your therapist on the 'same page as you'. Students also found that they were 'routinely questioned about the validity and accuracy' of their experiences of racism.

When I had CBT [Cognitive Behavioural Therapy] last year, a lot of the problems I had [were in] telling my CBT counsellor, who was a white man. I was like, a lot of the problems I have [are], you know, racism, sexism, that [affect] my mental health, so you know, it means I can't really make friends. And his answer was, 'Go to more society events, *make friends.*' – Fope

A general approach to mental health is not the best way to tackle the growing crisis. Marginalised groups, such as black women, will continue to be misaddressed by health services that are racialised. It is virtually impossible to disentangle structures such as race, class, gender, disability and sexuality from mental health. Individuals such as Dr Isha McKenzie-Mavinga, an integrative transcultural psychotherapist, recognise this, and actively try to carve out safe places for black women to share their experiences and 'not feel mad and isolated'. Using the term 'black empathic approach', McKenzie-Mavinga has created a safe space in which black women's experiences are not denied but are validated. Similarly, the Black, African and Asian Therapy Network (BAATN) helps to connect BAME people with counsellors of the same or similar ethnic origin.

Alternatively, first points of call may become lecturers or personal and academic tutors, who are immediately more accessible to students. This pushes the point that understandings of mental health need to extend beyond the student in an academic sense. There is often a disconnect between what is happening on campuses and what is happening in classrooms. Those who work at universities – lecturers, professors, personal tutors and support staff – regularly encounter students in distress, yet this is largely removed from the conversation of mental health.

A study completed by Student Minds found that 'responding to student mental health problems now appears to be an inevitable part of the role of an academic' – academics being 'all staff employed to teach, supervise or tutor students in a university'. It revealed that when some academics encountered mental health problems in a student, they were able to notify the relevant student services team. However, responses to this were 'variable'. Crucially, 'there were differences of opinion around what constitutes a crisis and the urgency with which students should receive formal support'. The majority of staff are unsure about the fine line between moral and professional duties which bind staff to reporting or recommending formal support. All of this ties into a wider safeguarding question of whether academics should have a duty to report incidents, and whether current guidelines are adequate. Yet it is clear from the Student Minds report that students are becoming more reliant on academics, especially those with whom they come into contact every week. With the alleviation of immediate pressures, you can manage your workload, shift deadlines and plead mitigating circumstances if needed.

I found the idea of speaking to an academic hard. I didn't want them to pity me, or to give anyone any reason to suggest that I couldn't cope with university life. I didn't want my blackness to be misconstrued into a form of weakness, so in typical black-woman style, I coerced myself into silence. How could I possibly tell the very people who let me in that I was struggling to keep up? Or that I truly believed that they had made a mistake in accepting me into university?

It would have been nice to have a black woman to speak to. This isn't to say that because she's a black woman we're going to have the same experiences because we're black, because I hate putting black people in boxes like that, but she might have been able to relate. – Adaobi

It shouldn't be assumed that BME friends, counsellors, therapists or academics will automatically understand our personal traumas. A black male counsellor may be able to relate to the racial strife of black people, but not necessarily how ideas of patriarchy intersect with race. Nonetheless, where professional help is available, using it to the best of our ability is a sure advantage. As shown by Micha's efforts, the act of introducing BAME counsellors is a huge step towards addressing issues of the inclusivity of black students within universities.

Self-Care 101

Besides counselling and university services, self-care includes taking productive steps to improving your lifestyle. The day after coffeegate, my neighbour Holly offered to walk forty-five minutes into town with me, as I was still too shaken to cycle to our American history lecture that morning, extreme sports helmet or no extreme sports helmet. We took the scenic route through the meadow, and tried to tactically dodge the cows in the middle of the path. Most importantly, she encouraged me to unpack my anxiety attack, and then was kind enough to share her own experiences with mental health. Don't get me wrong – the panic attacks didn't magically stop. But I learnt the best ways to manage them, and the positive steps I took after that day made my university experience a lot more pleasant.

Managing my anxiety at university was about pinpointing the main stressors and alleviating that stress as much as possible. If that meant unapologetically saying no, changing deadlines and putting myself first, then so be it. Mental health is important. Don't do what I did, and delay in addressing it.

To survive every single day in that environment is always going to be a struggle. So, self-care is like having a plant and keeping it alive. – Arenike

Your university room is likely to be pretty basic: desk, lamp, cupboard. It can feel impersonal and temporary at best, a little institutional at worst. At a time at which everything seemed to be strange and bewildering, bringing items from home helped me create my home away from home. By items, I mean *anything*. Before we left home, I would scavenge bits of wrapping paper, raid old family photo albums, and pile up my favourite throws and blankets. I forced my dad and my older brother to find space in the car for my fluffy red carpet, fairy lights and giant vanity mirror. It was quite a sight watching them lug everything in to my room. I would dedicate the first day of term to organising the furniture and furnishings, before venturing out in search of Blu-tac and a cute house plant or two. I stuck up photographs of my family and friends from home, especially all the important black women in my life, like my mum and my sister, and surrounded their faces with quotes and Ankara fabric. Whenever I felt low or down, going to my room always picked me up. I felt I wasn't alone.

I never had pictures up, not even a plant, not even a candle. Like, my friends used to come over all the time and be like, *not even a cheeky fairy light?* What's a fairy light? No, I want to lay my head, get up and go. Like it did not feel like home. I loved having my own space, but it wasn't home. I didn't feel settled in. – Courtney

Taking time to settle in to your new space can make a real difference in adjusting to university life – but even when your room is perfectly decorated, it can still feel as if something is missing. There was a general consensus among everyone we interviewed that surrounding yourself with not only familiar items, but also with people who are like you, online and offline, was crucial to maintaining good mental health.

This is what we say in every BAME network at the beginning of each session: 'Find your tribe.' – Fope

Sometimes, self-care just means protecting yourself from environments and people who you might find harmful. The moments you feel energised and alive will be with people who you can relate to the most. This doesn't have to be only one group; different groups or 'tribes' can serve different purposes in your life. In particular, online spaces have become invaluable for black women. In real life, there are not many safe spaces for us to meet, socialise, vent or simply have candid conversations. Black women around the world are waiting and eager to be connected, and to learn about each other's experiences. Finding your tribe is also about listening to the experiences of older black women, who are accessible thanks to the internet. Through common struggles, jokes and trends, there's something reassuring about knowing there's someone out there who looks like you *and* feels the same as you do. When asked where she found refuge at university, this is what Mikai had to say:

> **On YouTube! With my subscribers. On Instagram when I be writing those long [posts], when my head is going to fall off and my dissertation is coming to kill me everyone will be commenting, 'Same, sis!'**

Listening to podcasts was revolutionary for me when it came to discovering other online spaces. Schedule at least one hour a day when you can be still, listen and take on helpful tips. You can skip around and find topics that are most relevant to you. The 'Therapy for Black Girls' podcast is a weekly conversation with psychologist Dr Joy Harden Bradford. Also, Oprah's 'SuperSoul' podcast is designed to 'guide you through life's big questions and help bring you one step closer to your best self'. For around an hour, just listening to someone else talk, laugh and debate was enough to temporarily stop my thoughts. I didn't need to be stressed or feel particularly down to listen to podcasts, but found it a useful way to wind down and disconnect for a bit. By the end of term, I didn't care if the whole corridor could hear me screaming or laughing at Tolly T, Audrey, formally known as Ghana's Finest, and Mamacita Milena

Sanchez on the podcast 'The Receipts'. The girls have carved out their own online haven for women of colour, who have the opportunity to listen to conversations that are unapologetic and open. From 'The struggle is real but not necessary' to 'Role models and the price of virginity', it's like being in a WhatsApp group chat with people who feel like your older sisters.

Another outlet, you might be surprised to learn, is self-care apps. We're regularly told that the key to mental wellbeing and vitality is staying away from our phones and limiting our screen time. I agree that mindless scrolling and scrutinising the lifestyles of others can be really unhelpful when you're trying to focus on what is best for yourself. But downloading an app meant that self-care didn't have to be expensive or complicated; it also made information accessible, anywhere and anytime.

The Student Health App is free, and was founded by experienced doctors who want to support the self-care of students, 'which is about avoiding disease, maintaining health, handling illness and disability'. Bristol, UCL, Lady Margaret Hall at Oxford and St Andrews have partnered with the app. It provides a personalised service for students; with a click of a button, you're directed to your university's helplines and services. It's just one way of addressing the need for mental health services, at least preventative measures, to be more accessible. Apps like Headspace, the @tinycarebot on Twitter and Daylio are some other personal favourites that act as light reminders to address your mental health every day – not just when you're feeling low.

*

But sometimes decorating your room or finding a suitable app isn't enough. One of the questions I asked our interviewees was whether they ever felt like dropping out. Here's what some of them said.

> **Oh, only every day. Every single day. – Mikai**

> **No, I'll be honest and say no. I'm really grateful for that. – Eireann**

> **I felt like I wanted to drop out, but I knew I never would. I was going to change universities, but I was never going to drop out of university completely. – Kenya**

Personally, I really didn't think it was an option to take time out. Practically speaking, I didn't know anything about how I would even go about doing it. I was only familiar with taking a year out before university (gap yah) to have a short break before going back into education. It was only once I got to university that I heard of intermitting. The process of intermitting (sometimes referred to as intercalating) is designed to allow students to have a temporary break from studies for medical or non-medical reasons. It serves to reinforce the idea that university isn't going anywhere, despite being under the constant impression that we have to do things to a strict timeline.

Students have worked hard to make this process more transparent and ensure that support systems, such as providing a smooth transition back into university life, are in place for those who do decide to take a break from their studies. It offers a compromise, in that you don't have to completely drop out, but you can accept that your mental state or current situation is not conducive to you doing your best.

University self-care is fundamentally about striking a work-life balance. Learn to relax over any weekends, breaks, holidays or vacations you have away from the university environment. Time away is crucial to recouping your energy. Whether that means sleeping for a week straight, or taking part in hobbies or sports, it's a chance for you to do something that makes *you* feel good – because no one else will do it for you. Self-care doesn't have to be a sudden action that dramatically changes your life. Instead, slowly building on something you achieved yesterday and the days before can offer a big win.

Try and have a good time. Even if that does mean sacking off your work sometimes and taking a decent long nap. 'Cos that is fun, believe me. – Nathania

No one's going to kill you for going for a cheeky cider. – Barbara

Thinking Out Loud

University is a trying time, and the transition may or may not drain you. Especially when you're a black girl in a predominately white institution, your resilience will be slowly chipped away. Self-care will be a somewhat radical attempt to put yourself first. Not everyone will understand – and that doesn't matter. Most of the time, if you have mental health issues you don't want to have to constantly drag up deep and personal anecdotes all the time. Similarly, the onus shouldn't *always* be on you to 'speak up'. Instead, there needs to be a wider conversation about how and why the wider university system fails to incorporate student wellbeing into its fundamental structure.

You may be in a position where you don't have any existing issues with your mental health, or won't experience any at university. Where possible, ask how to help, and offer to be available for support to those around you who are experiencing issues. But never lose sight of the fact that prioritising your own mental health is more important. It may seem like a basic thing to say, but just as you have to pay attention to your physical health, you should do the same for your mental health. If you're in bed with the flu, you wouldn't go for a ten-mile run, you'd go to the doctor. If you're feeling particularly stressed or anxious, don't push yourself to work even harder – seek out someone to speak to about it, and give yourself a break. Never feel that you're alone. Everyone has to maintain their mental health to some degree. For me, this has meant that charting the good days is equally as important as charting the bad ones.

It may well be, though, that 'self-care' tips are hard to implement – especially if you're at crisis point. Little is said about mental health disorders such as bipolar disorder, psychosis and mania, and borderline personality disorders. We need to ask whether mental health conversations are truly becoming more open – or whether it's only those around anxiety and depression that are becoming more open. For most, mental health problems do not come in smooth, pre-packaged, manageable bouts. It's often irregular feelings of intense highs and extreme lows. Nothing in this chapter should be a substitute for seeking professional or medical advice and help.

Universities should not be seen as places only of education and academic excellence. They should utilise their positions to promote resources that help develop healthy students, staff and the wider community. Students across all universities have worked incredibly hard to address gaping holes in mental health provision. There really is no excuse. Students create the fabric of university life and therefore should be valued in a holistic sense.

4

Finding Spaces

Ọrẹ

Before I came to university, I had heard plenty about the infamous 'Freshers' Week'. Freshers' week refers to the first week (or few days) of university, during which a series of social events are planned by student groups to help first years, or freshers, mingle.

I had seen all my brother's pictures from his freshers' week at Newcastle, and heard about the foam parties, bar crawls and random fancy dress events. Freshers' week was sold to me as 'organised fun' that would be an interesting yet essential part of my university experience. I expected it to be where I would make my first and best friends, bond with everyone that I lived with, and consume copious amounts of alcohol that I knew I would later regret. Although I was nervous, the prospect of complete independence, with what seemed like no rules, excited me.

Luckily, I had made a few friends before I started university. At my college interview, I had met and befriended Alex, who had also got a place; he became my first friend – and eventually one of my best friends in those three years. We relied on each other for sanity in exam season and lifted each other up when the work got relentless. But Alex wasn't the only friend I had been lucky enough to meet before university. Chelsea and I have a cute love story too. At a careers event for 'high-achieving' black students in the weeks before we started university, I got busy networking with black students headed to universities across the country. On the way home, a group of us girls walked to the tube station together. Chelsea was one of them, and we began to talk about how scared we were to start Cambridge. We swapped numbers, as she was getting on the tube in the other direction, and for the next few days, we made plans ahead of freshers' week. We planned outfits, discussed where we were going to find plantain and looked for Cambridge hairstylists that could help us touch up our braids during term time.

But five days before I was due to start university, disaster struck. I was home alone in the kitchen. I had made a pot of jollof rice and another pot of chicken stew. After seeing a good deal on plantain outside West Croydon station, I said to myself, why not fry some plantain on the side? I got a bit excited in the kitchen, and whacked the whole pan of blazing hot oil and plantain onto both of my thighs. After waiting two hours for an ambulance, my neighbour put me in a cab to A&E with bad subdermal burns. The doctors ordered that I was to be in and out of hospital for two weeks. I managed to hobble up to Cambridge and into university for my college matriculation photo and a sexual consent workshop. But for the most part, my highly anticipated freshers' week was cancelled. I was distraught.

As it turned out, apparently I didn't miss much.

> [Freshers' week was] everything that I could imagine but ten times worse. – Kenya

> I remember I cried. Loads. I was super, super worried about friends. I really didn't meet many people that I thought I got on really well with. – Micha

> Oh my gosh, the memory of freshers' week makes me feel sick. It was objectively one of the worst things I've ever gone through in my entire life. – Renée

> I went out once, came back really early and have never been to a party again. – Adaobi

During freshers' week, some people have fun. Everyone else puts on a brave face and *acts* like they're having fun. Most people are terribly homesick, struggling to deal with their newfound independence, missing their old friends who are now spread to all four corners of the country, and surrendering themselves to an experience that for the most part is terribly awkward. In student forums online, many students will tell you that freshers' week is filled with 'lots of booze and sex' – and just as many will tell you that this is an overplayed stereotype and really isn't the case. Either way, most students agree that they only made their real friends in the weeks that followed.

However, even in those weeks afterwards, I personally still found it quite hard to settle into university. To try and fit in, and to catch up on missing freshers' week, I found myself engaging in habits that were very unlike me, simply because it felt as if that was what everyone else at university was doing. I would go to clubs with music that I hated and hang around the smoking areas (though I don't even smoke), having really long conversations with strangers in the freezing cold. Then I would head back to college, stinking of smoke and battling a cough. Nothing about it was enjoyable for me, but I would do it again and again, because I was led to believe that was the only way people were making friends. After weeks of this uncomfortable ritual, I still felt really lonely. It wasn't that the people I met weren't *nice* – but I just didn't think that they were my kind of people. I was looking for all the other black girls that I could stick to, who would stick up for me, and who would tell me that they could relate to what I was feeling. I remember telling my friends from home that I could die in my room and no one would know for days. I didn't feel that I had met anyone who genuinely cared about me.

Imposter syndrome, and the broader feeling that you are inadequate, is something that most students will experience in the early days. Pauline Clance and Suzanne Imes, the psychologists who coined the term, describe it as the 'internal experience of intellectual phoniness in people who believe that they are not intelligent, capable or creative despite evidence of high achievement'. While imposter syndrome is something that most students feel to some degree, you suffer from it uniquely when you are also made to stand out by your status as a racial minority. Your feeling like an 'imposter' is made visible, reinforced by the relative absence of people who look like you. A 2013 study by a group of American psychologists revealed that feelings of stress and minority-related depression in education were highest in black students. It's only in hindsight that I can understand that I was dealing with something similar. I was constantly censoring myself, having to be someone else in order to have a chance of being accepted. I felt that in order to thrive in this new university space, I would have to leave my full self – my *black* self – at the door. Only later would I realise how much of an emotional toll this had taken on me.

While it's common for those dealing with imposterism to struggle alone and in silence, I would learn from the friends I later made that I was not the only one feeling this, and that many had it worse than I did. These feelings of imposterism and minority-related depression manifest even more for black working-class students, who are marginalised by both their racial and class identities.

> **When I got to university, it was the task of juggling a sense of belonging in a very middle-to-upper-class higher education system and still existing in a working-class home that completely threw me. – Chelsea.**

While Chelsea was struggling on a student loan that almost always fell short every term, she would overhear other students talking about how they had spent over £600 in a month on brunch. For her, class was as significant an obstacle as race when it came to settling in. It exacerbated her experience of imposter syndrome, and she found herself retreating from university and college life.

If you've never really left a big city before, you may be surprised to discover that very few places in the UK have the same level of diversity as London, Manchester or Birmingham. Moving far away may mean that you're separated from those aspects of your culture that were so central to your life before university. To make up for the friends I had not made at Cambridge, I found myself going back to London (I will personally fight anyone who tells me Croydon is not in London) every week or two to see my old friends. I constantly felt the need to escape, to be in spaces where I could be my full self, not whatever weird version of myself I was trying to be in those early days at university.

At last, one evening in my second term, I had a long conversation with three people who would go on to become some of my best friends at university. After that conversation, I cried – and then called my mum, telling her that I had found my people, that for the first time I felt that if I died in my room, these were people who would care enough to check up on me. It was at this point that I felt I had finally settled in.

Fitting In

There is a lot of drinking at university. A *lot*. A whopping 79 per cent of respondents to a 2018 survey by the National Union of Students (NUS) said that drinking is a part of university culture. When you arrive at university, it may feel that everyone's idea of fun is to get really drunk, go clubbing, rinse and repeat. 'Pre-drinks', house parties and student nights at clubs are the main form of socialising, especially in the early days. And by drinking I don't just mean the odd glass of wine – it was more commonly situations like drinking beer out of a pipe attached to a keg and then spinning around several times until you vomited. And then going again. Arriving at lectures with hangovers is normalised, if not glamorised.

Young adults are the most likely age group to binge on alcohol (according to the Office for National Statistics), and this is partly due to drinking cultures at universities. We used the 'work hard, play hard' mantra to justify our alcohol intake in the new high-pressure environment of university, but for many, alcohol becomes not only a way to relax but an increasingly-turned-to means of coping with the challenges.

Drinking is so central to life at some universities that there are societies that revolve around it. I was in an all-girls drinking society at my college, the Black Widows. Historically, 'exclusive' drinking societies at Oxford and Cambridge such as the Bullingdon Club and the Pitt Club have been reserved for the wealthiest white, male students (David Cameron and Boris Johnson were both members of Oxford's Bullingdon Club). Most drinking societies are known for being very exclusionary, and allowing only people who went to private schools to be members. They are institutions that represent a marker of social privileges across identity groups and another context in which male privilege at university is perpetuated. I accepted an invitation to join the Black Widows at the end of my first year because it seemed like yet another opportunity to socialise and actually make some friends in my college and across the university. In events called 'swaps', female drinking societies and male drinking societies would go out to dinner together, and would aim to get as drunk as possible through drinking games and challenges. Although I never encountered such vile situations myself, the stories of sexual harassment, bullying, classism and racism in many other drinking societies make it clear that they are problematic. In the spring of 2018, a Cambridge-based Facebook page, known for anonymous submissions, became dedicated to exposing drinking societies, publishing the accounts of victims of bullying and sexual misconduct within them. People shared their horror stories, with some saying their drinks had been spiked, and others complaining about incidents in which male societies sang chants about rape.

While I soon realised that drinking societies weren't exactly my idea of fun, I still loved going clubbing, and I found out that there was more than one way to go about enjoying nightlife (and drinking) at university. I found a night called 'Fleek Fridays' that played all the Afrobeats and RnB that I wanted to hear. The friends who would turn up with me on most Fridays soon followed. It effectively became the 'black music' night and I loved it. I needed it.

We cannot ignore, though, that clubs are yet another place in which everyday racism manifests. It's not uncommon to hear stories of black students not being allowed into certain clubs, being randomly selected for bag searches, or even being followed by security. In 2017, a group of black students were refused entry to a nightclub in Cardiff because the club management didn't want an 'urban feel' to their club.

It doesn't always get much better when you are inside. Some nights are fun, and I have an incredible archive of Snapchat memories from my university years to testify to that. You're getting lit with your friends, catching all your whines, gassing your girls up when they're killing it on the dancefloor, and so on. But on other nights, the racist realities of the world permeate the club scene and turn a good night sour.

> **Clubbing was a massive source of upset and [discomfort] and something that made me feel really alienated in Cambridge. I remember going out with blonde friends who would get hit on by guys, and just feeling both undesirable and invisible, like you didn't even exist in this space. – Micha**

The constant reminders that no one was interested in you became draining. I can count on one hand the number of times I went out clubbing and a guy approached me. In a social context in which it seems as if lots of relationships are being forged, especially in the early days, this can be disheartening. It will be a frequent reminder of what it means as a black girl to not fall into society's standards of desirable.

Often, when you *are* approached, it's by people so in awe of your blackness that they fetishise you. Renee spoke to me about how 'creative' guys can get with their pickup lines:

> **There's 'brown sugar', all sorts of nonsense . . . I think the funniest one was 'chocolate mocha princess' . . . Like, sir, I just came to enjoy my martini in peace.**

Chocolate mocha princess?! While Renée laughs about it in hindsight, constantly being compared to food by drunk boys in the club can be exhausting. The ones who may not compare you to something edible may opt instead for the 'you're fit for a black girl' line or even, 'I've never been with a black girl before.' You are not some kind of experience or adventurous option to be tried. While I advise you to ignore these comments as best you can, rest assured I know how easily they can ruin your night.

*

The ubiquity of alcohol in university social spaces can be particularly isolating for people who don't drink. The NUS in 2018 asked universities to introduce more 'inclusive spaces' for teetotal students on campus because the centrality of drinking can be difficult to escape. Most student events, especially things like bar crawls in freshers' week, fall short when it comes to fully accommodating teetotal students. In addition to being excluded from certain events, these students often find themselves being quizzed by their peers on the reasons behind their sobriety.

I don't drink because I think alcohol tastes disgusting. But it was weird because people just don't get why you don't drink. I didn't ever feel

pressure to drink but I had friends who did feel like they had to drink to belong. – Ayomide

It is very possible to survive university without drinking. There will be hundreds of societies and other spaces that have a range of ways to keep you busy; I'll explore some of these spaces in the rest of this chapter. And if you do choose to go clubbing, find the nights you like. Don't end up like me, who spent a whole year dancing to dead Disney tunes two nights a week before I realised there were clubs that I liked and DJs that played all the Wizkid I needed to hear.

Unless you've been to boarding school, university is probably the first time you'll be living with a whole bunch of people your own age – and it will get messy. Most universities will offer you accommodation (in your first year, at least). On the one hand, this could be convenient – on the other, you will probably have little choice as to who you get to live with. If you're lucky, you'll get on with everyone in your halls of residence, but chances are, it won't always be bliss. For starters, I advise that you don't keep your plantain in the communal fridge just in case an unaware housemate mistakes it for a mouldy banana and throws it in the bin. True story, guys, I kid you not. You may also have to share bathrooms with people who don't know how to make good use of a toilet brush.

You will probably bump into your housemates on a daily basis (maybe weekly basis if you're particularly good at staying away from communal areas), and the proximity may make them convenient friends to have. However, living situations can also be a massive source of upset, socially speaking – and so if you find yourself feeling a bit left out, you're not alone, because I did too.

If you go to a university with a collegiate system, like Cambridge, Oxford, Durham and York, you'll find that roughly speaking, your academic life is controlled by your university departments or faculties, while everything social and residential is run by your college. We were told by other students that most of our friends would come from our college. It seemed to be true, for the most part. Everyone I lived with was buddying up. I couldn't understand why I was struggling to integrate. I just found college more isolating as time went on.

> **Cambridge really sells this idea of, you socialise in your college, or college is like your family. But I was the only black girl in my college for like three years. It's really, really hard, and it doesn't feel like a family. Towards the end of second year, I realised I didn't have to subscribe to the whole college lifestyle . . . I didn't have to keep being reminded that I was a minority. – Arenike**

There's nothing wrong with seeking out other options if life in college, or with people in your halls, isn't for you. In fact, I found that some of the most comfortable places for me were outside my college, in societies that I sought out on my own, where I found people who shared my feelings of isolation and minority representation.

Making Space

Some people have taken it upon themselves to respond to these feelings of isolation by making spaces of their own. For Saskia, this began in Cambridge's theatre world, which for a long time had been **'really white and inaccessible'** and **'a boys' club of nepotism'**, they told me. Despite having done no acting before university, the lack of accessibility for people of colour and non-private school students inspired them to start a Cambridge BME Theatre group on Facebook. Saskia eventually went on to direct many BME-only cast plays in Cambridge. Their first BME-only cast production, *Macbeth*, sold out every performance except the matinee.

> **Almost every show I've ever done is a refuge. I did Fences in my final year, and I've never seen so many black people in the audience for something before. It makes a massive difference to the atmosphere. It's so special. – Saskia**

Another example is Warwick's FlowSoc, created by Jeremiah Amoako-Gyapong:

> **'FlowSoc' was basically about music performance, poetry and spoken word. It was a lot of expressing yourself through creativity, and I**

thought it was very useful in terms of finding people to connect with and people that could support you, through poetry or through singing or whatever. – Mikai

For me, my refuge was my house. I would cook jollof rice or corned beef stew and invite all my favourite people round. Bonding over food that we loved and missed, food that played so much of a role in making up our cultural identities, was important. At home, we eat jollof at parties, with family and with friends. I would spend hours in the kitchen perfecting the dish, and I loved that I could recreate such an important space for people at university. We would laugh and cry about everything from relationships to school work until the early hours of the morning, before the reality of the next day's lectures reared its head. Being surrounded by people I loved, and people whom I felt truly loved me, gave me all the fire that I needed to get by. The solidarity that I found in such relationships was essential, the conversations we had unforgettable, and it's one of the things I miss the most about Cambridge.

Some people find that solidarity in online spaces too. Fope gave me some insight into how powerful online spaces can be:

> I used to moderate a group called Radical Black and Brown Hotties [RBBH], which had over 2,000 members at its peak. There's RBBH Brighton, Berlin, London and France. I know people who have started dating from the group and people who have definitely made friends from the group. They've even helped me write essays.

Online spaces are crucial, especially for marginalised communities. Facebook groups and black Twitter networks have been a central hub for both socialising *and* organising. They have been important sites for education and progressive conversations, away from those complicit in oppression. At Cambridge, we had a network called 'FLY', which was created to encourage this kind of solidarity. FLY, which I learned stands for 'Freedom. Love. You.', is a forum for women and non-binary people of colour (WNBPOC) to advise, support, or just listen, through an online Facebook group. It was created by BME women before us and has continued to be an important space for women and non-binary people of colour at Cambridge. FLY held weekly meetings in which WNBPOC from across the university could get together and be reminded that our experiences are valid.

> I went to FLY a lot, which was revolutionary for me. It kind of weirdly reminds me of having therapy at uni. – Micha

It was an incredible opportunity to talk to people who have been in your exact position, about this essay that you can't do, and which clubs to go to, and how to navigate Cambridge as a person of colour. – Saskia

Warwick's Anti-Racism Society, or WARSoc, is another example of a society that aims to provide a safe space for its members. Other such spaces include sexual assault survivor groups, disability groups and mental health groups. Safe spaces like these are heavily criticised for 'undermining free speech', but that's far from the point. They are a sanctuary in which minorities can engage in discourse without being silenced, places in which we are allowed to prioritise our own life experiences and histories of oppression, amid a society that often glosses over them. We can exhale, and find comfort in the knowledge that other people share these experiences; we are not alone.

However, it is important to bear in mind that not everyone has similar ideas of what safety looks or feels like. While for many, safe spaces allow us to be protected from the damaging opinions of communities that oppress us, they can also make it harder to disagree with those you share the space with.

I didn't like the hypocrisy. A lot of the time it was, 'You agree with our opinion or you're wrong' – and that to me is such a dangerous thing to do in a safe space. – Courtney

Safe spaces are useful and necessary, and this criticism should not undermine their importance. But for me, it was the first time that I realised that woman-of-colour solidarity is not a given, and that I could forgive myself for not feeling safe in a space where it seemed other black girls did. I say this for the other black women who have felt similarly isolated. A room full of other women sharing their experiences of racism may not be your idea of safety and solidarity, and you are allowed to feel that. FLY, like many other safe spaces, was an important source of education, therapy and refuge, and although it didn't quite work for me, there were other spaces that did. I came to realise that different societies served different purposes for me.

*

Without ACS, I don't know how I would have survived. – Courtney

Whatever university you go to, you will find a society for almost every activity under the sun (we even had a

Quidditch Society* at Cambridge). Societies are helpful for fostering a smaller sense of community with people who share your interests. However, a special mention goes out to the cultural societies that offer BME students a second home at university through events dedicated to sharing and celebrating their cultural communities. I found the ACS at Cambridge to be this and more.

I first encountered my university's ACS in November of my first year when I went to an event called 'Culture Fest'. There was jollof rice, music and spoken word performances, and lots of people were in traditional dress. Suddenly, I didn't feel I was in Cambridge any more. In fact, everything that seemed to make me stick out in the rest of Cambridge helped me fit right in. My first reaction was, 'Where have all these black people been hiding?' I was in a place where people understood all my cultural references, and shared my histories and, very importantly, my taste in music! I had found a society in Cambridge that felt like home. I went to almost every weekly ACS event that followed, from the parties to the talks – even the Valentine's Day 'Take Me Out'.

---

* It's that game they played in Harry Potter on the flying broomsticks. I cannot confirm that flying brooms are included in the society's membership.

The ACS is run by a small committee of elected students. I admired the group that had had such an impact on me and given me hope that I could truly enjoy Cambridge. In my second year, I decided to run for Events Officer, because I wanted to contribute to someone else's ACS experience and be more involved in what seemed to be a meaningful family.

I saw people who looked like me, and we could dance to Vybz Kartel and then talk about feminism. – Nathania

Being on the ACS Committee was . . . interesting. ACS committee drama seemed to be a thing everywhere, but we had it quite bad. We inherited a huge debt from our predecessors, and within three months, our president kicked someone off the committee. Halfway through the year, the president then resigned, for reasons that were not revealed to the rest of us. In spite of the pretty tempestuous start, under new leadership we managed to raise lots of sponsorship money, and even hold our first-ever ACS ball.

Most British universities have an ACS in some capacity. They're a particularly significant means for black students to engage with their own institutions and other universities. You may encounter events such as the 'Great Debate Tour' or the dance competition 'Big Clash', which involve many university ACSs. ACSs also have the potential to be an important political force, since they are the closest that we have to a country-wide black students union (especially since the NUS's 'Black Students Campaign' represents everyone who is 'politically black', or non-white). ACSs are generally known for having great parties and food, and embodying black British culture and diasporic identity within university life. Many corporate firms have noticed the value of these societies, and provide sponsorship to ACSs in the hope that black graduates will be attracted to their firms in the future. We would work for weeks perfecting shiny sponsorship proposals, detailing how many members we had, how much we had grown and how much we needed these corporations' help to keep that growth going.

Cambridge ACS is a bit different from other ACSs across the country in some respects. Having a very small black community meant that we often couldn't match what other ACSs were doing because we didn't have the manpower. We would look enviously at places like Warwick, which had a black community so large that both their ACS and their Nigerian Society could afford to throw huge balls every year. The more I met with black people from other universities, though, the more it became clear that this lack of black students wasn't only a Cambridge problem. Some universities don't even have enough black people willing to form an ACS committee. It was upsetting to learn that even though ACS had become so important to me, some people at other universities would never know what that felt like.

At the end of my second year, I ran for ACS president. I knew that there was nothing else that I would rather give my energy to for a whole year. I had become so invested in seeing this society grow because I saw how important it was for so many black people.

> **I think ACS will always come first. If I had to drop anything else for it, I would. I really give a shit about our community. – Nathania**

I had come to learn that although many ACSs in the UK are broadly about socialising, networking and getting black people into corporate jobs, Cambridge ACS *had* to be political in its aims.

> **Our ACS is inherently quite political because being black at Cambridge is political. – Chelsea**

For example, we had to address the fact Cambridge had an access problem and that black students were under-represented. The university's most recent admissions statistics revealed that twenty-five black men and thirty-three black women were accepted in 2017. While this is an improvement on the year of my intake, black applicants still have a lower *success* rate than white applicants. Essentially this means that even though more black people are applying, they are still less likely to receive an offer and then meet its terms. To counter this very specific problem, we introduced mentoring schemes and access conferences for black secondary school students. The goal was to pour all the knowledge we had about the process into potential black candidates so that they were better prepared and well-equipped not only to apply to Cambridge, but also to get in.

The increasing politicisation of ACSs seems to be a wider phenomenon. In my time at university, we were beginning to see many more ACSs hosting important discussions about black mental health and misogynoir; some were introducing LGBTQ+ officers to assist in the fight against homophobia and transphobia that often plague black communities. The ACS was *my* sanctuary, and I strongly recommend that black students at least give it a go while at university. You may have to pay a small membership fee to join – between £10 and £30 at most universities - but the memories I made were worth way more than the money.

Some people still felt isolated within this society, though. The focus on partying can exclude people who don't enjoy that kind of nightlife, or those who are more introverted. As is the case with many black spaces in the diaspora, ACSs tend to be dominated by West Africans, and particularly Nigerians, and many non-Nigerian black people often had a harder time identifying with that reality. ACSs need to make a more conscious effort to counter the overrepresentation of Nigerians in their societies – and I say that as a Nigerian who has been complicit in, and profited from, this overrepresentation! As an African-*Caribbean* Society, we have a duty to make sure that Caribbeans are also fairly represented.

The obsession with getting black students into corporate jobs in the city is one that is bigger than a student society. Yet we still have a responsibility to make sure that black students who want to pursue alternative career paths are equally supported. While it is the price that we pay for the corporate sponsorships that we receive, it reinforces the notion that there is only one path to success as a black graduate.

So yes, there's work to be done. But I know that the joy that I felt in this society was like nothing that I found anywhere else at university.

*

While I made myself at home socially in the ACS, I found a spiritual home in my Cambridge church. As a Christian, I hopped from church to church in my first year, trying to find what worked for me. Although I was born in a Christian household and have gone to church since I was a child, I made the personal decision to give my life to Christ early on in university. I was looking for somewhere where I would feel moved by the spirit, somewhere that reminded me of the churches that I was used to, but also somewhere that would support me in my baby Christian journey. I found it quite difficult to stay on my Christian path, especially in my first year, because I was in an academic environment that relied so much on proving everything, explaining everything and justifying everything. It seemed at odds with being Christian, which relies on faith that you can't really explain.

When you're in academic spaces, there's always an excuse of why God doesn't exist or why it's irrational to believe in God . . . but then I felt very lonely at university. – Courtney

By my second year, I had finally settled into a church which I loved. It was, I came to find, yet another community that reminded me of home. We would sing songs of praise that I had been singing since I was a child, the pastor was Nigerian and a lot of the congregation shared my background. It was a community that welcomed me with open arms, and it became a great comfort when university work really began to take its toll. Sometimes I would go to church and cry a little bit, and then I was good. It was a different kind of escape, a very personal one for me, and I don't think my friends really knew or understood why I needed it so much.

When I've not read my Bible in a long time, which happens a lot, it's just nice to always know that you can pray it will be fine. – Ayomide

Saredo is a Muslim, and found similar solace in religion while at university:

I always found religion was just a very personal thing. When it comes to faith, it's kind of letting you know that there is a path, whether or not I felt like I was on that path: in times of struggle and times of uncertainty, instead of seeing or viewing it as everything falling apart, just seeing it as everything coming together.

When you're homesick, or thinking about dropping out, or feeling like you have no one, a call from someone that they're praying for you might help. It was yet another support system that I didn't know I needed. I met people who would send me messages to check on me when I had exams coming up, or who would make sure I was okay if I had missed church for a few weeks.

I found a church and I met a lady, Aunty Sunkanmi. She took my number and she took me under her wing and it was like having a mother figure at university . . . She was constantly checking up on me and making me food. – Courtney

If you're a person of faith, find ways to keep that faith at university despite the pressure to explain why you believe what you believe. Church helped me stay grounded and was yet another comfort for me.

The Idea of a Black Sisterhood

I am grateful that I found spaces in university that I could thrive in. It may have taken me a while to settle in and to find my groove, but once I did, places like the ones I have discussed here kept me going. The support and solidarity that I found fuelled my fire.

There appears to be a running narrative in the circles I move in that black girls don't do enough to support each other. I'm not convinced that is true.

I always saw black girls really supporting each other in a way that was very unconditional.
– Micha

I am thankful for the black girls I found who just got it. They understood what I was going through without me having to explain. They would allow me to grow dependent on them, and they in turn on me, because we knew we needed each other. We would catch each other's eyes when we were the only black girls in the room, and feel the silent solidarity. They would understand exactly what about university was so difficult, and yet would also be the ones to try and make it a bit more bearable for you.

This whole book is written on exactly that premise: an inherent inclination to root for everyone black. It's a remarkable sisterhood that we're able to share in and that we should take pride in. So let's end that story here. Black girls do support each other, unapologetically so, and some of the greatest, most durable black sisterhoods will be formed in the trying times of university.

However, I question whether the idea that we *should* support and befriend every black girl ever is a fair expectation. One thing I wish I had learnt before I started university was that I could be both passionate about the importance of black spaces and the need for black girl solidarity, without feeling an obligation to be best friends with every black girl I encountered. In the first term, one black girl made a WhatsApp group for every black girl in our year which, I thought, was a clever idea. However, with time, it became clear that some of us didn't get along. The group offered a false sense of unity that masked deeper issues. I think I was mistaken, as were many others in the group, into thinking that we would all be friends by default.

It's interesting how we live in a climate [where] black women feel the need to always support each other, and I say this because when we got to Cambridge, there were a lot of black girls I just

simply didn't like. You're now stuck in this middle ground where, *I really don't like you, but I have to support you for the bigger cause* – which is a shame because you're not being genuine. – Chelsea

While it is important to find spaces in which you can escape and exhale, don't force it. You have no obligation to befriend and support every individual just because they're black. I tolerated a lot more than I should have from black girls in leadership positions because I felt I had to. I didn't want to allow others to use our own conflict against us. I yearned for a united front that didn't always exist, because I knew that we had bigger fights to fight together. But what use is false solidarity? I learned that it's possible to both believe in the necessity of a broad solidarity among black girls without feeling forced to like each and every single one as an individual.

Even if you magically do get along with every other black girl you find at university, what's to say that you will have the extra energy and time to consistently support them?

Black women have so much shit to deal with anyway. It's hard enough to just stay existing and surviving in a space like Cambridge. If you

don't have the extra energy to endlessly offer up labour to support other people, I think it's fair enough. – Micha

The Oxbridge context is tough because you're dealing with so much that it's hard to even check up on someone else. – Renée

Lastly, don't let the fantasy of the black sisterhood fool you into thinking that the only people who will be there to support you will be black and female. For the sake of time and space, I have made gross generalisations about men and non-black people; there were certainly people looking out for me who were neither black nor female, but offered up relentless support.

I understand that supporting other black girls isn't always easy or possible. I understand that the obligation isn't completely fair. But I also understand how fulfilling it is to know that there are black girls out there rooting for you. I felt that way in these spaces, with many of my university friends-turned-family who still stand by me today. So, black girls: when you get to university, I hope you find spaces you feel comfortable in, help make them if they don't exist, and forge sisterhoods that will root for you.

5

Desirability and Relationships

Chelsea

As daunting a prospect as university is, it is also a moment of exhilaration and liberation. We run away from the watchful eyes of our parents and family straight into an idealised playground of sweet *freedom*. You are granted your own space and your own schedule. You are surrounded by thousands of people your age and presented with the opportunity to meet and make friends with whoever you like. All of a sudden, you are master of your love life: free to test out romantic relationships without awkwardly having to sneak anyone into and out of your parents' house.

Dating at university can be life-changing for many students. Around 20 per cent of men and 18 per cent of women apparently find true love at university. The One Day University Love Survey stated that the top five universities in which to find that potential life-long partner are:

- Oxford (35 per cent of students)

- York (29 per cent)

- Durham (25 per cent)

- Liverpool (23 per cent)

- Manchester (21 per cent)

Now you all know where to apply if you want the best chance at finding long-term love. Call me Cupid Chelsea!

That's not to say that some people don't arrive at university already in relationships. I won't disguise the fact that maintaining existing relationships at university is hard and tiring, and requires a level of sacrifice few first-year students are able to commit to. I remember seeing a host of buzzing girlfriends helping settle their boyfriends in on the first day. Apart from a few heated arguments about missed twenty-minute FaceTime slots, I don't think I heard or saw any of them again.

Previous relationships withered away as people found that they couldn't maintain a degree *and* a relationship at the same time.

However, the dating scene for the majority of black girls at university is a minefield. To be honest, there isn't really much of a 'dating scene'; more, as Jasmine Lee-Zogbessou puts it, a 'dating puddle'. Despite carefully skirting around the people you definitely want to avoid, it's not long before you're hit with the reminder that ideas of desirability underline our very existence. Once you recognise this, it's hard to ignore the racism, misogynoir and prejudice that come with being black and seeking out relationships within university spaces.

The black female body has historically functioned as a scene of the doing and undoing of racial and gender-based structures of power. Representations and stereotypes of black women have been controlled by the media and society, who have served to reinforce a one-dimensional caricature. When we're not 'intimidating' and 'aggressive', we're 'hypersexual' and 'sassy'. We snap our fingers and bop our heads laced with fake hair, and are often seen as hostile and emasculating partners. To add to our woes, the fetishisation of black women has a long and deep history rooted in colonialism and slavery. Caren M. Holmes's essay 'The Colonial Roots of the Racial Fetishisation of Black Women' is a useful and short introduction to this topic.

She states that although women of all colours are 'reduced to sexual commodities by a patriarchal system', it is black women especially who find that their race, class and gender all contribute to their continued 'sexual debasement'.

> **I think people think they might look at me and be like, 'Oh yeah, I wanna bang her, but she would never be my girlfriend.' – Barbara**

University became the site where I was confronted with these issues head-on. When encountering students who had never spoken to a black girl, it was uncomfortable to think of all the preconceptions that existed before I even had a chance to open my mouth. I began to understand how desirability not only had a romantic dimension but also played a significant part in respectability politics, and how collapsed definitions of black women permeated every aspect of my university life. Widely believed stereotypes affected how we interacted with lecturers, tutors and also other students.

> **I think also a lot of people just didn't get that I was quite reserved. I feel like they expected me to be quite loud. – Kenya**

Through my own experiences and those of others in this book, it is clear that university is a trying time for most black girls and non-binary people when it comes to beauty, desirability and relationships. University can mean rejection, self-doubt and hopelessness. At the same time, it can also mean recognising your worth in its purest sense – not compromising for anyone and ultimately, knowing that there's nothing wrong with you, but something bigger with society.

Season of Singleness

In my first year, while sitting in the corridor of my halls with my new neighbours, a white male student felt the need to tell us all that 'personally, I don't find black women attractive. That's just not my preference.' I wasn't shocked, or offended. But you could bet that I was angry. Before he could finish his sentence, I shot back, 'What makes you think black women would find you attractive anyway?' Don't get me wrong, the validation of men is not the be-all and end-all. What hit a nerve was his air of confidence and privilege, which screamed, 'I'm at the top of the food chain.' Comments like these serve to reinforce the obvious reality that women of colour, especially black women, are right at the bottom of society's heterosexual desirability hierarchy.

The conversation about beauty and desirability starts way before university. I have many fond memories of running around in my primary school playground, playing the game all children either love or hate: kiss chase. I was the fastest runner out of the boys and girls, so I usually did quite well. One lunchtime, however, it was the boys' turn to chase the girls. All of a sudden, I wasn't the fastest in the field any more. I ran around the playground, deliberately slowing down so I could be caught, ready to fake outrage at being kissed. Instead, I found that a number of the boys tactfully avoided me. Why didn't they catch me? I was right there! I soon realised that even if it meant shooting up in the ranks of kiss chase, there was no desire to kiss me.

It doesn't stop there. My experience at secondary school wasn't an anomaly. The dark-skinned black girls were always *too* dark, *too* loud or had *too* much of an attitude. Instead, 'lighties' and white girls were preferred. An all-girl group at my school of around ten to fifteen pupils were the perfect example of this – they nicknamed themselves 'The Slags', reclaiming the intended insult. They were the girls who hit puberty early, doused themselves in Victoria's Secret PINK mist, wore the most makeup and were exclusively white or light. To their full knowledge, all the boys loved them, and all the girls in school despised them. The Slags formed the blueprint for 'desirability' for those who wanted them and those who wanted to *be* them. No one was interested in darker-skinned girls, and that was clear.

When I was in secondary school, I was always the ugly girl. People would call me 'gorilla', and it used to be so depressing because people would do their Facebook posts: 'Adaobi the Gorilla'. I internalised it around Year 9: I'm going to be ugly forever. – Adaobi

I felt the same as Adaobi. If whiteness was the standard that all women were judged by, I was going to be ugly forever. My hair was never going to be straight, my nose was never going to be narrow and my skin was never going to be fair. So where could I go from there? At the same time, the very characteristics that most black women were and still are ridiculed for such as full lips, curves or a big bum were worshipped on whiter and lighter women. You only have to look at the 'blackfishing' debate, with white Instagram models accused of extreme tanning, dark make-up and hair braids, to see that the racially ambiguous look is 'in' right now.

I left for university adamant that I was not going to get into a relationship – but also convinced that no one was going to find me attractive anyway. It was a win-win situation, in a way. I used it as the basis to focus on myself, and not to *expect* anything when I got to university. I feel that most black girls go to university with this same mindset.

Self-Love over Everything

Living in a world of edited images, algorithms and fake personalities, it becomes harder to believe that anyone truly loves themselves. I always believed that self-love was corny and embarrassing. What did it even mean? In my mind, it was an opportunity for those who extolled the message to write vague phrases like, 'You are worth it' or 'Love yourself', in pink, cursory calligraphy. Somehow the message was lost on me, and to an extent, still is.

To my surprise, going to university changed my understanding of self-love dramatically. University can be exciting for a number of reasons – one being that this will probably be your first time meeting such a wide range of new people. If you're like me, it will also be the time when you begin to realise the extent to which your personality, interests and likes have been defined by other people. I remember spending a lot of time in my first few months trying to work out who I was and most importantly, who I *wanted* to be. University is a fresh start.

Before anything, shatter your god complex and recognise that you are not perfect. In fact, you're very flawed. As black women, we often walk a fine line between false stereotypes or caricatures of the angry woman, the hypersexual woman, the flawless or magic 'Queen'. We are so used to working twice as hard for everything that neither failure nor having flaws is an option. We can't give anyone a reason to continue to deprive us of what we have worked hard for. This notion was detrimental to how I viewed myself – especially the idea that I wasn't *allowed* to have flaws. My actions at university would represent more than my own personal actions. There's a fear that your weaknesses and imperfections will be extrapolated as the prototype for all black students. Deconstructing this notion was refreshing, in that it reminded me that I'm a complex being, and one who makes mistakes.

> **My self-image has improved, but there's still such a long way to go – but I think I'm now looking at myself . . . trying to appreciate the best parts of me instead of always voicing the worst parts of me. Because the person I was before is the kind of person that could not take a compliment. – Ayomide**

After you're done with your god complex, you will truly understand that comparison is self-love's arch-nemesis. With social media representations, we're under constant pressure to define where we are and what we are doing at all times. Progress is now understood and measured against what *others* are doing in their lives and how they're doing it. At university, the stark reality will hit home that you're now in an environment where you're likely to be surrounded by girls who are, in the eyes of society, the epitome of beauty and desirability.

I used to say I wish[ed] I could be smaller, compact, petite, you know – more beautiful in the sense of adhering to those beauty standards. But then it just got to a point of, I back myself a hundred and ten per cent, I'm a good-looking girl, I don't need to look like this. – Renée

In line with challenging this standard of beauty, I found it best to develop a healthy relationship with my natural hair. Hair texture and styles have an immense power and ability to shape our lives as black women. With some workplaces even describing afro hair and hairstyles as 'unprofessional', there is a racialised hierarchy embedded in the language of hair – one that feeds into respectability politics.

Having a healthy relationship with your hair doesn't necessarily mean joining the natural hair movement and putting flowers in it, but moving past seeing having your natural hair 'out' as a transitional stage to your next hairstyle. The relationship between black women and hair runs a lot deeper than just *hair*. It's often memories of sitting in between someone's legs and having your hair yanked with an afro comb, or in my case, being tapped on the back in assembly to be told the girl behind me couldn't see because my hair was too big.

For most of my first year, I refused to change my hair style too much because I wanted it to be 'consistent' – AKA, I didn't want people to ask me about my hair. So I kept it black, straight and long-bob length, and rarely went more than two days with it in its natural state. I truly believed that this would help me blend in as much as I could. With my race already a talking point, I didn't have the energy for my hair to be one also. With no natural hairdressers in Cambridge, my curly edges would be screaming for help by the end of term. But I always tried to maintain my straight style because I wasn't ready to have a conversation about why my hair looked different every two weeks.

I remember when I had braids and I was nervous to change my hair – but I wanted to get a wig done, because it's easier. I remember just thinking, 'Oh, for fuck's sake, everyone's going to be talking about my hair tomorrow . . . it's going to be so long, I can't be bothered.' – Barbara

When I got braids . . . they'd be like, 'I love your dreadlocks' or, 'Wow, your hair grows so quickly.' – Eireann

Hopefully, university is also a radical time – in that you see for yourself how flawed and narrow this conception of beauty is. There is no point in comparing yourself to something that is virtually impossible, and most importantly, isn't *you*. Be selfish and radical in choosing how to discover self-love, because you will be the only person to do it justice. Surround yourself with positive representations you can relate to both visually and academically. Read books, journals and articles on topics that interest you, and cushion yourself with validating information. At the same time, be careful not to attribute significance and importance to noise on the internet that lacks nuance. We are complex beings – 'complex' not meaning 'difficult', but deserving of the time it takes to work us out.

The process of seeing myself as a desirable person only happened when I unlearned all the things that I was taught to learn throughout my life. So, desirability for me wasn't necessarily an external thing, I felt desirable once I desired myself. – Saredo

Notice how many 'I's are in Saredo's statement? There has to be a point where your self-worth starts and stops with you. Especially during my first few weeks at Cambridge, I wanted everyone to have a positive perception of me. If that meant changing my character slightly depending on who I was with, then so be it. It was always me adapting to suit them in the hope of the highest honour: validation. Thankfully, I got over that very soon, once I realised that the people who genuinely knew me appreciated who I really was. (Or it might have been when my best friend's dad told me to stop speaking like I had a plum in my mouth.)

Relationships at University

I think it's a very natural urge at that time in your life to get straight into quite a serious relationship, because it's like you're rebuilding your own family and your support systems in a new space. – Micha

The majority of black girls at university tended to look for relationships with people from the same racial or cultural background as them. There are very legitimate reasons why most of us choose to do this. You automatically assume – often rightly – that things will be a lot easier: same banter, same tastes, similar family backgrounds, all that good stuff. Most importantly, if there's a chance to skip the possibility of racism or fetishisation within your relationship – why not? With such a small number of black students in the overall university population, the potential pool of partners was always going to be small – so small that you had to check that your friend from ACS wasn't dating the same guy or girl. Can you imagine? A disaster waiting to happen. Oh, and the brutal truth was that most of the black boys just weren't interested in black girls at university. Everything society had told us so far about beauty, desirability and relationships didn't magically disappear; if anything, it was magnified tenfold.

No matter what we think, it seems that the external pressures from families and relatives also have an impact on how black girls view relationships at university. As Ọrẹ said in 'A Letter to my Fresher Self', many of us can relate to side-eyeing that one aunty who won't stop asking, 'When will you marry?' But can we really blame them? To our families on the outside, university is the perfect opportunity to find your potential partner, one who would have it all: a university degree, ambition, the prospect of a high-paying job. Of course, marriage and kids would shortly follow.

> **I was one of those people who before uni was like, *I'm coming to find my husband for sure.* Weren't we all? – Courtney**

Above all, our families love and want the best for us. In their eyes, it doesn't make sense that we are beautiful and smart, and yet cannot find anyone interested in us. Unsurprisingly, most black girls at university suddenly feel a sense of urgency. As a result, there is a strong sense of 'spouse-searching' at university, especially amongst those who choose to date exclusively within their own races. Going to universities with a tight-knit black community throws up plenty of opportunities to find black love – something that becomes even more important when your identity as a black student is politicised within predominately white institutions.

ACSs across the country host 'ACS Take Me Out' in a bid to pair up ACS members. This is based on the popular TV show *Take Me Out*, where contestants are on the lookout for one lucky girl to take to the Isle of Fernando's! Due to budgeting issues, our ACS committee could only afford to sponsor a trip to Nando's in the centre of town (see what we did there?). At UCL, the dress code for their version of ACS Take Me Out was 'Melanin Popping, Bae-merising Excellence'. I'm not sure how you dress up to be 'Bae-merising Excellence', but I respect it.

In first year, Orẹ and I went to our first ever ACS Take Me Out. Cambridge ACS had paired up with Anglia Ruskin's ACS because Cambridge had barely enough black people to be able to run consistently well-attended events. Orẹ and I were both picked to be one of the girls who popped their balloons when they weren't interested in a boy. From the beginning, Orẹ had her eyes on this tall, funny and very handsome guy from Cambridge. Did I mention he was a medic as well? Yeah. Anyway, she pulled me to the side to tell me that no matter how appealing this guy was to me, I had to pop my balloon and then she could get the date. I had just started seeing my boyfriend, which no one knew about yet, so this worked perfectly for me because I needed an out. Later, I watched her strut past the crowds in her black boob-tube dress and strappy heels, hand-in-hand with the medic as they walked out of the room to organise their date. Picture me beaming in the background like a proud mum on her wedding day.

As you can imagine, ACS Take Me Outs are a lot of fun, and a great sense of validation for heterosexual black women who are often left at the bottom when it comes to university dating.

Because people come to ACS looking for a partner, they come like, 'I've got three years! I need to find someone. I NEED TO GRAFT!' – Barbara

Funnily enough, Barbara met her current boyfriend through ACS when she least expected it. They had both applied to be on the committee for ACS, and got to know each other more through the society. In many ways, people viewed their union as sacred because of how little we see strong representations of black love. In Barbara's own words, 'It's like, "**Oh my gosh, two black medics, oh my gosh, your kids**." ' But she did mention that at the beginning it was hard because everyone wanted to know what was going on. When would they make it official? Were they arguing or fighting? Would it last? The tight-knit nature of the community of black students at university can sometimes be suffocating. It's like being in a large friendship group with dozens of off-shoot branches. You only have to tell a couple of people your business before everyone knows.

The dating scene and relationships also differ for black LGBTQ+ students. Almost all universities have their own LGBTQ+ societies, which can be a great way to meet new queer people and find a community. Bristol University's LGBTQ+ society hosts a BME mingle for freshers as an opportunity to meet other BME LGBTQ+ people. Or take FUSE Cambridge, for example, the network for LGBTQ+ people of colour, where students can attend socials and group movie nights to watch films or documentaries like *Moonlight* and *Tongues United*. It's an opportunity to become active within the queer community at Cambridge. Both are just some of the important spaces that allow BME LGBTQ+ people to safely express all overlapping aspects of their identity.

I prefer the queer community and it's a space I like to surround myself with, so I inevitably end up dating more women and non-binary people. – Saskia

So often, the stories of black LGBTQ+ students have been written out of the wider 'black experience' at university. The experiences of black LGBTQ+ students are often ones of navigating an environment that seeks to dehumanise your identity on both racial and sexual fronts. Stonewall's 'LGBT in Britain's Universities' Report asked 522 LGBT students about their experiences, highlighting what may be to some startling results. More than two in five LGBT students (42 per cent) hid or disguised the fact that they were LGBT at university due to fears of discrimination. Similarly, one in four non-binary students (24 per cent) and one in six trans students (16 per cent) didn't feel that they were able to wear clothes which offered a true reflection of their gender expression.

When we talk about 'black students', who do we mean? There is little to no discussion of black LGBTQ+ students, who are often faced with straddling multiple identities, rejecting one to accommodate another. Also, hardly spoken about or addressed is the rife homophobia, transphobia and biphobia within black communities, and specifically ACSs. The University of Oxford's 'Trans Report' in 2018 recognised that the 'transphobia experienced by trans people of colour is often racialised'. Prevailing notions of family, collective unity and the role of religion continue to have a large influence on most of our values today. Black LGBTQ+ students face the constant possibility of cultural estrangement from other black students within their own universities. Societies such as ACS can become stomping grounds for projecting a particular type of 'blackness', one that prioritises heterosexual black students.

The reality is that for anyone, sustaining a relationship at university is difficult and can be a pretty big commitment. They require time, sacrifice and, in most cases, selflessness on both ends if you really want the relationship to stand the test. It can be nice, though, to have someone at university who is specifically looking out for you backing your corner. It also relieved a lot of stress to have someone to binge-watch *House of Cards* and *How To Get Away With Murder* with after a long day. Just saying.

Interracial Dating at University

The first conversation I ever had with my now-boy-friend, Joe, was at a 90s-themed bop. Bops, Cambridge's equivalent of school discos, can be *very* interesting affairs. They're usually themed, play exclusively cheesy music, are stocked with VK Vodka Kicks, and are attended by almost everyone in college. At my college, bops were banned – much to the disappointment of many students – for the majority of my second year after wee, vomit and poo were found scattered across college grounds.

Needless to say, I wasn't looking forward to my first bop. I was probably most annoyed that the people on my corridor had actually convinced me to leave my room in a 90s bomber jacket and neon leg warmers. As expected, the bop was one of the worst things that I had ever experienced – but luckily Joe felt the same. He tapped me on the shoulder and asked if I wanted to join him outside for some fresh air. A bit confused, I agreed, and we sat on the stone step outside our accommoda-tion block. We spoke about a lot of things that night: our families, where we grew up, what our favourite col-ours were and what we expected from Cambridge.

Now is a good time to mention that Joe is a white Brit-ish boy, and this whole interaction came to me as a surprise. Growing up around Essex, attending a pre-dominately white school, I believed it to be a fact that both white *and* black boys did not find black girls attractive. I remember feeling tense and listing all of the other reasons why Joe might *want* to talk to me, but most of all I was worried that he would say some of the things that I had heard before. 'If you were a chocolate you would be Galaxy'; 'I like you because you're a coconut: black on the outside, white on the inside'; or 'You're different to *other* black girls.' I knew that university was supposed to be a time to experience and to explore. Maybe I, being a black girl, would be part of that 'experience' package. I promised myself that at any slight hint of 'Swirl YouTube', where interracial couples document their relationships, I'd be out.

For some, interracial relationships have become a lucrative lifestyle. Think Jamie and Nikki, an Australian couple with over 1.7 million YouTube subscribers, or HelloBianca, a channel amassing 55,000 subscribers. Maybe they're just living their lives, but it's really hard to ignore the obsession of their fans, who like to see black and white uniting as a sign that racism is well and truly over.

I've internalised to not even bother paying attention to white guys if you're looking at them romantically. Because in my head it was, *white guys are never going to like you*. – Ọrẹ

How do we, now that we're educated on institutional racism and oppressive structures, navigate something that is more emotionally based but still has that element pervasive within it? – Renée

Being in an interracial relationship isn't a pass to overlook the wider structures that politicise these very relationships, though.

When I was in a relationship with him, I was very clear that my blackness is not up for debate. – Fope

Fast-forward almost four years: Joe and I are still together, and in a relationship that prioritises conversations about race, not one that sweeps them under the carpet and pretends that we inhabit a post-racial society. Race colours the very fabric of everything we do, and it would be irresponsible to ignore that. But most importantly, I managed to find someone that I love, who respects my experiences, makes me belly-laugh and is committed to, in his own words, 'helping you live your best life'.

However, it wasn't all plain sailing and heart-shaped chocolates. I had a few black male students feel they could self-righteously comment on my relationship and what I should be doing. Often in all-black settings

I was told I didn't give any of the other black boys 'a chance' given that I got together with my boyfriend in my first year. There was a worrying sense of entitlement over my choices, but most of all I felt disrespected.

The sense of betrayal eroded the strong solidarity that is espoused between black students within predominately white institutions. Interracial relationships are complicated enough, but I found this factor complicated it even further. It became hard for others to accept the fact that I had just happened to find someone I really liked. I soon learnt that I wasn't obliged to jump through hoops to explain it to anyone, or bash anyone in the process of doing so. But it was frustrating that I didn't have the privilege of being in a regular relationship, where no one cared what we did and how we did it. Our relationship was collapsed into black and white – quite literally.

*

For the tough-skinned, it's easy to ignore the elephant in the room that is racism when it comes to interracial relationships. At university, it became hard to gloss over the blatant fetishisation of black men at predominately white institutions, from idolising their physical bodies and stature in a sporting context, to relationships and sex. For most black men, it is an uncomfortable reality that their bodies are commodified to the point that they are always expected to perform a certain standard of 'black masculinity'. Even more so, the masculine expectations are particularly hard to grapple with for black queer men or gender non-conforming people who may want to present or date in a way that doesn't necessarily meet a heterosexual standard. As such, many black queer men have found their experiences and existence simultaneously defined and erased by racism.

Yet it is no secret that black male students have a 'unique' appeal to women and men of all races and ethnicities and have the opportunity to capitalise on that. Among all those Ọrẹ and I interviewed, there was a collective sense of agreement that a select few black men at university simply didn't mind that most people were attracted to them – albeit some for the wrong reasons.

> **I think it also comes down to black men having a market, or a lot of choice – because they could still get with white girls very easily because of that fetishisation or that exploration of that interracial interaction. – Courtney**

> **I think the worst thing is when I have a crush on someone but – am I even his type? In terms of: is 'black girls' his type? Which I think a lot of white women just have never ever had to think about. – Fope**

Heterosexual black male privilege is well discussed in black feminist circles. There has never been a denial of the racism and unique prejudice that black men face, but a critical analysis of the contours of their privilege in relation to the experiences of black women is necessary. Within university walls, engaging in patriarchal rituals such as sports-related heavy drinking allows most black men to very conveniently buy into 'lad culture' and slip into 'cool' stereotypes.

When a black male student was pursued by a non-black woman, it was more likely to be deemed a sense of validation and acceptance – and a welcome one for some black male students, who were just trying to get by 'quietly' at university and blend in as much as possible. Many heterosexual black men were complicit in ignoring this issue, and chose to disengage. They didn't want to acknowledge that there was yet *another* thing that black students needed to be wary of. Any whiff of fetishisation was usually dismissed, in order to avoid 'unnecessary fuss'. In some cases, it was even spun into the age-old and tired story of black women feeling bitter or upset that black men were desired by non-black individuals. One black male student at my university even said that we black girls shouldn't be upset that he wasn't dating 'one of us' (for the record, no one was actually upset).

> **The class and prestige to get in with the white people carries on throughout society. Once you get to a certain level, you want to show that actually your whole life reflects that level, including your personal relationships. – Adaobi**

The very same interactions became validation tools for non-black students, who almost obsessively insisted that they were 'not racist' because they found black men attractive. In an article titled 'I'm not an object or a toy for your white gaze – don't fetishise me as a black man', Archie Mustow, a recent law graduate, explored what it was like to date as a black man:

> **It's almost as if white people feel guilty that they get to be white and I have to be black, so they take on the noble role of reminding me that there are some benefits to my negroness by being my mate or wanting to have sex with me.**

Lazing around on the grass one day, one of my favourite friends told me that he had been invited to an exclusive dinner at an all-girls college where each girl had been tasked to bring one boy with them. He told me that at the dinner most of the girls, all white, joked about *reserving* him and his brothers to have babies with. 'Our babies would be *so* cute,' they said.

I did a workshop for the [day] talking about online dating, and a lot of my group in the morning were white people. I was explaining that your preferences can be racist, and one girl was like, 'It's not my fault I like black guys because I like broad noses and flat foreheads.' I was like, 'You've just described Vin Diesel.' – Fope

When I've spoken to black guys about it . . . they've said that the black girls are the ones that they settle with after they're done having their fun. – Kenya

You think your black queen will just be waiting for you while you're doing your rubbish in university? – Renée

And that is it, isn't it? Kenya and Renée have said what a lot of us were thinking. It was known among black men at university that most black girls had little to no choice in a tiny pool of potential partners. Some black men exploited this fact, knowing that a few of us had no option but to wait around. But as I mentioned above, when I decided I was not going to entertain the idea of 'waiting around', I was suddenly treated like a traitor – despite black men having the agency and sexual freedom to have relationships with anyone.

I love black men, and I know I love black men, but I think that loving black men is a very painful process, because a lot of the time that kind of love is unrequited. Not just in a romantic sense, but I feel like I spend a lot of my time making sure that I'm being supportive to black men who don't put in the same kind of work to support me in return. – Ọrẹ

We saw how some black men acted at university, and for most of us, it was hurtful. That hurt wasn't only because they weren't interested – I truly believe that is something that shouldn't be forced. But most of them had failed to realise that by their internalising and accepting of racialised notions of desirability, us black women were affected very strongly. It was a reminder that interracial relationships and the structures of power around them are still contentious, and as always, vitally important to deconstruct.

Reclaiming Bodies

I think it's fair to say that you will often find the words 'university' and 'sex' in the same sentence. For most, university is an exciting time that allows for the agency to explore sexual relationships. Or perhaps, everything feels new and distant because of the lack of sex education. In my first sex education class in Year 6, one of my classmates ran out of the room straight to the toilets to be sick after watching our teacher awkwardly put a condom on a banana. Since that point, I have never been 'educated' on matters regarding sex, relationships or sexual assault. They all seemed to be things that you had to *experience* to really understand. Even now, when we watch sex scenes on TV, listen to relationship 'experts' and seek advice from our friends, their realities will never quite match our own.

A survey conducted by Hexjam looked at the sex lives of around 5,800 students up and down the UK, and revealed that around 25 per cent of students lost their virginity at university. This merely confirms what we all know: university is a prime time to explore sex and sexualities. Student unions across the country are prepped for the wave of excited freshers, issuing thousands of free condoms and pregnancy tests. All of a sudden, you're thrust into a world where the pressure to have sex is immense. You feel as if this is all everyone is doing all the time, and they all want someone to talk to about it – you know, the typical, 'I had to do the walk of shame last night' that forces you to ask all about your friend's antics.

**People just used to sleep around, and everyone is speaking to each other or like seeing each other, but no one's actually putting any god-damn labels on it, and I'm not here for that . . . The mixed messages, ugh: it's just annoying.
– Nathania**

A key component of my freshers' week was a compulsory session on consent, part of a long series of introductory talks about what college life would be like, and how to exit a building on fire. The session included a video called 'Tea and Consent', which compared sexual consent to making someone a cup a tea. 'If they say, "No, thank you,"' the narrator explained, 'then don't make them tea. *At all.*' Most of the people in the room laughed nervously. It seemed like such a gross oversimplification that it left most of us wondering how anyone could possibly *not* understand it?

'The body is an appropriate cultural symbol to explore the links between colonialism and patriarchal capitalism,' says Dr Akeia Benard, a professor from Wheelock College, Boston – meaning for black women, the conversation regarding sexual assault and harassment is particularly worrying when considering the historical trajectory of sexual violence and exploitation against black bodies. In my second year at university, I will never forget how the historian of racial and sexual violence Danielle L. McGuire detailed the case of Betty Jean Owens, an African American woman brutally raped by four white men in Tallahassee, Florida in 1959. Students mobilised for her cause when the student leader Buford Gibson 'universalised the attack', stating that 'you must remember it wasn't just one Negro girl that was raped, it was all of Negro womanhood in the South'. The exploitation of black women's bodies served as a reminder of white supremacy and a signpost of a social order that would continue to control black women's bodies.

Recently, we've seen the rise of the #MeToo movement, an online campaign supporting the survivors of sexual assault, abuse and harassment. The movement has reverberated across the globe, being joined by other hashtags such as #balancetonporc and #yotambien. #MeToo conjures images of glitzy Hollywood stars who defiantly wore all-black at the 2018 Golden Globes – with little consideration given to Tarana Burke, the black woman who launched the movement almost a decade ago. Burke told ESSENCE magazine, 'The world responds to the vulnerability of white women.

Our narrative has never been centred in mainstream media. Our stories don't get told and as a result, it makes us feel not as valuable.'

Every person Ọrẹ and I interviewed had been, or at least knew one other person who had been, sexually assaulted whilst at university. For those who don't understand or doubt the severity of sexual assault at university:

- 62 per cent of students and graduates have experienced sexual violence.

- Only 2 per cent of those experiencing sexual violence felt able to report it to their university and were satisfied with their university's reporting process.

- 33 per cent have no knowledge or very little knowledge about where to seek support if they experience sexual violence.

I think the right question would be: who *hasn't* been a victim? – Mikai

Universities across the UK have become grounds for assault, harassment and misconduct. This is a crisis affecting not only students, but also staff. It's not a new phenomenon to many of us, who are familiar with having to navigate conversations in fear of being blamed or further silenced. The conversation and language surrounding sexual assault and harassment continues to be part of a broader culture of victim blaming. Women are asked whether or not we were drunk, or what we were wearing, as a means of 'contextualising' sexual assault or harassment. It's as if the severity of the disciplinary procedure (or worse) is determined by whether or not the crime was in some way the victim's 'fault'.

This has widened the scope and range of what both students and staff deem to be sexual assault or harassment. In particular, lad culture, and its connection to social and educational privileges, has dramatically influenced the university environment. The NUS project 'That's What She Said' found that most students defined lad culture as 'a group or "pack" mentality residing in activities such as sport and heavy alcohol consumption, and "banter" which was often sexist, misogynist, and homophobic', and I would add, racist. With lad culture having such an influence on the social aspects of university, little effort is made to address the underlying cultural element of sexual abuse. Instead, most universities continue to address each report as it comes, rather than understanding how it fits into a wider and urgent conversation regarding university culture, sexual harassment and sexual violence. It is clear most universities are still not ready to address how this issue is embedded, rooted and perpetuated by the culture.

Men are often excused with the saying, 'boys will be boys', or 'just having a laugh'. Especially within the campus environment, sexual abuse and violence have been institutionally accepted and trivialised. In 2018, a group of eleven male students from the University of Warwick were revealed to have set up a group chat discussion in which they talked about raping and sexually assaulting other students. Comments included, 'Sometimes it's fun to just go wild and rape 100 girls', whilst one mentioned, 'Even the pakis??', and another 'I cannot wait to have surprise sex with some freshers.' In total, ninety-eight screenshots from the chat were sent to the University of Warwick as part of the complaint – enough, you would think, for the university to take appropriate action against the students? Well, no.

First of all, the university's director of press was appointed as the official investigator, a clear conflict of interests. Secondly, Vice-Chancellor Professor Stuart Croft wrote an open letter in which he spent two paragraphs detailing his 'shock', before setting out what the next steps would be. He went on to explain that 'we have a duty of care to all involved, as they are our students' and that the students involved will bear the brunt of the incident 'forward on their cvs [sic]'. Two of the men involved in the group chat would have an initial ten-year campus ban reduced to one. And still no mention of the students affected or their wellbeing, nor of the justification for such lenient disciplinary processes. Instead, there was an insistence on arbitrary terms such as 'the law', 'the courts' and 'justice'.

The university was apparently eager to put forward the notion that these students were an 'exceptional case' or 'bad apples'. Warwick students were not so easily placated, however. By 5 p.m. the next day, after an instant and sizeable backlash, the university performed an abrupt U-turn, and announced that two of the students would not be returning to Warwick at all. Its institutional culture was left unexamined, unchallenged and intact; it was only a media storm that forced it to change its position.

In 1994, the Zellick Report was published, an important guidance document regarding student disciplinary procedures such as the one at Warwick. The report suggested that universities should *not* take internal disciplinary action when it came to alleged misconduct. This has allowed universities to inadequately address a myriad of events that accompany sexual violence: disciplinary procedures, specialist aftercare and, most importantly, rebuilding the trust of students. Some of you may be surprised to find out that most universities still follow these very guidelines. This correlates with the sheer amount of sexual violence that goes unreported at universities. Compounded with sub-standard university regulations surrounding issues of sexual assault, it begs the question of how universities have managed to get away with being complicit in this manner.

As a result students, particularly women, feel unsupported, dismissed and disconnected from their universities. As That's What She Said rightly states, 'the growing individualism which is an aspect of corporate higher education may also prevent students, female and male, from reaching out for help when they experience difficulties'. Despite being published in 2013, the report still resonates today. As students, we often feel that our everyday issues and trials are miniscule in comparison to the bigger elements of university business, such as competition and privatisation. We're rarely seen as human beings with individual needs that are specific and complex, but rather as paying customers, existing within the university only for a short period.

Above all, it has taken generations of tireless women's officers and student activists on the ground to urge universities and, in some cases, to work with universities, to address this endemic crisis. When someone is a victim of sexual violence it reverberates across the student body. For every initiative, policy and campaign, it is clear that the main driving force is always from students.

Every year, University Student Unions organise a march entitled 'Reclaim the Night'. Reclaim the Night started in 1977 across England in Leeds, York, Bristol, Manchester and other cities. The Leeds Revolutionary Feminist group wanted to take collective action regarding male sexual violence against women, and to honour the histories of those who have come before us and the challenges they have faced throughout history. Manchester Student Union have rallied around the Night to encourage students to volunteer, write to the local council and sign a petition addressed to Manchester City Council to 'Make our Streets Safer'.

Reclaim the Night, amongst other ongoing campaigns by students, has contributed to a growing pressure on universities to admit responsibility. 'Where do you draw the line?' is a harassment prevention approach developed by UCL, Oxford, Cambridge and Manchester, all of which recognise that harassment within academia tends to be more nuanced and covert. Similarly, Cambridge's new 'zero tolerance' stance on harassment and abuse is conveyed in its 'Breaking The Silence' campaign. The university now has an anonymous reporting system embedded in its website, allowing any member of the university to report and record misconduct. However, this all comes only after women and non-binary students have worked to create spaces for themselves and for victims of sexual assault. Such actions have paved the way for the creation of standardised and comprehensive guidelines for alleged misconduct which prioritise victims/survivors first, rather than the reputations of institutions.

Under no circumstances is there an excuse for sexual violence. As stated by Rape Crisis, '100% of the responsibility for any act of sexual violence lies with the perpetrator'. As such, if you have ever been a victim, suspect you have been a victim or know someone who is a victim, where possible seek professional help from a professional organisation. Contact the Rape Crisis national freephone helpline on 0808 802 9999, or the National Domestic Violence Helpline on 0808 2000 247, or ring NHS 111. It's daunting and uncomfortable, but there are professionals out there who are trained, experienced and willing to help.

You may find yourself in a position where a friend or somebody close discloses to you that they have been a victim of sexual violence. First of all, it's important that you let them know that you care and that you believe what they are telling you. Despite the vilification of sexual assault victims in the media, it is *very* unlikely that someone will be lying about their experience of any form of sexual violence. It's about trust and allowing them to tell their own story when it is best for them. It could also be an idea to familiarise yourself with your university's disciplinary procedure and what steps your friend might want to take if they choose to do so. But above all, look after yourself and your needs. By all means you can be a supportive shoulder, but trust your friend to make the right decisions.

At the back of this book, you can find a small but useful directory of resources relating to sexual assault – for victims and supporters. From sharpening up your own understanding of consent and accessing helplines to supporting and organising, this can be a place to turn to if you're not sure where to start.

Choosing You

Getting to a stage of self-worth and self-love can be difficult and tiresome. It's easy to understand from all the above why we're more likely to experience feelings of self-hate and inadequacy. You're trying to be your best self – trying to be the most successful and empowered version of yourself – only to realise that it doesn't quite fit into this whole scale of desirability, palatability and subservience that women, especially black women, are often expected to adhere to.

If you take away anything from this chapter, let it be this: try to be kinder to yourself. *Please.* We are our own worst critics, and sometimes we need to cut ourselves some slack. It's about setting boundaries and practising good self-care – both acts which will put you first. Even though it sounds so simple, this strategy was revolutionary for me at university.

Taking a whistle-stop tour through everyone's university experiences was enough to witness the growth and constant learning curve that is involved in learning to love yourself with no excuses. It takes time, and there's no set blueprint for 'how to do it'. Don't expect to come into a university environment knowing everything.

Instead, you will grow, and you will learn. In my humble opinion, that's the best part about it.

Oh, and feel free to tell that one aunty all of this. I'm sure she'll understand!

TAKING*up*SPACE

6

Blacktivism

Ọrẹ

It was November 2015, my first term at Cambridge, and I had just got back from my first ACS event. I shared a cab with Amatey Doku, who was then the president of Jesus College's student union. As one of the few black students at Cambridge in an elected office, he was someone I looked up to from very early on in my time there. We were heading back to our rooms, and our saying goodbyes turned into an hour-long conversation about a whole range of things. I knew that his tenure as president would end that December, so I asked him what he was going to do afterwards. Then he told me about the cockerel. There was a bronze cockerel that sat in our college hall which had been taken during the 1897 Benin Expedition and bequeathed to the university by George William Neville. All of this was written on a plaque beneath the cockerel – in Latin, of course, because we know Cambridge loves some good old Latin!

I remember feeling shocked that this cockerel had been there and I hadn't noticed it. More shocking, though, was knowing that it was being displayed as if it were a trophy to be proud of, despite the knowledge of its history. The college couldn't feign ignorance about the circumstances surrounding when or how the artefact was acquired because they had engraved it on the plaque right below. The 1897 Benin Expedition was a British-led military expedition that became a pretext for the colonial occupation of what was once one of the most powerful West African kingdoms, the Benin Empire. The retaliatory expedition was intentionally meant to obliterate the Empire, and after burning and destroying the city, the British army looted the artefacts left in its wake, which are now held in museums and institutions across the Western world.

Amatey told me that once his presidency was over, he wanted to work to get the cockerel taken down and repatriated to Benin City (in modern-day Nigeria). As a Nigerian myself, I felt an obligation to get on board. If we couldn't fight for this, who would? Amatey made it sound so simple. We would write a proposal and spell out the already blatantly obvious injustice that was this cockerel's possession. There would be huge uproar, and it would be back in Benin in no time.

Little had we considered how much resistance we would encounter. Obviously, we were going up against an age-old institution, built, in certain respects, on imperialist legacies, and stuck in its traditional ways. We sought approval from the college student body to strengthen our case. We had to wait until the next Ordinary General Meeting (OGM) to raise a motion, present our proposal and then have the student body vote on it. Our team grew, and we worked on a proposal that outlined that keeping the cockerel was immoral in itself, particularly given how it made students from former colonies feel, and also that repatriation might turn out to be beneficial for the college. We added the second point because Amatey and I felt that a moral incentive alone wasn't enough, and that we had to negotiate with the college by showing them what was in it for them. This point in particular became a grave source of conflict within our team, and the night before the OGM, two people resigned from the group.

We thought that our biggest opposition would be from a few ignorant white students or empire nostalgics who were more concerned with the monetary value of the cockerel than with the history of its acquisition – but that wasn't the case. Instead, we faced opposition from a group of BME students who thought that we were stressing the material incentives for the college when actually the only reason that the college should have needed to repatriate the cockerel was moral. As far as they were concerned, it was stolen, so it should be returned. I do not entirely disagree – but as a first-year student, I was afraid of being seen as a troublemaker, and felt that I could be putting my place at Cambridge on the line. So I opted for what I thought would be the path of least resistance.

I learnt the hard way that just because people look like you or have comparable experiences with oppression doesn't mean that they will be on your side. We might all be minorities and we might all be engaged with activism, fighting to validate our voices in these oppressive circumstances, but we aren't a monolith. One of our members who had resigned showed up at the OGM, dressed as a Black Panther, with a whole team of friends who were also dressed all in black. The OGM turned into a mini-warzone.

As we were to discover, when you fight for things you believe in, you will make enemies. You expect enemies to be vicious, but when your friends turn on you, it takes on a different meaning. That's a pain that no one prepared me for. Attacks were made on my character. Having spent most of the meeting trying not to cry, when I couldn't hold it in any more, I wept.

After the two-hour-long OGM and a few days of team meetings, during which we revised the proposal, we presented a modified, extended proposal to the college. We were invited to meet with numerous college committees we had never heard of; the longer the process went on, the more unclear it became as to whether or not the college was actually going to do anything at all. Attempting to make any change at universities like Cambridge that are so stubbornly attached to 'tradition' takes forever. I think the expectation from the authorities was that we would be wearied by the wait, and that our fatigue would work in their favour.

We had to sit in lots of meetings with university officials who challenged our position that the plights of the Benin people, who had been requesting for over a century that their art be repatriated, were valid. They would ask questions like, 'But who's going to look after it?', as if the people from whom it was stolen hadn't been doing so perfectly well for centuries. Our well-researched responses never appeased them.

And that's how that story ended. (Or perhaps it hasn't ended yet.) After years of meetings, the cockerel has still not made it back to Benin in Nigeria, and neither the college nor the university ever gave us a reason as to why. Although it was taken down from the hall and the shelf removed, so we could be sure it wasn't going back up, we still have no clue where it has been kept.

However, my work on this campaign was not entirely fruitless. I raised considerable awareness about an underdiscussed issue that's very close to my heart as a Nigerian, and I set a ball in motion. It was a very steep learning curve for me. This was my first dip into Cambridge's 'activism' space, it was painful and tiring, and still we have not got the results that we wanted.

Fight the good fight – but be prepared for the difficult, less glamorous bits. Fighting for issues that affect people like us in white-dominated spaces will always be an uphill battle, but if we don't do it, who will? I had to constantly remind myself about the generation of black students who would come after me and never have to shudder at the sight of colonial war loot being celebrated in their dining hall.

We had to make our case in rooms full of white people who will never know what it is like to be black in an institution that seems to take pride in its ties with an imperialist history. And we had to make our case again, and again, and again, as everyone shifted in their shoes trying to decide who to pass us on to, so that they didn't have to be the ones to say no.

That's how they get away with stuff: institutional memory. Because everyone is here for like three years, then they leave – so any big issue, if you just wait long enough, it will be dead. – Arenike

Like most black girls at university, I didn't go in with a plan to engage in as much activism or political work as I did. But as a black woman in a white dominated space, I discovered that my very existence was an act of resistance. Although I wasn't looking for it, the political work found me.

The Burden of Obligation

Regardless of how hard it was and how fruitless it sometimes felt, I'm glad that I decided to get involved with the Benin Bronze repatriation campaign. Simply put, I made the initial decision to help because I felt like I *had to*; I felt obliged by my very identity as a Nigerian woman to do something. Since I had been given this privilege of being at such a renowned institution, the very least I could do was fight for every issue that concerned people like me, especially those who weren't there to fight their cases. I'm a black, Nigerian-British woman, and I realise that 'people like me' encompasses a significant percentage of the population.

As black girls, the activist instinct is bound up in our very identities. The more aware we become of our own oppression, the more we feel the need to fight for every cause. We have to stand up for black women and battle the insidious misogynoir we face, because other black women fought before us in order for us to be there. We have to fight for all women too, challenging gender-based violence and diversifying white feminist spaces while we're at it. Then we have to fight for the whole black community – even black men who, though they can be part of the problem, are still affected by racism in a unique way. Then we learn about the importance of intersectionality and the extent to which all the axes of oppression are mutually reinforcing and suddenly, we are carrying the plights of the whole world on our backs. Suddenly, we feel an obligation to fight everyone's corner. Suddenly, we are haunted by guilt if we do not.

To understand why the black experience is unique, it's important to examine why *we* feel the obligation to be politically active and engage in the ongoing fight for black progress, while our white counterparts have the privilege of choosing to jog on, oblivious to the realities of racism around them. Some white people may not be bothered; others may be afraid; but even those who do choose to man the trenches with us still have the privilege of choosing to ignore racism if they want to. When it's inextricably bound to every part of your life, as it is for black students, you don't.

To what extent are black students not privileged with mediocrity? Why must we feel the need, why are we obligated to make a difference? Why are we obligated to make an impact? – Renée

It's not merely an obligation that we feel within, it is an obligation that is placed on us. We're assumed to be the founts of all knowledge on everything concerning blackness, and to have an opinion on everything that affects black people everywhere. But what if you don't?

What if sometimes you just want to focus on your degree, and graduate? What if you just want to pursue other interests?

I had a really insightful conversation with Adaobi about how it is always assumed that the purpose of absolutely everything we do as black women is for the betterment of black people. Adaobi is very passionate about robotics, and has struggled with the fact that the white men she encounters in the tech world assume that her primary reason for entering the industry is to solve its very pertinent diversity problem.

> **I really am for black women, but I came here to be the CEO or the Team Lead – so why do I need to be the Diversity and Inclusion Officer? People think that all I do is driven by diversity and my life is no longer my own, my interests are no longer my own. I can't do something just because I enjoy it. – Adaobi**

The pressure of feeling as if you're obliged to constantly fight for your people can become a burden. Not everyone wants to be, or has to be, a community leader or a spokesperson in activist spaces. Try not to feel guilty for being passionate about things other than diversity quotas. Be an Adaobi and reclaim ownership over your interests.

Your interests may not be the only reason you choose to disengage with political work. The stress and fatigue can be a lot to manage alongside your studies. In my first year I chose the Benin Bronze campaign, and in my second and third years I focused on the ACS's access work. By the time our lecturers went on strike in the second term of my final year, following a drastic cut in their pensions, I was tired. By the time the Decolonise the Curriculum movement was picking up steam, with alternative reading lists being drafted and focus groups making real headway with department officials on diversifying the curriculum, I was exhausted. Regardless, people expected me, in my most stressful year at Cambridge, to keep showing up, and to have an opinion, and to be actively involved. I didn't know how to explain the fatigue without feeling bad for not being there to fight for a cause that might need me.

Fope can relate:

When someone knows you for always putting your opinion forward, being very bold with that, especially in political spaces, people tend to then ask you to do more and more and more. It's always, 'You know what, Fope will call this out, so I'll ask Fope to do this,' or 'Fope should go for this role because Fope would be really good at

it.' It's not taken into account that Fope has a life. Fope has very, very little energy to expend.

Learning to say no to this 'obligation' is difficult. Not only are we always expected to fight, it is assumed that all we care about is fighting, and that we will always want to fight. But sometimes, we want to rest and recover and focus on staying sane in what is already a troubling environment.

By my third year, I wasn't just physically and mentally tired of the struggle, I was also emotionally drained. The more engaged you try to be, the more aware you become of exactly how oppressed you are. I hate the way the word 'woke' is thrown around, but I appreciate how it helps us to conceptualise what it feels like to come to *see* your oppression. The awakening is painful and distressing. Every time you engage in the kind of activism that feels personal and proximal, you relive the anger, the frustration, and the helplessness of fighting a system of oppression so deeply entrenched that it's difficult to know where to begin. For some people, this pain is enough to dissuade them from doing any activism at all. But for those of us whose instinct to act is too strong to push back, remember that it's okay to stop, recover and look after yourself.

The power in solidarity can be very, very intoxicating, and you want to do everything, but you're going to burn out. – Fope

Choosing to opt out of political work and say no to student movements that might need you is not just self-care but also self-preservation. It's not everyday politics – sometimes rest, beloved. Rest.

The B in B(A)ME

This burden of obligation is something that BME (or BAME – black, Asian and minority ethnic) students feel especially. BME isn't a term that I had encountered before university, but much to the annoyance of almost everyone we interviewed for this book, it is often at the centre of these 'diversity' discussions. It's difficult to pinpoint when it became popularised. Some say it developed out of the notion of 'political blackness' used in British anti-racism movements in the 1970s. However, some suggest it didn't become used officially until the early 1990s, when the UK census categories used 'ethnic minority' to refer to everyone non-white. If you find yourself in political spaces, more often than not, you will be grouped under BME, or 'people of colour'.

The term BME is unhelpful. The idea of black *and* minority ethnic firstly implies that black is not an ethnic minority – but for now, that is beside the point. No one we spoke to had anything positive to say about the term.

Don't call me woman of colour. Don't call me BME. – Adaobi

Throw it in the bin or something. Bin it. – Mikai

The term is problematic because it lacks nuance. It conflates all non-white people, and treats them as a monolith. Yet our experiences of race and racism as people of colour are very different. The term speaks to the idea of white normativity – that every other race is constructed as deviant from whiteness, as 'lacking' in whiteness. The idea of political blackness has a similar effect. Eireann says, '**No group is in direct opposition to whiteness**,' but terms like BME and 'politically black' suggest that this is in fact the case.

> **I feel like black people are at the bottom of the totem pole and I don't feel like our issues are comparable to [other] racial groups. – Kenya**

> **I think at Cambridge specifically, black people face specific resistances and hostilities from the institution that I don't think can be applied to, let's say, Pakistani or Chinese international students. – Chelsea**

The term BME prevents us from having frank conversations about the unique ways in which black people in particular experience racism. It silences. Even in writing this book, I felt an initial need to apologise for not speaking directly to all women of colour – but why should I? Without trying to engage in 'oppression Olympics' here, when Kenya spoke about being at the bottom of the totem pole, it resonated with me. Even though we might all be bracketed under BME in research papers and articles, when are we going to talk about the fact that oppression replicates itself *within* the BME category as well?

Many do not realise that the idea of BME obscures the fact that racism can, and does, exist between people of colour. Anti-blackness, for instance, is present in many Arab and North African communities. The BME category suggests that white people are the only perpetrators of racism. It obscures the very sore, historical question of the role of Arabs, for example, in the slave trade. But where do you find spaces to have conversations about these issues when all the BME spaces at university are shared?

Anti-blackness is inherent in a lot of [non-black BME people's] cultures, and I don't think they want to acknowledge that. – Fope

Why are we all forcing unity that's not there? – Kenya

When you pander to this whole solidarity thing, you make it seem like we're best friends and we're not. Living on a council estate, it's just loads of people of colour, and a lot of people

**who are racist are also ethnic minorities.
– Courtney**

While I was at Cambridge, I was repeatedly asked by people I met if I went to the *other* university in Cambridge – because of course the notion that as a black woman, I might have earned a place at the best university in the country is difficult for some to conceive of. The first time I was ever asked this was by a boy of South Asian origin – even though I had just told him which Cambridge college I went to. His racialised assumptions about my academic abilities kicked in before his senses could, and he profiled me. Don't be deceived into thinking that the only racism that you're going to fight is going to come from white people. A lot of student political work and activism frames the conversation as white v. non-white – but be aware of what that lens obscures.

#BlackMenofCambridgeUniversity and the Gendered Aspect

These conversations often gloss over the ways in which patriarchal dynamics penetrate these spaces, too. A lot of political work, especially that concerning anti-racism movements, relies on the hard work of women and queer people, which often goes ignored. This isn't a phenomenon unique to student activism, or even to this period in modern history. However, our viral #BlackMenofCambridgeUniversity campaign was another reminder of what that looks like.

On 25 April 2017, a friend of mine, Hepsi Adeosun, WhatsApped me a screenshot of a tweet that had gone viral. It was a group of black boys from Yale University with the hashtag #BlackMenofYaleUniversity, and the text read 'Omg make this happen pls, for Cam haha'. I laughed it off, and said I would run it by the ACS committee. Before I knew it, the committee was loving the idea, Hepsi was brainstorming a list of boys who might be willing, and I was charging my camera because we had to jump on a trending wave that could end up being a very powerful access initiative for Cambridge.

In the end, we managed to get fourteen black boys together for what would become one of my favourite memories of my time at Cambridge. It was a warm afternoon on 1 May. I set up a little tripod on the lawns of St John's College, in front of a neo-gothic archway, hoping to capture a poignant juxtaposition between the old, quintessential Cambridge from which people like us had been excluded for so long, and its growing cohort of black students that were defining the new age. The boys all knew each other, even if vaguely. But in this moment, it felt different. This didn't feel like a random group of lads. There was a genuine camaraderie, fraternity and infectious joy that I was really keen to capture. It felt magical just being there.

I had a revision presentation right after the shoot, and so I had to rush off. I took my laptop out once I arrived, but I sat at the back, editing photos for about twenty minutes. After another ten minutes, I had to walk out – I was too excited to stay. I ran home, where Chelsea was waiting for me, ready to compose this make-or-break Facebook caption, decide on the hashtags, and prepare all our social media platforms. We knew there was no turning back after we hit that 'Post' button. We had to make sure that not a single word could be misinterpreted, twisted by any mischievous people or picked up by the *Daily Mail* in attempts to slander the ACS or Cambridge's black community more broadly. Chelsea thought we needed numbers in the caption to stress why these initiatives were so important, so we looked up the admissions statistics and found out that in the year that we joined the university, only fifteen black boys had matriculated alongside us. I find it quite telling that we weren't even shocked by the discovery.

Our carefully crafted caption, posted on the ACS Facebook page, read:

> **In 2015, only 15 black, male undergraduates were accepted into Cambridge.**
>
> **However, it is important that despite their under-representation, we let young black people know that this is something that they can aspire to.**
>
> **'Young black men don't grow up thinking they'll make it here. They should.' – Dami Adebayo (Robinson College)**
>
> **Inspired by the viral image of young black men from Yale, the Cambridge ACS decided to capture just some of the black men who contribute to one of the world's most innovative intellectual spaces.**
>
> **Representation matters.**
>
> **#BlackBoyJoy**
>
> **#BlackMenofCambridgeUniversity**

I don't exaggerate when I say 'carefully crafted'. We read it over again and again – and it paid off. We had about a thousand Facebook reactions within a few hours; we knew that this was going to be pretty big.

We posted the photos on the evening of 1 May. We wanted the campaign to go viral, so a media furore was welcomed. The morning after the pictures went out, I received a Twitter message from Victoria Sanusi, then at Buzzfeed. Thanks to her, Buzzfeed was the first publication to run a story on the photos on 2 May. As a black woman who has always used her voice to promote other black voices, we could trust that Victoria would do justice to the story.

One of the first people to write about me was Victoria Sanusi, and just seeing a black woman writing about me in such a great way on such a huge platform such as Buzzfeed . . . that to me was sisterhood. – Courtney

I remember being in a meeting and my phone kept ringing. I left the meeting, and listened to a string of voicemails from different newspaper outlets, asking for permission to use the pictures. Channel 4 followed Buzzfeed with a feature video for their online platform. Over the next few days, the pictures were broadcast on the BBC (online, World News and Victoria Derbyshire), the *Washington Post*, the *Evening Standard*, *Elle*, the *Mirror* and *The FADER*, to name just a few, and I and the boys featured did a variety of TV and radio interviews as well.

As the reach expanded, inevitably the criticisms got back to us. Numerous people were unhappy with the fact that there were no girls in the picture. We had a few explanations: firstly, we were just jumping on Yale's wave, but secondly, there were, and still are, unique issues that black boys face concerning representation, especially in the media. The news and mainstream media are much more likely to criminalise black boys than to show them thriving at an institution such as Cambridge. We weren't going to apologise for not focusing on black girls, who outnumbered black boys at Cambridge by over 50 per cent at the time. In 2015, the year of those fifteen black boys' admission, twenty-three black girls entered Cambridge. By 2017, in my final year, the figures stood at twenty-five black boys and thirty-three black girls. The underrepresentation of black students at Cambridge is poor – but it is worse still for black men, and we chose to focus on that.

Some people, however, weren't buying our explanations – and not because what we said wasn't true, but because for some, this campaign pointed to a broader underlying issue. Black women are used to doing the bulk of political work, while black men are the faces of the movements; black women are constantly taking it upon themselves to uplift black men, and address issues that affected them, with no reward or credit for them in return. The dynamic between who does the work and who gets credit for it falls along gendered lines.

This isn't a new phenomenon. 'Blacktivism', or race-related political work, has been riddled with this imbalance throughout history. When you think of 'Black Lives Matter', you're more likely to know who DeRay Mckesson is than the three women – Alicia Garza, Opal Tometi and Patrisse Cullors – who actually started the movement. Think further back to America's civil rights movements, and you think Martin Luther King Jr. – not the women who played key organisational roles in the movement. When you think of the Million Man March of 1995, you're more inclined to remember the prominent roles of the male speakers such as Jesse Jackson, and again, not the roles of women. The work of women such as Olive Morris, Funmilayo Ransome-Kuti and Claudia Jones is not lost on me. Women's labour is constantly being erased, while you don't have to look far to see how the legacies of men are memorialised.

In late September 2018, Cambridge held a month-long exhibition during Black History Month which featured portraits of ten notable black students and alumni. One of the boys I asked to feature in the Black Men of

Cambridge photos was included in the exhibition, simply because he had posed for my photos. But neither I, nor any other member of that Cambridge ACS committee who had organised the initiative, were honoured in the same way. Our ACS committee that year had eleven people on it, and ten of us were women, all of whom were elected. The only male member of the committee was not elected – we invited him to take up that role. Although the 2018–19 committee has more male committee members than I have ever seen in Cambridge ACS, and even a male president, the current president is the first male president that the society has had in ten years.

It's important to acknowledge that as black women in these spaces, we often outnumber black men. Aspiring for 50:50 representation in our activist work is hardly feasible. If there were more of us black women there, I shouldn't think that expecting us to use our platform to also lift up black men would be unreasonable. However, as black women, we spend a lot of time carrying the weight of everyone else, while finding our efforts ignored and unacknowledged.

For black queer people, this issue runs even deeper. Every single black queer person that I knew in Cambridge was engaged in political work. For the most part, they were the ones organising the protests, running the discussion groups and writing the open letters. I could never discuss the lack of representation in political work without honouring the black queer people who gave so much to fight for our black community in spite of the homophobia, transphobia and biphobia that they had to face.

The women of colour and queer people of colour and non-binary people of colour – those are the people I know who are consistently doing work and who never get shouted out for it. – Arenike

We are within our rights to question whether black, straight men in activist spaces are actively taking measures to resolve the erasure of black female voices. We must not forget that black men are still men, complicit in a patriarchal system that profits from the undervaluing of our labour. Some black men who share these spaces with us have not helped us when we're organising on the frontline, and have also not spoken up for us when our voices are silenced. Black men have male privilege in these spaces – but are they using that privilege to elevate the voices of the black women around them? Are the black men who can more easily adopt the 'cool' character in their groups of white friends speaking up for us? Are they challenging the misogynoir on our behalf in the rooms where we aren't present to defend ourselves?

It's easier for a crowd of black men to fade into the white school population in a way that black girls just simply couldn't. – Saredo

In my third year, a black mixed-race man in my year made a video in which he performed a freestyle (rap). He called out people like me who have spoken out extensively about the access issues facing black students in, and applying to, Cambridge. According to him, we were insinuating that 'you can't enjoy your time here [at university] if your skin is brown'. He was apparently very troubled by the fact that we were informing the rest of the world about the trials that come with being black at Cambridge because, he said, 'I enjoy Cambridge and I don't want a twisted version of my life being made money off by the papers.' Of *course* he was doing just fine; as a black (mixed-race) man, he could comfortably be the 'cool black guy' in his group of white friends in a way that I would never be able to. He just didn't see why black women like us might find Cambridge so hard. In response, I wrote a blog post entitled 'We need your support, not your freestyles'. I was also disappointed that, in spite of all his chat, it wasn't clear how he'd used his own relative privilege in Cambridge's spaces to uplift and empower those around him who struggle, or to offer help to those fighting our corner. Perhaps he did plenty that I don't know about. Whatever. One thing seems clear to me. It was easy for him to rap about 'the black experience' but I wished he would have matched that energy when we were looking for volunteers for our ACS Mentoring Scheme.

The gendered aspect of political work at university may infuriate you as it did me. I wanted to forgive black men for letting us down because they face their own challenges. After all, that was something that we tried to acknowledge with the Black Men of Cambridge campaign. My existence in this white space is hard enough – I don't want to have to fight black men too. And I don't think in-fighting does much to help the cause. On the other hand, I have had to accept that a lot of black men *will* let us down. I have learnt that there is work that we can do without them, and I have taken their presence, where it does exist, as an added bonus. I do my best to educate black men on how much the burden of this labour affects us, but I have stopped waiting for this to inspire them to speak up. So girls: if you choose to engage in political work, be prepared to take on an unfair amount of it – and be aware that if you are waiting for black men to lift you up too, you might be waiting a long time.

Hypervisibility and the Media

As a black girl in Cambridge, you can't really hide.

Being a black student in an elite space is being hypervisible because you are there. – Mikai

Whiteness as a category is powerful because of how it others non-white people. Whiteness is the normative position from which other races are defined, and being white therefore means that you can blend into the background in a way that black people can't. We are hypervisible and identifiable, and it's hard to avoid the media, especially if you are engaged in any form of activism.

With the Benin Bronze campaign, we tried very hard to avoid the press. The campaign came just after Oxford's 'Rhodes Must Fall' campaign had really taken off, and the media were practically waiting for a Cambridge sequel to erupt so that they could pursue this dramatic storyline of Oxbridge under attack from raging liberal snowflakes (as the media likes to characterise us). We had to be super careful about what we said to anyone. We released one statement, and decided that would be it – but of course, the press wasn't going to relent. The papers picked up a post from my personal blog (which I quickly deleted) in which I said how proud I was of the progress we had made as a student body, and there were articles about our proposal in the *Guardian* and *Daily Mail* within a few days. I stupidly thought it would be a good idea to read through the comment section under the *Guardian* article, which was filled with people telling me to go back to my country, to be grateful to Cambridge for even giving me a place, and calling us troublemakers and 'attention-seeking students'. After the incident of the college OGM, I thought I had developed a thicker skin, but it was still disheartening to see how many strangers were against us.

Another important reason why we chose to stay away from the media, apart from the fact that we needed to focus on our dialogue with the university, was that we wanted to retain control of the narrative. We knew how easy it was for student politics to be twisted in the mainstream media. This is a lesson that ended up being very helpful when the Black Men of Cambridge campaign came around.

The day after our post, I turned my phone off, because I really did have exams to revise for – but when I switched it on for a few minutes, I got a call from the BBC inviting me to be on *Victoria Derbyshire Live*, a huge morning show. I abandoned my revision for the day, did my makeup, put on a smart jacket and headed to the BBC Cambridge studios. While I was there, I ended up doing *BBC World News* as well. This, for me, was amazing, because it meant that my parents could watch from Nigeria. On my way to the interview, Chelsea prepared a research document with all our key facts and figures, and calmed me down in anticipation of my first-ever live TV interview. We were on a roll. The ACS was receiving heaps of messages from parents thanking us for being an inspiring image for their children, from teachers, from big sisters and big brothers, but also from people who had seen the pictures, and now felt embold-ened to make a Cambridge application. This was exactly the effect that we hoped the pictures would have.

A few days later, I got a call from an executive producer at Al Jazeera. (I still wonder how all these people got my number.) Al Jazeera for me has always been a news organisation that I admire because it challenges domin-ant narratives of non-Western countries in ways that I think are admirable. The producer wanted to bring me on to Femi Oke's show, *The Stream*. Femi Oke is one of the first black women I ever saw on TV when I was growing up, and as a fellow Nigerian, I was flattered by the request. This seemed like a big opportunity. How-ever, they wanted to run a thirty-minute feature, without me, pitting the Cambridge black boys against the boys from Yale in a discussion about how awful it was to be at an elite, white-dominated university, connecting their experiences with police brutality, microaggressions and everyday racism at university.

I instinctively turned it down; it was straying so far from the positive narrative that we had set out to pursue. How do we show people that Cambridge is a place where black people can thrive, and in the same breath tell them that it's awful? Al Jazeera wouldn't budge. Femi Oke called me personally, and I had to tell a lady that I had looked up to for effectively my whole life that I could not honour her request. Someone went behind my back and reached out to the boys personally – but luckily we were all on the same page; they knew that this was a bad idea too. As a budding broadcast journalist, it could have been one of the best opportunities of my life. But I had to refuse it in the pursuit of something bigger. We had a story to protect. We were intentional about the message that we wanted this campaign to represent and we stuck to it – even when it meant turning down significant coverage from a global news outlet.

Fortunately, most of the coverage of the Black Men of Cambridge campaign was positive. There were exceptions, though. In the days following the campaign, Camilla Turner, the *Telegraph*'s education editor, interviewed one of the boys we had photographed. The headline that ran with her story was 'Britain's top universities should not be "attacked" for admitting low numbers of ethnic minority students' – even though she knew that this was not the message of our campaign.

This would not be the last time that the *Telegraph* misrepresented the facts behind one of Cambridge's black-centred movements. Later in 2017, the Decolonise English working group at Cambridge sent its open letter to the English department, asking them to diversify their reading lists. Unfortunately, it fell into the hands of the press. On 25 October 2017, a photograph of Lola Olufemi, a black woman who was then the CUSU Women's Officer, was plastered on the cover of the *Telegraph*, with the headline on their print edition reading, 'Student forces Cambridge to drop white authors'. This was another Camilla Turner story. Lola was vilified for her role in the campaign. Although she was only one of over 100 people who had signed the open letter to the faculty, as a black woman who had been at the frontline of the campaign she was a visible, easy target.

Her efforts to diversify the curriculum were about more than just 'seeking to exclude white men' from the syllabus. Reducing the movement to this was a clear misrepresentation, which sought to frame Lola as a troublemaker who didn't appreciate the contributions of white men to English.

[The *Telegraph* was] misconstruing our claims for a more inclusive curriculum to be one of replacement or a kind of iconoclasm, which is

bullshit. I mean, I'm all for iconoclasm. We can literally shut Shakespeare off the curriculum – but that's not what the open letter said! – Arenike

By placing Lola in particular on the cover, the *Telegraph* opened her up to abuse from racist trolls online. The next day, following over forty complaints to the press regulator IPSO, it issued a fickle correction, a discreet square inside the paper:

> **The academics' proposals were in fact recommendations. Neither they nor the open letter called for the University to replace white authors with black ones and there are no plans to do so. We apologise to all concerned.**

But the damage had already been done. The *Telegraph* had succeeded in making Lola a scapegoat.

Many black students on the frontline have had similar experiences. Incidents like this force black activists to recede. Their rallying cries are reduced to whimpers by the fear of becoming the next target. As a black woman fighting to decolonise the curriculum, Lola represented both those who would benefit most from a diversified curriculum and those who had the most to lose from the fight.

> **For many black people and [people of colour],**
> **you can't just put yourself in the limelight. If**
> **you're black, you're very identifiable. I'm not**
> **gonna go and occupy anything! – Arenike**

Media attention may expose you to other silencing mechanisms, too. When Stormzy announced his Cambridge scholarship programme, Chelsea was interviewed on Sky News, and mysteriously received an email from the university's communications team with 'tips' on how to discuss Cambridge in the interview.

> **I just messaged him back: 'Hi. Thanks for these**
> **but I'm fine. Cheers. Chelsea.' He was basically**
> **telling me in a very coded way to be careful of**
> **what I say about Cambridge. – Chelsea**

When Mikai was featured on the BBC in a discussion about mental health at university, Warwick sent its university press officer to wait behind the scenes. '**I will say what I like, thank you very much!**' was her response to the university's attempt to stifle her. Universities are always working to make themselves look good. They even take credit for student labour that they've done next to nothing to meaningfully support, in order to make themselves look better. Regardless of their efforts to maintain their reputation, institutions have to be held accountable, and sometimes using the pressure of the media to speak up against them is the most power-ful tool you have to force a response. We're already being silenced by the press – but a university silencing you too? You have a right to speak out against your institution, and you should do so if you ever feel the need to – and you're brave enough.

I completely understand why black students choose to steer clear of media attention when they can, or even disengage from political work altogether. However, the media can also be used positively, and has played an important role in promoting black voices. While we were at Cambridge, Courtney and Renée made a video for Courtney's YouTube channel about their journey getting into Cambridge. Courtney was maligned by racists in the comments, and told that she was only accepted into the university to fulfil its diversity quota. When Courtney fought back, her comments went viral, she was able to use her interviews with media outlets such as Channel 4 and *Cosmopolitan* as a medium to continue to inspire black girls with her story.

Using the media in your political work can be fun sometimes – but be cautious or you'll risk becoming the media's black token. The Black Men of Cambridge campaign opened doors to many opportunities for me, particularly speaking ones. I had to try and make informed decisions about whether or not I was quali-fied to take up these opportunities, or whether I was being used by organisations hoping to tick their 'diversity' checklist. It became harder to tell whether *I* was using the media to get my message out there or the media was using me. I found myself winging a panel on 'Encountering Brexit', by the modern languages department, and was asked to do an interview on a BME orchestra coming to perform at a Cambridge music festival. Besides playing a few instruments when I was younger, nothing I had done indicated that I would be the most qualified person to speak on the importance of the orchestra's presence. It felt as if I was asked only because I was black and they had my phone number.

So, black girls, the chances of you finding yourself dealing with the press are higher than your white counterparts. It's the price of hypervisibility that no one prepared me for. It's up to you, but be aware of the potential risks before you make the call.

Allyship, Oppression and Privilege in Activist Spaces

Some people grow disenchanted with student activism due to the way oppression and privilege may be replicated in these spaces. Whiteness and white privilege permeate all aspects of our society, and activist spaces, even anti-racism ones, are no exception. There are some white people who think they can explain racism better than the people who are victims of it, and who speak over BME people in the process. It's not always conscious: sometimes, the mere presence of white people in these spaces can see BME people code-switch, and even stay silent out of concern for white people's feelings. The white privilege may manifest in very subtle ways, or it may show itself more overtly. Either way, white privilege is pervasive, and working actively to decentre whiteness in activism is an ongoing battle.

So much of these spaces are co-opted by white people. – Arenike

Feminist societies can be quite a good example of this. Most of the feminist society events that I went to at Jesus College did a good job of ensuring that the discussion was intersectional and aware of the extent to which other axes of identity (for example, race) might affect your experience of your gender and other systems of oppression. However, many black feminists have struggled when they have attempted to have painful, radical and necessary discussions about white feminism and the extent to which race is so often excluded from these discussions. Fope was the president of the Feminist Society at Newcastle University. Their attempts to dismantle racism within feminist spaces got them into more trouble than they deserved:

> I did workshops, like 'How to be an Ally' or like, 'Your Fave's a Racist'. I did one called 'The Suffragettes Were Racists, Sorry' – something like that. I did 'Jesus Wasn't White and Other White Lies' and stuff that clearly was meant to be provocative. And then I was reported to welfare [services] . . . I had a [Facebook] cover photo that said 'black pussy supremacy'. Someone reported me to welfare for that. – Fope

Although there were no serious repercussions for their actions, Fope told me how much of a toll it took on their mental health. Someone, somewhere felt threatened by their attempts to decentre white people in these discussions, even in feminist spaces where black women and non-binary people should expect a degree of safety.

Try and convince your friends, especially the white and male friends, who may have relative privilege in these spaces to make efforts to decentre themselves, and to use their white privilege to uplift you, not silence you. They may call themselves allies, and while their presence can be helpful and is often necessary, being an ally isn't about hijacking our voices or taking over our spaces.

But it's also more than standing by and holding our hands.

They don't understand that allyship is a doing word. You can't just call yourself an ally and like, that's the end of it. It's constantly unlearning problematic behaviours and a lot of them just don't have the time or range for it. – Fope

Allyship requires you to have difficult conversations and call out racism in the communities we can't reach – in your own households, for example. It means educating people in your everyday life and finding ways to relieve our burden. It also requires understanding that sometimes we invite you into our spaces to listen, not to speak over us or for us.

Budding activists: white people may feel threatened by your radicalism. When you highlight their complicity in racist structures, they may close off (or cry), but if they're going to try and be allies to the cause and support you in your fight without themselves taking up space, then they have some work to do too.

The A Word

Three years and a half-book later, I still don't know whether or not I would call myself an activist. I'm not alone in this internal battle. 'Activist' is an amorphous label that means something different to everyone. I've intentionally used the word quite loosely because I still don't know what it means. However, a common thread I have found is a sense of people feeling as if they have not done enough to earn the label. We hold activists to a higher moral standard. We expect them to always be ready to act. We expect them to always have the answers, and to be educated on the issues. Put that way, I see why some people may shy away from the term.

I would describe Fope as an activist, perhaps. Fope went to their first protest when they were in Year 10, and has worked tirelessly since secondary school creating spaces for women of colour, non-binary people of colour and queer people of colour, as well as educating people on the lack of diversity in white feminism. Yet they said to me, 'If I was going to write a bio, I don't know if I would say *activist*.'

There are also those who believe that to identify as an activist is to commit to a life of unyielding self-sacrifice for a larger cause.

I think the position of an activist and the idea of it has been hugely diluted and hugely romanticised. True activism to me is laying down your life for a cause. – Courtney

This is a standard so high that it's hard to imagine anyone realistically being able to measure up. There are also fears and risks attached to hypervisibility that not everyone is prepared to take on, and they disavow the label as a means of self-preservation. As a black activist, there is a lot at stake, and I hear that.

Despite the high standards to which we hold activists and the expectations we have of them, we must not undervalue contributions that may be less visible. Whether you're writing in resistance, or educating those around you, you have something to contribute to the movement.

It's about the small steps that you're taking towards the big picture of change. – Ayomide

The activist bar is always moving. You're going to come across people who think you haven't done enough groundwork, enough educating, or enough mobilising to be considered an activist. Whether or not you decide to call yourself an activist, *do activism*. It is so clichéd, but we literally own the future. University offers us a unique opportunity to be surrounded by equally passionate people, and the potential that students have as a group is both underestimated and extremely powerful. In whatever way you can, get involved and get on board.

We've got a system to fix.

Epilogue

University was a steep but rewarding learning curve for both of us, filled with opportunities that we could never have dreamt of elsewhere. Most of all, it was a new challenge in many ways. We were pushed to limits we didn't know we had, academically and mentally, and we were strengthened in the process. We were forced to find our voices in spaces in which people like us had often been silenced. But most importantly, university put us in a position to take these new lessons and inspire people, especially black girls, who would come after us.

We must think about how racist and gendered stereotypes are imposed on us before we even make our university applications, inevitably capping our aspirations. From the national curriculum that ignores or misrepresents our stories to university reading lists that don't go far enough to remedy this, everything is directly relevant to what 'inclusion' means for black girls at university. Minority underrepresentation, and being unable to always articulate how that affects us, is taking a toll on our mental wellbeing, quality of life and ultimately, what we can get out of our time at university. We are forced to carve out our own spaces for our own benefit and protection.

We want to show everyone that when we talk about diversity and inclusion at university, we're not just point-ing to abstract concepts, targets, theories and ideas. We are real people and these very conversations have a direct impact on our lives and university experiences. For once, we as students have decided to grab hold of this narrative and centre our voices in a conversation that only works if it is nuanced and critical. Black students across the country have been working tirelessly to address matters of diversity and inclusion for so long. We are not the first and we definitely will not be the last. We only hope that *Taking Up Space* will colour the existing conversation with the subjectivities of black students across the coun-try. This is what it *feels* like to be a black girl at university. These trying years have birthed our inner fighters, equipped us with critical ideas, networks and support systems for facing the outside world.

To round off our interviews with our contributors, we asked, 'Was university worth it?'

Well, a Cambridge degree, I'm hoping so! – Kenya

I absolutely do think it's worth it. It has inherent value, I believe, learning things and knowing things and just having options in your life. – Saredo

If you want to go 'big time corporate', yes. If you want to be a creative of any kind, it depends. – Mikai

No. Unless there's something you really, really want to study. I wouldn't say that I've ever been particularly challenged. And a lot of people I've talked to who didn't go to university and have apprenticeships, bitches got houses! – Fope

It's so worth it. It's expensive, but it's worth it. – Ayomide

I really think it is worth it if you do a degree that you care about. – Eireann

With all the pain, with all the sorrow, and all the joy mixed in, it was definitely worth it. – Renée

If you asked us, we'd say that of course university was worth it. Academically, it is simultaneously the most independence we have ever had and the hardest we have ever been pushed. The geeks deep inside us still miss being surrounded by library books and journal articles on a daily basis, and learning to develop and articulate our ideas in new, deeper ways. Like us, you may find that the friendships that survive some of your most horrible experiences at university become some of the most valuable.

Our memories of university are ultimately not consumed with our worst confrontations with racist ignorance and isolation, which we have tried to suppress for our own self-preservation. When we look back, the memories we treasure most are the nights we spent laughing and crying over jollof, dancing our asses off at house parties, and being there to celebrate with each other and all our friends on the days that we graduated. University was worth it for us because it helped us learn more about ourselves; it was an exploration of our identities in ways we couldn't have expected. For Ọrẹ, it was an encounter with the visibility of her blackness in a way that her life in Nigeria, and an extremely diverse boarding school, had shielded her from. For Chelsea, it was defying a false, reductive stereotype about what it means to be a working-class black woman at university.

Above all, at university we realised that the concept of space means a lot more to us as black women. We have never been afforded the luxury of simply existing and being able to blend into the background. We are constantly forced to navigate university spaces that claim to support us but rarely show positive action proving that. So what do we do?

We organise in, and most importantly, create spaces. They become centres of validation, sisterhood, and the epicentre of radical critique. For us, university shouldn't be about claiming authority over the intellectual and the academic. Instead, it should become a place where we can disrupt the ideas of knowledge and knowledge production.

Leaving university has only gone to show that many of the issues we faced as black girls at university are replicated, and often intensified, in the world beyond it. Imposter syndrome may become easier to handle, but is unlikely to disappear. The thinly-veiled racist incidents will not become less common in the life that you pursue afterwards, and unfortunately, no less common either will be the people who do not consider your voice valid. We only hope that you take all that we, and our interviewees, have shared with you to go into this world fearlessly, lighting it up and taking up all the space you truly deserve.

Now What?

Chelsea

'After taking up space'

Picture this. I'm at a house party, the kind of party you go to when you're twenty-two. It's loud, messy, and for some reason I'm anxious that an angry neighbour is going to come banging at the door, threatening to call the police at any minute. I find a quiet space and get chatting to this guy who seems nice enough. As usual, the conversation ventures into the typical questions: 'What do you do?', 'Do you enjoy it?' and 'What university did you go to?'. On autopilot, I mention Cambridge and his immediate question was 'Did you enjoy it?'. By the end of a long 'hmmmmm' in response, he went on to tell me about a book . . . written by two black girls from Cambridge . . . called Chelsea and Ọrẹ, and he recommended a book called *Taking Up Space* to me. For most, this is funny, cringe and probably really awkward, right? (Thank God he said something positive!) But, for me, it was a real full-circle moment.

When deciding the title of the book I co-authored with my best friend Ọrẹ Ogunbiyi, we decided on *Taking Up Space* because it captured so much, yet left room for debate and discussion surrounding the book. Currently the phrase 'taking up space' is associated with the body positivity movement mainly taking place on Instagram, where individuals aim to shatter impossibly narrow beauty ideals of how we should look and how we should feel about our bodies. It has also been used in various movements that urge women to be unapologetic in how they navigate the workplace, and public and private spheres. Within both movements, the message remains: to take up space is to know that your voice is valid, that you deserve to be in the room and, finally, celebrating all your wins first, rather than leading with your losses. However, Ọrẹ and I were told that for a book that was meant to be inspirational and positive, *Taking Up Space* as a title sounded overwhelmingly negative, even 'discouraging'. Without hesitation, I agreed and scrambled to find another phrase that could quickly replace the title that we had come to love and had planned purple and pink tote bags for(!). But then I stopped and took a moment to reflect. What drew me to the phrase 'taking up space' was that it conveyed everything that we were trying to achieve in the book. We wanted it to be honest, direct and, at times, painful – exactly what it feels like to take up space in institutions that were never made for you.

Between then and now, I've had time to think a lot about what 'taking up space' actually means to me as a young black woman. What does it really mean to take up space? How do we understand space and if we're 'taking it up', who occupies it in the first place? Are we reclaiming it or is the struggle less to do with 'taking' and more about creating the space in the first place?

I've come to terms with some uncomfortable truths.

It is said that black women will always be too loud in a world that never intended on listening to them. When I read the blogs and articles and listen to talks about taking up space, they make it sound so simple. They also never talk about what happens *after* you take up space. They say it's all about confidence and making your voice heard. But I couldn't shake the fact that I had been trying to do the exact opposite. By virtue of being a double minority, I have to deal with both an invisibility and visibility complex. In policy, articles and 'diversity' initiatives, my existence is ignored under the cushion of 'Black and Minority Ethnic' (BAME). Throughout my experience, the racial and gendered aspects of my identity have only made taking up space harder. Harder to accept the constant pushback, harder to ignore the overwhelming sense of helplessness, and harder to keep going when you felt like you have a different standard of proof to everyone else. Speaking up as black women is always going to come with risks. I fully understood the implications of this . . . Taking up space for me will always be inherently contentious and political because of how far my identity is drenched in a history of misogynoir (misogyny specifically directed towards black women), racism and classism.

However, sometimes when you speak, people actually do listen. Since publishing the book, it has been an incredible journey. People are riled up, speak passionately about change and, for once, are starting to imagine what a truly equal society will look like. I find glimmers of hope and optimism when people strive to learn and consider other experiences because they realise that we all need to shuffle to make sure there is room for everyone. In October 2019, the news broke that the University of Cambridge had admitted ninety-one Black British students – a 139% increase from 2015, when we were admitted. Major news outlets were quick to dub this the 'Stormzy Effect' in reference to the Stormzy Scholarship, set up in 2018, which saw two students fully funded (tuition and maintenance) at Cambridge. In his piece for *i-D*, which details the ways in which we need to change the narrative around elite university access, Jason Okundaye said it best: 'Rather than the "Stormzy effect" festering as a narrative that eclipses the tireless work of black students to reform the access systems and internal governance of the institutions they attend, the artist has placed the narrative directly in students' own hands.' Despite Stormzy paying accolades to those who have been fighting the good fight, many are still unable to see and give credit to the tireless black students behind the scenes. They are the ones who continue to speak up whilst universities engage with conversations about race in superficial and celebratory ways. Despite all this, the tenacity of black students continues to prevail.

Initially, we wanted this additional chapter to be a sweet and cute 'A Letter to Our Graduate Selves'. We wanted it to be an opportunity to follow up all the amazing things we have learnt since graduating; the incredible opportunities, partnerships and individuals we have met since publishing our book. It would be an opportunity to follow up on all our contributors, spread our pearls of wisdom and wrap up *Taking Up Space* on an inspiring, hopeful and positive note. But we realised that in writing a letter and centring on ourselves, we would be doing a massive disservice to the various student movements and developments in the face of the persistent inaction of universities. To tell the truth, it was never about Ọrẹ and I, and it's important to remember that we didn't start this 'movement'. At university, we both recognised the immense privilege that came with being welcomed into spaces that passionately discussed and debated the issues we speak about in *Taking Up Space*. I feel so glad that we've been able to share even an ounce of knowledge and conversation. We will forever be proud of *Taking Up Space*, what it's achieved, and what #Merky Books has done to and for the publishing industry. We opened up and demonstrated the very raw and human side of the statistics and headlines. Through *Taking Up Space* we created a comprehensive and detailed collation of sources, stories and emotions. But, in the process, we've been heralded as the two-young-black-Cambridge-graduates who have taken on racism within Higher Education by the horns and are taking it on a wild ride.

Although *Taking Up Space* has been significant for many across the UK, we recognise our place in a long history of wide-ranging responses to inaction within higher education. And that to us is key because *the book may have ended but the fight has not*. Most notably, the successful demands of those involved in the Goldsmiths Occupation in 2019 impassioned the little bit of fire left in me. Goldsmiths Anti-Racist Action (GARA) occupied Deptford Town Hall for 137 days over the institutional racism at Goldsmiths University. GARA is a Black, Minority

Ethnic, Muslim, LGBTQ and disabled student-led occupation that aims to 'inspire a new generation of anti-racist activists to build strength collectively and never back down in the fight of our collective liberation'. Demands to the university included allocation of £20,000 for Black History events annually, appointment of a researcher to support Dr Nicola Rollock (one a few black female professors) in her role as BAME attainment academic lead, and ensuring that all staff receive mandatory anti-racist training. They didn't ask for 'acknowledgement' or 'more conversations', they demanded commitments in a legally binding document. This delves into the heart of the campaign: that issues of oppression, institutional racism and anti-racist praxis are not negotiable.

Today, as I write this, the exit poll from the 2019 General Election has just been announced. In all honesty, right now in this exact moment, I feel deflated, emotional and vulnerable. But at times like this, you realise how much you rely on *hope* and just how far hope is an antidote for – to be blunt – a pretty messed-up world. The hope that your humanity will be valued and understood, the hope that people will feel a sense of urgency and, above all, the hope that one day we will all be able to see that we deserve transformative change.

I can only hope that *Taking Up Space* will in turn provide an element of hope to everyone who reads it.

Ọrẹ – Celebrating the small wins in the bigger war

It's 27 November 27 2019 and my phone is ringing. It's Chelsea. 'ỌRẸ, THEY'RE RETURNING THE COCKEREL', she screams via loudspeaker for my whole office to hear. 'EHN?', I replied. I hadn't heard yet and I was in disbelief. I vaguely remembered receiving an email notification from my old college earlier, which I had ignored. I scrambled to find it, had a quick glance on Twitter, and yes, it was true. Jesus College, Cambridge, had just announced that they would finally be repatriating the bronze cockerel which had been looted from the Benin Kingdom in 1897 and bequeathed to the college – *the* bronze cockerel that had kick-started my student activism at Cambridge.

The email, which had also been sent to other Jesus College alumni, was filled with updates on the progress of the 'Legacies of Slavery Working Party (LSWP)' – a newly formulated group of academics and students investigating the college's links to slavery. The email was written by our recently elected master, Sonita Alleyne, who a few months prior had become the first black person *ever* to head a college in Oxbridge history. In explaining the college's decision to finally repatriate the looted Benin bronze cockerel, she wrote simply,

'The statue is not, and never has been, owned by the College and therefore must be returned.' It was a relief to know that, finally, someone acknowledged that this fact alone was reason enough.

While this is not something she would have been able to enact alone, we cannot ignore the role that Sonita Alleyne's leadership played in this decision. It took her under two months to give us an answer that everyone had been too scared to give us for three years. It would have been easy for her to do nothing, to try not to ruffle too many feathers, to start the academic year with something less controversial, to take the path of least resistance. But she didn't. She picked up from where we left off and made a decision that generations of black students to come will thank her for. For me, the decision was about much more than the cockerel itself. It was inspiring to see a black woman in a leadership role not cowering to the pressures of an institution that is often reluctant to enact change. She was taking up space, visibly, unapologetically, and she wasn't being quiet about it. It was inspiring and exciting to see what positive representation looks like. I hope that other black women going into this space imbibe that same confidence and fearlessness because they've seen someone like Sonita do it before them.

The lesson here, though, goes far beyond Jesus College and Cambridge. Decisions like these are a reminder that the important work that we do while we are at university does not have to end there. Our fear when we left was that all the work we had done, all the meetings we had gone to, all the time spent drafting and redrafting proposals, was fruitless and would disappear from institutional memory. But this is why writing our stories and sharing them is so important. It means that just as we inherited the struggle from those before, we can also pass on the mantle to those who come after us. It means that our stories can live on, that legacies can be left behind, and that we can hope for a time when people like us are no longer erased from history books.

While I'm grateful for the small bursts of excitement that come with news like the cockerel's return, very often a lot of the work we do can feel like taking one step forward and two steps back. In October 2019, the Equality and Human Rights Commission (EHRC) led an inquiry into racial harassment in universities. On the surface, this report seems like something worth celebrating: finally, a government watchdog is holding institutions accountable and exposing the extent of the racism that we have been talking about for years. As expected, the document revealed that black students reported the highest rate of racial harassment. However, the same report also mentions that '9% of White students said they had experienced racial harassment since starting their course,' referring to 'anti-white sentiment'. From this point on, it was clear that in spite of all the work that student activists have continually done to try to explain, there are still people – even people as prominent as researchers for the EHRC – who don't fully understand the way in which institutional racism operates in the UK; that it is a question of white systemic power, and so to be a white victim of institutional racism is necessarily a contradiction in terms. By framing black and white students' experiences of 'racial harassment' as comparable, the report undermines the very claims made in this book: that as black students, especially black women, our experiences in higher education institutions are unique, and when it comes to racism, uniquely *worse*.

Fope Olaleye, the National Union of Students' Black Students Officer and an interviewee for this book, writes on this topic eloquently in the *Guardian*, stating: 'It is *exhausting* that we still cannot have a frank discussion about experiences of structural racism without positioning white people as equal victims of racial discrimination – and it shows the limitations of the language our legislative bodies are using.'

A whole book later, we still have to explain and re-explain our experiences, and unfortunately there are still people who don't get why this work is necessary, and why we focus specifically on black students – in our case, even more specifically black women.

You might also have slipped past the fact that the report chose to focus on 'racial harassment', not racism, thus focusing on specific interpersonal encounters as opposed to systems, structures and legacies that foster racist environments on a much wider level and in much more insidious, enduring ways. Until institutions, and the watchdogs that regulate them, are ready to go beyond the superficial in their research on race, we are going nowhere. *Taking Up Space* is a reminder of who is affected when you don't have these conversations in full, when you refuse to acknowledge and understand that racism in higher education is about more than one person's actions against you.

I hope that *Taking Up Space* is a reminder of why we need to keep going. The small wins, when they do come, are happening in a broader political context dominated by overtly racist rhetoric, and oftentimes leave us feeling as though all our work is in vain. Currently, our government is being run by a racist and misogynist homophobe and it's alarming. It's even more frightening to think that he garnered enough popular support to win a general election. It's hard to be hopeful in your activism in an environment where it is clear that so many people do not care about racism or the continual marginalisation of people who look like us. But these small wins, the minds we have changed, the people we have enlightened, the young people that we have helped find confidence, are a reminder to push on. They remind us to reignite our flames of hope because how else will we find our way forward?

We need to collectively keep going so that our black sisters and daughters eventually don't have to deal with the same imposter syndrome that we did, so that they can see themselves and their histories in their curricula, so that they can stand on our shoulders and thrive in spite of the systems that are trying to hold them back. We need to keep going so that they too can learn to unapologetically take up space.

Notes

To access the links below online, please visit the *Taking Up Space* page on the Penguin UK website (www.penguin.co.uk/takingupspace).

Introduction

8 'whitest universities in the country...'
https://www.undergraduate.study.cam.ac.uk/files/publications/ug_admissions_statistics_2017_cycle_2.pdf
Published May 2018.

Getting In

22 'In 2017-18, UK domiciled...'
https://www.advance-he.ac.uk/resources/2018_HE-stats-report-students.pdf
Published in 2018.

22 'But as Professor of Race and Gender Heidi Mirza states . . .'
Heidi Safia Mirza, Race, Gender and Educational Desire:
Why Black Women Succeed and Fail
Published 2009.

26 'But with black Caribbean students three times . . .' https://
www.bbc.co.uk/news/education-44886153 Published in July
2018.

28 'Recruit more students from exclusively . . .' https://www.
suttontrust.com/newsarchive/oxbridge-over-recruits-from-
eight-schools/
Published in December 2018.

28 'Around 7 per cent of all UK school pupils attend' https://
guidetoindependentschools.com/key-independent-school-
statistics/

30 'What it's like being black and working class at Cambridge'
http://www.bbc.co.uk/newsbeat/article/41696224/what-
its-like-being-black-and-working-class-at-cambridge
Published October 2017.

31 ' . . . university student in the UK receives around' https://
thetab.com/uk/2019/02/28/mum-can-you-send-me-100-the-
universities-where-students-get-the-most-money-from-
their-parents-94157
Published February 2019.

33 'Reni Eddo-Lodge sums this up perfectly . . .'
Reni Eddo-Lodge, *Why I'm No Longer Talking to White*
People About Race, p. 207.
Published June 2017.

34 'The Sutton Trust found that some groups . . .'
https://www.suttontrust.com/wp-content/uploads/2016/11/
Class-differences-report_References-available-online.pdf
Published November 2016.

35 'For example, in Northern Ireland, black ethnic groups . . .'
https://www.bbc.co.uk/news/education-44226434
Published May 2018.

37 'The three universities with the biggest black student . . .'
https://www.bbc.co.uk/news/education-44226434
Published May 2018 (as above).

37 'After students from Bangladeshi backgrounds . . .'
https://www.bath.ac.uk/publications/diverse-places-of-learning-home-neighbourhood-ethnic-diversity-ethnic-composition-of-universities/attachments/diverse-places-of-learning.pdf
Published August 2017.

38 'Social Market Foundation found that more than one in ten'
https://www.independent.co.uk/news/uk/home-news/black-students-drop-out-university-figures-a7847731.html
Published July 2017.

38 'This has led someone to claim a form of 'self-segregation . . .'
https://www.bbc.co.uk/news/education-40926117
Published August 2017.

39 'Coventry University, for example, is 54.5 per cent white and 44.5 per cent BME. From the outset, there's strength in numbers . . .'
https://www.coventry.ac.uk/globalassets/media/documents/equality-and-diversity/statistics-2017-18/eandd-web-statistics-all-students-31012018.pdf
Published January 2018.

40 'Professor David Gilborn, Director of the Centre . . .'
https://www.tes.com/news/tes-talks-todavid-gillborn
Published January 2017.

40 'Institutional racism can be defined as the collective . . .'
https://www.ucu.org.uk/media/9526/Investigating-higher-education-institutions-and-their-views-on-the-Race-Equality-Charter/pdf/Race_Equality_Charter_Kalwant_Bhopal_Clare_Pitkin.pdf
Published September 2018.

40 'In 2018, the independent reported on data which revealed . . .'

https://www.independent.co.uk/news/education/
education-news/black-students-university-uk-racism-
ucas-application-a8376501.html
Published May 2018.

41 'Black and minority ethnic students of all backgrounds . . .'
https://www.bbc.co.uk/news/education-44226434
Published May 2018 (as above).

43 'Strategic objectives from the University of York's Equality . . .'
https://www.york.ac.uk/admin/eo/EDIStrategy/EDandI-
Strategy-Nov2017.pdf
Published November 2017.

44 'If you think I'm being harsh, have a look at SOAS . . .'
https://www.soas.ac.uk/equality-diversity-and-inclusion-
strategy/file113520.pdf
Published July 2016.

45 'A report by Professor Kalwant Bhopal and Clare Pitkin . . .'
https://www.ucu.org.uk/media/9526/Investigating-
higher-education-institutions-and-their-views-on-the-
Race-Equality-Charter/pdf/Race_Equality_Charter_
Kalwant_Bhopal_Clare_Pitkin.pdf
Published September 2018.

45 'In 2016, 1.5 per cent of the Cambridge . . .'
https://www.bbc.co.uk/news/education-44226434
Published May 2018 (as above).

46 'The letter stated that Cambridge . . .'
https://www.cam.ac.uk/news/open-letter-on-diversity-
in-admissions
Published June 2018.

47 'At Pembroke College, a BME . . .'
https://www.varsity.co.uk/news/14897
Published February 2018.

48 'Oxford ACS's Annual Access Conference . . .'
https://annualaccessconference.co.uk/

48 'Oxford have increased by 24.1 per cent . . .'

https://www.huffingtonpost.co.uk/renee-kapuku/being-black-at-oxbridge-w_b_18368164.html?guccounter=1
Published September 2017.

49 'As Renée writes for the Huffington Post . . .'
As above.

51 'Target Oxbridge's partnership with both universities . . .'
http://www.ox.ac.uk/news/2018-02-16-success-and-expansion-target-oxbridge-programme-black-teenagers
Published February 2018.

#AcademiaSoWhite

55 'The history curriculum, for example . . .'
https://www.gov.uk/government/publications/national-curriculum-in-england-history-programmes-of-study
Published September 2013.

55 'Primary schools are only required . . .'
https://assets.publishing.service.gov.uk/government/uploads/system/uploads/attachment_data/file/239035/PRIMARY_national_curriculum_-_History.pdf
Published September 2013

60 'a black attainment gap at a university level that doesn't correlate with how well black students perform at GCSE stage . . .'
https://assets.publishing.service.gov.uk/government/uploads/system/uploads/attachment_data/file/439867/RR439B-Ethnic_minorities_and_attainment_the_effects_of_poverty_annex.pdf.pdf
https://www.advance-he.ac.uk/resources/2018_HE-stats-report-students.pdf
Published June 2015.

61 'Black students make up 7 percent . . .'
https://www.advance-he.ac.uk/resources/2018_HE-stats-report-students.pdf

Published September 2018

61 'Only 2.4 per cent of students [. . .] for the creative arts . . .'
https://royalhistsoc.org/wp-content/uploads/2018/10/
RHS_race_report_EMBARGO_0001_18Oct.pdf
Published October 2018.

64 'Over 10 per cent of students . . .'
As above.

64 'According to research by the Resolution Foundation . . .'
https://www.bloomberg.com/diversity-inclusion/blog/
people-ethnic-minorities-still-facing-major-jobs-gap-uk/
Published October 2018.

68 'Cambridge's Varsity newspaper featured a . . .'
https://www.varsity.co.uk/features/16174
Published October 2018.

70 'he was largely responsible for the deaths . . .'
https://www.independent.co.uk/news/world/world-
history/winston-churchill-genocide-dictator-shashi-
tharoor-melbourne-writers-festival-a7936141.html
Published September 2017.

73 'Academics such as Lundy Braun . . .'
https://journalofethics.ama-assn.org/article/avoiding-
racial-essentialism-medical-science-curricula/2017-06
Published June 2017.

74 'Chanda Prescod-Weinstein expands on this in her . . .'
https://medium.com/@chanda/decolonising-science-
reading-list-339fb773d51f#.0m5w2ivfq
Published June 2015, last updated May 2017.

74 'Akala spoke about it at the Oxford Union . . .'
https://www.youtube.com/watch?v=WUtAxUQjwB4
Published 26 November 2015.

75 'It is generally far more difficult . . .'
https://liberatingthecurriculumblog.wordpress.
com/2017/09/17/personal-experiences/
Published September 2017.

75 'According to a 2018 NHS report, "four times more likely to be 'sectioned" . . .'
https://digital.nhs.uk/data-and-information/publications/statistical/mental-health-act-statistics-annual-figures/2017-18-annual-figures
Published October 2018.

76 'That almost a third of UK graduate doctors . . .'
https://www.gmc-uk.org/static/documents/content/SoMEP-2017-final-executive-summary.pdf
Published December 2017.

88 'Data released by the Higher Educations Statistics Agency . . .'
https://www.hesa.ac.uk/news/19-01-2017/sfr243-staff
Published January 2017.

89 'A shockingly small 1.8 per cent . . .'
https://www.advance-he.ac.uk/resources/2018_HE-stats-report-staff.pdf
Published October 2018.

89 'Asian staff . . .'
As above.

89 'Considering just black women . . .'
As above and https://www.theguardian.com/education/2018/sep/07/uk-university-professors-black-minority-ethnic
Published September 2018.

92 'We welcomed the announcement in 2017 . . .'
https://www.theguardian.com/education/2017/may/28/oxford-students-to-get-exam-on-non-white-non-european-history
Published May 2017.

94 'ranked second in the country for sociology"'
The *Guardian* University Guide 2019: League Table for Sociology: https://www.theguardian.com/education/ng-interactive/2018/may/29/university-guide-2019-league-table-for-sociology

94 'in an online 'global social theory' reading list . . .'

https://globalsocialtheory.org/resources/reading-lists/

96 'In the same paper at Warwick . . .'
See 'Epic into Novel' paper. https://warwick.ac.uk/fac/arts/
english/undergraduate/uow_english_ug_prospectus_
online.pdf

98 'all but one of the countries tried by the International
Criminal Court . . .'
https://www.icc-cpi.int/pages/situations.aspx

101 'Chanda Prescod-Weinstein writes . . .'
https://medium.com/@chanda/making-meaning-of-
decolonising-35f1b5162509
Published February 2017.

103 'According to a 2018 report by Advance HE . . .'
https://www.advance-he.ac.uk/sites/default/files/2018_
HE-stats-report-students.pdf
Published October 2018.

Mental Health

109 'In 2015–16, over 15,000 first-year students (UK-based)
disclosed mental health issues . . .'
https://www.bbc.co.uk/news/education-41148704
Published September 2017.

109 'Yet a Freedom of Information request by the Liberal
Democrat . . .'
https://www.independent.co.uk/news/uk/politics/students-
mental-health-support-waiting-times-counselling-
university-care-diagnosis-treatment-liberal-a8124111.html
Published January 2018.

109 'At the University of Bristol alone, there were ten suspected
suicides . . .'
https://www.theguardian.com/uk-news/2018/may/10/
university-of-bristol-confirms-sudden-death-of-first-
year-student

Published May 2018.

110 'The University of Cumbria, for example . . .'
https://www.ippr.org/files/2017-09/1504645674_not-by-degrees-170905.pdf
Published September 2017.

113-4 'Black British and non-British women were both found to be more . . .'
https://www.mentalhealth.org.uk/statistics/mental-health-statistics-black-asian-and-minority-ethnic-groups
Published 2014.

113-4 'The *Guardian* began its Racial Bias series . . .'
https://www.theguardian.com/uk-news/2018/dec/03/from-football-to-dating-to-tv-10-areas-rife-with-racial-bias-in-uk
Published December 2018.

114 'From the words 'MONKEY' and 'NIGGA' found written on Warwick student Faramade Ifaturoti's bunch of bananas . . .'
https://www.theguardian.com/education/2016/apr/08/bananagate-highlights-racism-among-warwick-students
Published April 2016.

114 'to fellow students chanting 'we hate the blacks' outside Rufaro Chisango's room at Nottingham Trent University . . .'
https://www.theguardian.com/commentisfree/2018/mar/11/racist-universities-not-tolerant-rugaro-chisango-nottingham-trent
Published March 2018.

117 'At Bath Spa University, a photo exhibition . . .'
https://www.bathspasu.co.uk/opps/blackhistorymonth/blackexcellenceblog/

123 'For starters, black men and women are more likely to engage . . .'
https://www.mentalhealth.org.uk/a-to-z/b/black-asian-and-minority-ethnic-bame-communities

126 'came up more than once in students' testimonials . . .'
https://www.theguardian.com/commentisfree/2018/
may/21/identity-matters-black-students-black-
therapists-cambridge-university
Published May 2018.

127 'Similarly, the Black, African and Asian Therapy Network
(BAATN) . . .'
https://www.baatn.org.uk/

128 'A study completed by Student Minds found that . . .'
https://www.studentminds.org.uk/uploads/3/7/8/4/
3784584/180129_student_mental_health__the_role_and_
experience_of_academics__student_minds_pdf.pdf
Published January 2018.

Finding Spaces

145 'Pauline Clance and Suzanne Imes, the psychologists . . .'
https://psycnet.apa.org/record/1979-26502-001
Published 1978.

148 'A whopping 79 per cent of respondents to a . . .'
https://www.nus.org.uk/en/news/press-releases/new-survey-
shows-trends-in-student-drinking/
Published September 2018.

148 'Young adults are the most likely . . .'
https://www.ons.gov.uk/peoplepopulationandcommunity/
healthandsocialcare/drugusealcoholandsmoking/bulletins/
opinionsandlifestylesurveyadultdrinkinghabitsingreat
britain/2017
Published May 2018.

150 'In 2017, a group of black students . . .'
https://thetab.com/uk/cardiff/2017/04/28/they-said-
they-didnt-want-an-urban-feel-cardiff-students-tell-us-
their-experiences-of-racism-in-nightclubs-27092
Published 2017.

152 'The NUS in 2018 . . .'
https://www.nus.org.uk/en/news/press-releases/
new-survey-shows-trends-in-student-drinking/
Published September 2018.

158 'FLY, which I learned stands for . . .'
https://flygirlsofcambridge.com/

159 'Warwick's Anti-Racism Society . . .'
https://www.facebook.com/groups/warsoc.2015.2016/?fref=ts

164-5 'The university's most recent admissions . . .'
https://www.undergraduate.study.cam.ac.uk/sites/www.
undergraduate.study.cam.ac.uk/files/publications/ug_
admissions_statistics_2017_cycle_4.pdf
Published May 2018.

Desirability and Relationships

176 'The One Day University Love Survey stated that the top
five universities . . .'
https://tsrmatters.com/blog/one-fifth-of-british-students-
meet-the-love-of-their-life-on-campus/

177 'To be honest, there isn't really much of a dating scene . . .'
https://blackballad.co.uk/views-voices/navigating-the-
dating-scene-as-a-socially-conscious-black-woman?listId
s=590867cea8cobab2039c3ac5
Published February 2019.

177 'Caren M. Holmes's essay . . .'
https://openworks.wooster.edu/cgi/viewcontent.
cgi?referer=https://www.google.com/&httpsredir=1&artic
le=1026&context=blackandgold
Published 2018.

194 'Stonewall's LGBT in Britain's Universities Report . . .'
https://www.stonewall.org.uk/system/files/lgbt_in_
britain_universities_report.pdf
Published 2018.

194 'The University of Oxford's Trans . . .'
https://www.oxfordsu.org/resources/lgbtq/TRANS-
REPORT-2018/
Published November 2018.

197 'Think Jamie and Nikki . . .'
https://www.youtube.com/watch?v=46xhFCXBMJs
Published May 2013.

197 'or HelloBianca, a channel amassing 55,000 subscribers . . .'
https://www.youtube.com/watch?v=nmc9Fakbx1Q&t=1s
Published January 2018.

200 'As such, many black queer men . .'
https://metro.co.uk/2019/03/22/as-a-black-gay-man-i-am-
constantly-reduced-to-outdated-racist-stereotypes-when-
online-dating-8889330/
Published March 2019.

202 'in an article titled "I'm not an object or a toy for your
white gaze" . . .'
https://metro.co.uk/2018/09/18/im-not-an-object-or-a-toy-
for-your-white-gaze-dont-fetishise-me-as-a-black-man-
7957474/
Published September 2018.

205 'A survey conducted by Hexjam looked at the sex lives . . .'
https://www.bustle.com/articles/91951-7-things-to-know-
about-students-sex-lives-in-the-uk-according-to-a-new-
survey
Published June 2015.

206 'The session included a video called "Tea and Consent" . . .'
https://www.youtube.com/watch?v=oQbei5JGiT8
Published May 2015.

206 'The body is an appropriate cultural symbol . . .'
https://journals.sagepub.com/doi/full/10.1177/
2374623816680622
Published December 2016.

207 'In my second year at university, I will never forget . . .'

Danielle L. McGuire, "It Was Like All of Us Had Been Raped": Sexual Violence, Community Mobilisation, and the African American Freedom Struggle", JAH (2004), pp.910–920.
Published 2004.

207 'Burke told ESSENCE magazine . . .'
https://www.essence.com/videos/tarana-burke-explains-why-black-women-dont-think-metoo-is-for-them/
Published November 2018.

208 '62 per cent of students and graduates have experienced sexual violence . . .'
https://revoltsexualassault.com/research/
Published March 2018.

208 'Only 2 per cent of those . . .'
As above.

208 '33 per cent have no knowledge or very little knowledge'
As above.

209 'The NUS project "That's What She Said" found . . .'
https://www.nus.org.uk/Global/Campaigns/That's%20what%20she%20said%20full%20report%20Final%20web.pdf
Published 2013.

210 'Comments included, "Sometimes it's fun to just go wild and rape 100 girls" . . .'
https://theboar.org/2018/05/warwick-students-temporarily-suspended/
Published May 2018.

210 'First of all, the university's director of press was appointed . . .'
https://www.bbc.co.uk/news/uk-47090864?SThisFB&fbclid=IwAR1Gyg-lbX_MbeUvxxwmgLJ_vrQ5GF3bbafNhP8DhGzTaIoHeoXOdTe-Qxs
Published February 2019.

211 'In 1994, the Zellick Report was published . . .'
https://universityapp..co.uk/sites/default/files/field/
attachment/NUS%20Zellick%20report%20briefing.pdf
Published 2015.

213 'Manchester Student Union have rallied around the
night . . .'
https://manchesterstudentsunion.com/reclaimthenight

'Blacktivism'

232 'Some say it developed . . .'
https://www.bbc.com/news/uk-politics-43831279
Published May 2018.

238 'Our carefully crafted caption . . .'
https://www.facebook.com/cambridge.acs/posts/
in-2015-only-15-black-male-undergraduates-were-
accepted-into-cambridge-however-i/1881865065434347/
Published May 2017.

239 'Over the next few days . . .'
https://www.bbc.com/news/uk-39787690
https://www.washingtonpost.com/news/worldviews/
wp/2017/05/03/cambridge-has-a-problem-with-diversity-
these-black-men-just-illustrated-it-perfectly/?noredirect=
on&utm_term=.23e09f8b5aa9
https://www.standard.co.uk/lifestyle/london-life/why-a-
photo-of-14-young-black-cambridge-students-has-gone-
viral-a3529081.html
https://www.mirror.co.uk/news/real-life-stories/photo-
14-young-black-men-10347398
https://www.elle.com/uk/life-and-culture/news/
a35540/14-black-male-cambridge-students-pose-for-
photo-important-message/
https://www.thefader.com/2017/05/04/black-men-
cambridge-acs

All Published May 2017.

240 'We weren't going to apologise . . .'
https://www.undergraduate.study.cam.ac.uk/sites/www.
undergraduate.study.cam.ac.uk/files/publications/
undergrad_admissions_statistics_2015_cycle.pdf
Published May 2016.

240 'By 2017, in my final year . . .'
https://www.undergraduate.study.cam.ac.uk/sites/www.
undergraduate.study.cam.ac.uk/files/publications/ug_
admissions_statistics_2017_cycle_4.pdf
Published May 2018.

241 'One of the boys I asked to feature . . .'
https://www.cam.ac.uk/BlackCantabs
Published September 2018.

242 'Although the 2018-19 . . .'
https://cambridgeacs.org/committee/
Last updated in 2018.

244 'In response, I wrote . . .'
https://flygirlsofcambridge.com/2018/01/21/we-need-
your-support-not-your-freestyles-ore-ogunbiyi/
Published January 2018.

246 'The papers picked up . . .
https://www.theguardian.com/education/2016/feb/21/
cambridge-colleges-bronze-cockerel-must-go-back-to-
nigeria-students-say
https://www.dailymail.co.uk/news/article-3457159/After-
Cecil-Rhodes-s-Alcock-rooster-Students-call-bronze-
cockerel-sent-Africa-new-Oxbridge-college-row.html
Both published February 2016.

249 'In the days following the campaign . . .'
https://www.telegraph.co.uk/news/2017/05/03/dont-blame-
cambridge-lack-black-students-saysleading-students/
Published May 2017.

250 'On 25 October 2017 . . .'

https://www.telegraph.co.uk/education/2017/10/24/cambridge-decolonise-english-literature/
Published October 2017

251 'The next day, following . . .'
https://www.ipso.co.uk/rulings-and-resolution-statements/ruling/?id=19341-17
https://www.thedrum.com/news/2017/10/29/telegraph-story-which-claimed-cambridge-student-was-forcing-faculty-drop-white
Both published October 2017.

253 'While we were at Cambridge . . .'
https://www.youtube.com/watch?v=ICmuDCpDARQ
Published October 2015.

Now What?

272 https://i-d.vice.com/en_uk/article/evj75p/how-the-stormzy-effect-is-changing-the-narrative-around-elite-university-access

275 https://www.goldsmithssu.org/news/article/6013/A-public-statement-from-Goldsmiths-Anti-Racist-Action/

278 https://www.equalityhumanrights.com/en/publication-download/tackling-racial-harassment-universities-challenged

279 https://www.theguardian.com/commentisfree/2019/oct/28/agree-racism-anti-white-racial-harassment-ehrc

Our Favourite Reads

Fiction

Ayobami Adebayo, *Stay With Me*
Tomi Adeyemi, *Children of Blood and Bone*
Chimamanda Adichie, *Purple Hibiscus*
Bernardine Evaristo, *Girl, Woman, Other*
Sara Collins, *The Confessions of Frannie Langton*
Yaa Gyasi, *Homegoing*
Taiye Selasi, *Ghana Must Go*
Lola Shoneyin, *The Secret Lives of the Four Wives*
   (previously The Secret Lives of Baba Segi's Wives)

Chika Unigwe, *On Black Sisters' Street*
Alice Walker, *The Color Purple*

Non-Fiction

Sofia Akel, 'Insider-Outsider: The Role of Race in Shaping the Experiences of Black and Minority Ethnic Students'

Beverley Bryan, Stella Dadzie, and Suzanne Scafe, *Heart of the Race, Black Women's Lives in Britain*

Brittney Cooper, *Eloquent Rage: A Black Feminist Discovers Her Superpower*

Emma Dabiri, *Don't Touch My Hai*r

Jacquelyn Dowd Hall, 'The Long History of the Civil Rights Movement'

Reni Eddo-Lodge, *Why I'm No Longer Talking to White People About Race*

Frantz Fanon, *Black Skin, White Masks*

Tanisha C. Ford, 'Soul Style on Campus', from *Liberated Threads: Black Women, Style, and the Global Politics of Soul* (2015)

Patricia Hill Collins, *Black Feminist Thought: Knowledge, Consciousness and the Politics of Empowerment*

Afua Hirsch, *Brit-ish*

bell hooks, 'Is Paris Burning?'

C. L. R. James, *The Black Jacobins*

Jennie Livingston, *Paris is Burning* (docufilm: 1990)

Danielle L. McGuire, '"It Was Like All of Us Had Been Raped": Sexual Violence, Community Mobilisation, and the African American Freedom Struggle'

Walter Rodney, *How Europe Underdeveloped Africa*

Royal Historical Society Race Report https://royalhistsoc. org/racereport/

Global Social Theory Reading Lists https://globalsocial theory.org/resources/reading-lists/ (includes HSPS Alternative Reading List)

Support/Organise

1752 Group: https://1752group.com/
Black Girl Fest: https://www.blackgirlfest.com
FLY: https://flygirlsofcambridge.com/
Gal-Dem: https://gal-dem.com/
Imkaan: https://www.imkaan.org.uk/
Sisters Uncut: http://www.sistersuncut.org/

Resources

Black Girl Fest
https://www.blackgirlfest.com

Royal Historical Society Race Report
https://royalhistsoc.org/racereport/

Global Social Theory Reading Lists
https://globalsocialtheory.org/resources/reading-lists/
(includes HSPS Alternative Reading List)

FLY Cambridge
https://flygirlsofcambridge.com/

Gal-Dem
http://gal-dem.com/

My Body Back Project
http://www.mybodybackproject.com/notes-of-love/

The Elms, Cambridge
https://www.theelmssarc.org/

The Samaritans
https://www.samaritans.org/

Reporting Hate Crime
https://www.met.police.uk/true-vision-report-hate-crime/

Epigeum
https://www.epigeum.com/courses/support-wellbeing/consent-matters-boundaries-respect-and-positive-intervention/

Women Against Rape
www.womenagainstrape.net

The Runnymede Trust
https://www.runnymedetrust.org/projects-and-publications/education.html

Confident and Killing It
http://www.confidentandkillingit.com/

Click Relationships
https://clickrelationships.org/the-mix/

NHS Advice on Sexual Health for Young People
https://www.nhs.uk/live-well/sexual-health/
15-things-young-people-should-know-about-sex/

1752 Group
https://1752group.com/

Higher Educational Statistical Report 2018
https://www.ecu.ac.uk/publications/equality-higher-
education-statistical-report-2018/

Imkaan
https://www.imkaan.org.uk/

Sisters Uncut
http://www.sistersuncut.org/

Acknowledgements

Chelsea

Firstly, a huge thank you to Akua, Stormzy and the whole #Merky Team for making *Taking Up Space* possible. I will be forever grateful that you gave us this opportunity to tell such an important story and archive our history.

To our wonderful and amazing agent, Carrie, this whole book would never have taken off without you. Thank you for always fighting our corner, for your honesty and brilliant ideas.

To everyone at Penguin Random House, especially Tom, Kate, Alice and Natalia, for investing time, for your dedication and for matching Ọrẹ's and my energy every single time, right from the beginning. From edits to making sure everything surrounding us has stayed as authentic as possible. Most importantly, for understanding how urgent and important this conversation is. Thank you for letting us be US!

To Courtney, Arenike, Mikai, Micha, Kenya, Saredo, Adaobi, Ayomide, Barbara, Saskia, Fope, Renée, Eire-ann and Nathania. THANK YOU. Thank you for sharing your stories, experiences and past traumas. You're all brilliant and it goes without saying that this book wouldn't be possible without you.

To the Kwakye Krew, Mum, Dad, Jeanette, Louie, Toks and my biggest cheerleader, Joe, thank you for keeping me grounded, critical and unapologetic.

Finally, to my right-hand, best-friend and sister, Ore-oluwa. Our friendship has only strengthened throughout this whole process. We always said if we could survive Cambridge, we could do anything. Well . . . I'm sure this nearly pushed us to the edge. But, I wouldn't have it any other way! I love you.

Ọrẹ

First up, I need to thank God. I'm so grateful and so blessed to have had the opportunity to write this book and to share our stories with the world. I thank God for His grace and loving guidance throughout this whole process.

To my family, thank you for being behind me every step of the way. Thank you dad for staying up with me night after night to help me edit my chapters. Thank you mum for always answering my daily FaceTime calls, even when you're really busy. To Brother Toks, Anu, Aunty Dami and Mo for helping me make all the big decisions I was too indecisive to make myself. To the whole Ogunbiyi clan and beyond, I love you all.

To my friends who have had to put up with me while I've been stressed with deadlines, thank you for being understanding when I missed your calls, when I didn't have time to come out with you or if I ever forgot to check up on you. Now we can make up for all the lost time, I promise.

To the interviewees, you guys made this book. The interviews that we had made me feel nostalgic, happy, sad and every emotion in between. Thank you for sharing your experiences with us and with the world. Thank you for always replying to our annoying emails (and even the follow-ups). We really appreciate you.

However, none of this would have even been possible without the #Merky Books and Penguin squads. Stormzy, thank you for recognising that our stories need to be told and we hope we've done you proud. Akua, thank you for helping us bring our dream to life. Thank you for always letting us know that you're there if we need you. Thank you Tom Avery for giving up so much of your time to make sure that this book turned out the best it could be. To Kate, Natalia, Alice and everyone on the Penguin side, thank you for all your efforts.

To our agent turned wingwoman, Carrie. We knew from the first day we spoke to you that we'd be hard-pressed to find anyone who believed in this book more than you. Thank you for helping us through this new and sometimes scary process and for always having our best interests at heart.

TO MY OTHER HALF AND BESTIE BAE CHELS. We did it. I can't believe it. Thank you for not getting sick of me. Thank you for keeping me going. Thank you for going to all the meetings that couldn't wait and replying to emails when the time difference was killing me. We smashed it. It's me and you against the world babygirl.

For more information about *Taking Up Space*,
please follow:

Twitter: **@takingupspacebk**

Instagram: **@takingupspacebook**